SELLING

Building Partnerships

SELLING

Building Partnerships

Stephen B. Castleberry
University of Minnesota Duluth

John F. Tanner, Jr.
Baylor University

9

Mc
Graw
Hill
Education

SELLING: BUILDING PARTNERSHIPS, NINTH EDITION

Published by McGraw-Hill Education, 2 Penn Plaza, New York, NY 10121. Copyright © 2014 by McGraw-Hill Education. All rights reserved. Printed in the United States of America. Previous editions © 2011, 2009, and 2007. No part of this publication may be reproduced or distributed in any form or by any means, or stored in a database or retrieval system, without the prior written consent of McGraw-Hill Education, including, but not limited to, in any network or other electronic storage or transmission, or broadcast for distance learning.

Some ancillaries, including electronic and print components, may not be available to customers outside the United States.

This book is printed on acid-free paper.

3 4 5 6 7 8 9 0 QVS/QVS 1 0 9 8 7 6 5 4

ISBN   978–0–07–786100–1
MHID 0–07–786100–0

Senior Vice President, Products and Markets: *Kurt L. Strand*
Vice President, Content Production & Technology Services: *Kimberly Meriwether David*
Managing Director: *Paul Ducham*
Executive Brand Manager: *Shankha Basu*
Executive Director of Development: *Ann Torbert*
Development Editor: *Gabriela Gonzalez*
Senior Marketing Manager: *Donielle Xu*
Director, Content Production: *Terri Schiesl*
Project Manager: *Melissa M. Leick*
Buyer: *Nicole Baumgartner*
Media Project Manager: *Prashanti Nadipalli*
Cover Designer: *Studio Mondage, St. Louis, MO*
Cover Image: *Ariel Skelley/Getty Images*
Typeface: *10/12 Sabon*
Compositor: *S4Carlisle Publishing Services*
Printer: *Quad/Graphics*

All credits appearing on page or at the end of the book are considered to be an extension of the copyright page.

Library of Congress Cataloging-in-Publication Data
Castleberry, Stephen Bryon.
   Selling : building partnerships / Stephen B. Castleberry, University of Minnesota Duluth, John F. Tanner, Jr., Baylor University. —Ninth Edition.
      pages cm
   ISBN 978-0-07-786100-1—ISBN 0-07-786100-0   1. Selling. I. Tanner, John F. II. Title.
   HF5438.25.W2933 2013
   658.85—dc23
                                                                                2013008649

The Internet addresses listed in the text were accurate at the time of publication. The inclusion of a website does not indicate an endorsement by the authors or McGraw-Hill Education, and McGraw-Hill Education does not guarantee the accuracy of the information presented at these sites.

To Norah Grace Pederson, the cutest granddaughter in the world! And to my Creator, Redeemer and Friend, without whom I would be nothing.
—Steve Castleberry

To Karen—you make all the hard work worthwhile.
—Jeff Tanner

PREFACE

If you just looked at copyright dates, you would realize that this book was originally published over 20 years ago, but, truthfully, the work has been going on much longer than that. We took some time to reflect on how the sales profession and this book have changed over the years, much of it driven by technology. For example, we used to have a chapter on sales letters and written proposals—you can still find remnants of that material if you look hard enough, but most of that is obsolete. Now, we spend time on selling by email, when the use of texting is appropriate, and the influence of social media. Still, we've remained faithful to the premises that caused us to write the first edition more than 20 years ago:

- We don't want to teach the history of selling—we want our students to know how it is done now and why.
- Partnering skills are critical skills for all businesspeople.
- Adaptive communication skills—probing, listening, and presentation—are important in all areas of life but especially for salespeople.
- Students need to practice these skills through role playing.
- Helping people make the right decisions is not only the most ethical sales strategy but also the most effective strategy for long-term success.

At the same time, we've recognized that several factors are changing the face of selling:

- Increased use of multichannel go-to-market strategies, including inside sales.
- Changing roles for both technology and salespeople.
- Rapid economic change and the impact of the recession.
- Changing trends in how organizations buy, specifically the increasing use of technology, self-service, and presale search.

As we've revised the text, faithful adopters will see that we've held to the principles that made this book unique when it was launched and kept it in a leadership position. While others may have tried to copy role playing, partnering, or technology, none have truly captured the essence that makes this book the leading text.

WHAT'S NEW IN THE NINTH EDITION

- **Original examples** written specifically for this book, provided by current sales programs and salespeople, many of whom took the class and used this book.
- New chapter-opening **profiles**—all chapters open with a real salesperson or sales manager's perspective on the chapter. Each profile is new and original to this edition, and we've also integrated the profiles into each chapter as a running example to increase this feature's functionality.
- All new **"Building Partnerships"**—boxed features that provide more detailed examples of chapter material and present chapter material in a slightly different light.
- New **"Sales Technology"**—boxed features in each chapter, many new to this edition, that illustrate how technology is used. The result is a much better understanding of what professionals are calling Sales 3.0 or Sales in the Cloud (cloud computing). You'll find many types of technology, including knowledge management technology, CRM technology, and even GPS technology used in routing sales calls.
- All new **"From the Buyer's Seat"**—this feature was introduced in the last edition, and the feedback was overwhelmingly positive. Buyers, though, are no more stationary than salespeople, so we've created all new features for this edition, integrating the best of the last edition into the text.
- **Feature questions**—embedded in the end-of-chapter material are discussion questions that direct students back to the profiles, "Building Partnerships," "From the Buyer's Seat," and "Sales Technology" features so these features are read and used more fully.
- New **Role Plays**—we've written a new set of role plays featuring Stubbs and NetSuite. Stubbs is a

barbecue product line, and you can use this if you want to use simple role plays that span both trade sales and sales to users (institutions, restaurants, and so on). NetSuite is a hosted CRM application, and its Web site has role-based demonstrations so that students can learn what the product does for different people in the sales organization. This set of role plays can be a bit more complicated, but it also helps students understand what CRM software does for sales teams. At the end of most chapters, you will find a role play using NetSuite. Each set (Stubbs and NetSuite) have 10 prospect scenarios (with two buyer information sheets each in the Instructor's Manual) at the end of the book. If you would like to sell something different, Bob Erffmeyer has collaborated with Hormel to create a set of role plays that are available at www.sellingbuilding-partnerships.com.

- New **minicases**—each chapter has a new or significantly revised minicase as well as favorite minicases to choose from.

IMPORTANT FEATURES OF SELLING: BUILDING PARTNERSHIPS

Customer loyalty, customer lifetime value, the Challenger Model—all are influencing the way sales is done and taught. We believe that the partnering approach continues to be the best overall way to learn how to sell, particularly in the broader context of undergraduate education. Several unique features place this book at the cutting edge of sales technology and partnering research:

1. A continued emphasis on the partnering process, with recognition that multiple sales models may be appropriate in a company's total go-to-market strategy. We focus on the partnering process as the highest level of selling because the other models of transaction—focus, problem solver, and relational partner—still need to be learned as a foundation to partnering, and the partnering process fits the value-driven sales models currently in use in the field.

2. A thorough description of the partnering and buying processes used by business firms and the changes occurring in these processes. A number of important trends affecting buyers, such as more rigorous online research and social media use, also affect sellers.

3. A discussion of methods of internal and external partnering so that the value chain delivers the right value, in recognition of the salesperson's role in relationship management and value creation. This emphasis also broadens the applicability of the course for students who may not be interested in a sales career.

4. An emphasis throughout the text on the need for salespeople to be flexible—to adapt their strategies to customer needs, buyer social styles, and relationship needs and strategies.

5. A complete discussion of how effective selling and career growth are achieved through planning and continual learning.

6. An emphasis on the growing need for salespeople in organizations to carry the voice of the customer to all parts of the organization and beyond to suppliers and facilitators. This role is reflected in new product development, supply chain management, and many other functions in a customer-centric organization.

These unique content emphases are presented in a highly readable format, supported by the following:

- **Ethics questions**—at least two questions at the end of each chapter relate the chapter material to ethics.

- **Four-color exhibits and photographs** to support the examples highlighted in the book. Students find this book to be easy to read and use.

- **"Thinking It Through"**—these features embed discussion questions into the text itself; for this edition, we've also offered teaching suggestions to integrate this feature more fully. There are several of these features in each chapter.

- **Minicases**—two small cases are available at the end of each chapter. These are useful for in-class exercises or discussion or as homework. In this edition, you'll find one new or revised mini-case in each chapter, but if you can't find one from the eighth edition that you really like, check out www.sellingbuildingpartners.com to get a copy you can hand out.

- **Ethics icon**—because we've emphasized ethical partnering since the inception of this book, we highlight the integration of ethics by noting any ethics discussion with an icon in the margin. You'll find ethics discussed in every chapter.

- **Selling Yourself**—a feature at the end of each chapter that we introduced in the previous edition that relates the material in the chapter to the student's life *right now*. It's more than just the student's job search process, however. Selling Yourself helps students see the connections between chapter material and all aspects of their lives, such as how a student can sell an organization to new members, working with apartment managers to resolve issues, interacting with friends and family members, how to add value as a group member in a class team project, and so forth.

- **Key terms**—each key term defined in a chapter is listed at the end of the chapter, along with the page number on which the term is discussed. Key terms reflect current usage of sales jargon in the field, as well as academic terms.

- **Glossary**—key terms are also defined in a glossary at the end of the book.

FOR FACULTY

Instructor's manuals are available with any text, but the quality often varies. Because we teach the course to undergraduates and graduates, as well as presenting and participating in sales seminars in industry, we believe that we have created an Instructor's Manual (available at the Online Learning Center, www.mhhe.com/castleberry9e) that can significantly assist the teacher. We've also asked instructors what they would like to see in a manual. Based on their feedback, we include suggested course outlines, chapter outlines, lecture suggestions, and answers to questions and cases. On that site, you'll also find the slides, which are integrated into our teaching notes.

- **Slides** are available in PowerPoint, but given feedback from users (and our own experience), we've simplified their presentation. They are easily adapted to your own needs, and you can add material as you see fit.
- We also include many of the **in-class exercises** we have developed over the years. These have been subjected to student critique, and we are confident you will find them useful. You will also find a number of **additional role play scenarios.**
- Students need to practice their selling skills in a selling environment, and they need to do it in a way that is helpful. **Small group practice exercises, including role playing,** complete with instructions for student evaluations, are provided in the Instructor's Manual. These sessions can be held as part of class but are also designed for out-of-class time for teachers who want to save class time for full-length role plays.
- The **Test Bank** has been carefully and completely rewritten. Questions are directly tied to the learning goals presented at the beginning of each chapter and the material covered in the questions and problems. In addition, key terms are covered in the test questions. Application questions are available so students can demonstrate their understanding of the key concepts by applying those selling principles.
- The **Web site,** www.sellingbuildingpartnerships .com, is your Web site. This Web site is a place for

faculty to share materials, as well as a place where it is easy for us to quickly bring you up-to-date materials. Here you will find short slide decks (three to five slides) about current sales and sales management research that is template-free so you can integrate it into existing presentations as you see fit. You will also find new videos, presentation slide decks from other faculty and sales professionals, and other materials designed to support your teaching. Short cases from previous editions are also posted there if you would like to include these as essay questions on exams or in-class exercises. We hope you will also contribute to the site. Instructor materials are password-protected so students do not have access to them.

- **New chapters**—at www.sellingbuildingpartnerships .com you'll find several new chapters that students can access, such as Writing Proposals, Account Management, and others. We use these chapters ourselves in advanced selling classes, but you may find these necessary in your introductory sales course or in a sales management course. Students can access and download these chapters at no cost.

PARTNERING: FROM THE FIELD TO THE CLASSROOM

Faculty who use our book have reviewed it and offered suggestions, and we have taken their comments seriously. What is different is that sales executives and field salespeople who are locked in the daily struggle of adapting to the new realities of selling also reviewed *Selling: Building Partnerships*. They have told us what the field is like now, where it is going, and what students must do to be prepared for the challenges that will face them.

Students have also reviewed chapters. They are, after all, the ones who must learn from the book. We asked for their input prior to and during the revision process. And judging by their comments and suggestions, this book is effectively delivering the content. There are, however, several places where their comments have enabled us to clarify material and improve on its presentation.

As you can see in "About the Authors," we have spent considerable time in the field in a variety of sales positions. We continue to spend time in the field engaging in personal selling ourselves, as well as observing and serving professional salespeople. We believe the book has benefited greatly because of such a never-ending development process.

Acknowledgments

Staying current with the rapidly changing field of professional selling is a challenge. Our work has been blessed with the excellent support of reviewers, users, editors, salespeople, and students. Reviewers include the following:

Jill Attaway, Illinois State University
Robert Consenza, University of Mississippi
Karl Sooder, University of Central Florida
Carolyn Waits, Cincinnati State Technical and Community College
Vicki L. West, Texas State University

Readers will become familiar with many of the salespeople who contributed to the development of the ninth edition through various selling scenarios or profiles. But other salespeople, sales executives, buyers, and sales professors contributed in less obvious, but no less important, ways. For reviewing chapters, updating cases, providing material for selling scenarios, and other support, we'd like to thank the following:

Amber Fischer, Rehrig Pacific
Sally Cook, 3M
James Ellington, Tandy Brands
Angela Bertero, Liberty Mutual Insurance
Brett Georgulis, 3M
David Maebane, PepsiCo-FritoLay
Mike Buckland, NCR
Renee Miles, Johnson & Johnson
Evan Adonis, Dallas Cowboys
Carl Anderson, Powertex Group
Sean Anderson, Grainger
Matt Arneson, Buildings Xchange
Ronald N. Borrieci, COB Embry-Riddle Aeronautical University
Ken Bluedorn, Lake Superior Bottle Shop
Ashley Braine, Dell
Tracey Brill, Abbott Labs
Becky Burton, Automation Xchange
Heather Carr, Career Professionals
Caitlin Christoff, Process Technology Xchange
John E. Cicala, Texas A&M University
Sally Cook, 3M
Bruce Culbert, Pedowitz Group
Susan Denny, Cisco
Dr. Greg DiNovis, College of St. Catherine
Mike Donley, Opus Medical
Professor Susan Emens, Kent State University
Chris Evers, Swisher International
Danny Fernandez, KMBS

Gina Garuso, Meat Processing Xchange
Graham Gedmestad, Automation Xchange
Tom Gottschald, Team Goodyear Tire and Gemini Service Center
Amanda Gonzales, NetworkIP
Mary Gros, Teradata
Matt Haberle, Maximum Impact
Christina Harrod, Applied Medical Devices, Inc.
Dr. David Henard, North Carolina State University
Jim Keller, Teradata
Barbara Kellgren, Lutron Electronics
Michael Krause, Sales Sense Solutions, Inc.
Danielle Lord, U.S. Foodservice
Jeff Lynn, Hartford Insurance Group
Angie Main, Midwest Communications
Camille McConn, ACell Inc.
Dave Moore, ADP
Eddy Patterson, Stubb's Bar-B-Q
Terry Perrella, Sammy's United
Dr. Jim Prost, University of San Francisco
Neil Rackham, Huthwaite, Inc.
Jen Rennelt, Career Professionals
Dr. Rick Ridnour, Northern Illinois University
Leif Ringstad, Samsung Telecommunications
Mike Rocker, 3M
Spencer Ryan, Stryker
Kristen Scott, Oracle
Layne Skoyen, Process Technology Xchange
Professor Karl Sooder, University of Central Florida
Chad Stinchfield, Hospira
Dr. Jeff Strieter, State University of New York College–Brockport
Dan Termunde, Hilti
Dr. Brian Tietje, California Polytechnic State University
John Tanner, Concentra
Dr. Brian Vollmert, Northern Illinois University
Zac VonBank, University of Minnesota Duluth
Michael Wendinger, University of Minnesota Duluth
Kristy Wilke, Buildings Xchange

In addition to the support of these individuals, many companies also provided us with material. We'd like to express our sincere gratitude for their support.

The McGraw-Hill team, as is the usual, was wonderful to work with. Our greatest interaction during manuscript preparation was with Jean Smith, development editor, and we appreciate her quick response and dogged determination to make sure we turn out a great product. Melissa Leick, our production manager, is another important contributor to the physical product. Gabriela Gonzalez, editorial, rounds out the production triumvarate who makes sure that what you are holding in your hands meets the standards set so high in our previous editions. Sankha Basu, our brand manager, and Donielle Xu, our marketing manager, also make sure the product is excellent and then help us communicate that to the market. We really appreciate their efforts on our behalf.

Several people assisted in research and manuscript preparation, and we gratefully appreciate their help: Bryant Duong and W. T. Tanner. Students who made helpful comments and reviewed for us include Brooke Borgias, Anna Hoglund, and Zac VonBank. Many other students and teachers have made comments that have helped us strengthen the overall package. They deserve our thanks, as do others who prefer to remain anonymous.

—Steve Castleberry

—Jeff Tanner

ABOUT THE AUTHORS

STEPHEN B. CASTLEBERRY

Dr. Castleberry received his PhD from the University of Alabama in 1983. He taught at the University of Georgia for six years and for three years was UARCO Professor of Sales and Marketing at Northern Illinois University. Currently he is a professor of marketing at the University of Minnesota Duluth. He has received seven awards for teaching excellence, including the highest recognition by the University of Minnesota system of its most distinguished scholar teachers. His commitment to teaching has resulted in a number of cases, as well as articles in the *Journal of Marketing Education, Business Case Journal,* and *Marketing Education Review,* that describe his teaching style and methods.

Dr. Castleberry's research has been published in many journals, including the *Journal of Personal Selling and Sales Management, Industrial Marketing Management, Journal of Business Ethics, Journal of Selling and Major Account Management, Journal of Business and Industrial Marketing, Journal of Business to Business Marketing, Journal of Marketing Management, Journal of Consumer Marketing, Journal of Business Research, Journal of the Academy of Marketing Science,* and *International Journal of Research in Marketing.* He has also presented his work at the National Conference in Sales Management, as well as other national and regional conferences. He is past marketing editor of the *Journal of Applied Business Research* and serves on several journal editorial boards. He has received research grants and support from entities such as the London Business School, Gillette, Quaker Oats, Kimberly Clark, Proctor & Gamble, Coca-Cola Foods Division, and the Alexander Group/JPSSM.

Dr. Castleberry appeared as an academic expert in eight segments of *The Sales Connection,* a 26-segment video production shown on national PBS TV stations. He also appeared as the special guest on several broadcasts of *Sales Talk,* a nationally broadcast call-in talk show on the Business Radio Network.

Dr. Castleberry has held various sales assignments with Burroughs Corporation (now Unisys), Nabisco, and G.C. Murphy's and has worked as a consultant and sales trainer for numerous firms and groups. His interests outside academic life include outdoor activities (canoeing, hiking, bicycling, snowshoeing, skiing, and so on) and everything related to living on his 100-acre farm in northern Wisconsin. He is an elder in his church and a volunteer firefighter and first responder in the small township he lives in. He and his wife currently own and operate a publishing company, marketing and distributing popular press books internationally.

Stephen B. Castleberry

scastleb@d.umn.edu
www.d.umn.edu/~scastleb

JOHN F. TANNER, JR.

Dr. Tanner is Professor of Marketing, Baylor University. He earned his PhD from the University of Georgia. Prior to entering academia, Dr. Tanner spent eight years in industry with Rockwell International and Xerox Corporation as both salesperson and marketing manager.

Dr. Tanner has received several awards for teaching effectiveness and research. His sales teaching efforts have been recognized by student organizations, *Sales & Marketing Management,* and the *Dallas Morning News.* Dr. Tanner has authored or coauthored 13 books, including *Business Marketing: Connecting Strategy, Relationships, and Learning* with Bob Dwyer, and *The Hard Truth about Soft Selling* with George Dudley. His 14th book, *Dynamic Customer Strategy: Big Profits from Big Data*, is due out in the summer of 2013.

Research grants from the Center for Exhibition Industry Research, the Institute for the Study of Business Markets, the University Research Council, the Texas Department of

Health, and others have supported his research efforts. Dr. Tanner has published over 70 articles in the *Journal of Marketing, Journal of Business Research, Journal of Personal Selling and Sales Management,* international journals, and others. He serves on the review boards of several journals, including *Marketing Education Review, Journal of Personal Selling and Sales Management,* and *Industrial Marketing Management.*

Dr. Tanner writes a weekly blog, TannerismsonTuesday, about sales and sales management topics. He has been a featured presenter at executive workshops and conferences for organizations such as the Marketing Science Institute and the American Marketing Association. Since 2006 he has taught executive and graduate programs in India, Australia, Trinidad, Colombia, Canada, France, the United Kingdom, and Mexico, primarily as part of the CRM at the Speed of Light executive certification program. Jeff and his wife also breed and race thoroughbred horses on their farm.

Jeff_Tanner@BAYLOR.EDU
hsb.baylor.edu/html/tanner

Walkthrough

Selling: Building Partnerships remains the most innovative textbook in the Selling course area today with its unique role plays and partnering skills which are critical skills for all business people. The authors emphasize throughout the text the need for salespeople to be flexible–to adapt their strategies to customer needs, buyer social styles, and relationship needs and strategies. This is followed by a complete discussion of how effective selling and career growth are achieved through planning and continual learning. The 9th edition has been updated to continue its relevance in the Selling market today just as it was twenty years ago.

The **chapter opening profiles** in this edition are the product of strong selling partnerships. Faculty from around the country introduced Steve Castleberry and Jeff Tanner to their former students who had gone on to careers in sales. The results are exciting new profiles from sales professionals who were students with an earlier edition and understand the philosophy of this book. The profiles are also integrated into the chapter with additional examples involving the profiled salesperson and end-of-chapter questions. Students can easily relate to these young professionals who have benefited from wonderful faculty and *Selling: Building Partnerships*.

PROFILE

"It is important that my referral partners know what a good prospect looks like to me so that the leads they send me are actually qualified referrals."

Angela Bertero

PROFILE My name is Angela Bertero, and I graduated from Texas State University–San Marcos in 2008. I earned my master's in business administration and bachelor of business administration in marketing. While at Texas State University, I served as president of our national championship Students in Free Enterprise team and won quarter finalist at the National Collegiate Sales Competition, both of which were advised by Vicki West. Mrs. West introduced me to Liberty Mutual Insurance, which is where I was hired as a licensed sales representative.

Liberty Mutual offers a full line of high-quality insurance products and services. As the main contact for the company, it is my responsibility to develop and maintain client relationships as well as identify prospective customers and promote Liberty Mutual products.

While retention is key to a business's success, prospecting for new clients is crucial to growing my book of business. I have found success using the following methods of prospecting: referrals from satisfied clients and business partners, networking, and cross-selling to current clients. Referrals are by far the most important source of prospects.

Successful prospecting isn't about running around town and meeting everyone you can. It's about identifying your target market and knowing how to communicate that to your existing customers and referral partners. To do this, I often review the services I have provided for my clients and ask them if they know anyone in a similar situation that I may be able to help. I tell all of my clients that the greatest compliment I can receive is a referral from them.

I also work closely with a variety of referral partners to fill my pipeline with prospective new clients: mortgage brokers, realtors, financial advisors, auto dealerships, bankers, employers, school districts, and alumni associations, to name a few.

It is important that my referral partners know what a good prospect looks like to me so that the leads they send me are actually qualified referrals.

My networking group, Business Networking International (BNI), has given me the opportunity to give weekly educational moments to other professionals in different industries, or, as I like to call them, my marketing team. When I first joined BNI, I expected—or hoped for—immediate results. I have since learned that building personal relationships while becoming a trusted advisor to those around me is critical to building my network over time. After just a year, though, the partnerships I have made are a huge part of my weekly prospecting. We meet once a week to share ideas, help grow each other's businesses, and fill each other's pipelines with prospects. Then, we meet one to one to learn more about how we can work together for a mutually beneficial partnership.

To be a successful networker, make an effort to understand other people's businesses and connect with them on a personal level. Always follow up and thank your networking contact for the leads they send you and, if you can, send them leads as well.

Visit our Web site at:
www.libertymutual.com

Professional sales **ethics** have always been the hallmark of this text, and the new edition integrates ethics throughout each chapter, as well as in discussion questions devoted to this topic. Each chapter has separate ethics discussion questions, some of which were suggested by former students' experiences or current events.

ETHICS PROBLEMS

1. Suppose you're working at a trade show. You walk the floor of the show during one of your breaks, and you strike up a conversation with a sales rep from a competitor. She starts talking about their products and gives details on price breaks she offers to banks. She asks, "What kind of price deals do you give banks?" What would you say?
2. Suppose a spotter not only tells you about a potential prospect but also provides you with confidential memos and e-mails, detailing the people involved and what the issues are. However, all the e-mails and notes are marked with statements that prohibit the information from being shared with anyone outside of the company. What will you do with that confidential information that you're not supposed to have?

Current and continued emphasis on selling examples from China, India, Europe, and all around the globe reflects the reality of the global nature of selling.

This American salesperson needs to recognize the differences between communicating in an Arab culture and an American culture.

- Make a link to things you think prospects would find interesting, like articles and Web sites. Tweets should have real value to the receiver.
- Don't create spam with Twitter.
- You can schedule when the tweets will be sent with add-ons like Social Oomph.
- Share interesting things about your community and nonbusiness items to help make yourself real. Remember that you are trying to create a friendly relationship.
- Remember to listen, not just send out tweets. Respond to at least some of the replying tweets. Don't feel guilty if you don't read or respond to all tweets.

Because of the growing use of social networking, Chapters 6 and 7 will discuss ways to use these tools to prospect and learn more about new customers.

ADJUSTING FOR CULTURAL DIFFERENCES

Communication in international selling often takes place in English because English is likely to be the only language salespeople and customers have in common. To communicate effectively with customers whose native language is not English, salespeople need to be careful about the words and expressions they use. People who use English in international selling should observe the following rules:

- Use common English words that a customer would learn during the first two years of studying the language. For example, use *expense* rather than *expenditure* or *stop* instead of *cease*.
- Use words that do not have multiple meanings. For example, *right* has many meanings, whereas *accurate* is more specific. When you use words that have several meanings, recognize that nonnative speakers will usually use the most common meaning to interpret what you are saying.

Many technologies, including the sales cloud (or Sales 3.0 technology), pad computers, GPS, the Internet, and CRM software, have changed how salespeople operate. The ninth edition includes all new illustrations with its feature **"Sales Technology,"** which discusses how selling and technology interact within the context of each chapter.

SALES Technology

6.1

GENERATING LEADS THROUGH SOCIAL MEDIA

With the enormous presence that social media has in today's society, it is important for salespeople to consider their use. Here are a few quick yet astonishing facts about social media:

- Facebook has more weekly traffic than Google.
- If Facebook were a country, it would be the third largest in the world.
- The Ford Explorer launch on Facebook generated more traffic than a Super Bowl ad.

- There are more than 465 million Twitter accounts with 1 million more being added each day and 175 million tweets being tweeted daily.
- LinkedIn has two new members joining every second.
- There are over 57 million LinkedIn users in the United States alone.

When used correctly, social media has the potential to be an integral part of an organizations prospecting strategies.

"Thinking It Through" boxes (at least two per chapter) are engaging exercises that can inspire classroom dialogue or serve as a short-essay exam question to help students experience concepts as they read.

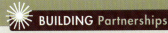

thinking **it** through Who is a center of influence for you right now? How could a salesperson who wanted to sell you something learn who your center of influence is?

"From the Buyer's Seat" is an all-new original feature that provides students with a buyer's inside perspective. **"Building Partnerships"** boxes examine how successful salespeople build relationships. All are original to the book—many using examples provided by former students and other sales professionals. And all are discussed as part of the end-of-chapter questions so that you can fully integrate them into the class.

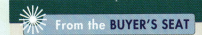

From the BUYER'S SEAT 4.1

PLEASE LEARN HOW TO COMMUNICATE!

As a senior buyer at Microsoft, I see many different types of salespeople. I receive numerous calls each day from salespeople trying to make appointments with me and there are usually one of two outcomes:

A. The salesperson that has done their research about my company prior to the call and has a very concise and clear message tends to have the best chance of actually getting the appointment that they are shooting for.

B. Often salespeople will say, "I didn't expect you to answer your phone!" The salespeople who have this response are caught completely off guard and stand very little chance of obtaining their desired appointment.

• Using active listening skills during a conversation with me and then remembering specifics from that conversation in future meetings. This proves to me that they really listen to what the objectives were, have retained this information, and then have acted on it to prepare for the next meeting.

• A salesperson who knows what situations are better to be handled via the telephone as opposed to e-mail. Under certain circumstances, sending an e-mail instead of making a phone call can make the problem worse, so knowing the proper means of communication can definitely help a salesperson build a relationship with me.

BUILDING Partnerships 5.1

CUSTOMIZE THE PRESENTATION

At ADP, we consider ourselves business consultants. We don't have a prescript sales pitch that is used on every call. The goal is to educate the owner on varying topics surrounding payroll to show them how a service like ADP can make them more efficient and compliant with state and federal employer laws. Because I meet with business owners who have anywhere from one employee to 49 employees in every industry thinkable, the needs of the businesses are never the same.

I have to customize my presentation depending on many factors. For example, a first-time restaurant owner who has 35 tipped employees will need me to explain everything we do in depth, from payroll taxes and new hire reporting to FICA tip reporting. Most new business owners are not aware of all their tax liabilities and ways they can get money back from the government for having tipped employees. The owners are very appreciative that I take the time to explain all these fiduciary responsibilities and the fines they could be liable for.

On the other hand, when I meet with a longtime owner of a nonprofit company with three employees, this presentation is completely different. In this situation, the owner wouldn't be interested in hearing about the "Payroll 101" I was telling the new business owner. Instead, he or she would want to know about payroll being directly tied to grant funding, ability to offer comprehensive benefits, and wage tracking for grant reporting.

Either way, I am selling the same service but simply customizing the presentation to the buyers' needs.

Source: Meggie Dominguez, personal correspondence, used with permission.

case 9.2

Miller Lite

On December 5, 1933, the U.S. Congress passed a bill that would repeal the Eighteenth Amendment and thus would end prohibition in this country. The implementation of prohibition had been linked to many negative social issues, such as organized crime, bootlegging, and racketeering. Some historians have commented that the alcohol industry accepted stronger regulation of alcohol in the decades after repeal as a way to reduce the chance that Prohibition would return.

Today, the American beer industry is the most heavily regulated industry in the country, even more than the tobacco industry, and Minnesota is a leader when it comes to heavy regulation and high taxes. For example, here are the beer laws in Minnesota:

1. All retailers must be offered the same price at all times.
2. Beer distributors cannot pay for any cooperative advertising.
3. Beer distributors cannot give any product for free.
4. Beer distributors have a maximum of $300 per brand, per year, to promote the brand within the account (using things like neon lights and point-of-sale items), but this can't be in the form of price cuts for an individual retailer.

I was the sales representative for a beer distributor in Minnesota. My territory volume was trending down, and I was told by my manager that I needed to secure incremental activity to promote Miller Lite. My largest customer, Bill, at Save-a-Lot Liquor, gave me an opportunity for an additional holiday ad in his weekly flyer. I knew this ad would yield a 200 percent lift in sales for the week and in turn would pay a nice commission to me.

Class-tested **minicases** at the end of each chapter work well as daily assignments and as frameworks for lectures, discussion, or small group practice. Each chapter includes at least one new minicase. The cases encourage students to apply theories and skills learned in the text to solve sales situations.

ROLE PLAY CASE

As a NetSuite salesperson, how can you help your buyer prospect better? Think about how NetSuite might be able to help your buyer develop a comprehensive prospecting system, from lead generation to making the first appointment. One way that NetSuite can help is to automate direct mail. Using the database that salespeople create, the marketing department can send mail to every contact who meets certain criteria. For example, it can select an industry and send a letter only to prospects in that industry. Similarly, NetSuite provides reporting capabilities. Salespeople can see how effective they are at each method of prospecting and

Students can practice their partnering skills in brand new **role play exercises** that encourage personal growth and experiential learning. Each role play features NetSuite, the software used in national collegiate sales competition. Also, comprehensive role plays are available at the end of the book, with additional role plays included in the Instructor's Manual.

Supplements

The **Online Learning Center** mhhe.com/castleberry9e houses the Instructor's Manual, PowerPoint slides, test bank, and a link to McGraw-Hill's course management system, PageOut for the Instructor. It also includes study outlines, quizzes, key terms, career information, video clips, and online resources for the student.

CONTENTS IN BRIEF

CONTENTS

chapter **1**

SELLING AND SALESPEOPLE

SOME QUESTIONS ANSWERED IN THIS CHAPTER ARE

- What is selling?
- Why should you learn about selling even if you do not plan to be a salesperson?
- What is the role of personal selling in a firm?
- What are the different types of salespeople?
- What are the rewards of a selling career?

PROFILE

PROFILE My name is Amber Fischer, and I am a 2004 graduate of the St. Catherine University (formerly known at College of St. Catherine) business-to-business sales program. I began my college career as a sociology major. I was fascinated by observing what factors influence people's decisions and behaviors as they relate to their surroundings and teachings. As I approached my junior year, it became evident that a career in the field of business was the right path for me. Lynn Schleeter, Marge Matheson-Hance, Mary Henderson, and Greg Dinovis did a great job of showing me that the sales program was a perfect fit, as it combined my love of understanding and interacting with people with my appreciation for commerce. I was fortunate enough to be selected at 3M Frontline sales intern for the summer of 2003. Throughout that summer and the subsequent school year, I was responsible for working with 3M sales reps throughout the organization and in a variety of industries to build customer-focused organization "maps" in an effort to increase sales through cross selling. In order to be successful, I needed to sell the 3M reps on giving me the time and exposure to Fortune 500 customers so that I could construct accurate maps that I would then present to a large number of reps. I then needed to sell them on using my maps to get in deeper with their customers and share their contacts with other 3Mers.

Over my postcollege career, I have been fortunate enough to work in sales in a variety of capacities. I have worked for a nationwide distributor, Interline Brands, to sell directly to end users. In this role, I had to learn to sell my ability to solve urgent customer problems as well as sell my capabilities to manufacturer reps so that they would entrust me with the best training and leads in order to grow my business. I was also fortunate enough to work for 3M as a manufacturer's rep. In this role, I sold through distributor reps to end users. Distributors sell a variety of lines, so I had to sell them on the reasons why they should focus on my products and promote them to the end user. I also needed to influence end users to request 3M products.

I currently work for Rehrig Pacific selling transport packaging to large retail and food and beverage customers (Walmart, Pepsi, and Target are a few key customers). In this role, I am responsible for influencing and directly selling our products to the end user. I must also sell internally, as I work directly with production to get my product manufactured and delivered quickly. We also have a great design team that I can work with to bring innovative solutions to our customers. Of course, I must sell my business case plan to our executives in order to get a design budget.

While I have had a variety of sales experiences in my career, there are some significant consistencies I can identify. Your customers, whether they are internal, end users, or distributors, are relying on you to help them get their job done. Understanding the business pressures that result in needs is vital to effectively communicating your value to the customer. This does not happen overnight. You must put in the time and hard work to really understand your customers. You must be reactive in responding to their needs, proactive in bringing creative ideas to their challenges, and consistent in your message that you are the person they should be relying on to meet their goals.

Visit our Web site at:
rehrigpacific.com

WHY LEARN ABOUT PERSONAL SELLING?

What's the first thing that pops into your mind when you hear the phrase "personal selling"? Do you conjure up images of fast-talking, nonlistening, pushy guys who won't take no for an answer? How about this definition: "Personal selling is the craft of persuading people to buy what they do not want and do not need for more than it is worth.[1]"

If that is your view of selling, we encourage you to study this book carefully. You're going to learn things about selling that you never knew before. Let's start with a more accurate definition of a professional salesperson, which is quite different from the one just mentioned. **Personal selling** is "the phenomenon of human-driven interaction between and within individuals/organizations in order to bring about economic exchange within a value-creation context."[2] Let's look at the definition more closely:

- It is more than just a set of sequential steps that a salesperson goes through with each buyer in order to get the order. It's not just about what a seller does but rather the *interaction* between sellers and buyers that makes selling work today. We will talk about steps in the selling process in this book, but remember that they are not necessarily sequential or all needed for all buying situations.

- It can often involve multiple people and organizations (not just one seller and one buyer, for example).

- Selling is all about creating **value**, which is the total benefit that the seller's products and services provide to the buyer. When describing this to prospects, the seller often refers to the collection of buyer-specific benefits as the **customer value proposition** (CVP), described more fully in Chapter 9. Just as our definition implies, this CVP is dynamic, evolving as time goes on and depends on the context of the situation.[3] In fact, success in future business often depends on enhancements to the original CVP.[4] Exhibit 1.1 provides examples of ways that salespeople create value.

- The goal of selling is to create economic exchange, not merely to promote the product or service. Customers today are very technology savvy and search enabled and no longer rely on salespeople alone to learn about products and services. Selling recognizes this fact and provides needed services to create the exchange that is in the best interests of both parties.

Exhibit 1.1

Examples of Ways That Salespeople Can Add Value in a Selling Situation

Provide an interface between the buying and selling companies.

Identify networks of key players in both the buying and the selling companies and then help to activate them to the task of cocreating value.

Encourage two-way communication and help to create effective bonds between people.

Help to create a climate of coleadership in the meetings rather than having the seller always take the leadership role.

Encourage both sides to learn from and understand each other.

Facilitate truly useful meetings and conversations between all parties.

Help to manage any situations that arise to bring everyone back to a value-adding perspective.

Help to foster conditions of trust and commitment between parties.

Be attuned to activities that increase value adding and help facilitate more of them.

Help key players to understand their own perceptions of what value is to them.

Create meaning out of situations that arise and conversations that occur.

Help to provide closure on solutions that provide value to all parties.

Source: Adapted from information found in Alexander Haas, Ivan Snehota, and Daniela Corsaro, "Creating Value in Business Relationships: The Role of Sales," *Industrial Marketing Management* 41, no. 1 (2012), pp. 94–105.

This economic exchange involves what we call profit for both parties. Everyone knows that sellers sell to make a profit. Why do buyers buy? Typically a student will say, "To satisfy a need or a want," and that is a good basic answer. More helpful is to recognize that buyers also buy to make a profit. But they calculate profit differently. A seller's profit is selling price minus cost of goods sold and selling costs. A buyer's profit, or value, is the benefit received minus the selling price and costs and hassles of buying, or time and effort, as noted in this equation:

$$\text{Personal Value Equation} = \text{Benefits received} - (\text{Selling price} + \text{Time and effort to purchase})$$

For example, when someone buys a product from a salesperson, the buyer's profit may be higher than that obtained by buying on the Internet due to the benefits received (expert knowledge in determining the appropriate product to purchase, assistance with installation, resolution of concerns, creation of new offerings based on the buyer's specific needs, and so forth). We'll explain more about benefits in Chapter 8.

EVERYONE SELLS

This text focuses on personal selling as a business activity undertaken by salespeople. But keep in mind that the principles of selling are useful to everyone, not just people with the title of salesperson. Developing mutually beneficial, long-term relationships is vital to all of us. In fact, the author team has taught the principles in this book to many groups of nonsalespeople. Let's look at some examples of how nonsalespeople sell ideas.

As a college student, you might use selling techniques when you ask a professor to let you enroll in a course that is closed out. When you near graduation, you will certainly confront a very important sales job: selling yourself to an employer.

To get a job after graduation, you will go through the same steps used in the sales process (discussed in Part 2, Chapters 6 through 14). First you will identify some potential employers (customers). On the basis of an analysis of each employer's needs, you will develop a presentation (as well as answers to questions you might encounter) to demonstrate your ability to satisfy those needs. You might even create a video resume, as Sales Technology 1.1 describes. During the interview you will listen to what the recruiter says, ask and answer questions, and perhaps alter your presentation based on the new information you receive during the interview. At some point you might negotiate with the employer over starting salary or other issues. Eventually you will try to secure a commitment from the employer to hire you. This process is selling at a very personal level. Chapter 17 reviews the steps you need to undertake to get a sales job.

Nonsalespeople in business use selling principles all the time. Engineers convince managers to support their R&D projects, industrial relations executives use selling approaches when negotiating with unions, and aspiring management trainees sell themselves to associates, superiors, and subordinates to get raises and promotions.

It's not just businesspeople who practice the art of selling. Presidents encourage politicians in Congress to support certain programs, charities solicit contributions and volunteers to run organizations, scientists try to convince foundations and government agencies to fund research, and doctors try to get their patients to adopt more healthful lifestyles. People skilled at selling value, influencing others, and developing long-term relationships are usually leaders in our society.

VIDEO RESUMES—THE NEW WAY TO SET YOURSELF APART

Employers receive hundreds of resumes for each sales position. You may meet all of the qualifications for the job and be a great candidate, but when it comes down to it, the people who review resumes and decide who will even get a call for an interview do not have the time to read through every aspect of each individual resume. You need to set yourself apart from the rest of the competition

With a video resume, you have the chance to instill your face in their minds. And why take the risk of having your resume read a way in which you did not intend for it to be read when you can verbally tell them your qualifications and why you are a great fit for the position; this limits the chance of communication errors. Here are some tips:

Do's of Video Resumes

- Practice and prepare what you are going to say.
- Dress professionally as if you were going in for an interview.
- Envision the camera as the eyes of the person viewing your video and maintain eye contact.
- Smile, smile, smile—your nonverbal cues can send a stronger message than you think.
- Ensure that the lighting in the room is as best as possible—dim lighting can lead to poor quality and also shows lack of preparedness.

- Edit your video, this is your opportunity to make it perfect. If you're not skilled with editing, check your campus for services that may be able to help you out.
- Keep the area that is being taped to no more than a head to waist shot.
- Film against a solid color—this will help to reduce "noise."
- Make sure that you are in a quiet area and free of distractions.

Don't of Video Resumes

- Get ahead of yourself and begin speaking too fast—you are talking to your computer, you have nothing to be nervous about.
- Chew gum—again, try to treat this entire process as if you are going in to the hiring manager's office for an interview.
- Avoid filler words, such as "umm," "ahh," "like," and "you know"—these words are a waste of time and show nervousness and lack of preparation, and if "they know," why would you have to tell them?

Source: Personal experience plus "Do's and Don'ts," Internships.com, http://www.internships.com/student/resources/prep/videointro/tips, August 30, 2012.

CREATING VALUE: THE ROLE OF SALESPEOPLE IN A BUSINESS

Companies exist only when their products and services are sold. It takes skill for salespeople to uncover exactly what a customer is looking for and how a potential product or service could add such value. Because this is so critical, this topic is covered in great detail in many chapters in this book.

Companies have many options in how they can approach customers as they add value, and the various methods are sometimes called **go-to-market strategies.** Strategies include selling through the Internet, field sales representatives, business partners, resellers, manufacturer agents, franchises, telemarketers, and others. Selling firms determine which strategy to use for each customer based on such factors as the estimated value of the customer over the lifetime of the relationship, often called **customer lifetime value.**[5] (Because this concept is so important, it is more fully discussed in Chapter 14.) Organizations whose go-to-market strategies rely heavily on salespeople are called **sales force–intensive organizations.**

Exhibit 1.2
Communication Methods

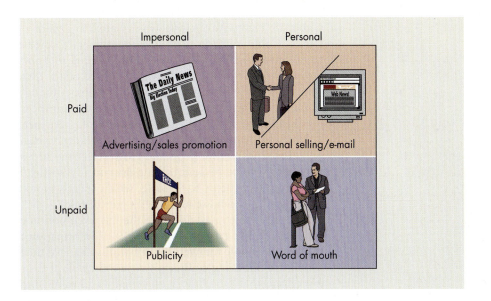

Naturally some firms use several strategies at the same time, and this is called **multichannel strategy.**[6] For example, Motorola uses the Internet for very small customers, telemarketers for midsized customers, and a field sales force for large, important customers.

Another way to view the role of salespeople in business is to realize that they are one element in the company's marketing communications program, as Exhibit 1.2 indicates.[7] Advertising uses impersonal mass media such as newspapers and TV to give information to customers, while sales promotions offer incentives to customers to purchase products during a specific period. Salespeople provide paid personal communication to customers, whereas publicity is communication through significant unpaid presentations about the firm (usually a news story). Finally, communication also occurs at no cost through word of mouth (communication among buyers about the selling firm).

Each of the communication methods in Exhibit 1.2 has strengths and weaknesses. For example, firms have more control when using paid versus unpaid methods. However, because publicity and word of mouth are communicated by independent sources, their information is usually perceived as more credible than information from paid communication sources. When using advertising, Internet sites, and sales promotions, companies can determine the message's exact content and the time of its delivery. They have less control over the communication delivered by salespeople and have very little control over the content or timing of publicity and word-of-mouth communication. Personal selling comes out on top in flexibility because salespeople can talk with each customer, discover the customer's specific needs, and develop unique presentations for that customer. Not surprisingly, personal selling is the most costly method of communication. The average cost of a sales call can be 10,000 times more expensive than exposing that single customer to a newspaper, radio, or TV ad.

Because each communication vehicle in Exhibit 1.2 has strengths and weaknesses, firms often use **integrated marketing communications,** which are communication programs that coordinate the use of various vehicles to maximize the total impact of the programs on customers.

For example, when Stouffer's introduced its new Spa Cuisine Classics, dinners that were inspired by chefs from wellness spas across the country, it used integrated marketing communications. Salespeople called on supermarkets and wholesale clubs. Advertising was created to generate awareness in consumers' minds. Coupons were offered to consumers to create interest and spur more rapid sales. Taste tests in stores were offered to build excitement and word of mouth. Publicity was generated that focused on the dinners' balance of great taste combined with the nutrition of whole grains. Although using salespeople in this example was an expensive part of the communication mix, it was important to do so to ensure that customers' precise needs were met.

Many students think—incorrectly—that advertising is the most important part of a firm's promotion program. However, many industrial companies place far more emphasis on personal selling than on advertising. Even in consumer product firms such as Procter & Gamble, which spends more than billions annually on advertising, personal selling plays a critical role.[8]

Students sometimes also have the mistaken notion that the growing world of e-commerce and the Web as a source of information are causing the demise of salespeople. While the Web has drastically changed the life of a salesperson, salespeople are not being completely replaced by all of the new technology. However, it is critical that the salesperson actually add value in this new reality.

Let's look at this from another perspective—your own life. Have you purchased anything from the Internet? Probably every student has—travel, music, clothing, books, and more. Have you noticed that, other than Internet services, everything you purchased on the Web existed in some form before the Web? Why, then, has the Web become such a ubiquitous place for commerce? Simple. The Internet makes information as well as products and services available the way the consumer wants them. Those who sell via the Web gain competitive advantage by selling the way the buyers (or at least some buyers in some situations) want to buy.

If salespeople want to sell effectively, they have to recognize that the buyer has needs that are met not only by the product but also by the selling process itself. These needs include time savings, shopping costs such as gas if they drive around, and others. Part of the salesperson's responsibility is to sell the way the buyer wants to buy.

WHAT DO SALESPEOPLE DO?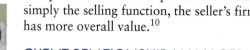

The activities of salespeople depend on the type of selling job they choose. The responsibilities of salespeople selling financial services for General Electric differ greatly from those of salespeople selling pharmaceuticals for Merck or paper products for Georgia-Pacific. Salespeople often have multiple roles to play, including client relationship manager, account team manager, vendor and channel manager, and information provider for their firms.[9] Studies have shown that when a salesperson's role encompasses more than simply the selling function, the seller's firm has more overall value.[10]

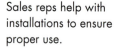
Sales reps help with installations to ensure proper use.

CLIENT RELATIONSHIP MANAGER

Sales jobs involve prospecting for new customers, making sales presentations, demonstrating products, negotiating price and delivery terms, writing orders, and increasing sales to existing customers. But these sales-generating activities (discussed in Chapters 6 through 14) are only part of the job. Although the numbers would vary greatly depending on the type of sales job, salespeople generally spend less than 50 percent of their time on-site in face-to-face meetings with customers and prospects. The rest of salespeople's time is spent in meetings, working with support people in their companies (internal selling), traveling, waiting for a sales interview, doing paperwork, and servicing customers.

Rather than buying from the lowest-cost suppliers, many buyers now are building competitive advantages by developing and maintaining close, cooperative relationships with a select set of suppliers, and salespeople play a key role in these relationships. Salespeople help customers identify problems, offering information about potential solutions and providing after-sale service to ensure long-term satisfaction. The phrase often used to describe this is **customer-centric**, which means making the customer the center of everything the salesperson does.[11] And buyers are demanding **24/7 service** (which means they expect a selling firm to be available for them 24 hours a day, 7 days a week). When salespeople fail in maintaining these relationships, the results are catastrophic. Research indicates that buyers worldwide are deserting firms they used to do business with in record numbers when their expectations are not met. For example, two-thirds of consumers surveyed cited poor service as the reason they left a provider in the last 12 months.[12]

The salesperson's job does not end when the customer places an order. Sales representatives must make sure customers get the benefits they expect from the product. Thus, salespeople work with other company employees to ensure that deliveries are made on time, equipment is properly installed, operators are trained to use the equipment, and questions or complaints are resolved quickly. Progressive selling firms like Standard Register and Johnson & Johnson's Ortho-Clinical Diagnostics are beginning to implement **six sigma selling programs,** which are designed to reduce errors introduced by the selling system to practically zero. Chapter 14 provides more insights on developing ongoing relationships through customer service.

ACCOUNT TEAM MANAGER

Salespeople also coordinate the activities within their firms to solve customer problems.[13] Many sales situations call for team selling, and studies show that salespeople who attempt to go it alone (sometimes called being "lone wolves") perform poorly, have lower job satisfaction, and have higher turnover intentions.[14] An example of team selling occurred when Dick Holder, president of Reynolds Metal Company, spent five years "selling" Campbell Soup Company on using aluminum cans for its tomato juice products. He coordinated a team of graphic designers, marketing people, and engineers that educated and convinced Campbell to use a packaging material it had never used before. Approaches for improving efficiency by working closely with other functional units in the firm are fully discussed in Chapter 16.

SUPPLY CHAIN LOGISTICS AND CHANNEL MANAGER

Sometimes it is necessary to interact with other partners and vendors to meet a customer's needs, and salespeople are often the key managers of these many relationships. With regard to **supply chain logistics**, the management of the supply chain, if a customer buys a new jet from Boeing, with features that will be added by a third-party vendor, the salesperson will need to coordinate the efforts of the vendor with Boeing. Glenn Price, who sells life and disability insurance with Northwestern Mutual, realizes the importance of working with channel partners. "Today the financial services industry is very complex, as are the needs of my clients, and I can't be all things to all people. I can, however, create a team of specialists. For areas outside of my expertise, all I have to do is identify which specialists are needed and bring them in. This approach allows me to operate at maximum efficiency while providing the highest level of expertise and service to my clients."[15]

INFORMATION PROVIDER TO THEIR FIRM

Salespeople are the eyes and ears of the company in the marketplace. For example, when Bob Meyer, a salesperson at Ballard Medical Products, was demonstrating a medical device, a surgeon commented that he could not tell whether the device was working properly because the tube was opaque. Meyer relayed this information to the vice president of engineering, and the product was redesigned, substituting a clear tube for the opaque tube.

To truly have effective impact on their organization, salespeople need to be skillful at disseminating the knowledge they have acquired from customers to

Salespeople share important market information with their boss and others in the firm.

other people in their companies. In their reporting activities, salespeople provide information to their firms about expenses, calls made, future calls scheduled, sales forecasts, competitor activities,[16] business conditions, and unsatisfied customer needs. It's not surprising, therefore, that the vice presidents of finance and manufacturing in most firms, for example, care greatly about the work and information provided by salespeople. Much of this information is now transmitted electronically to the company, its salespeople, and its customers and is contained in a **customer relationship management (CRM)** system. For example, each night salespeople at Curtin Matheson Scientific, a distributor of clinical and laboratory supplies, enter call report information and download all the ordering and shipping information for their customers from the company mainframe to their laptop computers. Chapter 16 discusses the relationship between salespeople and their companies in great detail.[17]

TYPES OF SALESPEOPLE

Almost everyone is familiar with people who sell products and services to consumers in retail outlets. Behind these retail salespeople is an army of salespeople working for commercial firms. Consider an iPad or MP3 player you might purchase in a store. To make the player, the manufacturer bought processed material, such as plastic and electronic components, from various salespeople. In addition, it purchased capital equipment from other salespeople to mold the plastic, assemble the components, and test the player. Finally, the player manufacturer bought services such as an employment agency to hire people and an accounting firm to audit the company's financial statements. The manufacturer's salespeople then sold the players to a wholesaler. The wholesaler purchased transportation services and warehouse space from other salespeople. Then the wholesaler's salespeople sold the players to a retailer.

SELLING AND DISTRIBUTION CHANNELS

As the MP3 player example shows, salespeople work for different types of firms and call on different types of customers. These differences in sales positions come from the many roles salespeople play in a firm's distribution channel. A **distribution channel** is a set of people and organizations responsible for the flow of products and services from the producer to the ultimate user. Exhibit 1.3

Exhibit 1.3
Sales Jobs and the
Distribution Channel

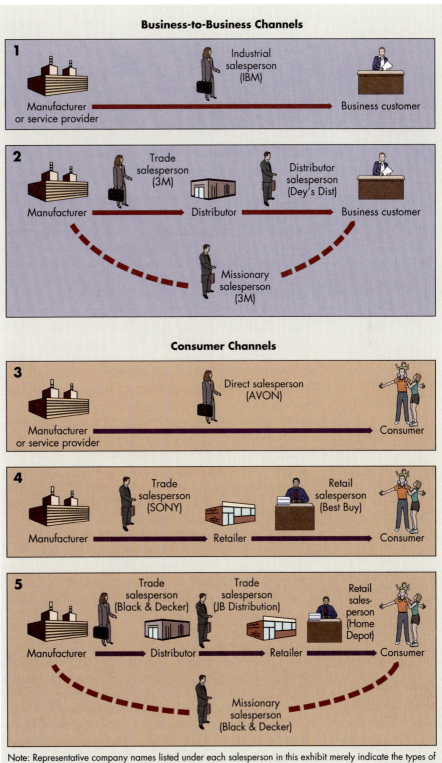

Note: Representative company names listed under each salesperson in this exhibit merely indicate the types of companies which are represented in that group.

shows the principal types of distribution channels used for business-to-business and consumer products and the varied roles salespeople play.

Business-to-Business Channels

The two main channels for producers and providers of business-to-business, or industrial, products, and services, are (1) direct sales to a business customer and (2) sales through distributors. In the direct channel, salespeople working for the manufacturer call directly on other manufacturers. For example, Nucor salespeople sell steel directly to automobile manufacturers, Dow Chemical salespeople sell plastics directly to toy manufacturers, and Nielsen salespeople sell marketing research services directly to business customers.

In the distributor channel the manufacturer employs salespeople to sell to distributors. These salespeople are referred to as **trade salespeople** because they sell to firms that resell the products (that is, they sell to the trade) rather than using them within the firm. Distributor salespeople sell products made by a number of manufacturers to businesses. For example, some Intel salespeople sell microprocessors to distributors such as Arrow Electronics, and Arrow salespeople then resell the microprocessors and other electronic components to customers such as Dell.

Many firms use more than one channel of distribution and thus employ several types of salespeople. For example, Dow Chemical has trade salespeople who call on distributors as well as direct salespeople who call on large companies.

Sales Jobs and the Distribution Channel

In the second business-to-business channel (see Exhibit 1.3), a missionary salesperson is employed. **Missionary salespeople** work for a manufacturer and promote the manufacturer's products to other firms. However, those firms buy the products from distributors or other manufacturers, not directly from the salesperson's firm. For example, sales representatives at Driltek, a manufacturer of mining equipment, call on mine owners to promote their products. The mines, however, place orders for drills with the local Driltek distributor rather than with Driltek directly. Normally missionary and local distributor salespeople work together to build relationships with customers.

Frequently missionary salespeople call on people who influence a buying decision but do not actually place the order. For example, Du Pont sales representatives call on Liz Claiborne and other clothing designers to encourage them to design garments made with Teflon, and Merck sales representatives call on physicians to encourage them to prescribe Merck pharmaceutical products.

Consumer Channels

The remaining channels shown in Exhibit 1.3 are used by producers and providers of consumer products and services. The third channel shows a firm, such as State Farm Insurance, whose salespeople sell insurance directly to consumers. The fourth and fifth channels show manufacturers that employ trade salespeople to sell to either retailers or distributors. For example, Revlon uses the fourth channel when its salespeople sell directly to Walmart. However, Revlon uses the fifth channel to sell to small, owner-operated stores through distributors. Missionary salespeople are also used in consumer channels. For example, a Black & Decker missionary salesperson may go to a Home Depot store to meet customers there and see how well Home Depot is serving its customers.

Some of the salespeople shown in Exhibit 1.3 may be manufacturers' agents. **Manufacturers' agents** are independent businesspeople who are paid a commission by a manufacturer for all products or services sold. Unlike distributors and retailers, agents never own the products. They simply perform the selling activities and then transmit the orders to the manufacturers.

DESCRIBING SALES JOBS

Descriptions of sales jobs often focus on six factors:

1. The stage of the buyer–seller relationship.
2. The salesperson's role.
3. The importance of the customer's purchase decision.
4. The location of salesperson–customer contact.
5. The nature of the offering sold by the salesperson.
6. The salesperson's role in securing customer commitment.

Stage of Buyer–Seller Relationship: New or Continuing

Some sales jobs emphasize finding and selling to new customers. Selling to prospects requires different skills than does selling to existing customers. To convince prospects to purchase a product they have never used before, salespeople need to be especially self-confident and must be able to deal with the inevitable rejections that occur when making initial contacts. On the other hand, salespeople responsible for existing customers place more emphasis on building relationships and servicing customers. For example, Lou Pritchett of Procter & Gamble, in a continuing relationship with Walmart, increased sales to Walmart from $400 million a year to over $6 billion a year by being creative and building partnerships. And the more important the buyer, the larger the group of sellers engaged in selling to that buyer. Hormel has a team of 50 who sell to Walmart in Bentonville, Arkansas.

Salesperson's Role: Taking Orders or Creating New Solutions

Some sales jobs focus primarily on taking orders. For example, most Frito-Lay salespeople go to grocery stores, check the stock, and prepare an order for the store manager to sign. However, some Frito-Lay salespeople sell only to buyers in the headquarters of supermarket chains. Headquarters selling requires a much higher level of skill and creativity. These salespeople work with buyers to develop new systems and methods and sometimes even new products to increase the retailer's sales and profits.[18] Some firms distinguish between salespeople who focus on one task versus another, as "Building Partnerships 1.1" describes.

Importance of the Purchase to the Customer

Consumers and businesses make many purchase decisions each year. Some decisions are important to them, such as purchasing a building or a computer Internet security system. Others are less crucial, such as buying candy or cleaning supplies. Sales jobs involving important decisions for customers differ greatly from sales jobs involving minor decisions. Consider a company that needs a computer-controlled drill press. Buying the drill press is a big decision. The drill press sales representative needs to be knowledgeable about the customer's needs and the features of drill presses. The salesperson will have to interact with a number of people involved in the purchase decision.

Even though many sales jobs do not involve building long-term partnerships, we stress the concept of developing partnering relationships throughout this textbook because the roles of salespeople in many companies are evolving toward a partnering orientation. As you'll see in Chapter 16, partnering orientations are important within one's own organization as well as with customers. Further, salespeople are called on to build partnerships with some accounts and other

HUNTER AND GATHERERS

There are many different types of salespeople and countless ways that they can be described. In our organization we like to classify our salespeople as either a hunter or a gatherer. A hunter can be thought of as one who is a high-energy salesperson that is the first contact with a potential customer. The hunter has skills and ability to set the foundation of a relationship for the gatherer. Once the foundation is set and the relationship has been established, the gatherer has the opportunity to go in. The gatherer's job is to now utilize the specifics that he or she knows about the potential customer and to cultivate the relationship in preparation to make sales. The gatherers ensure that they maintain a high service level with the customer and continue to build and strengthen the day-to-day relationship that they have.

Hunters in our company are expert at gaining new business leads that often come about unintentionally. For example, Philip, one of our hunters, was at a sporting event and struck up a conversation with the man sitting next to him. The conversation, naturally, started out about the hockey game they were attending. But as the game progressed, both parties started talking more and more, eventually leading to what both of them do for a living. Philip stated that he was a salesperson of industrial supplies, and immediately the other man indicated that he was a plant manager of a big account that our company had been trying to land for a while. With the new found information, we sent one of our gatherers to this man a few months later, closing the business.

There are needs for a variety of selling skills in our organization. We are glad to have both hunters and gatherers!

Source: Personal correspondence, used with permission, anonymous upon request.

Field salespeople go directly to the customer's place of business.

types of relationships with other accounts. The partnering orientation does not prevent salespeople from developing other types of relationships; rather, people who are good partners are likely to also be good at other types of relationships. Understanding partnerships is critical to understanding the professional selling process, as will become apparent as the book unfolds.

Location of Salesperson–Customer Contact: Field or Inside Sales

Field salespeople spend considerable time in the customer's place of business, communicating with the customer face-to-face. **Inside salespeople** work at their employer's location and typically communicate with customers by telephone or computer.

Field selling typically is more demanding than inside selling because the former entails more intense interactions with customers. Field salespeople are more involved in problem solving with customers, whereas inside salespeople often respond to customer-initiated requests.

thinking **it** through

Which do you think you would prefer: an inside sales job or a field sales job? What makes one more attractive to you than the other?

The Nature of the Offering Sold by the Salesperson: Products or Services

The type of benefits provided by products and services affects the nature of the sales job. Products such as chemicals and trucks typically have tangible benefits: Customers can objectively measure a chemical's purity and a truck's payload. The benefits of services, such as business insurance or investment opportunities, are more intangible: Customers cannot easily measure the riskiness of an investment.

Intangible benefits are harder to sell than tangible benefits. It is much easier to show a customer the payload of a truck than the benefits of carrying insurance.

The Salesperson's Role in Securing Customer Commitment: Information or Placing an Order

Sales jobs differ by the types of commitments sought and the manner in which they are obtained. For example, the Du Pont missionary salesperson might encourage a clothing designer to use Du Pont Teflon fibers. The salesperson might ask the designer to consider using the fiber but does not undertake the more difficult task of asking the designer to place an order. If the designer decides to use Teflon fabric in a dress, the actual order for Teflon will be secured by the fabric manufacturer salesperson, not the Du Pont salesperson.

THE SALES JOBS CONTINUUM

Exhibit 1.4 uses the factors just discussed to illustrate the continuum of sales jobs in terms of creativity. Sales jobs described by the responses in the far right column require salespeople to go into the field, call on new customers who make important buying decisions, promote products or services with intangible benefits, and seek purchase commitments. These types of sales jobs require the most creativity and skill and, consequently, offer the highest pay.

The next section examines the responsibilities of specific types of salespeople in more detail.

EXAMPLES OF SALES JOBS

The following are brief examples of several of the thousands of sales jobs that exist today. As you read each example, notice the vast differences in the type of compensation, the number of accounts, the length of an average sales call, the length of the order cycle, the need to prospect, and so forth. All are based on real salespeople and the sales jobs they got when they first graduated from college. As you read the examples, think about which would be more attractive to you personally.

Chris is a salesperson for IBM Large Systems, selling mainframe computers to organizations. She has five clients, provided to her by her company, and does no

Exhibit 1.4
Creativity Level of Sales Jobs

Factors in Sales Jobs	Lower Creativity	Higher Creativity
1. Stage of the customer–firm relationship	Existing customer	New customer
2. The salesperson's role	Order taking	Creating new solutions
3. Importance of the customer's purchase decision	Low	High
4. Location of salesperson–customer contact	Inside company	Field customer
5. Nature of the offering sold by the salesperson	Products	Services
6. Salesperson's role in securing customer commitment	Limited role	Significant role

prospecting for new accounts. She is paid a straight salary and travels by plane three to five days each week. Each visit to an account is roughly three hours long. For the first three years she had no sales. In her third year she made the largest sale in the company's history.

Lauree works for Standard Register selling business forms and document management solutions. She has 200 clients and does a good bit of searching for new accounts. She is paid salary plus commission and gets orders essentially every single day, with no overnight travel. Each visit lasts about 45 minutes.

Scott works for Pfizer, a pharmaceutical company, calling on 100 doctors to tell them about his company's drugs. He is paid a salary plus a year-end bonus and as a missionary salesperson never gets an actual order from a doctor (the patients buy the Pfizer drugs). He does no overnight travel and never searches for new accounts, and each call is about five minutes long.

Jim sells Makita power tools and serves 75 dealers. He is paid a salary plus commission and does very limited searching for new accounts. He gets orders every day and has little overnight travel. Each call is about 30 minutes long.

Jeff works for Hormel, selling refrigerated meat products as well as pantry products like canned chili, and has about 100 accounts. He does no searching for new accounts and is paid a salary plus a year-end bonus. Each call lasts about 10 minutes, and he has no overnight travel.

Niki works for MetLife, selling life, auto, home owners, long-term care, and disability insurance as well as investments (IRAs, mutual funds, annuities, and so forth). She has 250 clients, has no overnight travel, and is paid straight salary. She does a good bit of searching for new accounts, and here average first in-person sales call to a new account lasts about 30 minutes.

The next section reviews some of the skills required to be effective in the sales positions just discussed.

CHARACTERISTICS OF SUCCESSFUL SALESPEOPLE

The market is full of books and articles discussing why some people are successful in selling and others are not. Yet no one has identified the profile of the "perfect" salesperson because sales jobs are so different, as the examples just provided illustrated. In addition, each customer is unique. However, the following traits are generally associated with successful salespeople.

SELF-MOTIVATED

Salespeople work in the field without direct supervision and may be tempted to get up late, take long lunch breaks, and stop work early. But successful salespeople are self-starters who do not need the fear of an angry supervisor to get them going in the morning or to keep them working hard all day. Furthermore, successful salespeople are motivated to learn, and they work at improving their skills by analyzing their performance and using their mistakes as learning opportunities.

DEPENDABILITY AND TRUSTWORTHINESS

Customers develop long-term relationships only with salespeople who are dependable and trustworthy.[19] When salespeople say the equipment will perform in a certain way, they had better make sure the equipment performs that way! If it doesn't, the customer will not rely on them again. And dependability and trustworthiness can't just be a false front: Salespeople who are genuine and come across as authentic are better-performing salespeople. From the Buyer's Seat 1.1 illustrates the importance of building and maintaining trust.

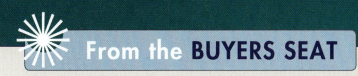

A TALE OF TWO SALESPERSONS: ONE GREAT, AND ONE...

For a salesperson to set him- or herself apart from the rest, it is crucial for one to prove to the buyer that he or she is a problem solver and is willing to be the buyer's front line with the seller's organization. Getting to know the buyer and the company is also an extremely important process for the salesperson to go through; he or she needs to know how to drill down and figure out the problem that the buyer's organization is facing and provide them with solutions to that problem. Honesty is huge when a salesperson is dealing with any buyer; any lie or false truth a salesperson may say to gain the business of the buyer will be uncovered at some point in time and will tarnish not only the relationship with that buyer but also the salesperson's credibility as a whole.

With the industry that I work in, it is essential for any salesperson to know who my end customer is. If a salesperson is able to really get to know who my end customer is and the trends that are hot in the industry, this is going to be a big factor when it comes to getting my company's business. Last but not least, to maintain a positive relationship with me as a buyer, follow-up skills are extremely important. Being able to check in and make sure that products have been received on time and that they are exactly what we had agreed on is huge. The following are two examples of recent situations I have encountered, one of which was over-the-top extraordinary and the other, well, you will find out.

First Example:

When getting ready to bring a new product in to our stores, we had all the dates set in stone for our marketing materials to be sent out to promote our new great product. We had strict terms with the manufacturer, and the product *had* to be delivered by a certain date. I received a phone call from the salesperson I had been working with, and when he said that a piece of the product had not been received at their manufacturing plant, all I could say was, "I don't care, it needs to be done; we agreed on the date, it needs to get done." Not knowing what was going to come of this, I was slightly worried. Little did I know that this salesperson went to his production manager and explained what was going on. He convinced his production manager to go to China to oversee the production of this product in order to do everything they could to get it done on time. This salesperson could have sat back and hoped that everything went alright, but he went above and beyond to do all in his power to make sure that we got our product on time—which we did!

Second Example:

Striving to carry products that consumers cannot find in other stores, we try to construct agreements with salespeople to ensure that we are the only store that will be selling certain products. When I was in a competitor's store and saw a product that I had just recently agreed to buy on their shelves, I was rather upset. I called my salesperson and asked her what was going on. She began by acting as though she had no clue what I was talking about, and finally, when we agreed that something needed to be done, I told her that I would work with her on product modifications to get the product the way I needed it to sell it in our stores. At the end of the conversation, she said, "Well, just let me know what you think we need to do." I could not believe that a salesperson would ask the buyer to solve a problem that the salesperson created in the first place. End result? No business!

Source: Personal correspondence, used with permission, anonymous upon request.

thinking it through

Take a minute and think about yourself. How dependable are you right now? Can people count on you to do what you say you will do? Or do they have to look you up and remind you of your promises? You don't start developing dependability when you graduate from college; it is something you should be working on right now. What can you do to start improving your dependability?

ETHICAL SALES BEHAVIOR

Honesty and integrity are critical for developing effective relationships. Over the long run, customers will find out who can be trusted and who cannot. Good ethics are good business.[20] Ethical sales behavior is such an important topic that much of Chapter 2 is devoted to it.

CUSTOMER AND PRODUCT KNOWLEDGE

Effective salespeople need to know how businesses make purchase decisions and how individuals evaluate product alternatives. In addition, effective salespeople need product knowledge—how their products work and how the products' features are related to the benefits customers are seeking. Chapter 3 reviews the buying process, and Chapter 5 discusses product knowledge.

ANALYTICAL SKILLS AND THE ABILITY TO USE INFORMATION TECHNOLOGY

Salespeople need to know how to analyze data and situations and use the Internet, databases, and software to effectively sell in today's marketplace.[21] **Selling analytics** is an attempt to gain insights into customers by using sophisticated data mining and analytic techniques.[22] Information technology will be discussed in every chapter in this book, and the use of analytical tools will be covered in Chapter 9 and other chapters.

COMMUNICATION SKILLS

The key to building strong long-term relationships is to be responsive to a customer's needs. To do that, the salesperson needs to be a good communicator. But talking is not enough; the salesperson must also listen to what the customer says, ask questions that uncover problems and needs, and pay attention to the responses.

To compete in world markets, salespeople need to learn how to communicate in international markets. Chapter 4 is devoted to developing communication skills, with considerable emphasis on communicating in other cultures.

FLEXIBILITY AND AGILITY

The successful salesperson realizes that the same sales approach does not work with all customers; it must be adapted to each selling situation. The salesperson must be sensitive to what is happening and agile enough to make those adaptations during the sales presentation.[23] Again, it is this flexibility that causes companies to spend so much money on personal selling instead of just advertising, which can't be tailored as easily or quickly to each individual.

CREATIVITY

Creativity is the trait of having imagination and inventiveness and using them to come up with new solutions and ideas. Sometimes it takes creativity to get an appointment with a prospect. It takes creativity to develop presentation that the buyer will long remember. It takes creativity to solve a sticky installation problem after the product is sold.

CONFIDENCE AND OPTIMISM

Successful salespeople tend to be confident about themselves, their company, and their products. They optimistically believe that their efforts will lead to success. Don't confuse confidence, however, with wishful thinking. According to research, truly confident people are willing to work hard to achieve their goals.

They are open to criticism, seek advice from others, and learn from their mistakes. They expect good things to happen, but they take personal responsibility for their fate. People who lack confidence, according to these same studies, are not honest about their own limits, react defensively when criticized, and set unrealistic goals.

Salespeople need emotional intelligence to be able to recognize customers' emotions.

EMOTIONAL INTELLIGENCE

Emotional intelligence (EI) is the ability to effectively understand and regulate one's own emotions and to read and respond to the emotions of others, and this is an important trait for salespeople.[24] EI has four aspects: (1) knowing one's own feelings and emotions as they are experienced, (2) controlling one's emotions to avoid acting impulsively, (3) recognizing customers' emotions (called empathy), and (4) using one's emotions to interact effectively with customers.[25] A recent study of over 6,000 people from a wide spectrum of industries found that good decision makers consistently score high in EI.[26] In marketing exchanges, EI is positively related to performance and retaining customers,[27] and TalentSmart notes that 90 percent of top performers have high EI.[28] Bad decisions result from a lack of EI, so it is not surprising that emotional immaturity plays a large role in many employee terminations.

What are some good first steps in improving your EI? Measure your own EI (see www.EIME-research.com) to learn where you currently stand. Learn to identify and understand your own emotions as they arise and recognize the fact that it is often in your best interest to step away from emotional situations and become more reflective. Engaging in most human interactions with just a keyboard (e.g., via texting or e-mailing) can reduce one's EI.[29]

Of course, one must realize that EI can be used in negative ways as well. People with high EI can use their skills to intimidate, manipulate, and spin outcomes to their own advantage.[30] We discuss aspects of EI as they relate to adaptive selling and effective verbal and nonverbal intelligence in Chapters 4 and 5.

ARE SALESPEOPLE BORN OR MADE?

On the basis of the preceding discussion, you can see that most of the skills required to be a successful salesperson can be learned. People can learn to work hard, plan their time, and adapt their sales approach to their customers' needs. In fact, companies show their faith in their ability to teach sales skills by spending billions of dollars each year on training programs. There is some evidence to suggest that students who take college courses in selling have higher placement rates in selling jobs.[31] The next section discusses the rewards you can realize if you develop the skills required for sales success.

REWARDS IN SELLING

Personal selling offers interesting and rewarding career opportunities. More than 8 million people in the United States currently work in sales positions, and the number of sales positions is growing. For the current number of salespeople in various types of sales jobs and to find average earnings, see the Occupational Outlook Handbook, created by the U.S. Department of Labor (www.bls.gov/ooh).

INDEPENDENCE AND RESPONSIBILITY

Many people do not want to spend long hours behind a desk, doing the same thing every day. They prefer to be outside, moving around, meeting people, and working on various problems. Selling ideally suits people with these interests. The typical salesperson interacts with dozens of people daily, and most of these contacts involve challenging new experiences.

Selling also offers unusual freedom and flexibility. It is not a nine-to-five job. Most salespeople decide how to spend their time; they do not have to report in. Long hours may be required on some days, and other days may bring fewer demands.

Because of this freedom, salespeople are like independent entrepreneurs. They have a territory to manage and few restrictions on how to do it. They are responsible for the sales and profits the territory generates. Thus, their success or failure rests largely on their own skills and efforts.[32]

FINANCIAL REWARDS

Salespeople tend to earn more money the longer they sell. Occasionally the top salespeople in a firm will even earn more than the sales executives in that firm. The average amount earned by salespeople depends somewhat on the annual revenues of the firm. Average starting salaries for students right out of college tend to range from $30,000 to $50,000, while experienced salespeople often make over $100,000 a year.[33]

The financial rewards of selling depend on the level of skill and sophistication needed to do the job. For example, salespeople who sell to businesses typically are paid more than retail salespeople. But salespeople usually don't earn overtime pay for working more than 40 hours.[34]

This young manager learned the ropes as a salesperson before moving into product management at his firm.

MANAGEMENT OPPORTUNITIES

Selling jobs provide a firm base for launching a business career. For example, Mark Alvarez started his sales career in the Medical Systems Division at General Electric (GE) selling diagnostic imaging equipment to hospitals in central Illinois. Over the years he held positions in the firm that included district and regional sales manager and product manager; at one point he had responsibility for all Medical Systems Division business in Latin America. Sixteen years later, he was in corporate marketing and was responsible for managing the relationships between GE's 39 divisions and key customers in the southeastern United States. These include such accounts as Federal Express, Disney, and Home Depot. Some of his businesses do more than $500 million worth of business with GE annually. His entry-level job in selling provided great experience for his current assignment. Many CEOs and chairmen of the board started their careers as salespeople.

THE BUILDING PARTNERSHIPS MODEL

This book is divided into three parts, as illustrated in Exhibit 1.5.

The knowledge and skills needed for successful partnerships are covered in Part 1. You will learn about the legal and ethical responsibilities of

Exhibit 1.5
The Building
Partnerships Model

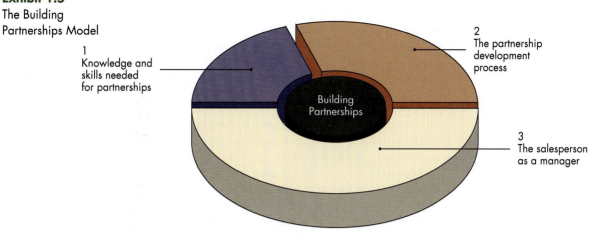

1
Knowledge and
skills needed
for partnerships

2
The partnership
development
process

Building
Partnerships

3
The salesperson
as a manager

Exhibit 1.6

Steps in the Selling
Process

Prospecting

Planning for the sales call

Making the sales call

Strengthening the presentation

Responding to objections

Obtaining commitment

Building partnering
relationships after the sale

salespeople, the buying process, the principles for communicating effectively, and methods for adapting to the unique styles and needs of each customer.

In Part 2 you will explore the partnership development process and the activities needed for this to occur. After completing this section, you should have enhanced skills and understanding about prospecting, planning, discovering needs, using visual aids and conducting demonstrations effectively, responding to objections, obtaining commitment, formally negotiating, and providing excellent after-sale service. Exhibit 1.6 provides a chart that summarizes the selling process.

Finally, Part 3 discusses the role of the salesperson as a manager. You'll learn how you can improve your effectiveness as a salesperson by managing your time and territory and by managing the relationships within your own company. This section also discusses ways to manage your career.

SELLING YOURSELF

The "Selling Yourself" sections of this book are designed to help you see the connections of the chapter material with all aspects of your life right now. Of course we're all different, with different interests and activities, so some of the examples might better fit you than others. But read them all and try to make a connection with something in your life. Selling is something you do all the time, and the ideas found in this book can help you now, not just after you graduate!

In all areas of life, we are looking to gain something from the activities we participate in and interactions we have. Whether it be convincing the elementary students you mentor to compete in the local spelling bee because you get a lot of joy seeing them succeed in an area that they previously struggled with or convincing the local deli to give you an extra pickle with your sandwich because you really love pickles, you need to give others a compelling reason to help you reach your goal. In both cases, you are simply the influencer. You have no say in the final decision. While the needs (tangible vs. intangible in this example) may be different with every interaction, the key ways to achieve your goals remain the same.

You must undercover and understand why the other party would want to help you as well as reasons why they would hesitate to work with you. In the case of your mentees, they may be excited at the prospect of competing yet don't have the self-confidence to practice and compete on their own. The deli owner may want to make a customer happy in order to get repeat business (a key technique in being successful in sales) yet may feel the crunch of rising costs and hesitate to provide more than what the price of the sandwich covers.

Once you determine this, you can start building your case of educating your customers on why they would want to work with you. In the case of your mentees, helping them put together a practice schedule and providing coaching while discussing with them the positives of participating in such event and validating their concerns would be great ways to get them to commit. In the case of the deli owner, it may be as simple of asking politely while conveying your love of pickles or tipping the cashier. You have to be invested in the outcome and willing to give something in order to reach your goal. In the case of your mentees, you have to give your time and effort to prepare them for the challenge. You may have to be a little more outgoing and chatty with the sandwich artist than you normally would when rushing to get lunch or have to wait an extra minute for that pickle.

You need to be confident and, more important, positive in your message in order to meet your goal. People are more likely to respond to and to be influenced by people who are enjoyable to be around. Your reputation usually spans more than just that one person or interaction. Your mentees may share your idea with the activity director and ask for you to mentor more students for next year's event, or the next time you go into that deli, they may have that extra pickle ready and waiting for you.

The world of business is a small one. No matter what industry or capacity you work in, word will spread about your consistent and positive techniques to help others reach their goals, and soon you will be called on to share your refreshing and innovative ideas with others. Conversely, word will spread if you are unreliable and unpleasant to work with. Whether the goal is big or small, it will take some work to meet. Make sure to choose the right attitude to reach your goal as quickly and easily as possible.

Happy selling!

Source: Amber Fischer, Rehrig Pacific, used with permission.

SUMMARY

You should study personal selling because we all use selling techniques. If you want to work in business, you need to know about selling because salespeople play a vital role in business activities. Finally, you might become a salesperson. Selling jobs are inherently interesting because of the variety of people encountered and activities undertaken. In addition, selling offers opportunities for financial rewards and promotions.

Salespeople engage in a wide range of activities, including providing information about products and services to customers and employees within their firms. Most of us are not aware of many of these activities because the salespeople we meet most frequently work in retail stores. However, the most exciting, rewarding, and challenging sales positions involve building partnerships: long-term, win–win relationships with customers.

The specific duties and responsibilities of salespeople depend on the type of selling position. But most salespeople engage in various tasks in addition to influencing customers. These tasks include managing customer relations, serving as the account team manager for their firm, managing the relationships with vendor and channel members, and providing information to their firm.

Sales jobs can be classified by the roles salespeople and their firms play in the channel of distribution. The nature of the selling job is affected by whom salespeople work for and whether they sell to manufacturers, distributors, or retailers. Other factors affecting the nature of selling jobs are the customer's relationship to the salesperson's firm, the salesperson's duties, the importance of the buying decision to the customer, where the selling occurs, the tangibility of the benefits considered by the customer, and the degree to which the salesperson seeks a commitment from customers.

Research on the characteristics of effective salespeople indicates that many different personality types can be successful in sales. However, successful salespeople do share some common characteristics. They are self-motivated, dependable, ethical, knowledgeable, good communicators, flexible, creative, confident, and emotionally intelligent. They also have good analytical skills and aren't afraid of technology.

KEY TERMS

creativity   18
customer-centric   9
customer lifetime value (CLV)   6
customer relationship management (CRM)   10
customer value proposition   4
distribution channel   10
emotional intelligence (EI)   19
field salespeople   14
go-to-market strategies   6
inside salespeople   14
integrated marketing communications   7

manufacturers' agents   11
missionary salespeople   11
multichannel strategy   7
personal selling   4
sales force–intensive organization   6
selling analytics   18
six sigma selling programs   9
supply chain logistics   9
trade salespeople   11
24/7 service   9
value   4

ETHICS PROBLEMS

1. Let's say you have excellent emotional intelligence. How can you avoid using that to your advantage if it is detrimental to the buyer (e.g., if you manipulate the buyer based on your skills)?

2. The chapter says that selling jobs can be a great way to get your foot in the door at an employer. Let's say you really want to be in product development, not sales, yet the position that is being offered at the company is in sales. You hope that after doing the sales job for six months to a year you'll get promoted to the product development job. Should you be honest and tell the interviewer (the sales manager) that now? Or should you act as though you want to be a career salesperson?

QUESTIONS AND PROBLEMS

1. There are many different go-to-market strategies. For which of the following products and services do you think a sales force–intensive strategy would probably not be used? Why? Make any assumptions needed and list your assumptions in your answer.
   a. Movie rentals.
   b. Home air-conditioning maintenance service.
   c. Shredding service for sensitive documents.
   d. Solar-powered compactor garbage cans for city use on city streets (the specially designed cans actually compact the garbage that is thrown into the can four times a day, using energy from the sun, reducing the number of times the can needs to be emptied).

2. In "Building Partnerships 1.1" you read how the company has hunters and gatherers. Which type of position appeals to you the most? Why?

3. Comment on each of the following statements:
   a. Salespeople rip people off.
   b. Salespeople are born, not made.
   c. Selling is just a big bag of tricks.
   d. A salesperson should never take no for an answer.
   e. A good salesperson can sell anything to anybody.

4. Carly Anderson has been working as a receptionist at her father's business for two years since graduating from college. She is considering taking a selling job with a pharmaceutical company. The job involves calling on doctors and explaining the benefits of the firm's products. What are the similarities and differences between her receptionist job and the selling job she is considering?

5. Nick Chattaway worked his way through college by selling home theater systems at Best Buy. He has done well on the job and is one of the top salespeople in the home electronics department. Last week Safety Harness Inc. offered him a job selling seat belt kits to school bus manufacturers. Explain the differences between selling in a consumer electronics store and the Safety Harness Inc. sales job.

6. Poll at least five students who are not taking your selling course (and who, better yet, are outside the business school or program). What are their opinions about salespeople? How accurate are their opinions based on what you've read in this chapter?

7. Think about what you want in your first job out of college. Based on what you know so far from this chapter, how well does selling match your desires in a job?

8. According to the text, some sales jobs are located as inside sales instead of field sales. Why would anyone want to be an inside sales rep?

9. "Sales Technology 1.1" described the use of video resumes to set yourself apart. Create a video resume for yourself and make it available to your instructor.

10. Assume you are a sales manager and you need to recruit someone for the following sales positions. For each position, list the qualities you would want in the recruit:
    a. Salesperson selling custom signage to small businesses.
    b. Salesperson calling on college bookstores, selling university logo backpacks.
    c. Used tractor salesperson.
    d. Salesperson selling janitorial services to a small local restaurant.

CASE PROBLEMS

case **1.1**

Chicago Blackhawks

Emily Hightower has been sales manager for Corporate Hospitality sales at the Chicago Blackhawks for the last three years. The Stanley Cup–winning Blackhawks are a National Hockey League franchise located in Chicago, Illinois. Blackhawks Corporate Hospitality is a unique way for businesses to entertain prospective clients or treat important customers to a special night out. The 20-person Executive Suites and 40- and 80-person Super Suites provide outstanding, panoramic views of the ice surface and can be rented on a per-game basis or a season basis. The all-inclusive packages (i.e., tickets to the event, parking passes, food and beverage, a private suite attendant, theater-style seating, easy access to elevators, multiple flat-screen televisions, and so on) make entertaining clients a breeze.

When Emily was promoted to the sales manager position, there were three full-time salespeople who called on businesses in the region. One quit right after she arrived, and Zach, a knowledgeable sports marketer with excellent connections in the business community, was hired as a replacement. Zach has been a real asset to the organization, building business in the financial and investment business community.

Emily thought everything was going smoothly until yesterday, when Chad, another salesperson, dropped a bombshell. He turned in his notice because he said he got a lucrative offer from the Chicago Bulls.

Emily sat in her office, mulling over the situation and halfheartedly working on the job description for Chad's position, when one of her most trusted administrative assistants, Amanda, walked in. After they chatted for a few minutes, the following conversation ensued:

Amanda: So why do you need a salesperson anyway? Why not just use our Web page to give prospective clients the information they need?

Emily: We have to have a salesperson, Amanda. I mean, there's always been three salespeople in our office.

Amanda: But I'm asking you to think outside the dots, Emily. Why do we need them? They cost the company a lot of money that we could save by just relying on Web advertising. Besides, the Chicago Blackhawks are already well known. There's no need for salespeople. The Blackhawks sell themselves!

The conversation continued in this vein for a few minutes, then Amanda left to work on some scheduling disputes. Emily sat there, thinking about what Amanda said. Who knows? Maybe Amanda had a good idea.

Questions

1. What impact would dropping one or more salespeople have on the Chicago Blackhawks Corporate Hospitality sales? You might want to review the section titled "What Do Salespeople Do?" as you answer this question.

2. If you were Emily, what would you do? Why?

case 1.2

Motion Industries, Inc.

Brandon Williams is a salesperson for J. B. Hunt Trucking. For the past three or four months, he has tried to get in to see Chris Menton, a transportation specialist at Motion Industries, Inc. Motion Industries is a large distributor, specializing in the sales of bearings and power transmission products. They distribute industrial MRO (maintenance, repair, and operation replacement) parts and have access to more than 4.3 million parts through 501 locations. Motion Industries also has over 40 repair and service centers that are fully equipped to handle field services, repairs, and modifications. Parts are transported between the various Motion Industries locations as well as to the final customer, using trucking companies as well as UPS and the U.S. Postal Service.

Brandon knows that Motion Industries uses the services of a number of trucking companies, and he would like Chris to consider adding J. B. Hunt as one of its primary transportation suppliers. J. B. Hunt uses state-of-the-art technology that offers customers real-time data to help them make real-time decisions about transportation. J. B. Hunt has won a number of awards for its outstanding supply chain visibility and offers the same stellar service regardless of the size of the buying organization.

Brandon has never actually been able to talk to Chris, not even for a few seconds. His voice mail is all he has ever gotten when making phone calls to Chris. Visits in person have resulted in Chris's secretary just taking Brandon's card and telling him that Chris will call if he is interested. Brandon is now under pressure from his sales manager because Brandon has placed Motion Industries Valley on his prospect list for the last three months and has nothing to show for all his efforts.

Questions

1. One of the skills that salespeople should possess is creativity. Come up with three creative and totally ethical methods Brandon can use to get Chris's attention.
2. Assume that Brandon does get Chris's attention with one of the methods you've described and Chris is willing to speak with Brandon on the phone the next time he is called. What should Brandon plan on saying, assuming that he has just two or three minutes of phone time?

ROLE PLAY CASE

At the end of each chapter, beginning just below this paragraph, you'll find a short role play exercise that focuses on the product NetSuite. NetSuite is a leading contact management software package. Contact management software is a form of software designed to help salespeople increase their productivity by helping them keep track of the customers they call. In addition to a calendar that tells them when to call on an account, the software can track account information concerning what has been bought, when it was bought, the decision-making process, and even personal information about each person in the account. In addition, sales managers can generate reports automatically when reps upload information to the company network. Reps don't have to type as many reports as they would otherwise, such as sales forecasts and call reports. Further, the system can tie into the company's ordering system, which helps save the salesperson paperwork time. You can learn more about NetSuite from its Web page: www.netsuite.com.

Congratulations, you've just graduated from college! Unfortunately you focused so much on your studies that you have not interviewed for any jobs. You moved back home, but you keep in touch with the school's Career Services Center, where you saw a job posting for NetSuite. Apparently it is some sort of software for salespeople. You've not had any serious interviews, so you thought you'd sign up. Today is your interview. Be yourself; interview honestly as if you were truly talking with NetSuite. To help you prepare for this job interview role play, you may want to take some time to find out about NetSuite by visiting www.netsuite.com for more information.

To the instructor: Additional information needed to complete the role play is available in the Instructor's Manual.

ADDITIONAL REFERENCES

Barnes, Cindy, Helen Blake, and David Pinder. *Creating and Delivering Your Value Proposition: Managing Customer Experience for Profit*. Philadelphia, PA: Kogan Page, 2009.

Bosworth, Michael T., John R. Holland, and Frank Visgatis. *CustomerCentric Selling*. McGraw-Hill, 2009.

Bradberry, Travis. *Emotional Intelligence 2.0*. TalentSmart: Har/Dig En edition, 2009.

Chan, Kimmy Wa, Chi Kin (Bennett) Yim, and Simon S. K. Lam. "Is Customer Participation in Value Creation a Double-Edged Sword? Evidence from Professional Financial

Services across Cultures." *Journal of Marketing* 74, no. 3 (May 2010), pp. 48–64.

Fox, Jeffrey J. *How to Be a Fierce Competitor: What Winning Companies and Great Managers Do in Tough Times.* Hoboken, NJ: Jossey-Bass, 2010.

Geigenmüller, A., and L. Greschuchna. "How to Establish Trustworthiness in Initial Service Encounters." *Journal of Marketing Theory and Practice* 19, no. 4 (2011), pp. 391–406.

Guenzi, Paolo, Luigi M. De Luca, and Gabriele Troilo. "Organizational Drivers of Salespeople's Customer Orientation and Selling Orientation." *Journal of Personal Selling and Sales Management* 31, no. 3 (Summer 2011), pp. 269–85.

Hackett, Joshua, and Dana Tebow. *Emotional intelligence: Complete Guide to Improving Your Emotional Intelligence.* Blue Shift Publishing, 2012.

Hansen, John D., Tanuja Singh, Dan C. Weilbaker, and Rodrigo Guesalaga. "Cultural Intelligence in Cross-Cultural Selling: Propositions and Directions for Future Research." *Journal of Personal Selling and Sales Management* 31, no. 3 (Summer 2011), pp. 243–54.

Hasson, Gil. *Brilliant Emotional Intelligence.* Pearson Life, 2012.

Heilman, T. "Implementing 'Extreme' Customer Service." *Evaluation Engineering* 48, no. 11 (November 2009), pp. 14–19.

Hsieh, Ming-Huei, and Wen-Chiung Chou. "Managing Key Account Portfolios across the Process of Relationship Development: A Value Proposition-Desired Value Alignment Perspective." *Journal of Business-to-Business Marketing* 18, no. 1 (January 2011), pp. 83–119.

Jambulingam, T., R. Kathuria, and J. Nevin. "Fairness-Trust-Loyalty Relationship under Varying Conditions of Supplier-Buyer Interdependence." *Journal of Marketing Theory and Practice* 19, no. 1 (2011), pp. 39–56.

Jaramillo, Fernando, Douglas B. Grisaffe, Lawrence B. Chonko, and James A. Roberts. "Examining the Impact of Servant Leadership on Salesperson's Turnover Intention." *Journal of Personal Selling and Sales Management* 29, no. 4 (Fall 2009), pp. 351–66.

Jelinek, Ronald, and Michael Ahearne. "Be Careful What You Look For: The Effect of Trait Competitiveness and Long Hours on Salesperson Deviance and Whether Meaningfulness of Work Matters." *Journal of Marketing Theory and Practice* 18, no. 4 (2010), pp. 303–21.

Krasnikov, Alexander, Satish Jayachandran, and V. Kumar. "The Impact of Customer Relationship Management Implementation on Cost and Profit Efficiencies: Evidence from the U.S. Commercial Banking Industry." *Journal of Marketing* 73, no. 6 (2009), pp. 61–76.

Kumar, V., and Bharath Rajan. "Nurturing the Right Customers: By Measuring and Improving Customer Lifetime Value, You'll Be Able to Grow Your Most Profitable Customers." *Strategic Finance* 91, no. 3 (2009), pp. 27–33.

Le Meunier-FitzHugh, Kenneth, and Nigel F. Piercy. "Exploring the Relationship between Market Orientation and Sales and Marketing Collaboration." *Journal of Personal Selling and Sales Management* 31, no. 3 (Summer 2011), pp. 287–296.

Lytle, Chris. *The Accidental Salesperson: How to Take Control of Your Sales Career and Earn the Respect and Income You Deserve.* New York: AMACOM, 2012.

McKee, Judy. *The Sales Survival Guide: Your Powerful Interactive Guide to Sales Success and Financial Freedom.* Bloomington, IN: AuthorHouse, 2009.

Menguc, Bulent, Seigyoung Auh, and Young Chan Kim. "Salespeople's Knowledge-Sharing Behaviors with Coworkers outside the Sales Unit." *Journal of Personal Selling and Sales Management* 31, no. 2 (Spring 2011), pp. 103–22.

Newell, S., J. Belonax, M. McCardle, and R. Plank. "The Effect of Personal Relationship and Consultative Task Behaviors on Buyer Perceptions of Salesperson Trust, Expertise, and Loyalty." *Journal of Marketing Theory and Practice* 19, no. 3 (2011), pp. 307–16.

Piercy, Nigel F. "Strategic Relationships between Boundary-Spanning Functions: Aligning Customer Relationship Management with Supplier Relationship Management." *Industrial Marketing Management* 38, no. 8 (November 2009), pp. 857–64.

Poujol, F. Juliet, and John F. Tanner. "The Impact of Contests on Salespeople's Customer Orientation: An Application of Tournament Theory." *Journal of Personal Selling and Sales Management* 30, no. 1 (Winter 2010), pp. 33–46.

Rich, David. "Create Your Own Upturn: A Shift from Managing Volume to Managing Relationships." *CRM Magazine* 13, no. 10 (2009), pp. 14–15.

Rouzies, Dominique, et al. "Determinants of Pay Levels and Structures in Sales Organizations." *Journal of Marketing* 73, no. 6 (2009), pp. 92–104.

Rust, Roland T., Christine Moorman, and Gaurav Bhalla. "Rethinking Marketing." *Harvard Business Review* 88, no. 1 (2010), pp. 94–101.

Stanley, Colleen, and Jill Konrath. *Emotional Intelligence for Sales Success: Connect with Customers and Get Results.* AMACOM, 2012.

Stanton, Michael, Catherine Dixon, and Tanya Back. *The Graduate's Guide to Sales.* Lilburn, GA: Fairmont Publishing, 2012.

Stein, Steve, and Liam O'Brien. *The EQ Edge: Emotional Intelligence and Your Success.* Newark, NJ: Audible, Inc., 2012.

Tähtinen, Jaana, and Keith Blois. "The Involvement and Influence of Emotions in Problematic Business Relationships." *Industrial Marketing Management* 40, no. 6 (2011), pp. 907–18.

Taulli, T. "Three Steps to a Sound Business Model." *BusinessWeek Online* 19 (March 2, 2009).

Temkin, Bruce. "7 Keys to Customer Experience: Big-Picture Advice for How to Improve the Customer Experience over the Next Year." *CRM Magazine* 13, no. 12 (2009), p. 12.

Thomson, D. "Essential No. 2: Redefine Your Market." *BusinessWeek Online* 17 (November 16, 2009).

Thomson, D. "No. 1: The Breakthrough Value Proposition." *BusinessWeek Online* 7 (November 9, 2009).

Walton, David. *Introducing Emotional Intelligence: A Practical Guide.* London: Icon Books, 2013.

Weinstein, Art. *Superior Customer Value: Strategies for Winning and Retaining Customers.* 3rd ed. New York: CRC Press, 2012.

Weinstein, Luke, and Ryan Mullins. "Technology Usage and Sales Teams: A Multilevel Analysis of the Antecedents of Usage." *Journal of Personal Selling and Sales Management* 32, no. 2 (2012), pp. 245–60.

Wieseke, Jan, Florian Kraus, Michael Ahearne, and Sven Mikolon. "Multiple Identification Foci and Their Countervailing Effects on Salespeople's Negative Headquarters Stereotypes." *Journal of Marketing* 76, no. 3 (2012), pp. 1–20.

chapter **2**

ETHICAL AND LEGAL ISSUES IN SELLING

SOME QUESTIONS ANSWERED IN THIS CHAPTER ARE

- Why do salespeople need to develop their own codes of ethics?
- Which ethical responsibilities do salespeople have toward themselves, their firms, and their customers?
- Do ethics get in the way of being a successful salesperson?
- What guidelines should salespeople consider when confronting situations involving an ethical issue?
- Which laws apply to personal selling?

PROFILE

I've always tried to put myself in the customer's shoes—how would I react as a customer to a statement made by the salesperson? What would I want? The only thing that matters is solving their problem—solve their problem, and your problems will be solved.

After 30 years as a salesperson, I'm retiring. Looking back over the years, I have to say that rarely did any pressure to do anything unethical really come from someone else. Most of the time, temptations seem to take shape because of pressure I could put on myself—answer a question when I didn't know the answer so I wouldn't look stupid, offer a solution that wouldn't really fit because I needed a sale, those types of pressures. But customers want the truth, and they want solutions. I quickly learned it was okay to say, "I don't know; let me research that question and get back to you." And when they trust you in the small things, they will put their trust in you for the big things.

Only once was I asked to do something that I couldn't—or rather wouldn't—do. I worked for a company with a reputation for being truthful, but in this instance, I was told to tell the customer something that just wasn't the truth. So I said to my boss, "There's the line. I don't cross it for you, this company, or anybody because this customer trusts me. Am I clear?" Shortly after, I got laid off. My attitude then, though, is the same as it is now. If it costs me, it costs me, but in the long run, it will come back to me. What I want to come back to me are good things.

A successful career in sales is built on a three-legged stool: the customer, the company, and the salesperson. The needs of all three should be balanced, and you have to keep in mind that you are in business for the long haul. It's not about making today's sale only—treat one of those three badly, and your business will suffer for a long time.

With Teradata, my one account has been FedEx, but I've sold to FedEx over my entire sales career while working for several companies. Things haven't always been peaches and cream; sometimes, no matter how hard we tried, we didn't get everything right. Once while working for another company, a FedEx manager got so mad that he told another person to escort me out, that he didn't want to talk to me even though I was standing right there. So I stepped in front of him and said, "Jimmy, I'm here to take my beating. Now can we get that over with so I can start fixing the problem?" For 90 minutes, he let me have it. But what he learned was that he could count on me to make it right because that's what I did.

A year ago, I told my boss I was going to retire and wanted them to have plenty of time to make a smooth transition. We hired someone in March to take my place, giving me about five months. Then in April, we told the customer and introduced the new account executive.

What's unusual is that when I mentioned my retirement to Rachel Harvey, assistant to Rob Carter, the chief information officer (CIO) and probably the most important person at FedEx for me, the two of them decided to organize my retirement luncheon. Once they had their plans in place, they asked me who I'd like to invite from Teradata, and along with my wife, we enjoyed a luncheon at a very nice restaurant with about 25 executive and senior FedEx vice presidents and others.

Rob gave everyone a nice and sincere history of my work and the impact on FedEx. As Rob said, "We always knew Jim bled purple" (the FedEx color). That was the highest compliment he could give, and he went on to say, "You always do the right thing for FedEx." Rob and I worked together from his time as director to now executive vice president and CIO. Then he presented me with a model Boeing 777, hand carved in wood and painted with the FedEx logo. He had autographed it, as had Fred Smith, the CEO. "We don't do this for everybody—this is very rare and very special."

The thing is, this type of tribute came about because I was always trying to do the right thing. And when you do that, sales can make for a wonderful career.

ETHICS AND SELLING

February 16, 2010: On the front page of the *Wall Street Journal* are four articles, two of which deal with business people acting unethically and probably illegally. One article focuses on a man who sold dreams of moving to America to Dutch dairy farmers, bilking them of millions. The other article centers on a plan to convince terminally ill individuals to purchase an investment product that pays the seller on the death of the patient. In return, the patient receives an upfront fee.[1] If all you ever saw about salespeople was that front page, you'd conclude that salespeople are all crooks. The reality, though, is that most sales transactions are aboveboard and free of ethical questions. These two stories are news precisely because such behavior is rare.

Ethics are the principles governing the behavior of an individual or a group. These principles establish appropriate behavior indicating what is right and wrong. Defining the term is easy, but determining what the principles are is difficult. What one person thinks is right another may consider wrong. For example, 58 percent of sales managers in one poll report believing that sales contests between salespeople do not generate unethical behavior—such as asking customers to take unwanted orders and then returning the merchandise after the contest is over—but 42 percent do believe that unethical behaviors are a consequence of sales contests.[2] So the feelings and experiences of sales managers are mixed when it comes to a commonly accepted practice.

What is ethical can vary from country to country and from industry to industry. For example, offering bribes to overcome bureaucratic roadblocks may be an accepted practice in Middle Eastern countries but is considered unethical and illegal in the United States. Further, while prevailing religions may influence ethics beliefs and practices, regional differences can occur. Both Egypt and Turkey, for example, are populated almost entirely by Muslims, yet in Egypt, the courteousness of the salesperson is an important indicator of ethical practices. Not so in Turkey, which is more like the United States in not placing so much emphasis on courtesy; rather, actual customer service is preferred.[3]

An ethical principle can change over time. For example, some years ago doctors and lawyers who advertised their services were considered unethical. Today such advertising is accepted as common practice. Similarly, providing free pens and other gifts to doctors was once considered standard business practice; now a growing number of doctors consider the practice unethical and have even banned some companies from their offices or medical centers.[4] In fact, the American Medical Association suggests that only gifts that benefit patients can be received. While that opinion can leave a lot of room for interpretation, the purpose is clear: gifts that benefit only the doctor are considered unethical.

THE EVOLUTION OF SELLING

The selling function has been a part of humankind since the beginning, perhaps when one person traded meat for berries. With the arrival of the Industrial Revolution in the 1800s, companies began to make more goods more cheaply. Even so, demand outstripped supply, and for many companies, the key issue in selling was to make people aware of the product and what it could do. Forward-thinking companies such as NCR and Singer Sewing Machines hired salespeople, called drummers or peddlers, and sent them across the country to sell. Then the companies brought the most effective salespeople back into the company office and wrote down their sales pitches. These **canned sales pitches** were distributed

Exhibit 2.1
The Evolution of
Personal Selling

	Production	Sales	Marketing	Partnering
Time Period	Before 1930	1930 to 1960	1960 to 1990	After 1990
Objective	Making sales	Making sales	Satisfying customer needs	Building relationships
Orientation	Short-term seller needs	Short-term seller needs	Short-term customer needs	Long-term customer and seller needs
Role of Salesperson	Provider	Persuader	Problem solver	Value creator
Activities of Salespeople	Taking orders, delivering goods	Aggressively convincing buyers to buy products	Matching available offerings to buyer needs	Creating new alternatives, matching buyer needs with seller capabilities

to all salespeople, who were expected to follow the scripts every time without deviation.

Since that time things have changed greatly. The nature of business evolved, necessarily changing how people sell. Exhibit 2.1 illustrates how the role of the salesperson has evolved from taking orders through persuading customers to building partnerships.[5]

As Exhibit 2.1 shows, the orientations of salespeople emerged in different periods. However, all these selling orientations still exist in business today. For example, inbound telephone salespeople working for retailers like Lands' End and Spiegel are providers with a production orientation. They answer a toll-free number and simply take orders. Many outbound telephone, real estate, and insurance salespeople are persuaders with a sales orientation. Partnering-oriented selling is becoming more common as companies make strategic choices about the type of selling best suited to their situation, but recent research indicates that even within partnerships, there are times when the buyer needs to hear persuasive messages that might be scripted.[6]

Even so, the move from a production orientation to a partnering orientation has affected the ethical perspective of the sales profession. The marketing orientation has created a customer-focused perspective that increases awareness of the buyer's needs. This customer awareness naturally leads to a less selfish seller and increases the importance of ethics. Further, the partnering orientation of the current period means long-term relationships are the norm. Salespeople who are less than ethical get caught in long-term relationships. The era of the peddler who can leave town and dupe the citizens of the next town is over.

ETHICS AND PARTNERING RELATIONSHIPS

Ethical principles are particularly important in personal selling. Most businesses try to develop long-term, mutually beneficial relationships with their customers. Salespeople are the official representatives of their companies, responsible for developing and maintaining these relationships, which are built on trust. Partnerships

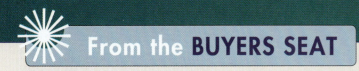

From the BUYERS SEAT

CLOSE ENCOUNTERS OF THE ETHICAL KIND

Most purchasing professionals don't often see blatant unethical behavior. Yes, they can quickly pierce through puffery, and sometimes they'll get a gift that raises an eyebrow, but by and large, most say that they usually encounter ethical salespeople.

As Rick Carlysle, regional contracts administrator for Granite Construction, says, setting the bar high by building a reputation for doing business in an ethical fashion stops many of the blatant unethical behaviors. "Dealings with other companies have been better than I thought they would be. Contractors in New York may not have the greatest image, but I've not had any under-the-table dealings and not seen anything funny. But that's likely to be as much due to our reputation, and when you have a reputation for being honest and ethical, you attract like-minded companies."

Ed Braig, purchasing director for Central Texas Iron Works, agrees. "Salespeople don't get a second chance. If they lie, that's it." Once you have a reputation for not putting up with unethical behavior, he believes you get better treatment in every category—better product, better pricing, and better service.

Some companies seek out ethical partners that share similar values. These similar values are important in building a partnering relationship. Mike Chuchmuch, an executive with Chevron, says, "One area of focus [for Chevron] is determining which companies operate in a manner that reflects our values and principles. We look for companies with a visible history of integrity, trust, diversity, ingenuity, protecting people and the environment, and delivering consistent high performance. We look for examples of these characteristics in those new companies we speak with as well as those with which we have history."

Buyers, individually and as organizations, want relationships with ethical people and organizations. They shed those of questionable reputation and concentrate on those who are trustworthy.

between buyers and sellers cannot develop when salespeople behave unethically or illegally.[7] Further, research shows that trust deteriorates rapidly even in well-established relationships if integrity becomes questionable.[8] As noted in "From the Buyer's Seat 2.1," companies and buyers seek out ethical salespeople and the companies they represent because they want relationships with trustworthy partners.

Legal principles guide business transactions. The issues governing buying and selling are typically straightforward when the transaction is simple and the purchase is a one-time deal. The terms and conditions can be well defined and easily written into a traditional contract. In longer-term relationships, though, legal principles cannot cover all behaviors between buyer and seller.

Ethical principles become increasingly important as firms move toward longer-term relationships. Many issues cannot be reduced to contractual terms. For example, a salesperson might make a concession for a buyer with a special problem, anticipating that the buyer will reciprocate on future orders. Yet there is no legal obligation for the buyer to do so; this type of give-and-take is exactly why trust is such an important part of relationships. Because of the high levels of investment and uncertainty, the parties in these relationships cannot accurately assess the potential benefits—the size of the pie—accruing from strategic investments in the relationships or the contributions of each party in producing those benefits. Thus, the parties in a longer-term relationship have to trust one another to divide the pie fairly. Further, many business settings require that the pie be divided among several suppliers or subcontractors, as well as with the customer.

A basic principle of ethical selling is that the customer remains free to make a choice. **Manipulation** eliminates or reduces the buyer's choice unfairly. Salespeople can persuade; but with **persuasion,** one may influence the buyer's decision, but the decision remains the buyer's. Manipulation is unethical; persuasion is not. Keep that difference in mind as you read the rest of this chapter.

Here are some examples of difficult situations that salespeople face:

- Should you give an expensive Christmas gift to your biggest customer?
- If a buyer tells you it is common practice to pay off purchasing agents to get orders in his or her country, should you do it?
- Is it acceptable to use a high-pressure sales approach when you know your product is the best for the customer's needs?
- Is it okay to *not* share information about your product that could cost you a sale?
- How do you handle a customer who has been lied to about your product by one of your competitors?

thinking it through
How would you respond to the situations in the preceding list? Why? How do you think your friends and your family would respond?

FACTORS INFLUENCING THE ETHICAL BEHAVIOR OF SALESPEOPLE

Exhibit 2.2 illustrates the factors that affect the ethical behavior of salespeople. The personal needs of salespeople, the needs of their companies and customers, company policies, the values of significant others, and the salesperson's personal code of ethics affect ethical choices.[9]

Personal, Company, and Customer Needs

Exhibit 2.3 shows how the personal needs of salespeople can conflict with needs of their firms and their customers. Both the salesperson's company and its customers want to make profits. But sometimes these objectives are conflicting. For example, should a salesperson tell a customer about problems his or her firm is having with a new product? Concealing this information might help make a sale, increase the company's profits, and enhance the salesperson's chances of getting a promotion and a bonus, but doing so could also decrease the customer's profits when the product does not perform adequately.

Companies need to make sales, and that need can drive some unethical behavior. One salesperson was recently asked by his boss to bid on a project that required all of the work to be done locally. Yet he knew that his company planned to have some of the work done in India. The CEO's justification was that the company needed the business, and the customer was going to get a better price. The sales rep decided to not bid the job and told the CEO that he didn't. Fortunately for him, the CEO did not get upset.

Resolving serious ethical problems is difficult, but companies that resolve ethical issues well experience many benefits. Research shows that a positive ethical climate is related to job satisfaction, commitment to the organization, and intention to stay among salespeople—especially better-performing salespeople.[10] Organizations that have a positive ethical climate also have salespeople more committed to meeting the organization's goals.

Exhibit 2.2
Factors Affecting Ethical
Behavior of Salespeople

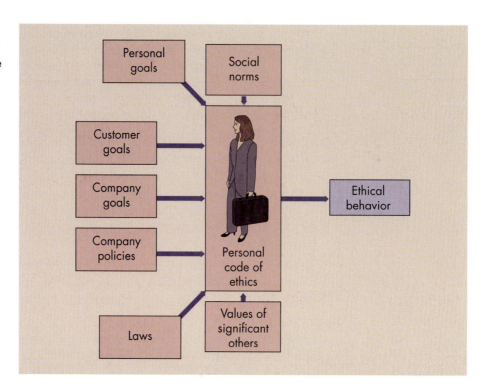

Exhibit 2.3
Conflicting Objectives

Company Objectives	Salesperson Objectives	Customer Objectives
Increase profits	Increase compensation	Increase profits
Increase sales	Receive recognition	Solve problems, satisfy needs
Reduce sales costs	Satisfy customers	Reduce costs
Build long-term customer relationships	Build long-term customer relationships	Build relationships with suppliers
Avoid legal trouble	Maintain personal code of ethics	Avoid legal trouble

Ethical conflicts often are not covered by company policies and procedures, and managers may not be available to provide advice. Thus, salespeople must make decisions on their own, relying on their ethical standards and understanding of the laws governing these situations.

Company Policies

To maintain good relationships with their companies and customers, salespeople need to have a clear sense of right and wrong so their companies and customers can depend on them when questionable situations arise. Many companies have codes of ethics for their salespeople to provide guidelines in making ethical decisions. An outline of Motorola's policy appears in Exhibit 2.4. Shell's ethics policy, however, is a book some 20 pages long! HP requires salespeople to take annual training courses regarding company policies, as well as laws and regulations, to ensure that they make informed decisions regarding ethics issues.

Values of Significant Others

People acquire their values and attitudes about what is right and wrong from the people they interact with and observe. Some important people influencing the

Exhibit 2.4

Ethics Policy for
Motorola Salespeople

Improper Use of Company Funds and Assets

The funds and assets of Motorola may not be used for influential gifts, illegal payments of any kind, or political contributions, whether legal or illegal.

The funds and assets of Motorola must be properly and accurately recorded on the books and records of Motorola.

Motorola shall not enter into, with dealers, distributors, agents, or consultants, any agreements that are not in compliance with U.S. laws and the laws of any other country that may be involved, or that provide for the payment of a commission or fee that is not commensurate with the services to be rendered.

Customer/Supplier/Government Relationships

Motorola will respect the confidence of its customers. Motorola will respect the laws, customs, and traditions of each country in which it operates but, in so doing, will not engage in any act or course of conduct that may violate U.S. laws or its business ethics. Employees of Motorola shall not accept payments, gifts, gratuities, or favors from customers or suppliers.

Conflict of Interest

A Motorola employee shall not be a supplier or a competitor of Motorola or be employed by a competitor, supplier, or customer of Motorola. A Motorola employee shall not engage in any activity where the skill and knowledge developed while in the employment of Motorola is transferred or applied to such activity in a way that results in a negative impact on the present or prospective business interest of Motorola.

A Motorola employee shall not have any relationship with any other business enterprise that might affect the employee's independence of judgment in transactions between Motorola and the other business enterprise.

A Motorola employee may not have any interest in any supplier or customer of Motorola that could compromise the employee's loyalty to Motorola.

Compliance with the Code of Conduct is a condition of employment. We urge you to read the complete code.

Should any questions remain, you are encouraged to consult your Motorola law department. In the world of business, your understanding and cooperation are essential. As in all things, Motorola cannot operate to the highest standards without you.

Source: Company document. Used with permission.

ethical behavior of salespeople are their relatives and friends, other salespeople, and their sales managers. Sales managers are particularly important because they establish the ethical climate in their organization through the salespeople they hire, the ethical training they provide for their salespeople, and the degree to which they enforce ethical standards.[11]

Some people hesitate to pursue a sales career because they think selling will force them to compromise their principles.[12] Research, though, suggests otherwise. One series of studies finds that salespeople are less prone to unethical behaviors like exaggeration than are politicians, preachers, and even professors![13] No matter the industry, research finds that ethical behavior leads to higher customer satisfaction, trust, loyalty, and repeat purchases. As one of our former students now selling commercial real estate told us, "Unethical reps are run out of our industry." Good ethics are good business, and sales managers and salespeople know that.

Laws

In this chapter we examine ethical and legal issues in personal selling. *Laws* dictate which activities society has deemed to be clearly wrong—the activities for which salespeople and their companies will be punished. Some of these laws are reviewed later in the chapter. However, most sales situations are not covered by laws. Salespeople have to rely on their own codes of ethics and/or their firms' and industries' codes of ethics to determine the right thing to do.

A Personal Code of Ethics

Values of significant others, such as spouses and family, can influence a salesperson's ethical choices.

Long before salespeople go to work they develop a sense of what is right and wrong—a standard of conduct—from family and friends. Although salespeople should abide by their own codes of ethics, they may be tempted to avoid difficult ethical choices by developing "logical" reasons for unethical conduct. For example, a salesperson may use the following rationalizations:

- All salespeople behave "this way" (unethically) in this situation.
- No one will be hurt by this behavior.
- This behavior is the lesser of two evils.
- This conduct is the price one has to pay for being in business.

Salespeople who use such reasoning want to avoid feeling responsible for their behavior and being bound by ethical considerations. Even though the pressure to make sales may tempt some salespeople to be unethical and act against their internal standards, maintaining an ethical self-image is important. Compromising ethical standards to achieve short-term gains can have adverse long-term effects. When salespeople violate their own principles, they lose self-respect and confidence in their abilities. They may begin to think that the only way they can make sales is to be dishonest or unethical, a downward spiral that can have significant negative effects.

Short-term compromises also make long-term customer relationships more difficult to form. As discussed earlier, customers who have been treated unethically will be reluctant to deal with those salespeople again. Also, they may relate these experiences to business associates in other companies.

Exhibit 2.5 lists some questions you can ask yourself to determine whether a sales behavior or activity is unethical. The questions emphasize that ethical behavior is determined by widely accepted views of what is right and wrong. Thus, you should engage only in activities about which you would be proud to tell your family, friends, employer, and customers.

Your firm can strongly affect the ethical choices you will have to make. What if your manager asks you to engage in activity you consider unethical? There are a

Exhibit 2.5
Checklist for Making Ethical Decisions

1. Would I be embarrassed if a customer found out about this behavior?
2. Would my supervisor disapprove of this behavior?
3. Would most salespeople feel that this behavior is unusual?
4. Am I about to do this because I think I can get away with it?
5. Would I be upset if a salesperson did this to me?
6. Would my family or friends think less of me if I told them about engaging in this sales activity?
7. Am I concerned about the possible consequences of this behavior?
8. Would I be upset if this behavior or activity were publicized in a newspaper article?
9. Would society be worse off if everyone engaged in this behavior or activity?

If the answer to any of these questions is yes, the behavior or activity is probably unethical, and you should not do it.

number of choices you can make that are discussed in greater detail in Chapter 16, when we focus on relationships with your manager. From a personal perspective, however, here are three of those choices:

1. *Ignore your personal values and do what your company asks you to do.* Self-respect suffers when you have to compromise principles to please an employer. If you take this path, you will probably feel guilty and quickly become dissatisfied with yourself and your job.

2. *Take a stand and tell your employer what you think.* Try to influence the decisions and policies of your company and supervisors.

3. *Refuse to compromise your principles.* Taking this path may mean you will get fired or be forced to quit. This is the path Jim Keller took (see Profile at the start of the chapter). Long-term benefits, though, can accrue as customers find that you are trustworthy.

You should not take a job with a company whose products, policies, and conduct conflict with your standards. Before taking a sales job, investigate the company's procedures and selling approach to see whether they conflict with your personal ethical standards. The issues concerning the relationship between salespeople and their companies are discussed in more detail in Chapter 16, and methods for evaluating companies are presented in Chapter 17.

SELLING ETHICS AND RELATIONSHIPS

The core principle at work in considering ethics in professional selling is that of fairness. The buyer has the right to make the purchase decision with equal and fair access to the information needed to make the decision; further, all competitors should have fair access to the sales opportunity. Keeping information from the customer or misrepresenting information is not fair because it does not allow the customer to make an informed decision. Kickbacks, bribes, and other unethical activities are unfair to both the customer's organization and to competitors. Those types of activities do not allow fair access to the sales opportunity. These and other situations can confront salespeople in their relationships with their customers, competitors, and colleagues (other salespeople).

RELATIONSHIPS WITH CUSTOMERS

The most common areas of ethical concern involving customers include using deception; offering gifts, bribes, and entertainment; divulging confidential information and rights to privacy; and backdoor selling.

Deception

Deliberately presenting inaccurate information, or lying, to a customer is illegal. Further, misleading customers by telling half-truths or withholding important information can also lead to legal consequences but is more often a matter of ethics. Some salespeople believe it is the customer's responsibility to uncover potential product problems. These salespeople answer questions, perhaps incompletely, and don't offer information that might make a sale more difficult. For example, a salesperson selling life insurance may fail to mention that the policy won't pay off under certain circumstances.

Customers expect salespeople to be enthusiastic about their firm and its products and recognize that this enthusiasm can result in a certain amount of exaggeration as part of the persuasion process. Customers also expect salespeople to emphasize the positive aspects of their products and spend little time talking about the negative aspects. But practicing **deception** by withholding information

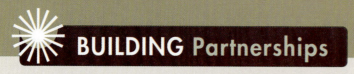

ON CONTRACTS, PERSONAL REPUTATIONS, AND SERVICE LEVEL AGREEMENTS

Trent Weaver, W Promotions, tells of one client that's a bit odd. Weaver's company has worked with companies all over the country, even supplying AAFES, the company that manages retail operations for the U.S. military the world over. But this one client was a little different.

"I was really nervous at first because they wouldn't sign a contract. The owner just walked away from it—literally, he'd get up and walk away," recalls Weaver. "But we'd bill them, and they would pay—and pay quickly."

In any services field, one reason the contract is so important is because the product isn't tangible. The contract specifies what the services are, when they will be delivered, when they are considered finished, and the like. This kind of contract is called a service level agreement,

and each level of service agreed to is called an SLA. If the SLA requires 24-hour turnaround, then 24 hours is the metric by which the service is measured.

"We put SLAs in the proposal we presented, and he verbally agreed to it, but nothing in writing." Finally, after a couple of attempts, one of the client's leadership team pulled Weaver aside and told him, "We pay weekly, so invoice us weekly. If there's a problem with SLAs, we'll both know it right away."

Weaver now says, "I'm still nervous, but you know, I've had contracts with other clients who either never paid us or slow-paid us. Yes, we could get fired at a moment's notice, but it's nice doing business with someone who operates on a handshake. I just know we have to deliver, and all's well."

---

or telling lies is clearly manipulative and therefore unethical. Such salespeople take advantage of the trust customers place in them. When buyers uncover these deceptions, they will be reluctant to trust such salespeople in the future. Not only that, but sophisticated buyers recognize such deceptions and assume the worst anyway.[14]

Salespeople who fail to provide customers with complete information about products lose an opportunity to develop trust. Trust is created through many actions, such as keeping all promises, especially the small promises like calling back when you say you will. In "Building Partnerships 2.1" we develop this concept of trust more completely.

Entertaining clients is an accepted business practice in most industries, and this is an acceptable way to build relationships as long as the entertainment is not too lavish.

Bribes, Gifts, and Entertainment

Bribes and kickbacks may be illegal. **Bribes** are payments made to buyers to influence their purchase decisions, whereas **kickbacks** are payments made to buyers based on the amount of orders placed. A purchasing agent personally benefits from bribes and kickbacks, but these payments typically have negative consequences for the purchasing agent's firm because the product's performance is not considered in buying decisions.

Taking customers to lunch is a commonly accepted business practice. Most salespeople take customers to lunch occasionally or frequently, and in many instances salespeople use this time to get to know the buyer better rather than pitch business. However, some companies take customers to sporting events, to play golf, or even on overnight trips to the company's plant or headquarters. In some cases these trips can become quite lavish; the pharmaceutical industry, for example, came under close governmental regulation for questionable practices regarding exotic and expensive trips for doctors who prescribe certain medications.

Determining which gifts and entertainment activities are acceptable and which are not brings up ethical issues. To avoid these issues, many U.S. companies have policies that forbid employees to accept gifts (more than pencils or coffee cups) or entertainment from suppliers. These firms require that all gifts sent to the employee's home or office be returned. IBM does not allow any gifts, even coffee cups; Walmart, the largest retailer in the world, makes no allowance for entertainment because all contact between buyers and vendors can occur only at business meetings at Walmart's or the vendor's headquarters. On the other hand, many companies have no policy on receiving gifts or entertainment. Some unethical employees will accept and even solicit gifts, even though their company has a policy against such practices.

To develop a productive, long-term relationship, salespeople need to avoid embarrassing customers by asking them to engage in activities they might see as unethical. If a salesperson wants to give a gift out of friendship or invite a customer to lunch to develop a better business relationship, she or he should phrase the offer so the customer can easily refuse it. For example, a salesperson with a large industrial firm might have this conversation with a customer:

SALESPERSON: John, we have worked well together over the last five years, and I would like to give you something to show my appreciation. Would that be OK?

BUYER: That's very nice of you, but what are you thinking of giving me?

SALESPERSON: Well, I want to give you a Mont Blanc pen. I really enjoy using my pen, and I thought you might like one also. Is that OK?

BUYER: I would appreciate that gift. Thank you.

Buyers typically are sensitive about receiving expensive gifts, according to Shirley Hunter, account manager for Teradata. "It's like getting five dozen roses after a first date. It's embarrassing if anyone finds out, and you have to wonder what's the catch?"[15] Some industries used promotional items frequently, but in pharmaceutical sales, government regulations have increasingly forbidden the use of gifts because no one wants the choice of a prescription to be influenced by a salesperson's gift to a doctor. Some guidelines for gift giving are as follows:

- Check your motives for giving the gift. The gift should be given to foster a mutually beneficial, long-term relationship, not to obligate or pay off the customer for placing an order.
- Make sure the customer views the gift as a symbol of your appreciation and respect with no strings attached. Never give customers the impression that you are attempting to buy their business with a gift.
- Make sure the gift does not violate the customer's or your firm's policies.
- The safest gifts are inexpensive business items imprinted with the salesperson's company's name or logo.

Even when customers encourage and accept gifts, lavish gifts and entertainment are both unethical and bad business. Treating a customer to a three-day fishing trip is no substitute for effective selling. Sales won this way are usually short lived. Salespeople who offer expensive gifts to get orders may be blackmailed into continually providing these gifts to obtain orders in the future. Customers who can be bribed are likely to switch their business when presented with better offers.

Special Treatment

Some customers try to take advantage of their status to get special treatment from salespeople. For example, a buyer asks a salesperson to make a weekly check on the performance of equipment even after the customer's employees have been thoroughly trained in the operation and maintenance of the equipment. Providing this extra service may upset other customers who do not get the special attention. In addition, the special service can reduce the salesperson's productivity. Salespeople should be diplomatic but careful about undertaking requests to provide unusual services.

Confidential Information

During sales calls salespeople often encounter confidential company information, such as new products under development, costs, and production schedules. Offering information about a customer's competitor in exchange for an order is unethical. Many times, though, the request is not that obvious. For example, a customer asks how well your product is selling, and you reply, "Great!" The customer then asks, "Well, how is it doing at HEB?" If the customer is told how many cases are sold at HEB, then HEB's right to confidentiality was violated. We discuss legal issues around privacy later in this chapter, but there are ethical issues regarding confidentiality that are not always covered by law.

Sometimes, salespeople have to sign an nondisclosure agreement (NDA). An NDA is a contract that specifies what information is owned by the customer and how or if that information can be shared with anyone. That's because salespeople may have access to information that, if it became public, could damage the customer. For example, a customer may be working on a new product, and if competitors found out, they might preempt the new product launch. Long-term relationships can develop only when customers trust salespeople to maintain confidentiality. By disclosing confidential information, a salesperson will get a reputation for being untrustworthy. Even the customer who solicited the confidential information will not trust the salesperson, who will then be denied access to information needed to make an effective sales presentation.

Backdoor Selling

Sometimes purchasing agents require that all contacts with the prospect's employees be made through them because they want to be fully informed about and control the buying process. The purchasing agent insists that salespeople get his or her approval before meeting with other people involved in the purchase decision. This policy can make it difficult for a new supplier to get business from a customer using a competitor's products.

Salespeople engage in **backdoor selling** when they ignore the purchasing agent's policy, go around his or her back, and contact other people directly involved in the purchasing decision. Backdoor selling can be risky and unethical. If the purchasing agent finds out, the salesperson may never be able to get an order. To avoid these potential problems, the salesperson needs to convince the purchasing agent of the benefits to be gained by direct contact with other people in the customer's firm.

Exhibit 2.6

One Doctor's Request
for Ethical Behavior

DO: Tell me why your drug is exceptional using the STEPS approach: safety, tolerability, efficacy, price, and simplicity.

DON'T: Say negative things about your competitors or their drugs.

DON'T: Tell me what and how much another physician in the area uses your drug.

DON'T: Invite me to dinner.

DO: Arrange for specialists to come to our office during lunch so I can pick their brains.

DON'T: Offer me pens, notepads, or any other "freebies" with your drug's name on it. The cost is in your company's budget, which raises the price you charge my patients.

Source: Adapted from Jason Evans, "Establishing Rules of the Road for Pharmaceutical Representatives," *Family Practice Management*, March 2005, pp. 10–11.

Exhibit 2.7

Buyers' View of
Unethical Sales
Behaviors

- Exaggerates benefits of product.
- Passes the blame for something he or she did to someone else.
- Lies about product availability.
- Misrepresents guarantees.
- Lies about competition.
- Sells products that people do not need.
- Makes oral promises that are not legally binding.
- Is not interested in customer needs.
- Answers questions even when he or she does not know the correct answer.
- Sells hazardous products.

Source: Adapted from William Bearden, Thomas Ingram, and Raymond LaForge, *Marketing: Principles and Perspectives* (New York: McGraw-Hill/Irwin, 2004).

Jason Evans, MD, wrote a letter to the pharmaceutical salespeople who called on him, and he posted it in several conspicuous places in his office building. This letter specifies his expectations for acceptable selling tactics; a few of his points are listed in Exhibit 2.6. He reports that many salespeople commented that they appreciated knowing his expectations for their behavior, and from his perspective, interactions with salespeople have improved. Yet salespeople we've interviewed find the list too restrictive. Whether fair or too restrictive, Evans's letter has caught on and can now be found in many doctors' offices.

Research on buyers in general suggests additional behaviors that they think are unethical or inappropriate. Exhibit 2.7 summarizes that research. The research suggests that buyers will go out of their way to avoid salespeople who engage in these practices.[16]

Sneaking in the back door to sell behind the purchasing agent's back directly to a user in the buying company is considered unethical and can get a company blacklisted, unable to sell to that buyer again.

RELATIONSHIPS WITH THE SALESPERSON'S COMPANY

Because salespeople's activities in the field cannot be closely monitored, their employers trust them to act in the company's best interests. Professional salespeople do not abuse this trust. They put the interests of their companies above self-interest. Taking this perspective may require them to make short-term sacrifices to achieve long-term benefits for their companies and themselves. Some problem areas in the salesperson–company relationship involve expense accounts, reporting work time information and activities, and switching jobs. "Sales Technology 2.1" illustrates some problems salespeople may have with use of the company computer.

TECHNOLOGY AND *THE HUNGER GAMES*

In *The Hunger Games,* Katniss Everdeen has a chip implanted that enables the game managers to know her every move. While that technology may exist now, companies aren't using it to track where their salespeople are. They don't need to, as there is other technology that they can use.

Sneaking out to the golf course? Busted by the company-issued cell phone! GPS technology in the phone can be used to identify where a salesperson is.

Waiting until the end of the month to create your reports? Busted! The software notes when you entered the data, and the sales manager assumes the data are, at best, a little fuzzy and perhaps not all that accurate. Or at worst the manager assumes the calls weren't made, and now someone is looking for a new job.

Spending work time on Facebook? Busted! But Facebook can be a real business tool, with its IM feature used between colleagues at work, and the social network aspects used for identifying prospects (finding friends) or sending a message. Just don't put this on your wall: "Work sucks! Three more days to the weekend!"

Sending risqué photos and jokes via e-mail? Busted again! Some companies closely monitor e-mail. While stories abound of salespeople accidentally copying customers on e-mail messages that make fun of those same customers, companies have cracked down on using work computers for personal activities. And it's not worth the possibility of getting fired to share jokes or pictures that some might think are funny but others think are sexual harassment.

Many salespeople complain of not being able to get away from work. Carrying a company-issued smartphone or iPad computer leads to answering e-mail and customer calls 24/7. Couple that around-the-clock availability with the fact that even though about 60 percent of salespeople reached quota last year, almost all companies increased quotas this year and the pressure is on to stay connected. Add to that the ability to track a salesperson's activity on the Web, e-mail, or even the phone, and it can feel like Seneca Crane is watching every move. When every move is the right move, though, it's no problem.

Source for survey data: "2012 Sales Compensation Trends," Alexander Group, January 6, 2012.

Expense Accounts

Many companies provide their salespeople with cars and reimburse them for travel and entertainment expenses. Developing a reimbursement policy that prevents salespeople from cheating and still allows them the flexibility they need to cover their territories and entertain customers is almost impossible. Moreover, a lack of tight control can tempt salespeople to use their expense accounts to increase their income.

To do their jobs well, salespeople need to incur expenses. However, using their expense accounts to offset what they consider to be inadequate compensation is unethical. A salesperson who cannot live within the company compensation plan and expense policies has two ethical alternatives: (1) persuade the company to change its compensation plan or expense policy or (2) find another job. Salespeople are given expense accounts to cover legitimate expenses, such as for travel. Act as though you are spending your own money; an expense account does not mean you should stay in the most luxurious hotel in town.

Reporting Work Time Information and Activities

Employers expect their salespeople to work full-time. Salespeople on salary are stealing from their employers when they waste time on coffee breaks, long lunches, or unauthorized days off. Even salespeople paid by commission cheat their companies by not working full-time. Both their incomes and company profits decrease when salespeople take time off. In "Sales Technology 2.1" we take a light hearted look at the reality of technology and the ever-increasing ability of companies to ensure accurate reporting and full use of company time.

To monitor work activities, many companies ask their salespeople to provide daily call reports. Most salespeople dislike this clerical task. Some provide false information, including calls they never made. Giving inaccurate information or bending the truth is clearly unethical. A failure to get an appointment with a customer is not a sales call. Providing a brief glimpse of a product is not a demonstration.

Switching Jobs

When salespeople decide to change jobs, they have an ethical responsibility to their employers. The company often makes a considerable investment in training salespeople and then gives them confidential information about new products and programs. Over time, salespeople use this training and information to build strong relationships with their customers.

For that reason, some companies require salespeople to sign a contract that contains a noncompete clause. While the legality of such a clause can vary from state to state, essentially the company wants to guard against your taking customers with you when you switch to a new company. If you switch jobs in the same industry, you may need to seek legal advice regarding any noncompete clauses. A salesperson may have good reasons to switch jobs. However, if a salesperson goes to work for a competitor, she or he should not say negative things about the past employer. Also, disclosing confidential information about the former employer's business is improper. The ethical approach to leaving a job includes the following:

- *Give ample notice.* If you leave a job during a busy time and with inadequate notice, your employer may suffer significant lost sales opportunities. Do not be surprised, though, if you are escorted out that day. Many companies are concerned about the loss of information by, as well as lack of productivity of, someone who has turned in notice, so the policy may be that you are turned out that day.

- *Offer assistance during the transition phase.* Help your replacement learn about your customers and territory, if given the opportunity, as Jim Keller did at Teradata (see Profile at the beginning of the chapter).

- *Don't burn your bridges.* Don't say things in anger that may come back to haunt you. Remember that you may want to return to the company or ask the company for a reference in the future. You may even find that the people you worked with move to a company you want to work for or sell to!

- *Don't take anything with you that belongs to the company.* That includes all your records and notes on companies you called on, even if you are going to a noncompeting company. In many states, customer records are considered **trade secrets,** or information owned by the company by which the company gains a competitive advantage. Trade secrets are protected by law, so if you take customer records with you, you could face a civil lawsuit.

RELATIONSHIPS WITH COLLEAGUES

To be effective, salespeople need to work together with other salespeople. Unethical behavior by salespeople toward their coworkers, such as engaging in sexual harassment and taking advantage of colleagues, can weaken company morale and harm the company's reputation.

Sexual Harassment

Sexual harassment includes unwelcome sexual advances; requests for sexual favors, jokes or graffiti; posting sexually explicit material on bulletin boards or cubicle walls; and physical conduct. Harassment is not confined to requests for sexual favors in exchange for job considerations such as a raise or promotion; creating a hostile work environment can be considered sexual harassment. Some actions that are considered sexual harassment are engaging in suggestive behavior, treating people differently because they are male or female, making lewd sexual comments and gestures, sharing by e-mail jokes that have sexual content, showing obscene photographs, alleging that an employee got rewards by engaging in sexual acts, and spreading rumors about a person's sexual conduct.

Customers as well as coworkers can sexually harass salespeople. Salespeople are particularly vulnerable to harassment from important customers who may seek sexual favors in exchange for their business. Following are some suggestions for dealing with sexual harassment from customers:

- Don't become so dependent on one customer that you would consider compromising your principles to retain the customer's business. Develop a large base of customers and prospects to minimize the importance of one customer—a good idea for a lot of reasons.

- Tell the harasser in person or write a letter stating that the behavior is offensive, is unacceptable, and must be stopped. Clearly indicate that you are in control and will not be passive.

- Use the sexual harassment policies of your firm and your customer's firm to resolve problems. These policies typically state the procedure for filing a complaint, the person responsible for investigating the complaint, the time frame for completing the investigation, and the means by which the parties will be informed about the resolution.

Research indicates that sexual harassment is rare; one study found only an average of 1.3 cases per year per company in all areas of the company, not just sales.[17] That study also found that companies are much more worried about making sure their employees have a safe environment in which to work than any fear of lawsuits; in other words, executives want to make sure their people have a good environment in which to work because it is the right thing to do, not because they may get sued if they fail to do so.

Taking Advantage of Other Salespeople

Salespeople can behave unethically when they are too aggressive in pursuing their own goals at the expense of their colleagues. For example, it is unethical to steal potential customers from other salespeople. This practice is called **poaching.** In some companies, sales territories are defined by a customer list, and customers are open to being called on until they are on the list. Should the account go dormant, it can become open again. But some salespeople will try to take over accounts, while others will try to make dormant accounts look active in order to keep them. Colleagues usually discover such unethical behavior and return the lack of support. If the company has policies protecting customers or territories, such behavior can lead to immediate termination.

RELATIONSHIPS WITH COMPETITORS

Making false claims about competitors' products or sabotaging their efforts is clearly unethical and often illegal. For example, a salesperson who rearranges the display of a competitor's products in a customer's store to make it less appealing is being unethical. This type of behavior can backfire. When customers detect these practices, the reputations of the salespeople and their companies may be permanently damaged.

Another questionable tactic is criticizing a competitor's products or policies. Although you may be tempted to say negative things about a competitor, this approach usually does not work. Customers will assume you are biased toward your own company and its products and discount negative comments you make about the competition. Some customers may even be offended. If they have bought the competitor's products in the past, they may regard these comments as a criticism of their judgment.

LEGAL ISSUES

Society has determined that some activities are clearly unethical and has created a legal system to prevent people from engaging in these activities. Salespeople who violate these laws can cause serious problems for themselves and their companies—problems more serious than being considered unethical by a buyer. By engaging in illegal activities, salespeople expose themselves and their firms to costly legal fees and millions of dollars in fines.

The activities of salespeople in the United States are affected by three forms of law: statutory, administrative, and common. **Statutory law** is based on legislation passed either by state legislatures or by Congress. The main statutory laws governing salespeople are the Uniform Commercial Code and antitrust laws. **Administrative laws** are established by local, state, or federal regulatory agencies. The Federal Trade Commission (FTC) is the most active agency in developing administrative laws affecting salespeople. However, the Securities and Exchange Commission regulates stockbrokers, and the Food and Drug Administration regulates pharmaceutical salespeople. Finally, **common law** grows out of court decisions. Precedents set by these decisions fill in the gaps where no laws exist.

This section discusses current laws affecting salespeople, but every year important new laws are developed and court decisions rendered. Thus you should contact your firm for advice when a potential legal issue arises.

UNIFORM COMMERCIAL CODE

The **Uniform Commercial Code (UCC)** is the legal guide to commercial practice in the United States. The UCC defines a number of terms related to salespeople.

Agency

A person who acts in place of his or her company is an **agent.** Authorized agents of a company have the authority to legally obligate their firm in a business transaction. This authorization to represent the company does not have to be in writing. Thus, as a salesperson, your statements and actions can legally bind your company and have significant financial impact.

Sale

The UCC defines a **sale** as "the transfer of title to goods by the seller to the buyer for a consideration known as price." A sale differs from a **contract to sell.** Any time a salesperson makes an offer and receives an unqualified acceptance, a contract exists. A sale is made when the contract is completed and title passes from the seller to the buyer.

The UCC also distinguishes between an offer and an invitation to negotiate. A sales presentation is usually considered to be an **invitation to negotiate.** An **offer** takes place when the salesperson quotes specific terms. The offer specifically states what the seller promises to deliver and what it expects from the buyer. If the buyer accepts these terms, the parties will have established a binding contract.

Salespeople are agents when they have the authority to make offers. However, most salespeople are not agents because they have the power only to solicit written offers from buyers. These written offers, called **orders,** become contracts when they are signed by an authorized representative in the salesperson's company. Sometimes these orders contain clauses stating that the firm is not obligated by its salesperson's statements. However, the buyer usually can have the contract nullified and may even sue for damages if salespeople make misleading statements, even though they are not official agents.

This buyer is inspecting a shipment of various products in a restaurant. Because the products were shipped FOB destination, the buyer is not responsible for the merchandise until it shows up at the buyer's location. The buyer can even turn down the sale now if the products are not up to standard.

Title and Risk of Loss

If the contract terms specify **free on board (FOB) destination,** the seller has title until the goods are received at the destination. In this case any loss or damage incurred during transportation is the responsibility of the seller. The buyer assumes this responsibility and risk if contract terms call for **FOB factory.** The UCC also defines when titles transfer for goods shipped cash on delivery (COD) and for goods sold on consignment. Understanding the terms of the sale and who has title can be useful in resolving complaints about damaged merchandise.

thinking **it** through

If a salesperson is not an agent, then what is the salesperson? Does not being an agent change the salesperson's obligations to the company in any way? Or to the customer?

Oral versus Written Agreements

In most cases oral agreements between a salesperson and a customer are just as binding as written agreements. Normally, written agreements are required for sales over $500. Salespeople may be the legal representatives of their firms and thus must be careful when signing written agreements.

Obligations and Performance

When the salesperson and the customer agree on the terms of a contract, both firms must perform according to those terms in "good faith," which means they have to try to fulfill the contract. In addition, both parties must perform according to commonly accepted industry practices. Even if salespeople overstate the performance of their products, their firms have to provide the stated performance and meet the terms of the contract.

Warranties

A **warranty** is an assurance by the seller that the products will perform as represented. Sometimes a warranty is called a *guarantee.* The UCC distinguishes between two types of warranties: expressed and implied. An **expressed warranty** is an oral or a written statement by the seller. An **implied warranty** is not actually stated but is still an obligation defined by law. For example, products sold using an oral or a written description (the buyer never sees the products) carry an implied warranty that the products are of average quality. However, if the buyer inspects the product before placing an order, the implied warranty applies only to any performance aspects that the inspection would not have uncovered. Typically an implied warranty also guarantees that the product can be used in the manner stated by the seller.

Problems with warranties often arise when the sale is to a reseller (a distributor or retailer). The ultimate user—the reseller's customer—may complain about a product to the reseller. The reseller, in turn, tries to shift the responsibility to the manufacturer. Salespeople often have to investigate and resolve these issues.

MISREPRESENTATION OR SALES PUFFERY

In their enthusiasm salespeople may exaggerate the performance of products and even make false statements to get an order. Over time, common and administrative laws have defined the difference between illegal misrepresentation and sales puffery. Not all statements salespeople make have legal consequences. However, misrepresentation, even if legal, can destroy a business relationship and may involve salespeople and their firms in lawsuits.

Glowing descriptions such as "Our service can't be beat" are considered to be opinions or **sales puffery**. Customers cannot reasonably rely on these statements. Following are some examples of puffery:

- This is a top-notch product.
- This product will last a lifetime.
- Our school bus chassis has been designed to provide the utmost safety and reliability for carrying the nation's most precious cargo—schoolchildren.
- The most complete line of reliable, economical gas heating appliances.

However, statements about the inherent capabilities of products or services, such as "Our system will reduce your inventory by 40 percent," may be treated as statements of fact and become warranties. Here are examples of such statements found to be legally binding:

- Mechanically, this oil rig is a 9 on a scale of 10.
- Feel free to prescribe this drug to your patients, doctor. It's nonaddicting.
- This equipment will keep up with any other machine you are using and will work well with your other machines.

Rich Kraus owned a company providing document shredding services using special trucks that contain high-speed shredders. When purchasing a new truck, he looked to another small company. The salesperson was the owner's son, and his pride came through as he gave a demo and rattled off the capabilities of the equipment. Compared to Kraus's current model, this shredder was 40 percent faster and had 30 percent more capacity for storing shredded material, so he placed an order for the $250,000 truck.

Unfortunately he quickly realized the truck was capable of holding only 60 percent of the paper that the salesperson said it could. When the problem was discussed with the engineer, he admitted that the salesperson had provided incorrect information. However, he didn't want to correct the owner's son in front of a prospective customer. He added that the salesperson was a good honest person and that his enthusiasm probably just got the best of him.

Only after threatening legal action did Kraus get his money back and order a truck from his original vendor. Since then, Kraus sold his company to a larger company that purchases an average of 50 trucks per year, all from Kraus's original vendor.

As Kraus says, "Since that time we have had dozens of associates in the industry ask us about our experience with this company. It's hard to fathom how many orders it lost as a result." Risking the reputation of the company for even a single unit just wasn't worth it.[18]

The **False Claims Act,** or Lincoln Law, was passed in 1863 during the Civil War to encourage citizens to press claims against vendors that fraudulently sold to the U.S. government (all states now have their own version, too). During the war, defense contractors were selling all manner of products (including mules) that could not live up to the claims made by the salespeople. As a result, the government was losing money and the war. This law enabled a person bringing a claim of fraud to share in the proceeds if the contractor was found guilty and damages are assessed. Although this law is well over 100 years old, as you read in the opening profile, today's businesspeople like Jim Keller at Teradata still have to ensure that their claims are accurate, especially when selling to the government.

U.S. salespeople need to be aware of both U.S. laws and laws in the host country when selling internationally. All countries have laws regulating marketing and selling activities. In Canada all claims and statements made in advertisements and sales presentations about comparisons with competitive products must pass the **credulous person standard.** This standard means the company and the salesperson have to pay damages if a reasonable person could misunderstand a statement. Thus, a statement like "This is the strongest axle in Canada" might be considered puffery in the United States but be viewed as misleading in Canada unless the firm had absolute evidence that the axle was stronger than any other axle sold in Canada.

To avoid legal and ethical problems with misrepresentation, you should try to educate customers thoroughly before concluding a sale. You should tell the customer as much about the specific performance of the product as possible. Unless your firm has test results concerning the product's performance, you should avoid offering an opinion about the product's specific benefits for the customer's application. If you don't have the answer to a customer's question, don't guess. Say that you don't know the answer and will get back to the customer with the information.

ILLEGAL BUSINESS PRACTICES

The Sherman Antitrust Act of 1890, the Clayton Act of 1914, the Federal Trade Commission Act of 1914, and the Robinson-Patman Act of 1934 prohibit unfair business practices that may reduce competition. The Federal Trade Commission is often tasked with enforcing these laws, though the Justice Department may also bring cases. The courts use these laws to create common law that defines the illegal business practices discussed in this section.

Business Defamation

Business defamation occurs when a salesperson makes unfair or untrue statements to customers about a competitor, its products, or its salespeople. These statements are illegal when they damage the competitor's reputation or the reputation of its salespeople.

Following are some examples of false statements made about competitors that have been found to be illegal:

- Company X broke the law when it offered you a free case of toilet paper with every 12 cases you buy.

- Company X is going bankrupt.
- You shouldn't do business with Company X. Mr. Jones, the CEO, is really incompetent and dishonest.

You should avoid making negative comments about a competitor, its salespeople, or its products unless you have proof to support the statements.

Reciprocity

Reciprocity is a special relationship in which two companies agree to buy products from each other. For example, a manufacturer of computers agrees to use microprocessors from a component manufacturer if the component manufacturer agrees to buy its computers. Such interrelationships can lead to greater trust and cooperation between the firms. However, reciprocity agreements are illegal under the Sherman Antitrust Act if one company forces another company to join the agreement. Reciprocity is legal only when both parties consent to the agreement willingly.

Tying Agreements

In a **tying agreement** a buyer is required to purchase one product in order to get another product. For example, a customer who wants to buy a copy machine is required to buy paper from the same company, or a distributor that wants to stock one product must stock the manufacturer's entire product line. Because they reduce competition, tying agreements typically are illegal under the Clayton Act. They are legal only when the seller can show that the products must be used together—that is, that one product will not function properly unless the other product is used with it.

Tying agreements are also legal when a company's reputation depends on the proper functioning of equipment. Thus, a firm can be required to buy a service contract for equipment it purchases, although the customer need not buy the contract from the manufacturer.

Conspiracy and Collusion

An agreement between competitors before customers are contacted is a **conspiracy,** whereas **collusion** refers to competitors working together while the customer is making a purchase decision. For example, competitors are conspiring when they get together and divide up a territory so that only one competitor will call on each prospect. Collusion occurs when competitors agree to charge the same price for equipment that a prospect is considering. These examples of collusion and conspiracy are illegal because they reduce competition.

Interference with Competitors

Salespeople may illegally interfere with competitors by doing the following:

- Trying to get a customer to break a contract with a competitor
- Tampering with a competitor's product
- Confusing a competitor's market research by buying merchandise from stores

Restrictions on Resellers

Numerous laws govern the relationship between manufacturers and resellers—wholesalers and retailers. At one time it was illegal for companies to establish a minimum price below which their distributors or retailers could not resell their products. Today this practice, called **resale price maintenance,** is legal in some situations.

Manufacturers do not have to sell their products to any reseller that wants to buy them. Sellers can use their judgment to select resellers if they announce their selection criteria in advance. One sales practice considered unfair is providing special incentives to get a reseller's salespeople to push products. For example, salespeople for a cosmetics company may give a department store's cosmetics salespeople prizes based on sales of the company's product. These special incentives, called **spiffs** (or **push money**), are legal only if the reseller knows and approves of the incentive and it is offered to all the reseller's salespeople. *Spiff* stands for "special promotion incentive fund" and dates back to a time when there was more selling by retail salespeople. Even if they are legal, though, not everyone agrees that spiffs are ethical.[19]

Price Discrimination

The Robinson-Patman Act became law because independent wholesalers and retailers wanted additional protection from the aggressive marketing tactics of large chain stores. Principally, the act forbids price discrimination in interstate commerce. Robinson-Patman applies only to interstate commerce, but most states have passed similar laws to govern sales transactions between buyers and sellers within the same state.

Court decisions related to the Robinson-Patman Act define **price discrimination** as a seller giving *unjustified* special prices, discounts, or services to some customers and not to others. To justify a special price or discount, the seller must prove that

Using spiffs to promote one product over another, such as one brand of oven, is legal, but research shows consumers believe the practice to be unethical.

it results from (1) differences in the cost of manufacture, sale, or delivery; (2) differences in the quality or nature of the product delivered; or (3) an attempt to meet prices offered by competitors in a market. Different prices can be charged, however, if the cost of doing business is different or if a customer negotiates more effectively. For example, a customer who buys in large volume can be charged a lower price if the manufacturing and shipping charges for higher-volume orders are lower than they are for smaller orders.

In general, firms also may not offer special allowances to one reseller unless those allowances are made available to competing resellers. Because most resellers compete in limited geographic areas, firms frequently offer allowances in specific regions of the country. However, recent Supreme Court decisions allow some leeway in offering discounts to resellers who are engaged in competitive bids. These discounts do not necessarily have to be offered uniformly to all resellers for all customers but can be selectively offered to meet specific competitive situations. In one case a Volvo truck dealer sued Volvo, citing discounts given to other Volvo dealers in situations where the dealers were all bidding on the same customer's contract. The Supreme Court ruled that these instances did not violate the law because they were negotiated individually to meet bids from non-Volvo providers.

Privacy Laws

Privacy laws limit the amount of information that a firm can obtain about a consumer and specify how that information can be used or shared. The Gramm-Leach-Bliley Act, passed in 1999, requires written notification of customers regarding privacy policies. Note that the law does not discriminate in how the information was obtained. In other words, the law is the same for a customer who fills out a credit application or a customer who responds to questions from a salesperson. Although this law applies primarily to financial institutions, a second phase of the act became law in 2003, broadening its application. Further, any company that publishes a privacy policy is expected, by regulation of the FTC, to follow that policy and is liable to prosecution if it uses customer information inappropriately.

European Union (EU) law is even more stringent than U.S. law. The application of privacy applies to many more settings, and transfer of information is forbidden in nearly all circumstances. Further, the law can apply to information that could be shared among non-EU subsidiaries, which means that in some instances an account manager in Europe cannot share information with an American colleague.

Do-Not-Call Law

The federal Do-Not-Call Registry originally took effect in 2003 and was strengthened in 2007 and limits the conditions under which anyone on the registry may be telephoned at home or on a cell phone. A salesperson, for example, cannot call the number of someone on the registry if the person is not already a customer. This registry was set up by the FTC under its ability to set rules for commerce, and is an administrative law. However, the FTC can levy fines against companies and individuals that violate the rules, as some companies have already learned. The rules do not apply to business phones.

INTERNATIONAL ETHICAL AND LEGAL ISSUES

Ethical and legal issues are complex for selling in international markets. Value judgments and laws vary widely across cultures and countries. Behavior that is commonly accepted as proper in one country can be completely unacceptable in another country. For example, a small payment to expedite the loading of a truck is considered a cost of doing business in some Middle Eastern countries but may be viewed as a bribe in the United States. Walmart recently got into trouble by allegedly bribing officials in Mexico in order to expedite the company's growth in that country. While the case is currently pending, it is an example of how an American company has to follow U.S. law, even when in another country.[20]

Many countries make a clear distinction between payments for lubrication and payments for subordination. **Lubrication** involves small sums of money or gifts, typically made to low-ranking managers or government officials, in countries where these payments are not illegal. The lubrication payments are made to get the official or manager to do the job more rapidly—to process an order more quickly or to provide a copy of a request for a proposal. For example, Halliburton, the company hired to rebuild Iraq, says, "Sometimes the company [Halliburton] may be required to make facilitating or expediting payments to a low-level government employee or employee in some other countries than the United States to expedite or secure the routine governmental action. . . . Such facilitating payments may not be illegal. . . . Accordingly, facilitating payments must be strictly controlled, and every effort must be made to eliminate or minimize such payments."[21] The policy goes on to say that any such payments must have advance authorization from the company's legal department so there will be no question whether the payment is lubrication or subordination. **Subordination** involves paying larger sums of money to higher-ranking officials to get them to do something that is illegal or to ignore an illegal act. Even in countries where bribery is common, subordination is considered unethical.[22]

RESOLVING CULTURAL DIFFERENCES

What do you do when the ethical standards in a country differ from the standards in your country? This is an old question. Cultural relativism and ethical imperialism are two extreme answers to this question. **Cultural relativism** is the view that no culture's ethics are superior. If the people in Indonesia tolerate bribery, their attitude toward bribery is no better or worse than that of people in Singapore who refuse to give or accept bribes. When in Rome, do as the Romans do. But is it right for a European pharmaceutical company to pay a Nigerian company to dispose of the pharmaceutical company's highly toxic waste near Nigerian residential neighborhoods, even though Nigeria has no rules against toxic waste disposal?

On the other hand, **ethical imperialism** is the view that ethical standards in one's home country should be applied to one's behavior across the world. This view suggests, for example, that Saudi Arabian salespeople working for a U.S. firm should go through the same sexual harassment training U.S. salespeople do, even though the strict conventions governing relationships between men and women in Saudi Arabia make the training meaningless and potentially embarrassing.

Adopting one of these extreme positions is probably not the best approach. To guide your behavior in dealing with cultural differences, you need to distinguish between what is merely a cultural difference and what is clearly wrong. You must respect not only core human values that should apply in all business situations but also local traditions and use the cultural background to help you decide what is right and what is wrong. For example, exchanging expensive gifts is common in Japanese business relationships, although it may be considered unethical in Western cultures. Most Western firms operating in Japan now accept this practice as an appropriate local tradition.

Research indicates that salespeople, particularly those who operate in foreign cultures, need significant corporate support and guidance in handling cultural ethical differences. Even a high level of personal morality may not prevent an individual from violating a law in a sales context, so it is imperative that companies establish specific standards of conduct, provide ethical training, and monitor behavior to enforce standards as uniformly as possible around the globe.[23]

LEGAL ISSUES

Regardless of the country in which U.S. salespeople sell, they are subject to U.S. laws that prohibit participating in unauthorized boycotts, trading with enemies of the United States, or engaging in activities that adversely affect the U.S. economy. The **Foreign Corrupt Practices Act** (FCPA) makes it illegal for U.S. companies to pay bribes to foreign officials; however, an amendment to the act permits small lubrication payments when they are customary in a culture. Violations of the law can result in sizable fines for company managers, employees, and agents who knowingly participate in or authorize the payment of such bribes. Recently 22 people were arrested at a conference for arms industry executives when they allegedly attempted to bribe a senior government minister in an African country. Included among those arrested was a vice president for sales with Smith & Wesson. Note that the individuals were charged with violating the law, while their companies were not indicted.[24] Siemens, a company indicted under the FCPA, paid a fine of over $1.6 billion, as well as the cost of over 100 attorneys and 1,300 forensic accountants.[25] One method companies can use to protect themselves, in the event an employee does violate the law, is to include the FCPA in the company's code of ethics. If the company takes specific steps, such as mentioning the law in company policy, the government's assumption is that the employee acted on his or her own and is individually responsible.[26]

The U.S. laws concerning bribery are much more restrictive than laws in other countries. For example, in Italy and Germany bribes made outside the countries are clearly defined as legal and tax deductible.

SELLING YOURSELF

Most college students do not give much thought to their reputations, at least in terms of a professional reputation. Yet your actions in class and around campus add up to a professional reputation in the sense that faculty form an opinion that is shared with recruiters and others who make important decisions. For example, faculty recommendations may be necessary for scholarships, membership in prestigious organizations, and, of course, jobs. Professors and instructors base their recommendations not only on what they observe but also on what they hear.

Carrying your weight in group projects, contributing your share in study groups, and doing your own work are actions that exhibit more than a professional work ethic; they also show your integrity. Other small things, like coming to class and leaving your cell phone silent in your backpack during class, can also contribute to a professor's estimation of a student's overall professional demeanor.

Of course, obvious actions such as claiming illness without any documentation, cheating on an exam (or even giving the appearance of cheating), or collaborating too closely with another student on an independent exercise can damage your credibility. Students may believe they can get away with such actions in classes not in their major and still get good faculty recommendations, but in reality reputation is much bigger than that. Although not every faculty member will learn a student's complete reputation, most of us learn enough from our colleagues and our students to know whom to recommend and whom to avoid.

When you meet guest speakers, when you work on projects that involve companies, and when you completed that internship, your professional reputation was being added to. What does it say about a student, for example, who accepts a job but continues to interview? The professional reputation is significantly damaged if that first job ends up getting turned down. Start working on your professional reputation now. Whether or not you decide to create one intentionally, you are building that reputation anyway.

SUMMARY

This chapter discussed the legal and ethical responsibilities of salespeople. These responsibilities are particularly important in personal selling because salespeople may face conflicts between their personal standards and the standards of their firms and customers. However, the evolution of selling has raised ethical standards and expectations; building long-term relationships with customers doesn't allow for unethical behavior.

Salespeople's ethical standards determine how they conduct relationships with their customers, employers, and competitors. Ethical issues in relations with customers involve the use of entertainment and gifts and the disclosure of confidential information. Ethical issues in relations with employers involve expenses and job changes. Finally, salespeople must be careful in how they talk about competitors and treat competitive products.

Many companies have ethical standards that describe the behavior expected of their salespeople. In evaluating potential employers, salespeople should consider these standards.

Salespeople also encounter many situations not covered by company statements and therefore must develop personal standards of right and wrong. Without personal standards, salespeople will lose their self-respect and the respect of their company and customers. Good ethics are good business. Over the long run, salespeople with a strong sense of ethics will be more successful than salespeople who compromise their own and society's ethics for short-term gain.

Statutory laws (such as the Uniform Commercial Code) and administrative laws (such as Federal Trade Commission rulings) guide the activities of salespeople in the United States. Selling in international markets is complex because of cultural differences in ethical judgments and laws that relate to sales activities in various countries.

KEY TERMS

QUESTIONS AND PROBLEMS

1. There are certainly many ethical and legal issues in selling, as this chapter demonstrates. Do you think there are more ethical and legal issues in selling than other jobs, such as accounting, finance, retail store management, or the like? Which issues raised in the chapter are likely to be present, no matter the job, and which are likely to be specific to sales jobs?

2. Do you think that the Internet has made companies more or less ethical? Why or why not?

3. For centuries the guideline for business transactions was the Latin term *caveat emptor* (let the buyer beware). This principle suggests that the seller is not responsible for the buyer's welfare. Is this principle still appropriate in modern business transactions? Why or why not? How has the evolution of selling influenced ethics in professional selling?

4. What's the difference between manipulation and persuasion? Give two examples of what would be considered manipulation and alternatives of acceptable persuasion. Then describe how your examples of manipulation might fall into the realm of illegal activity and under which law or laws.

5. Some professors believe that ethics cannot be taught; only laws need to be taught. Do you agree? Why or why not? What do you think Jim Keller's (in the opening profile) answer would be to this question? Why? Would his answer differ from that of someone who sells to consumers?

6. Your customer asks you what you think of a competitor's product. You know from experience with other customers that it is unreliable and breaks down frequently. Further, given this particular customer's needs, you expect that this issue would be an even bigger problem if the customer chose this product. How do you respond? Be specific about what you would say.

7. Your company has a contact management software system in which you enter all the information you can about your customers. The company wants to partner with another firm in marketing products. Your company wants to give your database to the other firm so the other firm can create marketing pieces and e-mail them to your clients. Is this legal? Is it ethical? Why or why not?

8. One of our students shared the story of how his family was able to spend their vacation on a

private Caribbean island—no exaggeration—as a guest of one of his father's clients. While that may be extreme, what might the ethical issues be with accepting a gift from a customer? How should you respond if offered a gift?

9. For each of the following situations, evaluate the salesperson's action and indicate what you think the appropriate action would be:

   a. In an electronics store, salespeople are offered an extra $50 for each sale of HDTV models that are being closed out. The manufacturer is offering the extra spiff, and management is fully aware of it. Salespeople, though, are encouraged to not mention either the spiff or the fact that these are closeout models.

   b. A customer asks if you can remove a safety feature because it slows down the operators of the equipment.

   c. The custom of the trade is that competitive firms submit bids based on specifications provided by the buyer, then the buyer places an order with the firm offering the lowest bid. After a salesperson submits a bid, the purchasing agent calls him and indicates that the bid is too high; the lowest bid so far is almost 8 percent lower than that. The buyer asks the salesperson to submit another bid at a price at least 10 percent lower.

   d. A few months after joining a company, you learn about a credit card that gives you a 20 percent cash refund on meals at certain restaurants. You get the card and start taking clients to restaurants offering the rebate, pocketing the rebate.

   e. A customer gives a salesperson a suggestion for a new service. The salesperson does not turn in the idea to her company, even though the company's policy manual states that all customer ideas should be submitted with the monthly expense report. Instead, the salesperson quits her job and starts her own business using the customer's suggestion.

CASE PROBLEMS

case **2.1**

Plaxico

Jesse Fernandes joined Plaxico, a major provider of engineering services in the plastics industry, straight out of college in sales support. After a couple of years of working on proposals and bids, she moved into the field, calling directly on manufacturers who could use Plaxico's services. Things went well—the territory she took over had not been worked very hard, so she was able to show some significant increases in the first year.

But shortly after the first of the year, she began to get the same e-mail from client after client. "Jesse, please explain your firm's pricing to us, line item by line item." After the fifth such e-mail, she forwarded it to her manager, Marty.

As soon as he saw the e-mail, Marty picked up the phone and called Jesse. "Looks like you've got Notelli & Associates moving in," he told her. "Their strategy is to tell customers our prices are higher and prove it by showing a line-item comparison. But actually, it's how they define each line that differs, and when you add it up, we're less expensive by some 15 to 20 percent."

"How do I prove that we're not more expensive?" asked Jesse.

"It's hard because they won't show the client a full price list. To make matters worse, we also have filed a lawsuit against them because they keep telling clients we're going out of the environmental engineering business."

"Oh, that explains why I've gotten that question a few times recently."

Questions

1. How do you respond to the pricing issue if you can't actually prove Notelli is lying until a customer tries them and then realizes it is more?

2. How do you respond to the question about leaving the business? What if a client asked about the lawsuit directly, saying, "I hear your company filed suit against Notelli. Wasn't that a cheap shot at a competitor?"

Note: This scenario is based on a situation faced by one of our former students. The names and industry have been changed, but the situation is real.

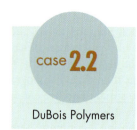

DuBois Polymers manufactures and distributes chemicals in the northwestern United States and western Canada. Usually the company sells to a distributor, which sells to the customer that uses the chemicals. Mitch Thompson is Betsy Briles's biggest customer. His business, which distributes chemicals in British Columbia and Washington State, represents nearly 15 percent of Betsy's annual sales. Recently Betsy acquired a new account in the same area, Crago Chemicals, which has the potential to be just as large. Her most recent meeting with Mitch, though, went like this:

"Look, Crago Chemicals underbid us on the Canuck contract by 10 percent. You must be offering them a better price than us, and I want to know why," said Mitch.

Betsy knew that Crago bid that job with no profit in order to expand into Vancouver and that the price she quoted them was actually 5 percent more than Mitch's. "Mitch, I'm not giving them a better price—they don't buy as much as you do from us, so I can't."

"Huh. You'll have to do better than that. You know that the Farley contract is coming up, and it is going to be big. I want to know what they intend to do about it."

"Mitch, if I told you their pricing strategy, as if I knew it, why would you ever trust me with your information?"

"C'mon. I'm your biggest customer. We have to stick together."

"Well, I don't know their strategy."

"Try to find out. And while you're at it, I think I can get the Hudson Pulp and Paper account away from National if you'll give me just a 5 percent discount on those products."

Betsy knew she was as low as she could go pricing wise. But if she gave him a few barrels a month free and marked it down as a sample, then she would effectively lower the price and get away with it. And National was not one of her accounts—if Mitch won the Hudson account, she would see another $100,000 in revenue per month.

Questions

1. What should she do about the Farley situation? Should she try to find out if Canuck plans to bid on the Farley contract and, if so, what its strategy is?
2. What should she do about the Hudson account?
3. Describe her relationship with Mitch. Where should she go with this account in the future?

ROLE PLAY CASE

(Note: If you've not completed the Role Play Case in Chapter 1, you should review it before starting this role play.) XBM is a national records management company. You are calling on the CEO, and everything seems to be going well. XBM has 48 salespeople, managed by six sales managers who report directly to the CEO. Currently they e-mail sales call reports to their managers at the end of each week, and sales are forecast for the following week. The CEO uses these forecasts to manage inventory, but always orders less than forecast because salespeople are overly optimistic. Sales are also slower than she would prefer, and she thinks with better knowledge of what is happening in each account, she could help salespeople perform better.

It's time to ask for the order. You should summarize how NetSuite lets the manager summarize the sales team's activities daily. Salespeople no longer have to e-mail their reports; they simply have to log into NetSuite and enter the day's activities. Not only will NetSuite give the managers a forecast daily, but it will also summarize each rep's performance by level of the sales process. The manager can then use that information to pinpoint how to improve each rep's performance. Once you've summarized, ask for an order of 55 units. Each buyer will be given a sheet with information about how to respond.

ADDITIONAL REFERENCES

Agnihotri, Raj, Michael Krush, and Rakesh K. Singh. "Understanding the Mechanism Linking Interpersonal Traits to Pro-Social Behaviors among Salespeople: Lessons from India." *Journal of Business and Industrial Marketing* 27, no. 3 (2012), pp. 211–27.

Agnihotri, Raj, Adam Rapp, Prabakar Kothandaraman, and Rakesh K. Singh. "An Emotion-Based Model of Salesperson Ethical Behaviors." *Journal of Business Ethics* 109, no. 2 (August 2012), pp. 243–57.

Bellizi, Joseph A. "Honoring Accounts of Top Sales Performers and Poor Sales Performers Who Have Engaged in Unethical Selling Behavior." *Journal of Global Business Issues* 2, no. 2 (2010), pp. 207–15.

Bush, Victoria, Al Bush, and L. Orr. "Monitoring the Ethical Use of Sales Technology: An Exploratory Investigation." *Journal of Business Ethics* 95, no. 2 (2009), pp. 239–57.

Cadogan, John Nick Lee, Anssi Tarkiainen, and Sanna Sundqvist. "Sales Manager and Sales Team Determinants of Salesperson Ethical Behavior." *European Journal of Marketing* 43, no. 7/8 (2009), pp. 907–22.

Calderaro, Fabio, and Anne T. Coughlan. "Spiffed-Up Channels: The Role of Spiffs in Hierarchical Selling Organizations." *Marketing Science* 26, no. 1 (2007), pp. 31–52.

DeConinick, James B. "The Effects of Ethical Climate on Organizational Identification, Supervisory Trust, and Turnover among Salespeople." *Journal of Business Research* 64 (2011), pp. 617–24.

Donoho, Casey, and Timothy Heinze. "The Personal Selling Ethics Scale: Revisions and Expansions for Teaching Sales Ethics. *Journal of Marketing Education* 33, no. 1 (2011), pp. 107–22.

Donoho, Casey, Timothy Heinze, and Christopher Kondo. "Gender Differences in Personal Selling Ethics Evaluations: Do They Exist and What Does Their Existence Mean for Teaching Sales Ethics?" *Journal of Marketing Education* 34, no. 1 (2012), pp. 55–70.

Hansen, John D., and Robert J. Riggle. "Ethical Salesperson Behavior in Sales Relationships." *Journal of Personal Selling and Sales Management* 29, no. 2 (2009), pp. 151–66.

Hunt, C. Shane. "The Emerging Influence of Compensation Plan Choice on Salesperson Organizational Identification and Perceived Organizational Support." *Journal of Leadership, Accountability and Ethics* 9, no. 1 (February 2012), pp. 71–80.

Kaynak, Ramazan, and Tuba Sert. "The Impact of Service Supplier's Unethical Behavior to Buyer's Satisfaction: An Empirical Study." *Journal of Business Ethics* 109, no. 2 (August 2012), pp. 219–26.

Lin, Su-Hsiu. "Effects of Ethical Sales Behavior Considered through Transaction Cost Theory: To Whom Is the Customer Loyal?" *Journal of International Management Studies* 7, no. 1 (April 2012), pp. 31–40.

Martin, Craig A. "An Empirical Examination of the Antecedents of Ethical Intentions in Professional Selling." *Journal of Leadership, Accountability and Ethics* 9, no. 1 (February 2012), pp. 19–26.

Moberg, Christopher R., and Megan Leasher. "American Preview: Examining the Differences in Salesperson Motivation among Different Cultures." *Journal of Business* 26, no. 2 (2011), pp. 145–60.

Neale, Larry, and Sam Fullerton. "The International Search for Ethics Norms: Which Consumer Behaviors Do Consumers Consider (Un)Acceptable?" *Journal of Services Marketing* 24, no. 6 (2010), pp. 476–86.

Ou, Wei-Ming, Chia-Mei Shih, Chin-Yuan Chen, and Chih-Wei Tseng. "Effects of Ethical Sales Behaviour, Expertise, Corporate Reputation, and Performance on Relationship Quality and Loyalty." *Service Industries Journal* 32, no. 5 (2012), p. 773.

Perry, James. "Managing Moral Distress: A Strategy for Resolving Ethical Dilemmas." *Business Horizons* 54, no. 5 (2011), pp. 393–97.

Pettijohn, Charles E., Nancy K. Keith, and Melissa S. Burnett. "Managerial and Peer Influence on Ethical Behavioral Intentions in a Personal Selling Context." *Journal of Promotion Management* 17, no. 2 (2011), p. 133.

Pullins, Ellen Bolman, Michael L. Mallin, Richard E. Buehrer, and Deirdre E. Jones. "How Salespeople Deal with Intergenerational Relationship Selling." *Journal of Business and Industrial Marketing* 26, no. 6 (2011), pp. 443–55.

Schwepker, Charles H., and David J. Good. "Moral Judgment and Its Impact on Business-to-Business Sales Performance and Customer Relationships." *Journal of Business Ethics* 98, no. 4 (February 2011), pp. 609–25.

Valentine, Sean, and Tim Barnett. "Perceived Organizational Ethics and the Ethical Decisions of Sales and Marketing Personnel." *Journal of Personal Selling and Sales Management* 27, no. 4 (2007), pp. 373–89.

Watkins, Alison, and Ronald Paul Hill. "Morality in Marketing: Oxymoron or Good Business Practice?" *Journal of Business Research* 64 (2011), pp. 921–27.

Zhuang, Guijun, and Alex Tsang. "A Study of Ethically Problematic Selling: Methods in China with a Broaden Concept of Gray-Marketing." *Journal of Business Ethics* 79, no. 1–2 (2008), pp. 85–101.

Zoltners, Andrew, P. Sinha, and S. Lorimer. "Breaking the Sales Force Incentive Addiction: A Balanced Approach to Sales Force Effectiveness." *Journal of Personal Selling and Sales Management* 32, no. 2 (2012), pp. 171–86.

chapter **3**

BUYING BEHAVIOR AND THE BUYING PROCESS

SOME QUESTIONS ANSWERED IN THIS CHAPTER ARE

- What are the different types of customers?
- How do organizations make purchase decisions?
- Which factors do organizations consider when they evaluate products and services?
- Who is involved in the buying decision?
- What should salespeople do in the different types of buying situations?
- Which changes are occurring in organizational buying, and how will these changes affect salespeople?

PROFILE I knew everything about this surgeon. I knew what surgeries he performed, how he performed them, the frequency he performed, even his favorite scrub cap. You could say I had done my homework. So when I began discussing the benefits of my company's product with him in the hallway of the hospital one day, I was a little frustrated when his response was, "That's crap, I don't believe you." I knew this product would work for him and work well. I told him, "You're going to call me in a week when you have a patient and nothing has worked on him, and you're going to want to try our product." Imagine my delight a week later when I did get that call, and sure enough he bought our product.

Understanding your buyer's behavior is the first step to a successful sale. I have discovered four types of buyers. There are the early adopters—those who are eager to try new products and step out of the box to see what's new in the market. These buyers look for new ways to improve their business practices. Then there are the late adopters. These buyers buy products and services early on in the product life cycle but are not quite as eager to jump on the buying train as first adopters. After the late adopters come what you may call "trend followers." When everyone else starts using a product and they see their colleagues buying it, then they too will become buyers. Lastly, there is the group that will never buy. They are not interested, nor will they ever be interested no matter how wonderful your product is. They are set in their ways and have no interest to change.

Knowing what type of buyer you have is not all that difficult. I have found that I can pretty much tell which type I'm dealing with within in the first 20 seconds. Reading your buyers' verbal and nonverbal body language can help you determine what category of buyer you are dealing with and how to approach them. In my industry of selling medical devices, figuring out your buyer type and then getting him or her on your team is critical for success

in the buying process. Unfortunately, getting a "yes, I want to buy" is not enough for a sale.

The buying process is more intricate than that. I not only have to get the support of the surgeon, but the hospital must be on board as well. To make matters more complicated, many times the contracting department must get involved too. Our medical products must be approved at the hospitals we sell to in order for the surgeons to be able to use them. So getting the surgeon's support helps immensely when it comes time to sell to the hospital. If the surgeon will go up to bat for me, the process becomes a whole lot easier. The hospital is more likely to work with the contracting department to approve the product if their own surgeons are the ones backing the product.

Not surprisingly, building a strong relationship with your buyer is critical not only to gain support from everyone in the buying center but also to continuing sales. Most buyers are not one-time buyers. Instead, many customers come back to me with new needs. I constantly work to make my relationships with my buyers more communicative and more supportive. As unfortunate as it may be in the medical field, it's not always about product superiority. Even though I may have the better product, I must constantly compete to maintain strong relationships with my buyers to keep their business. There is always a competitor trying to build a relationship, and more often than not, the sales representative with the better relationship will land the deal.

Understanding the buying process will also lead to success. Every doctor and potential buyer is different, so each buying process differs slightly too. Doing your homework is therefore incredibly important. I research their surgeries, their procedures, what instruments they use, what they like, everything down to the last scalpel on the operating table. After background research, I am ready for the approach. I will only be able to catch some doctors in the hall or in a surgery. Some will want to schedule a meeting. And some will just refuse any contact until a colleague has urged them to take a look at my product. Understanding which approach I will need to use makes a difference. When I do get in front of the buyer, I know I only have the length of time of an elevator pitch to catch their attention and spark interest. Once I do, it is time to meet with them and discuss how the product works and what it can do for them and their patients. Then I ask for their business by inquiring how they would like to try it out or which surgeries they would want to use it in. After they try the product out, the decision is up to them. I have found that buyers weigh what I believe about the product heavily in the buying decision. Buyers can tell from the way I talk, my voice, and my body language that I really believe in our products. This knowledge fuels them to sit down and actually look at the science behind what I am saying. But if I don't illustrate my belief in the product, why would they?

What's most rewarding is the impact I have on people's lives. After coming out of surgery one day, I learned an elderly man was going to have to have surgery on his nose due to devastating skin cancer. The procedure required gruesome steps, including cutting, stitching, and other grisly processes. With this procedure, the normal outcome was ending up looking like Frankenstein. After speaking with the patient and the surgeon in charge, I knew one of my company's products could really make a difference. Our product could actually regrow tissue! The surgeon did decide to use our product as an alternative. When Frankenstein failed to appear after the procedure, everyone was delighted, and I had gained a customer (the surgeon) for life. But what was really rewarding was that the patient would not have to face life with a grotesque, patched-up face.

By understanding the buyer and the buying process, I have made a difference in the lives of many end users. Whether it has been watching a surgeon perform an open-heart surgery with our new product or regrowing a nose, understanding the buyer's behavior and the buying process is a critical step to helping your customer and your customer's customer.

Visit our Web site at:
www.acell.com.

WHY PEOPLE BUY

In general, people buy to satisfy a want or desire, to solve a problem, or to satisfy an impulse. Even in situations where people are buying as part of their jobs, like all people, buyers have personal goals and aspirations. They want to get a raise, be promoted to a high-level position, have their managers recognize their accomplishments, and feel they have done something for their company or demonstrated their skills as a buyer or engineer. These needs can complicate buying decisions that are made on behalf of an employer, not forgetting that there are also the basic needs that the product or service solves.

To complicate matters further, there may needs associated with how the person wants to buy. Think, for a moment, about what you have purchased for yourself via the Internet. You may have many reasons for using the Internet, none of which have anything to do with the product you purchased. But the way you bought met certain needs. As salespeople, we have to be acutely aware of the needs we are solving: the needs that the product solves directly, the individual's needs that are served indirectly, and the needs that are solved by selling the way the buyer wants to buy.

TYPES OF CUSTOMERS

Business is full of a wide variety of customers, including producers, resellers, government agencies, institutions, and consumers. Each of these customer types has different needs and uses a different process to buy products and services. In many situations salespeople will have only one type of customer, but in other territories they may have many different types of customers. Thus salespeople may need to use different approaches when selling to different types of customers.

PRODUCERS

Producers buy products and services to manufacture and sell their products and services to customers. Buyers working for producers are involved in two types of buying situations: buying products that will be included in the products the company is manufacturing or buying products and services to support the manufacturing operation.

OEM Purchasers

Buyers for **original equipment manufacturers (OEMs)** purchase goods (components, subassemblies, raw and processed materials) to use in making their products. For example, when a distributor sells pizza toppings to a restaurant, that it is an OEM purchase. The pizza topping is a processed material used in making the restaurant's product, pizza. Another example of an OEM buyer would be Dell. Dell is an OEM purchaser. It may use Intel processors in its computers, but Dell is the OEM. Sometimes, though, Dell sells computers to other OEM manufacturers. For example, when you use a kiosk at the airport to print your boarding pass, the computer inside it is a Dell, but the kiosk is put together and sold by someone else.

Salespeople selling OEM products need to demonstrate that their products help their customers produce products that will offer superior value. For example, Tim Pavlovich, OEM salesperson for Dell, says that one reason why Dell gets contracts like the kiosk contract is because Dell has a nationwide service team already in place and can fix the computers anywhere in the world.

Most OEM products are bought in large quantities on an annual contract. The purchasing department negotiates the contract with the supplier; however, engineering and production departments play a major role in the purchase decision. Engineers evaluate the products and may prepare specifications for a custom design. The production department works with the supplier to make sure the OEM products are delivered "just in time."

OEM customers are building long-term relationships with a limited number of OEM suppliers. Thus, relationship building with more than one department in a customer firm is particularly important when selling OEM products.

End Users

When producers buy goods and services to support their own production and operations, they are acting as **end users.** End-user buying situations include the purchase of capital equipment; maintenance, repair, and overhaul (MRO) supplies; and services. **Capital equipment** items are major purchases, such as mainframe computers and machine tools that the producer uses for a number of years. **MRO supplies** include paper towels and replacement parts for machinery. **Services** include Internet and telephone connections, employment agencies, consultants, and transportation.

Because capital equipment purchases typically require major financial commitments, capital equipment salespeople need to work with a number of people involved in the purchase decision, including high-level corporate executives. These salespeople need to demonstrate the reliability of their products and their support services because an equipment failure can shut down the producer's operation. Capital equipment buying often focuses on lifetime operating cost rather than the initial purchase price because the equipment is used over a long period. Thus, capital equipment salespeople need to present the financial implications as well as the operating features and benefits of their products.

MRO supplies and services are typically a minor expense and therefore are usually less important to businesses than are many other items. Purchasing agents typically oversee MRO buying decisions. Because they often do not want to spend the time to evaluate all suppliers, they tend to purchase from vendors who have performed well in the past, creating functional relationships.

Although the cost of MRO supplies is typically low, availability can be critical. For example, the failure of a $10 motor in an industrial robot can shut down an entire assembly line. Some professional services, such as accounting, advertising, and consulting, also are important to the company and may be purchased in a manner similar to capital equipment purchases.

RESELLERS

Resellers buy finished products or services with the intention to resell them to businesses and consumers. Hormel sells precooked meats, such as pepperoni for pizza toppings, to resellers—distributors who then sell to restaurants. Other examples of resellers include McKesson Corporation, a wholesaler that buys health care products from manufacturers and resells those products to drugstores; Brazos Valley Equipment, a dealer for John Deere, selling tractors, harvesters, combines, and other agricultural implements to farmers; and Dealer's Electric, selling lighting, conduit, and other electrical components to electricians and contractors. All these are resellers, and they buy for similar reasons.

Resellers consider three elements when making decisions about which products to sell: profit margin, turnover, and effort. Resellers want to maximize their return on investment (ROI), which is a function of **profit margin,** or how much they make on each sale; **turnover,** or how quickly a product will sell; and how much effort it takes to sell the product. Buyers for resellers often simplify their decisions by a focus on either profit margin or turnover, but all resellers are interested in putting together an assortment of products that will yield the greatest overall ROI.

Salespeople work with resellers to help them build their ROI. Not only do salespeople help resellers choose which products to sell, but they also train

resellers on how to sell and service products and build point-of-purchase displays and promotions and may also help resellers with developing advertising and marketing campaigns to boost sales. For example, with increasing competition between grocery chains, retailers are asking suppliers to create excitement and generate traffic in stores.

"Retailers' expectations for our products' performance continue to escalate. Price is important but not the only thing retailers are demanding," Eddy Patterson, of Stubb's Legendary Kitchen, said. "We need to look at innovative ways that not only help sell our products and create brand awareness but also ways to contribute to the success of our customers, the retailers who sell our products." For example, Stubb's Bar-B-Q has sold its line of barbecue sauces and marinades in supermarkets and has created a loyal following. In fact, the following is so loyal that they created the "Que Crew," a loyalty marketing program for consumers. The program helps local retailers increase their sales of Stubb's products and helps consumers find new and creative uses for Stubb's products.

Stubb's partners with grocers to cross-promote the full line of Stubb's products with in-store displays, building sales for both Stubb's and the retailer.

Note that the same customer can act as an OEM manufacturer, an end user, and a reseller. For example, Dell Computer makes OEM buying decisions when it purchases microprocessors for its computers, acts as an end user when it buys materials handling equipment for its warehouse, and functions as a reseller when it buys software to resell to its computer customers when they place orders.

GOVERNMENT AGENCIES

The largest customers for goods and services in the United States are federal, state, and local governments, which collectively purchase goods and services valued at more than $1 trillion annually. Including government-owned utilities, federal, state, and local governments purchase the equivalent of 12 percent of the country's entire gross domestic product, making it the largest customer in the world.[1] Government buyers typically develop detailed specifications for a product and then invite qualified suppliers to submit bids. A contract is awarded to the lowest bidder. The government has also developed procedures for small purchases without a bid, streamlining the process and reducing costs.

Effective selling to government agencies requires a thorough knowledge of their unique procurement procedures and rules. Salespeople also need to know about projected needs so they can influence the development of the buying specifications. For example, Harris Corporation worked for six years with the Federal Aviation Administration and finally won a $1.7 billion contract to modernize air traffic communication systems.

Some resources available to salespeople working with the federal and state governments are the following:

- The *Commerce Business Daily* provides notice of new federal sales opportunities each day at www.cbd-net.com. Companies can sign up to be notified of opportunities in specific product categories.

- The National Association of State Purchasing Officials in Washington, D.C., which publishes information for all 50 states, including the availability of vendor guides, registration fees, and how to get on bidder lists (see www.NASPO.org).

- The Small Business Administration offers a Web site (www.sba.gov) that educates small businesses on how to sell to governments and also lists sales opportunities specifically available only to small businesses.

- FedBizOpps.gov, a Web site listing all business opportunities greater than $25,000. At any given time, there are over 40,000 open sales opportunities described on this Web site.

Many international salespeople are selling to government agencies, even though private companies may be the biggest buyers of these products and services in the United States. For example, Alcatel-Lucent, a French company that manufactures telephone equipment, sells not only to private companies such as Verizon and AT&T in the United States but also to the post, telephone, and telegraph (PTT) government agencies in many countries in Europe, Asia, and Africa. In fact, PTTs can represent as much as 40 percent of the government's purchases in countries such as the Netherlands and the Slovak Republic.[2]

Selling to foreign governments is challenging. The percentage of domestic product (countries may require that a certain percentage of the product be manufactured or assembled locally) and exchange rates (the values of local currencies in U.S. dollars) are as important as the characteristics of the product. Different economic and political systems, cultures, and languages also can make international selling difficult.

INSTITUTIONS

Another important customer group consists of public and private institutions such as churches, hospitals, and colleges. Often these institutions have purchasing rules and procedures that are as complex and rigid as those used by government agencies.

Packaged goods manufacturers, such as Stubbs and Hormel, sell to both resellers (supermarkets) and institutional customers (restaurants and hospitals). These customers have different needs and buying processes. In some instances, institutions purchase more like resellers, worrying about the same needs, such as how fast the product will sell or be consumed. In other ways, institutions can be like producers, concerned with how their clients will view their services.

CONSUMERS

Consumers purchase products and services for use by themselves or by their families. A lot of salespeople sell insurance, automobiles, clothing, and real estate to consumers. However, college graduates often take sales jobs that involve selling to business enterprises, government agencies, or institutions. Thus, the examples in this text focus on these selling situations, and this chapter discusses organizational rather than consumer buying behavior.

In the next section we contrast the buying processes of consumers and organizations. Then we describe the buying process that organizations use in more detail, including the steps in the process, who influences the decisions, and how salespeople can influence the decisions.

ORGANIZATIONAL BUYING AND SELLING

Salespeople who sell to consumers and salespeople who call on organizations have very different jobs. Because the organizational buying process typically is more complex than the consumer buying process, selling to organizations often requires more skills and is more challenging than selling to consumers. Relationships, too, can differ because of the size of the organizations involved.

COMPLEXITY OF THE ORGANIZATIONAL BUYING PROCESS

The typical organizational purchase is much larger and more complex than the typical consumer purchase. Organizations use highly trained, knowledgeable purchasing agents to make these decisions. Many other people in organizations are involved in purchase decisions, including engineers, production managers, business analysts, and senior executives.

Organizational buying decisions often involve extensive evaluations and negotiations over time. The average time required to complete a purchase is five months, and during that period salespeople need to make many calls to gather and provide information.

Ashley Anderson, salesperson for "The Ranch" country-western radio station in the Dallas–Fort Worth area, worked for over a year with one account before getting the sale. The account is an eye surgeon promoting his Lasik surgery practice. Ashley worked with his PR agency and him, calling at least twice a month on one or both. "I think three factors finally won him over," says Ashley. "First, over the course of the year, I built a strong relationship with him and he began to trust me. Second, I was able to show him that advertising with us would reach a market no one else was going after. And third, I leveraged a free month of advertising to create an urgency to make a decision." Two years later he still advertises with "The Ranch."

The complexity of organizational purchase decisions means salespeople must be able to work effectively with a wide range of people working for their customer and their company. For example, when selling a new additive to a food processor such as Nabisco, an International Flavors and Fragrances salesperson may interact with advertising, product development, legal, production, quality control, and customer service people at Nabisco. The salesperson needs to know the technical and economic benefits of the additive to Nabisco and the benefits to consumers.

In addition, the salesperson coordinates all areas of his or her own firm to assist in making the sale. The salesperson works with research and development to provide data on consumer taste tests, with production to meet the customer's delivery requirements, and with finance to set the purchasing terms. (Working effectively within the salesperson's organization is discussed in more detail in Chapter 16.)

The complexity of organizational selling is increasing as more customers become global businesses. For example, Deere and Company has a special unit to coordinate worldwide purchases. The unit evaluates potential suppliers across the globe for each of its product lines and manufacturing facilities. Further, the company wants to standardize products made in different plants. A harvester made in Ottumwa, Iowa, should have the same belt as the same model harvester made at Arc-les-Gray, France. Thus, a salesperson selling belts to Deere must work with the special corporate buying unit as well as with the employees at each manufacturing location around the world.[3] There's no doubt that global competitiveness is a key factor increasing the complexity of organizational buying, but global sourcing is also a key factor for achieving a sustainable competitive advantage.[4]

If you want to sell a part such as a belt for a John Deere harvester made in Ottumwa, Iowa, then you must be able to sell and service this plant in Arc-les-Gray, France, too.

DERIVED VERSUS DIRECT DEMAND

Salespeople selling to consumers typically can focus on individual consumer or family needs. Organizational selling often requires salespeople to know about the customer's customers. Sales to OEMs and resellers are based on derived rather than direct demand. **Derived demand** means that purchases made by these customers ultimately depend on the demand for their products—either other organizations or consumers. For example, Apple's iPad has not only increased sales for touch screens made by Wintek and computer chips made by Samsung; the demand for the equipment that makes touch screens and computer chips has also been affected.[5]

HOW DO ORGANIZATIONS MAKE BUYING DECISIONS?

To effectively sell to organizations, salespeople need to understand how organizations make buying decisions. This section discusses the steps in the organizational buying process, the different types of buying decisions, and the people involved in making the decisions.

STEPS IN THE BUYING PROCESS

Exhibit 3.1 shows the eight steps in an organizational buying process.

Exhibit 3.1

Steps in the Organizational Buying Process

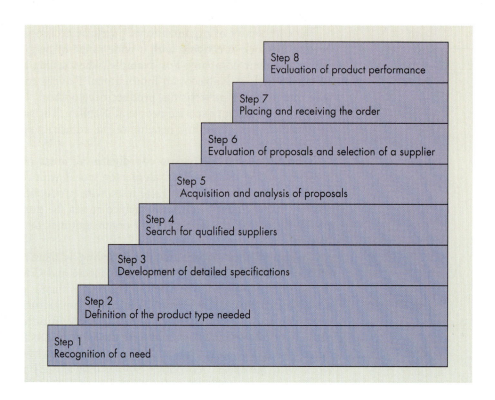

Step 8
Evaluation of product performance

Step 7
Placing and receiving the order

Step 6
Evaluation of proposals and selection of a supplier

Step 5
Acquisition and analysis of proposals

Step 4
Search for qualified suppliers

Step 3
Development of detailed specifications

Step 2
Definition of the product type needed

Step 1
Recognition of a need

Recognizing a Need or a Problem (Step 1)

The buying process starts when someone realizes a problem exists. Employees in the customer's firm or outside salespeople can trigger this recognition. For example, a supermarket cashier might discover that the optical scanner is making mistakes in reading bar code labels. Salespeople often trigger the buying process by demonstrating how their products can improve the efficiency of the customer's operation.

Defining the Type of Product Needed (Step 2)

After identifying a problem, organization members develop a general approach to solving it. For example, a production manager who concludes that the factory is not running efficiently recognizes a problem, but this insight may not lead to a purchase decision. The manager may think the inefficiency is caused by poor supervision or unskilled workers.

However, a production equipment salesperson might work with the manager to analyze the situation and show how efficiency could be improved by purchasing some automated assembly equipment. Thus, the problem solution is defined in terms of purchasing a product or service—the automated assembly equipment needed—and the buying process moves to step 3. If the decision to continue requires senior management participation, research suggests that these executives will approve the manager's request to consider the purchase, then leave it up to the manager to cover the next few steps before stepping back in when a final decision is made.[6]

Developing Product Specifications (Step 3)

In step 3 the specifications for the product needed to solve the problem are prepared. Potential suppliers will use these specifications to develop proposals. The buyers will use them to objectively evaluate the proposals.

Steps 2 and 3 offer great opportunities for salespeople to influence the outcome of the buying process. Using their knowledge of their firm's products and the customer's needs, salespeople can help develop specifications that favor their particular product. For example, a Hyster forklift might have superior performance in terms of a small turning radius. Knowing this advantage and the customer's small, tightly packed warehouse, the Hyster salesperson might influence the customer to specify a very small turning radius for forklifts—a turning radius that only Hyster forklifts can provide. Competing salespeople, who first become aware of this procurement after the specifications are written, will be at a severe disadvantage.

Searching for Qualified Suppliers (Step 4)

After the specifications have been written, the customer looks for potential suppliers. The customer may simply contact previous suppliers or go through an extensive search procedure: do a Web search, read customer reviews online, download case studies and position papers, and call customers found on a list on the potential supplier's Web site.

Acquiring and Analyzing Proposals (Step 5)

In step 5 qualified suppliers are asked to submit proposals. Salespeople work with people in their company to develop their proposal. In many instances, proposals are slide presentations delivered by the salesperson over the Web through Webex, Skype, or some other form of online conference call.

Evaluating Proposals and Selecting a Supplier (Step 6)

Next, the customer evaluates the proposals. After a preferred supplier is selected, further negotiations may occur concerning price, delivery, or specific performance features.

Placing an Order and Receiving the Product (Step 7)

In step 7 an order is placed with the selected supplier. The order goes to the supplier, who acknowledges receipt and commits to a delivery date. After the product is shipped, the buying firm inspects the received goods and then pays the supplier for the product. During this step salespeople need to make sure the paperwork is correct and their firm knows what has to be done to satisfy the customer's requirements. In many instances, the customer may be responsible for placing the order through a secure Web site.

Evaluating Product Performance (Step 8)

In the final step of the purchasing process, the product's performance is evaluated. The evaluation may be a formal or informal assessment made by people involved in the buying process. The supplier is also evaluated on such characteristics as whether the billing was accurate, how quickly service calls were handled, and similar criteria.

Salespeople play an important role in this step. They need to work with the users to make sure the product performs well. In addition, salespeople need to work with purchasing agents to ensure that they are satisfied with the communications and delivery.

This after-sale support ensures that the salesperson's product will get a positive evaluation and that he or she will be considered a qualified supplier in future procurement. This step is critical to establishing successful long-term relationships. (Building relationships through after-sale support is discussed in more detail in Chapter 14.)

CREEPING COMMITMENT

Creeping commitment means a customer becomes increasingly committed to a particular course of action while going through the steps in the buying process. As decisions are made at each step, the range of alternatives narrows; the customer becomes more and more committed to a specific course of action and even to a specific vendor. Thus, it is vital that salespeople be involved in the initial steps so they will have an opportunity to participate in the final steps.

In instances involving purchasing components or materials as part of new product development, buyers are more interested in early involvement by possible vendors than when buying other types of products. Called *early procurement involvement* or *early supplier involvement,* this strategy has potential suppliers participate in the actual design process for a new product. BASF, the giant German chemical company, engages in early vendor involvement to ensure that the proper levels and quality of supply are available.[7] Other companies use supplier involvement to aid in designing a more effective new product.[8] Whatever the reason, each design decision represents a creeping commitment to a final set of decisions that are difficult to undo.

thinking it through

What steps did you go through in making the choice to attend this university? How can you relate your decision-making process to the eight steps in the organizational buying process? Did any decisions you made early in the process affect decisions you made later in the process? What roles did your family and friends play in the decision process?

TYPES OF ORGANIZATIONAL BUYING DECISIONS

Many purchase decisions are made without going through all the steps just described. For example, a Frito-Lay salesperson may check the supply of his or her products in a supermarket, write a purchase order to restock the shelves, and present it to the store manager. After recognizing the problem of low stock, the manager simply signs the order (step 6) without going through any of the other steps. However, if the Frito-Lay salesperson wanted the manager to devote more shelf space to Frito-Lay snacks, the manager might go through all eight steps in making and evaluating this decision.

Exhibit 3.2 describes three types of buying decisions—new tasks, modified rebuys, and straight rebuys[9]—along with the strategies salespeople need to use in each situation. In this exhibit the "in" company is the seller that has provided the product or service to the company in the past, and the "out" company is the seller that is not or has not been a supplier to the customer.

NEW TASKS

When a customer purchases a product or service for the first time, a **new-task situation occurs.** Most purchase decisions involving capital equipment or the initial purchase of OEM products are new tasks.

Because the customer has not made the purchase decision recently, the company's knowledge is limited, and it goes through all eight steps of the buying process. In these situations customers face considerable risk. Thus, they typically seek information from salespeople and welcome their knowledge. Two studies found that organizational buyers rate salespeople as a more important information source than the Internet, particularly when the success of the purchase is likely to be difficult to achieve and to evaluate.[10]

Exhibit 3.2

Types of Organizational
Buying Decisions

	New Task	Modified Rebuy	Straight Rebuy
Customer Needs			
Information and risk reduction	Information about causes and solutions for a new problem; reduce high risk in making a decision with limited knowledge.	Information and solutions to increase efficiency and/or reduce costs.	Needs are generally satisfied.
Nature of Buying Process			
Number of people involved in process	Many	Few	One
Time to make a decision	Months or years	Month	Day
Key steps in the buying process (Exhibit 3.1)	1, 2, 3, 8	3, 4, 5, 6, 8	5, 6, 7, 8
Key decision makers	Executives and engineers	Production and purchasing managers	Purchasing agent
Selling Strategy			
For in-supplier	Monitor changes in customer needs; respond quickly when problems and new needs arise; provide technical information.	Act immediately when problems arise with customers; make sure all of customer's needs are satisfied.	Reinforce relationship.
For out-supplier	Suggest new approach for solving problems; provide technical advice.	Respond more quickly than present supplier when problem arises; encourage customer to consider an alternative; present information about how new alternative will increase efficiency.	Convince customer of potential benefits from reexamining choice of supplier; secure recognition and approval as an alternative supplier.

From the salesperson's perspective, the initial buying process steps are critical in new-task situations. During these steps the alert salesperson can help the customer define the characteristics of the needed product and develop the purchase specifications. By working with the customer in these initial steps, the salesperson can take advantage of creeping commitment and gain a significant advantage over the competition. The final step, postpurchase evaluation, is also vital. Buyers making a new purchase decision are especially interested in evaluating results and will use this information in making similar purchase decisions in the future.

STRAIGHT REBUYS

In a straight rebuy situation, the customer buys the same product from the same source it used when the need arose previously. Because customers have purchased the product or service a number of times, they have considerable knowledge about their requirements and the potential vendors. MRO supplies and services and reorders of OEM components often are straight rebuy situations.

Typically, a straight rebuy is triggered by an internal event, such as a low inventory level. Because needs are easily recognized, specifications have been developed, and potential suppliers have been identified, the latter steps of the buying process assume greater importance.

Some straight rebuys are computerized. For example, many hospitals use an automatic reorder system developed by Baxter, a manufacturer and distributor of medical supplies. When the inventory control system recognizes that levels of supplies such as tape, surgical sponges, or IV kits have dropped to prespecified levels, a purchase order is automatically generated and transmitted electronically to the nearest Baxter distribution center.

When a company is satisfied and has developed a long-term supplier relationship, it continues to order from the same company it has used in the past. Salespeople at in-companies want to maintain the strong relationship; they do not want the customer to consider new suppliers. Thus, these salespeople must make sure that orders are delivered on time and that the products continue to get favorable evaluations.

Salespeople trying to break into a straight rebuy situation—those representing an out-supplier—face a tough sales problem. Often they need to persuade a customer to change suppliers, even though the present supplier is performing satisfactorily. In such situations the salesperson hopes the present supplier will make a significant mistake, causing the customer to reevaluate suppliers. To break into a straight rebuy situation, salespeople need to provide compelling information to motivate the customer to treat the purchase as a modified rebuy.

MODIFIED REBUYS

In a **modified rebuy** situation, the customer has purchased the product or a similar product in the past but is interested in obtaining new information. This situation typically occurs when the in-supplier performs unsatisfactorily, a new product becomes available, or the buying needs change. In such situations sales representatives of the in-suppliers need to convince customers to maintain the relationship and continue their present buying pattern. In-suppliers with strong customer relationships are the first to find out when requirements change. In this case customers give the supplier's salespeople information to help them respond to the new requirements.

Salespeople with out-suppliers want customers to reevaluate the situation and to actively consider switching vendors. The successful sales rep from an out-supplier will need to influence all the people taking part in the buying decision.

WHO MAKES THE BUYING DECISION? ●────

As we discussed previously, a number of people are involved in new-task and modified rebuy decisions. This group of people is called the **buying center**, an informal, cross-department group of people involved in a purchase decision. People in the customer's organization become involved in a buying center because they have formal responsibilities for purchasing or they are important sources of information. In some cases the buying center includes experts who are not full-time employees. For example, consultants usually specify the air-conditioning equipment that will be used in a factory undergoing remodeling. Thus, the buying center defines the set of people who make or influence the purchase decision.[11]

Salespeople need to know the names and responsibilities of all people in the buying center for a purchase decision, and sometimes they need to make sure the right people are participating. For example, one of Bill Dunne's prospects for a customer relationship management software application was certain that the company would buy Bill's offering, a customized version of SugarCRM. Yet when it came time to buy, the CEO, who had not been involved in any prior meetings, stepped in and selected another vendor. Why? There was one key feature about the other vendor's product that he really liked, and while Bill had uncovered the CEO's interest in the feature, he didn't realize it would be a deal killer for him. "The lesson I learned," says Bill, "is to meet with every person who uses the system at least once."

USERS

Users, such as the manufacturing personnel for OEM products and capital equipment, typically do not make the ultimate purchase decision. However, they often have considerable influence in the early and late steps of the buying process—need recognition, product definition, and postpurchase evaluation. Thus users are particularly important in new-task and modified rebuy situations. Salespeople often attempt to convert a straight rebuy to a modified rebuy by demonstrating superior product performance or a new benefit to users.

INITIATORS

Another role in the buying process is that of initiator, or the person who starts the buying process. A user can play the role of the initiator, as in "This machine is broken; we need a new one." In fact, often it is users' dissatisfaction with a product used by the organization that initiates the purchase process.[12] In some instances, though, such as in OEM product decisions, the initiator could be an executive making a decision such as introducing a new product, which starts the buying process.

INFLUENCERS

People inside or outside the organization who directly or indirectly provide information during the buying process are influencers. These members of the buying center may seek to influence issues regarding product specifications, criteria for evaluating proposals, or information about potential suppliers. For example, the marketing department can influence a purchase decision by indicating that the company's products would sell better if they included a particular supplier's components. Architects can play a critical role in the purchase of construction material by specifying suppliers, even though the ultimate purchase orders will be placed by the contractor responsible for constructing the building. Influence can be technical, such as in product specifications, but can also involve finances and how a decision is made.

Miller and Heiman, two noted sales consultants, assert that there are four types of influencers. One is the economic influencer, or person who is concerned about the financial aspects of the decision. Another is the user, which we will discuss later. A third is the technical influencer, a person who makes sure the technical requirements (including logistics, terms and conditions, quality measurements, or other specifications) are met. Miller and Heiman state that these people usually have the authority only to say no (meaning the salesperson did not meet the specifications, so the proposal is rejected), so they play a gatekeeping role (discussed more in a moment). The fourth role or type of influencer is the coach. The coach is someone in a buying organization who can advise and direct you, the salesperson, in maneuvering through the buying process in an effective fashion, leading to a sale. In addition, this person may advocate for you in private conversations among members of the buying center. As you can imagine, finding a coach is an important factor when decision processes are complex and involve a lot of people.[13]

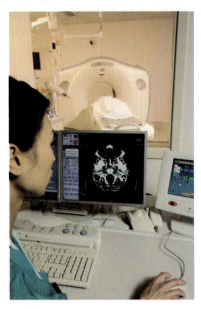

The buying center for radiology equipment includes (clockwise from lower left) the technicians operating the equipment (users), the radiologists (gatekeepers and influencers), and the hospital administrator (the decision maker).

GATEKEEPERS

Gatekeepers control the flow of information and may limit the alternatives considered. For example, the quality control and service departments may determine which potential suppliers are qualified sources.

Purchasing agents often play a gatekeeping role by determining which potential suppliers are to be notified about the purchase situation and are to have access to relevant information. In some companies all contacts must be made through purchasing agents. They arrange meetings with other gatekeepers, influencers, and users. Such gatekeeping activity is not a power play; rather, it ensures that purchases are consolidated under one contract, thus reducing costs and increasing quality. These single contracts are growing in popularity as a way to reduce costs globally.[13] When dealing with such companies, salespeople may not be allowed to contact members of the buying center directly. When purchasing agents restrict access to important information, salespeople are tempted to bypass the purchasing agents and make direct contact. This backdoor selling approach can upset purchasing agents so much that they may disqualify the salesperson's company from the purchase situation. In Chapter 7 we discuss ethical strategies that salespeople can use to deal with this issue.

DECIDERS

In any buying center one or more members of the group, **deciders,** make the final choice. Determining who actually makes the purchase decision for an organization is often difficult. For straight rebuys the purchasing agent usually selects the vendor and places the order. However, for new tasks many people influence the decision, and several people must approve the decision and sign the purchase order.

In general, senior executives get more involved in important purchase decisions that have a greater effect on the performance of the organization. For example, the chief executive officer (CEO) and chief financial officer (CFO) play an important role in purchasing a telephone system because this network has a significant impact on the firm's day-to-day operations.

Exhibit 3.3

Importance of Hospital
Buying Center Members
in the Buying Process
for Intensive Care
Monitoring Equipment

Step in Buying Process	Physicians	Nurses	Hospital Administrators	Purchasing Engineers	Agents
Need recognition (step 1)	High	Moderate	Low	Low	Low
Definition of product type (step 2)	High	High	Moderate	Moderate	Low
Analysis of proposal (step 5)	High	Moderate	Moderate	High	Low
Proposal evaluation and supplier selection (step 6)	High	Low	High	Low	Moderate

To sell effectively to organizations, salespeople need to know the people in the buying center and their involvement at different steps of the buying process. Consider the following situation. Salespeople selling expensive intensive care monitoring equipment know that a hospital buying center for the type of equipment they sell typically consists of physicians, nurses, hospital administrators, engineers, and purchasing agents. Through experience, these salespeople also know the relative importance of the buying center members in various stages of the purchasing process (see Exhibit 3.3). With this information the intensive care equipment salespeople know to concentrate on physicians throughout the process, nurses and engineers in the middle of the process, and hospital administrators and purchasing agents at the end of the process.

SUPPLIER EVALUATION AND CHOICE

At various steps in the buying process, members of the buying center evaluate alternative methods for solving a problem (step 2), the qualifications of potential suppliers (step 4), proposals submitted by potential suppliers (step 5), and the performance of products purchased (step 8). Using these evaluations, buyers select potential suppliers and eventually choose a specific vendor.

The needs of both the organization and the individuals making the decisions affect the evaluation and selection of products and suppliers (see Exhibit 3.4). Often these organizational and personal needs are classified into two categories: rational needs and emotional needs. **Rational needs** are directly related to the performance of the product. Thus, the organizational needs discussed in the next section are examples of rational needs. **Emotional needs** are associated with the personal rewards and gratification of the person buying the product. Thus, the personal needs of buying center members often are considered emotional needs.

ORGANIZATIONAL NEEDS AND CRITERIA

Organizations consider a number of factors when they make buying decisions, including economic factors such as price, product quality, and supplier service. In addition, organizations also consider strategic objectives, such as sustainability (choosing vendors and products that are good for the planet) and social diversity.

Economic Criteria

The objective of businesses is to make a profit. Thus, businesses are very concerned about buying products and services at the lowest cost. Organizational buyers are now taking a more sophisticated approach to evaluating the cost of equipment. Rather than simply focusing on the purchase price, they consider

Exhibit 3.4

Factors Influencing
Organizational Buying
Decisions

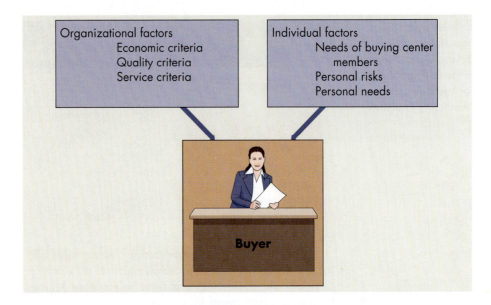

Organizational factors
  Economic criteria
  Quality criteria
  Service criteria

Individual factors
  Needs of buying center
    members
  Personal risks
  Personal needs

Buyer

Exhibit 3.5

Life-Cycle Costing

	Product A	Product B
Initial cost	$35,000	$30,000
Life of machine	10 years	10 years
Power consumption per year	150 MWh*	180 MWh*
Power cost at $30/MWh	$45,000	$54,000
Estimated operating and maintenance cost over 10 years	$25,000	$30,000
Life-cycle cost	$105,000	$114,000

Note: A more thorough analysis would calculate the net present value of the cash flow associated with each product's purchase and use.

*MWh = megawatt-hour.

installation costs, the costs of needed accessories, freight charges, estimated maintenance costs, and operating costs, including forecasts of energy costs. Retail buyers also consider other financial factors, such as promotion plans, as described in Building Partnerships 3.1.

Life-cycle costing, also referred to as the total cost of ownership, is a method for determining the cost of equipment or supplies over their useful lives. Using this approach, salespeople can demonstrate that a product with a higher initial cost will have a lower overall cost. An example of life-cycle costing appears in Exhibit 3.5. (Approaches, that salespeople can use to demonstrate the value of their products to customers are discussed in more detail in Chapter 9.)

Quality Criteria

Many firms recognize that the quality and reliability of their products are as important to their customers as price. Firms expect their suppliers to support their efforts to provide quality products. A recent study in Japan indicates that suppliers are evaluated on both the quality of their service and the quality of their products because both impact the quality that the buyer can deliver to its customer.[14] Salespeople often need to describe how their firms will support the customer's quality objectives.

ADAPTING TO BUYERS

Jenna Weber followed up a college internship with Hormel Foods with a sales position with the company. Selling meat products like HORMEL® chili, DINTY MOORE® beef stew, and even SPAM®, she calls on retailers. Each retailer has a corporate buyer that she has to convince to allow Hormel products into the store, but then it is up to each store manager to decide if and how many to carry. As she says, her role is "to give the consumer every opportunity to purchase Hormel products by getting the products on the shelf and supporting the products through promotions."

"I currently work with a regional retail customer that has over 100 stores in the Northeast. I must sell products, promotions, and strategies for each one of my categories. However, the most difficult part of my job is dealing with different buyers. Some categories have the same buyer. For example HORMEL® chili, DINTY MOORE® beef stew, and SPAM® are all purchased by the same grocery buyer. But there are five different buyers overall, and each buyer has a different style. For example, my meat buyer is very relationship oriented and appreciates that I bring him donuts and coffee. We talk about his children, his plans for the weekend, and, of course, the business. He doesn't like long presentations with data-filled pages. He just wants to know, "Will this item sell?" He is easy to deal with, especially on promotions that are run annually (such as hams during the holidays).

Another buyer is the complete opposite. He wants to know every detail of the item, including pages of analytical data that support the success of the product. He takes longer to make a decision and needs data to prove his choice. This can be good and bad. For example, we were running a bacon promotion, and I argued with my meat buyer that one truckload wasn't enough. It didn't matter to him that I had past history of similar promotions that proved he needed more; he simply refused. Conversely, for a large promotion in grocery, I used multiple analytical tools to prove the volume my grocery buyer needed. By showing him the facts, I successfully sold him three truckloads of displays. As you can see, it's important to understand your buyer's personality and the most effective way to connect with him or her.

The end consumer is also very important in the buying process. While I do not sell to consumers directly, they play a key role in my decision making. When planning a promotion, does it make the most sense to present a deal at two for $4 or one at $1.99? In making that choice, I have to decide which price point seems like the best deal to my end user. For an item that a customer may already buy multiples of, CHI-CHI'S® salsa, for example, two for $4 makes the most sense. However, most people won't purchase more than one 38-ounce DINTY MOORE® beef stew, so that item is better left at a single price point. Along with deciding price, I also have to choose which products are items that should be displayed. Most of Hormel's products are impulse items, but it is up to the retailer if they are worthy of an end cap or aisle display. My job is to ensure that Hormel products are highly visible to our end user, thus encouraging increased sales."

Whether it is the corporate buyer or the end consumer, the purchasing process is very complex. A lot of planning goes into how Jenna approaches each buyer and presents a promotion. Whatever Hormel comes up with for her to offer, it is still up to her to adapt it to the needs and buying style of each of her individual buyers.

To satisfy customer quality needs, salespeople need to know what organizational buyers are looking for. Quality criteria can include such objective measures as the number of defects per thousand products, the amount of time a machine operates before needing service, or the number of items a system can process in a given period of time. Some buyers also utilize subjective measures, such as if a piece of office furniture looks sturdy or if the vendor has great ratings on the Web. Either way, the salesperson has to identify what criteria will be used to determine quality.

Service Criteria

Organizational buyers want more than products that are low cost, that perform reliably, and that are aesthetically pleasing. They also want suppliers that will work with them to solve their problems. One primary reason firms are interested in developing long-term relationships with suppliers is so they can learn about each other's needs and capabilities and use this information to enhance their products' performance. **Value analysis** is an example of a program in which suppliers and customers work together to reduce costs and still provide the required level of performance.[15]

Representatives from the supplier and the purchasing department and technical experts from engineering, production, or quality control usually form a team to undertake the analysis. The team begins by examining the product's function. Then members brainstorm to see whether changes can be made in the design, materials, construction, or production process to reduce the product's costs but keep its performance high. Some questions addressed in this phase are the following:

- Can a part in the product be eliminated?
- If the part is not standard, can a standard (and presumably less expensive) part be used?
- Does the part have greater performance than this application needs?
- Are unnecessary machining or fine finishes specified?

Salespeople can use value analysis to get customers to consider a new product. This approach is particularly useful for the out-supplier in a straight rebuy situation. David Lenling, a sales representative for Hormel, used value analysis to sell pepperoni to a 35-unit group of pizzerias in the Cincinnati area. The owner had been using the same pepperoni and bacon topping for over 15 years and was reluctant to switch. Lenling showed how the Hormel pepperoni product cost $5 per case more but offered 1,200 more slices in a case with the same weight, which equated to an additional $12 of pepperoni, or a $7 per case net savings, enough to make about 35 more pizzas per case. The owner of the chain was unaware of these differences until Lenling actually weighed his current product. Through value analysis, Lenling was able to interrupt a straight rebuy. Further, Lenling's buyer agreed that the Hormel product tasted better and was less greasy, resulting in a better-looking and tastier pizza, which might result in customers coming back more often. Because Hormel products are of high quality and sell at a premium price, Lenling and other sales representatives have to prove that the products are worth the extra money. They use value analysis to help purchasing agents determine how much it costs to use the product rather than how much the product costs. That's why Lenling was able to win that large pizza chain's business.[16]

INDIVIDUAL NEEDS OF BUYING CENTER MEMBERS

In the preceding section we discussed criteria used to determine whether a product satisfies the needs of the organization. However, buying center members are people. Their evaluations and choices are affected by their personal needs as well as the organization's needs.

Types of Needs

Buying center members, like all people, have personal goals and aspirations. They want to get a raise, be promoted to a high-level position, have their managers recognize their accomplishments, and feel they have done something for their company or demonstrated their skills as a buyer or engineer.

Salespeople can influence members of the buying center by developing strategies to satisfy individual needs. For example, demonstrating how a new product will reduce costs and increase the purchasing agents' bonus would satisfy the purchasing agents' financial security needs. Encouraging an engineer to recommend a product employing the latest technology might satisfy the engineer's need for self-esteem and recognition by his or her engineering peers.

Risk Reduction

In many situations, members of the buying center tend to be more concerned about losing benefits they have now than about increasing their benefits. They place a lot of emphasis on avoiding risks that may result in poor decisions, decisions that can adversely affect their personal reputations and rewards as well as their organization's performance. Buyers first assess the potential for risk and then develop a risk reduction strategy.[17] To reduce risk, buying center members may collect additional information, develop a loyalty to present suppliers, or spread the risk by placing orders with several vendors.

Because they know suppliers try to promote their own products, customers tend to question information received from vendors. Customers usually view information from independent sources such as trade publications, colleagues, and outside consultants as more credible than information provided by salespeople and company advertising and sales literature. Therefore, they will search for such information to reduce risk when a purchase is important.

When making a buying decision, this [woman]'s performance is being judged by others in the organization. Thus, she will seek to find ways to reduce her risk, while also reducing risk to the organization.

Advertising, the Internet, and sales literature tend to be used more in the early steps of the buying process. Word-of-mouth information from friends and colleagues is important in the proposal evaluation and supplier selection steps. Word-of-mouth information is especially important for risky decisions that will have a significant impact on the organization or the buying center member. "Sales Technology 3.1" illustrates the importance of the Internet for word-of-mouth information.

Another way to reduce uncertainty and risk is to display vendor loyalty to suppliers—that is, to continue buying from suppliers that proved satisfactory in the past. Converting buying decisions into straight rebuys makes the decisions routine, minimizing the chances of a poor decision. One name for this is lost for good; for all the out-suppliers, this account can be considered lost for good because the in-supplier has cemented this relationship for a long time. Organizations tend to develop vendor loyalty for unimportant purchase decisions, though they will often look to vendors who have proved trustworthy when beginning to search in a risky situation. In these situations the potential benefits from new suppliers do not compensate for the costs of evaluating these suppliers.

TODAY'S WEB-EMPOWERED CUSTOMER

Customers today have greater power than ever before. In the past, an upset customer might have told 20 friends about a bad experience. But if you've tweeted about a store or restaurant giving you bad service, how many more people have you told?

If you've purchased a night at a hotel at Hotels.com, you're probably like most who read other consumers' reviews of the hotel first. The Web makes product and supplier information readily available to anyone who will look for it. Deitra Pope, for example, was looking for a CRM solution for her company. The first consultant who called on her, though, had such a bad reputation online that she wanted nothing to do with him or his company. She's not alone. One study found that 87 percent of business buyers turn to the Internet for information on important purchases (and, frankly, we're surprised that it wasn't 100 percent).

Recently, a new service was launched called Decide.com, which aggregates and summarizes all of the consumer reviews that it can find on the Web. The company cites one example of how vendor information on the Web can provide only part of the story. A leading television on Amazon's Web site looks like a great buy, but the broader array of information from Decide.com suggests that you should look for another.

Buyers also use the Web to offer input into new product development. IdeaStorm, for example, is a platform that Dell uses to allow users to post ideas for new products or features (see www.ideastorm.com), and other users can then vote for the ideas. Submissions earn points for good ideas that submitters can then redeem for prizes. A recent review of the site indicated that Dell had implemented over 500 of the ideas submitted.

Buyers are using the Web to engage with each other and with companies. Smart companies participate in these interactions in many ways to grow their business.

Sources: Deitra Pope, personal interview, August 29, 2012; Richard Bush, "The Changing Face of B2B," *Marketing*, January 14, 2009, p. 5; www.decide.com, accessed August 29, 2012; www.ideastorm.com, accessed August 29, 2012.

The consequences of choosing a poor supplier can be reduced by using more than one vendor. Rather than placing all orders for an OEM component with one supplier, for example, a firm might elect to purchase 75 percent of its needs from one supplier and 25 percent from another. Thus, if a problem occurs with one supplier, another will be available to fill the firm's needs. If the product is proprietary—available from only one supplier—the buyer might insist that the supplier develop a second source for the component. Such a strategy is called "always a share," which means the buyer will always allocate only a share to each vendor.

These risk reduction approaches present a major problem for salespeople working for out-suppliers. To break this loyalty barrier, these salespeople need to develop trusting relationships with customers. They can build trust by offering performance guarantees or consistently meeting personal commitments. Another approach is to encourage buyers to place a small trial order so the salesperson's company can demonstrate the product's capabilities. On the other hand, the salesperson for the in-supplier wants to discourage buyers from considering new sources, even on a trial basis.

PROFESSIONAL PURCHASING'S GROWING IMPORTANCE

The purchasing profession is undergoing dramatic changes. Companies have recognized the impact that effective purchasing can make on the bottom line. For example, if a company can save $5,000 on a purchase, $5,000 is added to net income. If sales go up $5,000, of which most is additional costs, only $500 may be added to net income. Most large firms have elevated their directors of purchasing to the level of senior vice president to reflect the increasing importance of this function. For example, Alcoa's profits have recently been so strategically tied to sourcing that the purchasing function is given direct attention by the CEO. Combine recognition of the power of purchasing with technology, and you can see why trends in professional purchasing are changing the business environment. The overall strategy is called supply chain management.

SUPPLY CHAIN MANAGEMENT

Supply chain management (SCM) began as a set of programs undertaken to increase the efficiency of the distribution channel that moves products from the producer's facilities to the end user. More recently, however, SCM has become more than just logistics; it is now a strategy of managing inventory while containing costs. SCM includes logistics systems, such as just-in-time inventory control, as well as supplier evaluation processes, such as supplier relationship management systems.

The **just-in-time (JIT) inventory control** system is an example of a logistics SCM system used by a producer to minimize its inventory by having frequent deliveries, sometimes daily, just in time for assembly into the final product. In theory each product delivered by a supplier must conform to the manufacturer's specifications every time. It must be delivered when needed, not earlier or later, and it must arrive in the exact quantity needed, not more or less. The ultimate goal is to eventually eliminate all inventory except products in production and transit.

To develop the close coordination needed for JIT systems, manufacturers tend to rely on one supplier. The selection criterion is not the lowest cost, but the ability of the supplier to be flexible. As these relationships develop, employees of the supplier have offices at the customer's site and participate in value analysis meetings with the supplier. The salesperson becomes a facilitator, coordinator, and even marriage counselor in developing a selling team that works effectively with the customer's buying center. Resellers are also interested in managing their inventories more efficiently. Retailers and distributors work closely with their suppliers to minimize inventory investments and still satisfy the needs of customers. These JIT inventory systems are referred to as **quick-response system** or **efficient consumer response** (ECR) systems in a consumer product distribution channel. (Partnering relationships involving these systems are discussed in more detail in Chapter 14.)

Automatic replenishment is a form of JIT where the supplier manages inventory levels for the customer. The materials are provided on consignment, meaning the buyer doesn't pay for them until they are actually used. These types of arrangements are used in industrial settings, where the product being consumed is a supply item used in a manufacturing process, as well as in retail settings. Efficient consumer response systems use automatic replenishment technology through **electronic data interchange (EDI)**, or computer systems that share data across companies. Exhibit 3.6 illustrates the communications associated with placing orders and receiving products that are transmitted electronically through EDI. Recent research has indicated that adopting systems involving both EDI and quick response or JIT delivers a number of benefits to the firm, in addition to lower costs. These benefits include greater flexibility in manufacturing, improved stability of supply, and other operating benefits. Though EDI has been around a long time, global sourcing challenges still exist that influence EDI, as you can see in "From the Buyer's Seat 3.1."

Exhibit 3.6
EDI Transactions

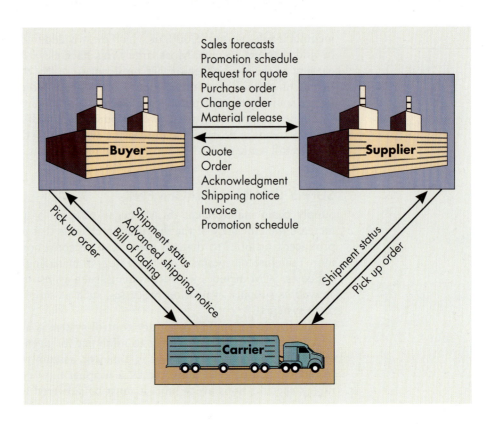

Material requirements planning (MRP) systems are an important element in JIT programs. These systems are used to forecast sales, develop a production schedule, and then order parts and raw materials with delivery dates that minimize the amount of inventory needed, thereby reducing costs. Effective JIT requires that customers inform suppliers well in advance about production schedules and needs.

SUPPLIER RELATIONSHIP MANAGEMENT

Supplier relationship management (SRM) is a strategy by which organizational buyers evaluate the relative importance of suppliers and use that information to determine with whom they want to develop partnerships. The first step is to identify the annual spend, or amount that is spent with each vendor and for what products. One outcome is the ability to consolidate purchases and negotiate better terms. After the relative importance is identified, organizational buyers frequently use a formal method, called vendor analysis, to summarize the benefits and needs satisfied by a supplier. When using this procedure, the buyer rates the supplier and its products on a number of criteria, such as price, quality, performance, and on-time delivery.[18] Note that the ratings of suppliers can be affected by the perceptions and personal needs of the buyers. Then the ratings are weighted by the importance of the characteristics, and an overall score or evaluation of the vendor is developed. Exhibit 3.7 shows a vendor evaluation form used by Chrysler Corporation. The next section describes the multiattribute model, which is useful in analyzing how members of the buying center evaluate and select products. The model also suggests strategies salespeople can use to influence these evaluations.

SRM software is being used by companies like Kingfisher plc, a company with some 1,400 stores across 17 countries and leading European retail brands, such

From the BUYER'S SEAT

CHALLENGES IN GLOBAL SOURCING

Ten years ago, mention global sourcing to a business executive, and you'd start a conversation about finding low-cost sources in other countries. Now the topic isn't always about the lowest cost; rather, it's about getting global organizations on the same page.

The Web promised to make all of the world easier to access, and you might expect such tools as electronic data interchange (EDI) to be ubiquitous. But while the basic advantages of EDI haven't changed—that is, assured supply and lower operating costs due to automatic ordering and inventory management—global supply chain management systems have added so many layers of complexity that global EDI systems simply don't exist—at least not yet.

Working on a global EDI system for Nestlé, Sean Gardner, cadre director of B2B strategies, explains the challenges. "One size doesn't fit all, not when you have so many markets and so many countries, each with their own computer network systems and their own preferred ways of doing things, some of which work very efficiently and some of which are not so efficient."

Marvin Wagner, global engineering director for John Deere, agrees that global sourcing faces many local challenges. "Local engineers want to use the same local suppliers they've always used. But that means facing significant redundancy to supply chain management systems." When Deere is able to standardize a part the world over, not only do costs go down because of the larger quantity purchased, so do costs associated with managing inventory and even for simple functions, like reordering.

Gardner notes, "Some units might be paying 20 times what they would pay on a global contract, while others may only be paying five times." That may sound like a great saving is possible for everyone, but, as Gardner notes, "Any change that changes how people operate is not easy."

When you process millions of transactions a month, the lure of global sourcing solutions is awfully tempting. But realizing the benefits can take years. Gardner estimates that it may take as long as four years to fully implement an EDI system throughout all of Nestlé. "If you want to compete in an environment where your customers want to work with fewer suppliers, you have to do what they want. And that includes trimming costs all throughout the supply chain," states Gardner. Wagner agrees but also adds, "It's not just about trimming costs throughout the supply chain. We're also interested in making sure we have a healthy supply chain, one that is innovative and profitable for everyone involved. That way, we have suppliers who help us stay competitive."

as Castorama and BUT. The company's Asia sourcing office in Hong Kong buys over 8,000 products from more than 150 suppliers. SRM software enables the company to identify problems, such as a delivery problem with one vendor in particular. Caterpillar, the construction and agriculture equipment manufacturer, instituted SRM software and training for all employees involved in purchasing. The training, created by Accenture, was more than just about the software; it was also about the strategy so the company could maximize its return on the software investment.[19]

SRM isn't always about improving profits. Sustainability, for example, is an important trend in purchasing and means making purchasing decisions that do not damage the environment. Bell Inc., a Sioux Falls, South Dakota, manufacturer of packaging products, worked with the U.S. Postal Service to develop sustainable packaging products. The project required Bell to work with its suppliers, but the important element that allowed the project to flourish was the trust already built by actively managing relationships with suppliers. As Ben Graham, vice president for sales and supply chain, notes, "The project required us to work with a

Exhibit 3.7

Sample Vendor Analysis Form

Supplier Name: _____   Type of Product: _____

Shipping Location: _____   Annual Sales Dollars: _____

	5 Excellent	4 Good	3 Satisfactory	2 Fair	1 Poor	0 N/A
Quality (45%)						
Defect rates	___	___	___	___	___	___
Quality of sample	___	___	___	___	___	___
Conformance with quality program	___	___	___	___	___	___
Responsiveness to quality problems	___	___	___	___	___	___
Overall quality	___	___	___	___	___	___
Delivery (25%)						
Avoidance of late shipments		___	___	___	___	___
Ability to expand production capacity	___	___	___	___	___	___
Performance in sample delivery	___	___	___	___	___	___
Response to changes in order size	___	___	___	___	___	___
Overall delivery	___	___	___	___	___	___
Price (20%)						
Price competitiveness	___	___	___	___	___	___
Payment terms	___	___	___	___	___	___
Absorption of costs	___	___	___	___	___	___
Submission of cost savings plans	___	___	___	___	___	___
Overall price	___	___	___	___	___	___
Technology (10%)	___	___	___	___	___	___
State-of-the-art components	___	___	___	___	___	___
Sharing research & development capability	___	___	___	___	___	___
Ability and willingness to help with design	___	___	___	___	___	___
Responsiveness to engineering problems	___	___	___	___	___	___
Overall technology	___	___	___	___	___	___

Buyer: _____   Date: _____

Comments: _____

Source: Chrysler Corporation.

third-party accrediting agency that went back to our supply chain to understand the impact of the components of our packaging on the waste stream. It's a huge process, and it's not easy to go back to a supplier asking it to share its recipes. That takes confidentiality, trust, and understanding." Key for suppliers, Graham says, is to recognize the direction Bell's business is taking, the company's goals in the marketplace, and how they as suppliers fit in that strategy. "Once they understand that and see the opportunity they get very excited," he says. "Suppliers take part in our success."[20]

thinking it through

Review the stages in the decision-making process described earlier in the chapter. Do you go through those stages when making an important purchase? How does the Internet affect the way you buy products and services? What effect does it have on each stage of the process?

MULTIATTRIBUTE MODEL OF PRODUCT EVALUATION AND CHOICE

The multiattribute model is a useful approach for understanding the factors individual members of a buying center consider in evaluating products and making choices. The multiattribute model is one approach that companies can take to making purchases and is most often used in complex decisions involving several vendors.[21] Many business decisions are straight rebuys, but the original vendor selection decision may have involved a multiattribute approach. The vendor analysis form used by Chrysler (see Exhibit 3.7) illustrates the use of this model in selecting vendors. The model also provides a framework for developing sales strategies.

The multiattribute model is based on the idea that people view a product as a collection of characteristics or attributes. Buyers evaluate a product by considering how each characteristic satisfies the firm's needs and perhaps their individual needs. The following example examines a firm's decision to buy laptop computers for its sales force. The computers will be used by salespeople to track information about customers and provide call reports to sales managers. At the end of each day, salespeople will call headquarters and upload their call reports.

PERFORMANCE EVALUATION OF CHARACTERISTICS

Assume the company narrows its choice to three hypothetical brands: Apex, Bell, and Deltos. Exhibit 3.8 shows information the company has collected about each brand. Note that the information goes beyond the physical characteristics of the product to include services provided by the potential suppliers.

Each buying center member (or the group as a whole in a meeting) might process this objective information and evaluate the laptop computers on each characteristic. These evaluations appear in Exhibit 3.9 as ratings on a 10-point scale, with 10 being the highest rating and 1 the lowest.

How do members of the buying center use these evaluations to select a laptop computer? The final decision depends on the relationship between the

Exhibit 3.8
Information about Laptop Computers

Characteristic/Brand	Apex	Bell	Deltos
Reliability rating	Very good	Very good	Excellent
Weight (pounds)	3.0	4.5	7.5
Display size (inches)	15.0	13	10.1
Display visibility	Good	Very good	Excellent
Speed (clock rate in gigahertz)	2.4	3.0	2.4
RAM (memory in gigabytes)	2	2	4
Number of U.S. service centers	140	60	20

Exhibit 3.9
Performance Evaluation
of Laptop Computers

Characteristic/Brand Rating	Apex	Bell	Deltos
Reliability	5	5	8
Weight	8	5	2
Display size	8	6	4
Display visibility	2	4	6
Speed	4	8	4
RAM	3	3	8
Service availability	7	5	3

performance evaluations and the company's needs. The buying center members must consider the degree to which they are willing to sacrifice poor performance on one attribute for superior performance on another. The members of the buying center must make some trade-offs.

No single product will perform best on all characteristics. For example, Apex excels on size, weight, and availability of convenient service; Bell has superior speed; and Deltos provides the best reliability and internal memory.

IMPORTANCE WEIGHTS

In making an overall evaluation, buying center members need to consider the importance of each characteristic. These importance weights may differ from member to member. Consider two members of the buying center: the national sales manager and the director of management information systems (MIS). The national sales manager is particularly concerned about motivating his salespeople to use the laptop computers. He believes the laptops must be small and lightweight and have good screen visibility. On the other hand, the MIS director foresees using the laptop computers to transmit orders and customer inventory information to corporation headquarters. She believes expanded memory and processing speed will be critical for these future applications.

Exhibit 3.10 shows the importance these two buying center members place on each characteristic using a 10-point scale, with 10 representing very important and 1 representing very unimportant. In this illustration the national sales manager and the MIS director differ in the importance they place on characteristics; however, both have the same evaluations of the brands' performance on the characteristics. In some cases people may differ on both importance weights and performance ratings.

OVERALL EVALUATION

A person's overall evaluation of a product can be quantified by multiplying the sum of the performance ratings by the importance weights. Thus, the sales manager's overall evaluation of Apex would be as follows:

$$4 \times 5 = 20$$
$$6 \times 8 = 48$$
$$7 \times 8 = 56$$
$$1 \times 4 = 4$$
$$1 \times 3 = 3$$
$$8 \times 2 = 16$$
$$3 \times 7 = \underline{21}$$
$$168$$

Exhibit 3.10

Information Used to Form an Overall Evaluation

Characteristic	Importance Weights		Brand Ratings		
	Sales Manager	MIS Director	Apex	Bell	Deltos
Reliability	4	4	5	5	8
Weight	6	2	8	5	2
Display size	7	3	8	6	4
Display visibility	8	5	2	4	6
Speed	1	7	4	8	4
RAM	1	6	3	3	8
Service availability	3	3	7	5	3
Overall evaluation					
Sales manager's			168	150	141
MIS director's			137	157	163

Exhibit 3.11

Value Offered by Each Brand

	Overall Evaluation (Benefits Points)	Assigned Value	
		Computer Cost	Benefit/Cost
Sales manager			
Apex	167	$1,600	$0.10
Bell	152	1,800	0.08
Deltos	143	1,800	0.08
MIS director			
Apex	130	$1,600	0.08
Bell	169	1,800	0.09
Deltos	177	1,800	0.10

Using the national sales manager's and MIS director's importance weights, the overall evaluations, or scores, for the three laptop computer brands appear at the bottom of Exhibit 3.10. The scores indicate the benefit levels the brands provide as seen by these two buying center members.

VALUE OFFERED

The cost of the computers also needs to be considered in making the purchase decision. One approach for incorporating cost calculates the value—the benefits divided by the cost—for each laptop. The prices for the computers and their values are shown in Exhibit 3.11. The sales manager believes Apex provides more value. He would probably buy this brand if he were the only person involved in the buying decision. On the other hand, the MIS director believes that Bell and Deltos offer the best value.

SUPPLIER SELECTION

In this situation the sales manager might be the key decision maker, and the MIS director might be a gatekeeper. Rather than using the MIS director's overall evaluation, the buying center might simply ask her to serve as a gatekeeper and determine whether these computers meet her minimum acceptable performance standards on speed and memory. All three laptops pass the minimum levels she established of a 2-gigahertz clock rate and a 3-gigabyte internal memory. Thus, the company would rely on the sales manager's evaluation and purchase Apex laptops for the sales force.

Even if a buying center or individual members do not go through the calculations described here, the multiattribute model is a good representation of their product evaluations and can be used to predict product choices. Purchase decisions are often made as though a formal multiattribute model were used.

thinking it through

If you were selling the Bell computer to the national sales manager and MIS director depicted in the text and in Exhibits 3.10 and 3.11, how would you try to get them to believe that your computer provides more value than Apex or Deltos does? What numbers would you try to change?

IMPLICATIONS FOR SALESPEOPLE

How can salespeople use the multiattribute model to influence their customers' purchase decisions? First, the model describes the information customers use in making their evaluations and purchase decisions. Thus, salespeople need to know the following information to develop a sales strategy:

1. The suppliers or brands the customer is considering
2. The product characteristics being used in the evaluation
3. The customer's rating of each product's performance on each dimension
4. The weights the customer attaches to each dimension

With this knowledge salespeople can use several strategies to influence purchase decisions. First, salespeople must be sure their product is among the brands being considered. Then they can try to change the customer's perception of their product's value. Some approaches for changing perceived value follow:

1. Increase the performance rating for your product.
2. Decrease the rating for a competitive product.
3. Increase or decrease an importance weight.
4. Add a new dimension.
5. Decrease the price of your product.

Assume you are selling the Bell computer and you want to influence the sales manager so he believes your computer provides more value than the Apex computer. Approach 1 involves altering the sales manager's belief about your product's performance. To raise his evaluation, you would try to have the sales manager perceive your computer as small and lightweight. You might show him how easy it is to carry—how well it satisfies his need for portability. The objective of this demonstration is to increase your rating on weight from 5 to 7 and your rating on size from 6 to 8.

You should focus on these two characteristics because they are the most important to the sales manager. A small change in a performance evaluation on these characteristics will have a large impact on the overall evaluation. You would not want to spend much time influencing his performance evaluations of speed or memory because these characteristics are not important to him. Of course your objectives when selling to the MIS director would be different because she places more importance on speed and memory.

This example illustrates a key principle in selling. In general, salespeople should focus primarily on product characteristics that are important to the customer—characteristics that satisfy the customer's needs. Salespeople should not focus on the areas of superior performance (such as speed in this example) that are not important to the customer.

Approach 2 involves decreasing the performance rating of Apex. This strategy can be dangerous. Customers prefer dealing with salespeople who say good things about their products, not bad things about competitive products.

In approach 3 you try to change the sales manager's importance weights. You want to increase the importance he places on a characteristic on which your product excels, such as speed, or decrease the importance of a characteristic on which your product performs poorly, such as display visibility. For example, you might try to convince the sales manager that a fast computer will decrease the time salespeople need to spend developing and transmitting reports.

Approach 4 encourages the sales manager to consider a new characteristic, one on which your product has superior performance. For example, suppose the sales manager and MIS director have not considered the availability of software. To add a new dimension, you might demonstrate a program specially developed for sales call reports and usable only with your computer.

Approach 5 is the simplest to implement: Simply drop your price. Typically firms use this strategy as a last resort because cutting prices decreases profits.

These strategies illustrate how salespeople can adapt their selling approach to the needs of their customers. Using the multiattribute model, salespeople decide how to alter the content of their presentation—the benefits to be discussed—based on customer beliefs and needs. (Chapter 4 describes adaptive selling in more detail and illustrates it in terms of the form of the presentation—the communication style the salesperson uses.)

SELLING YOURSELF

When you are selling your ideas or selling yourself in a job search, recognize that there is a buying center. Although a sales manager may make the final decision on whether you are hired, chances are that you'll interview with at least four people before the job offer will come. Who is the gatekeeper, who is the decider, and who are influencers? Similarly, once you have the job and you have an idea for a new program or product, you will have to sell that idea to management. That decision will likely include someone from finance, someone from operations, and so on, creating a buying center. Each member of the center will take on different roles and may be present for only part of the decision. Each member may also have different criteria.

Further, you need to understand the process by which the decision is made. In a job search, the decision to hire someone has been made before anyone talks to you. At that point your concern is making it from the large pool of college students they've interviewed at six different campuses to the group they bring into the office, to the final selection of new employees. Similarly, management approval of your idea is likely to follow a process not unlike that of any organizational purchase. Keep in mind that your idea is competing against other ideas from other people, just as your candidacy for a sales job is compared to other college students from your school and others. Therefore, take some time to understand who is involved in the decision, what criteria they will use, and what process they will use to reach a decision.

SUMMARY

Salespeople sell to many different types of customers, including consumers, business enterprises, government agencies, and institutions. This text focuses on selling to organizations rather than to consumers. Selling to organizations differs from selling to consumers because organizations are more concentrated, demand is derived, and the buying process is more complex.

The organizational buying process consists of eight steps, beginning with the recognition of a need and ending with the evaluation of the product's performance. Each step involves several decisions. As organizations progress through these steps, decisions made at previous steps affect subsequent steps, leading to a creeping commitment. Thus, salespeople need to be involved in the buying process as early as possible.

The length of the buying process and the role of various participants depend on the customer's past experiences. When customers have had considerable experience in buying a product, the decision becomes routine—a straight rebuy. Few people are involved, and the process is short. However, when customers have little experience in buying a product—a new task—many people are involved, and the process can be lengthy.

The people involved in the buying process are referred to as the buying center. The buying center is composed of people who are initiators, users, influencers, gatekeepers, and deciders. Salespeople need to understand the roles buying center members play to effectively influence their decisions.

Individuals in the buying center are concerned about satisfying the economic, quality, and service needs of their organization. In addition, these people have personal needs they want to satisfy.

Organizations face an increasingly dynamic and competitive environment. Purchasing is becoming a strategic weapon with the development of supply chain management and supplier relationship management strategies.

The Internet is playing a much more important role in business-to-business transactions than it plays in the widely publicized business-to-consumer e-businesses. Business-to-business applications of the Internet are designed to support salespeople's ability to build relationships with major customers.

KEY TERMS

always a share 78
annual spend 80
automatic replenishment 79
buying center 70
capital equipment 61
coach 71
creeping commitment 68
deciders 72
derived demand 65
economic influencer 71
efficient consumer response 79
electronic data interchange (EDI) 79
emotional needs 73
end users 61
gatekeepers 72
influencers 71

initiators 71
just-in-time (JIT) inventory control 79
life-cycle costing 74
lost for good 77
material requirements planning 80
modified rebuy 70
MRO supplies 61
new-task 68
original equipment manufacturer (OEM) 61
producers 61
profit margin 62
quick-response system 79
rational needs 73
resellers 62
services 61
straight rebuy 69

supplier relationship management (SRM)   80
supply chain management (SCM)   79
technical influencer   71
turnover   62

users   71
value analysis   76
vendor analysis   80
vendor loyalty   77

ETHICS PROBLEMS

1. You know that both American Airlines and Delta Airlines have goals for purchasing from women- and minority-owned businesses. You have a product that is innovative and patented, and it will save airlines like American and Delta over 30 percent in fuel costs. But your business does not qualify as woman or minority owned because you are a white male, so you are thinking of bringing a partner into the business—your sister. Is this appropriate? Or would it be better to license the product to an already certified minority-owned business?

2. You are talking about this class to someone who isn't familiar with business. When you mention you are studying how people make buying decisions and that this information will help you become a better salesperson, your friend says you are just trying to learn how to manipulate people more effectively. How do you respond?

QUESTIONS AND PROBLEMS

1. Assume that the federal government is going to make reducing obesity a major priority. The process it has adopted includes reducing sugar content in children's cereals, making vegetables more palatable, and reducing fat in the overall diet. Identify three product categories (not including vegetables) for which derived demand would influence manufacturers and producers of consumer packaged goods (foods sold to be cooked or heated and eaten at home). Include at least one product affected positively and one product affected negatively.

2. Read "Building Partnerships 3.1." Jenna Weber, salesperson for Hormel®, described two buyers. One was friendly and easy to get along with, while the other was tough, hard to get an appointment with, and impatient during the meeting and demanded proof of almost everything she said. Are these the only two types of personalities she might run into? What could she have done better with the bacon promotion?

3. Assume you work for a division of 3M that makes medical monitoring systems. How would the purchasing decision process differ in the following situations? Which situation is a new task? A modified rebuy? A straight rebuy? How likely is the buyer to get other people in the organization involved? Which types of people are likely to get involved in each decision? Which situation is likely to produce the slowest decision?

   a. The organization is purchasing a custom-designed machine to be used in the manufacturing of metal racks that house multiple monitoring systems.

   b. An organization reorders plastic shields that it uses in making medical monitoring equipment from a regular supplier, a supplier that it has bought from in the past.

   c. The organization is designing a new line of medical monitoring equipment and wants an improved and updated microprocessor. It is considering its past suppliers as well as some suppliers that it has not bought from before.

4. Review each purchase in question 3. What information would you need to conduct a value analysis for each? Note: You will need some different and some similar information in each situation.

5. A chain of restaurants wants to purchase a new order entry computer system tied into an accounting system that manages food inventory and automatically replenishes

food items. Which criteria for evaluating supplier proposals might be used by (a) the purchasing agent, (b) the information systems department, (c) a store manager, and (d) the head of the legal department? How would this purchase differ from a purchase of the same products by a company that resells store fixtures and equipment to small restaurants?

6. Dub Oliver runs the maintenance department at the paper mill, and he buys lots of hardware to fix equipment. Right now, he orders most of it through a Web site at NCH. If you work for Home Depot, how would you try to make a sale to Oliver? Assume you have a Web site he can order through, too.

7. When is vendor loyalty important? Find at least one example in the chapter (there are several) where vendor loyalty would prove to be important and discuss why it was important in that particular instance. What can buyers do to improve vendor loyalty? When might vendor loyalty be inefficient or wasteful?

8. Create a matrix of types of needs and types of customers. Which customer types share the same types of needs or express needs in the same way? Which ones differ? Why? Relate your chart to the multiattribute matrix. How would your chart help you prepare to sell?

9. Mitchell's Metal Shop is considering the purchase of a new press, a machine that bends sheet metal. The cost is $10,000, which is about 25 percent of the firm's profit for the quarter. Ford Motor Company is also considering buying new presses—30 of them. Discuss how risk is different for Frank Mitchell, owner of Mitchell's Metal Shop, and Ford.

10. How would your multiattribute matrix for a new car differ from that of your parents? How is it that you might have some of the same desires (such as high gas mileage) yet consider completely different cars?

CASE PROBLEMS

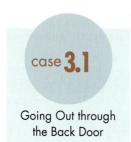

case **3.1**

Going Out through the Back Door

Travis Bruns is a sales representative for Crown Lift Services in Houston, Texas. In his own words, he describes an ethics issue with a buyer.

Last year I was in a real cutthroat bidding war for a $300,000-plus sales opportunity. Over the course of two months the competitive field had been narrowed down to two organizations, mine and the incumbent organization. The customer had set up a set of strict guidelines for the bidding process. One of those was that they had designated a "point of contact" (POC) that was to be the liaison through which all bids and proposals were to channel through to the VP. My organization and I had truly put our best foot forward on pricing and proposed service after the sale, and although the negotiations had been rough, we were able to sell the value of our solution, retain a fair amount of profit, and were told we had the deal: a true win–win. On the final day that the bid was open, I received a call from the point of contact asking me to lower my price. I was confused. I inquired about the previous discussions that had taken place in which we had mutually agreed that the price of our proposal was fair and good. I could hear some level of discomfort if not embarrassment in the POC's voice, so I came right out and asked him, "I get the sense that you are not comfortable with what is happening here either. What happened?"

He replied, "Well, Travis, [your competitor] called one of the other managers in the office and was able to find out the pricing in your proposal. He then went around me and called the VP directly and offered a much lower price. The VP then called me and asked me to get you to lower your price or the other company will get the business."

I was dumbfounded. I asked the customer, "If I cannot lower my price, are you telling me this deal is over for me?"

"I think so," he replied.

Source: Travis Bruns. Used with permission.

Questions

1. What would you do? Do you lower your price or walk away? Why? Write out specifically what you would say next.
2. Do buyers have to follow the same ethics principles as sellers? For example, sellers have to fully disclose all information. Do buyers? Why or why not? What ethical principle violation occurred here?

case 3.2

Heritage Health

Frank Briles, account executive and his boss, Kylie Martinez, were talking over one of his accounts, Parker Pet Products. Frank was describing his initial meeting with Shirley Parker, CEO of the family pet food manufacturer.

"She said that Mark Davis, the company's HR director, asked her if he could look into getting health care for the company. She said he was having trouble finding new employees because there were so few benefits. But she also said that the CFO was against adding more costs," Frank reported.

"Do you think she was serious about the costs?" asked Shirley.

"I think so." Frank's face showed his lack of confidence in knowing the answer. "What I do know is that they have no budget set aside for it."

"How will they determine a budget? And what will their process be in making a decision?"

Frank looked at his computer for notes he had taken on the meeting. "Well, we're lucky in the sense that they've not really set up a process. So we can help them determine what's important, assuming I can get to the right people fast enough. As for budget, that will be decided by Shirley and the CFO."

Kylie gave Frank a sharp look. "Right people? What do you mean?"

"They're setting up a committee," said Frank. "I've asked to have an opportunity to meet with them and just talk through options and process. I know that there will be two employee representatives, one from each plant, along with the HR guy, the CFO, Shirley, and the two plant managers. What I don't know is how they will make the decision or what they want."

Questions

1. What is the likely makeup of the buying center? Who plays or has played which roles?
2. What type of purchase situation is this? What are the implications for Frank?
3. How can Frank use the multiattribute matrix to guide his sales plan?

ROLE PLAY CASE

During much of the rest of the semester, you will be calling on one of three accounts. The accounts are listed here with some information. Information that you gain on each call can be used in subsequent calls as you practice the skills and apply the concepts introduced in each chapter.

BancVue: BancVue works with community banks to enable these smaller banks provide big-bank products and services. They are a marketing agency that has built its own brands for products and services that community banks can then sell as their own.

GelTech: Originally just a manufacturer of firefighting systems, this company began by selling fire suppression products to fire departments and to commercial property owners and builders. Now international, the company also manufactures other chemical products that serve the agriculture market (including forestry and golf course maintenance) and the fishing industry.

HighPoint Solutions: HighPoint Solutions is a business services company. They are a midsize company that can provide complete outsourced human resource solutions or software and support. With offices in 30 major cities, they do everything from managing the hiring/separation processes and payroll to administering benefit packages and more.

Today, you have an appointment with a sales manager whom you met at a workshop sponsored by the American Marketing Association. You were presenting a case study of how one of your clients improved sales productivity through your CRM software. Start the sales call from the beginning as if you were entering the sales manager's office. Reintroduce yourself and your company, thank the person for the appointment, and then tell the buyer you'd like to ask some questions. Your questions should be about the buying process and who is involved. Afterward, see if you can chart the buying center and the company's organizational structure.

ADDITIONAL REFERENCES

Andersson, Svante, and Per Servais. "Combining Industrial Buyer and Seller Strategies for International Supply and Marketing Management." *European Business Review* 22 (2010), pp. 64–82.

Autry, Chad W., and Susan L. Golicic. "Evaluating Buyer-Supplier Relationship-Performance Spirals: A Longitudinal Study." *Journal of Operations Management* 28 (March 2010), pp. 87–104.

Briggs, Ellen, and Douglas Grisaffe. "Service Performance-Loyalty Intentions Link in a Business to Business Context: The Role of Relational Exchange Outcomes and Customer Characteristics." *Journal of Service Research* 13 (2010), pp. 37–52.

Brown, B., Alex Zablah, and Danny Bellenger. "When Do B2B Brands Influence the Decision Making of Organizational Buyers? An Examination of the Relationship between Purchase Risk and Brand Sensitivity." *International Journal of Research Marketing* 28, no. 3 (2011), pp. 194–204.

Geigenmüller, Anja, and Harriette Bettis-Outland. "Brand Equity in B2B Services and Consequences for the Trade Show Industry." *Journal of Business and Industrial Marketing* 27, no. 6 (2012), pp. 428–35.

Kotabe, Masaaki, Michael J. Mol, and Janet Y. Murray. "Outsourcing, Performance, and the Role of E-Commerce: A Dynamic Perspective." *Industrial Marketing Management* 37, no. 1 (2008), pp. 37–49.

Leach, Mark. "Examining Exchange Relationships among High-Tech Firms in the Evolving Global Economy." *Journal of Business and Industrial Marketing* 24 (2009), pp. 78–94.

Lindgreen, Adam, Balazs Revesz, and Mark Glynn. "Purchasing Orientation." *Journal of Business and Industrial Marketing* 24 (2009), pp. 148–72.

Lucero, Carrete. "A Relationship Model between Key Problems of International Purchasing and the Post-Purchase Behavior of Industrial Firms." *Journal of Business and Industrial Marketing* 23 (2008), pp. 332–47.

Makkonen, Hannu, Rami Olkkonen, and Aino Halinen. "Organizational Buying as Muddling Through: A Practice Theory Approach." *Journal of Business Research* 65, no. 6 (June 2012), pp. 773–81.

Miocevic, Dario, and Biljana Crnjak-Karanovic. "The Mediating Role of Key Supplier Relationship Management Practices on Supply Chain Orientation: The Organizational Buying Effectiveness Link." *Industrial Marketing Management* 41, no. 1 (2012), pp. 115–25.

Pels, Jaqueline, Kristian Moller, and Michael Saren. "Do We Really Understand Business Marketing?" Getting beyond the RM and BM Matrimony." *Journal of Business and Industrial Marketing* 24 (2009), pp. 322–49.

Rutherford, Brian N., Nwamaka Anaza, and Adrienne Hall Phillips. "Predictors of Buyer-Seller Firm Conflict." *Journal of Marketing Theory and Practice* 20 (Spring 2012), pp. 161–71.

Saini, Amit. "Purchasing Ethics and Inter-Organizational Buyer-Supplier Relationship Determinants: A Conceptual Framework." *Journal of Business Ethics* 95, no. 3 (2010), pp. 439–55.

Sashi, C. M. "Buyer Behavior in Business Markets: A Review and Integrative Model." *Journal of Global Issues* 3 (Summer 2009), pp. 129–38.

Skarmeas, Dionysis, Constantine S. Katsikeas, Stavroula Pyropoulou, and Esmail Salehi-Sangari. "Market and Supplier Characteristics Driving Distributor Relationship Quality in International Marketing Channels of Industrial Products." *Industrial Marketing Management* 27, no. 1 (2008), pp. 23–29.

Spekman, Robert, and R. Thomas. "Organizational Buying Behavior: Where We Have Been and Where We Need to Go." Darden Business School Working Paper No. 1993207, Georgetown McDonough School of Business Research Paper No. 2012-05, 2011. Retrieved from http://papers.ssrn.com/sol3/papers.cfm?abstract_id=1993207, September 27, 2012.

Svahn, Senja, and Mika Westerlund. "Purchasing Strategies in Supply Relationships." *Journal of Business and Industrial Marketing* 24 (2009), pp. 173–89.

Van Der Rhee, Brian, R. Verma, and G. Plaschka. "Understanding Trade-Offs in the Supplier Selection Process: The Role of Flexibility, Delivery, and Value-Added Services/Support." *International Journal of Production Economics* 120, no. 1 (2009), pp. 30–31.

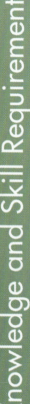

chapter **4**

USING COMMUNICATION PRINCIPLES TO BUILD RELATIONSHIPS

SOME QUESTIONS ANSWERED IN THIS CHAPTER ARE

- What are the basic elements in the communication process?
- Why are listening and questioning skills important?
- How can salespeople develop listening skills to collect information about customers?
- How do people communicate without using words?
- What are some things to remember when communicating via technology like phones, e-mail, and social media?
- How does a salesperson adjust for cultural differences?

PROFILE

PROFILE My name is Sally Cook, and I graduated from St. Catherine University in 2011 with a bachelor of science degree in health care sales. One of the very first key takeaways from my first sales course taught by Lynn Schleeter was about effective communication. It is more and more apparent to me how communication with customers has dramatically changed in the last decade.

It used to be imperative to get that face-to-face meeting, but now I rely equally on other technology platforms in order to get myself, my company, and my products in front of my customer. Almost every buyer has a cell phone that can receive e-mails and text messages for shipping information and so on. Plus, with other technology, such as Skype and Facebook, businesses and their owners are constantly on the go. With that being said, how can we, as current and future sales professionals, get our foot in the door? By asking the right questions, actively listening, and mastering the use of technology, each one of us has an opportunity to make our mark on our customer. Companies and corporations alike are looking for that diverse sales talent that can provide these skills.

At St. Catherine's, one of my professor's requirements for his class was to do telesales for the alumni association, which is definitely no easy feat. I found myself calling on a variety of previous St. Kate students whose graduation from the school ranged from 1 year to 50 years. With the small amount of background information given about these possible donors, I had to call on them and figure out how I could help these individuals see the benefit in donating to their alma mater. The first calls didn't go as smoothly as hoped, but as I continued to make calls, I discovered that by tailoring my questioning and listening actively, I was actually having more "luck" in creating the sale.

Not every customer has the same story, and with that not every customer wants to hear the same story. This is the reality of almost every sales call: Your customers want to be treated as individuals. This requires the sales professional to adjust and adapt to each customer's needs and wants. In order to do that, the sales professional needs to be actively listening to each customer to identify what it is that may be important to them. The sales professional would not be calling on said customer if they didn't think that they had a product or service that would benefit the customer. It is up to the sales professional to identify the key points to drive the sale forward, which again all comes back to actively engaging yourself in the conversation.

Visit our Web site at:
www.3m.com

BUILDING RELATIONSHIPS THROUGH TWO-WAY COMMUNICATION

As we will discuss further in Chapter 13, open and honest communication is a key to building trust and developing successful relationships. To develop a good understanding of each other's needs, buyers and sellers must effectively communicate with each other by actively talking and listening.

THE COMMUNICATION PROCESS

Exhibit 4.1 illustrates the **two-way communication** process. The process begins when the sender, either the salesperson or the customer, wants to communicate some thoughts or ideas. Because the receiver cannot read the sender's mind, the sender must translate these ideas into words. The translation of thoughts into words is called **encoding**. Then the receiver must decode the message and try to understand what the sender intended to communicate. **Decoding** involves interpreting the meaning of the received message.

Consider a salesperson who is describing a complex product to a customer. At one point, a perplexed look flits across the customer's face. The salesperson receives this nonverbal message and asks the customer what part of the presentation needs further explanation. This **feedback** from the customer's expression tells the salesperson that the message is not being received. The customer then sends verbal messages to the salesperson in the form of questions concerning the operation and benefits of the product.

COMMUNICATION BREAKDOWNS

Communication breakdowns can be caused by encoding and decoding problems and the environment in which the communications occur. The following sales interaction between a copier salesperson and a prospect illustrates problems that can arise in encoding and decoding messages:

What the salesperson means to say: We have an entire line of Toshiba copiers. But I think the Model 900 is ideally suited for your needs because it provides the basic copying functions at a low price.

What the salesperson actually says (encodes): The Model 900 is our best-selling copier, and it's designed to economically meet the copying needs of small businesses like yours.

Exhibit 4.1
Two-Way Flow of Information

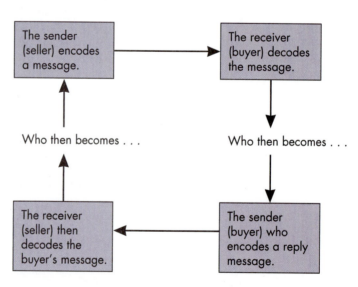

Background noise from traffic can hinder effective communication. The salesperson should attempt to move the discussion to a quieter location so the noise will not distract the customer.

What the customer hears: The Model 900 is a low-priced copier for small businesses.

What the customer thinks (decodes): This company makes cheap copiers with limited features, probably for businesses that don't have much money. But I need a copier with more features. I think I'd better look elsewhere for a better copier.

What the customer actually says: I don't think I'm interested in buying a copier now.

In this situation the salesperson assumed that price was very important to the prospect, and the prospect thought (incorrectly) that the salesperson's company made only low-priced, low-performance copiers.

Communication can also be inhibited by the environment in which the communication process occurs. For example, noises can distract the salesperson and the customer. **Noises** are sounds unrelated to messages being exchanged by the salesperson and the customer, such as ringing telephones or other conversations nearby. To improve communication, the salesperson should attempt to minimize noises in the environment by closing a door to the room or suggesting that the meeting move to a quieter place.

Other environmental issues must be dealt with before effective communication can occur. For example, people communicate most effectively when they are physically comfortable. If the room is too hot or too cold, the salesperson should suggest changing the temperature controls or moving to another room. These types of environmental issues and possible solutions are discussed in Chapters 7 and 8. For now, realize that effective communication can't occur without the proper environment.

Finally, it is important to note that buyers do not always follow this communication model perfectly.[1] Some buyers—and sellers for that matter—have agendas that do not always result in honest, straightforward attempts to reveal truth. Rather, they may at times use communication as a tool to mask their true motives and intentions. You have probably done this yourself—when caught doing something wrong and wishing to avoid detection or punishment, you masked the truth or said things you hoped would be interpreted in ways that were favorable to you.

thinking **it** through

Think of a big disagreement you had with someone recently (perhaps with a boyfriend, girlfriend, professor, or parents). Did any miscommunication occur? Why was the communication poor? Was it due to noise, poor feedback, poor encoding, poor decoding, or what?

SENDING VERBAL MESSAGES EFFECTIVELY

A basic reason that salespeople communicate is to simply provide information to the buyer. Salespeople also often attempt to engage in **persuading,** the process by which the salesperson attempts to convince other people (e.g., buyers) to change their attitudes or behaviors regarding an issue while understanding that the other person is free to accept or reject the idea. This section will explore methods of communicating via verbal communication.

CHOICE OF WORDS

As Quintilion, the famous Roman orator, said, "Choice of words is the origin of eloquence." Salespeople don't have to be eloquent, but most could use some pointers to develop their skills in word choice. Use short words and phrases to demonstrate strength and force (like *accelerated* and *intervened*) or to provide charm and grace (like *crystal clear* and *crisp copies*). Avoid trite words[2] such as *nice* and *good* and phrases that make you sound like an overeager salesperson such as *a great deal, I guarantee you will . . .* , and *No problem!* Also avoid using off-color language, slang, and foul language, even with established customers.

Every salesperson should be able to draw on a set of words to best help present the features of a product or service. The words might form a simile, such as *This battery backup is like a spare tire;* a metaphor, such as *This machine is a real workhorse;* or a phrase drawing on sensory appeal, such as *smooth as silk* or *strong as steel*. To find the best way to use words, it often helps to listen to the way your customer talks.

Be careful about using words that have become so common in business conversations as to be almost meaningless. Words like *core competence, value added, enterprisewide, fault-tolerant,* and *mission-critical* are often cited as examples. Avoid them because they can make you come across as phony.

Words have different meanings in different cultures and even in different subcultures of the United States. In England the hood of a car is called the *bonnet*, and the trunk is called the *boot*. In Boston a milkshake is simply syrup mixed with milk, whereas a frappe is ice cream, syrup, and milk mixed together.

VOICE CHARACTERISTICS

A salesperson's delivery of words affects how the customer will understand and evaluate his or her presentation. Poor voice and speech habits make it difficult for customers to understand a salesperson's message. **Voice characteristics** include rate of speech, loudness, inflection, and articulation.

Customers tend to question the expertise of salespeople who talk much slower or faster than the normal rate of 140 words per minute. Salespeople should vary their rate of speech depending on the nature of the message and the environment in which the communication occurs. Simple messages can be delivered at faster rates, and more difficult concepts should be presented at slower rates.

Loudness should be tailored to the communication situation. To avoid monotony, salespeople should learn to vary the loudness of their speech. Loudness can also be used to emphasize certain parts of the sales presentation, indicating to the customer that these parts are more important.

Inflection is the tone or pitch of speech. At the end of a sentence, the tone should drop, indicating the completion of a thought. When the tone goes up at the end of a sentence, listeners often sense uncertainty in the speaker. Use inflection to reduce monotony. If you speak with enthusiasm, it will help your customer connect emotionally. However, don't forget to be yourself. The buyer can be turned off if you're obviously just trying to copy the successful communication traits of someone else.

Articulation refers to the production of recognizable sounds. Articulation is best when the speaker opens his or her mouth properly; then the movements of the lips and tongue are unimpeded. When the lips are too close together, the enunciation of certain vowels and consonants suffers.

In order for the salesperson to communicate with this buyer, he must use words and stories that are meaningful and interesting to the buyer.

STORIES

While they are entertaining, stories can also make points most effectively. Great stories often include conflicts, trials, and crises and help the listener think through choices and outcomes of those decisions. Of course salespeople cannot assume all customers are familiar with trade jargon, and thus they need to check with their customers continually to determine whether they are interpreting sales messages and stories properly.

Salespeople can paint word pictures to help customers understand the benefits or features of a product. A **word picture** is a graphic or vivid story designed to help the buyer easily visualize a point. To use a word picture effectively, the salesperson needs to paint as accurate and reliable a picture as possible.[3] Exhibit 4.2 provides an example of a word picture that a Toyota Highlander salesperson might use when calling on the owner of a real estate firm.

Effective stories often include an **analogy,** which is when the speaker attempts to draw a parallel between one thing and another. For example, to explain how a new machine controller is always monitoring and is ready to respond instantly, the seller could say this:

> It's kind of like a broadband Internet connection. It's always on. This controller never goes to sleep, never hangs up. This controller is sitting there, 24 hours a day, 7 days a week, 365 days a year, watching for the smallest malfunction and then taking immediate action to resolve the problem.

KEEP OPEN LINES OF COMMUNICATION

Although this might seem obvious, sometimes the obvious needs to be stated: As a salesperson you must always keep the lines of verbal communication with the buyer

Exhibit 4.2
Example of a Word Picture

Situation

A Toyota salesperson is calling on Jill, the owner of a commercial real estate firm. The goal of the word picture is to demonstrate the value of the four-wheel-drive option.

Word Picture

Jill, picture for a moment the following situation. You have this really hot prospect—let's call him Steve—for a remote resort development. You're in your current car, a Cadillac XTS. You've been trying to get Steve up to the property for months, and today is his only free day for several weeks. The property, up in the northern Georgia mountains, is accessible only by an old logging road. The day is bright and sunny, and Steve is in a good mood. When you reach the foot of the mountains, the weather turns cloudy and windy. As you wind up the old, bumpy road, a light rain begins. You've just crossed a small bridge when a downpour starts; the rain is pelting your windshield. Steve looks a little worried. Suddenly your car's tires start spinning. You're stuck in the mud.

Now let's replay the story, assuming that you buy the Toyota Highlander we've been talking about. [Salesperson quickly repeats the first paragraph of this story, substituting "Toyota Highlander" for "Cadillac XTS."] Suddenly your car tires start spinning. You're stuck in the mud. Calmly you reach down and shift into four-wheel drive. The Toyota pulls out easily, and you reach the destination in about five minutes. Although it's raining, the prospect looks at the land and sees great potential. On the way back down the mountain, you discuss how Steve should go about making an offer on the property. Jill, I hope I've made a point. Can you see why the four-wheel-drive option is important for you, even though it does add to the base price of the car?

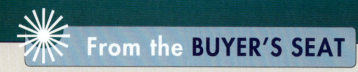

PLEASE LEARN HOW TO COMMUNICATE!

As a senior buyer at Microsoft, I see many different types of salespeople. I receive numerous calls each day from salespeople trying to make appointments with me and there are usually one of two outcomes:

A. The salesperson that has done their research about my company prior to the call and has a very concise and clear message tends to have the best chance of actually getting the appointment that they are shooting for.

B. Often salespeople will say, "I didn't expect you to answer your phone!" The salespeople who have this response are caught completely off guard and stand very little chance of obtaining their desired appointment.

With many means options of communication methods that a salesperson has, I believe that their choice should strongly rely on the message being delivered. When it is a salesperson who is new to me and with who I don't have a relationship, I feel as though a phone call is sufficient. In this phone call, I will usually share my e-mail with the salesperson so that he or she can send me a profile of his or her company. Once a relationship has been established and we have begun doing business together, I tend to prefer to call my salespeople when a problem or issue arises. After this phone call, I will then follow-up with an e-mail that outlines the problem and solution.

I personally feel it is important for salespeople to avoid texting a buyer. However, once you have developed a very strong relationship and have asked the buyer if he or she is okay with an occasional text, then I would say it is deemed acceptable.

The following are examples I have personally experienced that have helped salespeople strengthen their relationship with me:

- Using active listening skills during a conversation with me and then remembering specifics from that conversation in future meetings. This proves to me that they really listen to what the objectives were, have retained this information, and then have acted on it to prepare for the next meeting.

- A salesperson who knows what situations are better to be handled via the telephone as opposed to e-mail. Under certain circumstances, sending an e-mail instead of making a phone call can make the problem worse, so knowing the proper means of communication can definitely help a salesperson build a relationship with me.

The following are two examples of things that I have personally experienced with salespeople that have hindered our relationship:

- I was facing a quality issue, and I felt as though Jerry, my salesperson, had disappeared. We had discussed the problem on the phone, and when I followed up later that day and the next day, I received no response, not even an "I'm working on it; allow me time to get back to you." Instead, each time I called, I was told Jerry was in a meeting.

- When a salesperson does not know how to respectfully use means of communications, it can lead to a poor relationship. For example, a salesperson with whom I had not worked in the past, Tyler, received my e-mail address from one of my coworkers. That was fine with me. However, Tyler sent me nine e-mails within one hour in attempts to set up a meeting!

Source: Maria Longori, personal correspondence, used with permission, names changed on request.

open. That means you must contact buyers often, keep them fully informed, and make sure you are accessible for their contact, as "From the Buyer's Seat 4.1" indicates.

ACTIVE LISTENING

Many people believe effective communication is achieved by talking a lot. Inexperienced salespeople often go into a selling situation thinking they have to out-talk the prospect. They are enthusiastic about their product and company, and

Exhibit 4.3
Levels of Listening

Level	Name	Characteristics
1	Hearing	Tuning in and tuning out. Mainly paying attention to yourself. Not responding to the speaker. Often just pretending to listen.
2	Passive listening	Not making a great effort to understand what the speaker is trying to convey. Not listening to the deeper meaning of what the speaker is saying. More concerned with content of the message than the speaker's feelings. Speaker may think the listener is really listening.
3	Active listening	Actively tries to put self in the speaker's place. Sees things from the speaker's point of view, including feelings. Reading speaker's body language carefully. Avoids all distractions.

they want to tell the prospect all they know. However, salespeople who monopolize conversations cannot find out what customers need. One authority suggests an **80–20 listening rule:** Salespeople should listen 80 percent of the time and talk no more than 20 percent of the time.[4] Studies have shown that salespeople with outstanding communication skills actually support the value creation process.[5]

People can speak at a rate of only 120 to 160 words per minute, but they can listen to more than 800 words per minute. This difference is referred to as the **speaking–listening differential.** Because of this differential, salespeople often become lazy listeners. They do not pay attention and often remember only 50 percent of what is said immediately after they hear it.

Effective listening is not a passive activity. There are three levels of listening, as Exhibit 4.3 illustrates. Salespeople who practice **active listening** project themselves into the mind of the speaker and attempt to feel the way the speaker feels. Firms are spending millions of dollars on speech analytics technology for their call centers so they can discover the customer's emotions during a phone conversation. Salespeople should be able to do that more effectively because they are face-to-face with the customer. If a customer says she needs a small microphone, a Sony salesperson needs to listen carefully to find out what the term *small* means to this particular customer—how small the microphone has to be, why she needs a small microphone, and what she will be willing to sacrifice to get a small microphone. Active listening enables the salesperson to recommend a type of microphone that will meet the customer's specific needs.

Active listeners think while they listen. They think about the conclusions toward which the speaker is building, evaluate the evidence being presented, and sort out important facts from irrelevant ones. Active listening also means the listener attempts to draw out as much information as possible. Gestures can motivate a person to continue talking. Head nodding, eye contact, and an occasional *I see, Tell me more,* or *That's interesting* all demonstrate an interest in and understanding of what is being said. Take a moment to complete the questionnaire in Exhibit 4.4 to rate your active listening skills.

Suggestions for active listening include (1) repeating information, (2) restating or rephrasing information, (3) clarifying information, (4) summarizing the conversation, (5) tolerating silences, and (6) concentrating on the ideas being communicated.

Exhibit 4.4
Test Your Active
Listening Skills

During a typical conversation:	My performance could be improved substantially			My performance needs no improvement	
1. I project an impression that I sincerely care about what the person is saying.	1	2	3	4	5
2. I don't interrupt the person.	1	2	3	4	5
3. I don't jump to conclusions.	1	2	3	4	5
4. I ask probing questions.	1	2	3	4	5
5. I ask continuing questions like "Could you tell me more?"	1	2	3	4	5
6. I maintain eye contact with the person.	1	2	3	4	5
7. I nod to show the person that I agree or understand.	1	2	3	4	5
8. I read the person's nonverbal communications.	1	2	3	4	5
9. I wait for the person to finish speaking before evaluating what has been said.	1	2	3	4	5
10. I ask clarifying questions like "I'm not sure I know what you mean."	1	2	3	4	5
11. I restate what the person has stated or asked.	1	2	3	4	5
12. I summarize what the person has said.	1	2	3	4	5
13. I make an effort to understand the person's point of view.	1	2	3	4	5
14. I try to find things I have in common with the person.	1	2	3	4	5

Scoring: 60–70 = Outstanding; 50–59 = Good; 40–49 = Could use some improvement; 30–39 = Could definitely use some improvement; Under 30 = Are you listening?

Source: An adaptation of the ILPS scale, Stephen B. Castleberry, C. David Shepherd, and Rick E. Ridnour, "Effective Interpersonal Listening in the Personal Selling Environment: Conceptualization, Measurement, and Nomological Validity," *Journal of Marketing Theory and Practice*, Winter 1999, pp. 30–38.

REPEATING INFORMATION

During a sales interaction the salesperson should verify the information he or she is collecting from the customer. A useful way to verify information is to repeat, word for word, what has been said. This technique minimizes the chance of misunderstandings:

CUSTOMER: I'll take 20 cases of Nestlé milk chocolate hot cocoa and 12 cases of the rich chocolate.

SALESPERSON: Sure, Mr. Johnson, 20 cases of milk chocolate and 12 cases of rich chocolate.

CUSTOMER: Wait a minute. I got that backward. The rich chocolate is what sells the best here. I want 20 cases of the rich chocolate and 12 cases of the milk chocolate.

SALESPERSON: Fine. Twelve milk chocolate, 20 rich chocolate. Is that right?

CUSTOMER: Yes. That's what I want.

Salespeople need to be careful when using this technique, however. Customers can get irritated with salespeople who echo everything.

RESTATING OR REPHRASING INFORMATION

To verify a customer's intent, salespeople should restate the customer's comment in his or her own words. This step ensures that the salesperson and customer understand each other:

CUSTOMER: Your service isn't what I had expected it would be.

SALESPERSON: I see, you're a bit dissatisfied with the financial advisor services I've been giving you.

CUSTOMER: Oh, no. As a matter of fact, I've been getting better service than I thought I would.

CLARIFYING INFORMATION

Another way to verify a customer's meaning is to ask questions designed to obtain additional information. These can give a more complete understanding of the customer's concerns:

To be an effective listener, the salesperson demonstrates an interest in what the customer is saying and actively thinks about questions for drawing out more information.

CUSTOMER: Listen, I've tried everything. I just can't get this drill press to work properly.

SALESPERSON: Just what is it that the drill press doesn't do?

CUSTOMER: Well, the rivets keep jamming inside the machine. Sometimes one rivet is inserted on top of the other.

SALESPERSON: Would you describe for me the way you load the rivets onto the tray?

CUSTOMER: Well, first I push down the release lever and take out the tray. Then I push that little button and put in the rivets. Next, I push the lever again, put the tray in the machine, and push the lever.

SALESPERSON: When you put the tray in, which side is up?

CUSTOMER: Does that make a difference?

This exchange shows how a sequence of questions can clarify a problem and help the salesperson determine its cause.

SUMMARIZING THE CONVERSATION

An important element of active listening is to mentally summarize points that have been made. At critical spots in the sales presentation, the salesperson should present his or her mentally prepared summary. Summarizing provides both salesperson and customer with a quick overview of what has taken place and lets them focus on the issues that have been discussed:

CUSTOMER: So I told him I wasn't interested.

SALESPERSON: Let me see whether I have this straight. A salesperson called on you today and asked whether you were interested in reducing your costs. He also said he could save you about $125 a month. But when you pursued the matter, you found out the dollar savings in costs were offset by reduced service.

CUSTOMER: That's right.

SALESPERSON: Well, I have your account records right here. Assuming you're interested in getting more for your company's dollar with regard to cell service costs, I think there's a way we can help you—without having to worry about any decrease in the quality of service.

CUSTOMER: Tell me more.

TOLERATING SILENCES

This technique could more appropriately be titled "Bite your tongue." At times during a sales presentation, a customer needs time to think. This need can be triggered by a tough question or an issue the customer wants to avoid. While the customer is thinking, periods of silence occur. Salespeople may be uncomfortable during these silences and feel they need to say something. However, the customer cannot think when the salesperson is talking. The following conversation about setting a second appointment demonstrates the benefits of tolerating silence:

SALESPERSON: What day would you like me to return with the samples and give that demonstration to you and your team?

CUSTOMER: [*obviously thinking*]

SALESPERSON: [*silence*]

CUSTOMER: OK, let's make it on Monday, the 22nd.

CONCENTRATING ON THE IDEAS BEING COMMUNICATED

Frequently what customers say and how they say it can distract salespeople from the ideas the customers are actually trying to communicate. For example, salespeople may react strongly when customers use emotion-laden phrases such as *bad service* or *lousy product*. Rather than getting angry, the salesperson should try to find out what upset the customer so much. Salespeople should listen to the words from the customer's viewpoint instead of reacting from their own viewpoint, as "Building Partnerships 4.1" discusses.

READING NONVERBAL MESSAGES FROM CUSTOMERS

In addition to asking questions and listening, salespeople can learn a lot from their customers' nonverbal behaviors.[6] When two people communicate with each other, spoken words play a surprisingly small part in the communication process. Words are responsible for only 40 percent of the information people acquire in face-to-face communication. Voice characteristics account for 10 percent of the message received, and the remaining 50 percent comes from nonverbal communications.[7] In this section we discuss how salespeople can collect information by observing their customers' **body language**. Later in the chapter we examine how salespeople can use the three forms of **nonverbal communication**—body language, space, and appearance—to convey messages to their customers. Note that experts don't always agree on what nonverbal cues mean. The examples provided in this chapter are those commonly accepted by sales trainers.

Studies have shown that the brain can actually lose it's ability to understand nonverbals if face-to-face contact decreases. One fear of over-use of social media is that people will lose their nonverbal reading skills.[8]

USE COMMUNICATION PRINCIPLES TO BUILD STRONG RELATIONSHIPS

As a salesperson for Sadelco, Inc., a manufacturer of digital signal meters, I am in such an industry that I rarely walk out of a sales call with an order in hand. I must rely on my customer to come to me when he or she has a need for my category of products. Communicating with my clients on a regular basis provides me the opportunity to keep them abreast of the latest product changes, special promotions, and other information that is essential for their company to be successful.

My customers are very busy, and I must have their trust that if they are to take my phone call or accept my invitation to meet. They must realize that when I contact them that I am bringing something useful to them that is necessary for them to do their job effectively. Listening to my customers is the starting point to understanding their needs and motivations. Their needs are the only thing that I should be focused on as I begin to establish a strong business relationship. The more quickly one masters the ability to listen, the faster you will build the level of trust and lead to your greater success as a salesperson.

Examples of important information that my customers appreciate in a very timely manner are the following:

- Informing them of new pricing that will affect products that they are reselling in the marketplace and giving them the option to place an order prior to new pricing taking effect.

- Informing them when one of my products is out of stock and unable to fill their orders as needed. This includes offering viable alternatives of replacement products to fill their orders until the requested products are available.

- Changes in the technical specifications of my products that could have an impact for their customers.

- Suggesting complementary accessories or other products that would work well with products already being purchased.

- Situations with one of my factories that could have an adverse effect on lead times, trying to prevent an unhappy customer on their end.

I feel if I do a great job in communication many of these important matters to enable my customer to make more informed decisions, they are more likely to come to me with their business versus my competition.

Occasionally, I must tell my customers information that they don't want to hear (e.g., that products will not ship in time or that I cannot get them the pricing they need to make a project work). Communicating the bad news in a timely manner will lead to their trusting me more and greatly strengthening the critical trust level that is so vital in sales.

One of the most satisfying parts of my business is when a customer comes to me looking for a solution to a problem or a specific need for a product. It tells me that I have done my job and that my customers trust me to help them solve a problem. I may not profit in the immediate future, but I know I have a good customer and often a good friend who will help me to be successful in my job.

Source: RDM, personal correspondence, used with permission, names changed on request.

BODY ANGLE

Back-and-forth motions indicate a positive outlook, whereas side-to-side movements suggest insecurity and doubt. Body movements directed toward a person indicate positive regard; in contrast, leaning back or away suggests boredom, apprehension, or possibly anger. Changes in position may indicate that a customer wants to end the interview, strongly agrees or disagrees with what has been said, or wants to place an order.

FACE

The face has many small muscles capable of communicating innumerable messages. Customers can use these muscles to indicate interest, expectation, concern,

The customer in the upper panel is giving negative nonverbal signals of arms crossed and no smile. Both buyers and the seller in the lower panel are giving positive, nonverbal signals.

disapproval, or approval. The eyes are the most important area of the face. The pupils of interested or excited people tend to enlarge. Thus, by looking at a customer's eyes, salespeople can often determine when their presentations have made an impression. For this reason many Chinese jade buyers wear dark glasses so they can conceal their interest in specific items and bargain more effectively. Even the rate at which someone blinks can tell a lot about a person. The average blink rate for a relaxed person is 10 to 20 blinks per minute (bmp). During normal conversation, it increases to about 25 bmp. A bmp rate over 50, and particularly over 70, indicates high stress levels.

Eye position can indicate a customer's thought process. Eyes focused straight ahead mean a customer is passively receiving information but devoting little effort to analyzing the meaning and not really concentrating on the presentation. Intense eye contact for more than three seconds generally indicates customer displeasure. Staring indicates coldness, anger, or dislike.

Customers look away from the salesperson while they actively consider information in the sales presentation. When the customer's eyes are positioned to the left or right, the salesperson has succeeded in getting the customer involved in the presentation. A gaze to the right suggests the customer is considering the logic and facts in the presentation, and gazing to the left suggests more intense concentration based on an emotional consideration. Eyes cast down offer the strongest signal of concentration. However, when customers cast their eyes down, they may be thinking, *How can I get my boss to buy this product?* or *How can I get out of this conversation?* When customers look away for an extended period, they probably want to end the meeting.

Skin color and skin tautness are other facial cues. A customer whose face reddens is signaling that something is wrong. That blush can indicate either anger or embarrassment. Tension and anger show in a tightness around the cheeks, jawline, or neck.

ARMS

A key factor in interpreting arm movements is intensity. Customers will use more arm movement when they are conveying an opinion. Broader and more vigorous movement indicates the customer is more emphatic about the point being communicated verbally. Always remember cultural differences. For example, it's rude to cross your arms in Turkey.

HANDS

Hand gestures are very expressive. For example, open and relaxed hands are a positive signal, especially with palms facing up. Self-touching gestures typically indicate tension. Involuntary gestures, such as tightening of a fist, are good indicators of true feelings. The meanings of hand gestures differ from one culture to another. For example, the thumbs-up gesture is considered offensive in the Middle East, rude in Australia, and a sign of OK in France. In Japan the OK sign

The open hands on the left are a positive signal by a salesperson. The intertwined fingers in the middle indicate that the salesperson is expressing his power and authority. On the right the salesperson is playing with his hands, indicating underlying tension. Source: Stephen B. Castleberry, used with permission

made by holding the thumb and forefinger in a circle symbolizes money, but in France it indicates that something is worthless.

LEGS

When customers have uncrossed legs in an open position, they send a message of cooperation, confidence, and friendly interest. Legs crossed away from a salesperson suggest that the sales call is not going well. Note that crossing your feet and showing the bottoms of your shoes are insulting in Japan.

BODY LANGUAGE PATTERNS

Exhibit 4.5 illustrates the patterns of signals that generally indicate the customer is reacting positively or negatively to a salesperson's presentation. However, no single gesture or position defines a specific emotion or attitude. To interpret a customer's feelings, salespeople need to consider the pattern of the signals via a number of channels. For example, many men are comfortable in informal conversations with their arms crossed. It doesn't necessarily mean they're against you or what you're saying.

In business and social situations, buyers often use nonverbal cues to try to be polite. As a result salespeople often have difficulty knowing what a customer is really thinking. For example, smiling is the most common way to conceal a strong emotion. Salespeople need to know whether a customer's smile is real or just a polite mask. The muscles around the eyes reveal whether a smile is real or polite.

Exhibit 4.5
Patterns of Nonverbal
Reactions to Presentation

Positive Signals	Negative Signals
Uncrossed arms and legs	Crossed arms or legs
Leaning forward	Leaning backward or turned away from you
Smiling or otherwise pleasant expression	Furrowed brow, pursed lips, frowning
Nodding	Shaking head
Contemplative posture	Fidgeting, distracted
Eye contact	No eye contact
Animated, excited reaction	Little change in expression, lifeless

When a customer is truly impressed, the muscles around the eyes contract, the skin above the eyes comes down a little, and the eyelids are slightly closed.

Here are some other signals that customers may be hiding their true feelings:

- *Contradictions and verbal mistakes.* People often forget what they said previously. They may leak their true feelings through a slip of the tongue or a lapse in memory.
- *Differences in two parts of a conversation.* In the first part of a conversation, a customer may display some nervousness when asked about the performance of a competitor's product and then respond by outlining the competitor's product's faults. Later in the conversation, the evaluation of the competitor's product may be much more positive.
- *Contradictions between verbal and nonverbal messages.* For example, a facial expression may not match the enthusiasm indicated by verbal comments. Also, a decrease in nonverbal signals may indicate that the customer is making a cautious response.
- *Nonverbal signals.* Voice tone going up at the end of a sentence, hesitation in the voice, small shrugs, increased self-touching, and stiffer body posture suggest that the customer has concerns.

When customers disguise their true feelings, they are often trying to be polite, not deceptive. To uncover the customer's true feelings and build a relationship, the salesperson needs to encourage the customer to be frank by emphasizing that she or he will benefit from an open exchange of information. Here are some comments a salesperson can make to encourage forthright discussion:

- Perhaps there is some reason you cannot share the information with me.
- Are you worried about how I might react to what you are telling me?
- I have a sense that there is really more to the story than what you are telling me. Let's put the cards on the table so we can put this issue to rest.

SENDING MESSAGES WITH NONVERBAL COMMUNICATION

The preceding section described how salespeople can develop a better understanding of their customers by observing their body language. Salespeople can also use their own body language, spacing, and appearance to send messages to their customers. This section explores that aspect of body language.

USING BODY LANGUAGE

During a 30-minute sales call around 800 nonverbal signals are exchanged.[9] Astute salespeople use these signals to communicate more effectively with customers.[10] For example, salespeople should strive to use the positive signals shown in Exhibit 4.5. Cooperative cues indicate to customers that the salesperson sincerely wants to help them satisfy their needs. Obviously salespeople should avoid using negative cues. In fact, salespeople should consider engaging in **mirroring,** which is where one person copies the nonverbals of another. In this case, salespeople should use their nonverbals carefully, hoping that the buyer will mirror their positive and open nonverbals.

Remember this word of warning: The most effective gestures are natural ones, not those you are forcing yourself to perform. A buyer can spot nongenuine nonverbals. Use as much of this information as you can, but don't become so engrossed in following all the rules that you can't be yourself.

Facial Muscles

Nonverbal communication is difficult to manage. Facial reactions are often involuntary, especially during stressful situations. Lips tense, foreheads wrinkle, and eyes glare without salespeople realizing they are disclosing their feelings to a customer. Salespeople will be able to control their facial reactions only with practice.

As with muscles anywhere else in the body, the coordination of facial muscles requires exercise. Actors realize this need and attend facial exercise classes to learn to control their reactions. Salespeople are also performers to some extent and need to learn how to use their faces to communicate emotions.

Nothing creates rapport like a smile.[11] The smile should appear natural and comfortable, not a smirk or an exaggerated, clownlike grin. To achieve the right smile, stand before a mirror or a video camera and put your lips in various smiling positions until you find a position that feels natural and comfortable. Then practice the smile until it becomes almost second nature.

Eye Contact

Appropriate eye contact varies from situation to situation.[12] People should use direct eye contact when talking in front of a group to indicate sincerity, credibility, and trustworthiness. Glancing from face to face rapidly or staring at a wall has the opposite effect. However, staring can overpower customers and make them uncomfortable.

Gestures and Handshaking

Gestures can have a dramatic impact.[13] For example, by exposing the palm of the hand, a salesperson indicates openness and receptivity. Slicing hand movements and pointing a finger are very strong signals and should be used to reinforce only the most important points. In most cases pointing a finger should be avoided. This gesture will remind customers of a parent scolding a child. When salespeople make presentations to a group, they often use too few hand gestures. Gestures should be used to drive home a point. But if a salesperson uses too many gestures, acting like an orchestra conductor, people will begin to watch the hands and miss the words.

The location of your hands during gestures can have a huge impact on the message received.[14] For example, imagine a salesperson standing and giving a presentation to a small group of businesspeople. If she drops her hands down by her sides while presenting and keeps them there, she will come across as passive and lacking enthusiasm. Hand gestures presented at about the height of her navel help the salesperson come across as truthful. Gestures at chest level suggest she has real passion about a topic, while those above the head are interpreted as great passion. Try each of these locations of gestures in front of a mirror while saying "I love you" to see what impact the location of gestures has on the interpretation of the spoken words.

In terms of shaking hands, salespeople should not automatically extend their hands to prospects, particularly if a prospect is seated.[15] Shaking hands should be the prospect's choice. If the prospect offers a hand, the salesperson should respond with a firm but not overpowering handshake while maintaining good eye contact. Chances are that you have experienced both a limpid handshake—a hand with little or no grip—and a bone-crunching grip. Either impression is often lasting and negative. Also, if you tend to have sweaty hands, carry a handkerchief.

Women should shake hands in the same manner men do. They should avoid offering their hand for a social handshake (palm facing down and level with the ground, with fingers drooping and pointing to the ground). Likewise, a man should not force a social handshake from a woman in a business setting.

The salesperson selling in an international context needs to carefully consider cultural norms regarding the appropriateness of handshaking, bowing, and other forms of greeting. For example, the Chinese prefer no more than a slight bow in their greeting, whereas an Arab businessperson may not only shake hands vigorously but also keep holding your hand for several seconds. A hug in Mexico communicates a trusting relationship, but in Germany such a gesture would be offensive because it suggests an inappropriate level of intimacy. Germans tend to pump the hand only once during a handshake. Seventy-four percent of British adults admit they no longer reach out a hand to greet friends or colleagues.[16] Some African cultures snap their fingers after shaking hands, but other Africans would see this act as tasteless. And some Eastern cultures use the left hand for hygienic purposes, so offering a left hand to them would insult them.

Posture and Body Movements

Shuffling one's feet and slumping give an impression of a lack of both self-confidence and self-discipline. On the other hand, an overly erect posture, like that of a military cadet, suggests rigidity. Salespeople should let comfort be their guide when searching for the right posture.

To get an idea of what looks good and feels good, stand in front of a mirror and shift your weight until tension in your back and neck is at a minimum. Then gently pull your shoulders up and back and elevate your head. Practice walking by taking a few steps. Keep the pace deliberate, not halting; deliberate, controlled movements indicate confidence and empathy. Note cultural differences like the fact that Japanese people value the ability to sit quietly and can view a fidgety American as uncontrolled.

This buyer and seller are in the intimate zone.

THE ROLE OF SPACE AND PHYSICAL CONTACT

The physical space between a customer and a salesperson can affect the customer's reaction to a sales presentation. Exhibit 4.6 shows the four distance zones people use when interacting in business and social situations. The **intimate zone** is reserved primarily for a person's closest relationships, the **personal zone** for close friends and those who share special interests, the **social zone** for business transactions and other impersonal relationships, and the **public zone** for speeches, teachers in classrooms, and passersby. The exact sizes of the intimate and personal zones depend on age, gender, culture, and race. For example, the social zone for Latinos is much closer than that for North Americans. Latinos tend to conduct business transactions so close together that North Americans feel uncomfortable.

Customers may react negatively when they believe salespeople are invading their intimate or personal space. To show the negative reaction, customers may assume a defensive posture by moving back or folding their arms. Although approaching too close can generate a negative reaction, standing too far away can create an image of aloofness, conceit, or unsociability.

In general, salespeople should begin customer interactions at the social zone and not move closer until an initial rapport has been established. If the buyer indicates that a friendlier relationship has developed, the salesperson should move closer.

In terms of touching, buyers fall into two touching groups: contact and noncontact. Contact people usually see noncontact people as cold and unfriendly. On the other hand, noncontact people view contact people as overly friendly and obtrusive. People who like to be touched tend to respond to touch with increased

Exhibit 4.6

Distance Zones for Interaction

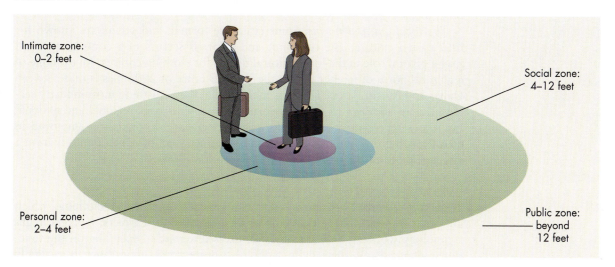

Intimate zone: 0–2 feet

Social zone: 4–12 feet

Personal zone: 2–4 feet

Public zone: beyond 12 feet

persuasion and liking for the salesperson. Although some customers may accept a hand on their backs or a touch on their shoulders, salespeople should generally limit touching to a handshake. Touching clearly enters a customer's intimate space and may be considered rude and threatening—an invasion.

APPEARANCE

Physical appearance, specifically dress style, is an aspect of nonverbal communication that affects the customer's evaluation of the salesperson. Two priorities in dressing for business are (1) getting customers to notice you in a positive way and (2) getting customers to trust you. If salespeople overdress, their clothing may distract from their sales presentation. Proper attire and grooming, however, can give salespeople additional poise and confidence. One salesperson for Smith & Nephew, a medical equipment company, says he always dresses like a chameleon. "Dress like your doctor," is his motto. If the doctor is in suit and tie, he wears a suit and tie; if the doctor prefers casual dress, the seller does likewise.

At one time dressing for work was simple: You just reached in the closet and picked from your wardrobe of blue, gray, and pinstripe suits. Today things are not that simple. With casual days and dress-down Fridays, styles and dress codes vary considerably from office to office. Salespeople should learn the norms for dress in their field and follow them closely.

During a given day a salesperson may have to visit his or her company's and customers' offices, each of which may have a different dress code. And sometimes the buyer will have dress codes that even visiting salespeople must follow. For example, Target has dress codes that apply to salespeople who want to make presentations at its company offices.

Vicki West has developed five timeless principles for a salesperson wanting to dress for success.[17] We describe these here.

Principle 1: Consider the Geography

The temperature: Clothing choices are obviously influenced by temperature trends and variations. San Francisco is different from Minneapolis, which differs from Austin, Texas, in humidity, temperature, and weather patterns. These factors dictate the fiber and type of clothing worn. Although linen and cotton are cool, warm-weather fabrics suitable almost the entire year in the southern part of the United States, they would be appropriate only in the late spring and summer in other locales.

The local cultural norms: Some cities are formal, and others are known for their casual culture. The economic and business sectors of a community often play a pivotal role in the local cultural norms for clothing choices. An example of a cultural norm difference within the short distance of 200 miles is that between Dallas and Austin, Texas. Dallas is more formal than Austin in most industry sectors. Dallas is known as a "headquarters" town with large regional and national businesses represented. Austin has a large segment of population employed in education, high technology, and the music industry, all of which typically have a younger, more casual workforce.

Principle 2: Consider Your Customers

Their appearance: Customers wear many different types of clothing, which are often dictated by the demands of their profession. Farmers, bankers, high-technology workers, and educators all dress differently depending on the functional demands of their daily work. A salesperson's appearance is certainly impacted by the customers' industry.

Their expectations for your appearance, however, generally reflect their impression of your industry. Salespeople representing the banking industry would be expected to dress differently from salespeople in the music recording industry.

Principle 3: Consider Your Corporate Culture

Norms for your industry should dictate the general parameters for appearance choices. It is obvious that corporate cultures change from time to time. The trend has been to dress more casually in the hot-weather months, even in conservative industries such as banking and finance. However, the consensus of many industry groups is that it is important to wear professional business attire regularly, with some exceptions based on geography and a salesperson's customer base.

Principle 4: Consider Your Aspirations

Top levels of your organization generally set the tone for an entire organization. If you aspire to reach a high level in the organization, it's important to note what expectations your organization might have for your general appearance.

An old rule is to dress *one level above your position.* Watch your immediate superior, who will decide whom to promote. If you want a promotion to the next level in the organization, dress as if you already have the position; then you will be perceived as a good fit for the job.

Principle 5: Consider Your Own Personal Style

Wait until you have the halo effect before making a personal style statement. The "halo effect" refers to the tendency to generalize one positive aspect of your behavior to all aspects of your behavior. This phenomenon can work to your benefit. No one wants to look like a corporate drone with no individual style, but the first week on the job may not be the best time to make your personal appearance statement. Wait until you have proved your professional skills, no matter what the industry, before wearing clothing that may be deemed inappropriate to your particular industry.

Be reasonable in your wardrobe choices. Being individualist and memorable can be a positive decision, depending on the range of choices that are acceptable to a specific industry group. However, choosing outrageous or completely unsuitable clothing is probably not in the best interests of your personal career development. Like it or not, large jewelry, piercings, tattoos, heavy perfumes and colognes, short skirts, shorts, revealing blouses or shirts, pink or turquoise hair, and so forth are simply considered inappropriate in most sales situations.

COMMUNICATING VIA TECHNOLOGY

In addition to face-to-face interactions, salespeople communicate with customers by using the telephone, fax, e-mail, and voice mail. As shown in Exhibit 4.7, these methods vary in the interactivity of the communications, the ability to use verbal and nonverbal communication channels, and the quantity of information that can be conveyed. **Response time** is the time between sending a message and getting a response to it. Salespeople should use the communication method preferred by the buyer and should not overdo communicating with the buyer to the point of being a nuisance.[18]

TELEPHONE AND VOICE MAIL COMMUNICATIONS

Salespeople need to use the phone correctly and effectively. All of us have used telephones since childhood; many of us have developed bad habits that reduce our effectiveness when talking over the phone.[19] Perfect your phone style by practicing alone before making any calls. Make sure you know what you want to say before placing the call. Many would argue that it is a polite gesture to start by asking, "Is this a good time to talk?" Don't be too rushed to be nice; it is never acceptable to be rude. And don't forget to smile as you talk. Even though the prospect won't see it, he or she will hear it in your enthusiastic tone of voice.

Active listening is as important when conversing over the phone as when conversing in person. Take notes and restate the message or any action you have agreed to undertake. In addition, you will need to encourage two-way communication. If you have ever talked with two-year-olds over the phone, you know that if you ask them a yes-or-no question, they tend to shake their heads yes or no rather than verbalize a response. Similarly, you cannot nod your head to encourage someone to continue talking on the phone. Instead you must encourage conversations with verbal cues such as *Uh-huh, I see,* or *That's interesting.* Finally, just as in face-to-face conversation, you must be able to tolerate silences so customers have an opportunity to ask questions, agree or disagree, or relate a point to their circumstances.

Exhibit 4.7

Comparison of Various Methods of Salesperson Communications*

	Face-to-Face	Telephone	Voice Mail	Fax	E-Mail
Response time	Fast	Fast	Slow	Slow	Slow
Salesperson can use verbal communications	Yes	Yes	Yes	No	No
Salesperson can hear buyer's verbal communications	Yes	Yes	No	No	No
Salesperson can read buyer's nonverbal communications	Yes	No	No	No	No
Quantity of information seller can send	Highest	Average	Lowest	Varies	Varies
Quantity of information buyer can send	Highest	Average	None	None	None

*Ratings can vary greatly given the situation.

It is important to set objectives for your phone call and strategize what you're going to say and why. Here is an example of using the phone to make an appointment:

1. [*State customer's name.*] Hello, Mr. Peterson? (*Pause.*)

2. [*Introduce yourself and show preparation.*] This is Amanda Lowden with Cisco Systems. I was talking to your director of operations, Marvin Schepp, and he suggested I talk with you.

3. [*Politely check time.*] I hope I didn't catch you in the middle of something urgent or pressing? (*Pause.*)

4. [*State purpose and build credibility.*] I'm calling to let you know about our new carrier routing system. I've shown it to several other systems engineers in town, and they found its self-healing and self-defending operating system to be something they wanted to explore further.

5. [*Commitment to action.*] I'd like to meet with you and share some feedback from your business associates. Could you put me on your calendar for 30 minutes next Monday or Tuesday?

6. [*Show appreciation and restate time, or keep door open.*] Thank you, Mr. Peterson. I'll be at your office at 9 a.m. on Tuesday. [*or*] I appreciate your frankness, Mr. Peterson. I'd like to get back to you in a couple of months. Would that be all right?

Use proper techniques and etiquette when leaving voice mail messages:[20]

- If making a cold call to set up an appointment, don't leave a message. Just call back later.

- Leave a clear, concise message that includes a suggested time for a return call (so you can be prepared for that call).

- Speak slowly and distinctly.

- A little casual conversation up front is acceptable, but don't waste the prospect's time.

- Ask for a callback.

- Slowly repeat your name and phone number at the end of your message.

For your own voice mail system, use a fresh greeting on your system each day. Tell callers if a time limit exists for your voice mail, and if possible, offer the option to talk to someone immediately.

E-MAIL COMMUNICATIONS

Technology makes the transfer of information fast and easy. But it also holds the salesperson at arm's length and makes it difficult to develop rapport. High tech doesn't replace face-to-face interactions; it merely supplements and enhances personal exchanges. Following are some suggestions for salespeople with regard to e-mail communication:

- Don't be lulled into thinking that immediacy (fast) means the same thing as intimacy (close, friendly relationship) in communication. Buyers generally prefer face-to-face communications over other media types. When asked, most buyers said face-to-face communication builds high trust, reduces confusion and misunderstanding, and is easier to understand. And sometimes snail mail still works the best.

Developments in technology enable salespeople to improve their communications with customers.

- For the subject line, use important information to avoid having the e-mail deleted unread (for example, don't use "hello" as your subject line). And make it sound easy to deal with (such as "Two Short Questions").
- Make sure the first few lines of the e-mail are important. Many people read only the first few lines before deleting a message. Use a heading and bullets to help the reader follow a longer e-mail message.
- It is hard for buyers to read your nonverbal messages in e-mail because they can't see them (and you can't read theirs). Studies show that many users do not grasp the tone or intent of e-mail, and using smiley faces or other emoticons just makes it more confusing.
- Learn the customer's preferences for e-mail. Adapt the content to the customer's preferred communication style. For example, some firms have instituted "no e-mail Fridays." And never be viewed by your prospect as a spammer!
- Avoid "techno overkill." Written communication (such as letters and printed brochures or catalogs) may be better when the customer wants to study the information at his or her leisure.
- Customers are drowning in information. Don't send long e-mail messages or large attachments unless the buyer is expecting them. If you decide to send a PowerPoint presentation via e-mail, use special software that will help ensure that it gets through the virus and spam filters.
- Use speed to impress customers—especially for damage control. Exceed a customer's expectations, such as responding immediately to urgent calls via e-mail. E-mail sent to you by customers should be answered by the end of the workday.
- Don't deliver bad news via e-mail; rather, use e-mail to arrange a meeting to discuss the issue.
- If you want your e-mail read, at least according to one study, send it on Wednesdays around 11:00 a.m. The worst time to send is (not surprisingly) Saturday and Sunday. See Sales Technology 4.1 for more hints on successful e-mailing.

SOCIAL NETWORKING

Social networking is the use of Web tools that allow users to share content, interact, and develop communities around similar interests. Salespeople are using social networking, like blogs, LinkedIn, Twitter, Pinterest, and Facebook, to communicate with customers and prospects.[21] While many of the suggestions already covered in this chapter apply to these networks, salespeople should consider other issues as well. Some suggestions for networking sites like LinkedIn and Facebook include the following:

- Fill out your profile completely to build trust and establish common bonds. Spend the time and money to get a great head shot photo and include it on your site. Make sure it is appropriate for business purposes. Update your profile regularly to keep it current and interesting. Remember that many members get updates every time someone changes his or her profile, so you're getting more exposure with every adjustment to your profile.
- Create contacts/friends lists such as "Family" and "Work Related" so you can better control the privacy of your profile and information.
- Follow all rules for the networking sites.
- Share articles and links to presentations and other information that might be helpful to prospects. Posting comments from experts will improve your credibility. Studies show that 55 percent of buyers use social media when looking for informatiion.[22]

E-MAILS: TEN EASY RULES TO FOLLOW

With technology being a prominent piece of today's business world, it is essential that one know the proper way to construct a professional business e-mail. The following is a list of things to consider to help ensure proper e-mail etiquette:

1. Have a meaningful subject line. For a deadline, do not just put "important" or "product 'x.'" Instead use, "Deadline approaching for product 'x.'"

2. Don't beat around the bush; you have a reason for the e-mail, so state it right away in the opening sentence.

3. Use specifics in your opening—avoid using words such as "this" or "that."

4. Use proper capitalization and punctuation—use correct uppercase and lowercase. Maybe write your e-mail first in a word processing document; this will give you the ability to utilize its spelling and grammar-check function.

5. Do not use chat room abbreviations, such as "LOL."

6. Be concise and detailed. The use of bullet points will help organize the information and make it easier and quicker for the recipient to read.

7. Be polite. "Please" and "thank you" can go a long way.

8. Create a signature block that will go on the end of the e-mail with good contact information.

9. Proofread, proofread, and proofread—the small things you may not notice when you are writing the e-mail may translate to carelessness in the eyes of the reader.

10. When receiving an important e-mail, be sure to respond quickly. If more than 24 hours will be needed to provide a response, it is a great idea to send a quick reply explaining your delay.

Failing to follow these simple rules may make it seem as though the recipients were not worth your time, and in turn they may feel as though you should not be worth their time.

Sources: Kitty O. Locker and Stephen Kyo Kaczmarek, *Business Communication: Building Critical Skills*, 5th ed. (New York: McGraw-Hill, 2011); Richard Nordquist, "Ten Tips on How to Write a Professional Email," *About.com Grammar & Composition*, August 30, 2012, http://grammar.about.com/od/developingessays/a/profemails.htm.

- Remember to post updates on your wall about your business. Tell about upcoming events like webinars and conferences where you will be speaking.
- Combine your Facebook/LinkedIn account with other social media sites you participate in, like Twitter and Pinterest.
- Respond quickly to posts and queries.
- Add your Facebook/LinkedIn URL to your e-mail signature so prospects can learn more about you.

Businesses are starting to build relationships and stay connected to their customers and prospects with microblogging tools like Twitter. The 140-or-less character messages are called tweets. Due to the nature of Twitter, some additional considerations apply:[23]

- Build your account and include a picture.
- Use a Twitter search tool to listen for your name, the name of your product, or your company.
- Use a friendly and casual tone in messages. But make sure your tweets reflect the culture of your company.

This American salesperson needs to recognize the differences between communicating in an Arab culture and an American culture.

- Make a link to things you think prospects would find interesting, like articles and Web sites. Tweets should have real value to the receiver.
- Don't create spam with Twitter.
- You can schedule when the tweets will be sent with add-ons like Social Oomph.
- Share interesting things about your community and nonbusiness items to help make yourself real. Remember that you are trying to create a friendly relationship.
- Remember to listen, not just send out tweets. Respond to at least some of the replying tweets. Don't feel guilty if you don't read or respond to all tweets.

Because of the growing use of social networking, Chapters 6 and 7 will discuss ways to use these tools to prospect and learn more about new customers.

ADJUSTING FOR CULTURAL DIFFERENCES

Communication in international selling often takes place in English because English is likely to be the only language salespeople and customers have in common. To communicate effectively with customers whose native language is not English, salespeople need to be careful about the words and expressions they use. People who use English in international selling should observe the following rules:

- Use common English words that a customer would learn during the first two years of studying the language. For example, use *expense* rather than *expenditure* or *stop* instead of *cease*.
- Use words that do not have multiple meanings. For example, *right* has many meanings, whereas *accurate* is more specific. When you use words that have several meanings, recognize that nonnative speakers will usually use the most common meaning to interpret what you are saying.
- Avoid slang expressions peculiar to American culture, such as *slice of life, struck out, wade through the figures,* and *run that by me again.*
- Use rules of grammar more strictly than you would in everyday speech. Make sure you express your thoughts in complete sentences, with a noun and a verb.
- Use action-specific verbs, as in *start the motor,* rather than action-general verbs, as in *get the motor going.*
- Never use vulgar expressions, tell off-color jokes, or make religious references.

Even if you are careful about the words you use, misunderstandings can still arise because terms have different meanings, even among people from different English-speaking countries.[24] For example, in the United States *tabling a proposal* means "delaying a decision," but in England it means "taking immediate action." In England promising to do something by the end of the day means doing it when you have finished what you are working on now, not within 24 hours. In England *bombed* means the negotiations were successful, whereas in the United States this term has the opposite meaning.

International salespeople need to understand the varying perceptions of time in general and the time it takes for business activities to occur in different countries. For example, in Latin American and Arab countries people are not strict about keeping appointments at the designated times. If you show up for an appointment on time in these cultures, you may have to wait several hours for the meeting to start. Lunch is at 3:00 p.m. in Spain, 12:00 noon in Germany, 1:00 p.m. in England, and 11:00 a.m. in Norway. In Greece no one makes telephone calls between 2:00 p.m. and 5:00 p.m. The British arrive at their desks at 9:30 a.m. but like to do paperwork and have a cup of tea before getting any calls. The French, like the Germans, like to start early in the day, frequently having working breakfasts. Restaurants close at 9:00 p.m. in Norway—just when dinner is starting in Spain. The best time to reach high-level Western European executives is after 7:00 p.m., when daily activities have slowed down and they are continuing to work for a few more hours. However, Germans start going home at 4:00 p.m.

Significant cultural differences dictate the appropriate level of eye contact between individuals. In the United States salespeople look directly into their customers' eyes when speaking or listening to them. Direct eye contact is a sign of interest in what the customer is saying. In other cultures looking someone in the eye may be a sign of disrespect:

- In Japan looking directly at a subordinate indicates that the subordinate has done something wrong. When a subordinate looks directly into the eyes of his or her supervisor, the subordinate is displaying hostility.
- In Muslim countries, eye contact is not supposed to occur between men and women.
- In Korea eye contact is considered rude.
- Brazilians look at people directly even more than Americans do. Americans tend to find this direct eye contact, when held over a long period, to be disconcerting.

SELLING YOURSELF

You've been applying for jobs and recently heard back from HR at one of your top choices. After e-mailing back and forth, you have finally set up a time for the two interviews with two different professionals from the business. The surprising element was that each of these interviews will be via phone.

Communication is vital not only to obtaining a sale but also to obtaining a job. Because the first two rounds of the interview are conducted on the phone, you will not be able to identify nonverbal cues, which makes being actively engaged in the conversation even more important. You can do this by asking clarifying questions and restating key points, which will help to keep the conversation flowing. Again, you want to make sure you have an understanding of who your audience is and what may be important to them. The first round may be a screening with HR, while the second round could be with a potential manager. A good point of reference for job objectives can always be found in the job description. It would also be a good idea to have a notebook and pencil so you can take notes during the interview for reference and also for future interviews you may have. These notes could really help you develop good, key questions.

One of the hardest things to remember, especially when you are used to talking to family and friends on the telephone, is to speak slowly and concisely. You want to make sure that whatever message you are trying to convey is a true reflection of who you are as a professional. This means adapting to your audience and leaving the slang and abbreviations at home.

With all of these tools at your side, the tele-interview will seem less daunting. Your confidence will shine through, and the flow of the conversation will be as if you were at a face-to-face meeting.

Source: Sally Cook, used with permission.

SUMMARY

This chapter discussed the principles of communication and how they can be used to build trust in relationships, improve selling effectiveness, and reduce misunderstandings. The communication process consists of a sender, who encodes information and transmits messages, and a receiver, who decodes the messages. A communication breakdown can occur when the sender does a poor encoding job, when the receiver has difficulty decoding, and when noise and the environment interfere with the transmission of the message.

Effective communication requires a two-way flow of information. At different times in the interaction, both parties will act as sender and receiver. This two-way process enables salespeople to adapt their sales approach to the customer's needs and communication style.

When communicating verbally with customers, salespeople must be careful to use words and expressions their customers will understand. Effective communication is facilitated through the use of word pictures and by appropriate voice characteristics like inflection, articulation, and the proper rate of speech and loudness.

Listening is a valuable communication skill that enables salespeople to adapt to various situations. To listen effectively, salespeople need to actively think about what the customer is saying and how to draw out more information. Some suggestions for actively collecting information from customers are to repeat, restate, clarify, summarize the customer's comments, and demonstrate an interest in what the customer is saying.

About 50 percent of communication is nonverbal. Nonverbal messages sent by customers are conveyed by body language. The five channels of body language communication are body angle, face, arms, hands, and legs. No single channel can be used to determine the feelings or attitudes of customers. Salespeople need to analyze the body language pattern composed of all five channels to determine how a customer feels.

Salespeople can use nonverbal communication to convey information to customers. In addition to knowing how to use the five channels of body language, salespeople need to know the appropriate distances between themselves and their customers for different types of communications and relationships. Salespeople should learn to use their physical appearance and dress to create a favorable impression on customers.

Learning how to communicate effectively with technology is critical in today's marketplace. Not only should salespeople learn how to use the phone and e-mail effectively; they should also master the use of social networking like Facebook and LinkedIn, as well as Twitter and blogs, to connect with their customers and prospects.

Finally, two-way communication increases when salespeople adjust their communication styles to the styles of their customers. In making such adjustments, salespeople need to be sensitive to cultural differences when selling internationally and in diverse subcultures.

KEY TERMS

ETHICS PROBLEMS

1. In an effort to improve relationships and open communications, is it OK to enjoy a few beers on the golf course with your clients?
2. Assume you are making a call on a person of the opposite sex in a culture where direct eye contact between the sexes is not supposed to occur. Much to your amazement, the buyer continues to look intently into your eyes. You are in an office alone with the buyer. What should you do?

QUESTIONS AND PROBLEMS

1. As a student in a college classroom, you may encounter many distractions that affect your listening ability.
   a. List three things you have seen professors do that are distracting to you.
   b. What can you do to reduce each of these distractions?
2. Have a friend score you using the listening test (See Exhibit 4.4) found in this chapter.
   a. Compare your friend's score with the one you gave yourself.
   b. What did this exercise teach you about your listening skills?
3. Make a chart with three columns: *Items, What I Want This Item to Communicate to Others*, and *What Others Will Think My Item Is Communicating*. In the first column list the following: *my hairstyle, the clothing I'm wearing today*, and *any jewelry or body accents* (like earrings or tattoos). In the second column describe the message you want to communicate with each item. Have someone else fill in the third column, describing what the items communicate to him or her.
4. Develop a word picture that helps explain to a 60-year-old the merits of buying a smartphone, assuming the person doesn't own a cell phone currently.
5. What do the following body language cues indicate?
   a. Looking at something out the window while you're talking.
   b. Tapping the feet on the floor rhythmically.
   c. Leaning back in a chair with arms folded across the chest.
   d. Sitting on the edge of the seat.
6. Word choice is important. Some words, by themselves, may be perceived negatively. Come up with a better word choice that could be more positive for each of the following words: *cost, down payment, deal, objection, cheaper, appointment, commission*.
7. In "From the Buyer's Seat 4.1" you learned about Jerry, who was always "in a meeting"

when the buyer called. Assume you are Jerry and you didn't get any of the buyer's messages until now. How will you communicate to the buyer that you didn't receive her messages?

8. Closely examine 10 e-mail messages you receive. Evaluate them on the basis of the suggestions offered in this chapter for the proper use of e-mail.

9. Assume you sell football tickets for a nearby NFL team and you wish to use Twitter to build relationships with potential season ticket holders. Create two tweets that you would post to accomplish this objective.

CASE PROBLEMS

case **4.1**

Denmark Interiors

Ben Alan, a salesperson for Yellow Book USA, has just entered the elaborate office of Laura C. Curran, owner of Denmark Interiors, an upscale interior decorator in Louisville. Laura is seated behind a vast mahogany desk in a high-backed stylish executive chair working on some paperwork. She doesn't look up as Ben enters the room.

Ben: [walking around Laura's desk and extending his hand] Good morning, Laura! It's sure nice to finally get a chance to meet you. [laughing] Forgive me for saying so, but I'll have to admit this is the nicest office, and you're the prettiest person I've called on this week!

Laura: [not looking up from her paperwork or extending her hand as she finally responds] Please have a seat, Mr. ... what was your name?

Ben: [dragging up a seat from the side of the room and placing it on the same side of the desk as Laura, then plopping down in the seat] Ben. Ben Alan. I believe it's one of the hottest days in Louisville this summer! Say, here's a good joke I heard yesterday. A man fainted in the middle of a busy intersection, and traffic quickly piled up in all directions, so a woman rushed to help him. When she knelt down to loosen his collar, a man emerged from the crowd, pushed her aside, and said, "It's all right honey, I've had a course in CPR!" The woman stood up and watched as he took the ill man's pulse and prepared to administer artificial respiration. At this point she tapped him on the shoulder and said, "When you get to the part about calling a doctor, I'm already here." Ha ha ha!

Laura: [not laughing but pushing her paperwork away from her and crossing her arms] What can I do for you, Mr. Alan?

Ben: Well, Laura, I'd like to see your company take out a bigger ad in the Yellow Pages. Can't beat the Yellow Pages for business, now can you?

Laura: [turning in her chair to look out the window while looking at her watch] We provide professional interior decorating to high-end clients, depending mostly on word-of-mouth recommendations for new clients, Mr. Alan.

Ben: [taking out a pad of paper from his shirt pocket and searching his pockets for a pen] Now that's news to me, Laura. I thought you were like all the rest, desperately seeking ugly homes to make them prettier. Ha ha ha!

Laura: [making a steeple with her hands while still looking out the office window] I would guess you would, Mr. Alan. [swiveling in her chair to face Ben] Yes, I would guess you would. [pressing a button on her desk] Ms. Deramus, Mr. Alan has completed his interview with me. Will you kindly escort him out? [eyeing Ben with a triumphant look on her face] Have a good day, Mr. [strongly emphasizing the word Mr.] Alan.

Questions

1. Evaluate the exchange.

2. What would you do differently if you were Ben?

case 4.2

Case IH Agricultural

Joel Winnes is a sales rep for Case IH Agricultural, a global leader in agricultural equipment. Headquartered in the United States, Case IH has a vast network of more than 4,900 dealers and distributors that operates in over 160 countries. Case IH sells tractors, planting and seeding equipment, application and harvesting equipment, skid steers, attachments, and other farming-related equipment.

Joel, who grew up in central Minnesota and who has been selling for Case IH in northern Iowa for the past three years, was just transferred to the Case IH office in Mexico City. Joel has never lived or worked in Mexico before and is thinking about what changes he might need to make as he works with farmers in that country.

Questions

1. Investigate the culture of Mexico in more detail by viewing Web pages and reading articles about how business salespeople can best sell there. Briefly summarize four key findings.

2. What changes should Joel consider making (compared to how he probably sold to clients in Iowa) as he calls on prospects in Mexico? Make any assumptions necessary.

Source: www.pwm.com/pwm/pwm_lang_select.htm.

ROLE PLAY CASE

In this chapter's role play interaction, you are still meeting with the same person you did for Chapter 3. (If you did not do the role play at the end of Chapter 3, you will need to review that information now.) That person is telling you about the business. Feel free to ask questions, but your main objective is to listen and understand all you can about the business environment in which he or she operates. Practice active listening skills; after the role play, identify which listening techniques you used. Further, identify the three most important elements about the person's business that you need to understand. Interpret the buyer's body language. Finally, any time you hear jargon, write the word or phrase down.

Note: For background information about these role plays, see page 26.

To the instructor: Additional information needed to complete the role play is available in the Instructor's Manual.

ADDITIONAL REFERENCES

Brooks, Bill. "The Power of Active Listening." *American Salesman* 55, no. 12 (December 2010), pp. 28–30.

Bowden, Mark. *Winning Body Language: Control the Conversation, Command Attention, and Convey the Right Message without Saying a Word.* New York: McGraw-Hill, 2010.

Curtis, Joan C., and Barbara Giamanco. *The New Handshake: Sales Meets Social Media.* Santa Barbara, CA: Praeger, 2010.

Feigon, Josiane Chriqui, and Jill Konrath. *Smart Selling on the Phone and Online: Inside Sales That Gets Results.* New York: AMACOM, 2009.

Ferrari, Bernard T. *Power Listening: Mastering the Most Critical Business Skill of All.* Penguin Group, New York, 2012.

Ghosh, Rishab Aiyer. "There Are 200 Million People Tweeting: Are You Listening?" *Forbes.com,* October 10, 2011, p. 19.

Goulston, Mark, and Keith Ferrazzi. *Just Listen: Discover the Secret to Getting through to Absolutely Anyone.* New York: AMACOM, 2009.

Graham, John R. "What It Takes to Make the Sale: Making Sense Out of Buyer Behavior in a Wired World." *American Salesman* 54, no. 12 (December 2009), pp. 24–30.

Groves, Eric. *The Constant Contact Guide to E-Mail Marketing.* Hoboken, NJ: Wiley, 2009.

Hartley, Gregory, and Maryann Karinch. *The Body Language Handbook: How to Read Everyone's Hidden Thoughts and Intentions.* Pompton Plains, NJ: Career Press, 2010.

Hayden, C. J. "In Marketing and Sales, It Pays to Listen." *American Salesman* 57, no. 8 (August 2012), pp. 8–10.

Hollenbeck, Candice R., George M. Zinkhan, Warren French, and Ji Hee Song. "Collaborative Networks: A Case Study on the New Role of the Sales Force." *Journal of Personal Selling and Sales Management* 29, no. 2 (Spring 2009), pp. 125–36.

Knapp, Mark L., Judith A. Hall, and Terrence G. Horgan. *Nonverbal Communication in Human Interaction.* New York: Wadsworth Publishing, 2013.

Marker, Scott. *Let's Get It On! Realistic Strategies for Winning the Sales Game.* Ogden, UT: MSA Publishing, 2009.

McPheat, Sean. *Eselling: The Alternative Way to Prospect and Sell for Sales Professionals: How to Use the Internet for Prospecting, Personal Branding, Networking and for Engaging the C-Suite Decision Maker.* Leicester, England: Troubador Publishing, 2011.

Mychals, Brandy. *How to Read a Client from Across the Room: Win More Business with the Proven Character Code System to Decode Verbal and Nonverbal Communication.* McGraw-Hill, 2012.

Nelson, Audrey, and Claire Damken Brown. *The Gender Communication Handbook: Conquering Conversational Collisions between Men and Women.* San Francisco: Pfeiffer, 2012.

Raghavan, Anita. "Watch Your Body Language." *Forbes,* March 2009, p. 92.

Sobel, Andrew. *Power Questions: Build Relationships, Win New Business, and Influence.* Hoboken, NJ: Wiley, 2012.

Solomon, Denise H., and Jennifer Theiss. *Interpersonal Communication: Putting Theory into Practice.* New York: Routledge, 2013.

Wollan, Robert. "Knowing Your Customers in the Digital Age." *CRM Magazine* 16, no. 5 (May 2012), p. 8.

Wolvin, Andrew D. *Listening and Human Communication in the 21st Century.* Hoboken, NJ: Wiley-Blackwell, 2010.

chapter **5**

ADAPTIVE SELLING FOR RELATIONSHIP BUILDING

SOME QUESTIONS ANSWERED IN THIS CHAPTER ARE

- What is adaptive selling?
- Why is it important for salespeople to practice adaptive selling?
- What kind of knowledge do salespeople need to practice adaptive selling?
- How can salespeople acquire this knowledge?
- How can salespeople adapt their sales strategies, presentations, and social styles to various situations?

PROFILE I am James Ellington, a May 2003 graduate of Texas State University–San Marcos, where I earned a BBA in marketing. I served as lead presenter on the presentation team for Students in Free Enterprise (SIFE) after having been recruited by my professional selling professor, Mrs. Vicki West. I credit both the sales program and the SIFE program at Texas State and Mrs. West for launching me into the career I have today, as it was through an introduction by Mrs. West that I began a successful career in consumer products.

Now, as director of sales and analytics for Tandy Brands Accessories, building relationships with both my internal and my external customers is essential to my success. With multiple roles and responsibilities on both teams, I have to adjust my sales approach dependent on the audience I am meeting with at any particular time. I have learned that despite my best efforts to customize my message to my customers' needs, inevitably I have to be prepared for the fact that they may have different or additional agenda points for our meeting. It helps to understand the social styles of the various professionals involved so that my presentations can be quick and to the point with key benefits and quick action for a driver or more deliberate with logical, fact-based research and solutions for an analytical.

In meetings with buyers who may be responsible for multiple businesses, I keep my sales analysis presentations to high-level overviews to ensure that they are aware of the current sales successes and opportunities. I keep them up to speed on the latest trends in the marketplace as well as what my company has to offer with regard to new product development and other resources to grow the overall business. Meetings with the typically more analytical financial planners and inventory managers require a very different approach. These meetings focus more around inventory levels and sales performance versus various metrics. Often, this audience is more interested in the lower levels of detail that illustrate how the business is performing and what the financial implications are at a more granular level.

It is always critical to remember that every opportunity for face time with my customers is an opportunity to further our business relationship and ultimately leads to increased sales volume and profits for my company. Therefore, I must continually earn the trust of my customers by providing my category and product expertise and ensuring that I maintain the most up-to-date product and company knowledge. Retailers' buying teams in my industry rely heavily on suppliers' analytical resources to guide their decision-making process with regard to new products, merchandising, and inventory. It is my responsibility to understand the sales situations and the customers' needs in order to develop the most relevant, meaningful, and actionable analysis and presentations possible.

The most successful salespeople in my industry are those who are able to adapt to the various social styles in each selling situation, whether they are selling products, services, or just an idea. Understand your customer's needs, adapt your approach to their social style, and be the expert on your business, and you will develop long-lasting business partnerships that lead to your mutual success. Best of luck and happy selling!

Visit our Web site at:
www.tandybrands.com

Personal selling is the most effective marketing communication medium because it allows salespeople to tailor their presentations to each customer. They use their knowledge of the customer's buying process (Chapter 3) and finely tuned communication skills (Chapter 4) to learn about their customers and select effective sales strategies. Effective salespeople adapt their selling strategies and approaches to the selling situation. This chapter examines how salespeople can communicate effectively with their customers by practicing adaptive selling.

TYPES OF PRESENTATIONS

Salespeople can choose from a number of presentation types, which vary in the extent to which salespeople adapt to the circumstance. This text examines the three most common: (1) the standard memorized presentation, (2) the outlined presentation, and (3) the customized presentation.

STANDARD MEMORIZED PRESENTATION

The **standard memorized presentation,** also called a *canned presentation,* is a completely memorized sales talk. The salesperson presents the same selling points in the same order to all customers. Some companies insist that their inside telemarketing salespeople, for example, memorize the entire presentation and deliver it word for word. Others believe that salespeople should be free to make some minor adjustments.

The standard memorized presentation ensures that the salesperson will provide complete and accurate information about the firm's products and policies. Because it includes the best techniques and methods, the standard memorized presentation can help bring new salespeople up to speed quickly and give them

Exhibit 5.1
Example of an Outlined Presentation

Scenario: A Procter & Gamble Salesperson Calling on a Grocery Store Manager	
Step in Outlined Sales Presentation	**Say Something Like This**
1. Reinforce past success.	Good morning, Mr. Babcock. I was talking with one of your stockers, and he said that our Crest end-of-aisle display was very popular with customers last weekend. He said that he had to restock it three times. Looks like you made a wise decision to go with that program.
2. Reiterate customer's needs.	I know that profits and fast turns are what you are always looking for.
3. Introduce new Sure antiperspirant campaign.	We have a new campaign coming up for our Sure line.
4. Explain ad campaign and coupon drops.	We will be running a new set of commercials on all three network news programs.... Also, we'll be adding an insert in the Sunday coupon section with a 35-cents-off coupon.
5. Explain case allowances.	We are going to give you a $1.20 case allowance for every case of Sure you buy today.
6. Ask for end-of-aisle display and order of cases.	I propose that you erect an end-of-aisle display on aisle 7... and that you order 20 cases.
7. Thank manager for order.	Thank you, and I know the results will be just as good as they were for our Crest promotion.

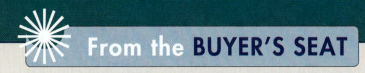

From the BUYER'S SEAT

PLEASE ADAPT TO MY NEEDS

I'm a fashion buyer for Dillard's. To me, adaptive selling starts from the very beginning, even before I meet with the salesperson. They must find out who my end customers are and be able to figure out what exactly it is that they want. Being in the fashion industry, a truly adapted presentation includes a modified product that the seller has created specifically for my organization and our end customer.

When salespeople come to me with products that I have seen in numerous stores already, this screams to me that they do not care who my end customer is, nor do they know much of anything about the way my company does business.

To truly adapt a sales presentation to me, the seller must know the nitty-gritty details about not only my company but also the industry trends, what is hot in the industry, and what my end customers are actually looking for. If a salesperson is able to do all of this research before meeting with me and adapt their product for me, this is a huge plus and a great stepping-stone to a strong business relationship.

Finally, the salesperson must know that they are selling to me, Jill, with my own personal needs and presentation preferences. They must also know to change how they approach the presentation depending on what members of my organization are in the meeting. A presentation should be different if it is being given to my boss and myself as opposed to a store manager and myself.

It all boils down to this: knowing who your audience is and adapting your selling to them.

Source: Jill McNally, personal correspondence, used with permission, names changed as requested.

---

confidence. However, the effectiveness of the standard memorized presentation is limited because it offers no opportunity for the salesperson to tailor the presentation to the needs of the specific customer.

OUTLINED PRESENTATION

The **outlined presentation** is a prearranged presentation that usually includes a standard introduction, standard answers to common objections raised by customers, and a standard method for getting the customer to place an order. An example of an outlined presentation appears in Exhibit 5.1.

An outlined presentation can be very effective because it is well organized. It is more informal and natural than the standard memorized presentation and provides more opportunity for the customer to participate in the sales interaction. It also permits some flexibility in the approach used to present the key points.

CUSTOMIZED PRESENTATION

The **customized presentation** is a written and/or oral presentation based on a detailed analysis of the customer's needs. This type of presentation offers an opportunity to use the communication principles discussed in Chapter 4 to discover the customer's needs and problems and propose the most effective solution for satisfying those needs. The customer recognizes the sales representative as a professional who is helping solve problems, not just selling products, as "From the Buyer's Seat 5.1" describes. The customized presentation lets the salesperson demonstrate empathy. Cultivating this view is an important step in developing a partnering relationship.

Each of the presentation types just discussed involves a different level of skill, cost, and flexibility. Standard memorized presentations can be delivered at a low cost by unskilled salespeople with little training. On the other hand, the customized presentation can be costly, requiring highly skilled people to analyze the customer's needs. Salespeople have the greatest opportunity to adapt their presentations to customer needs when using the customized presentation and the least opportunity when using the standard memorized presentation. The next section discusses the importance of adapting sales presentations.

ADAPTIVE SELLING AND SALES SUCCESS

Salespeople practice **adaptive selling** when they react to different sales situations by changing their sales behaviors. An extreme example of nonadaptive selling is using the standard memorized presentation, in which the same presentation is used for all customers. The customized presentation illustrates adaptive selling because the presentation is tailored to the specific needs of the customer.

Adaptive selling is featured in this textbook because this approach forces the salesperson to practice the marketing concept. It emphasizes the importance of satisfying customer needs. And being adaptable increases buyer trust and commitment and results in higher sales performance. It's important for salespeople to take the initiate and be adaptive. The communication principles described in Chapter 4 are required to practice adaptive selling successfully. For example, a Kohler sales representative may believe that a portable generator manufacturer is interested in buying an economical, low-horsepower gasoline motor. While presenting the benefits of a low-cost motor, the sales rep discovers, by observing nonverbal behaviors, that the customer is interested in discussing overall operating costs. At this point the rep asks some questions to find out whether the customer would pay a higher price for a more efficient motor with lower operating costs. Based on the customer's response, the rep may adopt a new sales strategy: presenting a more efficient motor and demonstrating its low operating costs.

It is sometimes hard for people to realize that the world is not made up of people just like them. Many people are much older than you, while some are younger than you. They practice different religions, enjoy different foods, and shop at stores where you would never think of shopping. They have different moral beliefs and different ideas about "the perfect product" and were raised in a totally different way. Their hopes and aspirations don't match yours. Many of them would be shocked to hear what your life's dreams and goals are.

We are not just talking about differences in people in other countries. We are talking about people who live next door to you, who are sitting next to you in your classroom. Men and women often react differently to presentations.[1] Generation Xers are different from baby boomers, who differ from the generations before them. One salesperson reported that grocery stores that cater to migrant farmers in the San Francisco area want a different product mix (such as more demand for Hormel SPAM) than a grocery store in midtown San Francisco (more demand for upscale, specialty Hormel meat products like Cure81 ham). The sooner you realize that your world is made up of diverse people, the sooner you will realize the importance of becoming adaptive. Selecting the appropriate sales strategy for a sales situation and making adjustments during the interaction are crucial to successful selling.

Salespeople should also adapt to the customer's desire for a specific type of relationship. For example, if a customer is not interested in developing a strong, long-term relationship and is more interested in maintaining a less involved relationship, the salesperson should adapt to this desire.

CUSTOMIZE THE PRESENTATION

At ADP, we consider ourselves business consultants. We don't have a prescript sales pitch that is used on every call. The goal is to educate the owner on varying topics surrounding payroll to show them how a service like ADP can make them more efficient and compliant with state and federal employer laws. Because I meet with business owners who have anywhere from one employee to 49 employees in every industry thinkable, the needs of the businesses are never the same.

I have to customize my presentation depending on many factors. For example, a first-time restaurant owner who has 35 tipped employees will need me to explain everything we do in depth, from payroll taxes and new hire reporting to FICA tip reporting. Most new business owners are not aware of all their tax liabilities and ways they can get money back from the government for having tipped employees. The owners are very appreciative that I take the time to explain all these fiduciary responsibilities and the fines they could be liable for.

On the other hand, when I meet with a longtime owner of a nonprofit company with three employees, this presentation is completely different. In this situation, the owner wouldn't be interested in hearing about the "Payroll 101" I was telling the new business owner. Instead, he or she would want to know about payroll being directly tied to grant funding, ability to offer comprehensive benefits, and wage tracking for grant reporting.

Either way, I am selling the same service but simply customizing the presentation to the buyers' needs.

Source: Meggie Dominguez, personal correspondence, used with permission.

Practicing adaptive selling does not mean salespeople should be dishonest about their products or their personal feelings. It does mean salespeople should alter the content and form of their sales presentation so customers will be able to absorb the information easily and find it relevant to their situation. As "Building Partnerships 5.1" illustrates, sometimes a salesperson has to adapt to a difficult situation.

thinking it through Do you act and talk differently to your professor than when you talk to your friends? Why do you adapt in that way?

The advantages and disadvantages of the three types of sales presentations illustrate the benefits and drawbacks of adaptive selling. Adaptive selling gives salespeople the opportunity to use the most effective sales presentation for each customer. However, uncovering needs, designing and delivering different presentations, and making adjustments require a high level of skill. The objective of this textbook is to help you develop the skills and knowledge required to practice adaptive selling.

ADAPTIVE SELLING: THE IMPORTANCE OF KNOWLEDGE

A key ingredient to be adaptive is knowledge. Salespeople need to know about the products they are selling, the company they work for, and the customers they will be selling to. Knowledge enables the salesperson to build self-confidence,

This salesperson has acquired extensive knowledge of the customer's systems.

gain the buyer's trust, satisfy customer needs, practice adaptive selling, and have greater performance.[2]

PRODUCT AND COMPANY KNOWLEDGE

Salespeople need to have a lot of information about their products, services, and company. Purchasing agents rate product knowledge as one of the most important attributes of good salespeople. Effective salespeople need to know how products are made, what services are provided with the products, how the products relate to other products, and how the products can satisfy customers' needs. Salespeople also need to know about their competitors' products as well as their own because they are frequently asked to compare their products to competitors' offerings.

KNOWLEDGE ABOUT SALES SITUATIONS AND CUSTOMERS

Equally important with product and company knowledge is detailed information about the different types of sales situations and customers salespeople may encounter, as "Building Partnerships 5.1" discusses. For example, T-Mobile salespeople need to be knowledgeable about networking and information technology and have overall expertise in how businesses operate in order to sell cell phone service to their unique customer types.

By developing categories of customer types or types of sales situations, salespeople reduce the complexity of selling and free up their mental capacity to think more creatively. The categories salespeople use can focus on the benefits the customer seeks, the person's role in the buying center, the stage in the buying process, or the type of buying situation. For example, a Colgate-Palmolive salesperson might divide buyers into several categories based on their decision-making style. When selling to emotional buyers, this salesperson might need to be more enthusiastic and engage in visual storytelling. When selling to rational buyers, this salesperson might want to stress the financial benefits of purchasing the new toothpaste.

HOW TO CREATE KNOWLEDGE

One source of knowledge would be top salespeople in the company you work for. Some firms will collect and share this information with you. For example, AT&T conducted in-depth interviews with its top performers.[3] Through these interviews, it learned about the types of situations these salespeople encountered and what strategies they used in each situation. The company developed role plays for each sales situation and used them when training new salespeople. Such role playing enabled the new salespeople to experience the variety of situations they would actually encounter on the job. The strategies recommended by the top salespeople served as a starting point for the trainees to develop their own sales methods for handling these situations.

Salespeople also create knowledge by getting feedback from sales managers. This can be in the form of **performance feedback** ("Did you achieve the goals you set for this call?") or **diagnostic feedback** ("Let's talk about why you didn't achieve your goals"). Diagnostic feedback provides information about what you're doing right and wrong instead of just whether you made a sale.

The following example illustrates diagnostic feedback:

SALESPERSON: Why do you think I didn't make the sale?

SALES MANAGER: You stressed the low maintenance cost, but he wasn't interested in maintenance cost. Did you see how he kept looking around while you were talking about how cheap it is to maintain the product?

SALESPERSON: What do you think I should do next time?

SALES MANAGER: You might try spending more time finding his hot button. Maintenance cost isn't it.

Other sources of knowledge include the Web, company sales manuals and newsletters, experts in the salesperson's firm, sales meetings, plant visits, and business and trade publications. Salespeople also collect information about competitors from customers, by visiting competitor displays at trade shows, and from viewing competitors' Web pages.

RETRIEVING KNOWLEDGE FROM THE KNOWLEDGE MANAGEMENT SYSTEM

Successful sales managers give their salespeople diagnostic feedback.

Salespeople store much of their acquired knowledge in their memory, and, as such, retrieval is merely accessing information in that memory.[4] Many companies, like Charles Schwab, described in "Sales Technology 5.1," also have customer relationship management (CRM) systems and knowledge management software to support their salespeople. Salespeople use programs like NetSuite to store and retrieve critical knowledge about accounts, products, and competitors. For example, salespeople for the Houston Aeros hockey franchise use NetSuite to store and access information about its customers. They use this knowledge when interacting with customers to develop sales strategies and purchase recommendations. Studies have shown that using a CRM system has a positive impact on being adaptive while selling.

It is important for salespeople to be able to retrieve brochures and other business collateral from the knowledge management system. But perhaps more important is the ability to tap the knowledge of in-house experts. One writer calls this "genius management," which implies going beyond document management to the realm of tapping knowledge from genius within your firm. Social computing tools are important in this regard.[5] Progressive firms are encouraging in-house experts, like engineers, product development specialists, and financial staff, to develop in-house blogs, wikis, and Web pages that are easily accessible and searchable by the sales force. Social networking sites like LinkedIn and Facebook can also be used to connect in-house experts with salespeople. Finally, firms are experimenting with tagging, which is including key words with a person's name in company documents and on internal Web pages. The key words indicate the areas of expertise for which that person can be contacted. The goal in all of this is to make it easier for salespeople to connect to experts in their own firms for ideas and assistance.

THE SOCIAL STYLE MATRIX: A TRAINING PROGRAM FOR BUILDING ADAPTIVE SELLING SKILLS

To be effective, salespeople need to use their knowledge about products and customers to adapt both the content of their sales presentations—the benefits they emphasize to customers and the needs they attempt to satisfy—and the style they use to communicate with customers. The **social style matrix** is a

MANAGE KNOWLEDGE USING SOFTWARE

Being able to effectively access a large amount of information provides salespeople a competitive advantage. Interspire bills itself as the "World's #1 Best Selling FAQ & Knowledge Base Software" and is used by a wide range of companies, including Xerox, Siemens, AT&T, Charles Schwab, Shell, Dell, Virgin Blue, and Kraft Foods, just to name a few. Their Knowledge Management Software aids companies by reducing inbound customer support inquiries, sharing company documents and procedures, and helping to reduce/eliminate training time.

The software enables customers to search a salesperson's database for solutions to their own problems. By reducing the number of inbound customer support inquiries, the personal support that needs to be provided to customers can be cut by as much as 50 percent. This has the added benefit of giving customers the chance to quickly solve their own problems, often increasing their overall satisfaction.

With centralized information, all salespeople have access to the company's information no matter where they are. The Knowledge Management Software greatly increases the productivity of salespeople and also makes it easier for a company to standardize their policies and procedures. For example, if a company wants to make sure that certain files are accessible to only a select group of salespeople, they are able to restrict the categories.

The implementation of Interspire's Knowledge Management Software can also help to reduce the amount of time that it takes to train in new salespeople. All training aides (e.g., cases, readings, video instruction, and so on) are in one location that is easy for new hires to access.

Source: www.interspire.com.

---

popular training program that companies use to help salespeople adapt their communication styles.

David Merrill and Roger Reid discovered patterns of communication behaviors, or social styles, that people use when interacting with one another.[6] Merrill and Reid found that people who recognize and adjust to these behavior patterns have better relationships with other people. The company Wilson Learning conducts training using these concepts.[7]

Here is a quick preview of what you will learn about the social style training program. As you know, the world is made up of diverse people. For example, some are fast decision makers, whereas others are slow to make just about any kind of decision; some like to talk, whereas others are quiet. To make it easier, this system divides all people into four different types or categories that are based on two dimensions. Your goal as a salesperson is to first identify which of the four types you are. Next you figure out which of the four types your customer is. Finally you adjust your behavior to mirror or match that of your customer. This adaptation is often called **style flexing.** Now that you have a general idea of how the system works, let's look at it in more detail.

DIMENSIONS OF SOCIAL STYLES

This training program uses two critical dimensions to understand social behavior: assertiveness and responsiveness.

Assertiveness

The degree to which people have opinions about issues and publicly make their positions clear to others is called **assertiveness.** Simply having strong convictions

Exhibit 5.2
Indicators of
Assertiveness

Less Assertive	More Assertive
"Ask" oriented	"Tell" oriented
Go-along attitude	Take-charge attitude
Cooperative	Competitive
Supportive	Directive
Risk avoider	Risk taker
Makes decisions slowly	Makes decisions quickly
Lets others take initiative	Takes initiative
Leans backward	Leans forward
Indirect eye contact	Direct eye contact
Speaks slowly, softly	Speaks quickly, intensely
Moves deliberately	Moves rapidly
Makes few statements	Makes many statements
Expresses moderate opinions	Expresses strong opinions

Exhibit 5.3
Indicators of
Responsiveness

Less Responsive	More Responsive
Controls emotions	Shows emotions
Cool, aloof	Warm, approachable
Talk oriented	People oriented
Uses facts	Uses opinions
Serious	Playful
Impersonal, businesslike	Personable, friendly
Moves stiffly	Moves freely
Seldom gestures	Gestures frequently
Formal dress	Informal dress
Disciplined about time	Undisciplined about time
Controlled facial expressions	Animated facial expressions
Monotone voice	Many vocal inflections

does not make a person assertive; assertive people express their convictions publicly and attempt to influence others to accept these beliefs.

Assertive people speak out, make strong statements, and have a take-charge attitude. When under tension, they tend to confront the situation. Unassertive people rarely dominate a social situation, and they often keep their opinions to themselves. Exhibit 5.2 shows some verbal and nonverbal behavioral indicators of assertiveness.

Responsiveness

The second dimension, **responsiveness,** is based on how emotional people tend to get in social situations. Responsive people readily express joy, anger, and sorrow. They appear to be more concerned with others and are informal and casual in social situations. Less responsive people devote more effort toward controlling their emotions. They are described as cautious, intellectual, serious, formal, and businesslike. Exhibit 5.3 lists some indicators of responsiveness.

Exhibit 5.4
Social Style Matrix

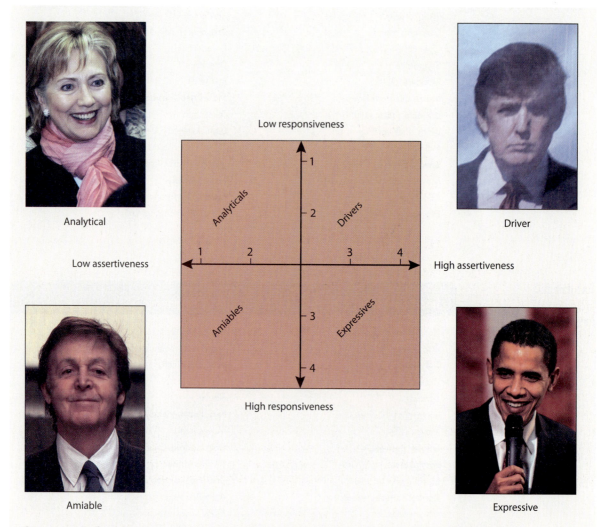

Some example of social styles (Donald Trump, Barack Obama, Paul McCartney, Hilary Clinton). Do you agree with where they are placed? Note that all these people may switch to a different style under certain conditions.

CATEGORIES OF SOCIAL STYLES

The two dimensions of social style, assertiveness and responsiveness, form the social style matrix shown in Exhibit 5.4. Each quadrant of the matrix defines a social style type.

Drivers

Drivers are high on assertiveness and low on responsiveness. The slogan of drivers, who are task-oriented people, might be "Let's get it done now, and get it done my way." Drivers have learned to work with others only because they must do so to get the job done, not because they enjoy people. They have a great desire to get ahead in their companies and careers.

Drivers are swift, efficient decision makers. They focus on the present and appear to have little concern with the past or future. They generally base their decisions on facts, take risks, and want to look at several alternatives before making a decision. As compared to analyticals, who also like facts and data, drivers want to know how the facts affect results—the bottom line. They are not interested in simply technical information.

To influence a driver, salespeople need to use a direct, businesslike, organized presentation with quick action and follow-up. Proposals should emphasize the effects of a purchase decision on profits.

Expressives

Expressives are high on assertiveness and high on responsiveness. Warm, approachable, intuitive, and competitive, expressives view power and politics as important factors in their quest for personal rewards and recognition. Although expressives are interested in personal relationships, their relationships are primarily with supporters and followers recruited to assist expressives in achieving their personal goals.

People with an expressive style focus on the future, directing their time and effort toward achieving their vision. They have little concern for practical details in present situations. Expressives base their decisions on their personal opinions and the opinions of others. They act quickly, take risks, but tend to be impatient and change their minds easily.

When selling to expressives, salespeople need to demonstrate how their products will help the customer achieve personal status and recognition. Expressives prefer sales presentations with product demonstrations and creative graphics rather than factual statements and technical details. Also, testimonials from well-known firms and people appeal to expressives' need for status and recognition. Expressives respond to sales presentations that put them in the role of innovator, the first person to use a new product.

Amiables

Amiables are low on assertiveness and high on responsiveness. Close relationships and cooperation are important to amiables. They achieve their objectives by working with people, developing an atmosphere of mutual respect rather than using power and authority. Amiables tend to make decisions slowly, building a consensus among people involved in the decision. They avoid risks and change their opinions reluctantly.

Salespeople may have difficulty detecting an amiable's true feelings. Because amiables avoid conflict, they often say things to please others despite their personal opinions. Therefore, salespeople need to build personal relationships with amiables. Amiables are particularly interested in receiving guarantees about a product's performance. They do not like salespeople who agree to undertake activities and then do not follow through on commitments. Salespeople selling to amiables should stress the product's benefits in terms of its effects on the satisfaction of employees.

Analyticals

Analyticals are low on assertiveness and low on responsiveness. They like facts, principles, and logic. Suspicious of power and personal relationships, they strive to find a way to carry out a task without resorting to these influence methods.

Because they are strongly motivated to make the right decision, analyticals make decisions slowly, in a deliberate and disciplined manner. They systematically analyze the facts, using the past as an indication of future events.

Salespeople need to use solid, tangible evidence when making presentations to analyticals. Analyticals are also influenced by sales presentations that recognize their technical expertise and emphasize long-term benefits. They tend to disregard

Exhibit 5.5

Cues for Recognizing Social Styles

Analytical	Driver
Technical background. Achievement awards on wall. Office is work oriented, showing much activity. Conservative dress. Likes solitary activities (e.g., reading, individual sports).	Technical background. Achievement awards on wall. No posters or slogans on office walls. Calendar prominently displayed. Furniture is placed so that contact with people is across desk. Conservative dress. Likes group activities (e.g., politics, team sports).
Amiable	**Expressive**
Liberal arts background. Office has friendly, open atmosphere. Pictures of family displayed. Personal momentos on wall. Desk placed for open contact with people. Casual or flamboyant dress. Likes solitary activities (e.g., reading, individual sports).	Liberal arts background. Motivational slogans on wall. Office has friendly, open atmosphere. Cluttered, unorganized desk. Desk placed for open contact with people. Casual or flamboyant dress. Likes group activities (e.g., politics, team sports).

personal opinions. Both analyticals and amiables tend to develop loyalty toward suppliers. For amiables, the loyalty is based on personal relationships; analyticals' loyalty is based on their feeling that well-reasoned decisions do not need to be reexamined.

IDENTIFYING CUSTOMERS' SOCIAL STYLES

Exhibit 5.5 lists some cues for identifying the social styles of customers or prospects.[8] Salespeople can use their communication skills to observe the customer's behavior, listen to the customer, and ask questions to classify the customer. Merrill and Reid caution that identifying social style is difficult and requires close, careful observation. Salespeople should not jump to quick conclusions based on limited information. Here are some suggestions for making accurate assessments:

- Concentrate on the customer's behavior and disregard how you feel about the behavior. Don't let your feelings about the customer or thoughts about the customer's motives cloud your judgment.

- Avoid assuming that specific jobs or functions are associated with a social style ("He must be an analytical because he is an engineer").

- Test your assessments. Look for clues and information that may suggest you have incorrectly assessed a customer's social style. If you look for only confirming cues, you will filter out important information.

- Create, join, and participate in social media groups (e.g., LinkedIn, Twitter) to learn more about the social style of the buyer.[9]

Exhibit 5.6

Self-Assessment of Social Styles

Assertiveness Ratings I perceive myself as:				Responsiveness Ratings I perceive myself as:			
Quiet . . . . Talkative				Open . . . . Closed			
1	2	3	4	4	3	2	1
Slow to decide . . . . Fast to decide				Impulsive . . . . Deliberate			
1	2	3	4	4	3	2	1
Going along . . . . Taking charge				Using opinions . . . . Using facts			
1	2	3	4	4	3	2	1
Supportive . . . . .Challenging				Informal . . . . Formal			
1	2	3	4	4	3	2	1
Compliant. . . . . Dominant				Emotional . . . . Unemotional			
1	2	3	4	4	3	2	1
Deliberate. . . . . Fast to decide				Easy to know . . . . Hard to know			
1	2	3	4	4	3	2	1
Asking questions . . . . Making statements				Warm . . . . .Cool			
1	2	3	4	4	3	2	1
Cooperative . . . . .Competitive				Excitable . . . . .Calm			
1	2	3	4	4	3	2	1
Avoiding risks . . . . Taking risks				Animated . . . . Poker-faced			
1	2	3	4	4	3	2	1
Slow, studied. . . . . .Fast-paced				People-oriented . . . . Task-oriented			
1	2	3	4	4	3	2	1
Cautious. . . . . Carefree				Spontaneous. . . . . Cautious			
1	2	3	4	4	3	2	1
Indulgent. . . . . Firm				Responsive . . . . Nonresponsive			
1	2	3	4	4	3	2	1
Nonassertive. . . . . Assertive				Humorous. . . . . Serious			
1	2	3	4	4	3	2	1
Mellow. . . . . Matter-of-fact				Impulsive . . . . Methodical			
1	2	3	4	4	3	2	1
Reserved. . . . . Outgoing				Lighthearted . . . . Intense			
1	2	3	4	4	3	2	1

Mark your answers above. Total the score for each side and divide each by 15. Then plot your scores on Exhibit 5.4 to see what social style you are. For fun, you may want to have several friends also score you.

Sources: Based on work by David Merrill and Roger Reid, *Personal Styles and Effective Performance* (Radnor, PA: Chilton, 1981). See also Tom Kramlinger and Larry Wilson, *The Social Styles Handbook: Adapt Your Style to Win Trust,* 2nd ed. (Herentals, Belgium: Nova Vista Publishing, 2011).

SOCIAL STYLES AND SALES PRESENTATIONS

In addition to teaching trainees how to assess social style, the Merrill and Reid program also assesses the trainees' social styles. Each person is asked to have a group of his or her customers complete a questionnaire and mail it to the director of the training program. These responses are used to determine the trainee's style. Trainees frequently are surprised by the difference between their self-perceptions and the perceptions of their customers. To get a rough idea of your own social style, you can complete the assessment in Exhibit 5.6.

Exhibit 5.7
Customer Expectations Based on Social Styles

Area of Expectation	Customer's Social Style			
	Driver	Expressive	Amiable	Analytical
Atmosphere in sales interview	Businesslike	Open, friendly	Open, honest	Businesslike
Salesperson's use of time	Effective, efficient	To develop relationship	Leisurely, to develop relationship	Thorough, accurate
Pace of interview	Quick	Quick	Deliberate	Deliberate
Information provided by salesperson	Salesperson's qualifications; value of products	What salesperson thinks; whom he/she knows	Evidence that salesperson is trustworthy, friendly	Evidence of salesperson's expertise in solving problem
Salesperson's actions to win customer acceptance	Documented evidence, stress results	Recognition and approval	Personal attention and interest	Evidence that salesperson has analyzed the situation
Presentation of benefits	What product can do	Who has used the product	Why product is best to solve problem	How product can solve the problem
Assistance to aid decision making	Explanation of options and probabilities	Testimonials	Guarantees and assurances	Evidence and offers of service

Interpreting self-ratings requires great caution. Self-assessments can be misleading because we usually do not see ourselves the same way others see us. When you rate yourself, you know your own feelings, but others can observe only your behaviors. They don't know your thoughts or your intentions. We also vary our behavior from situation to situation. The indicators listed in Exhibits 5.2 and 5.3 merely show a tendency to be assertive or responsive.

Is there one best social style for a salesperson? No. None is "best" for all situations; each style has its strong points and weak points. Driver salespeople are efficient, determined, and decisive, but customers may find them pushy and dominating. Expressives have enthusiasm, dramatic flair, and creativity but can also seem opinionated, undisciplined, and unstable. Analyticals are orderly, serious, and thorough, but customers may view them as cold, calculating, and stuffy. Finally, amiables are dependable, supportive, and personable but may also be perceived as undisciplined and inflexible.

The sales training program based on the social style matrix emphasizes that effective selling involves more than communicating a product's benefits. Salespeople must also recognize the customer's needs and expectations. In the sales interaction, salespeople should conduct themselves in a manner consistent with customer expectations. Exhibit 5.7 indicates the expectations of customers with various social styles.

Although each customer type requires a different sales presentation, the salesperson's personal social style tends to determine the sales technique he or she typically uses. For example, drivers tend to use a driver technique with all customer types. When interacting with an amiable customer, driver salespeople will be efficient and businesslike, even though the amiable customer would prefer to deal with a more relationship-oriented and friendlier salesperson.

This sales training program emphasizes that to be effective with a variety of customer types, salespeople must adapt their selling presentations to customers' social styles. Versatility is the key to effective adaptive selling.

Exhibit 5.8
Adjusting Social Styles

| Dimension | Adjustment | |
	Reduce	Increase
Assertiveness	Ask for customer's opinion.	Get to the point.
	Acknowledge merits of customer's viewpoint.	Don't be vague or ambiguous.
	Listen without interruption.	Volunteer information.
	Be more deliberate; don't rush.	Be willing to disagree.
	Let customer direct flow of conversation.	Take a stand.
		Initiate conversation.
Responsiveness	Become businesslike.	Verbalize feelings.
	Talk less.	Express enthusiasm.
	Restrain enthusiasm.	Pay personal compliments.
	Make decision based on facts.	Spend time on relationships rather than business.
	Stop and think.	Socialize; engage in small talk.
		Use nonverbal communication.

VERSATILITY

The effort people make to increase the productivity of a relationship by adjusting to the needs of the other party is known as **versatility.** Versatile salespeople—those able to adapt their social styles—are much more effective than salespeople who do not adjust their sales presentations. Here is a comparison of behaviors of more versatile and less versatile people:

How can a salesperson improve his or her versatility? Many companies have sales training programs, using tools like the social style matrix that help teach salespeople the differences in buyers. Role playing is also used extensively for managers to spot problems in salesperson versatility and to teach new ways to help improve it. For example, sales training might suggest that effective salespeople adjust their social styles to match their customers' styles. In role plays, salespeople with a driver orientation need to become more emotional and less assertive when selling to amiable customers. Analytical salespeople must increase their assertiveness and responsiveness when selling to expressive customers. Exhibit 5.8 shows some techniques for adjusting sales behaviors in terms of assertiveness and responsiveness.

Less Versatile	More Versatile
Limited ability to adapt to others' needs	Able to adapt to others' needs
Specialist	Generalist
Well-defined interests	Broad interests
Sticks to principles	Negotiates issues
Predictable	Unpredictable
Looks at one side of an issue	Looks at many sides of an issue

RECAP: THE ROLE OF KNOWLEDGE IN ADAPTING

The social style matrix illustrates the importance of knowledge, organized into categories, in determining selling effectiveness through adaptive selling. Sales training based on the social style matrix teaches salespeople the four customer categories or types (driver, expressive, amiable, and analytical). Salespeople learn the cues for identifying them. Salespeople also learn which adjustments they need to make in their communication styles to be effective with each customer type.

SYSTEMS FOR DEVELOPING ADAPTIVE SELLING SKILLS

The social style matrix developed by Merrill and Reid is one of several sales training methods based on customer classification schemes. Rather than using assertiveness and responsiveness, other classification schemes by other sales trainers use dimensions like the following:

- Warm–hostile and dominant–submissive
- Dominance and sociability
- Relater, socializer, thinker, and director
- Logical (yellow), emotional (blue), conceptual (orange), and analytical (green)
- Skeptics, charismatics, thinkers, followers, and controllers
- Hawk, owl, dove, and peacock

Regardless of the training system used, it is imperative that salespeople adjust to their audience. Salespeople adjust for types of customers. They also adjust their style when selling to diverse cultures even within their own country. For example, Hispanic salespeople may need to alter their communication style when selling to Anglo-American customers.

Training methods such as the social style matrix are simply a first step in developing knowledge for practicing adaptive selling. They emphasize the need to practice adaptive selling—to use different presentations with different customers—and stimulate salespeople to base their sales presentations on an analysis of the customer. But these methods are limited; they present only a few types of customers, and classification is based on the form of communication (the social style), not on the content of the communication (the specific features and benefits stressed in the presentation).

In addition, accurately fitting customers into the suggested categories is often difficult. Customers act differently and have different needs in different sales encounters: A buyer may be amiable in a new task buying situation and be analytical when dealing with an out-supplier's salesperson in a straight rebuy. Amiable buyers in a bad mood may act like drivers. By rigidly applying the classification rules, salespeople may actually limit their flexibility, reducing the adaptive selling behavior these training methods emphasize.

SELLING YOURSELF

The topics discussed in this chapter involve recognizing and adjusting to the social dynamics of a selling or presentation situation. The same applies to your first job interviews coming out of college. It is imperative to research and prepare for job interviews just as you would final exams. The interviewer is looking for certain qualities, such as drive, determination, dynamic personality, and integrity. However, the first impression from a prepared candidate sets the tone for the entire interview.

You must quickly determine the type of communication style your interviewer is going to use and adjust to them. Beware, however, that they are probably doing the same thing, so this could be a moving target. Confidence in your abilities goes a long way to showing your potential employer that you are up to the task in stressful or high-pressure situations. If you come to the interview prepared with questions about the opportunity and the company, you will be able to showcase that you have thought through taking on the job. Consider all of the reasons that you would be a good fit for the particular position you are interviewing for and for the company. Use these as examples throughout the conversation to demonstrate your abilities as a businessperson and presenter.

Especially in a challenged economy, each job interview should be treated as a precious commodity. Take the extra time to thoroughly prepare by taking advantage of your college's career center resources, your business professors' advice, and, of course, the wealth of information available on the Internet. If you can find out with whom you will be interviewing, research them as well. Both Facebook and LinkedIn are both excellent resources. Read through any recent Securities and Exchange Commission filings by the company to pull out some nuggets of information you can use and search for any articles on the company in national business publications, such as the *Wall Street Journal* or *Business Weekly*. Weave any key findings into the interview conversation to illustrate your business acumen and your interest in the company.

Above all, when you take the time to apply for and go after a job that you really want, make sure to set yourself up for the most successful interview possible. So many candidates seemingly try to wing it in an interview, but rest assured that winging it will almost always get your name thrown into the same pile as the others. Set your goal to stand out among the other candidates through confidence, preparedness, a positive attitude, and clear communication. Let's face it: You are selling yourself, and who knows you better than you do?

Best of luck in reaching your goals and finding the job of your dreams.

Source: James Ellington, used with permission.

SUMMARY

Adaptive selling uses one of the unique properties of personal selling as a marketing communication tool: the ability to tailor messages to individual customers and make on-the-spot adjustments. Extensive knowledge of customer and sales situation types is a key ingredient in effective adaptive selling.

To be effective at adapting, salespeople need considerable knowledge about the products they sell, the companies for which they work, and the customers to whom they sell. Experienced salespeople organize customer knowledge into categories. Each category has cues for classifying customers or sales situations and an effective sales presentation for customers in the category.

The social style matrix, developed by Merrill and Reid, illustrates the concept of developing categorical knowledge to facilitate adaptive selling. The matrix defines four customer categories based on a customer's responsiveness and assertiveness in sales interactions. To effectively interact with a customer, a salesperson needs to identify the customer's social style and adapt a style to match. The sales training program based on the social style matrix provides cues for identifying social style as well as presentations salespeople can use to make adjustments.

KEY TERMS

adaptive selling   128
amiable   135
analytical   135
assertiveness   132
customized presentation   126
diagnostic feedback   130
driver   134
expressive   135

outlined presentation   126
performance feedback   130
responsiveness   133
social style matrix   131
standard memorized presentation   126
style flexing   132
versatility   139

ETHICS PROBLEMS

1. Your boss tells you about one of your buyers, Julie: "Just talk about Julie's children. If you do, she'll like you and buy anything. Even more than she needs because she hates to say no to someone she likes!" What will you do in that situation?

2. You have a buyer who is a real jerk. She is in constant battles with all the salespeople who call on her as well as with her own staff. Her business is important to you, and you don't want to lose it because you love the commissions on the sales you make. How should you adapt to her social style?

QUESTIONS AND PROBLEMS

1. A salesperson stated, "I just can't stand to deal with buyers who shout at me and tell me in no uncertain terms what they hate about me or my product." Based on this limited amount of information, what social style would you guess the salesperson to be? What would be your response to this salesperson?

2. Some salespeople, far from using the benefits of technology, are still writing call notes on the back of envelopes. What would be your response to a salesperson who says, "I don't need a bunch of fancy technology. My system of taking hand notes works just fine for me"?

3. A salesperson made the following comment: "I hate it when my sales manager makes calls with me. I do so much better when I'm by myself. After the call, she is always telling me what I did wrong." Based on what you learned in this chapter about knowledge systems, what would be your response to this salesperson?

4. "A good salesperson can sell any customer." Do you agree? Why or why not?

5. Would a person with an amiable social style be better at selling than a person with a driver or an expressive style? Why?

6. Some people object to the social style matrix training system because they don't want to "act." That can be a valid concern. What would you say to them?

7. What social styles would you assign to the following people?
   a. David Letterman.
   b. Your favorite instructor last term.
   c. The person who sits next to you in this class.
   d. Katy Perry.

8. The salesperson in "Building Partnerships 5.1" changes her presentation depending on the customer. If you were a salesperson for ADP like her, how would you know what a specific situation called for?

9. Suppose that during a sales call, a customer says, "I don't think iPads are going to continue to be a best-selling item in the future!" How should you respond if this customer is a driver? An analytical?

10. Market research by a company specializing in designing and installing swimming pools identified two types of hotels. Type I is concerned only about the ambiance of the pool area since most guests just sit by the pool while they socialize. Type II is concerned about providing a good fitness option for its guests. How would you adapt the selling of your pools to each type?

CASE PROBLEMS

case **5.1**

I'm in a Hurry!

I'm in a buyer role at a Fortune 100 firm. Let me tell you a true story that happened to me last month. I was in my doorway about to leave my office to meet with a vice president. I had ended a meeting in my office about three minutes early to give myself the time to get up the three flights of stairs to her (the VP's) office in time.

A salesperson whom I had never met before stopped me in my doorway, and I explained that I was on my way to an important meeting. The salesperson said he understood but proceeded to take my hand and shake it and introduce himself. He continued to say that he was asked to meet with me by a coworker to introduce his services. I continued to explain that I needed to go to my meeting, but I would take his card and call him later.

He would not clear the doorway and continued to explain his services, which was "only going to take a minute." I explained that I really didn't have a minute and that I would call him later. He continued to explain his services after I said I didn't have the time. I interrupted him and explained that he needed to allow me to leave my office. His disregard for my time and his desire "to only take a minute of my time" resulted in my standing there longer than I needed to and my being two minutes late for my meeting.

Questions

1. Based on the limited amount of information provided, what would you guess is the social style of the buyer? How about the social style of the seller? Explain your reasoning.

2. Make a list of five "rules" you could set for yourself as a salesperson to avoid making a buyer like this angry at you.

Source: Tracey Brill, used with permission.

case **5.2**

Smith & Nephew
Hip Replacements

I sell orthopedic products, like hip and knee replacements, for Smith & Nephew. One aspect of my selling job requires me to service what I sell, and in the case of replacement joints, that means going into the operating room with the surgeon and taking on the role of a technical expert when it comes to the capabilities, function, and surgical technique used with my company's hardware.

This scenario occurred during a total hip replacement on an 80-year-old woman. The doctor involved was a new customer, so I had brought in a wide variety of options (i.e., hip replacement systems) for him to use, as I wasn't very familiar with his preferences and I wanted to be prepared for anything.

The case was going smoothly until the surgeon was deciding which component to use in the femur. There are two different types when it comes to the method of fixation of the new joint: cemented stems and press-fit stems. The stem is inserted into the intermedullary, or IM, canal, and if it is a round stem, it is secured to the bone using bone cement. If it is a press-fit stem, it is squared off, and you are essentially sticking a square peg into a round hole. The press-fit stem is pounded in such a manner that the four corners dig into the surrounding bone, and that provides fixation. It also leaves some open gaps in the IM canal.

The doctor decided to use a press-fit stem but decided that the bone quality wasn't what he wanted, and he didn't feel like it was secure. He told me he wanted to cement the press-fit stem in place. I knew that this was not typically done, and my training told me that it shouldn't be done in order to avoid having bone cement leak down into the IM canal, which could potentially cause a number of problems down the road. At the same time, if it was done very carefully, it could work without any issues.

Questions

1. If you were the sales rep in this situation, what would you do?
2. How would you discuss the situation with the doctor?

Source: Brendan Brooks, Smith & Nephew, used with permission.

ROLE PLAY CASE

This role play requires some before-class preparation. Write a brief outline of how you would describe NetSuite to someone who has never seen it. Identify three features of NetSuite that you think would benefit your buyer, based on the information you've learned so far this semester. Then write down what you would want to say about each feature. You will take turns presenting your sales presentations to your buyer. After you give your presentation, determine what the other person's social style was. Identify the hints the buyer gave you.

If you have been using NetSuite role plays all along, you can use the same customer you have called on. If not, you will need to review the role play material at the end of Chapter 3. You can also review material about NetSuite in the role play case at the back of this book to understand NetSuite and what it does.

When you play the buyer, pick a social style different from your own. Interact with the seller in ways that give clues about your social style. Before the role play starts, think of at least five things you will do to hint at your new social style. Keep in mind that a social style includes both responsiveness and assertiveness, so make sure your hints combine both dimensions. After each role play, the salesperson should say what the other person's social style was and what clues were used to make that determination.

Note: For background information about these role plays, please see page 26.

To the instructor: Additional information needed to complete the role play is available in the Instructor's Manual.

ADDITIONAL REFERENCES

Amyx, Douglas, and Shahid Bhuian. "The Salesperson Service Performance Scale." *Journal of Personal Selling and Sales Management* 29, no. 4 (Fall 2009), pp. 367–76.

Aramo-Immonen, Heli, and Pasi Porkka. "Shared Knowledge in Project-Based Companies' Value Chain." *International Journal of Knowledge Management Studies* 6 (October 2009), p. 364.

Chakrabarty, Subhra, Gene Brown, and Robert E. Widing. "Closed Influence Tactics: Do Smugglers Win in the Long Run?" *Journal of Personal Selling and Sales Management* 30, no. 1 (Winter 2010), pp. 23–32.

Dickson, Peter R., Walfried M. Lassar, Gary Hunter, and Samit Chakravorti. "The Pursuit of Excellence in Process Thinking and Customer Relationship Management." *Journal of Personal Selling and Sales Management* 29, no. 2 (Spring 2009), pp. 111–24.

Dietvorst, Roeland C., et al. "A Sales Force-Specific Theory-of-Mind Scale: Tests of Its Validity by Classical Methods and Functional Magnetic Resonance Imaging." *Journal of Marketing Research* 46, no. 5 (2009), pp. 653–68.

Dungy, Tony, Jim Caldwell, and Nathan Whitaker. *The Mentor Leader: Secrets to Building People and Teams That Win Consistently.* Carol Stream, IL: Tyndale House Publishers, 2010.

Erickson, G. Scott, and Helen N. Rothberg. "Intellectual Capital in Business-to-Business Markets." *Industrial Marketing Management* 38, no. 2 (February 2009), pp. 159–65.

Goldsmith, Marshall, and Louis Carter. *Best Practices in Talent Management*. San Francisco: Pfeiffer, 2009.

Guenzi, Paolo, Laurent Georges, and Catherine Pardo. "The Impact of Strategic Account Managers' Behaviors on Relational Outcomes: An Empirical Study." *Industrial Marketing Management* 38, no. 3 (April 2009), pp. 300–11.

Lamont, J. "Past and Future: Closing the Knowledge Loop." *KM World* 19, no. 1 (January 2010), pp. 8–19.

Liao, S, and C. Wu. "System Perspective of Knowledge Management, Organizational Learning, and Organizational Innovation." *Expert Systems with Applications* 37, no. 2 (March 2010), pp. 1096–1103.

Liebowitz, Jay, ed. *Knowledge Management Handbook: Collaboration and Social Networking*. 2nd ed. CRC Press, 2012.

Lohtia, Ritu, Daniel C. Bello, and Constance Elise Porter. "Building Trust in US–Japanese Business Relationships: Mediating Role of Cultural Sensitivity." *Industrial Marketing Management* 38, no. 3 (April 2009), pp. 239–52.

Lytle, Chris. *The Accidental Salesperson: How to Take Control of Your Sales Career and Earn the Respect and Income You Deserve*. 2nd ed. New York: AMACOM, 2012.

Meehan, Joanne, and Gillian H. Wright. "The Origins of Power in Buyer–Seller Relationships." *Industrial Marketing Management* 41, no. 4 (2012), pp. 669–79.

O'Dell, Carla, and Cindy Hubert. *The New Edge in Knowledge: How Knowledge Management Is Changing the Way We Do Business*. Hoboken, NJ: Wiley, 2011.

Román, Sergio, and Dawn Iacobucci. "Antecedents and Consequences of Adaptive Selling Confidence and Behavior: A Dyadic Analysis of Salespeople and Their Customers." *Journal of the Academy of Marketing Science* 38, no. 3 (Summer 2010), pp. 363–82.

Spraggon, Martin, and Virginia Bodolica. "A Multidimensional Taxonomy of Intra-Firm Knowledge Transfer Processes." *Journal of Business Research* 65, no. 9 (September 2012), pp. 1273–82.

Taylor, James, Stephen Kraus, and Doug Harrison. *Selling to the New Elite: Discover the Secret to Winning Over Your Wealthiest Prospects*. New York: AMACOM, 2011.

Van Hulse, J., and T. Khoshgoftaar. "Knowledge Discovery from Imbalanced and Noisy Data." *Data and Knowledge Engineering* 68, no. 12 (December 2009), pp. 1513–42.

Voldnes, Gøril, Kjell Grønhaug, and Frode Nilssen. "Satisfaction in Buyer–Seller Relationships—Influence of Cultural Differences." *Industrial Marketing Management* 41, no. 7 (October 2012), pp. 1081–93.

Wachner, Trent, Christopher R. Plouffe, and Yany Grégoire. "SOCO's Impact on Individual Sales Performance: The Integration of Selling Skills as a Missing Link." *Industrial Marketing Management* 38, no. 1 (January 2009), pp. 32–44.

Wang, Mei-Ling. "How Does the Learning Climate Affect Customer Satisfaction? *Service Industries Journal* 32, no. 8 (2012), pp. 1283–303.

chapter **6**

PROSPECTING

SOME QUESTIONS ANSWERED IN THIS CHAPTER ARE

- Why is prospecting important for effective selling?
- Are all sales leads good prospects? What are the characteristics of a qualified prospect?
- How can prospects be identified? How can social media be used?
- How can the organization's promotional program be used in prospecting?
- How can an effective lead qualification and management system aid a salesperson?
- How can a salesperson overcome a reluctance to prospect?

PROFILE

PROFILE My name is Angela Bertero, and I graduated from Texas State University–San Marcos in 2008. I earned my master's in business administration and bachelor of business administration in marketing. While at Texas State University, I served as president of our national championship Students in Free Enterprise team and won quarter finalist at the National Collegiate Sales Competition, both of which were advised by Vicki West. Mrs. West introduced me to Liberty Mutual Insurance, which is where I was hired as a licensed sales representative.

Liberty Mutual offers a full line of high-quality insurance products and services. As the main contact for the company, it is my responsibility to develop and maintain client relationships as well as identify prospective customers and promote Liberty Mutual products.

While retention is key to a business's success, prospecting for new clients is crucial to growing my book of business. I have found success using the following methods of prospecting: referrals from satisfied clients and business partners, networking, and cross-selling to current clients. Referrals are by far the most important source of prospects.

Successful prospecting isn't about running around town and meeting everyone you can. It's about identifying your target market and knowing how to communicate that to your existing customers and referral partners. To do this, I often review the services I have provided for my clients and ask them if they know anyone in a similar situation that I may be able to help. I tell all of my clients that the greatest compliment I can receive is a referral from them.

I also work closely with a variety of referral partners to fill my pipeline with prospective new clients: mortgage brokers, realtors, financial advisors, auto dealerships, bankers, employers, school districts, and alumni associations, to name a few.

It is important that my referral partners know what a good prospect looks like to me so that the leads they send me are actually qualified referrals.

My networking group, Business Networking International (BNI), has given me the opportunity to give weekly educational moments to other professionals in different industries, or, as I like to call them, my marketing team. When I first joined BNI, I expected—or hoped for—immediate results. I have since learned that building personal relationships while becoming a trusted advisor to those around me is critical to building my network over time. After just a year, though, the partnerships I have made are a huge part of my weekly prospecting. We meet once a week to share ideas, help grow each other's businesses, and fill each other's pipelines with prospects. Then, we meet one to one to learn more about how we can work together for a mutually beneficial partnership.

To be a successful networker, make an effort to understand other people's businesses and connect with them on a personal level. Always follow up and thank your networking contact for the leads they send you and, if you can, send them leads as well.

Visit our Web site at:
www.libertymutual.com

An important activity for nearly all salespeople is locating qualified prospects. This chapter provides resources to help you prospect effectively and efficiently.

THE IMPORTANCE OF PROSPECTING

Prospecting, the process of locating potential customers for a product or service, is the most important activity that many salespeople do.[1]

Why is it so important? Salespeople must find new customers to replace those that switch to competitors, go bankrupt, move out of the territory, merge with noncustomers, or decide to do without a product or service. A salesperson often needs to prospect even in existing accounts because of downsizing, job changes, or retirements of buyers. Sales trainer Joe Girard uses a Ferris wheel metaphor to describe the important process of adding new customers (loading new accounts onto the Ferris wheel) to replace customers you lose (people getting off the Ferris wheel). Without replacing lost accounts, your Ferris wheel will soon be running with no one on board.

Of course, prospecting is more important in some selling fields than in others. For example, the office products salesperson, stockbroker, financial advisor, or real estate sales representative with no effective prospecting plan usually doesn't last long in the business. Sales positions such as these may require 100 contacts to get 10 prospects who will listen to presentations, out of which one person will buy. Each sale, then, represents a great deal of prospecting. It is also important in these fields to prospect continually. Some sales trainers relate this process to your car's gas tank: You don't wait until the gas gauge is on empty before you fill up!

Some sales positions require less emphasis on locating new contacts. For example, a Lockheed Martin salesperson assigned exclusively to sell the F-16 tactical fighter jet to Taiwan, South Korea, Greece, and Singapore would not spend any time trying to locate new governments to call on. For these types of sales positions, prospecting as we normally think of it (that is, looking for new leads) is not an important part of the sales process. Nevertheless, salespeople cannot ignore these obvious leads, as the next section discusses. Salespeople still have to assess whether leads are good prospects.[2]

Exhibit 6.1
The Sales Funnel

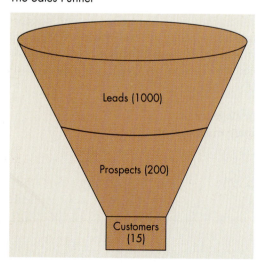

Leads (1000)

Prospects (200)

Customers (15)

CHARACTERISTICS OF A GOOD PROSPECT

Prospecting actually begins with locating a **lead** (sometimes called a "suspect")—a potential prospect that may or may not have what it takes to be a true prospect. Some salespeople mistakenly consider every lead a prospect without first taking the time to see whether these people really provide an opportunity to make a sale.

To avoid that mistake, the salesperson must **qualify the lead.** Qualifying is the process of determining whether a lead is in fact a **prospect.** If the salesperson determines that the lead is a good candidate for making a sale, that person or organization is no longer considered a lead and instead is called a prospect. Note that many leads do not become prospects. Exhibit 6.1 illustrates this process. One thousand leads might be needed, for example, to generate 200 prospects, of which only 15 might become prospects. Some companies break down this **sales funnel** into more levels, depending on how complex the purchase process and sales cycle are.

The following five questions are used by many organizations to help qualify leads and pinpoint the good prospects:

DOES A WANT OR NEED EXIST?

Research has supplied no infallible answers to why customers buy, but it has found many reasons. As we pointed out in Chapter 3, customers buy to satisfy practical needs as well as intangible needs, such as prestige or aesthetics.

By using high-pressure tactics, sales attempts may be made to those who do not need or really want a product. Such sales benefit no one. The buyer will resent making the purchase, and a potential long-term customer will be lost.

DOES THE LEAD HAVE THE ABILITY TO PAY?

For example, the commercial real estate agent usually checks the financial status of each client to determine the price range of office buildings to show. A client with annual profits of $100,000 and cash resources of $75,000 may be a genuine prospect for office space in the $30,000 to $50,000 annual rental bracket. An agent would be wasting time, however, by showing this client space listed at $100,000 annual rent. The client may have a desire for the more expensive setting, but the client is still not a real prospect for the higher-priced office space if he or she doesn't have the resources to pay for it.

Ability to pay includes both cash and credit. Many companies subscribe to a credit-rating service offered by firms such as Dun & Bradstreet. Salespeople use information from these sources to determine the financial status and credit rating of a lead. They can also qualify leads with information obtained from local credit agencies, consumer credit agencies such as Experian, noncompetitive salespeople, and the Better Business Bureau. Salespeople are sometimes surprised at their leads' credit ratings. Some big-name firms have poor ratings.

DOES THE LEAD HAVE THE AUTHORITY TO BUY?

Knowing who has the authority to make a purchase saves the salesperson time and effort and results in a higher percentage of closed sales. As discussed in Chapter 3, many people can be involved in a purchase decision, and it can be unclear who has the authority to buy.

Because of downsizing, some firms are delegating their purchasing tasks to outside vendors. These service vendors, called **systems integrators,** have the authority to buy products and services on behalf of the delegating firm. Systems integrators usually assume complete responsibility for a project from its beginning to follow-up servicing. An example would be Lockheed Martin acting as a systems integrator for the complete mail-processing system of a new postal sorting facility in Germany. In that scenario every potential vendor would actually be selling to Lockheed Martin, not to the German government. When systems integrators are involved, salespeople need to delineate clearly who has the authority to purchase. Sometimes the overall buyer (the German government in this example) will retain veto power over potential vendors.

CAN THE LEAD BE APPROACHED FAVORABLY?

Some leads simply are not accessible to the salesperson. For example, the president of an international bank, a major executive of a large manufacturing company, or the senior partner in a well-established law firm normally would not normally be accessible to a young college graduate starting out as a financial advisor for Edward Jones. Getting an interview with these people may be so difficult and the chances of making a sale may be so small that the sales representative should eliminate them as possible prospects.

IS THE LEAD ELIGIBLE TO BUY?

Eligibility is an equally important factor in finding a genuine prospect. For example, a salesperson who works for a firm that requires a large minimum order should not call on leads that could never order in such volume. Likewise, a representative who sells exclusively to wholesalers should be certain the individuals he or she calls on are actually wholesalers, not retailers.

Another factor that may determine eligibility for a particular salesperson is the geographic location of the prospect. Most companies operate on the basis of **exclusive sales territories,** meaning that a particular salesperson can sell only to certain prospects (such as doctors in only a three-county area) and not to other prospects. A salesperson working for such a company must consider whether the prospect is eligible, based on location or customer type, to buy from him or her.

Salespeople should also avoid targeting leads already covered by their corporate headquarters. Large customers or potential customers that are handled exclusively by corporate executives are often called **house accounts.** For example, if Marriott Hotels considers Ingersoll Rand a house account, a Marriott Hotel salesperson (who sets up events and conventions at the hotel) located in New York City should not try to solicit business from one of Ingersoll Rand's divisions located in New York City. Instead all Ingersoll Rand business would be handled by a Marriott executive at Marriott corporate headquarters.

OTHER CRITERIA

Leads that meet the five criteria are generally considered excellent prospects by most companies. Some sellers, however, add other criteria. For example, DEI Management Group instructs its salespeople to classify leads by their likelihood of buying.

Some firms look at the timing of purchase to determine whether a lead is really a good prospect. Relevant questions to consider include these: When does the prospect's contract with our competitor expire? Is a purchase decision really pending? How do we know? Still other firms look at the long-term potential of developing a partnering relationship with a lead. Here are some questions to ponder: What is the climate at the organization—is it looking to develop partnering relationships with suppliers? Do any of our competitors already have a partnering relationship there?

The Corporate Executive Board takes an entirely different approach to prospecting and qualifying leads, which they term **insight selling.**[3] Under this approach, salespeople evaluate prospects who do not necessarily have a clear understanding of what they need but are in a state of flux and have been shown to be quite agile in making changes (that is, they are able and willing to act quickly when a compelling case is made to them). This approach also encourages salespeople to interact with people in the buying firm who are skeptical rather than friendly information providers and then coach these skeptical decision makers how to buy the seller's solution. Why this approach? Proponents claim that buyers today already know a great deal about the marketplace and understand many of their options and that salespeople who follow the proposed approach are more successful in gaining commitment.

HOW AND WHERE TO OBTAIN PROSPECTS •

Prospecting sources and methods vary for different types of selling. A sales representative selling corrugated containers for Citation Box & Paper Company, for example, may use a system different from what banking or office products

Exhibit 6.2

Overview of Common
Sources of Leads

Source	How Used
Satisfied customers	Current and previous customers are contacted for additional business and leads.
Endless chain	Salesperson attempts to secure at least one additional lead from each person he or she interviews.
Networking	Salesperson uses personal relationships with those who are connected and cooperative to secure leads.
Center of influence	Salesperson cultivates well-known, influential people in the territory who are willing to supply lead information.
Social media	Salesperson uses online tools like LinkedIn, Facebook, and Twitter to prospect for new customers and maintain contact with existing customers.
Other Internet uses	Salesperson uses Web sites, e-mail, listservs, bulletin boards, forums, roundtables, and newsgroups to secure leads.
Ads, direct mail, catalogs, and publicity	Salespeople use these forms of promotional activities to generate leads.
Shows, fairs, and merchandise markets	Salespeople use trade shows, conventions, fairs, and merchandise markets for lead generation.
Webinars and seminars	Salespeople use seminars and online webinars to generate leads.
Lists and directories	Salesperson uses secondary data sources, which can be free or fee-based.
Databases and data mining	Salespeople use sophisticated data analysis software and the company's databases to generate leads.
Cold calling	Salesperson tries to generate leads by calling on totally unfamiliar organizations.
Spotters	Salesperson pays someone for lead information.
Telemarketing	Salesperson uses phone and/or telemarketing staff to generate leads.
Sales letters	Salesperson writes personal letters to potential leads.
Other sources	Salesperson uses noncompeting salespeople, people in his or her own firm, friends, and so on to secure information.

salespeople would use. Exhibit 6.2 presents an overview of some of the most common lead-generating methods. Note that there is some overlap among the methods.

SATISFIED CUSTOMERS

Satisfied customers, particularly those who are truly partners with the seller, are the most effective sources for leads. In fact some trainers argue that successful salespeople should be getting about 75 percent of their new business through referrals from customers, and firms are now encouraged to calculate **customer referral value,** which is the monetary value of the these referrals as well as the costs to get and maintain the referrals.[4] Referrals of leads in the same industry are particularly useful because the salesperson already understands the unique needs of this type of organization (If you have sold to a bank already, you have a better understanding of banks' needs). Referrals in some cultures, like Japan, are even more important than they are in North America.

To maximize the usefulness of satisfied customers, salespeople should follow several logical steps. First they should make a list of potential references (customers who might provide leads) from among their most satisfied customers. This task will be much easier if the salespeople have maintained an accurate and detailed database of customers. Some current customers could be called **promoters** or evangelists. These are your most loyal customers who not only keep buying from you but also urge their friends and associate to do the same.[5] Next

Salespeople use referral events to generate leads.

salespeople should decide what they would like each customer to do (such as have the customer write a personal letter or e-mail message of introduction to a specific prospect, see whether the customer would be willing to take phone inquiries, have the customer directly contact prospects, or have the customer provide a generic letter of reference or write a recommendation for you on LinkedIn). Finally salespeople should ask the customer for the names of leads and for the specific type of help she or he can provide.

Salespeople sometimes gather leads at **referral events,** which are gatherings designed to allow current customers to introduce prospects to the salesperson. For example, a Merrill Lynch financial advisor might invite a group of current clients to a ski resort for a weekend. The skiing weekend is free for clients who bring one or more prospects. Other events that salespeople use include sporting events, theater visits, dinner at a nice restaurant, a short cruise, or golf lessons by a pro. The key is that the gathering should be fun and sociable and a way for a salesperson to gather leads. The name of a lead provided by either a customer or a prospect, known as a **referred lead,** is generally considered the most successful type of lead.

Satisfied customers not only provide leads but also are usually prospects for additional sales. This situation is sometimes referred to as **selling deeper** to a current customer. Salespeople should never overlook this profitable opportunity. Sales to existing customers often result in more profits than do sales to new customers. For example, if a midsized company increased its customer retention by just 5 percent, its profits would double in only 10 years. Customers that buy a lot from the selling firm at a lower service cost are sometimes affectionately referred to as "star clients."[6] Chapter 15 explores selling deeper more fully. Of course it is also possible that a customer could be the other kind of a referrer—one who tells others about how poorly you or your product performed. This **negative referral** is not the kind of referral a salesperson likes to get, and every effort should be made to ensure that the customer is satisfied and stays satisfied with the solution offered by the salesperson. This also will be discussed in more detail in Chapter 14.

Finally, salespeople who leave one company can bring their sales clients with them to the new company for which they work. Phil Birt did that when he was laid off from Seagate Technology during the recent recession and went to work for Bell Micro. At Bell Micro, Birt grew the revenue of one customer by $400,000 in four months and that of another customer by $100,000 in a single month.[7] Of course salespeople who change jobs must always follow the agreements signed with their first employers before transferring such business.

ENDLESS-CHAIN METHOD

In the **endless-chain method** sales representatives attempt to get at least one additional lead from each person they interview. This method works best when the source is a satisfied customer and partner; however, it may also be used even when a prospect does not buy. Exhibit 6.3 illustrates how a sales representative successfully used the endless-chain method.

NETWORKING

Networking is the utilization of personal relationships by connected and cooperating individuals for the purpose of achieving goals. In selling, networking simply

Exhibit 6.3
Example of the Endless-Chain Method of Prospecting

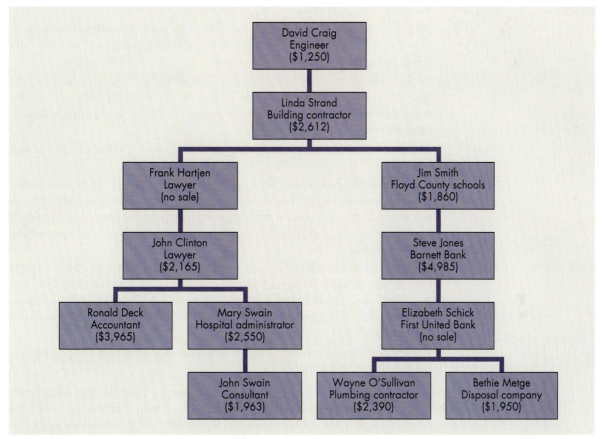

The sales representative used the endless-chain method to produce $25,690 in business (selling fax machines) within a 30-day period. All the sales resulted directly or indirectly from the first referral from an engineer to whom the sales rep had sold a mere $1,250 worth of equipment.

means establishing connections to other people and then using those networks to generate leads, gather information, generate sales, and so on. Networking can, and often does, include satisfied customers.

Networking is crucial in many selling situations.[8] For example, trying to sell in China without successful networking, called *guanxi* in China, would be disastrous.

Successful networkers offer a number of practical suggestions:[9]

- Call at least two people per day, and go to at least one networking event every week to increase your exposure and time with your contacts.
- Make a special effort to move outside your own comfort zone in a social setting. Learn to mingle with people you don't already know. One expert calls this behavior acting like a host instead of like a guest.
- Spend most of your initial conversation with a new contact talking about his or her business, not yours, and don't forget to learn about the person's nonbusiness interests.
- Follow up with your new contact on a regular basis with cards, notes of congratulations about awards or promotions, and articles and information that might help her or him.

- Whenever you receive a lead from your contact, send a handwritten, personal note thanking the person for the information, regardless of whether the lead buys from you.
- Whenever possible, send your networking contact lead information as well. Don't make your contact feel like she or he is just being used and the only thing you care about is leads for yourself.
- Make free use of your business cards. Consider having something on the back of your business card (such as humor, an inspirational quote, or an endorsement) that will encourage the person to keep it and perhaps share it with others.
- Monitor the performance of your networking to see what's working and what's not.
- Consider joining Business Network International (BNI). With over 3,600 chapters worldwide, BNI is the largest business networking organization in the world and offers members the opportunity to share ideas, contacts, and, most importantly, referrals. There are thousands of other local networking organizations.
- Be prepared to introduce yourself succinctly in social settings. Some experts suggest you create a 30-second commercial (also called an "elevator speech") in which you introduce yourself and provide some pertinent information (such as education, general work history, a significant accomplishment, and a future goal).[10]
- Remember that the goal of networking events is to prospect. Don't start trying to sell the lead at the event.

In one form of networking, the **center-of-influence method,** the salesperson cultivates a relationship with well-known, influential people in the territory who are willing to supply the names of leads. Here is how an industrial cleaning service salesperson used the center-of-influence method when meeting with a well-known and respected maintenance engineer:

> Now that you've had the opportunity to learn more about me and my service, I wonder if you will do me a favor? You mentioned that it was probably the best-designed package you've ever seen. I know that as an engineer you wouldn't personally need my services, but can you think of any of your business associates who could benefit from such a plan? Does one come to mind?

thinking **it** through   Who is a center of influence for you right now? How could a salesperson who wanted to sell you something learn who your center of influence is?

In industrial sales situations the centers of influence are frequently people in important departments not directly involved in the purchase decision, such as quality control, equipment maintenance, and receiving. The salesperson keeps in close touch with these people over an extended period, solicits their help in a straightforward manner, and keeps them informed about sales that result from their aid.

The Roper Organization, which has studied centers of influence for more than 45 years, states that they are consistent in one aspect: their degree of activity. Centers of influence tend to be those who enjoy being very socially involved in their communities. And people in the community not only trust these individuals but also seek their advice.

One true story illustrates the method's use. A Xerox representative found that decision makers from several companies would get together from time to time. These accounts formed a **buying community:** a small, informal group of people in similar positions, often from several companies, who communicate regularly, both socially and professionally. The salesperson also found that one particular decision maker in that group, or community, would share the results of any sales call with the other members of the community. Thus a call on that account had the power of seven calls. By working carefully with this center of influence, the salesperson closed nine orders from the seven accounts, with sales that totaled more than $450,000.

SOCIAL MEDIA

Social media has been defined as "the technological component of the communication, transaction, and relationship building functions of a business that leverages the network of customers and prospects to promote value co-creation."[11] As described in Chapter 4, salespeople are using social media, like LinkedIn, Facebook, blogs, and Twitter, to communicate with buyers. Given the growing importance of these channels (see "Sales Technology 6.1"), these types of tools can also be used to prospect for new customers.

Salespeople should first determine their overall approach for using social media, involving either a push or a pull strategy.[12] As salespeople, are we trying to push ourselves, our companies, and our products to prospects? If so, then the seller can use social media tactics, such as live question-and-answer sessions on the seller's Facebook page, using LinkedIn to gather prospect names, and so forth. As salespeople, are we trying to pull customers toward us and our products? If so, tactics might include the use of seller blogs, wikis, video blogs (called vlogs), microblogs like Twitter, and so forth.

Here are some social networking tips from Mike Krause,[13] a pro on the use of social networking for salespeople, and others:[14]

- Go to the prospect's Web site. Read blogs posted there and register yourself to receive any type of material the prospect might occasionally send out.
- Go to LinkedIn and search for the company and the person you want to call on. Try to get connected to the individual through a connection you already have.
- Once you are connected, review the prospect's LinkedIn page carefully. Look for things you have in common. See what organizations and groups your prospect belongs to or follows. Follow the same procedure for other social networking sites like Facebook, as well as specialized networking sites like CFOZone (www.cfozone.com), and make sure you tailor messages to fit the mission and tone of each specific networking site.
- Follow the prospect (both the company and the individual you will be calling on) on Twitter. Sometimes a prospect won't have a Twitter account showing on the company Web site, so you will need to do a company search on Twitter to find the prospect (search.twitter.com). Also, see whom your prospect is following on Twitter.
- Search for special interest groups that your prospect belongs to on Twitter, and read those tweets.
- If the prospect decides to follow you on Twitter, send her or him a direct message. If the prospect doesn't follow you on Twitter, you can still send a message by commenting on one of his or her tweets using Twitter's @ feature.
- Search for the prospect and the company on other networking sites like YouTube and SlideShare.
- If your company has just launched a new product or service, ask users what they think about it via Twitter. Or ask any question. Twitter is great for getting opinions from people.
- Upload your contacts from your e-mail program (like Microsoft Outlook and Gmail) to LinkedIn and Facebook to search for more connections.
- Use Find Friends in Facebook to find other people whom you might be able to add to your network.
- Look at your friends' lists of friends. Invite them to link to you or ask your friend to initiate this linking.
- Start a group page for your product in Facebook.
- Use Search to find groups and fan pages that might be related to your business.
- Use the search updates feature in LinkedIn and data intelligence tools like InsideView to see if prospects have secured any new business, are developing new products, and so forth.
- Create a blog that includes your opinions, educates prospects, provides news, and encourages reactions and postings from prospects. Carefully establish a personal brand identity for yourself in all social media venues.
- Follow competitors' social media postings to gather competitor intelligence.
- Monitor your social media sites for comments/postings by competitors and unsatisfied customers.
- Use the TweetDeck feature to be alerted whenever a key word (like your company name or your product) has appeared in any tweet. Use other social media monitoring tools, like HootSuite, to pick up when someone needs help or is dissatisfied.

As an example of the effectiveness of using social networking, Madeline's Catering in Rochester, New York, redesigned its Web page to fully integrate with Facebook, LinkedIn, and Twitter.[15] As a result, in only six weeks Web site traffic grew by 41 percent and phone inquiries doubled, increasing sales and profits tremendously. As another example, an employee of SoftBrands was trying to find a way to connect with the software giant SAP. The employee decided to start following the tweets of a local SAP worker, and this resulted in some small talk via tweets about sports. Eventually this moved to a face-to-face meeting with the prospect and a profitable sale.[16] As a final example, IBM has set up Web sites that allow their sales reps to create blogs with feeds tied directly to LinkedIn and Twitter.[17] IBM reps also use Twitter to provide customers information about events and news.

OTHER INTERNET USES

Successful salespeople are using their companies' Web sites, e-mail, listservs, bulletin boards, forums, roundtables, and newsgroups to connect to individuals and companies that may be interested in their products or services.

For example, John Deere, which sells construction and agriculture equipment, uses its Web site to give leads information about products, show them where the nearest dealers are located, and gather their names and addresses if they desire more information. One advantage of Web-based promotions is the number of international leads that can be secured, and John Deere realizes this benefit by making its Web site available in many different languages.

Personal Medicine, a start-up company that is bringing the house call back to medicine, had trouble enlisting both doctors and patients. Its solution was to use LeadShare, a Web tool offered by SlideShare. With LeadShare marketers post interesting and important information online (in the form of PowerPoint slides, PDF documents, and so forth). To review that information, the viewer must supply contact information. That information is then sent to the organization posting the information and forms the basis for sales leads.

Firms are also developing **extranets**—Internet sites that are customized for specific target markets. Extranets are usually used to build relationships with current customers, but some companies are also using these sites to generate leads. For example, Turner, a TimesWarner Company, owns CNN, TNT, Cartoon Network, Adult Swim, truTV, and NBA on TNT. Turner set up an extranet that is accessible only to media buyers. Buyers can access programming information, cable research data, and Turner's salespeople from the site.

ADS AND DIRECT MAIL

Firms have developed sophisticated systems to generate inquiries from leads by using advertising and direct mail. For example, Fiskars, a Finnish scissors manufacturer, used a direct marketing campaign targeted at purchasing managers and directors at high-volume German hardware stores. The company sent a special package to each individual that included a unique form of a letter, with each word carefully cut out letter by letter in a single piece of paper, along with a pair of Fiskars to clip out a redeemable coupon for more information. The result was a 19 percent increase in orders during that month.[18] As another example, health insurer Anthem sent mailers to health benefit consultants and brokers who help companies choose health insurance plans. A group of brochures, all with a food-theme background, were bound in a white tablecloth to gain attention. Nearly a third of recipients visited the Anthem Web site, and 74 percent became leads for salespeople.[19]

SHOWS, FAIRS, AND MERCHANDISE MARKETS

Many companies display or demonstrate their products at trade shows, conventions, fairs, and merchandise markets. Sales representatives, usually stationed at booths, as shown in the following picture, are present to demonstrate products to visitors, many of whom salespeople have not called on before. In some cases a manufacturer lives or dies by how well it does in these special selling situations. MeadWestVaco, a company that manufactures office products such as calendars, depends heavily on the annual national office products association show. Its salespeople report that selling year-round is easier due to the impression the company makes on prospects at the show. And don't forget that one way to prospect is to simply "walk" the show and meet and learn about people who are working at other booths.

Trade shows are short (usually less than a week), temporary exhibitions of products by manufacturers and resellers. In Europe trade shows are called **trade fairs.** Once the show is over, all vendors pack up and leave. The Consumer Electronics Show showcases electronics products each year. The more than 2,500 vendors at this show are all manufacturers looking for dealers for their products; the end users of the products are not admitted. Dealers often make an entire year's worth of purchases at the show, so the show is a make-or-break situation for many manufacturers. The New York National Boat Show differs in that it has a dual audience: Vendors exhibit to end users (the boating public) as well as to resellers.

Trade shows and fairs help salespeople discover and qualify leads.

Even firms that do not use resellers may have salespeople involved in trade shows. At many trade shows all attendees are customers. For example, when the National Association of Legal Career Professionals holds its annual convention, it also invites manufacturers of office equipment and other products to exhibit wares. The trade show is an adjunct of the convention, with the audience composed entirely of end users. Progressive companies, like Thomson Reuters, create elaborate booths, develop contests and interesting takeaways, and do on-site demonstrations at trade shows. Its Camp Thomson, a whimsical summer camp–themed booth at the American Association of Law Libraries annual meeting, was very successful in generating buzz and produced over 4,000 actual demonstrations of its offerings.[20]

Merchandise markets are places where suppliers have sales offices and buyers from resellers visit to purchase merchandise. The Dallas Market Center, for example, hosts more than 50 separate markets for children's wear, western apparel, linens, and other soft goods. The sellers are the manufacturers or distributors, and they sell only to resellers, not to the public. Sellers may lease showroom space permanently or only during market weeks. Sellers who lease space permanently usually bring in buyers during off-market periods or when no markets are being held.

Buyers visit many vendors during markets, selecting the products they will carry for the next season. In some industries, almost all sales to resellers occur during markets.

Instead of mechanically asking, Are you enjoying the show? or Can I help you with something today? sharp salespeople try to discover whether the lead has a need or a want they can meet. The seller then gives the lead helpful information and gathers information that will be used later in further qualifying the lead and preparing for a sales call. Timely follow-up of leads is critical if sales are to follow a show.

WEBINARS AND SEMINARS

Many firms use seminars and **webinars** (online seminars) to generate leads and to provide information to prospective customers.[21] For example, a local pharmaceutical representative for Bristol-Myers Squibb will set up a seminar for 8 to 10 oncologists and invite a nationally known research oncologist to make a presentation. The research specialist usually discusses some new technique or treatment being developed. During or after the presentation, the pharmaceutical representative for Bristol-Myers Squibb might describe how Squibb's drug Taxol helps in the treatment of ovarian and breast cancer.

What are some key things to keep in mind when planning a webinar or seminar? Make sure your seminar appeals to a specialized market and invite good prospects, especially those prospects who might not be willing to see you one-on-one. The subject should be something your attendees have a strong interest in, while your speaker must be considered an authority on the topic. Try to go as high quality as possible (remember, you're building an image) and consider serving food. Finally, you should take an active role before, during, and after the seminar.

LISTS AND DIRECTORIES

Individual sales representatives can develop prospect lists from sources such as public records, telephone directories, chamber of commerce directories, newspapers, trade publications, club membership lists, and professional or trade membership lists. Secondary sources of information from public libraries also can be useful. For example, industrial trade directories are available for all states. It is often useful to know the **standard industrial classification (SIC)** code or the **North America industry classification system (NAICS)** code, which is a uniform classification for all countries in North America, when researching using secondary sources.[22]

Salespeople can purchase a number of prospecting directories and lead-generating publications. You can purchase mailing lists for all gerontologists (specialists in geriatrics), Lions clubs, T-shirt retailers, yacht owners, antique dealers, Catholic high schools, motel supply houses, multimillionaires, pump wholesalers, and thousands of other classifications. These lists can be delivered as printed mailing labels or secured directly from the Web from such sources as www.salesgenie.com.

Salespeople should keep in mind that lists may not be current and may contain inaccurate information regardless of any guarantee of accuracy. In international selling situations, procuring lists can be much more difficult.

DATABASES AND DATA MINING

Sophisticated firms are developing interactive **databases** that contain information about leads, prospects, and customers. For example, Pioneer, one of the country's largest producers of seed corn, has a dynamic database of 600,000 farm operators in the United States and Canada that everyone in the firm can access. The system has resulted in better sales prospecting and more tailored sales presentations.

Companies are using **data mining,** which consists of artificial intelligence and statistical tools, to discover insights hidden in the volumes of data in their databases. For example, Eagle Equipment of Norton, Massachusetts, uses iMarket software to target its sales calls to the best prospects. Using the company's

From the BUYERS SEAT

I'm an assistant buyer for Macy's. My company does our best to attend trade shows. Through these trade shows, we are actually the ones prospecting suppliers for potential products. If we see a product from a supplier that we feel matches our needs, we will then get in contact with that supplier and salesperson.

In my industry, it is also common for salespeople to prospect and develop leads through cold calling. For a salesperson to make the most efficient use of their time, it is a *must* that they do their homework on my company so that they know at least the basics (the more the better). Here are a few things that salespeople have done in the past that have really set them apart from the competition:

- Knowing what Macy's provides to our end customer before cold calling me by a salesperson being able to tell me how my end customer will perceive their product.

- When a salespeople send samples of their product to our office to be reviewed. If a salesperson really thinks out the product that they are sending us and ties it in to what they have learned about our company, it sends the message that they really are looking to build a relationship and not just make a sale.

There are also those salespeople who just come in, do the minimum they need to do to get their paycheck, and get out. To me, this is very evident. An example of this revolves around pricing. Even if a product that is brought to me is of exceptional quality, we still need to stick to our pricing range and not venture out of that to maintain our organizational goals. Salespeople should come to me knowing something about the structure of our organization before trying to sell us on products that are outside of our price range.

Source: Brooke Downey, Macy's; names changed as requested; used with permission.

database, the software identifies prospects most likely to buy something and then matches that profile against a database of 12 million businesses. Chapter 15 more fully examines the use of data mining and databases.

COLD CALLING

Before learning about other prospecting methods, college students often assume that salespeople spend most of their time making cold calls. In using the **cold canvass method,** or **cold calls** (by call we usually mean a personal visit, not a telemarketing call), a sales representative tries to generate leads for new business by calling on totally unfamiliar organizations. Cold calling can waste a salesperson's time because many companies have neither a need for the product nor the ability to pay for it. This fact stresses the importance of qualifying the lead quickly in a cold call so as not to waste time. Also, today cold calling is considered rude by many purchasing agents and other professionals.

Salespeople often rate making cold calls as the part of the job they like least. Thus, as mentioned earlier, most firms now encourage their salespeople to qualify leads instead of relying on cold calls. In fact, Ameriprise banned cold calling for its salespeople nationwide years ago. This policy forced the reps to use other methods, such as networking and referrals. But sometimes firms requires their salespeople to start making cold calls, especially in downtimes. For example, Ted Sperides, a customer service rep at Bankcard Associates, was required, as were all employees, to start making cold calls on prospects during the recent recession. He found that the key to successful cold calling was to generate attention immediately, which he did by claiming that his firm could help the buyer save money in credit card processing fees.[23] From the Buyer's Seat 6.1 shares some thoughts from one buyer about salespeople who cold call.

Still, some companies use cold calling. And some companies use a selective type of cold calling they refer to as a **blitz:** A large group of salespeople attempts to call on all the prospective businesses in a given geographical territory on a specified day. For example, an office machine firm may target a specific four-block area in Guadalajara, Mexico; bring in all the salespeople from the surrounding areas; and then have them, in one day, call on every business located in that four-block area. The purpose is to generate leads for the local sales representative as well as to build camaraderie and a sense of unity among the salespeople.

SPOTTERS

Some salespeople use **spotters,** also called **bird dogs.** These individuals will, for a fee, provide leads for the salesperson. The sales rep sometimes pays the fee simply for the name of the lead but more often pays only if the lead ends up buying the product or service. Spotters are usually in a position to find out when someone is ready to make a purchase decision. For example, a janitor who works for a janitorial service company and notices that the heating system for a client is antiquated and hears people complaining about it can turn this information over to a heating contractor.

A more recent development is the use of outside paid consultants to locate and qualify leads. Small firms attempting to secure business with large organizations are most likely to use this approach. For example, Synesis Corporation, a small firm specializing in computerized training, used the services of a consultant to identify and develop leads. The result of one lead was a major contract with AT&T.

Use caution, however, when offering a cash payment to a customer for spotting. Your action may be misconstrued by the customer as exploiting the relationship. Also, some customers' firms may prohibit such behavior. Sometimes it is better to send a personal thank-you note or small gift to the customer instead.

TELEMARKETING

Increasingly, firms are relying on telemarketing to perform many functions that field sales representatives used to perform. **Telemarketing** is a systematic and continuous program of communicating with customers and prospects via telephone. Telemarketing is now used to sell everything from 25-cent supplies to $10 million airplanes.

In **outbound telemarketing** telephones are used to generate and then qualify leads. These calls may be initiated directly by the salesperson, by inside sales representatives (inside sales reps were discussed in Chapter 1), or by third-party vendors. **Inbound telemarketing** uses a telephone number (usually a toll-free number) that leads and customers can call for additional information. Again, the call may be answered by several types of people: the salesperson, an inside salesperson, or a customer service representative.[24]

Firms combine outbound and inbound telemarketing to prospect effectively. For example, Motorola's government division, which sells mobile communication systems to such entities as police stations and fire departments, can use outbound telemarketing to generate and then qualify leads for its sales force. Qualified leads are turned over to field sales representatives if the order is large enough to warrant a personal visit to the company. If the prospect needs a smaller system, a separate telemarketing salesperson will handle the account. Motorola also uses inbound telemarketing by providing a toll-free number for people who

Progressive firms use telemarketers to qualify leads before sending a salesperson on a call.

want more information about a product or service Motorola offers. Because of this excellent telemarketing organization, Motorola's field reps have more time to spend with qualified prospects and more time to develop long-term customer relations.

Although the telephone is a wonderful tool that can enhance productivity, it also has some limitations. Customers often find telephone calls an annoying inconvenience, which is why a huge percent use voice mail to screen their calls. When telephoning customers—in fact, at all times—salespeople need to respect the customers' privacy concerns and the do-not-call rules, as discussed in Chapter 2. Attracting and maintaining the customer's attention and interest is harder over the telephone than it is in person, and prospects may even continue to work or read a report or magazine. While it is true that is it much easier for a prospect to say no over the phone than in person, salespeople should often take that "no" to mean exactly what they say—no, rather than continue to try to badger the prospect into complying.

BECOMING AN EXPERT

Salespeople can prospect by becoming recognized experts in their field, resulting in prospects seeking information from them. Admittedly, that won't happen for most salespeople when they first graduate from college, but over time they can develop their expertise and seek avenues to showcase their talent.

Salespeople have many ways to demonstrate their expertise in a particular subject. Some will engage in public speaking on topics related to their expertise. Speeches at industry conventions, at luncheons and dinners hosted by prospects and industry representatives, and on college campuses provide outlets for expertise to be disseminated.

Salespeople can also demonstrate their expertise in writing. This can take many forms, including writing journal articles, publishing articles in trade publications, hosting a blog, posting on other's blogs, and so forth. One study found that technical buyers often read white papers before making decisions.

SALES LETTERS

Prospecting sales letters can be integrated into an overall prospecting plan. For example, Xerox salespeople who handle smaller businesses send prospecting sales letters every day. They follow up three days later with a telephone prospecting call and ask for an appointment for a personal visit. The telephone call begins with a question about the letter.

One way to make sales letters stand out is to include a promotional item with the mailer. Here are some good examples:[25]

- First National Bank of Shreveport, Louisiana, targeted certified public accountants (CPAs) for one mailer. The bank timed the mailers to arrive on April 16, the day after the federal income tax filing deadline. Included in each mailer was a small bottle of wine, a glass, and cheese and crackers—a party kit designed to celebrate the end of tax season. The bank followed up with telephone calls two days later and ultimately gained 21 percent of the CPAs as new customers.

- OfficeMax sent top executives at a large bank a metal suitcase filled with piles of fake money. The box also contained an MP3 player that included videos of how OfficeMax could meet that bank's specific needs.

- Sprint sent top decision makers a personal meeting invitation housed in a specially designed attractive box with a Louisville Slugger bat enclosed. Those who agreed to meetings would receive professional baseball jerseys for their favorite baseball teams.

thinking **it** through

What would be your reaction if you received the Louisville Slugger bat just described as part of a direct mail piece? Would there be a better way to gain your attention in such a mailing? If so, how could a salesperson learn what that would be?

The salesperson must first consider the objective of any written communication (like a sales letter or e-mail message) and the audience. What action does the salesperson desire from the reader? Why would the reader want to undertake that action? Why would the reader not want to undertake the action? These questions help guide the salesperson in writing the letter.

The opening paragraph must grab the reader's attention, just as a salesperson's approach must get a prospect's attention in a face-to-face call. The opening gives the readers a reason to continue reading, drawing them into the rest of the letter. Another way to gain attention is to have a loyal client whom the prospect respects write the introduction (or even the entire letter) for the salesperson. Here's an example of an opening paragraph:

> Thanks for stopping by the Datasource booth at the VON San Jose IP Communications Show. I hope you enjoyed the show and had some fun shooting hoops with us! Were you there when one highly energetic attendee shot the basketball clear over into the Mac booth and knocked the presenter's iPhone right out of his hand? You won't believe what he did next! I'll fill you in on the details in a moment, but first I'd like to invite you to something I know you're not going to want to miss.

The next paragraph or two, the body of the letter, considers why the reader would and would not want to take the desired action. Benefits of taking the action should be presented clearly, without jargon, and briefly. The best-presented benefits are tailored to the specific individual, especially when the salesperson can refer to a recent conversation with the reader. A reference such as the following example can truly personalize the letter:

> As you said during our visit at the show, you're looking for a software firm that can work with a small business like yours without making you feel like a second-class citizen. At Datasource, we've committed ourselves to working exclusively with small to midsized firms like yours.

If the salesperson and the buyer do not know each other, part of the body of the letter should be used to increase credibility. References to satisfied customers, market research data, and other independent sources can be used to improve credibility:

> You may have heard that last year we won the prestigious Youcon Achievement Award, presented by the Tennessee Small Business Development Center in recognition for outstanding service specifically to small businesses. In fact, the small businesses themselves are the voters for the award. We're proud of that award because it tangibly reflects the commitment we've shown. And we have dedicated ourselves to continue in that tradition.

The final paragraph should seek commitment to the desired course of action. Whatever the action desired, the letter must specifically ask that it take place. The writer should leave no doubt in the prospect's mind about what he or she is supposed to do. The writer should make the action for the prospect easy to accomplish, fully explain why it should be done now, and end with a positive picture. Here's an example:

> So I want to personally invite you to a free lunch seminar at Datasource. You'll hear from our partners about the very latest solutions to your technology challenges. The food promises to be great, and the information will be presented in a casual, small group setting. Please take a moment to reserve your spot at the lunch by visiting our Web site, www.datasource.com, or calling 800-343-8764. You'll be glad you did.

A postscript (or PS) can also be effective. Postscripts stand out because of their location and should be used to make an important selling point. Alternatively, they can be used to emphasize the requested action, such as pointing out a deadline.

While you are writing, remember to check your work carefully for misspelled words and grammar problems. And read it carefully because you often don't see problems in a quick glance, as the following paragraph illustrates:[26]

> i cdnuolt blveiee taht I cluod aulaclty uesdnatnrd waht I was rdanieg. The phaonmneal pweor of the hmuan mnid, aoccdrnig to a rscheearch at Cmabrigde Uinervtisy, it dseno't mtaetr in waht oerdr the ltteres in a wrod are, the olny iproamtnt tihng is taht the frsit and lsat ltteer be in the rghit pclae. The rset can be a taotl mses and you can sitll raed it whotuit a pboerlm. Tihs is bcuseae the huamn mnid deos not raed ervey lteter by istlef, but the wrod as a wlohe.

And of course spell check won't catch everything; the following passed with flying colors:[27]

> I have a spelling checker, it came with my PC. It plainly marks four my revenue mistakes I cannot sea. I've run this poem threw it, I'm sure your pleased too no, its letter perfect in it's weigh, my checker tolled me sew.

OTHER SOURCES OF LEADS

Many salespeople find leads through personal observation, as "Building Partnerships 6.1" describes. For example, by reading trade journals carefully, salespeople can learn the names of the most important leaders (and hence decision makers) in the industry. Sellers also read general business publications (such as the *Wall Street Journal*) and local newspapers.

Nonsales employees within the salesperson's firm can also provide leads. Some companies strongly encourage this practice. For example, Computer Specialists Inc., a computer service firm, pays its nonsales employees a bonus of up to $1,000 for any names of prospective customers they pass along. In one year the program resulted in 75 leads and 9 new accounts.

Government agencies can also supply lead information. The FedBizOpps site, for example, provides information about federal government bid opportunities and can be viewed at www.fbo.gov.

Leads can be found in many other places as well. Some prospect while doing something they enjoy, such as belonging to a cycling club. Salespeople for noncompeting but related products can often provide leads, as can members of trade associations. You can find leads while volunteering in your community, doing things like helping build a house for Habitat for Humanity. Good friends can also provide leads. Of course one of the best ways to learn about new business opportunities is to keep up with regional, national, and world trends from sources such as *World Watch* magazine and industry surveys (Manufacturing USA, Service USA, Standard & Poor's Industry Surveys, U.S. Industrial Outlook, and the like).

BUILDING Partnerships

As an independent distributor of building supplies, BlueLinx has more than 10,000 products and 70,000 SKUs of interest to contractors and builders. These include siding and trim, metal products, structural framing products, and molding and millwork, to name just a few. We have a broad array of the most well respected brands in the industry.

In terms of prospecting, we at BlueLinx do our best to come in contact with any possible client that we can. Our motto is "keep your feet on the streets and meet folks face to face." When our salespeople learn about a potential customer, they enter the information into our CRM system. Our system consists of many drop-down boxes, making the information easy to input for our salespeople and taking as little time as possible for them to store valuable information. This not only helps salespeople keep track of what they have done with each of their potential customers but also builds our database with information that others can check to see what their coworkers are doing.

The information in our CRM system is not only valuable to current salespeople while they are in their current positions; once they move on to other positions, this information is extremely valuable to their successors. Nothing is worse than wasting a client's time asking for information that has already be contacted by BlueLinx. With the vast information in our database, new salespeople can see what has previously been done with current clients.

Other ways that prospecting done in our organization is through trade shows and by our salespeople just stopping at a job site that they see while out making their sales calls. When stopping at a job site, it gives our salespeople the opportunity to assess firsthand the types of products we offer that may benefit the company. Also, this enables us to put a face to the name.

Source: Jason Ungar, BlueLinx, names have been changed at the request of the provider, used with permission.

LEAD QUALIFICATION AND MANAGEMENT SYSTEMS

Salespeople need to develop a process for qualifying leads, often called a **lead qualification system.** As mentioned early in this chapter, salespeople must ensure that their leads meet the five basic criteria of a prospect. Let's look more closely at this process.

Many firms view prospecting as a funneling process in which a large number of leads are funneled (or narrowed down) into prospects and some, finally, into customers. Marketing often generates these leads, but it is interesting that most leads thus generated by marketing departments are not followed up by salespeople.

To help salespeople use their time wisely and to increase the number of leads that sellers actually follow up with, some firms engage in **prequalification** of leads before turning them over to the field sales force. Sometimes the prequalification process is as simple as purchasing a prequalified list. At other times a firm will use the resources of telemarketers to prequalify leads. Many lead qualification systems assign points to a prospect, rather than simply designating them as hot or cold, offering the salesperson more insight into the lead's value.

Salespeople can get leads during volunteering activities.

Salespeople must not only qualify leads but also carefully analyze the relative value of each lead. This part of the process is called a **lead management system,** which is discussed more fully in Chapter 15. Part of the decision process often includes a valuation of the prospects' expected customer lifetime value or return on investment, as well as an appraisal of what types of value the selling firm can add to the prospect. Grading prospects and establishing a priority list result in increased sales and the most efficient use of time and energy. There is even an association dedicated to helping companies manage their leads more effectively: the Sales Lead Management Association.[28]

The use of technology makes lead qualification and management more efficient and effective. For example, IBM has tied its lead generation and management system into its CRM system. The results have been better tracking and prioritization of leads and prospects. The scoring system recommended by the Corporate Executive Board rates leads on five traits (organizational basics, operating environment, view of the status quo, receptivity to new or disruptive ideas, and potential for emerging needs) and then, based on the score, offers suggestions on whether to pursue the opportunity.[29]

Any good lead management system, like IBM's, should evaluate the profitability of sales resulting from various lead-generating activities instead of just counting the number of names a particular method yields. Analysis may show that the present system does not produce enough prospects or the right kinds of prospects. Salespeople may, for example, depend entirely on referred names from company advertising or from the service department. If these two sources do not supply enough names to produce the sales volume and profits desired, other prospecting methods should be considered.

Salespeople must learn how to overcome a reluctance to prospect.

OVERCOMING A RELUCTANCE TO PROSPECT

People often stereotype salespeople as bold, adventurous, and somewhat abrasive. But salespeople often struggle with a reluctance to prospect that persists no matter how well they have been trained and how much they believe in the products they sell.

Research shows a number of reasons for reluctance to call, including worrying about worst-case scenarios; spending too much time preparing; being overly concerned with looking successful; being fearful of making group presentations, of appearing too pushy, of losing friends or losing family approval, and of using the phone for prospecting; feeling intimidated by people with prestige or power or feeling guilt at having a career in selling; and having a compulsive need to argue, make excuses, or blame others.

Reluctance to call can and must be overcome to sell successfully. Several activities can help:

- Start by listening to the excuses other salespeople give to justify their call reluctance behavior. Evaluate their validity. You'll usually be surprised to find that most excuses really aren't valid.

- Engage in sales training and role-playing activity to improve your prospecting skills and your ability to handle questions and rejections that arise.

- Make prospecting contacts with a supporting partner or sales manager. Just their presence will often provide additional needed confidence (you won't feel so alone).

- Set specific goals for all your prospecting activity. Put them in your "to do" list. Chapter 15 will provide more direction in this activity.

- Realize the economic value of most prospecting activities. For example, if you keep good records, you may discover that every phone call you make (regardless of whether that particular prospect buys) results in an average of $22 commission in the long run.

- Stop negative self-evaluations from ruling your behavior. Learn to think positively about the future instead of focusing on your past blunders.

- Remember that you are calling on prospects to solve their needs, not just so you can line your pocket with money. You are performing a vital, helpful, important service to your prospects by calling on them. (If this isn't true, maybe you should find another sales job.)

- Control your perceptions of what prospects might say about you, your company, or your products. You don't know what their reactions will be until you meet with the prospects. Leads do buy from salespeople.

- Learn and apply relaxation and stress-reducing techniques.

- Recount your own prospecting successes or those of others.

SELLING YOURSELF

It's time to put the material in this chapter to practical use. Getting your first job out of college can seem like a full-time job in itself. If you find yourself in a job-hunting rut, it may be time to stop simply looking for a job and start actively *prospecting* for one. Many potential employers can be completely overlooked without prospecting because often jobs are not advertised.

As the chapter discussed, leads are not automatically prospects and must be qualified first. This means that not all jobs are going to be good prospects for you. When researching your job leads, ask yourself these important questions: Does the company have a want or need that I can satisfy?, Do I have the skills and experience necessary to bring value to the company?, Is the salary within an acceptable range?, and Does my contact have the authority to make a hiring decision? Answering these questions can help you sort through the job leads out there so that you can make the most of your time and theirs by applying only for jobs that are a good fit.

There are many sources of prospects for a job, including internships, business organizations, job fairs, and networking. College internships and prior jobs would be obvious choices for prospective careers. Current and previous employers can be contacted for leads. Getting involved in business organizations, such as the American Marketing Association and Students in Free Enterprise, can expose you to executives and hiring managers that may be impossible to access otherwise. Attending job fairs can be priceless, allowing face-to-face interaction with hiring managers before the interview. A bonus to job fairs is that there are often employees manning the booths who can give you additional insight into the career you are looking into. Networking through social media (i.e. LinkedIn), your school's alumni group, family and friends, volunteer groups, and other organizations will help get the word out that you are looking for a career. People like helping others and making connections; you've heard the saying, "It's not what you know, but who you know."

As the chapter relates, you can be the perfect candidate for a job, but if you are applying to the wrong companies, you are letting your skills go to waste. Prospecting is important for nearly all salespeople, and, after all, you are *selling yourself*.

Source: Angela Bertero, Liberty Mutual, used with permission.

SUMMARY

Locating prospective customers is the first step in the sales process. New prospects are needed to replace old customers lost for a variety of reasons and to replace contacts lost in existing customers because of plant relocations, turnover, mergers, downsizing, and other factors.

Not all sales leads qualify as good prospects. A qualified prospect has a need that can be satisfied by the salesperson's product, has the ability and authority to buy the product, can be approached by the salesperson, and is eligible to buy.

Many methods can be used to locate prospects. The best source is a satisfied customer. Salespeople can also use the endless-chain method, networking, social media, lists and directories, cold canvassing (including blitzes), spotters, and becoming known as experts via blogs, speeches, and so forth. Companies provide leads to salespeople through promotional activities such as the Internet, inquiries from advertising and direct mail, telemarketing, trade shows, merchandise markets, and webinars/seminars.

Effective prospecting requires a strong plan that hinges on developing a lead qualification and management system and overcoming reluctance to prospect.

KEY TERMS

bird dog   161
blitz   161
buying community   155
center-of-influence method   154
cold call   160
cold canvass method   160
customer referral value   151
databases   159
data mining   159
endless-chain method   152
exclusive sales territories   150
extranet   157
house accounts   150
inbound telemarketing   161
insight selling   150
lead   148
lead management system   166
lead qualification system   165
merchandise market   158
negative referral   152
networking   152

North America industry classification system (NAICS)   159
outbound telemarketing   161
prequalification   165
promoters   151
prospect   148
prospecting   148
qualify the lead   148
referral event   152
referred lead   152
sales funnel   149
selling deeper   152
social media   155
spotter   161
standard industrial classification (SIC)   159
systems integrator   149
telemarketing   161
trade fairs   158
trade show   158
webinars   159

ETHICS PROBLEMS

1. Suppose you're working at a trade show. You walk the floor of the show during one of your breaks, and you strike up a conversation with a sales rep from a competitor. She starts talking about their products and gives details on price breaks she offers to banks. She asks, "What kind of price deals do you give banks?" What would you say?

2. Suppose a spotter not only tells you about a potential prospect but also provides you with confidential memos and e-mails, detailing the people involved and what the issues are. However, all the e-mails and notes are marked with statements that prohibit the information from being shared with anyone outside of the company. What will you do with that confidential information that you're not supposed to have?

QUESTIONS AND PROBLEMS

1. Describe a referral event that could be created, assuming you are a member of a service club in your college. Your target market for new leads consists of students not currently members in any service club.

2. Think of a time when you acted as a negative referral for a product or service or company. Why did you do it? What could the company or salesperson have done to cause you to not be a negative referral?

3. What things would concern you about prospecting? How will you deal with those concerns?

4. Assume you are a landscape contractor, and you specialize in planting quality trees and plants. Whom might you use as paid spotters to generate leads?

5. Reluctance to prospect is a real phenomenon. What can you do now (and avoid doing now), while you're in school, to avoid being reluctant to prospect when you become a salesperson?

6. Assume you sell restaurant supplies, such as cooking equipment, tabletop accessories, tables, and chairs. Locate at least one merchandise mart and one trade show or fair where you might be able to display your products.

7. How would you develop a prospect list under the following situations?
   a. You belong to a Lions Club that needs to recruit new members.
   b. You sell carpet-cleaning services to businesses.

8. "Building Partnerships 6.1" describes how salespeople for BlueLinx look for prospects as they drive in their territory. Would there be any risks to relying exclusively on that technique?

9. "From the Buyer's Seat 6.1" described how some sellers try to get Macy's to buy clothing products that are too expensive. Assume that you are a seller who is selling clothing that is above Macy's price lines. What would you do?

10. If you were a salesperson for the following, how would you develop a prospect list?
    a. A new line of doors that are energy efficient.
    b. A travel agency specializing in vacations to Chile.
    c. A manufacturer of a theft deterrent device for Blue Ray players.

CASE PROBLEMS

case **6.1**

Federated Insurance

A few years back, I was a Federated Insurance salesperson and had a large Redi-Mix Concrete contractor I was quoting. This was the second time I had quoted this account, and I had built a good relationship there. My price was $159,000 for their property and casualty insurance. I knew they paid only $150,000 the year before, but I had uncovered many coverage disadvantages and issues in their current program. I had a really great shot at selling this account. The commission rate on P&C is about 15 percent, so I would make about $23,000 if I made the sale.

The buyer said that I was to stop by on Friday morning and that his current agent was coming later that afternoon with a quote. The insurance expiration day was that Saturday.

I gave my proposal, and it went very well. I gave the buyer a list of 10 things to ask the other agent in which I had coverage advantages. The buyer said he wanted to do business with me, but because his current agent was already coming in that afternoon, he felt like he should see what she had to offer and go through the issues I had pointed out.

I left and set an appointment for first thing Monday morning. On Monday at 8:00, I was there, and the owner said that I had earned the business! I was pumped! He pulled out his checkbook and gave me a check for $15,900 as a down payment. I called my underwriter to tell him the great news, and he said, "Awesome!" He asked, "When is it effective?" I said, "As of last Saturday." He said to have them sign a form saying they had not had any claims since Saturday.

I asked the owner, and he said he didn't have any claims. Then he said, "Oh, I forgot, Joe hit a deer on the way home from a job on Saturday in the company truck. It wasn't bad, though, about $1,200 in damages we are guessing. Joe wasn't hurt or anything."

I was devastated! What were my options? I could call the underwriter and tell him about the claim, knowing that he most likely would tell me to give the check back and that I could not bind an account that already had a claim pending. And I'd lose $23,000 in commission. Or I could tell the owner not to worry about it, knowing that Federated would pay the claim if I pretended I didn't know about the accident and bind the account. Or I could tell the owner that I would pay for the $1,200 claim out of my pocket because I would earn a hefty $23,000 commission check.

Questions

1. What should the salesperson do?
2. How should the salesperson communicate that decision to his customer? To his own company, Federated?

Source: Jim Sodoma, district manager, Federated Insurance; used with permission.

case 6.2

Chicago Marriott Downtown Magnificent Mile

The Chicago Marriott Downtown Magnificent Mile is a Windy City landmark on Michigan Avenue's Magnificent Mile. Located in the heart of world-class shopping and dining, this hotel is within walking distance of top attractions, including the Navy Pier, Shedd Aquarium, Millennium Park, as well as the landmark Chicago Theater District. The hotel rooms and suites have state-of-the-art flat-screen TVs, deluxe bedding, and ergonomic furnishings. With 66,400 square feet of event space, including 54 meeting rooms, this luxury hotel creates a distinguished venue for business engagements, social gatherings, and elegant wedding receptions. The largest meeting room is the Grand Ballroom with maximum meeting space of 19,193 square feet and a maximum seating capacity of 2,200. The hotel is known for its outstanding service coupled with magnificent style.

Assume that you are a salesperson for the Chicago Marriott Downtown Magnificent Mile. Your goal is to book meetings and conventions from businesses and not-for-profit organizations.

Questions

1. Provide a list of company names and addresses of five actual leads for the Chicago Marriott Downtown Magnificent Mile. You don't have to know whether the leads already have used the hotel. Explain where you got the list of leads.
2. Develop the details of an appropriate referral event for the Chicago Marriott Downtown Magnificent Mile. Provide information about the place of the event as well as what should happen during the event. Be creative. Remember that referral events should be fun for current clients as well as leads.

Source: www.marriott.com/hotels/travel/chidt-chicago-marriott-downtown-magnificent-mile.

ROLE PLAY CASE

As a NetSuite salesperson, how can youhelp your buyer prospect better? Think about how NetSuite might be able to help your buyer develop a comprehensive prospecting system, from lead generation to making the first appointment. One way that NetSuite can help is to automate direct mail. Using the database that salespeople create, the marketing department can send mail to every contact who meets certain criteria. For example, it can select an industry and send a letter only to prospects in that industry. Similarly, NetSuite provides reporting capabilities. Salespeople can see how effective they are at each method of prospecting and then focus their efforts on the methods that work the best. These are only some ideas—you may want to visit the Web site for more or think about how the concepts in the chapter can help your account.

Using the same account you've been selling to (BancVue, GelTech, HighPoint Solutions), write out some questions you'd like to ask your buyer to determine how he or she prospects now and how NetSuite might help. (*Note:* If you have not done role plays before, you will need to review the information about the various role play customers that can be found at the end of Chapter 3.)

Then role-play with your buyer, trying to determine her or his needs for assistance with prospecting. Once you've identified those needs, give a short presentation about how NetSuite can help. Your professor will pass out buyer sheets.

Note: For background information about these role plays, please see page 26.

To the instructor: Additional information needed to complete the role play is available in the Instructor's Manual.

ADDITIONAL REFERENCES

Allen, Jeff F., and Gary D. McGugan. *NEEDS Selling Solutions.* Bloomington, IN: Trafford Publishing, 2009.

Bachrach, Anne M. "Getting to the Right People." *American Salesman* 57, no. 5 (May 2012), pp. 27–30.

Bednarz, Timothy F., and Monika Pawlak. *Productive Sales Networking: Pinpoint Sales Skill Development Training Series.* Stevens Point, WI: Majorium Business Press, 2011.

Blythe, Jim. "Trade Fairs as Communication: A New Model." *Journal of Business and Industrial Marketing* 25, no. 1 (2010), pp. 57–62.

Brogan, Chris. *Social Media 101: Tactics and Tips to Develop Your Business Online.* Hoboken, NJ: Wiley, 2010.

Brynko, Barbara. "Hoover's Links Up with LinkedIn." *Information Today* 28, no. 2 (February 2011), p. 32.

Caramanico, Dan, Marie Maguire, and Dave Kurlan. *The Optimal Salesperson: Mastering the Mindset of Sales Superstars and Overachievers.* Great Falls, VA: LINX Corp., 2009.

Carter, Brian. *LinkedIn for Business: How Advertisers, Marketers and Salespeople Get Leads, Sales and Profits from LinkedIn.* Indianapolis, Indiana: Que, 2012.

Chase, Landy. "Value, Selling, and the Social Media Sales Revolution." *American Salesman* 56, no. 7 (July 2011), pp. 3–5.

Cole, Tony, and John Graham. "Prospecting—The Only 'A' Priority." *American Salesman* 57, no. 3 (March 2012), pp. 18–27.

Curtis, Joan C., and Barbara Giamanco. *The New Handshake: Sales Meets Social Media.* Westport, CT: Praeger, 2010.

Eggert, Andreas, and Murat Serdaroglu. "Exploring the Impact of Sales Technology on Salesperson Performance: A Task-Based Approach." *Journal of Personal Selling and Sales Management* 31, no. 2 (Spring 2011), pp. 169–85.

Gitomer, Jeffrey H. *Social BOOM!* FT Press, 2011.

Godson, Mark. *Relationship Marketing.* New York City: Oxford University Press, 2009.

Good, Bill. Hot *Prospects: The Proven Prospecting System to Ramp Up Your Sale.* New York City: Scribner, 2011.

Greenberg, Kevin. "Managing Social Customers for Profit." *CRM Magazine* 13, no. 8 (August 2009), p. 1

Handley, Ann. "Uncovering New Territories." *Entrepreneur* 40, no. 4 (April 2012), p. 62.

Jaffe, Joseph. *Flip the Funnel: How to Use Existing Customers to Gain New Ones.* Hoboken, NJ: Wiley, 2010.

Kahle, Dave. "7 Power-Packed Prospecting Pointers." *American Salesman* 57, no. 8 (August 2012), pp. 23–27.

Lager, M. "Looking to SCORE." *CRM Magazine* 13, no. 3 (March 2009), pp. 38–42.

Marshall, Greg W., William C. Moncrief, John M. Rudd, and Nick Lee. 2012. "Revolution in Sales: The Impact of Social Media and Related Technology on the Selling Environment." *Journal of Personal Selling and Sales Management* 32, no. 3 (2012), pp. 349–63.

Meyerson, Mitch. *Success Secrets of Social Media Marketing Superstars.* New York City: Entrepreneur Press, 2010.

Misner, Ivan, David Alexander, and Brian Hilliard. *Networking Like a Pro: Turning Contacts into Connections.* New York City: Entrepreneur Press, 2010.

Mitrega, Maciej, Sebastian Forkmann, Carla Ramos, and Stephan C. Henneberg. Networking Capability in Business Relationships—Concept and Scale Development. *Industrial Marketing Management* 41, no. 5 (July 2012), pp. 739–51.

Peppers & Rogers Group. "Turning Prospects into Profits: Using Lead Management Innovation to Win Customers" (white paper). Retrieved from http://www.peppersandrogers group.com, March 5, 2010.

Schep, Brad. *How to Find a Job on LinkedIn, Facebook, Twitter, MySpace, and Other Social Networks.* New York City: McGraw-Hill, 2009.

Stevens, Ruth P. *Maximizing Lead Generation: The Complete Guide for B2B Marketers.* Indianapolis, Indiana: Que, 2011.

Weinberg, Mike, and S. Anthony Iannarino. *New Sales. Simplified: The Essential Handbook for Prospecting and New Business Development.* New York City: AMACOM, 2012.

Wilson, David James. *Prospecting 101: The Ultimate Guide to Prospect Successfully to Super Grow Your Pipeline or Business.* Seattle, WA: CreateSpace, 2009.

Xu, Jun, and Mohammed Quaddus. *E-Business in the 21st Century: Realities, Challenges and Outlook.* Hackensack, NJ: World Scientific Publishing, 2010.

chapter 7

PLANNING THE SALES CALL

SOME QUESTIONS ANSWERED IN THIS CHAPTER ARE

- Why should salespeople plan their sales calls?
- What precall information is needed about the individual prospect and the prospect's organization?
- How can this information be obtained?
- What is involved in setting call objectives?
- Should more than one objective be set for each call?
- How can appointments be made effectively and efficiently?

2

PART

PROFILE

PROFILE My name is Brett Georgulis, and I graduated from Texas State University–San Marcos in 2011 with a bachelor's degree in marketing and a master's degree in business administration. My experience in "Professional Selling," taught by Mrs. Vicki West, has impacted my life more than any other course. "Professional Selling" provided an in-your-face perspective of how to prepare yourself for nearly any business situation, no matter what field you entered. Throughout the course work were real-world scenarios that reinforced textbook and lecture material, including role play sales calls, mock sales presentations, and interactive interview preparation. The knowledge and experienced I gained from the professional selling class has benefited me during my first year as a sales rep for 3M's Electrical Markets Division.

With a broad and diverse end-user and distributor client base encompassing an endless array of needs, sales call preplanning is an absolute must for me to be successful. There are several things to consider when planning for a sales call. Possibly the most important part of my planning is to know my audience and understand their needs. Gathering information about personality, attitude, relationships, past decisions, and current business environment, among other information, helps me tailor my sales approach and know what to say in any given situation. But just as important, this information helps me know what not to say. As the information about my customer is gathered, I am able to get a clearer view of what his or her needs are.

Just as important as understanding you audience and their needs is understanding what you want to accomplish while making the call. Using the information collected, I create call objectives to help me organize what goals I want to accomplish. Creating these call objectives keeps me on track and uses the time I have with the customer in the most efficient and effective way possible. These objectives must be specific, measurable, and attainable. Do they have to be extravagant? No. For example, if I am meeting a job site superintendent for the first time, my primary goal may be to simply introduce myself, gain an understanding of the project, and secure a second call. On a large construction project, it may be the seventh or eighth call, when a number of factors align, that the customer has all the information they need to be comfortable in their purchasing decision.

Because of the nature of my job with 3M, I could be making a pitch in an office setting, on a construction site to a job foreman, or at a trade show in a distributor warehouse. In each situation, planning the sales call helps me to be as prepared as possible in any given situation.

Visit our Web site at:
www.mmm.com/electrical

Exhibit 7.1
A Flow Diagram of the
Planning Process

| Gathering information about the prospect and firm | Setting objectives for the call | Making an appointment |

WHY PLAN THE SALES CALL?

Successful salespeople know that advance planning of the sales call is essential to achieve in selling. The salesperson should remember that the buyer's time is valuable. Without planning the sales call, a salesperson may cover material in which the buyer has no interest, try to obtain an order even though that is an unrealistic expectation for this sales call, or strike off into areas that veer from what the buyer needs to hear. The results are wasted time and an annoyed prospect. However, by having a clear plan for the call, the salesperson more likely will not only obtain commitment but also win the buyer's respect and confidence.

Salespeople should also remember the value of their own time. Proper planning helps them meet their call objectives efficiently and effectively. They then have more time to make additional calls, conduct research on customers, fill out company reports, and complete other necessary tasks. The result is better territory management. (See Chapter 15 for more discussion of time and territory management.)

Of course planning must fit into the salesperson's goals for the account. Some accounts have greater strategic importance and thus require more planning. (See Chapter 13 for a discussion of the types of relationships that a seller can have with a buyer and Chapter 15 about classifying accounts and prospects.) Accounts with which a firm is partnering obviously need the most planning, whereas smaller accounts may warrant less planning. Also, salespeople must not make planning an end in itself and a way to avoid actually making calls. Exhibit 7.1 shows how the concepts in this chapter are related.

OBTAINING PRECALL INFORMATION

Often the difference between making and not making a sale depends on the amount of homework the salesperson does before making a call. The more information the salesperson has about the prospect, the higher the probability of meeting the prospect's needs and developing a long-term relationship. However, the salesperson must be aware of the costs involved in collecting information. At some point, the time and effort put into collecting information become greater than the benefits obtained. And of course, for some cold calls, there will be little if any precall information collected.

Clearly a salesperson who has been calling regularly on a prospect or customer may not need to collect a lot of additional information; records and notes from prior calls may be adequate to prepare for the sales call. The same holds true for a new salesperson if the previous one kept good records. But beware! In this fast-paced world, things are changing every day. Consider the following dialogue:

SALESPERSON [*walking up to the receptionist of one of his best customers*]: Hello, Jim. I'm here

Gathering information from individuals in the prospect's firm before making a call on the prospect is often a wise investment of time.

to see Toby. I have some information I promised to share with her about our new manufacturing process. She was pretty excited about seeing it!

RECEPTIONIST [*looking tired*]: Sorry, Jeff. Toby was transferred last week to our Toronto plant. Haven't you heard about our latest reorganization? Just went into effect two weeks ago. I'm still trying to figure it out. It seems that all our engineering people are moving to the Toronto site.

The key: Don't assume that your knowledge about the account is automatically up to date.

Of course, before you make an initial call on an important prospect, you will often expend considerable effort in collecting precall information about both the individual prospect and the prospect's company. Don't expect this information gathering to be quick, easy, or cheap.

It is important to learn and maintain current knowledge about both the prospect as an individual and his or her firm. The sections that follow examine these areas more closely. Of course the salesperson should keep in mind privacy concerns, as related in Chapter 2.

THE PROSPECT/CUSTOMER AS AN INDIVIDUAL

Salespeople should attempt to learn the following types of information about a prospect or a customer:

Personal (Some of This Information Can Be Confidential)

- Name (including pronunciation).
- Family status.
- Education.
- Aspirations.
- Interests (such as hobbies) and disinterests.
- Social style (driver or another category—see Chapter 5).

Attitudes

- Toward salespeople.
- Toward your company.
- Toward your product.

Relationships

- Formal reporting relationships.
- Important reference groups and group norms.
- Bonds that the prospect has already formed with other salespeople.

Evaluation of Products/Services

- Product attributes that are important.
- Product evaluation process (see Chapter 3 for details).

THE PROSPECT'S/CUSTOMER'S ORGANIZATION

Information about the prospect's or customer's company obviously helps the salesperson understand the customer's environment. This type of information lets the salesperson identify problem areas more quickly and respond accordingly.

For example, in a modified rebuy situation, it would not be necessary to educate the prospect about general features common to the product class as a whole. Using the prospect's valuable time by covering material he or she already knows is minimized. Information like the following about the prospect's organization would be helpful:

Demographics

- Type of organization (manufacturing, wholesaling, retailing).
- Size; number of locations.
- Products and services offered.
- Financial position and its future.
- Overall culture of the organization (risk averse, highest ethical standards, forward thinking).

Prospect's Customers

- Types (consumers, retailers, wholesalers).
- Benefits they seek from the prospect's products and services.

Prospect's Competitors

- Who they are.
- How they differ in their business approaches.
- Prospect's strategic position in the industry (dominant, strong, weak).

Historical Buying Patterns

- Amount purchased in the product category.
- Sole supplier or multiple suppliers. Why?
- Reason for buying from present suppliers.
- Level of satisfaction with suppliers.
- Reasons for any dissatisfaction with suppliers or products currently purchased.

Current Buying Situation

- Type of buying process (new task, straight rebuy, or modified rebuy—see Chapter 3).
- Strengths and weaknesses of potential competitors.

People Involved in the Purchase Decision

- How they fit into the formal and informal organizational structure.
- Their roles in this decision (gatekeeper, influencer, or the like).
- Who is most influential.
- Any **influential adversaries** (carry great influence but are opposed to us)?
- Current problems the organization faces.
- Stage in the buying cycle.

Policies and Procedures

- About salespeople.
- About sales visits.
- About purchasing and contracts.

SOURCES OF INFORMATION

Gathering all the information listed in the preceding sections for every prospect and organization is initially impossible. The goal is to gather what is both possible and profitable. Remember, your time is valuable! Also, you don't want to fall into the trap sometimes referred to as **analysis paralysis,** which can occur if you prefer to spend practically all your time analyzing situations and finding information instead of making sales calls. Salespeople must strike a proper balance between time spent in acquiring information and time spent making calls. The Marine Corps teaches what it calls the 70 percent solution: If you've got 70 percent of the information, have done 70 percent of the analysis, and feel 70 percent confident, then act!

It is important to gather useful information—not just piles of trivial facts about a prospect, as "From the Buyer's Seat 7.1" illustrates. In addition, salespeople need to check the quality of any data gathered rather than assuming they are good. Salespeople must also be concerned about information overload, which can be detrimental to their jobs.

RESOURCES WITHIN YOUR COMPANY

One of the best sources of information can be the records in your own company, especially if your firm has developed a sophisticated CRM database, as described in Chapter 6.[1] The most useful databases include (in addition to standard demographic information) information about any direct inquiries made by the prospect (from direct mail inquiries, telemarketing, online requests, social media contact, or the like), a sales history for the firm, whether anyone from your company has called on the prospect, and the results of any sales meetings.

Firms are devising many ways to keep the field sales force well informed. Some are using **sales portals:** online databases that include many sources of information in one place. This information can include items like account data, competitor intelligence, and news about the company, the industry, and the economy. All the salesperson has to do is use a single log-on to access all this information. For example, Delta Airlines salespeople can log into their company's portal and quickly and easily access key insights about their business customers.

Even if your firm doesn't have such a database, you should try to gather information about your prospect. For example, wouldn't it be nice to find out before, as opposed to during, a sales call that the prospect used to be a big customer of your firm but quit for some reason?

From the BUYER'S SEAT

PLAN BEFORE SELLING ME

I'm a buyer for ACME Tools. For me personally, I receive many sales calls each and every day, and at the end of the week it is not uncommon for a majority of them to blend together in my mind. Those that stand out typically have put time and effort into the plans of their sales call. I find that the amount of time salespeople dedicate in preparation of a sales call is a good indicator as to how they will handle my account if we give them our business.

Knowing background information about my company is a great way to stand out against competitors, but knowing who they are calling on is also going to help give them the upper hand. For salespeople to find information about me as a buyer, I would recommend they look at our Web site and my social media sites, whether that be LinkedIn to find my professional past or Facebook to see some things that interest me other than work. Also, salespeople can visit some of our brick-and-mortar locations

and ask around to figure out things that may be beneficial when calling on me.

It is very easy to tell when a salesperson has been on our Web site, researched our Facebook page, and know who exactly our target demographic is. As a buyer, it can be very frustrating when a salesperson comes to me pitching a product that is nowhere near our target demographic. For example, all too often during a phone call from a prospective salesperson, I will give her a brief history of the company and ask her to send me some samples of the products or services that the company can provide us with. When the samples arrive, I see that they in no way match the needs of our organization. So, please, salesperson, do your homework before calling on me!

Source: James Nickerson, ACME Tools; all names and titles have been changed on request; used with permission.

For important sales, you may well be working with a sales team that interacts with a prospect (a topic more fully addressed in Chapter 16). This team, sometimes called a **selling center,** consists of all the people in the selling organization who participate in a selling opportunity. Members of the team may be able to provide or help you secure needed information.

THE INTERNET

A first place to look for information would be the prospect company's own Web page. It is amazing what you can find on company Web pages.

Don't forget to use social media like LinkedIn and Facebook to learn more about prospects, as described in Chapter 6. And there are many business information providers online, like InsideView, Pipl.com, and ZoomInfo, that salespeople can use to extract information about companies and people from million of published sources. Some of this information is free, and some requires payment for more exact information.

SECRETARIES AND RECEPTIONISTS

ethics

Secretaries and receptionists in the prospect's firm usually are a rich source of information. Be courteous, however, because secretaries and receptionists are accustomed to having salespeople pry for all sorts of free information. Prioritize your questions and provide justification for asking them. Above all, treat secretaries and receptionists with genuine respect. Dawn Hedges, a Zimmer salesperson who sells surgical joint replacements, has built tremendous relationships with the receptionists she calls on. For example, she knows one receptionist who doesn't let Dawn's competitors in to see the doctors. And the receptionist collects any brochures left with her by competitors and then calls Dawn and gives her the information.[2]

NONCOMPETING SALESPEOPLE

Another source for precall information is noncompeting salespeople. In fact, one of the best sources of information is the prospect's own salespeople because they empathize with your situation.

TRADITIONAL SECONDARY SOURCES

Traditional secondary data sources can also be helpful. Firms such as Standard & Poor's, Hoover's, and Moody's publish a number of informative documents in print and online that are available in many public libraries. These sources can help answer questions about brand names, key contacts, historical information, the current situation and outlook for the firm and the industry, location of plants and distribution centers, market shares, and so on.

THE PROSPECT

Much information can be gleaned directly from the prospect. However, don't expect prospects to sit down and answer any and all questions you might have, especially for topics where the information is fairly easy to get (like what products the prospect makes or sells). Prospects don't have time to fill you in on all the details of their business. If you don't know the basics, many prospects will justifiably refuse to deal with you.

It is also worth mentioning that just as you are gathering information about the prospect prior to a meeting, the prospect often does collect information about you. Even before the sale your prospect can request price quotes via e-mail. He or she can also view your Web page as well as your competitors' Web pages. And the prospect can easily chat with colleagues and read about you on newsgroups, blogs, and social media sites to learn about you and your firm. Any salesperson who doesn't understand these realities won't be prepared for the kinds of questions a prospect might ask or for comments a prospect might make.

OTHER SOURCES

Many other sources can provide information. Some information may have been gleaned at a trade show the prospect attended. Much information will be in the lists and directories from which the prospect's name came. For example, a center of influence will often be able to provide information to a Merrill Lynch financial advisor about his friends. Your current customers can often provide information about new clients. Occasionally a prospect will be important enough to warrant hiring an outside consultant to collect information, especially if you are gathering precall information for international selling. Although some information about foreign companies is available, much will not be obtainable. Salespeople in the United States are often amazed at the lack of information about foreign companies. Two good sources are the U.S. government's export portal and the U.S. Commercial Service market research library.

SETTING CALL OBJECTIVES

The most important step in planning is to set objectives for the call. Merely stating the objective "I want to make a sale" or "to tell her about my product" will not suffice. The customer's decision-making process (see Chapter 3) involves many steps, and salespeople need to undertake many activities as they guide customers through the process.

Yet, as Neil Rackham, an internationally respected sales researcher, notes, "It's astonishing how rarely salespeople set themselves call objectives of any kind—let alone effective ones. Although most books on selling emphasize the importance of clear call objectives, it's rare to see these exhortations turned into practice."[3] Why? Probably because many salespeople want to start doing something instead of "wasting time" planning. But without a plan, they actually increase their chances of wasting time.

As a first step in setting objectives, the salesperson should review what has been learned from precall information gathering. Any call objectives should be based on the results of this review. Also, the seller must keep in mind the relationship the firm wishes to have with the prospect. Not all prospects will or should become strategic partners with the seller's firm. Call objectives should not be created in a vacuum. They should be developed while taking into account the firm's goals, the sales team's goals, and the salesperson's goals. Regardless of the type of goal you are referring to, the old adage is true: If you don't know where you're going, you may wind up somewhere else.

In their well-received sales training books about strategic selling, Miller and Heiman stress the importance of sales call planning being related to the firm's strategic goals for the account.[4] This important topic is covered in Chapter 15. For now, realize that call objectives are based on strategic decisions about the account.

CRITERIA FOR EFFECTIVE OBJECTIVES

All objectives should be specific, realistic, and measurable. A call objective that meets only one or two of these criteria will be an ineffective guide for the salesperson. We now examine each criterion in more detail.

An objective must be specific to be effective. It should state precisely what the salesperson hopes to accomplish, what the objective targets are, and any other details (suggested order quantity, suggested dates for future meetings, length of time needed for a follow-up survey, or the like). Specific objectives help the salesperson avoid "shooting from the hip" during the presentation and perhaps moving the prospect along too rapidly or too slowly.

Objectives must also be realistic. Inexperienced salespeople often have unrealistic expectations about the prospect's or customer's response in the sales call. For example, if Kia Motors currently uses Sony radios in all of its models, a Philips salesperson who expects Kia to change over to Philips radios in the first few sales calls has an unrealistic objective. It is important for sellers to plan objectives for a call that can be accomplished within the time allocated for that sales call. That doesn't mean the objectives should be easy. In reality, challenging but reachable goals tend to lead to better performance.

For objectives to be realistic, the salesperson needs to consider factors such as cultural influences. For example, some firms have an extremely conservative corporate culture. Creating change in such a culture is time consuming and often frustrating for the seller. The national culture is important in selling to international prospects. When selling to Arab or Japanese businesses, salespeople should plan to spend at least several meetings getting to know the other party. Developing relationships with Chinese businesspeople requires a great deal of entertaining. Selling in Russia is often slowed because of bureaucracy and incredible amounts of red tape. As these examples illustrate, culture is an important consideration in attempts to set realistic call objectives.

Finally, call objectives must be measurable so salespeople can objectively evaluate each sales call at its conclusion and determine whether the objectives were met. This suggests they should be written down. If a salesperson's stated objective is to get acquainted with the prospect or to establish rapport, how can the salesperson assess whether this goal was achieved? How can someone measure "getting acquainted"? To what extent would the salesperson have to be acquainted with the prospect to know that he or she achieved the sales call objective? A more measurable sales call objective (as well as a more specific and realistic one) is something like the following: to get acquainted with the prospect by learning which clubs or organizations she or he belongs to, which sports the prospect follows, what his or her professional background is, and how long the prospect has held the current position. With this revised call objective, a salesperson can easily determine whether the objective was reached.

A simple way to help ensure that objectives are measurable is to set objectives that require a buyer's response. For example, achievement of the following objective is easy to measure: to make a follow-up appointment with the buyer.

Successful salespeople in almost every industry have learned the importance of setting proper call objectives. Pharmaceutical salespeople for Novartis set clear objectives for each sales call they make to a physician. Then they lay out a series of objectives for subsequent calls so they know exactly what they hope to accomplish over the next several visits. One industrial products sales manager recommends that her salespeople keep their call objectives in view while they are on the sales call, helping them focus on the true goals of the sales call. Both these examples share a common theme: The salesperson needs to set specific, realistic, measurable call objectives. Exhibit 7.2 lists examples of call objectives that meet these criteria.

Some trainers use the acronym SMART to help salespeople remember how to set proper call objections. SMART suggests that call objectives should be specific, measurable, and achievable but realistic and time based.

SETTING MORE THAN ONE CALL OBJECTIVE

Salespeople have learned the importance of setting multiple objectives for a sales call. Not only do they set a **primary call objective** (the actual goal they hope to achieve) before each sales call; they also set a **minimum call objective** (the

Exhibit 7.2
Examples of Call Objectives

Objectives Related to the Process Leading Up to the Sale

- To have the prospect agree to come to the Atlanta branch office sometime during the next two weeks for a hands-on demonstration of the copier.
- To set up another appointment for one week from now, when the buyer will allow me to do a complete survey of her printing needs.
- To inform the doctor of the revolutionary anticlotting mechanism that has been incorporated into our new drug and have her agree to read the pamphlet I will leave.
- To have the buyer agree to pass my information along to the buying committee with his endorsement of my proposal.
- To have the prospect agree to call several references that I will provide to develop further confidence and trust in my office-cleaning business.
- To have the prospect agree on the first point (of our four-point program) and schedule another meeting in two days to discuss the second point.
- To have the prospect initiate the necessary paperwork to allow us to be considered as a future vendor.

Objectives Related to Consummating the Sale

- To have the prospect sign an order for 100 pairs of Levi's jeans.
- To schedule a co-op newspaper advertising program to be implemented in the next month.
- To have the prospect agree to use our brand of computer paper for a trial period of one month.
- To have the retailer agree to allow us space for an end-of-aisle display for the summer promotion of Raid insect repellent.

Even a salesperson who fails to achieve the primary call objective will be encouraged to at least achieve the minimum call objective.

minimum they hope to achieve) because they realize the call may not go exactly as planned (the prospect may be called away or the salesperson may not have all the necessary facts).[5] On the other hand, the call may go better than the salesperson originally thought it would. Thus, although rarely achieved, an **optimistic call objective** (the most optimistic outcome the salesperson thinks could occur) is also set. The optimistic call objective will probably relate to what the salesperson hopes to accomplish for the account over the long term (that is, the account objectives—see Chapter 15).

The primary call objective, for example, of a Nestlé rep might be to secure an order from a grocer for 10 cases of Nestlé Morsels for an upcoming coupon promotion. That is what the seller realistically hopes to accomplish in the call. A minimum call objective could be to sell at least 5 cases of Morsels, whereas an optimistic call objective would be to sell 20 cases, set up an end-of-aisle display, and secure a retail promotional price of $5.68.

Multiple call objectives have many benefits. First, they help take away the salesperson's fear of failure because most salespeople can achieve at least their stated minimum objective. Second, multiple objectives tend to be self-correcting. Salespeople who always reach their optimum objective realize they are probably setting their sights too low. On the other hand, if they rarely meet even their minimum objective, they probably are setting their goals too high.

It is possible to have more than one primary call objective for a single call. For example, several primary objectives a salesperson might hope to accomplish in a single meeting are to sell one unit, be introduced to one other member of the buying center, and have the prospect agree to send along a packet of information to an executive. In this example, if the salesperson genuinely hopes and expects to achieve all three objectives in the next meeting, they will all be considered primary call objectives. To aid in planning the call, some trainers suggest that the salesperson further prioritize these primary objectives into two groups: The most important primary objective is called the primary call objective, whereas the remaining ones become **secondary call objectives.** So, in this example, if selling the product is the most important thing to accomplish in the next meeting, the objectives will be as follows:

Primary call objective	Sell one unit.
Secondary call objectives	Be introduced to one other member of the buying center.
	Have the prospect agree to send along a packet of information to an executive.

SETTING OBJECTIVES FOR SEVERAL CALLS

By developing a series of specific objectives for future calls, the salesperson can develop a comprehensive strategy for the prospect or customer. This approach is especially important in a partnering relationship. To illustrate the use of multiple call objectives, Exhibit 7.3 gives a set of call objectives for visits over a period of time. The left side of the exhibit contains the long-term plan and each call objective that the Samsung salesperson developed for Johnson Electronics. Note the logical strategy for introducing the new product, the F104 DVD player. The right side of Exhibit 7.3 shows the actual call results.

The salesperson was not always 100 percent successful in achieving the call objectives. Thus, several subsequent objectives needed to be modified. For example, because the meeting on October 10 resulted in the buyer dropping F92 DVD

Exhibit 7.3

Multiple Call Objectives of a Samsung Salesperson Selling to Johnson Electronics

Overall Plan Developed on Oct. 1		Actual Call Results	
Expected Date of the Call	Call Objective	Date of Call	Call Results
Oct. 10	Secure normal repeat orders on F88 and F92. Increase normal repeat order of F100 DVD player from three to five units. Provide product information for new DVD product F104.	Oct. 10	Obtained normal order of F88. Steve decided to drop F92 (refused to give a good reason). Purchased only four F100 players. Seemed responsive to F104 but needs a point-of-purchase (POP) display.
Oct. 17	Erect a front-counter POP display for F104 and secure a trial order of two units.	Oct. 18	Steve was out. His assistant didn't like the POP (thought it was too large!). Refused to use POP. Did order one F104. Told me about several complaints with F100.
Nov. 10	Secure normal repeat orders for F88, F92, and F100. Schedule one co-op newspaper ad for the next 30 days featuring F104. Secure an order for F104s.	Nov. 8	Obtained normal orders. Steve agreed to co-op ad but bought only five F104s. Thinks the margins are too low.
Nov. 17	Secure normal repeat orders of F88, F92, and F100. Secure an order for F104s.	Nov. 18	Obtained normal order on F88, but Steve refused to reorder F100. Claimed the competitor product (Sony) is selling much better. Obtained an order of 15 units of F104.

players, the call objectives on November 10 and November 17 need to reflect that Johnson Electronics no longer carries the F92 DVD players. The seller may also want to add a call objective for October 17: to discuss more about the situation with the F92 (because of the outcome of the October 10 meeting) and perhaps try to reintroduce it. This example illustrates the importance of keeping good records, making any necessary adjustments in the long-term call objectives, and then preparing for the next sales call. One sales vice president for a large sales force has some specific advice about setting multiple call objectives:

> The primary objective of the first session is to have another chance to visit. What this allows you to do is have your standards relatively low because you are trying to build a long-term relationship. You should be very sensitive to an opportunity to establish a second visit. What you want to do is identify aspects of the business conversation that require follow-up and make note of them. . . . The key is not the first visit . . . it is the second, the third, the twenty-second visit.[6]

Some industries typically have a long interval between when a prospect is first visited and when an actual sale is consummated. If so, this factor needs to be considered when setting up multiple call objectives and may imply that others get involved in the selling cycle. For example, the typical sale of a Kodak Image Sensor scanner (an image sensor for automated inspection applications in industrial plants) could take several years to close. After having its field sales force demonstrate the image-sensing scanner, the company can use inside sales reps (see Chapter 1 for a description of inside salespeople) to keep the prospects updated in a fashion that is consistent with the prospects' buying time frames. Kodak may also send out newsletters several times a year to prospects. It is important for salespeople to consider the company's other promotional efforts when developing multiple call objectives for a prospect.

When setting multiple call objectives, the salesperson should obviously consider whom to call on in upcoming meetings. Although it seems obvious that the decision maker (who is often a middle manager for many products and services) should be included in those calls, visiting briefly with senior-level managers may also make sense. But what information would you share with the CEO, for example? As discussed in Chapter 1, the answer is the **customer value proposition:** a written statement (usually one or two sentences) that clearly states how purchasing your product or service can help solve the customer's perceived business issue ("BI"). Further, the CVP focuses on what an individual manager needs to address and resolve to be able to better contribute to overall company objectives. The customer value proposition will be more fully discussed in Chapter 9 and will include numerous examples. Frequently the problem needing assistance involves a significant impediment to the firm's revenues and profits. Four common "BI's" include the following:[7]

- Increase revenue, market share, and shareholder value
- Increase efficiency and productivity
- Manage costs
- Control quality and reliability

Appointments increase the chances of seeing the right person and having uninterrupted time with the prospect.

Often a very important consideration is the success of the individual who is your contact within the customer's firm. And there needs to be a struggle (distinct emotion) associated with it.

BUYERS ARE SETTING GOALS ALSO

Salespeople must understand that buyers may also be setting objectives for the salesperson's sales call. These objectives are based on perceptions of how the salesperson's product or service can add value, as described in Chapters 1 and 3. Salespeople's job is to discover what customers value and then find ways to improve customer value relative to their own products or services.

What are some things that buyers look for to increase value? Purchasing managers continually point to the following areas: on-time delivery, products that are exactly to specifications, competitive pricing, proper packaging/paperwork, technical support/service, quality of sales calls, level of technological innovation, and good emergency response. Thus, sellers can expect that buyers may set goals for sales calls in these areas.

MAKING AN APPOINTMENT

After gathering precall information and setting objectives, the salesperson's next step is generally to make an appointment. Many sales managers insist that their salespeople make appointments before calling on prospects or customers. Appointments dignify the salesperson and help get the sales process off to a good start by putting the salesperson and the prospect on the same level—equal participants in a legitimate needs solution process. Appointments also increase the chances of seeing the right person and having uninterrupted time with the prospect.

Experienced sales representatives use different contact methods for different customers. It's also important to point out that attitude (and the salesperson's mood) can have a tremendous impact on success in making appointments. This section describes how to see the right person at the right time and the right place, how to interact with gatekeepers, and how to gain an appointment.

THE RIGHT PERSON

Some experts emphasize the importance of going right to the top and making the first call on the highest-level decision maker. After carefully studying more than 35,000 sales calls, Neil Rackham offers a radically different view.[8] His research suggests that a salesperson should initially try to call on the **focus of receptivity**—the person who will listen receptively and give the seller needed valuable information. Note that this person may not be the decision maker or the one who understands all of the firm's problems. In fact, this person might not even be in the buying center. (See Chapter 3 for details about various people who serve as buying center members.) But this person will talk to the salesperson and provide information.

The focus of receptivity, according to the research, will then lead the salesperson to the **focus of dissatisfaction:** the person who is most likely to perceive problems and dissatisfactions. Finally, the focus of dissatisfaction leads to the **focus of power:** the person who can approve, prevent, and/or influence action. Getting to the focus of power too quickly can lead to disaster because the seller has not yet built a relationship and does not really know the buyer's needs. In summary, Rackham notes, "There's a superstition in selling that the sooner you can get to the decision maker the better. Effective selling, so it's said, is going straight to the focus of power. That's a questionable belief."[9]

Recent research has indicated that a salesperson should work with specific types of individuals because they are better at generating consensus in the buying firm.[10] These include "go-getters," those who are always on the lookout for good ideas; "teachers," those who love to share insights and ideas with others in the firm; and "skeptics," those who tend to be cautious and generally slow down the adoption of new processes. These three groups, collectively called "mobilizers," will question, be skeptical, yet help the firm move in the right direction when convinced.

Often someone needs to introduce you to the decision maker, especially in some cultures. For example, to do business with companies in Mideast countries, it is often necessary to have introductions by trusted individuals. Former senators, ambassadors, and even celebrities provide this role.

Frequently in industrial selling situations, as Chapter 3 described, no single person has the sole authority to buy a product because it is a team buying decision. For example, a forklift sales representative for Clarke may have to see the safety engineer, the methods engineer, the materials-handling engineer, and the general superintendent before selling the product to a manufacturing company. In this case the salesperson should usually try to arrange a meeting with the entire group as well as with each individual.

THE RIGHT TIME

There is little agreement on the subject of the best time for a sales interview; obviously the most opportune time to call will vary by customer and type of selling. The salesperson who calls on wholesale grocers, for example, may find from experience that the best times to call are from 9 a.m. to 11 a.m. and from 1:30 p.m.

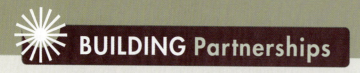

MAKE SURE YOU ACTUALLY MEET WHERE YOU CLAIMED TO MEET

When my brother was a doctor, he once told me about a pharmaceutical representative who worked for a large drug company that had provided their sales representatives with GMC Yukons, complete with the OnStar navigation system. What the reps didn't know was that the company was using OnStar to keep track of vehicle locations during work hours. Several salespeople were terminated when the vehicle OnStar report did not sync with the rep's call reports. Other reps felt betrayed by this and began plotting ways to beat the system, such as parking the vehicles at a hospital and having someone else pick them up in a noncompany car or taking the vehicle to a dealership for servicing so as to justify not using it.

I later asked a pharmaceutical sales rep friend how likely she thought this was. She told me it wouldn't surprise her at all, pointing out that "Big Pharma is equal to Big Brother, and as companies consolidate, they are all becoming Big Pharma." She thought it was more likely among companies that provide reps with drug samples than those that don't or if a company was looking to fire someone; they could see if the car even left the driveway that week. She explained that a lot of firms that use samples also typically provide reps with iPads or other handheld devices and require doctor signatures and time/date stamps to verify when and where the reps are. She added that a friend of hers works for a company that checks company gas cards to ensure that sales reps are getting gas within assigned territories as a way of verifying that the vehicle is not driven outside of its designated area.

She even shared that once when she worked for a "Big Pharma" company and was picking up her new company vehicle, she "called ahead to the dealership and told them that if there was a GPS tracking device in the car, I'd pay whatever it took to disable it."

Source: John E. Cicala, assistant professor, Texas A&M University, Kingsville, personal correspondence, used with permission.

to 3:30 p.m. A hospital rep, on the other hand, may discover that the most productive calls on surgeons are made between 8:30 a.m. and 10 a.m. and after 4 p.m. Car washes are busiest in the winter months, with spring being the second-busiest time of year. For most types of selling, the best hours of the day are from approximately 9 a.m. to 11:30 a.m. and from 1:30 p.m. to 4 p.m. For companies that call on Web-generated leads, the best days are Wednesdays and Thursdays between 4 p.m. and 6 p.m. and as soon as possible after the lead is generated.[11]

THE RIGHT PLACE

Meetings can occur just about anywhere, including by video on the Internet. The sales call should take place in an environment conducive to doing business. Such is not always the case, however. For example, some salespeople still take customers to topless bars. In addition to distractions, topless bars present a number of problems for the salesperson who uses them to achieve sales. For example, is it ethical to gain business by using such tactics? Also, once a buyer has purchased on the basis of this entertainment, chances are the seller will have to keep it up or lose the customer. Salespeople should also understand that their companies do care about where they meet a client and are tracking that information for a number of purposes, as "Building Partnerships 7.1" illustrates.

"Sales Technology 7.1" provides the experience of one company that used online Webcasting to its advantage.

Videoconferencing—meetings in which people are not physically present in one location but are connected via voice and video—is growing in usage. In a variant on videoconferencing, called **Webcasting** or **virtual sales calls,** the meeting

SALES Technology

USING WEBEX TO SELL EDUCATIONAL PRODUCTS

CEV Multimedia creates educational tools (e.g., DVDs, PowerPoint presentations, lesson plans, activities, and assessments) for students from junior high school through college. The company needed a way to showcase its more than 1,800 titles to teachers and principals, and with a geographically disbursed sales force, this was quite a challenge.

The solution is to demonstrate their products using WebEx. Through online video sales calls, salespeople are able to demonstrate videos, graphics, and all other elements of their titles. CEV Multimedia also uses WebEx to provide customer support and train teachers if they are having trouble with the materials.

The result has been that salespeople have reached more customers and increased the volume of prospects greatly. WebEx has also allowed CEV to reach out to a wider range of schools, including smaller, sometimes remote school districts. The technology has reduced travel expenses and avoided the need to hire additional salespeople. Finally, the technology has made it easier for salespeople to collaborate between themselves, resulting in efficiencies and a greater sense of community.

Sources: http://www.cevmultimedia.com and http://www.webex.com/includes/documents/case-studies/cev-multimedia.pdf.

is broadcast over the Internet.[12] For example, due to downsizing, emWare, Inc., has only eight salespeople. According to Michael Nelson, CEO of emWare, the use of virtual sales calls is now necessary and is actually quite successful. Salespeople should learn how to plan for such meetings. One key is to carefully plan all technical elements of the presentation and to rehearse them as much as possible. (Chapter 9 provides more insight into practicing and avoiding problems.)

Videoconferencing makes it easy for a U.S. salesperson to make a presentation in Germany.

CULTIVATING RELATIONSHIPS WITH SUBORDINATES

Busy executives usually have one or more subordinates who plan and schedule interviews for them. These **screens** (or **barriers,** as salespeople sometimes call them) often make seeing the boss difficult. These screens can also take on the role of gatekeepers for the buying center (Chapter 3 discusses gatekeepers).

Sales strategists have identified several ways to interact with a screen:

- The salesperson can work "through the screen." The seller has to convince the gatekeeper that a meeting with the boss is in the boss's best interests.

- The salesperson can go "over the screen." While talking to the screen, the seller drops names of people higher up in the organization. The screen may allow the seller in to see the boss right away for fear of getting into trouble.

- The salesperson can go "under the screen" by trying to make contact with the prospect before or after the screen gets to work (or while the screen is taking a coffee break). This is a strategy that can easily backfire. For example, Oracle learned, the hard way, the impact of having pushy, aggressive salespeople who constantly bypassed screens and formal committees. The result was great customer dissatisfaction.

Salespeople should work to achieve friendly relationships with the prospect's subordinates.

TELEPHONING FOR APPOINTMENTS

The telephone is most often used to make an initial appointment. Salespeople can save many hours by phoning, or having others phone for them, to make appointments. Chapter 4 provided many insights on how to use the phone effectively and suggested a way to gain an appointment with a prospect.

The goal of the telephone call is to make an appointment, not to sell the product or service. Exhibit 7.4 shows appropriate responses to common objections that Xerox copier salespeople encounter when making appointments. Salespeople need to anticipate objections and decide exactly how to respond, as Chapter 10 will more fully discuss.

ADDITIONAL PLANNING

A successful salesperson thinks ahead to the meeting that will occur and plans accordingly. For example, salespeople should plan how they intend to make a good first impression and build credibility during the call. It is also important to plan how to further uncover the customer's needs and strengthen the presentation. Salespeople should anticipate the questions and concerns the prospect may raise and plan to answer them helpfully. These issues are discussed in detail in the next several chapters. For now, be aware that these activities should be planned before the meeting begins.

Exhibit 7.4
Responses to Objections concerning Appointments

Objection from a Secretary	Response
I'm sorry, but Mr. Wilkes is busy now.	What I have to say will take only a few minutes. Should I call back in a half hour, or would you suggest I set up an appointment?
We already have a copier.	That's fine. I want to talk to Mr. Wilkes about our new paper flow system design for companies like yours.
I take care of all the copying.	That's fine, but I'm here to present what Xerox has to offer for a complete paper flow system that integrates data transmission, report generation, and copiers. I'd like to speak to Mr. Wilkes about this total service.

Objection from the Prospect	Response
Can't you mail the information to me?	Yes, I could. But everyone's situation is different, Mr. Wilkes, and our systems are individually tailored to meet the needs of each customer. Now . . . [benefit statement and repeat request for appointment].
Well, what is it you want to talk about?	It's difficult to explain the system over the telephone. In 15 minutes, I can demonstrate the savings you get from the system.
You'd just be wasting your time. I'm not interested.	The general objection is hiding a specific objection. The salesperson needs to probe for the specific objection: Do you say that because you don't copy many documents?
We had a Xerox copier once and didn't like it.	Probe for the specific reason of dissatisfaction and have a reply, but don't go too far. The objective is to get an appointment, not sell a copier.

Source: Courtesy of Xerox Corporation. Used by permission.

Before making the sales call, it is important to practice. How long should a rep spend practicing? Longer than many would think. As Mark Twain wrote, "It usually takes more than three weeks to prepare a good impromptu speech." Some have even suggested that for very important presentatons, the seller spend 30 minutes preparing and practicing for each minute of presentation time. While often broken, the rule does indicate the importance of planning and practicing the presentation. Of course the time spent in practicing would depend on how much time the seller has and on the goals of the presentation.

One other thing that salespeople do is **seeding**—that is, sending the customer important and useful information. For example, a rep can constantly search newspapers, blogs, and social media postings for material that may be useful for a prospect. This material is sent to the prospect with a note saying something like, "Jim, I thought you would find this article useful!" The material does not include the selling firm's catalogs, brochures, pricing, and so on. Rather, it is good, useful information that will help the prospect's business. The result? The buyer views the seller as someone trying to be truly helpful and as someone who really understands the buyer's business.

SELLING YOURSELF

The information learned about planning the sales call can be applied to more than just business settings. Using the same approach in your personal life can pay dividends, regardless if the decision you are making is large or small. For example, when purchasing a new car, you should use the same concepts about planning before you visit a dealership. Most people probably do this without thinking. You start by obtaining precall information about the dealerships you will visit and about the type of vehicle that you want to purchase. Using the Internet, friends, and other sources, you gather all the relevant information for your call. Then some call objectives are set. The first visit might entail only getting a feel for which dealerships have the best deals, where the best financing options are, and so on. Setting the appointment follows. Maybe you think just before or just after lunch might be the best time to get the best deal. Regardless, it is easy to see how this information can be translated to everyday life.

As graduation approaches and the job hunt begins, it would be smart to apply this strategy to the interviewing process. When looking at potential employers, it makes sense to collect information about the company to understand if it is a leader in the marketplace, what kind of reputation the company has, and whether there are opportunities for advancement. That information will help to determine if the company is a proper fit. Setting call objectives is a must so that you know what you want to accomplish from the interview. You probably want to understand more about the job position, what they expect from potential candidates, what benefits the company provides, and so on. I'm assuming that most of you will be setting a primary goal of moving to the next step in the interview process or securing the position. Precall planning could make the difference between success and failure in today's job market. Putting the effort in up front, much like in sales, will help you achieve your goals.

A job in sales may not be for everyone, but everyone is going to be selling regardless of professional focus. Selling your ideas to your boss/coworker and selling yourself for a promotion are two situations where knowing how to sell can be valuable. My advice is to gain a thorough understanding of all the steps in the sales process, from precall planning to asking for the business. The better you understand the process, the easier it will be for you to apply it in any situation.

Source: Brett Georgulis; used with permission.

SUMMARY

This chapter stressed the importance of planning the sales call. Developing a clear plan saves time for both salespeople and customers. In addition, it helps salespeople increase their confidence and reduce their stress.

As part of the planning process, salespeople need to gather as much information about the prospect as possible before the first call. They need information about both the individual prospect and the prospect's organization. Sources of this information include lists and directories, secretaries and receptionists, noncompeting salespeople, and direct inquiries made by the prospect.

To be effective, a call objective should be specific, realistic, and measurable. In situations requiring several calls, the salesperson should develop a plan with call objectives for each future call. Also, many salespeople benefit from setting multiple levels of objectives—primary, minimum, and optimum—for each call.

As a general rule, salespeople should make appointments before calling on customers. This approach enables the salesperson to talk to the right person at the customer's site.

A number of methods can be used to make appointments. Perhaps the most effective is the straightforward telephone approach.

KEY TERMS

analysis paralysis 177
barriers 187
customer value proposition 184
focus of dissatisfaction 185
focus of power 185
focus of receptivity 185
influential adversaries 176
minimum call objective 181
optimistic call objective 182

primary call objective 181
sales portals 177
screens 187
secondary call objectives 182
seeding 189
selling center 178
videoconferencing 186
virtual sales call 186
Webcasting 186

ETHICS PROBLEMS

1. Suppose that during your information-gathering phase you identify a hostile influential adversary named Larry. You know that Larry will do everything possible to see your competitor get the business. In talking about this with your sales manager, she suggests that you find some way to covertly strip Larry of his credibility and thus cause him to be a nonissue. Would you follow your manager's advice? What kinds of things would you be willing to do? What would you be uncomfortable doing?

2. During precall planning, you learn that an important prospect enjoys being treated by salespeople to visit strip clubs, of which there are several in your town. Your firm doesn't have any policy about whether you can visit one of these clubs with a client. You've never visited one with a client before. How will these facts affect your planning for your upcoming sales visit to this prospect? What will you do?

QUESTIONS AND PROBLEMS

1. Think about a teacher you have had in college. Assume that a salesperson wanted to sell that teacher an important product or service. Who would be a good focus of receptivity for this salesperson? Do you think the focus of receptivity would cooperate with the salesperson?

2. In "Sales Technology 7.1" you learned how one firm uses WebEx to give presentations. Can you think of any negative aspects of using such technology for giving sales presentations to prospects?

3. This chapter listed a number of information items that a salesperson should find out about a prospect/customer as an individual. Assume you are going to sell your best friend a new iPod. See how much information you can supply from the list in the text.

4. Evaluate the following objectives for a sales call:

   a. Show and demonstrate the entire line of 10 squash racquets.

   b. Find out more about competitors' offerings under consideration.

   c. Make the buyer believe what I say.

   d. Determine which service the prospect is currently using for furniture cleaning and how much it costs.

   e. Have the buyer agree to hold our next meeting at a quieter location.

   f. Get an order for 15 carpet cleanings.

   g. Make the buyer not worry about the fact that our newspaper has been in business only two years.

5. Think for a moment about trying to secure a job. Assume you are going to have your second job interview next week with Fastenol for a sales position. The interview will take place over the phone with the senior recruiter. You've already had one informational interview on campus. Most candidates go through a set of four interviews. List your primary objective, minimum objective, and optimistic objective for your second interview.

6. In "Building Partnerships 7.1" you learned that some firms use technology to keep tabs on their salespeople, like where they have driven their company cars and when they have given out samples. What would you say if a manager asked you why you used the company car to visit a mall in the middle of the day? Assume that you stopped at the mall to get your hair cut.

7. Evaluate the following approach for getting an appointment: Ms. Stevens, I've not got any calls on my calendar for next Thursday. Would it be OK if I stopped by for a few minutes, say, sometime between 1:00 and 4:00?

8. Although there is no firm rule, list what you think to be the best time of day to call on the following individuals:

   a. A college bookstore manager (to sell water bottles).

   b. A manager at an automotive glass replacement company (to sell a new tool to remove broken glass shards).

   c. An apartment complex manager (to sell a new lawn watering system).

   d. A heating contractor (to sell a new model of heating system).

9. Review the list of prospects in Question 8 and identify the following:

   a. The worst time of day to call on each individual.

   b. The worst time of year to call on each individual.

10. Suppose you have graduated and you belong to the alumni association of your school. Your association plans to raffle off a number of donated items to raise funds for a new multimedia center at your school. To be a success, the event will need many donated raffle prizes.

   a. Which sources will you use to identify potential sponsors?

   b. What information do you need to qualify them properly?

CASE PROBLEMS

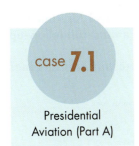

case **7.1**

Presidential Aviation (Part A)

Presidential Aviation has provided charter flights to a wide array of customers, including business travelers worldwide. Thanks to the Presidential online booking system, business travelers can secure reliable quotes and book both domestic and international flights. Presidential has a sizable fleet of aircraft, including jets (light, midsize, and large jets) and turboprops.

The company is known for its ability to cater to passengers' every desire, including gourmet meals, special beverages, entertainment while in the air, and other luxury accommodations. Presidential also staffs a full-service VIP jet concierge program, similar to what major airlines offer.

Santiago Diego is a salesperson for Presidential Aviation. He is currently planning an important first visit to Juan Espinosa, a procurement officer at

Regent Seven Seas Cruises. Company officials travel across the country a great deal in their work. Santiago would like to tell Juan how Presidential can provide outstanding benefits to the Regent Seven Seas Cruises. Some of the special features for business travelers include the following:

- Privacy—you have the entire aircraft to yourself and can travel with passengers you know and enjoy.
- Comfort—including extra-roomy leather seats, in-flight movies, fully stocked bar, and gourmet meals that you choose.
- Ease—no time-consuming check-in process. You drive right up to the plane, and your luggage goes from your car into the plane.
- Point-to-point travel—there are no set schedules, so you fly when you want. Presidential uses 10 times more airports than commercial airlines, so you can fly from less congested airports closer to where you live.

Questions

1. What kind of information should Santiago gather about Juan before their meeting?
2. What kind of information should Santiago gather about Regent Seven Seas Cruises before his meeting?
3. Which sources can Santiago use to gather that needed information?

Sources: http://www.rssc.com and http://www.presidential-aviation.com.

case 7.2

Underground Construction Magazine

Underground Construction magazine is a publication with special appeal for any contractor, municipal manager, or engineering professional involved in the construction, rehabilitation, and remediation of underground pipeline systems. The magazine covers the entire underground utilities infrastructure market, including water/wastewater, oil, gas, telephone, cable, and power. Each issue of the magazine includes latest news, changes in technology, and significant innovations that can be used by industry professionals in managing their underground construction projects.

Andres Orrino is a salesperson for *Underground Construction*, and his territory includes all of states each of the Mississippi River in the United States. In a few weeks, Andres will be calling on Takeuchi, a company that makes track loaders. Track loaders are used in underground construction projects for a variety of tasks. Takeuchi has never advertised in *Underground Construction* magazine. Andres is not sure if anyone from his magazine has ever even called on Takeuchi.

Questions

1. Assume that you are Andres Orrino. List your call objectives for your first call with the marketing director for Takeuchi. Develop a three-call follow-up schedule and list the objectives for each call.
2. What kind of information would you like to have before your first meeting? How could you obtain that information?

Sources: http://www.undergroundconstructionmagazine.com and http://www.takeuchi-us.com.

ROLE PLAY CASE

This role play continues with the same customer firm you have been selling to: BancVue, GelTech, or HighPoint Solutions. (If you have not done role plays before, you will need to review the information about the various role play customers that can be found at the end of Chapter 3.)

Your buyer has agreed to allow you to meet with the rest of the buying center. Now it is time to plan the sales call. Write out your sales call objectives. In case you need assistance, here is some additional information from your previous calls, and feel free to ask your buyer for additional information. In addition to your call objectives, outline an agenda, or what you plan to do step-by-step.

BancVue: You are planning for a sales call with the VP of sales and marketing. You know that the company is growing about 15 percent per year. There are 45 salespeople, managed by four regional sales managers.

GelTech: Your sales call will be with the same person plus some of the agents who have contact management software that they bought. The ultimate decision will be made by Mr. McLane, but he is likely to buy whatever this group recommends.

HighPoint Solutions: You are going to meet with the two VPs of sales. Recall that one manages a sales force of 59 salespeople and sells to distributors, while the other has institutions and government agencies as accounts, with 18 salespeople.

Once you've written your objectives, review them with your group. Make sure they meet the criteria for objectives as specified in the chapter.

Note: For background information about these role plays, please see page 26.

To the instructor: Additional information needed to complete the role play is available in the Instructor's Manual.

ADDITIONAL REFERENCES

Adams, Susan. "The New Rules of Business Etiquette." *Forbes.* Retrieved from http://www.forbes.com/sites/susanadams/2011/10/05/the-new-rules-of-business-etiquette, October 15, 2012.

Bachrach, Anne M. "Getting to the Right People." *American Salesman* 57, no. 5 (May 2012), pp. 27–30.

Barnes, Cindy, Helen Blake, and David Pinder. *Creating and Delivering Your Value Proposition: Managing Customer Experience for Profit.* Philadelphia, PA: Kogan Page, 2009.

Boulton, C. "Web Conferencing Fills Void in Tight Times." *eWeek* 26, no. 1 (January 5, 2009), pp. 14–16.

Chang, Man-Ling, Cheng-Feng Cheng, and Wann-Yih Wu. "How Buyer-Seller Relationship Quality Influences Adaptation and Innovation by Foreign MNCs' Subsidiaries." *Industrial Marketing Management* 41, no. 7 (October 2012), pp. 1047–57.

Ivens, Björn Sven, Catherine Pardo, Robert Salle, and Bernard Cova. "Relationship Keyness: The Underlying Concept for Different Forms of Key Relationship Management." *Industrial Marketing Management* 38, no. 5 (July 2009), pp. 513–19.

Kahle, Dave. "Creating a Powerful Sales Plan." *American Salesman* 56, no. 11 (November 2011), pp. 3–7.

Lewin, Jeffrey E., and Jeffrey K. Sager. "An Investigation of the Influence of Coping Resources in Salespersons' Emotional Exhaustion." *Industrial Marketing Management* 38, no. 7 (October 2009), pp. 798–805.

Macdivitt, Harry, and Mike Wilkinson. *Value-Based Pricing: Drive Sales and Boost Your Bottom Line by Creating, Communicating and Capturing Customer Value.* New York: McGraw-Hill, 2011.

Mayo, M., and M. Mallin. "The Impact of Sales Failure on Attributions Made by 'Resource-Challenged' and 'Resource-Secure' Salespeople." *Journal of Marketing Theory and Practice* 18, no. 3 (2010), pp. 233–47.

Shelton, Robert. "Integrating Product and Service Innovation: Industry Leaders Complement Their Product Offerings with Service Innovations to Boost Overall Customer Value." *Research-Technology Management* 52, no. 3 (2009), pp. 38–44.

chapter **8**

MAKING THE SALES CALL

SOME QUESTIONS ANSWERED IN THIS CHAPTER ARE

- How should the salesperson make the initial approach to make a good impression and gain the prospect's attention?

- How can the salesperson develop rapport and increase source credibility?

- Why is discovering the prospect's needs important, and how can a salesperson get this information?

- How can the salesperson most effectively relate the product or service features to the prospect's needs?

- Why is it important for the salesperson to make adjustments during the call?

- How does the salesperson recognize that adjustments are needed?

- How can a salesperson effectively sell to groups?

2

PART

PROFILE

PROFILE My name is David Maebane. I graduated with a BS in marketing and a certificate in professional selling from Northern Illinois University, where I had the privilege of studying principles of selling from professors Ridnour, Weilbaker, and Vollmert. On graduation, I took a position as a district manager for PepsiCo-Frito Lay.

I lead a territory of 11 salespeople who drive sales and increase market share in a very competitive consumer foods industry. My primary focus is to grow territory and reduce costs.

The responsibility of my sales team is to create profit and customized solutions for buyers and decision makers in the grocery retail industry. It is very important that we create effective sales calls and deliver value-added strategies to increase our customer's profits. Having a prepared and fact-based call is the most strategic way to grow a win–win relationship in my industry and across other functions in business.

When making a sales call, I do my homework on that company, identifying opportunities and strengths as well as what value proposition my company can offer in order to give them a competitive advantage in their industry. It's important that I am professional and prepared for each sales call because I am representing not only myself but also PepsiCo-FritoLay. I want to be genuinely myself, showing that I will build a long-term relationship based on values and good business ethics.

When addressing competition in a sales call, I always want to be professional and never voice negative opinions about the other company. Price sometimes can be a very sensitive topic in a sales call. I try to remain consistent and confident and know what my company specifies on price. I make sure that I do not compromise on my personal ethics or those of my company by promising things that I cannot deliver. During each sales call, I always check for understanding and ask questions to make sure the person I'm selling to is following along and is not confused. As I ask for feedback and follow through on everything after the sale, only then am I providing true relationship selling and not just a one-time business transaction.

Visit our Web site at:
www.pepsico.com/brands/frito_lay-brands.html

Exhibit 8.1

Essential Elements of the
Sales Call

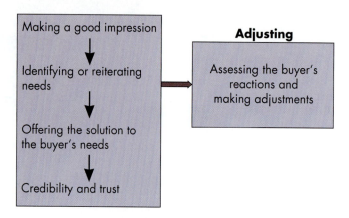

At this point in the sales process, we assume that an appointment has been made, sufficient information about the prospect and his or her organization has been gathered, and the salesperson has developed strong objectives for the call. In this chapter we discuss how to make the actual sales call. The content of a sales call depends on the specific situation the salesperson encounters as well as the extent of the relationship the salesperson has already established with the other party.[1] Exhibit 8.1 provides an organizing framework for our discussion. We start by considering how to make a good impression and begin to develop a long-term relationship. We then examine the initial needs assessment phase of a relationship and how to relate solutions to those needs. Finally, we discuss the relationship between adaptability and successful sales calls. Recent research echoes past research in showing that knowledge, adaptability, and trust are critical for successful sales to occur.[2]

There are, of course, many conceptualizations of the selling process. For example, one trainer finds value in describing the selling process as the **Four A's** (*a*cknowledge, *a*cquire, *a*dvise, and *a*ssure).[3] First the seller acknowledges the buyer by greeting/welcoming/honoring and building trust. Next the seller acquires information via needs analysis and a summary of that analysis outlining the agreement between buyer and seller about the current situation and the desired solution. Advising comes next, during which the seller narrows the possible choices to specific options, sells benefits of those options (not just features), watches for buying signals, and asks for the order. Finally, the seller assures the buyer after the sale by enhancing satisfaction with the buying decision and giving proper follow-up and referrals.

MAKING A GOOD IMPRESSION

When salespeople arrive late, make a poor entrance, fail to gain the buyer's interest, or lack rapport-building skills, it is difficult for them to secure commitment and build partnerships.[4] This section discusses how salespeople can manage the buyer's impression of them, a process termed **impression management**. Most of the information presented here assumes that the salesperson is making a first call on a prospect. However, impression management continues throughout calls.

One of the most important ways to ensure a good first impression is to be well prepared (as we discussed in Chapter 7). Some salespeople prepare a checklist of things to take to the presentation so they won't forget anything.

WAITING FOR THE PROSPECT

Being on time for a scheduled sales call is critical to avoid giving the buyer a negative impression. With cell phones, there is no good reason for not calling if you're

Salespeople should use waiting time effectively.

going to be a few minutes late to the appointment.

Every salesperson must expect to spend a certain portion of each working day waiting for sales interviews. Successful salespeople make the best possible use of this time by working on reports, studying new product information, checking e-mail and text messages, planning and preparing for their next calls, and obtaining additional information about the prospect. (Chapter 15 covers time management more fully.)

Some trainers suggest that salespeople not wait for any prospect, under normal circumstances, more than 15 minutes after the appointment time. Why? To demonstrate that the seller's time is also important. Exceptions are necessary, of course, depending on the importance of the customer, the reason the customer is running late, and the distance the salesperson has traveled. In all cases salespeople should keep the sales call in perspective, realizing that their time is also valuable. Chapter 15 discusses just how valuable that time really is.

When the salesperson arrives, the receptionist may merely say, "I'll tell Ms. Schimpf that you are here." After the receptionist has spoken with Ms. Schimpf, the salesperson should ask approximately how long the wait will be. If the wait will be excessive or the salesperson has another appointment, it may be advisable to explain this tactfully and to ask for another appointment. Usually the secretary either will try to get the salesperson in to see the prospect more quickly or will arrange for a later appointment.

FIRST IMPRESSIONS

In the first meeting between a salesperson and a prospect or customer, the first two or three minutes can be very important. Making a favorable first impression usually results in a prospect who is willing to listen. A negative first impression, on the other hand, sets up a barrier that may never be hurdled.

Salespeople may make a poor impression without realizing it. They may know their customer's needs and their own product but overlook seemingly insignificant things that can create negative impressions. As Chapter 5 related, how you dress can affect the message you send to the buyer. Also, studies have shown that the physical attractiveness and gender of salespeople can influence purchase intentions of buyers. And don't forget that according to generation gap experts, it is often quite difficult for a Generation X (born 1965–1978) salesperson to relate to a baby-boom (born 1946–1964) buyer and even harder to relate to a traditionalist (born 1922–1946) buyer.

So what should a seller do to create a good first impression? You should be well groomed and enter confidently (but not arrogantly) by using erect posture, lengthy stride, and a lively pace, and among the first words out of your mouth should be something like, "Thanks for seeing me." And don't forget to smile. Watch what happens when you look at someone and smile. In 99 out of 100 cases, you will receive a smile in return.

But here's a caveat to the counsel just offered: Observe the prospect's state and modify your behavior as needed. When customers are in a bad mood, the last thing they want is a happy, bouncy salesperson. In fact, in such a situation, the prospect might be inattentive or even refuse to meet with such a salesperson. Adapt and even ask if this is not a good time to meet if you perceive that the buyer is very stressed. Also, be aware that many buyers are repulsed by a salesperson who enters the room with exaggerated and false enthusiasm that her product is for sure going to solve all of the buyer's problems. It's better to be humble than to be cocky.[5]

It is also important to remember prospects' names and how to pronounce them (www.hearnames.com provides verbal pronunciation of many hard-to-say names). There are many ways to try to remember someone's name—such as giving your full attention when you hear it and then repeating the name immediately, associating it with someone else you know with the same name, associating it with the person's most prominent feature or trait, using it during the conversation, and writing it down phonetically.

Some experts argue that the customer's name should be used in the opening statement. Dale Carnegie, a master at developing relationships, said a person's name is "the sweetest and most important sound" to that person. Using a person's name often indicates respect and a recognition of the person's unique qualities. Others disagree with this logic, claiming that using the person's name, especially more than once in any short time, sounds phony and insincere. A compromise is to use the prospect's name in the opening and then to use it occasionally during the rest of the call.

thinking it through

You walk into a prospect's office confidently. Even though you've never met her before, you aren't nervous. You've done your homework and have strong objectives for this meeting. After you introduce yourself to the prospect and sit down, you suddenly remember that you left your iPad in your car. And in that iPad is your entire presentation! Your car is several blocks away. What should you do? What would you say to the prospect?

SELECTING A SEAT

When selecting a seat, it is a good idea to look around and start to identify the prospect's social style and status (see Chapter 5). For example, in the United States important decision makers usually have large, well-appointed, private offices. But this isn't always true. In Kuwait a high-ranking businessperson may have a small office and lots of interruptions. Don't take that environment to mean he or she is a low-ranking employee or is not interested. Walmart buyers interview salespeople in rough conditions to help instill the idea that they want the lowest prices they can get.

Asking permission to sit down is usually unnecessary. The salesperson should read the prospect's nonverbal cues to determine the right time to be seated. And note that many calls will not involve sitting down at all, such as talking to a store manager in a grocery store aisle, conversing with a supervisor in a warehouse, or asking questions of a surgeon in a post-op ward.

GETTING THE CUSTOMER'S ATTENTION

Recall from Chapter 5 that there are several types of sales presentations, including standard memorized, outlined, and customized. In this chapter we assume that the salesperson has chosen a customized presentation.

Getting the customer's attention is not a new concept. It is also the goal of many other activities you are familiar with, such as advertising, making new friends, writing an English composition, giving a speech, or writing a letter to a friend. Also, gaining the prospect's attention can be started before the sales call via social media tools (like sending surveys and polls via LinkedIn to generate interest in your idea).[6]

Time is valuable to prospects, and prospects concentrate their attention on the first few minutes with a salesperson to determine whether they will benefit from the interaction. The prospect is making a decision: Do I want to give this salesperson 15 minutes of my time? Thirty minutes of my time? None of my time? This decision is made even while the salesperson is walking in the door and selecting a seat. Some claim that salespeople have less than six minutes to establish credibility with a client. The first few words the salesperson says often set the tone of the entire sales call. The **halo effect** (how and what you do in one thing changes a person's perceptions of other things you do) seems to operate in many sales calls. If the salesperson is perceived by the prospect as effective at the beginning of the call, he will be perceived as effective during the rest of the call and vice versa. There are many ways to open a presentation. An **opening** is a method designed to get the prospect's attention and interest quickly and to make a smooth transition into the next part of the presentation (which is usually to more fully discover the prospect's needs). Because each prospect and sales situation is unique, salespeople should be adaptable and be able to use any or a combination of openings. Again, keep in mind that openings are generally less important with partnering customers whom the salesperson has already met. Exhibit 8.2 provides details about a number of possible openings. But remember, many prospects won't like what they deem to be "canned" approaches and will react negatively.

Exhibit 8.2

Openings That Salespeople Can Use to Gain Attention

Opening Method	Example	Things to Consider
Introduction opening (simply introduce yourself).	Ms. Hallgren, thank you for seeing me today. My name is Daniel Mundt, and I'm with ServiceMaster.	Simple but may not generate interest.
Referral opening (tell about someone who referred you to the buyer).	Mr. Schaumberg, I appreciate your seeing me today. I'm here at the suggestion of Ms. Fleming of Acumen Ornamental Iron Works. She thought you would be interested in our line of wrought iron products and railings.	Always get permission. Don't stretch the truth.
Benefit opening (start by telling some benefit of the product).	Mr. Penney, I would like to tell you about a color copier that can reduce your copying costs by 15 percent.	Gets down to business right away.
Product opening (actually demonstrate a product feature and benefit as soon as you walk up to the prospect).	[Carrying an iPad into an office] Ms. Hemming, you spend a lot of time on the road as an investigative lawyer. Let me show you how this little handheld item can transform your car (or any place you go) into an efficient, effective office.	Uses visual and not just verbal opening; can create excitement.
Compliment opening (start by complimenting the buyer or the buyer's firm).	I was calling on one of your customers, Jackson Street Books, last week, and the owner couldn't say enough good things about your service. It sure says a lot about your operation to have a customer just start praising you out of the blue.	Must be sincere, not just flattery. **ethics**
Question opening (start the conversation with a question).	Ms. Borgelt, what is your reaction to the brochure I sent you about our new telemarketing service?	Starts two-way communication.

DEVELOPING RAPPORT

Rapport in selling is a close, harmonious relationship founded on mutual trust. You build rapport when the prospect perceives you to be like him or her in some way. Ultimately the goal of every salesperson should be to establish rapport with each customer. Often salespeople can accomplish this with some friendly conversation early in the call. Part of this process involves identifying the prospect's social style and making necessary adjustments (see Chapter 5).

The talk about current news, hobbies, mutual friends, and the like that usually breaks the ice for the actual presentation is often referred to as **small talk.** One of the top traits of successful salespeople is the ability to be sociable. Examples include the following:[7]

> I understand you went to Nebraska? I graduated from there with a BBA in 2007.

> Did you see the Houston Rockets game on TV last night?

> I read in the paper that you won the bass fishing tournament last weekend. I bet that was pretty exciting!

> So did you have trouble getting home from work last week with that snowstorm?

> Your receptionist was very helpful when I set this appointment. I never would have found this building if she hadn't told me where to park.

> You don't happen to remember Marla Jones, do you? She said she went to college with you and said to say hi.

Sharing letters from satisfied customers helps a salesperson establish credibility.

Customers are more receptive to salespeople with whom they can identify—that is, with whom they have something in common. Thus, salespeople will be more effective with customers with whom they establish such links as mutual friends, common hobbies, or attendance at the same schools. Successful salespeople engage in small talk more effectively by first performing **office scanning:** looking around the prospect's environment for relevant topics to talk about. "Sales Technology 8.1" describes how several salespeople use social networking sites to learn about appropriate topics of conversation.

Be careful, however, when engaging in small talk because it can be to your detriment.[8] One salesperson told of a client who asked her opinion about the economic outlook. The seller said she thought it was going down. The buyer had a different opinion, and it took months to repair the relationship. It is generally best to avoid controversial topics like politics and religion. Don't talk about your personal problems in an effort to get sympathy. Don't complain about others (boss, wife) or gossip about your competitors. Also, especially for first calls on prospects, you want to avoid using trite phrases like "How are you doing today?" because they don't sound sincere.

SALES Technology

USING INFORMATION FOUND IN SOCIAL MEDIA IN A SALES CALL

Everyone always says that you need to make a great first impression, and it is true. With all of the social media sites out there today, it is very easy to gain valuable information that will assist you in making a great first impression on your prospective client. Finding something in common with your potential buyer can help you develop a common ground with them and possibly give you the upper hand against competition.

For example, imagine you are working for an appliance company and are preparing for a sales call to the senior buyer of major appliances at Best Buy. When you go to LinkedIn, you can search for that exact person and get an extensive background on what he or she has done and where he or she is coming from. If you can find a similarity in interest, this can be a great way to break the ice and get the meeting off to a great start.

Being current on company initiatives can greatly increase your ability to present information that will be valuable to your client. With many businesses being involved in social media these days, you can find a lot of very current information. For example, on April 23, 2012, Best Buy tweeted, "No matter where you bought it, we'll recycle it!" This tweet linked with the recycling page on Best Buy's Web site. Knowing that Best Buy is making a big effort to become more "green" by offering a recycling service to their customers, you can now take this into account during your presentation by making sure that you stress the way your organization is making efforts to produce the product that you are attempting to sell them in a "green" way. For example, if you are selling them a large home appliance and if your product beats current offerings at Best Buy in energy usage, this may help you win their business over competitors.

Social media offer endless information; you just need to put in the time and effort to find it. By doing your research about a potential company and buyer, you are not being "creepy" as some may think of it; rather, you are being proactive, and many buyers will be impressed with the fact that you have put forth the extra effort to get to know them and their company before you ever even meet them.

Of course salespeople should consider cultural and personality differences and adapt the extent of their nonbusiness conversation accordingly. For example, an AT&T rep would probably spend considerably less time in friendly conversation with a New York City office manager than with, say, a manager in a rural Texas town. Businesspeople in Africa place such high value on establishing friendships that the norm calls for a great deal of friendly conversation before getting down to business. Chinese customers want a lot of rapport building before they get down to business. Amiables and expressives tend to enjoy such conversations, whereas drivers and analyticals may be less receptive to spending much time in nonbusiness conversation. Studies show that salespeople who adapt and mirror their prospects are more successful in gaining desired results.[9] Also, there could be less need for small talk if the salesperson uses a question or product opening when getting the customer's attention.

At this point in the sales call, after gaining the prospect's attention and establishing some rapport, a salesperson will often share his or her goals or agenda for the meeting with the prospect. This step can help build further rapport and trust. For example:

> Just so you know, my goal today is simply to verify what your needs might be and then, as I promised in the phone call, to share with you the results of the lab test we conducted last fall.

WHEN THINGS GO WRONG

Making and maintaining a good impression is important. How nice it would be if the beginning of every call went as smoothly as we have described here. Actually, things do go wrong sometimes. The best line of defense when something goes wrong is to maintain the proper perspective and a sense of humor. It's not the first thing you have done wrong and won't be your last.

For example, assume that a seller accidently scratched a prospect's desk with her portfolio. The worst response by this salesperson would be to faint, scream, or totally lose control. A better response would include a sincere apology for the scratch and an offer to pay for any repairs.

What if you say something that is truly embarrassing? According to Mark Twain, "Man is the only animal that blushes, or needs to." For example, one salesperson calling on an older buyer motioned to a picture of a very young lady on the buyer's desk. "Is that your daughter?" the seller asked, smiling. "That's my wife," the buyer replied, frowning. In another sales call, the salesperson saw a picture on the prospect's desk and said, "Oh wow! What a great picture! How'd you ever get a picture of yourself with John Madden, the football guy!" The buyer replied angrily, "That's not John Madden, that's my wife!"[10] Obviously both sellers made major blunders. The first thing you should do in such a situation is to apologize sincerely. Then change the subject or move on in your presentation. Try to relax and put the incident behind you. And learn this lesson: Think before you speak!

Of course you can get into trouble without even saying a word. As Chapter 4 indicated, you must be careful when using gestures in other cultures because they often take on different meanings.

IDENTIFYING THE PROSPECT'S NEEDS: THE POWER OF ASKING QUESTIONS

Once the salesperson has entered and captured the buyer's attention, it is time to identify the buyer's needs. Remember that this might have occurred in the preapproach and might involve more than one buyer and more than one sales call. To begin this process, a salesperson might use transition sentences like the following (assuming a product approach was used to gain attention):

> Well, I'm glad you find this little model interesting. And I want to tell you all about it. But first I need to ask you a few questions to make sure I understand what your specific needs are. Is that okay?

If the buyer gives permission, the salesperson begins to ask questions about the buyer's needs. Don't be surprised if the buyer is reluctant to provide confidential information. There are many people out there trying to steal valuable company information. The seller has to establish credibility and trust.

Occasionally a salesperson makes the mistake of starting with product information rather than with a discussion of the prospect's needs. The experienced salesperson, however, attempts to uncover the prospect's needs and problems at the start of the relationship. In reality, discovering needs is still a part of qualifying the prospect.

Research continually demonstrates the importance of needs discovery. An analysis by Huthwaite, Inc., of more than 35,000 sales calls in 23 countries over a 12-year period revealed that the distinguishing feature of successful salespeople was their ability to discover the prospect's needs.[11] Discovering needs was more important than opening the call strategically, handling objections, or using closing techniques effectively.

Exhibit 8.3
Discovering the Root Cause of the Need

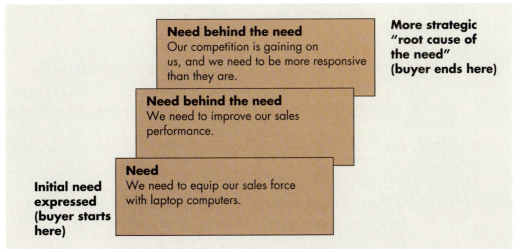

Need behind the need
Our competition is gaining on us, and we need to be more responsive than they are.

More strategic "root cause of the need" (buyer ends here)

Need behind the need
We need to improve our sales performance.

Need
We need to equip our sales force with laptop computers.

Initial need expressed (buyer starts here)

There is an underlying reason for every customer need, and the salesperson must continue probing until he or she uncovers the root problem or need. This process could be called "discovering the root cause of the need" and is graphically illustrated in Exhibit 8.3.

This salesperson is discovering the prospect's needs before describing the services he offers.

As you discover needs, keep in mind that this process can be uncomfortable for the prospect. The prospect may resent your suggesting that there could be a problem or a better way to do things. When faced with direct evidence that things could be better, the prospect may express fear (fear of losing her job if things are not corrected or of things changing and the situation getting worse than it is now). Also, remember that the time needed to discuss needs varies greatly depending on the type of industry, the nature of the product, how well the salesperson and buyer know each other, and so forth. We will come back to this issue after we examine methods of identifying needs.

Chapter 4 covered most of the important communication principles regarding how to effectively ask questions of the prospect and be a better listener. Remember to speak naturally while asking questions. You don't want to sound like a computer asking a set of rote questions. Nor do you want to appear to be following a strict word-for-word outline that you learned in your sales training classes.

We now briefly describe two of the most widely used systems of needs identification taught to salespeople today.

ASKING OPEN AND CLOSED QUESTIONS
In the first method of needs discovery, salespeople are taught to distinguish between open and closed questions and then encouraged to utilize more open questions. Many highly respected sales training organizations, such as Wilson Learning and Achieve Global, use this type of approach. **Open questions** require

the prospect to go beyond a simple yes-or-no response. They encourage the prospect to open up and share a great deal of useful information. For example:

> What kinds of problems have the new federal guidelines caused for your division?
>
> What projects are crucial for your company right now?
>
> What are your decision-making criteria for choosing the successful vendor?

Closed questions require the prospect to simply answer yes or no or to offer a short, fill-in-the-blank type of response. Examples include the following questions:

> Have you ever experienced computer downtime as a result of an electrical storm?
>
> Do you have a favored vendor?
>
> Did you make the decision that resulted in your current vendor?
>
> Who else will be involved in the decision-making process?

In most cases salespeople need to ask both open and closed questions. Open questions help paint the broad strokes of the situation, whereas closed questions help zero in on specific problems and attitudes. Some trainers believe simple, closed questions are best at first. Prospects become accustomed to talking and start to open up. After a few closed questions, the salesperson moves to a series of open questions. At some point he or she may revert back to closed questions.

Angie Main, a radio advertising salesperson, likes to ask her prospects the following two open questions to discover their needs:

> What misconceptions do people have about your business?
>
> If you could tell people one thing about your business, what would you want to tell them?[12]

Notice how these questions focus on the needs of the prospect rather than the solution (how her radio station can meet those needs).

Exhibit 8.4 contains an illustrative dialogue of a bank selling a commercial checking account to a business. In this sales presentation the salesperson's questions follow a logical flow. Note that follow-up probes are often necessary to clarify the prospect's responses. At the conclusion of asking open and closed questions, the salesperson should have a good feel for the needs and wants of the prospect.

One final suggestion is to summarize the prospect's needs:

> So let me see if I have this right. You write about 35 checks a month, you keep about a $5,000 balance, and you are looking for a checking account that pays interest on your unused balance and has overdraft protection. ... Is that correct?

Summarizing helps solidify the needs in the prospect's mind and ensures that the prospect has no other hidden needs or wants.

SPIN® TECHNIQUE

The SPIN method of discovering needs was developed by Huthwaite, an international research and training organization, after analyzing thousands of actual sales calls.[13] The results indicated that successful salespeople go through a logical needs identification sequence, which Huthwaite labeled **SPIN**: *s*ituation questions, *p*roblem questions, *i*mplication questions, and *n*eed payoff questions. SPIN works for salespeople involved in a **major sale**: one that involves a long selling cycle, a large

Exhibit 8.4
Using Open and Closed
Questions to Discover
Needs

Salesperson's Probe	Prospect's Response
Have you ever done business with our bank before? [closed]	No, our firm has always used First of America Bank.
I assume, then, that your checking account is currently with First of America? [closed]	Yes.
If you could design an ideal checking account for your business, what would it look like? [open]	Well, it would pay interest on all idle money, have no service charges, and supply a good statement.
When you say "good statement," what exactly do you mean? [open]	It should come to us once a month, be easy to follow, and help us reconcile our books quickly.
Uh-huh. Anything else in an ideal checking account? [open]	No, I guess that's about it.
What things, if any, about your checking account have dissatisfied you in the past? [open]	Having to pay so much for our checks! Also, sometimes when we have a question, the bank can't answer it quickly because the computers are down. That's frustrating!
Sure! Anything else dissatisfy you? [open]	Well, I really don't like the layout of the monthly statement we get now. It doesn't list checks in order; it has them listed by the date they cleared the bank.
Is there anything else that I need to know before I begin telling you about our account? [open]	No, I think that just about covers it all.

customer commitment, an ongoing relationship, and large risks for the prospect if a bad decision is made. Major sales can occur anywhere but often involve large or national accounts. For example, both SC Johnson and Bridgestone have used SPIN for their major accounts but may use other techniques for smaller accounts.

SPIN actually helps the prospect identify unrecognized problem areas. Often, when a salesperson simply asks an open question, such as, "What problems are you having?" the prospect replies, "None!" The prospect isn't lying; he or she may not realize that a problem exists. SPIN excels at helping prospects test their current opinions or perceptions of the situation. Also, SPIN questions may be asked over the course of several sales calls, especially for large or important buyers. An abbreviated needs identification dialogue appears in Exhibit 8.5; it demonstrates all components of SPIN for a salesperson selling cell phone services.

Situation Questions

Early in the sales call, salespeople ask **situation questions,** which are general data-gathering questions about background and current facts. The goal of these questions is to better understand the prospect's current situation. Because these questions are broad, successful salespeople learn to limit them; prospects quickly become bored or impatient if they hear too many of them. Inexperienced and unsuccessful salespeople tend to ask too many situation questions. In fact, many situation-type questions should be answered through precall information gathering and planning. If a salesperson asks too many situation questions, the prospect will think the salesperson is unprepared. Here are some examples of situation questions:

What's your position? How long have you been here?

How many people do you employ? Is the number growing or shrinking?

What kind of handling equipment are you using at present? How long have you had it?

Exhibit 8.5
Using the SPIN
Technique to Sell Cell
Phone Internet Access

Salesperson: Do your engineers use cell phones in their work? [situation question]

Prospect: Yes, we supply each field engineer with a cell phone.

Salesperson: Do you have many problems with cell calls being lost while an engineer is talking? [problem question]

Prospect: Not really. Most of our engineers work in the city, and there are plenty of towers here to take care of calls.

Salesperson: Sure. Have you ever had engineers who need to access the Internet for details about a client's situation while on-site? Or a need to access files from your central server? [problem question]

Prospect: Well, now that you mention it, that is starting to be a problem. Most engineers like to carry paper copies of the documents they will need, but there are times when a document is back at the office.

Salesperson: What happens if an engineer doesn't have the document she needs while at a client's location? [implication question]

Prospect: That happened just last week to Carlee. She was at a client and thought she had all the paperwork. Turns out there was a spreadsheet she needed but didn't have. She had to drive back to the office to get it. Our client got pretty upset because their staff had to just stand around and wait for Carlee to get back.

Salesperson: If I can show you a way to make sure your engineers have access to all of their important files as well as complete Internet access while at the clients' locations and do so for no more than 10 percent above what you're paying for cell service now, would you be interested? [need payoff question]

Prospect: Sure. The more I think about it, the more I realize that we need to give our engineers the tools that our competitors are using. I'd hate to lose business because we're too cheap to invest in the right tools.

Problem Questions

When salespeople ask about specific difficulties, problems, or dissatisfactions the prospect has, they are asking **problem questions**. The goal is to discover a problem. Here are some examples of problem questions:

Is your current machine difficult to repair?

Do your operators ever complain that the noise level is too high?

Do you get fast turnaround when you outsource your work?

Is the cost of maintaining your own server becoming an issue?

If a seller can't discover a problem using problem questions, then she might need to ask additional situation questions first to uncover more issues that might lead to better problem questions.

Implication Questions

Questions that logically follow one or more problem questions and are designed to help the prospect recognize the true ramifications of the problem are **implication questions**. Implication questions cannot be asked until some problem area has been identified (through problem questions). The goal of implication questions is for the prospect to see that the identified problem has some serious ramifications and implications that make the problem worthy of being resolved. These questions attempt to motivate the prospect to search for a solution to the problem.

Implication questions relate back to some similar issues that were described in the multiattribute model in Chapter 3. In the multiattribute model, customers weigh various attributes differently in terms of importance. In the same way, some problems that are identified by problem questions have more weight (are more serious in the eyes of the buyer) than others. The goal of the salesperson is to identify problems that have high importance to the buyer.

Examples of implication questions include these:

What happens if you ship your customer a product that doesn't meet specs?

What does having to pay overtime do to your price, as compared to your competitors'?

Does the slowness of your present system create any bottlenecks in other parts of the process?

What happens if you miss a deadline?

Could that situation have repercussions for your job security?

Do you think competitors will notice what is going on and attempt to gain market share at your expense due to the problem?

If the buyer answers these questions in a way that indicates she doesn't see serious implications of the problem identified, the seller would have to go back and ask additional implication questions, problem questions, and maybe even situation questions. The seller doesn't move ahead to need payoff questions until the prospect sees that there are serious ramifications if he does not solve the problem.

Need Payoff Questions

When salespeople ask questions about the usefulness of solving a problem, they are asking **need payoff questions.** In contrast to implication questions, which are problem centered, need payoff questions are solution centered:

If I can show you a way to eliminate paying overtime for your operators and therefore reduce your cost, would you be interested?

Would you like to see a reduction in the number of products that don't meet quality specifications?

Would an increase in the speed of your present system by 5 percent resolve the bottlenecks you currently experience?

If the prospect responds negatively to a need payoff question, the salesperson has not identified a problem serious enough for the prospect to take action. In that case, the salesperson should probe further by asking additional problem questions, implication questions, and then a new need payoff question.

Conclusions about SPIN

One critical advantage of SPIN is that it encourages the prospect to define the need. During the questioning phase the salesperson is focusing on problems and isn't focusing on her product. As a result, the prospect views the salesperson more as a consultant trying to help than as someone trying to push a product. "Building Partnerships 8.1" describes the importance of being a consultant and discovering needs before talking about solutions.

SPIN selling has been taught to thousands of salespeople. Many salespeople quickly master the technique, whereas others have more difficulty. The best advice is to practice each component and to plan implication and need payoff questions before each sales call. SPIN works well for buyers that have a real problem (like inventory piling up). It is perhaps more difficult to use when the seller is only discussing an opportunity (no real problems, but "my solution could help you make more money").

MY POORLY CONDUCTED MEETING

I had a meeting recently that I conducted somewhat poorly in my opinion. I wanted to share some mistakes I made in order to help everyone learn from them. First, I think it's best to understand my interpretation of some background research on the psychology of making major decisions.

In buying situations or in other situations involving a decision or changing mind, Huthwaite (a research firm that focuses primarily on sales technique) found that decision makers goes through four phases: recognition of needs, evaluation of options, resolution of concerns, and implementation. In the first phase, people are realizing that the status quo has problems. Then they graduate from the first phase to the second phase once they realize both that they have problems and that they want to change those problems and take action. In the second stage, decision makers are deciding which actions to take. The third phase involves resolving any worries about side effects their decisions may cause, and the fourth involves implementing solutions the decision makers choose. Most decision makers bounce around from one phase to the next, sometimes moving forward, sometimes backward, but it's always important for anyone coaching a person through a decision to empathize with what phase the decision maker is in.

I believe my meeting yesterday went poorly because I spent 90 percent of the meeting talking about what our company does with little regard to what my customers were feeling. I think a lot of sales reps love to talk about their companies, and there is a time and place for this. However, there is also a great deal of hard research verifying that the "recognition of needs" phase is not that time. In fact, sales reps who do talk about themselves or their solutions within that phase are proven to be considerably less likely to win the decision maker's agreement.

The "recognition of needs" phase should be reserved for talking about decision makers' problems and helping decision makers come to their own realization that those problems need to change. *Our job as salespeople during the first part of the buying process is not to discuss our solutions but rather to uncover and grow problems that can best be solved by our solutions.*

What I did in my recent meeting was skip that phase altogether and move to a discussion about solutions. It doesn't make sense to do this because the buyer probably doesn't care about solutions for problems he or she doesn't want to solve. For example, with the advancement of medical science, there are some amazing cosmetic dental treatments. My insurance might get me a $10,000 treatment for a very low deductible, so I'd get great value on a technologically advanced service. I can get an incredible service and a great value, but because I think my teeth look fine, I'm going to be pretty irritated with the dentist who tries to me sell a procedure I don't want.

We're all subjected to this behavior from time to time by unlearned sales reps, but then we carry on one-sided conversations with our own clients without first taking the time to understand them and to let them grow a need for our products. It's hard to fight this personal demon. It takes patience, empathy, and self-control—three tools that aren't much fun to use. It might take many meetings to fully exhaust the scope of a decision maker's problems and to build a genuine mutual desire to fix them. Waiting will conflict with our desire to close business right away and also conflict with pressures that we might face from others inside and outside our organizations.

Perhaps in the future, I'll do a better job of remembering that, as sales reps, we're the final defense against actions that might not be best for our companies and our customers. This means controlling our own desire to skip forward to a later phase of the sale. First focusing on the customer and later creating a dialogue about my company at the appropriate time is the right move for everyone involved. It will have the highest probably of winning business and the highest probability of finding a solution that will best help our customers.

Source: Karl Anderson, Powertex Group, personal correspondence, used with permission.

REITERATING NEEDS YOU IDENTIFIED BEFORE THE MEETING

The salesperson may fully identify the needs of the prospect before making the sales call. In that case reiterating the needs early in the sales call is advisable so that both parties agree about the problem they are trying to solve. For example:

> Mr. Reed, based on our several phone conversations, it appears that you are looking for an advertising campaign that will position your product for the rapidly growing senior citizen market, at a cost under $100,000, using humor and a well-known older personality, and delivered in less than one month. Is that an accurate summary of your needs? Has anything changed since we talked last? Is there anything else I need to know at this point?

Likewise, in multiple-call situations, going through a complete needs identification at every call is unnecessary. But it is still best to briefly reiterate the needs identified to that point:

> In my last call we pretty much agreed that your number one concern is customer satisfaction with your inventory system. Is that correct? Has anything changed since we met last time, or is there anything else I need to know?

ADDITIONAL CONSIDERATIONS

How many questions can a salesperson ask to discover needs? It depends on the situation. Generally, as the buyer's risk of making the wrong decision goes up, so does the amount of time the salesperson can spend asking the prospect questions.

Occasionally the prospect will refuse to answer important questions because the information is confidential or proprietary. The salesperson can do little except emphasize the reason for asking the questions. Ultimately the prospect needs to trust the salesperson enough to divulge sensitive data. Chapters 13 and 14 discuss trust-building strategies.

At times buyers do not answer questions because they honestly don't know the answers. The salesperson should then ask whether the prospect can get the information. If the prospect cannot do so, the salesperson can often ask the buyer's permission to probe further within the prospect's firm.

On the other hand, some buyers will not only answer questions but also appear to want to talk indefinitely. In general, the advice is to let them talk, particularly in many cultures. For example, people in French-speaking countries tend to love rhetoric, the act and art of speaking; attempts to cut them off will only frustrate and anger them.

ethics

thinking it through

> Prospects often provide sensitive and confidential information when they reveal facts about their situations and needs. Assume that a prospect at Allied reveals to you her firm's long-term strategy for taking business away from her number one competitor, Baker's. You are close friends with the buyer at Baker's, which is one of your biggest customers. Will you share the confidential information with the Baker's buyer?

DEVELOPING A STRATEGY FOR THE PRESENTATION

Based on the needs identified, the salesperson should develop a strategy for how best to meet those needs. This process includes sorting through the various options available to the seller to see what is best for this prospect. To do so, the salesperson usually must sort out the needs of the buyer and prioritize them. Decisions have to be made about the exact product or service to recommend, the optimal payment terms to present for consideration, service levels to suggest, product or service features to stress during the presentation, and so on. Chapter 7 also talks about developing a strategy.

Products have many, many features, and one product may possess a large number of features that are unique and exciting when compared to competitive offerings. Rather than overload the customer with all the great features, successful salespeople discuss only those that specifically address the needs of the prospect. Talking about lots of features of little interest to the customer is a waste of time and is sometimes called **feature dumping.**

OFFERING VALUE: THE SOLUTION TO THE BUYER'S NEEDS

After developing a strategy for the presentation based on a customer's needs, it is time to relate product or service features that are meaningful to the buyer, assess the buyer's reaction to what is being said, resolve objections (covered in Chapter 10), and obtain commitment (the topic of Chapter 11). As one best-selling author stated, "Ditch the canned 1-2-3, sometimes pushy, usually insensitive, and almost always repetitive sales strategies glamorized in the past. ... We must be willing to learn, adapt, and listen to our customers."[14]

The salesperson usually begins offering the solution with a transition sentence, something like the following: "Now that I know what your needs are, I would like to talk to you about how our product can meet those needs." The seller's job is then to translate product features into benefits for solving the buyer's needs. To do this effectively, the salesperson must know the metrics of the prospect's decision; that is, on what criteria and in what way is the prospect evaluating possible solutions? This will be discussed more in Chapter 9 and in other chapters.

RELATING FEATURES TO BENEFITS

A **feature** is a quality or characteristic of the product or service. Every product has many features designed to help potential customers. A **benefit** is the way in which a specific feature will help a particular buyer and is tied directly to the buying motives of the prospect.[15] A benefit helps the prospect more fully answer the question "What's in it for me?" Exhibit 8.6 shows a list of features and sample benefits for a product. The way in which a salesperson shows how a product addresses the buyer's specific needs is sometimes called the **customer benefit proposition.** This concept will be described more fully in Chapter 9.

The salesperson usually includes a word or a phrase to make a smooth transition from features to benefits:

> This china is fired at 2,600°F, and what that means to you is that it will last longer. Because it is so sturdy, you will be able to hand this china down to your children as an heirloom, which was one of your biggest concerns.

> Our service hotline is open 24 hours a day, which means that even your third-shift operators can call if they have any questions. That should be a real help to you because you said your third-shift supervisor was inexperienced in dealing with problems.

Some trainers suggest going beyond mentioning features and benefits. One variation, **FAB,** has salespeople discussing *f*eatures, *a*dvantages (why that feature would be important to anyone), and *b*enefits. For example:

> This car has antilock brakes [*feature*], which help the car stop quickly [*advantage*], which provides the safety you said you were looking for [*benefit*].

Exhibit 8.6

An Example of Features and Benefits

THE HURON TRI-PANE CUSTOM PROFILE.

4 Tri-pane units
The air between the panes of glass is your insulation from heat and cold, not the glass. Tri-pane windows are essential to maximizing energy savings on an ongoing basis. As well, they greatly reduce exterior noise filtration and allow for a comfortable level of humidity in your home. Remember to look for a true 1/2" air space, for the ideal insulating value.

WHEN ONLY THE BEST WILL DO

Huron's Quality Construction Features have been developed to maximize the quality and performance benefits of our windows. Understanding what each feature does and the importance of reducing air infiltration is essential in making the best decision for your window needs.

HURON CONSTRUCTION ADVANTAGES

1 Provisions for steel reinforcement
Every Huron vinyl window is made with a heavy walled extrusion that is 25% thicker than the industry standard. Structural cavities, steel reinforced (when needed), ensure that Huron windows never warp, twist, sag or bow. In fact, even with the heaviest triple glazed awning windows, Huron Windows always keep their shape and remain easy to open and will retain their beauty and high performance for many years.

2 Count the cavities
More cavities (air spaces) means greater insulation value, strength and rigidity. Compare this to the competition's construction.

3 Co-extruded gasket seals
For long-term guaranteed window performance, the double gasket is extruded into the frame and welded in the corners. These gaskets are an integral part of the frame so they can't shrink away and fail. This means there is no shrinkage in the corners and never a need to caulk, for lasting energy performance. Wind and water resistant, tests conducted on our operating windows indicate they are just as airtight as a sealed picture window.

5 Glass units are set deeper in the frame
By setting the glass units deeper in the frame, air filtration is reduced dramatically. With the Super Spacer® seals set deeper within the frame towers, the insulating air spaces help reduce heat loss through the spacer bars at the edge of the glass. This is an important feature in reducing energy costs and helping eliminate condensation on the windows.

6 Built-in drain channel
Huron Windows have a special molded drain channel should moisture ever get past the co-extruded gasket seals. The moisture is quickly drained to the outside of the sealed unit, eliminating potential damage to the sealed glass unit and the walls of your home. Glass units sit on shims, so they never sit in water.

7 Count the seals on the opening unit
Huron window opening units are triple sealed to ensure low air infiltration rates that exceed CSA standards for a standard, non-opening unit. Huron weather stripping is a build style design, that is secured in an extruded cavity that provides a fail-safe compressed fit. The weather stripping is manufactured from a special synthetic compound that remains pliable, even at -40°C. Fusion welded corners means they can't shrink away and fail.

8 Super Spacer® Edgetech Warm Edge Technology
Edgetech manufactures the industry leading Super Spacer® line of thermal resistant, flexible tape insulating glass edge-seals, ensuring a long-lasting seal on every Huron Window.

Super Spacer SEALED

In another variation, **FEBA** (*f*eatures, *e*vidence, *b*enefits, *a*greement), salespeople mention the feature, provide evidence that the feature actually exists, explain the benefit (why that feature is important to the buyer), and then ask whether the buyer agrees with the value of the feature and benefit. For example:

> This car has the highest-quality antilock brakes on the market today [*feature*] as proved by this test by the federal government [*evidence*]. They will provide the safety you said you were looking for [*benefit*]; don't you agree [*agreement*]?

Buyers are not interested in facts about the product or the seller's company unless those facts help solve their wants or needs. The salesperson's job is to supply the facts and then point out what those features mean to the buyer in terms of benefits and value creation. Neil Rackham, noted sales training leader, emphasizes this theme:

> The world has changed and so has selling. Today, the primary sales job is to create value—to add problem solving and creativity, so that the customer buys the advice and expertise of the salesperson as much as they buy the product . . . [in a survey] product pitches were the number one complaint from customers, with comments such as "It's quicker, more convenient, and more objective to go to the Internet than to listen to a product pitch."[16]

Exhibit 8.7
The Problem/Solution
Model

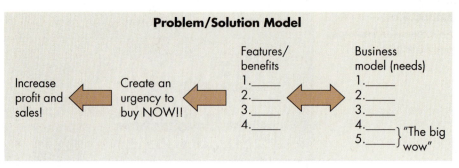

Source: Carl Sooder, used with permission.

Exhibit 8.7 illustrates how one trainer incorporates these concepts into a problem/solution model. The customer's needs are called "business model." The salesperson knows some, but not all, of the buyer's needs before the sales call, represented by the first three lines under "Business model." However, by actively listening (see Chapter 4), the seller learns more needs during the presentation, represented by lines 4 and 5 under "Business model." Using all identified needs, the seller talks about the relevant features and benefits. While doing this, the salesperson offers proof of these assertions, based on the customer's social style (see Chapter 5). The salesperson also engages in activities to help the buyer realize the importance of meeting his or her needs sooner, providing reasons to buy now. The end result is increased sales and profits for the seller.

Buyers typically consider two or more competitive products when making a purchase decision. Thus, salespeople need to know more than just the benefits their products provide. They need to know how the benefits of their products are superior or inferior to the benefits of competitive products. Of course, as you explain the benefits of your service, you must make sure the prospect is looking for those benefits.

Sometimes, when selling certain commodities, it is important to sell the features and benefits of the seller's firm instead of the product. For example, Ray Hanson of Fastenal sells fasteners such as bolts and nuts. He states, "In the fastener industry I have found that a generic product, such as a nut or bolt, doesn't have too many features and benefits. We talk to our potential customers about the features our company has and how these features could benefit them as our customers."[17]

When selling to resellers, salespeople have two sets of benefits to discuss with the prospect: what the features of the product will do for the reseller and what the product features will do for the ultimate consumer of the product. Covering both sets of features and benefits is important. Exhibit 8.8 illustrates the two sets of features.

ASSESSING REACTIONS

While making a presentation, salespeople need to continually assess the reactions of their prospects. The prospect needs to agree that the benefits described would actually help his or her company. By listening to what buyers say and observing their body language (see Chapter 4 to review how to be a better listener), salespeople can determine whether prospects are interested in the product. If buyers react favorably to the presentation and seem to grasp the benefits of the proposed solution, the salesperson will have less need to make alterations or adjustments. But if a prospect does not develop enthusiasm for the product, the salesperson will need to make some changes in the presentation.

Exhibit 8.8

Features and Benefits of Yummy Earth Organic Gummy Bears, as Presented to a Grocery Store

Features	Benefits
Important to the Final Consumer	
Organic.	You want organic products, and this product is certified organic.
Only 90 calories per serving.	You can enjoy a treat without worrying about its effect on your weight.
100 percent of daily need for Vitamin C in every serving.	You are getting needed nutrition from a snack.
Important to the Grocery Store	
Test marketed for two years.	Because of this research, you are assured of a successful product and effective promotion; thus, your risk is greatly reduced.
$500,000 will be spent for consumer advertising in the next 18 months.	Your customers will come to your store looking for the product.
40-cent coupon with front positioning in the national Sunday insert section.	Your customers will want to take advantage of the coupon and will be looking for the product in your store.

Nonverbal cues help salespeople know when to make adjustments. Can you interpret the cues provided by members of this buying team (the three on the right side)?

Using Nonverbal Cues

An important aspect of making adjustments is interpreting a prospect's reactions to the sales presentation. By observing the prospect's five channels of nonverbal communication, salespeople can determine how to proceed with their presentations. Chapter 4 provides more detailed information about nonverbal cues.

Verbal Probing

As salespeople move through a presentation, they must take the pulse of the situation. This process, often called a **trial close,** is more fully described in Chapter 11. For example, the salesperson should say something like the following:

How does this sound to you?

Can you see how these features help solve the problem you have?

Have I clearly explained our program to you?

Do you have any questions?

The use of such probing questions helps achieve several things. First, it allows the salesperson to stop talking and encourages two-way conversation. Without such probing, a salesperson can turn into a rambling talker while the buyer becomes a passive listener. Second, probing lets the salesperson see whether the buyer is listening and understanding what is being said. Third, the probe may show that the prospect is uninterested in what the salesperson is talking about. This response allows the salesperson to redirect the conversation to areas of interest to the buyer. This kind of adjustment is necessary in almost every presentation and underscores the fact that the salesperson should not simply memorize a canned presentation that unfolds in a particular sequence.

Salespeople must listen. Often we hear only what we want to hear. This behavior is called **selective perception,** and everyone is guilty of it at times. For example, read the following sentence:[18]

> Finished files are the result of years of scientific study combined with the experience of years.

Now go back and quickly count the number of *f*'s in that sentence. Most non-native English speakers see all six *f*'s, whereas native English speakers see only three (they don't count the *f*'s in *of* because it is not considered an important word). The point is that once salespeople stop actively listening, they miss many things the buyer is trying to communicate.

Making Adjustments

Salespeople can alter their presentations in many ways to obtain a favorable reaction. For example, a salesperson may discover during a sales presentation that the prospect simply does not believe the seller has the appropriate product knowledge. Rather than continue with the presentation, the salesperson should redirect her or his efforts toward establishing credibility in the eyes of the prospect.

Other adjustments might require collecting additional information about the prospect, developing a new sales strategy, or altering the style of presentation. For example, a salesperson may believe a prospect is interested in buying an economical, low-cost motor. While presenting the benefits of the lowest-cost motor, the salesperson discovers the prospect is interested in the motor's operating costs. At this point the salesperson should ask some questions to find out whether the prospect would be interested in paying a higher price for a more efficient motor with lower operating costs. On the basis of the prospect's response, the salesperson can adopt a new sales strategy, one that emphasizes operating efficiency rather than the motor's initial price. In this way the sales presentation is shifted from features and benefits based on a low initial cost to features and benefits related to low operating costs.

BUILDING CREDIBILITY DURING THE CALL

To develop a close and harmonious relationship, the salesperson must be perceived as having **credibility**—that is, he or she must be believable and reliable. A salesperson can take many actions during a sales call to develop such a perception.[19] From the Buyer's Seat 8.1 provides examples of when sellers did and did not achieve that goal.

To establish credibility early in the sales call, the salesperson should clearly delineate the time she or he thinks the call will take and then stop when the time is up. How many times has a salesperson said, "This will take only 5 minutes!" and 30 minutes later you still can't get rid of him? No doubt you would have perceived the salesperson as more credible if, after 5 minutes, he or she stated, "Well, I promised to take no more than 5 minutes, and I see our time is up. How would you like to proceed from here?" One successful salesperson likes to ask for half an hour and take only 25 minutes.[20]

Another way to establish credibility is to offer concrete evidence to back up verbal statements. If a salesperson states, "It is estimated that more than 80 percent of the households in America will own tablet computers by 2018," he or she should be prepared to offer proof of this assertion—for instance, hand the prospect a

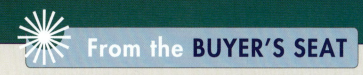

From the BUYER'S SEAT

PLEASE REMEMBER WHAT I'VE ALREADY TOLD YOU

I'm a buyer at Home Depot. For the products I buy, many of the sales presentations are actually done in the offices of the companies that are attempting to sell me their products. Before most of my planned meetings with salespeople, I do my best to send them literature to show them what we have been doing as an organization and where we are looking to go in the future. In this information there are also things regarding the different trends that we see going on. There are two ways a salesperson can use this information: They can either use it to their advantage or completely disregard it. Let me share a few examples.

A few weeks back, I went in to visit a salesperson, and when I walked in, I could tell that they were not prepared. They were flying around the office trying to grab different products to show me, like they had forgotten I was coming. When I referred to the information that I sent them, they looked at me like I was speaking a foreign language. I asked them if they had received the information, and they said yes, but they were not able to take a look at it. To me this really made it seem as though my business was unimportant to them.

Now here's a different example. I had a planned meeting with a salesperson and had sent them the exact same information with the exact same amount of time for them to prepare for the meeting. When I walked in to their office, they were standing and waiting for me with various products lined up for me to look at. When I mentioned something in the information that I had sent them, they said, "Yeah hold on, let me grab that." They had printed off the information that I had sent them and had notes all over the pages. This proved to me that our business meant a lot to them and that they were really going to give it their all to gain our business and work not only with us but also for us and our customers to provide quality products.

Source: Antonio Alfonso, Home Depot; all names changed for anonymity; used with permission.

letter or an article from a credible source. Ways to establish credibility are discussed in greater detail in Chapter 9.

Some trainers suggest adding a **credibility statement** early in the sales call that includes features of yourself and your company.[21] The purpose of the statement is to help the buyer realize you are capable of meeting her needs. The statement can be strengthened by proving its assertions with such items as testimonials and test results (more about these in the next chapter). Here's an example of a credibility statement:

> Hank, I don't know how much you may know about Apple Valley Savings and Loan. We were founded by a Swedish immigrant back in 1932 whose stated goal was to offer the best service in the Midwest. We've now grown into the third-largest savings bank in the upper Midwest with assets exceeding $23 billion and are the only savings bank in the Midwest earning the coveted Pinnacle Award for Excellent eight years in a row. We have over 32 branches in the five-state region. I've been with the bank for the last 14 years and have spent the last 6 years working closely with higher education institutions like yours. In terms of investments, we have focused a great deal of effort on higher education. For example, we recently provided a $2.3 million loan to West Valania State University to expand its ice hockey rink.

Of course, one way to establish credibility is to avoid making statements that do not have the ring of truth to them. For example, some suggest you should avoid using a phrase like "We're the best" or "We're number one." As one skeptical buyer noted, "Just how many number ones are there in the world, anyway?" Salespeople should also remember that, in addition to damaging credibility, truth-stretching comments can come back to haunt them in the form of legal liability (see Chapter 2 for a review of legal issues).

Many salespeople have found that the most effective way to establish credibility is to make a **balanced presentation** that shows all sides of the situation—that is, to be totally honest. Thus, a salesperson might mention some things about the product that make it less than perfect or may speak positively about some exclusive feature of a competitor's product. Will this approach defeat the seller's chances of a sale? No. In fact, it may increase the chances of building long-term commitment and rapport. Salespeople can keep customers happy and dedicated by helping them form correct, realistic expectations about a product or service.

Salespeople can build credibility by recognizing cultural differences, not only in foreign markets but also in North America. How? By demonstrating sensitivity to the needs and wants of specific subcultures and avoiding biased or racist language. See Chapter 4 for more information about cultural differences.

In selling complex products, sales representatives often must demonstrate product expertise at the beginning of the sales process—for example, by telling the customer, without bragging, about their special training or education. They can also strengthen credibility with well-conceived, insightful questions or comments.

When selling complicated technical products and services, Todd Graf notes, "You have to keep it simple. Teach as you go. Make transitions slow and smooth and always ask if they understand (half the time they don't). This is key because they may have to go back and explain some of your features to the decision maker who isn't present in this meeting."[22]

Being willing to say, "I'm sorry, I was wrong on that," or "I don't know the answer to that, but I'll get it to you," will also go a long way toward establishing credibility. A seller should never use a word if he or she doesn't know the exact definition. Some buyers may even test the salesperson. Here's an example from a real salesperson who was calling on a doctor:[23]

> SALESPERSON: Because product X acts as an agonist at the kappa receptor, miosis will occur.
>
> DOCTOR: What does *miosis* mean?
>
> SALESPERSON: It means the stage of disease during which intensity of signs and symptoms diminishes.
>
> DOCTOR: No! *Miosis* means contraction of the pupils.

At this point the doctor walked out of the room, and the seller thought she had lost all credibility. Actually, he had just gone out and grabbed a dictionary. The first definition was the contraction of the pupils, and the second was the seller's definition. The salesperson's definition, not the doctor's, fit the use of the term for this medication. The doctor then shook the seller's hand and thanked her for teaching him a new definition of the word. The salesperson's credibility certainly increased.

SELLING TO GROUPS

Selling to groups can be both rewarding and frustrating. On the plus side, if you make an effective presentation, every member of the prospect group becomes your ally. On the down side, groups behave like groups, with group standards and norms and issues of status and group leadership.

When selling to groups, the salesperson must gather information about the needs and concerns of each individual who will attend. Salespeople should discover (for each prospect group member) member status within the group, authority, perceptions about the urgency of the problem, receptivity to ideas, knowledge

Selling to groups requires special skills in monitoring several individuals at once, as well as being able to respond to customers with occasionally conflicting needs.

of the subject matter, attitude toward the salesperson, major areas of interest and concern, key benefits sought, likely resistance, and ways to handle this resistance. Chapter 3 discusses many things that salespeople should consider about buying centers.

It is important to develop not only objectives for the meeting but also objectives for what the seller hopes to accomplish with each prospect present at the meeting. Planning may include the development of special visual aids for specific individuals present. The seller must expect many more objections and interruptions in a group setting compared to selling to an individual.

An informal atmosphere in which group members are encouraged to speak freely and the salesperson feels free to join the group's discussion usually works best in these situations. Thus an informal location (such as a corner of a large room as opposed to a formal conference room) is preferred. Formal presentation methods, such as speeches, that separate buyers and sellers into them-versus-us sides should be avoided. If the group members decide that the meeting is over, the salesperson should not try to hold them.

Of course most things you have learned about selling to individuals apply equally to groups. You should learn the names of group members and use them when appropriate. You should listen carefully and observe all nonverbal cues. When one member of the buying team is talking, it is especially important to observe the cues being transmitted by the other members of the buying team to see whether they are, in effect, agreeing or disagreeing with the speaker.

There are several types of group selling situations. If the group meeting is actually a negotiation session, many more things must be considered. As a result, we devote an entire chapter (Chapter 12) to the topic of formal negotiations. Also, sometimes a salesperson makes a call on a prospect as part of a selling team from his firm (for example, the team might consist of his sales manager, someone from technical support, someone from customer support, and a sales executive from the firm). These situations require coordination and teamwork. Because of the importance of the various selling team scenarios, the issue of selling teams is more fully discussed in Chapter 16.

SELLING YOURSELF

It's a fact. You're going to be selling yourself while trying to get that first job right out of college. Don't forget to use everything you've read in this chapter as you do so. Otherwise you'll look and sound like the thousands of other students who merely *hope* that the company will hire them without really keying in on what the hiring company is looking for.

Always attempt to build rapport with an interviewer. Find something you have in common with her, based on information you learned from her LinkedIn profile, from your professor, or even from the staff in the career services center at your school. Someone is bound to know something about the person. Use that information to break the ice and build a sense of "liking" between the two of you. You'll be surprised how much that simple act calms you down as you realize you really do have some things in common.

Make sure you discover interviewers' needs. What exactly are they looking for in a job candidate? If you've not already discovered it, and the information is not available on their Web site, then go ahead and ask. The interviewers won't think you're weird; they'll think you are sharp. Once you find out what those needs are, sell yourself by explicitly showing how your "features" meet their needs. For example, your résumé might state the following:

> Reading with Champions Volunteer, Birchwood Elementary School: read to elementary school students two times a week to help them gain a love for books.

You're interviewing for a sales job, not a job to read books to small children. So it's your job to convert that feature into a benefit to the interviewers with something like the following:

> You said you were looking for someone with a hard work ethic and also for someone with an ability to interact with lots of different kinds of clients. Well, my volunteer work demonstrates my work ethic because I did this activity for six months, all while I was also taking 18 credits at school. I never missed a reading at that school, either! Also, the children I interacted with at that school were not like me at all. Most came from poor backgrounds and broken families. Many had never had a book read to them before. Anyway, what all of this means to you is that I am able to interact with people who are very different from me. In fact I enjoy it. I'm sure I'll be able to adapt to the many different types of customers you say you have at your firm. Did that example help you see that I am a hard worker and that I can interact with different types of people?

Finally, establish credibility by bringing your portfolio with you to the interview. The portfolio should include copies of papers you wrote, videos of presentations you gave, and any other evidence that will demonstrate that you have the skills they are looking for.

Source: David Maebane, used with permission.

SUMMARY

Salespeople need to make every possible effort to create a good impression during a sales call. The first few minutes with the prospect are important, and care should be taken to make an effective entrance by giving a good first impression, expressing confidence while standing and shaking hands, and selecting an appropriate seat.

The salesperson can use any of several methods to gain the prospect's attention. Salespeople should adopt the opening that is most effective for the prospect's personality style. Also critical is the development of rapport with the prospect, which can often be enhanced by engaging in friendly conversation.

Before beginning any discussion of product information, the salesperson can establish the prospect's needs by using open and closed questions. The SPIN technique is very effective for discovering needs in a major sale. In subsequent calls the salesperson should reiterate the prospect's needs.

When moving into a discussion of the proposed solution or alternatives, the salesperson translates features into benefits for the buyer. The salesperson also makes any necessary adjustments in the presentation based on feedback provided by the buyer's nonverbal cues and by verbal probing.

A close, harmonious relationship will enhance the whole selling process. The salesperson can build credibility by adhering to stated appointment lengths, backing up statements with proof, offering a balanced presentation, and establishing his or her credentials.

When selling to groups, the salesperson must gather information about the needs and concerns of each individual who will attend. The seller should also uncover the ego involvement and issue involvement of each group member. It is important to develop objectives not only for the meeting but also for what the seller hopes to accomplish with each prospect present at the meeting.

Now that you know how to start the sale, discover needs, relate features to specific benefits for the buyer, and build credibility, it is time to look more closely at how to communicate your ideas more effectively. That's the topic of the next chapter.

KEY TERMS

ETHICS PROBLEMS

1. You're an account executive for Wells Fargo Financial in Minnesota. You had an initial appointment with a customer, June, to find out what her goals were financially. The meeting went just as a typical first meeting should go, and there was a beneficial product you could create for her. However, her husband could not meet with you. After weeks of work and preparation, you have a loan that makes sense. The loan meets the goals June wanted, so you have a second appointment with her to go over exact terms, again without her husband. You asked when her husband could come in and sign the loan documents, and she discloses to you that her husband is not aware of the $35,000 of credit card debts the loan is going to pay off. Both the husband and the wife must be present at the time of the loan. Legally you can call the husband and tell him about the loan application. What should you do?

   Source: Erik Abrahamson, Wells Fargo Financial; used with permission.

2. You're calling on an important prospect in the sportswear industry, and she starts asking you how other sportswear retailers are handling a specific problem. You know that this is important competitive information and that you should not provide details about a competitor. Instead you decide to give the prospect the information without specifics (like the name of the sportswear retailer you're talking about). Is that OK?

QUESTIONS AND PROBLEMS

1. Think for a moment about trying to secure a sales job. Assume you are going to have an interview with a district manager of a consumer products firm next week for a sales position. What can you do to develop rapport and build credibility with her?

2. "I don't need to discover my prospect's needs. I sell frozen pizzas to grocery stores and convenience stores. I know what their needs are: a high profit margin and fast turnover of products!" Comment.

3. Develop the FEBA for one of the features shown in Exhibit 8.8.

4. Assume that you are selling swimming pool maintenance services to a small hotel. Develop a series of open and closed questions to discover the prospect's needs.

5. Assume that you represent your school's placement service. You are calling on a large business nearby that never hires graduates from your college. Generate a list of SPIN questions, making any additional assumptions necessary.

6. Prepare a list of features and benefits that could be used in a presentation to other students at your college. The objective of the presentation is to encourage them to declare the same major you are taking.

7. "Sales Technology 8.1" told about the use of social networking to gain information and hence do a better job of gaining the prospect's attention. Look at the profiles of two of your friends or contacts on LinkedIn, Facebook, or some other social networking site. Using strictly the information you find there, what are some ways you could gain that person's attention in a sales call, assuming you didn't actually know them before the call?

8. In "Building Partnerships 8.1" you read about a salesperson who admitted that he performed poorly in a sales meeting. Even though he knew what to do, he didn't do it. Why do you think that happened?

9. In which situations should a salesperson use a prospect's first name? When should a more formal salutation be used?

10. You're selling a new line of candy to a grocery store (choose some brand of candy). Write a list of features and benefits for the grocery store, as well as a list of features and benefits for the store's customers (the shoppers who come in and buy candy).

11. In "From the Buyer's Seat 8.1" you heard a buyer describe one good and one poor salesperson. What can a company do to ensure that salespeople act more like the good salesperson profiled?

CASE PROBLEMS

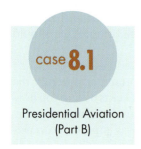

case **8.1**

Presidential Aviation
(Part B)

Presidential Aviation has provided charter flights to a wide array of customers, including business travelers worldwide. The company is known for its ability to cater to passengers' every desire, including gourmet meals, special beverages, entertainment while in the air, and other luxury accommodations. Santiago Diego is a salesperson for Presidential Aviation. Today he will be making his first visit to Juan Espinosa, a procurement officer at Regent Seven Seas Cruises.

For more details about Presidential Aviation and Regent Seven Seas Cruises, see Case 7.1 in Chapter 7.

Questions

1. Develop a set of open and closed questions to fully discover Juan Espinosa's needs.

2. Develop a set of SPIN questions to discover Juan Espinosa's needs.

Sources: http://www.rssc.com and http://www.presidential-aviation.com.

case 8.2

Citrix Systems

Jamie Skrbis of Citrix Systems had an important appointment with a senior buyer and her assistant at a pharmaceutical company. It had taken Jamie three months to get the appointment, and she was excited about the chance to finally demonstrate her company's new cloud networking system. As Jamie was leaving her office, her sales manager learned where Jamie was going and asked to come along. Jamie had no option but to say, "Sure." However, she was worried because his manager often took control of meetings and sometimes wasn't a good listener.

When the sales team got there, the buyer, Tracey, stated that she could participate for only about 30 minutes but that her assistant, Sally, would be staying for the remainder of the time. Before Jamie could begin talking, Kyle, her sales manager, began taking the buyers through his sales binder that had a presentation in it. It began with the history of the company.

Tracey politely interrupted and explained that she was already familiar with Citrix Systems, but there were certain things that she was interested in learning about their services. Tracey asked the sales team if they could produce two items for her.

Again, before Jamie could answer, Kyle jumped in with, "Yes, we could, and I'm going to get there in a minute." Tracey patiently waited as he continued to take her through the company history. By now, almost 10 minutes had passed.

Next, Kyle talked about the work that Citrix Systems had done for other companies. This is something that many buyers are usually interested in. However, Tracey interrupted again and said that they were really looking for a vendor for a couple of specific projects and that she wanted to see what they could do for those specific situations. Kyle replied, "Hang on, Tracey. I'm almost there! I promise to get there soon."

After Kyle finished showing the work Citrix Systems did for other companies, he began to explain the benefits of working with his company because of reputation, pricing, service, and so on. Tracey asked again about the two projects, and instead of answering her questions, Kyle continued to follow his canned presentation. Tracey was becoming noticeably upset and agitated, although Sally seemed quite interested.

Questions

1. You are Jamie. What will you do now?

2. How can you avoid a situation like this in future calls with your manager?

Source: Tracey Brill; used with permission.

ROLE PLAY CASE

Today we are going to start over again, "from the top" as they say in the theater. Start from the beginning of the sales call, from when you knock on the door through the needs identification stage, ending just before your presentation. All that you have learned in previous role plays about the account continues to hold true. If you've been selling to Banc/Vue, you'll continue to do so, but you are now meeting with a different member of the buying center. The same is true for GelTech and HighPoint Solutions. New buyer sheets will be passed out. You can have the same person play the new role or someone else in class. (*Note:* If you have not done role plays before, you will need to review the information about the various role play customers that can be found at the end of Chapter 3.)

If your class is divided into groups of three, the person who is watching should create a check sheet. Write *S, P, I,* and *N* down the left side of the paper. As the salesperson asks a question, check whether it is a situation, problem, implication, or needs payoff question. Also note if and how he or she identified or verified the decision process. *Don't forget:* At the start of the sales call, identify the type of opening used (introduction, benefit, product, curiosity, or some other form).

> *Banc/Vue:* You will meet with the VP of sales and marketing. This is an appointment that was set up by the regional sales manager you called on earlier. You've never talked to this person before.

> *GelTech:* Mr. McLane has asked to see you. You weren't expecting this from your earlier sales calls, but you welcome the opportunity to meet the decision maker. His secretary called and made the appointment.

> *HighPoint Solutions:* You are meeting with one of the VPs of sales. The other VP was fired, but you don't know why. The meeting was set up by the regional sales manager you called on earlier, who also told you about the firing, but she didn't know what had happened.

Note: For background information about these role plays, please see page 26.

To the instructor: Additional information needed to complete the role play is available in the Instructor's Manual.

ADDITIONAL REFERENCES

Ahearne, Michael, Scott B. MacKenzie, Philip M. Podsakoff, John E. Mathieu, and Son K. Lam. "The Role of Consensus in Sales Team Performance." *Journal of Marketing Research* 47, no. 3 (2010), pp. 458–69.

Badrinarayanan, Vishag, Sreedhar Madhavaram, and Elad Granot. "Global Virtual Sales Teams (GVSTs): A Conceptual Framework of the Influence of Intellectual and Social Capital on Effectiveness." *Journal of Personal Selling and Sales Management* 31, no. 3 (Summer 2011), pp. 311–24.

Bednarz, Timothy F. Bednarz. *Consultative Sales Strategies.* Steven's Point, WI: Majorium Business Press, 2011.

Blocker, Christopher P., Joseph P. Cannon, Nikolaos G. Panagopoulos, and Jeffrey K. Sager. "The Role of the Sales Force in Value Creation and Appropriation: New Directions for Research." *Journal of Personal Selling and Sales Management* 32, no. 1 (2012), pp. 15–28.

Burn, Brian. *The Maverick Selling Method: Simplifying the Complex Sale.* Bloomington, IN: Xlibris Corporation, 2009.

Cassell, Jeremy, and Tom Bird. *Brilliant Selling: What the Best Salespeople Know, Do, and Say.* Upper Saddle River, New Jersey: FT Press, 2009.

Chan, Elaine, and Jaideep Sengupta. "Insincere Flattery Actually Works: A Dual Attitudes Perspective." *Journal of Marketing Research* 47, no. 1 (February 2010), pp. 122–33.

Cole, Tony. "7 Steps to Start the Sale." *American Salesman* 56, no. 11 (November 2011), pp. 8–11.

Freedman, David H. "On the Road with a Supersalesman." *Inc* 32, no. 3 (April 2010), pp. 84–91.

Graham, John R. "A Sales Strategy That Works!" *American Salesman* 55, no. 6 (June 2010), pp. 17–21.

Griffin, Jill G., and Susan M. Broniarczyk. "The Slippery Slope: The Impact of Feature Alignability on Search and Satisfaction." *Journal of Marketing Research* 47, no. 2 (April 2010), pp. 323–34.

Jakob, Rehme, and Svensson Peter. "Credibility-Driven Entrepreneurship: A Study of the First Sale." *International Journal of Entrepreneurship and Innovation* 12, no. 1 (February 2011), pp. 5–15.

Johnson, Mark S., Eugene Sivadas, and Vishal Kashyap. "Response Bias in the Measurement of Salesperson Orientations: The Role of Impression Management." *Industrial Marketing Management* 38, no. 8 (November 2009), pp. 1014–24.

Kahle, Dave. "The Three Biggest Mistakes in Sales Presentations." *American Salesman* 56, no. 8 (August 2011), pp. 3–6.

Keh, Hean Tat, and Yi Xie. "Corporate Reputation and Customer Behavioral Intentions: The Roles of Trust, Identification, and Commitment." *Industrial Marketing Management* 38, no. 7 (October 2009), pp. 732–42.

Lager, Marshall. "The Psychology of the Sale: There's a Lot Going on inside the Customer's Head, Whether You Put It There or Not. What Are Salespeople Up Against?" *CRM Magazine* 13, no. 5 (2009), pp. 34–37.

Lovas, Michael, and Pam Holloway. *Axis of Influence: How Credibility and Likeability Intersect to Drive Success.* New York City: Morgan James Publishing, 2009.

Malcolm, Jack. *Strategic Sales Presentations*. Seatlle Washington Editions, 2012.

Malone, Tim. "Improve through Consultative Selling." *JCK* 181, no. 4 (April 2010), p. 49.

Pullins, Ellen Bolman, Michael L. Mallin, Richard E. Buehrer, and Deirdre E. Jones. "How Salespeople Deal with Intergenerational Relationship Selling." *Journal of Business and Industrial Marketing* 26, no. 6 (2011), pp. 443–55.

Read, Nicholas A. C., and Stephen J. Bistritz. *Selling to the C-Suite: What Every Executive Wants You to Know about Successfully Selling to the Top*. New York City: McGraw-Hill, 2009.

Sundtoft Hald, Kim, Carlos Cordón, and Thomas E. Vollmann. "Towards an Understanding of Attraction in Buyer–Supplier Relationships." *Industrial Marketing Management* 38, no. 8 (November 2009), pp. 960–70.

chapter **9**

STRENGTHENING THE PRESENTATION

SOME QUESTIONS ANSWERED IN THIS CHAPTER ARE

- How can salespeople use verbal tools to strengthen a presentation?
- Why do salespeople need to augment their oral communication through tools such as visual aids, samples, testimonials, and demonstrations?
- What methods are available to strengthen a presentation?
- How can salespeople use visual aids and technology most effectively?
- What are the ingredients of a good demonstration?
- Is there a way to quantify the salesperson's solution to a buyer's problem?
- How can salespeople reduce presentation jitters?

PROFILE

PROFILE I was not "sold" on a career in sales until taking "Fundamentals of Selling" with Professor John Kratz at the University of Minnesota–Duluth. He sold the concept of being able to control your work schedule and, ultimately, your performance. Nowhere is that more evident than in a sales presentation.

In my current role as an account executive with the NCR Corporation, I manage NCR's relationship with retailers based in the upper Midwest as we develop collaborative technology solutions consisting of software, services, and hardware. Due to the potential complexity of the both the technology and the retailer's existing environment, finding ways to convey the benefits of the end solution is one the most pivotal elements in determining the success of the sales process. There are five ways I focus on strengthening a presentation:

Know Your Audience—Conservative or laid back? Old or young? Male or female? Concept driven or fact driven? Interactive or stoic? These are just some of the elements that must be considered in crafting the structure and messaging of your sales presentation. For example, if you are calling on a group of people 50 years old or older, premeeting rapport-building conversation should not focus around the Justin Bieber concert coming to town.

Audience Participation—The most common mistake I see is salespeople who talk far more than their prospect or customer. Remember, nearly all people like to talk and share their opinions. This uncovers additional information for the salesperson and keeps the audience engaged in the dialogue. Also, collaboration through the customer's or prospect's participation creates a sense of ownership on their side that can allow for dramatic advancement of the sales process.

Feature/Function/Benefit—Far too many salespeople get down in the weeds, focused on bits and bites. If you are selling to the most desirable level (the C-Suite), you must explain your product or service in a way that communicates what something is, what it does, and what the end result or positive outcome is.

Tell Them What You Will Tell Them, Tell Them, and Tell Them What You Told Them—Remember, although you may know every minute detail of the concepts you are describing, some of the people you will be presenting to will be hearing it for the first time. While it may seem simplistic, repeating the key points of your message and confirming their understanding will increase the chances of their retention and the ability to move forward.

Customization—If I have learned anything in terms of successful sales presentations, it is the power of customization. It is far too easy to take a standard PowerPoint deck from your company's marketing department and show it "as is" to your customer. However, what are the odds that this is dead-on to what your customer wants to take away from your discussion? You must operate with this concept in mind because the time you are spending is *all* about them. With proper research and planning prior to the meeting, you can find ways to demonstrate that you have learned about their company and listened to what they have told you. There is no greater way to earn respect and credibility.

In summary, strengthening the presentation boils down to one question: Are you willing to invest the time and energy *before* the meeting to ensure success? In the words of renowned sales trainer Jeffrey Gitomer, "Most salespeople are not willing to do the hard work it takes to make selling *easy*!"

Visit our Web site at:
www.ncr.com

CHARACTERISTICS OF A STRONG PRESENTATION

Communication tools such as visual aids, samples, testimonials, demonstrations, and the use of humor are important ingredients in most sales calls. Use of such tools focuses the buyer's attention, improves the buyer's understanding, helps the buyer remember what the salesperson said, offers concrete proof of the salesperson's statements, and creates a sense of value.

KEEPS THE BUYER'S ATTENTION

How many times has your mind wandered during classroom lectures while the instructor earnestly discussed some topic? What happened? The instructor lost your attention. In contrast, your attention probably remains more focused in a class when the instructor uses visuals and humor effectively, brings in guest speakers, and finds ways to get you actively involved in the discussion.

The same is true of buyer–seller interactions. Unless you can get the buyer actively involved in the communication process and doing more than just passively hearing you talk, the buyer's attention will probably turn to other topics. "Building Partnerships 9.1" illustrates how important it is to make sure you are giving the prospect the exact information that she wants if you want to keep her attention.

The buyer's personality can also affect his or her attention span. For example, one would expect an amiable to listen more attentively to a long presentation than, say, a driver would. Thus an effective salesperson should consider the social style of the prospect and adapt the use of communication aids accordingly (see Chapter 5 for more about personality styles).

IMPROVES THE BUYER'S UNDERSTANDING

Many buyers have difficulty forming clear images from the written or spoken word. An old Chinese proverb says, "Tell me—I'll forget. Show me—I may remember. But involve me, and I'll understand." Appeals should be made to as many of the senses (hearing, sight, touch, taste, and smell) as possible. Studies show that appealing to more than one sense with **multiple-sense appeals** increases understanding dramatically, as Exhibit 9.1 illustrates. For example, in selling Ben & Jerry's ice cream novelties to a grocery store manager, the salesperson may describe the product's merits (an appeal to the sense of hearing) or show the product and invite the merchant to taste it (appeals to sight, touch, and taste). Appeals to the grocer's fifth sense, smell, are also possible. On the other hand, salespeople who sell machinery are limited to appeals that will affect the buyers' senses of hearing, sight, and touch.

HELPS THE BUYER REMEMBER WHAT WAS SAID

On average, people immediately forget 50 percent of what they hear; after 48 hours they have forgotten 75 percent of the message. This is unfortunate because securing an order often requires multiple visits, and in many situations the prospect must relay to other people information learned in a sales call. In these circumstances it becomes more critical for the seller to help the buyer remember what was said.

Even selling situations involving one call or one decision maker will be more profitable if the buyer remembers what was said. Vividly communicated features create such a strong impression that the buyer remembers the seller's claims and is more likely to tell others about them.

Lasting impressions can be created in many ways. One salesperson swallows some industrial cleanser to show that it is nontoxic; another kicks the protective

BUILDING Partnerships

9.1

KNOW YOUR AUDIENCE

You have to keep the prospect's attention throughout your presentation. To do that, you really need to "know your audience" and sell to their specific needs. I sell gas monitors and transmitters to industrial firms. These monitors detect the exact level of all sorts of gases present in the building, including O_2, CO, H_2S, NH_3, NO, NO_2, methane, propane, butane, and hydrogen.

If I am giving a sales presentation to an engineer who will be using my product to get her day-to-day tasks completed, she is going to care very little about the cost. The key things they want to know about are reliability and accuracy. So, in this type of scenario, I go more in depth on how my products can make the engineer's job easier

and more efficient as opposed to doing the same job with the competitor's product.

On the other hand, if I am giving a presentation about the exact same product to the plant manager, I am going to highlight how it will save the plant money in the long run and possibly the short run as well if we are able to beat prices of similar competitor products. Going into a call knowing who you are presenting to and their specific needs will not only keep their attention but also make it easier to build the relationship and prove to the client that you really care about helping them out.

Source: Industrial Scientific Company; all names changed for anonymity; used with permission.

Exhibit 9.1

How We Learn and Remember

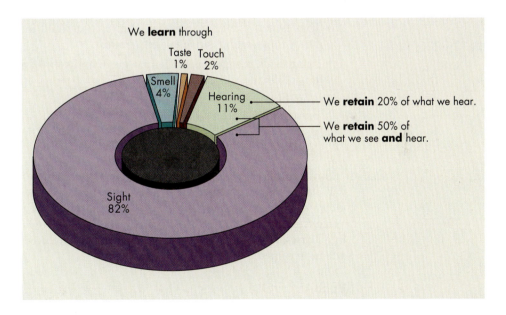

glass in the control panel of a piece of machinery to show that it is virtually unbreakable in even the roughest conditions. Whatever the method used, the prospect is more likely to remember a sales feature if it is presented skillfully in a well-timed demonstration.

OFFERS PROOF OF THE SALESPERSON'S ASSERTIONS

Let's face it: Most people won't believe everything a salesperson tells them. Many of the communication tools we discuss in this chapter provide solid proof to back up a salesperson's claims. For example, a salesperson can easily claim that a liquid is nontoxic, but the claim is much more convincing if the salesperson drinks some of the liquid in front of the prospect.

CREATES A SENSE OF VALUE

The manner in which a product is handled suggests value. Careful handling communicates value, whereas careless handling implies that the product has little value. For example, a delicate piece of china will be perceived as more valuable if the salesperson uses appropriate props, words, and care in handling it.

HOW TO STRENGTHEN THE PRESENTATION

Salespeople should ask themselves the following questions: How can I use my imagination and creativity to make a vivid impression on my prospect or customer? How can I make my presentation a little different and a little stronger? With this frame of mind, salespeople will always try to do a better and more effective job of meeting their customers' needs. In this section we explore the many tools available to strengthen a presentation.

Before we describe the various methods, it is important to reiterate a point made in the preceding chapter. A seller should not grab a method because it sounds trendy or because it worked in a previous sales call or because it is highly entertaining. Rather, a seller should strategically select methods and media that will helpfully address the needs of the buyer. This process includes responding to the buyer's unique style (see Chapter 5 to review social styles):

- Expressives like to see strong, intense colors and lots of photos, cartoons, fancy fonts, and positive images (smiles).
- Analyticals prefer visuals that are clean and simple, a list of references, and lots of details.
- Amiables prefer visuals with people in them and a relatively slow-moving presentation.
- Drivers want crisp, professional visuals with bold lettering to highlight important points.

Strategizing also includes considering such elements as how many people will attend the presentation, which stage of the buying process they are in, what information they need, what type of situation this is (new task, modified rebuy, straight rebuy), and so on (see Chapter 3 for more buying factors to consider). In all cases, it is important to get your prospects involved and keep the focus of attention centered on them.

VERBAL TOOLS
Word Pictures and Stories

The power of the spoken word can be phenomenal. To communicate effectively, the salesperson needs to remember all the hints and tools found in Chapter 4. The latest neuroscience tells us that there are basically three paths to the subconscious mind (habits, beliefs, and emotions), and stories are ways to tap into all of those paths.[1] Word pictures and stories of all types can be effective.[2] Here are some points to keep in mind when using stories:

- It is best to use stories from your own life. If you borrow one, don't act as if it is your personal story.
- Make sure you have a reason for telling the story.

- Consider using a prop, like a glove or a suitcase or something that helps tell the story and will help the prospect remember the story.
- Use the "hook" of the story to tie back directly into your presentation.
- Be accurate and vivid with the words you choose. Learn to paint a clear picture.
- Pace the story, watching your audience for cues. Use silence, loudness, softness, and pauses.
- Choose stories that fit your own style. Don't try to be someone you're not.
- Remember, stories can be short—even a few sentences.

Humor

Another way a salesperson can help keep the buyer's attention is through the use of humor. The wonderful effects of laughter will put everyone more at ease, including the salesperson. Use humorous stories from your own experience, borrowed humor, or humor adapted from another source. Here are some things to keep in mind:

- Don't oversell the joke (Here's one that'll really break you up!).
- Don't apologize before telling a joke (I wasn't ever good at telling a joke, but here goes).
- Identify any facts that are absolutely necessary for the punch line of the story to make sense (Jerry Joyner, my next-door neighbor who was always sticking his nose in other people's business, . . .).
- Use humor from your own life. Most have already heard jokes circulating in e-mail or on the Web.
- Enjoy yourself by smiling and animating your voice and nonverbals.
- Practice telling the joke different ways to see which exact wording works best.
- Make sure your punch line is clear.

Beware of overdoing humor or using off-the-wall or offensive humor. Both can backfire, as one presenter found out when he used the following opening line about an overweight attendee: "Pull up two chairs and have a seat." The presenter knew right away that it was a big mistake. Always be cautious about using insider jokes, especially if you're still considered an outsider.

thinking it through What humor have you seen backfire? How can you be sure the humor you are using isn't going to offend someone?

Also, understand that what is funny to one person or group may not be funny to others. For example, a foreigner from Egypt may not appreciate someone from America making fun of Egyptian culture—but someone from Egypt can tell that same joke and get plenty of laughs.

VISUAL TOOLS

A salesperson can use various visually oriented tools to strengthen a presentation. This section explores the content and use of those tools, followed by a discussion of the various media available to display the results.

Salespeople should use humor to get and keep the customer's attention.

Graphics and Charts

Graphics and charts help illustrate relationships and clearly communicate large amounts of information. Charts may show, for example, advertising schedules, a breakdown of typical customer profiles, details of product manufacture, profit margins at various pricing points, or the investment nature of purchasing a product.

Here are hints for developing charts and related visuals:

- Know the single point a visual should make, and then ensure that it accomplishes that point.
- Charts should be customized by including the name of the prospect's company in one corner or by some other form of personalization.
- Use current, accurate information.
- Don't place too much information on a visual; on text visuals, don't use more than five or six words per line or more than five lines or bullets per visual. Don't use complete sentences; the speaker should verbally provide the missing details.
- Use bullets (dots or symbols before each line) to differentiate issues and to emphasize key points.
- Don't overload the buyer with numbers. Use no more than five or six columns, and drop all unnecessary zeros.
- Clearly label each visual with a title. Label all columns and rows.
- Recognize the emotional impact of colors, and choose appropriate ones. An abundance of green connected to a humorous graph might be offensive in Islamic countries because green is a religious color. In Brazil and Mexico, purple indicates death. In America, blue indicates confidence and safety, black connotes a strong sense of power, and white indicates sophistication and formality.[3]
- If possible, use graphics (like diagrams, pie charts, and bar charts) instead of tables. Tables are often needed if actual raw numbers are important; graphics are better for displaying trends and relationships.
- Use high-quality drawings and photographs instead of clip art if possible.
- Use consistent art styles, layouts, and scales for your collection of charts and figures. Consistency makes it easier for the buyer to follow along.
- For PowerPoint slides, use 28-point type for the titles and 24-point type for the text, using Arial or Helvetica. And use transition effects and sound clips sparingly.
- Check your visuals closely for typographical errors, misspelled words, and other errors.
- Know and obey copyright laws. You can't just grab images off the Web and use them.

Models, Samples, and Gifts

Visual selling aids such as models, samples, and gifts may be a good answer to the problem of getting and keeping buyer interest. For example, Mul-T-Lock salespeople carry along a miniature working model of the company's electronic door locks when calling on prison security systems buyers. The model allows the salesperson to show how the various components work together to form a fail-safe security network.

Other salespeople use cross-sectional models to communicate with the buyer. For example, salespeople for Motion Industries use a cutaway model of a power transmission friction reduction product. This model helps the buyer, usually an industrial engineer, to clearly see how the product is constructed, resulting in greater confidence that the product will perform as described.

Depending on the service or product, samples and gifts can make excellent sales aids and help maintain the prospect's interest after the call. Loctite displayed the superior holding power of its glue by suspending a man by his shoes at a trade show, held in place by the Loctite adhesive.[4] In a Johnson's Wax sales campaign, salespeople called on buyers of major chains to describe the promotion. Salespeople walked into each buyer's office with a solid oak briefcase containing cans of aerosol Pledge, the product to be highlighted during the promotion. During the call the sales representative demonstrated the Pledge furniture polish on the oak briefcase. At the conclusion of the visit, the rep gave the buyer not only the cans of Pledge but also the briefcase. Of course gift giving must be done with care and not violate the rules of the buyer's company.

ethics

Catalogs and Brochures

Catalogs and brochures can help salespeople communicate information to buyers effectively. The salesperson can use them during a presentation and then leave them with the buyer as a reminder of the issues covered. Brochures often summarize key points and contain answers to the usual questions buyers pose.

Firms often spend a great deal of money to develop visually attractive brochures for salespeople. Exhibit 9.2 shows an example of a brochure used by salespeople. Creatively designed brochures usually unfold in a way that enables the salesperson to create and maintain great interest while showing them.

Exhibit 9.2
A Brochure with Great Visual Appeal

Photos, Illustrations, Ads, and Maps

Photos are easy to prepare, are inexpensive, and permit a realistic portrayal of a product and its benefits. Photographs of people may be particularly effective. For example, leisure made possible through savings can be communicated via photographs of retired people at a ranch, a mountain resort, or the seashore. Illustrations drawn, painted, or prepared in other ways also help dramatize needs or benefits. Copies of recent or upcoming ads may contribute visual appeal. Detailed maps can be easily developed, for example, to show how a magazine's circulation matches the needs of potential advertisers.

Testimonials and Test Results

Testimonials are statements written by satisfied users of a product or service. For example, company representatives who sell air travel for major airlines have found case histories helpful in communicating sales points. Air Canada recounts actual experiences of business firms, showing the variety of problems that air travel can solve.

The effectiveness of a testimonial hinges on the skill with which it is used and a careful matching of satisfied user and prospect. In some situations the testimony of a rival or a competitor of the prospective buyer would end all chance of closing the sale; in other cases this type of testimony may be a strong factor in obtaining commitment. As much as possible, the person who writes the testimonial should be above reproach, well respected by his or her peers, and perhaps a center of influence (see Chapter 6). For example, when selling to certified public accountants (CPAs), a good source for a testimonial would be the president of the state's CPA association.

Before using a testimonial, the salesperson needs to check with the person who wrote it and frequently reaffirm that he or she is still a happy, satisfied customer. One salesperson for Unisys routinely handed all prospects a testimonial from a satisfied customer of a new software package. But unknown to the salesperson, the "satisfied customer" became an unsatisfied one and actually returned the software. The salesperson kept handing out the letter until one of his prospects alerted him to the situation. He will never know how many other prospects lost interest after contacting that customer.

Salespeople should not hand out a testimonial to every prospect. Such letters should be used only if they help to address the buyer's needs or concerns. Also, be aware that prospects probably discount testimonials, thinking that the seller is presenting letters only from very satisfied customers.

Salespeople can also use test results to strengthen the presentation. Tests on the product or service may have been conducted by the seller's firm or some third-party organization (such as Consumer Reports or Underwriters Laboratories). Generally, tests conducted by independent, recognized authorities have more credibility for the prospect than tests done by the seller.

Using Media to Display Visuals

Many media are available to display the types of items just mentioned. New media and improvements to existing media are being introduced almost every week (like 3D interactive viewing, the use of Flash for presentations, and so forth). Salespeople are encouraged to choose media that are appropriate for the exact situation and not merely choose a tool because it is new or exciting. "Sales Technology 9.1" describes the use of one tool that salespeople incorporate.

Most salespeople have developed a **portfolio**, which is a collection of visual aids, often placed in a binder or on a computer. Salespeople do not intend to use everything in the portfolio in a single call; rather, the portfolio should contain a broad spectrum of visual aids the salesperson can find quickly should the need arise. When showing visuals in your portfolio, make sure the portfolio is turned

IPADS—WAYS TO INCREASE SALES POTENTIAL?

Many companies have turned to the use of iPads to help their sales force excel, including such firms as IBM, General Mills, Sears, and ADT. According to a vice president of sales at ADT, there are four main ways in which, by using an iPad, sellers' jobs are becoming easier and more efficient:

- iPad gives salespeople the ability to show prospects firsthand how their "ADT Pulse mobile app" works. This app enables users to control things in their buildings, such as heating and cooling as well as lights and video cameras.

- ADT iPads are equipped with a customer relationship management (CRM) app. This app helps to increase the overall productivity of ADT's sales force by allowing them to view their appointments as well as their locations and also retrieve valuable information regarding their customers that has previously been obtained by ADT.

- The camera on the iPad gives the sales representative the chance to take pictures of the potential devices that the customer may want to link with the Pulse mobile app. These pictures are then sent to the ADT office and paired with notes from the salesperson about the particular business that they are selling to.

- The iPad's capability to show the prospect current crime rates in the area helps the salesperson drive home the point that the ADP security system will truly be beneficial to them.

With the use of iPads, ADT's sales force has been able to decrease the time that it takes to make each sales call. This decrease in time per call increases the maximum number of sales calls each representative can make during a given workday. With the implementation of iPads, ADT salespeople in Texas have been able to double their total revenue.

Going forward, ADT plans to have their entire sales force of 4,000 representatives equipped with iPads. Also, they plan on adding two more apps for the iPads; one will give salespeople the chance to obtain a signed contract on their iPad, and the second will be an easy-to-use price configurator.

Source: Eric Lai, "IPads Have Helped Some of This Company's Salespeople DOUBLE Their Sales," *Forbes Magazine*, March 19, 2012, http://www.forbes.com/sites/sap/2012/03/19/ipads-have-helped-some-of-this-companys-salespeople-double-their-sales/2, October 23, 2012.

so the buyer can see it easily. The portfolio should not be placed, like a wall, between you and the buyer. Remember to look at the buyer, not at your visual; maintaining eye contact is always important.

Video is another tool salespeople can use. Salespeople use video to help buyers see how quality is manufactured into a product (showing the production process at the manufacturing plant), how others use a product or service (showing a group of seniors enjoying the golf course at a retirement resort), promotional support offered with the product (showing an upcoming TV commercial for a product), and even testimonials from satisfied users. When using video, make sure the video is fast paced and relatively short. Don't show more than four minutes of a video at one time.

Salespeople have adopted laptops, iPads, and other portable devices for use in sales calls. For example, Merck pharmaceutical salespeople carry laptops with a database of technical information, as well as complete copies of articles from medical journals. Progressive firms, like Aetna, are investing in **digital collateral management systems** (also called **sales asset management systems**) to archive, catalog, and retrieve digital media and text. **Collateral** is a collection of documents that are designed to generate sales, such as brochures, sales flyers and fact sheets, and short success stories. Digital collateral management systems simplify the collection and make it possible for salespeople to easily secure and adapt these selling tools for specific situations. For example, salespeople using the SAVO digital collateral management system (www.savogroup.com) can easily call up photos, videos, audio files, PowerPoint templates, Web pages, legal documents, streaming media, and just about anything else that has been digitally entered into the system.

Some salespeople use PowerPoint to give presentations. However, it is critical that salespeople not merely progress from one slide to the next. Presentations should use visuals that encourage two-way conversation rather than an endless group of slides.

thinking **it** through

You turn the lights down for a PowerPoint computer slide presentation. A few minutes later, you start to panic when your eye catches an unusual jerking movement made by the buyer—she's falling asleep! What do you do now?

Computers not only offer excellent visuals and graphics but also allow the salesperson to perform what-if analyses. For example, when a grocery buyer asked a Procter & Gamble rep what would happen if a new product were sold for $3.69 instead of the $3.75 suggested retail price, the salesperson was able to easily change this number in the spreadsheet program. Instantly all charts and graphs were corrected to illustrate the new pricing point, and comparisons with the competitor's product were generated.

When using computers, be prepared. Have backup batteries, adapters, and copies of any DVDs. Really get to know your hardware and software so you can recover if the system crashes. And make sure both you and your customer can comfortably view the output.

Images can also be displayed using other media. **Document cameras,** also called **visual presenters,** are capable of displaying any three-dimensional object without the use of a transparency. **Electronic whiteboards,** commonly referred

Examples of sales collateral for an industrial product.

Salespeople use electronic tools to display important information.

to as SMART boards or digital easels, are used by salespeople, especially when working with customers who prefer to brainstorm an issue or problem. These are great at encouraging a group to interact with a presentation rather than merely watching it.

PRODUCT DEMONSTRATIONS

One of the most effective methods of appealing to a buyer's senses is through product demonstrations or performance tests.[5] Customers and prospects have a natural desire to prove a product's claims for themselves. For example, orthopedic surgeons are like carpenters for human bodies: They repair damage and build new skeletons. They don't want a salesperson merely to tell them about new products; these surgeons want to touch them, feel them, and use them to see if they are good. When selling hip replacements to such doctors, sales reps demonstrate their products right in the surgery room. Because there is a definite sterile field, sales reps have to stand outside that field and use a green laser pointer to show where the surgeon should place the appliance.

One enterprising sales representative was having trouble convincing the buyer for a national retailer that the salesperson's company could provide service at all the retailer's scattered outlets. On the next trip to the buyer, the sales representative brought along a bag of darts and a map marked with the chain's hundreds of stores and service locations. The buyer was invited to throw darts at the map and then find the nearest stores. The test pointed out that the nearest location for service was always within 50 miles. This "service demonstration" helped win the representative's company a multimillion-dollar order.

Another salesperson was selling feeding tubes to a hospital. A nurse took the salesperson to a patient's bed and stated, "Here, you do it. You said it was easier to insert. Let me see you insert it."[6]

Some products can be sold most successfully by getting the prospect into the showroom for a hands-on product demonstration. Showrooms can be quite elaborate and effective. For example, Kohler operates a marketing showroom in Kohler, Wisconsin. Prospects (architects and designers) from across the world can view and try all of Kohler's kitchen and bath fixtures. **Executive briefing centers,** which are rooms set aside to highlight a company's products and capabilities, are the ultimate presentation room.

Here are a number of helpful hints for developing and engaging in effective demonstrations:

- Be prepared. Practice your demonstration until you become an expert. Plan for everything that could possibly go wrong.

- Secure a proper place for the demonstration, one free of distractions for both you and the buyer. If the demonstration

An executive briefing center.

is at the buyer's office, make sure you have everything you need (power supply, lighting, and so on). Remember, it can even be an online presentation as Chapters 7 and 8 described.

- Check the equipment again to make sure it is in good working order prior to beginning the presentation. Have necessary backup parts and supplies (like paper or bulbs).

- Get the prospect involved in a meaningful way. In a group situation, plan which group members need to participate.

- Always relate product features to the buyer's unique needs.

- Make the demonstration an integral part of the overall presentation, not a separate, unrelated activity.

- Keep the demonstration simple, concise, and clear. Long, complicated demonstrations add to the possibility that the buyer will miss the point. Limit technical jargon to technically advanced buyers who you know will understand technical terms.

- Plan what you will do during any dead time—that is, time in which the machine is processing on its own. You can use these intervals to ask the buyer questions and have the buyer ask you questions.

- Find out whether the prospect has already seen a competitor's product demonstration. If so, strategically include a demonstration of features the buyer liked about the competitor's product. Also, plan to show how your product can meet the prospect's desires and do what the competitor's product will not do.

- Find out whether any buyers present at your demonstration have used your product before. Having them assist in the demonstration may be advantageous if they view your product favorably.

- Probe during and after the demonstration. Make sure buyers understand the features and see how the product can help them. Also, probe to see whether buyers are interested in securing the product.

Remember Murphy's law: What can go wrong will go wrong! If a demonstration "blows up" for any reason, your best strategy usually is to appeal to fate with a humorous tone of voice: "Wow, have you ever seen anything get so messed up? Maybe I should run for Congress!" Don't let technical glitches embarrass or frustrate you. Life is not perfect, and sometimes things just don't work out the way you plan them. If it will help, remember that prospects also are not perfect, and sometimes they mess things up as well. Maintaining a cool and level head will probably impress the prospect with your ability to deal with a difficult situation. It may even increase your chances of a sale because you are demonstrating your ability to handle stress (something that often occurs during the after-sale servicing of an account).

HANDOUTS

Handouts are written documents provided to help buyers remember what was said. A well-prepared set of handouts can be one of the best ways to increase buyer retention of information, especially over longer periods. A common practice is to make a printed copy of the presentation visuals and give that to the buyers at the conclusion of the presentation.

Others would argue that your use of handouts should be more strategically focused. Thus, handouts are not a last-minute thought but rather are a tool that

Getting the buyer actively involved during the call is important.

needs to be carefully planned while you are preparing your presentation. For example, you could draw a line on a piece of planning paper and on the left side list the things you will do and say during the presentation while on the right side listing the items that should go into the handout. In that way the two will work together and be complementary.

What things can go into a handout? Complex charts and diagrams can be included. Because you want to keep your presentation visuals relatively simple (see the preceding hints), your handouts can supply more complete, detailed information. You may also want to include some company reports or literature. However, to avoid making the buyer wade through a lot of nonrelevant information, include only important sections. Other items to include are addresses with a description of each studies, magazine articles, and a copy presentation visuals themselves (with room to take notes if you're going to buyer your handout during the presentation). Whatever you choose, the tips:

- Avoid talking while the handout is passed out.
- Consider highlighting important the handout.
- Don't forget the goal of your should drive all your decisions about what to include in your
- Make sure the handouts look Use graphics instead of text whenever possible.
- Don't cram too much information on a page. White space is fine. Try not to fill more than two-thirds of any page with information.
- Don't drown your prospect in information. Include only helpful information in your handouts.
- Handouts are even more important for foreign buyers, especially those who are nonnative English speakers. You might even consider giving them a copy of your handouts before your meeting so they can become more comfortable and familiar with concepts and phrases. Including a glossary, with definitions, will also be appreciated by foreign buyers.

WRITTEN PROPOSALS

In some industries written proposals are an important part of the selling process. Some proposals are simple adaptations of brochures developed by a corporate marketing department. But in industries that sell customized products or require competitive bidding (as many state and local governments do), a written proposal may be necessary for the buyer to organize and compare various offerings.

The RFP Process

A document issued by a prospective buyer asking for a proposal may be called a **request for proposal (RFP)**, request for quote (RFQ), or request for bid (RFB). For brevity's sake, we will refer to all of these as RFPs.

The RFP should contain the customer's specifications for the desired product, including delivery schedules. RFPs are used when the customer has a firm idea of the product needed. From the salesperson's perspective, being a part of the specifying process makes sense. Using the needs identification process, the salesperson can help the customer identify needs and specify product characteristics.

Writing Proposals

Proposals include an **executive summary**—a one- or two-page summary that provides the total cost minus the total savings, a brief description of the problem to be solved, and a brief description of the proposed solution. The summary should satisfy the concerns of an executive who is too busy or unwilling to read the entire proposal. The executive summary also piques the interest of all readers by allowing a quick glance at the benefits of the purchase.

The proposal also includes a description of the current situation in relation to the proposed solution and a budget (which details costs). Some firms have even developed computer programs to automatically generate sales proposals in response to a set of questions the salesperson answers about a particular customer.[7] This is especially helpful because sometimes buyers use RFPs to keep their current suppliers in check. In such a case, a seller might want to minimize the amount of time spent responding to an RFP. (A familiar saying in sales is "You can't cash an RFP.")

When writing proposals, remember to use your most polished writing skills. Skip buzzwords, focusing on actual results that the prospect can gain from going with your proposal.

Presenting the Proposal

Prospects use proposals in many different ways. Proposals can be used to convince the home office that the local office needs the product, or proposals may be used to compare the product and terms of sale with those of competitors. As we mentioned earlier, the intended use will influence the design of the proposal; it will also influence how the salesperson presents the proposal.

When the proposal is going to be sent to the home office, it is wise to secure the support of the local decision maker. Although that person is not the ultimate decision maker, the decision may rest on how much effort that person puts into getting the proposal accepted. Buying centers often use proposals to compare competitive offerings, and the salesperson is asked to present the proposal to the buying committee.

There are several options if you are going to give an oral presentation of your proposal. First, you can give the buyers a copy of the complete proposal before your presentation. During the meeting you would spend about 5 to 10 minutes summarizing the proposal and then ask for questions. Second, if you choose to give the written proposal to the buyers during the oral presentation, you may want to distribute the proposal a section at a time to avoid having them read ahead instead of listening to your oral presentation.

VALUE ANALYSIS: QUANTIFYING THE SOLUTION

To recap what we've described throughout this book, salespeople are selling value. As mentioned in Chapter 3, one of the trends in buying is more sophisticated analyses by buyers. This section explores methods available to help the buyer conduct these types of analyses.

Quantifying a solution is more important in some situations than in others. Some products or services (like replacement parts or repairs) pose little risk for the prospect. These products are so necessary for the continuation of the prospect's business that little quantifying of the solution is usually needed. Other products pose moderate risk (such as expanding the production capacity of a plant for an existing successful product) or high risk (like programs designed to reduce costs or increase sales; these present higher risk because it is hard to calculate the exact magnitude of the potential savings or sales). For moderate-risk and high-risk situations, quantifying the solution becomes increasingly important. Finally, certain products pose super-high risk (brand-new products or services, which are riskier because no one can calculate costs or revenues with certainty). Attempts at quantifying the solution are imperative in super-high-risk situations. In summary, the higher the risk to the prospect, the more attention the salesperson should pay to quantifying the solution.

Salespeople can strengthen a presentation by showing the prospect that the cost of the proposal is offset by added value; this process is often called **quantifying the solution** or **value analysis.** Some of the most common ways to quantify a solution are value propositions, cost–benefit analysis, return on investment, payback period, net present value, and opportunity cost. For retail buyers, the seller usually must prove turnover and profit margins. The key is to offer information that will help buyers evaluate your offering based on their metrics. Thus, if a buyer is evaluating proposals on the basis of ROI, that's the metric you should focus on in your presentation.

Customer Value Proposition

A **customer value proposition,** also called a *value proposition,* is the way in which your product will meet the prospect's needs and how that is different from the offerings of competitors, especially the next-best alternative.[8] Honeywell sales reps create basic value propositions for each market segment and then further refine them for each individual customer. The value bundle contained in a solid customer value proposition includes the features and benefits (financial and emotional) tailored to the prospect, the proof that those benefits actually exist, and the value of the seller and the seller's firm as the solutions provider. Simply having a superior product or delivering on your promises is no longer sufficient. Rather, what distinguishes you is how you make your customers feel while using your product. The experience is what bonds your customers to you.

As you write your customer value proposition, remember that what it contains is tailored to the individual prospect, so it needs to address three key issues: What is important to this specific prospect (which requires we understand the customer's business model)? How does our solution create value for this specific prospect? And how can we demonstrate our capability (which means we have to communicate the value to the customer)?[9]

Here are some weak examples of customer value proposition statements, none of which tell how the prospect is really going to benefit or how the seller can demonstrate that she is able to accomplish the goals for the account:

- It's the most technologically advanced system on the market today.
- We reduce training time more than any of our competitors.
- Our service was rated number one by an independent service lab.

Now here are examples of good customer value proposition statements, which include the elements discussed:[10]

- According to your CFO, dispatching multiple service vans to a customer site has been costing an estimated $20,000 a year in extra fuel costs. When you add that to the cost of unproductive personnel time and missed revenue, the loss is $850,000 per year. When you implement our Call Tracker system you will be able to reduce repeat customer service calls by 20 percent, resulting in a monthly savings of $250,000. This will require an investment of $2 million, which will be returned in only eight months. We implemented a similar solution at Acme Transfer, which began achieving a monthly savings of $500,000 within 90 days of installation. And I have personally overseen 15 such installations and will be there to ensure that all parties are fully trained in use of the new system.

- In this era of heightened airport security concerns, Advanced Engineering, a leading manufacturer of state-of-the-art explosives detective devices, offers a unique solution. The complete "Senso-37 Detection System" for major airports like yours requires a $200,000 investment, fully installed. Our superior system has been shown to save lives, lower human security guard costs, and decr___ passenger processing time. My analysis reveals that Orlando Interna___ ___ort will decrease its general security guard expenses at the majo___ ___ening area by $80,000 per year for the next four years, gi___ ___ in just 2.5 years and also giving you and your passeng___ ___hat ALL passengers are being screened with state-of-th___ ___hen you install the system you also get an added adv___ ___tment and supervision, as one of the top salespeople i___ ___at your system will be installed at Orlando Internationa___ ___ and as promised and that your security staff will be trai___ ___ effectively.

Customer val___ ___s should contain four main parts:

- One or more key fe___es of the product/service complete with external proof
- The benefits, both economical and emotional
- Positioning your company as the prospect's long-term partner
- Offering yourself as the personal problem solver

How do you create a customer value proposition?[11] Having solid, clear information is critical, as "From the Buyer's Seat 9.1" illustrates. Try brainstorming with your sales team and look for statements that truly tell your customers how your solution is going to solve their problems. Every time you write one down, keep asking, "So what difference does that make?" For example, if you write "saves time," ask, "So what does it matter if it saves time?" By doing so, you will eventually be able to reach the core value that your customer will achieve by adopting your product. Another helpful way to create a customer value proposition is by talking to your customers. They know what value you can bring to a prospect because they have experienced it firsthand and are usually willing to offer suggestions.

Cost–Benefit Analysis

Perhaps the simplest method of quantifying a solution is to list the costs to the buyer and the savings the buyer can expect from the investment, often called a **simple cost–benefit analysis.** For this analysis to be realistic and meaningful, information needed to calculate savings must be supplied by the buyer. Exhibit 9.3 shows how one salesperson used a chart to compare the costs and benefits of purchasing a two-way radio system.

In many situations the salesperson does a **comparative cost–benefit analysis** by comparing the present situation's costs with the value of the proposed solution or the seller's product with a competitor's product. For example, a company with

From the BUYER'S SEAT

I LOVE TO SEE SELLER'S PLAN!

I'm comanager at an Independent Grocers Alliance (IGA) grocery store located in Iowa. IGA was founded in 1926 to bring together independent grocers across the nation to help ensure that the local grocery store remained strong in the face of growing chain competition. My store is actually one of six that are owned by a single owner. Many of the new products that we carry in our six stores must first be presented during one of our store meetings. During these meetings, managers from all locations are present, along with the owners of the organization and a few other individuals. After salespeople pitch their products to us during our meetings, the floor opens for questions from anyone who may have an objection or question.

There are some simple ways that salespeople can prepare for their sales presentation not only to strengthen their overall presentation but also to increase the chances that our stores will begin to carry their products and/or product lines. First, they should visit as many stores as possible to get a better feel as to the types of people they will be attempting to sell to and to get a better sense of the overall culture of the store (what we currently carry, our current prices, how our current products are packaged, and so on). Second, we are not going to consider bringing a product into our stores that we have never tried ourselves, so sellers should provide enough samples for everyone who wishes to try the product a chance to try it.

I'll never forget the impression made by one particular salesperson from Pepsi. As I was finishing up all of the nightly tasks before closing, she walked into my store carrying a clipboard, a notebook, and a pen in hand. I asked her if there was anything that I could help her with, and she responded, "Well, to be honest, I am going to be presenting a new soft drink line at your managers meeting tomorrow, and I just wanted to see how my current competition is looking in your stores. If you have a little bit of time, I'd love to run a few things by you and see if we're on the same page." We talked for a while, and by the end of our conversation she had taken over two pages of notes on things that we had talked about, from what I feel was missing in our current offerings as well as their strengths.

The next day when she was making her sales pitch, she took into account all the things that we had talked about and tailored her presentation toward the areas that we had discovered were the most weaknesses and how her product was going to help us in those areas. Everything that she had learned about our stores in that short time period was put into her sales presentation and ultimately helped her strengthen his presentation and tailor it to our needs. Needless to say, she got the business!

Source: Herberto Aguila, IGA; all names have been changed for anonymity; used with permission.

---

a premium-priced product may justify the higher price on the basis of offsetting costs in other areas. If productivity is enhanced, the increased productivity has economic value.

Return on Investment

The **return on investment (ROI)** is simply the net profits (or savings) expected from a given investment, expressed as a percentage of the investment:

$$\text{ROI} = \text{Net profits (or savings)} \div \text{Investment}$$

Thus, if a new product costs \$4,000 but saves the firm \$5,000, the ROI is 125 percent (\$5,000 ÷ \$4,000 = 1.25). Many firms set a minimum ROI for any new products, services, or cost-saving programs. Salespeople need to discover the firm's minimum ROI or ROI expectations and then show that the proposal's ROI meets or exceeds those requirements. For an ROI analysis to be accurate, it is

Exhibit 9.3

Cost–Benefit Analysis for a Mobile Radio

Monthly Cost

Monthly equipment payment (five-year lease/purchase)*	$1,555.18
Monthly service agreement	339.00
Monthly broadcast fee	+ 533.60
Total monthly cost for entire fleet	$2,427.78

Monthly Savings

Cost savings (per truck) by eliminating backtracking, unnecessary trips (based on $.36/mile × 20 miles × 22 days/month)	$158.40
Labor cost savings (per driver) by eliminating wasted time in backtracking, etc. ($8.00/hour × 25 minutes/day × 22 days/month)	+ 73.33
Total cost savings per vehicle	231.73
Times number of vehicles	× 32
Total monthly cost savings for entire fleet	$7,415.36

	Years 1–5	Year 6+
Monthly savings	$7,415.36	$7,415.36
Less: monthly cost	− 2,427.78	− 872.85
Monthly benefit	4,987.58	6,542.51
Times months per year	× 12	× 12
Annual benefit	$59,850.96	$78,510.12

*Payment reflects ongoing cost of service agreement and broadcast fees.

important for the seller to collect meaningful data about costs and savings that the buyer can expect.

Payback Period

The **payback period** is the length of time it takes for the investment cash outflow to be returned in the form of cash inflows or savings. To calculate the payback period, you simply add up estimated future cash inflows and divide them into the investment cost. If expressed in years, the formula is as follows:

$$\text{Payback period} = \text{Investment} \div \text{Savings (or profits) per year}$$

Of course the payback period could be expressed in days, weeks, months, or any other period.

As an example, suppose a new machine costs $865,000 but will save the firm $120,000 per year in labor costs. The payback period is 7.2 years ($865,000 ÷ $120,000 per year = 7.2 years).

Thus, for the buyer, the payback period indicates how quickly the investment money will come back to him or her and can be a good measure of personal risk. When a buyer makes a decision, his or her neck is "on the line," so to speak, until the investment money is at least recovered. Hence, it's not surprising that buyers like to see short payback periods.

We have kept the discussion simple to help you understand the concept. In reality the calculation of

For large capital outlays, the prospect usually needs to see the return on investment, payback period, and/or net present value.

the payback period would take into account many other factors, such as investment tax credits and depreciation.

Net Present Value

As you may have learned in finance courses, money left idle loses value over time (a dollar today is worth more than a dollar next week) because of inflation and the firm's cost of capital. Thus, firms calculate the value of future cash inflows in today's dollars (this process is called *discounting the cash flows*). One tool to assess the validity of an opportunity is to calculate the **net present value (NPV)**, which is simply the net value today of future cash inflows (discounted back to their present value today at the firm's cost of capital) minus the investment. The actual method of calculating NPV is beyond the scope of this book, but many computer programs and calculators can calculate NPV quickly and easily:

$$\text{Net present value} = \text{Future cash inflows discounted into today's dollars} - \text{Investment}$$

As an example of the preceding formula, let's assume that a $50 million investment will provide annual cash inflows over the next five years of $15 million per year. The cash inflows are discounted (at the firm's cost of capital), and the result is that they are actually worth $59 million in today's dollars. The NPV is thus $9 million ($59 million − $50 million).

As with ROI and payback period, many firms set a minimum NPV. In no case should the NPV be less than $0. Again, we have kept this discussion simple to help you understand the basic concept.

Opportunity Cost

The **opportunity cost** is the return a buyer would have earned from a different use of the same investment capital. Thus, a buyer could spend $100 million to buy any of the following: a new computer system, a new production machine, or a controlling interest in another firm.

Successful salespeople identify other realistic investment opportunities and then help the prospect compare the returns of the various options. These comparisons can be made by using any of the techniques we have already discussed (cost–benefit analysis, ROI, payback period, NPV). For example, a salesperson might help the buyer determine the following information about the options identified:

	NPV	Payback Period
Buying a new telecommunications system	$1.6 million	3.6 years
Upgrading the current telecommunications system	0.4 million	4.0 years

Salespeople should never forget that prospects have a multitude of ways to invest their money.

Selling Value to Resellers

When resellers purchase a product for resale, they are primarily concerned with whether their customers will buy the product and how much they will make on each sale. For example, when an Xbox salesperson meets with Walmart to sell video games, he is armed with data showing how much profit is made every time Walmart sells a game and how fast the games sell. The Walmart buyer uses this information to compare the performance of Xbox video games with objectives and with other products sold in the same category, such as Sony's PlayStation.

PROFIT MARGIN Profit margin is the net profit the reseller makes, expressed as a percentage of sales. It is calculated, and thus influenced, by many factors. For example, if Linz Jewelers bought 100 rings for $1,000 each ($100,000), spent $45,000 in expenses (for advertising, salesperson commission, store rent, and other items), and sold them all at an average price of $3,000 ($300,000 in revenue), the profit would be $155,000, with a profit margin of 52 percent ($155,000 ÷ $300,000 = .52).

INVENTORY TURNOVER Inventory turnover is typically calculated by dividing the annual sales by the average retail price of the inventory on hand. Thus it measures how fast a product sells relative to how much inventory has to be carried—how efficiently a reseller manages its inventory. The reseller would like to have in the store only the amount needed for that day's sales because inventory represents an investment. Thus, large retailers such as Cub Foods receive daily delivery of some products. If the reseller is able to reduce its inventory level, it can invest this savings in stores or warehouses or in the stock market.

For example, if Linz Jewelers usually kept eight rings in stock, inventory turnover would be calculated by dividing total sales in units (100 rings) by average inventory (8 rings). Thus inventory turnover would be 100 ÷ 8, or 12.5 times. The answer represents the number of times that Linz sold the average inventory level. Another way to calculate this is to divide total sales ($300,000 in the Linz example) by the average price of inventory (8 units at $3,000, or $24,000). The answer is the same: 12.5 times.

A reseller does not necessarily want to increase inventory turnover by reducing the amount of inventory carried. Several negative consequences can result. For example, sales may fall because stockouts occur more frequently and products are not available when customers want to buy them. Expenses can increase because the reseller has to order more frequently. Finally, the cost of goods sold may increase because the reseller pays higher shipping charges and does not get as big a quantity discount.

Sellers provide resellers with information to prove that inventory turnover can be improved by buying from them. They describe their **efficient consumer response (ECR), quick response (QR), automatic replenishment (AR),** and just-in-time (JIT) inventory management systems designed to reduce the reseller's average inventory and transportation expenses but still make sure products are available when end users want them. Chapter 3 described the use of these information systems in depth.

As an example, the September 11, 2001, tragedy created an outpouring of patriotic feelings among Americans. Within 24 hours there was a shortage of American flags, and there is only one major American flag manufacturer. The company had 80,000 flags in inventory on September 11. By the close of business September 12, both Target and Walmart had completely sold out of flags—over 150,000 each. When the stores opened September 13, Walmart had 80,000 more flags, whereas Target had none. How? Walmart's QR system was updated every five minutes, whereas Target didn't update its inventory system until the stores were closed in the evening. Walmart had an order placed with expedited shipping before the stores closed and before Target knew it was out of flags! Similar situations occurred in other product categories, such as flashlights, batteries, battery-powered radios, bottled water, guns, ammunition, and other products that frightened Americans wanted. As you can see, EDI and ECR systems can give resellers significant competitive advantage.

Electronic data interchange (EDI) is a computer-to-computer transmission of data from a reseller, such as Walmart, to vendors (such as American Flag Company) and back. Resellers and vendors that have ECR or QR relationships use EDI to transmit purchase orders and shipping information.

RETURN ON SPACE A key investment [...] ake is in space—retail store space and warehouse space. A meas[...] use to assess the return on their space investment is sales per s[...] per shelf foot. In a grocery store or a department store, shelf o[...] a finite asset that is used to capacity. Products therefore must [...] how well they use the space allocated to them. For example, [...] erates $200 per square foot in sales with Tommy Hilfiger merch[...] y $150 selling Ralph Lauren merchandise, it may increase the sp[...] o Tommy Hilfiger and reduce the space allocated to Ralph Laure[...]

DEALING WITH THE JITTERS

Let's face it. For many people giving a presentation is a frightening experience. Even seasoned salespeople can get the jitters when the presentation is for a very important client or when the prospect has been rude in an earlier meeting. It all comes down to fear: the fear of being embarrassed or failing, the fear of exposing our lack of knowledge in some area, or the fear of losing our train of thought. The reasons don't even have to be valid. If you have the jitters, you need to help resolve them.

Here are some tips from the experts on how to reduce presentation jitters:

- Know your audience well.
- Know what you're talking about. Keep up to date.
- Prepare professional, helpful visuals. These not only help your audience understand the presentation, but also can help you remember important points.
- Be yourself. Don't try to present like someone else.
- Get a good night's sleep.
- For presentations to groups, feed off the energy and enthusiasm of several friendly, happy-looking people in your audience. (Note: That's what professors often do!)
- Recognize the effect of fear on your body and reduce the accompanying stress manifestations by stretching, taking deep breaths to relax breathing, and so on.
- Visualize your audience as your friends—people who are interested and eager to hear what you have to say.

- Psych yourself up for the presentation. Think of the successes you have had in your life (previous presentations that went well or other things you have done well).

- Realize that everyone gets nervous before a presentation at times. It is natural. In fact, it can help you keep from being cocky.

- *Practice, practice, practice!* And finally, practice.

SELLING YOURSELF

To be successful in selling, customizing the material and method of communication is vital to your success. These points may seem high level, but they act as the foundation of any sales motion. Remember, selling is present in nearly all areas of your life, and preparation can dramatically increase your probability of success. Consider this scenario.

As the school year approaches an end, you are hopeful to land a high-paying internship in an area of business that interests you. You find the marketing research internship of your dreams, but it requests a recommendation from your college or university.

"Marketing Research" was a class in which you excelled, and your goal is to convince John, a professor of marketing at your university, to sponsor you for the opportunity. From your past experiences, John is clearly analytic by nature. As you learned in Chapter 5 on social styles, analytics have several tendencies you can use to best position your request.

Knowing John's background as a market researcher tends to drive his focus to quantitative figures over opinions or concept based information, what would be the best way to sell this professor on recommending you for the internship?

As the chapter suggests, analytics "prefer visuals that are clean and simple, a list of references, and lots of details." Therefore, your request is likely to be accepted if it focuses on specifics and detailed information with proper citing. Be sure to leave no stone unturned in terms of how you describe why would be successful in the role. An analytic will appreciate the detail because this allows for a development of comfort associated with his pending recommendation. While it may feel overdrawn, keep in mind that an analytic tends to review and appreciate full information before making a decision.

While an expressive or amiable professor may be more receptive to a referral from a high-achieving peer student or even another professor, John is more likely to connect with a printed transcript or validated certifications that demonstrate achievement. Be sure to provide information with sources to ensure his comfort with the information presented and, thus, your request.

When creating a value proposition for this professor, what is worth focusing on? Because John appreciates facts, detail, and proper sourcing, he needs to see facts about how your experience will lead to success in the internship. While your personality may be perfect for the internship, this opinion should not lead the sales motion with John. Stay focused on the importance of conscious consideration of who you are selling to because it may be the most vital element but an unnoticed factor in a sales motion.

In summary, strengthening the presentation revolves around first knowing your audience and then creating materials and communication strategies that are most likely to be positively accepted. Good selling!

Source: Mike Buckland; used with permission.

SUMMARY

Strengthening communication with the buyer is important. It helps focus the buyer's attention, improves the buyer's understanding, helps the buyer remember what was said, and can create a sense of value.

Many methods of strengthening communication are available. These include such items as word pictures, stories, humor, charts, models, samples, gifts, catalogs, brochures, photos, ads, maps, illustrations, testimonials, and test results. Media available include portfolios, video, computers, and visual projectors.

A backbone of many sales presentations is the product demonstration. It allows the buyer to get hands-on experience with the product, something most other communication methods do not offer. Handouts and written proposals can also strengthen presentations.

It is often important to quantify a solution so the buyer can evaluate its costs in relation to the benefits he or she can derive from the proposal. Some of the more common methods of quantifying a solution include simple cost–benefit analysis, comparative cost–benefit analysis, return on investment, payback period, net present value, and calculation of opportunity cost, turnover, and profit margins. Salespeople should be prepared to present a clear customer value proposition that offers real value to the customer.

All communication tools require skill and practice to be used effectively. Outstanding salespeople follow a number of guidelines to improve their use of visuals, demonstrate their products more effectively, and reduce their nervousness.

KEY TERMS

automatic replenishment (AR) 244
collateral 233
comparative cost–benefit analysis 240
customer value proposition 239
digital collateral management 233
document cameras 234
efficient consumer response (ECR) 244
electronic data interchange (EDI) 245
electronic whiteboard 234
executive briefing center 235
executive summary 238
handouts 236
inventory turnover 244
multiple-sense appeals 226

net present value (NPV) 243
opportunity cost 243
payback period 242
portfolio 232
profit margin 244
quantifying the solution 238
quick response (QR) 244
request for proposal (RFP) 237
return on investment (ROI) 241
sales asset management system 233
simple cost–benefit analysis 240
testimonials 232
value analysis 239
visual presenters 234

ETHICS PROBLEMS

1. Men tend to respond more to jokes involving sexual innuendo than women do. Assume this statement is true for a male buyer you are going to call on next Tuesday. You learn that he loves jokes with a sexual bent. Is there any reason you should avoid using a joke with a sexual theme when calling on him?

2. Is encouraging buyers to order a large quantity so they can get a better quantity discount always a good idea? Why or why not?

QUESTIONS AND PROBLEMS

1. Assume you plan a demonstration to prove some of the claims you have made for a new riding lawnmower. How would the demonstration differ for each of these three individuals: a person who is very concerned about the environment, an economy-minded person, and a safety-minded person?

2. How could you demonstrate the following products?
   a. A new Wilson basketball to a high school coach.
   b. The strength of a fiberglass stepladder to an industrial construction contractor.
   c. A line of stay-sharp cutlery to a chef at a five-star restaurant.

3. Which communication tools would you use to provide solid proof to address the following concerns expressed by prospects?
   a. I don't think that type of carpet would sell well in a store like ours.
   b. No one eats popcorn anymore, so I don't need your Nostalgia old-fashioned popcorn cart.
   c. That Tonka steel dump truck won't hold up under rough play with three-year-old boys.
   d. You look too old to know what the younger customers who shop in my store are looking for.

4. This chapter generally accepts the use of Power-Point presentations as a positive, useful tool for salespeople. Are there any times when the use of PowerPoint could actually be detrimental to communication effectiveness? Explain.

5. Which communication tools would you use to communicate the following facts?
   a. We have been in business for over 10 years.
   b. This driver is going to help you get more distance with the golf ball.
   c. These bedsheets will not pill or wear out even after 100 washings.
   d. This scale is accurate to plus or minus .00015 ounces.
   e. This camera produces extra-high-quality resolution.

6. Assume that you are selling a complete line of canoes and kayaks to a large outfitter to replace all of their current units. The total costs will be $125,000. You expect that repairs will drop by $25,000 a year over the next 10 years. At the outfitter's cost of capital, the discounted cash inflows have a value today of $215,000. Use this information to calculate the following:
   a. Return on investment.
   b. Payback period.
   c. Net present value.

7. Assume that ACME Tools buys 100 portable generators for $425 each and then spends $1,000 in expenses for advertising, salesperson commission, and store rent. The generators sell for $695 each. ACME keeps 100 generators in stock at all times. Average annual sales are 500 generators. Calculate the following:
   a. Profit margin
   b. Inventory turnover

8. Are there any retail situations for which return on space is not a big deal? How about situations where return on space is extremely important?

9. In "Building Partnerships 9.1" you read how the salesperson varied his presentation depending on the customer's job title. Using the various methods described in this chapter, exactly how would you suggest strengthening the presentation to an engineer as described in "Building Partnerships 9.1?"

CASE PROBLEMS

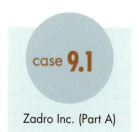

case **9.1**

Zadro Inc. (Part A)

There are many harmful germs found in the home, in public places, and in hotels while traveling. The Programmable UV Sanitizing Wand, made by Zadro, can effectively kill up to 99.99 percent of germs and viruses in just 10 seconds. It can also kill dust mites in mattresses, pillows, and carpets. Since the wand is portable, it can travel with you wherever you travel, removing harmful substances regardless of where you are. The user simply waves the scanner within a quarter inch of the surface for 10 seconds to kill the substances.

The scanner is 1½ inches high × 20 inches wide × 1¾ inches deep and runs on three C batteries. An optional AC adapter is sold separately. The scanner includes an electronic child lock to prevent misuse. A stand is provided and is used to go over keyboards, butcher blocks, and so on for hands-free operation. The programmable unit can be set for 10-, 20-, 40-, and 60-second times as well as two to five minutes, depending on the surface area that needs to be scanned. The unit is not designed to be used on humans or animals. The scanner, which is laboratory certified and tested, retails for $99, and all units come with a 90-day limited warranty. Resellers are offered the units for $60, with a quantity discount price of $50 for all units over 100 in a single order.

Questions

1. Describe how you would use the communication tools described in this chapter to sell the Programmable UV Sanitizing Wand to Target. Target would then resell to its consumers. Make any assumptions necessary.
2. Develop a short (five-minute) slide show that you can use to introduce the product to potential buyers at a retailer trade show.

Source: http://www.zadroinc.com/health-solutions-nano-technology-c-43_44.html; discount information is for illustration purposes only.

case **9.2**

Miller Lite

On December 5, 1933, the U.S. Congress passed a bill that would repeal the Eighteenth Amendment and thus would end prohibition in this country. The implementation of prohibition had been linked to many negative social issues, such as organized crime, bootlegging, and racketeering. Some historians have commented that the alcohol industry accepted stronger regulation of alcohol in the decades after repeal as a way to reduce the chance that Prohibition would return.

Today, the American beer industry is the most heavily regulated industry in the country, even more than the tobacco industry, and Minnesota is a leader when it comes to heavy regulation and high taxes. For example, here are the beer laws in Minnesota:

1. All retailers must be offered the same price at all times.
2. Beer distributors cannot pay for any cooperative advertising.
3. Beer distributors cannot give any product for free.
4. Beer distributors have a maximum of $300 per brand, per year, to promote the brand within the account (using things like neon lights and point-of-sale items), but this can't be in the form of price cuts for an individual retailer.

I was the sales representative for a beer distributor in Minnesota. My territory volume was trending down, and I was told by my manager that I needed to secure incremental activity to promote Miller Lite. My largest customer, Bill, at Save-a-Lot Liquor, gave me an opportunity for an additional holiday ad in his weekly flyer. I knew this ad would yield a 200 percent lift in sales for the week and in turn would pay a nice commission to me.

To secure the ad, Bill was asking me to lower the price of my product by 50 cents per case to cover the cost of the ad. Bill also stated that if I decided not to participate, my competition had already committed to the ad. I believed that my competition had lowered the price in the past, and there had never been any repercussions from the authorities. What should I do? I had totally lost the interest of Bill, who would turn elsewhere to buy the bulk of his beer!

I had several options. I could write a personal check for the amount of the ad, but that would have repercussions down the road, and I was sure I'd be asked to do so again and again. I could try to see if Bill really did have the competitor's agreement to cut the price, but that could backfire on me and make the customer think I didn't trust his word. I could give all the other liquor stores in my territory the same 50-cent discount, but that would cut into our profit margins.

Questions

1. What should the salesperson do at this point?
2. What will be the repercussions of your answer to question 1?

Source: Amir Permeh, Bernick's Beverages & Vending, personal correspondence; used with permission; names of buyer changed to protect confidentiality.

ROLE PLAY CASE

Today you will present to the same person whose needs you identified in Chapter 8. (If you have not done role plays before, you will need to review the information about the various role play customers that can be found at the end of Chapter 3. If you did not do the role play at the end of Chapter 8, choose one of the three companies to sell to.) If you sold to BancVue, you'll do so again; the same goes for GelTech and HighPoint Solutions. Begin by summarizing the buyer's needs and gaining agreement that these are all the needs. Then make your presentation.

As a buyer, do not offer any objections today. Just listen, add your thoughts on how the product might help if asked, and agree. Ask questions if something seems vague or confusing. Further, ask for proof. For example, if the salesperson says everyone loves it, ask to see a testimonial letter or something of that sort.

When you are the odd person out and observing, look for the following:

- Did the seller tie the features to the buyer's needs? Or did the seller present features that were not needed?
- Did the seller try to gain agreement that the buyer recognized and valued the benefit?
- Did the seller use visual aids as proof sources effectively?
- Did the seller use specific language versus general or ambiguous language (for example, "It's the best")?

Note: For background information about these role plays, please see page 26.

To the instructor: Additional information needed to complete the role play is available in the Instructor's Manual.

ADDITIONAL REFERENCES

Boe, John. "Harness the Power of Your Customers' Testimonials." *American Salesman* 56, no. 10 (October 2011), pp. 3–5.

Bradford, Kevin D., and Barton A. Weitz. "Salespersons' Management of Conflict in Buyer–Seller Relationships." *Journal of Personal Selling and Sales Management* 29, no. 1 (Winter 2008–2009), pp. 25–42.

Frey, Robert S. *Successful Proposal Strategies for Small Businesses: Using Knowledge Management to Win Government, Private-Sector, and International Contracts.* 6th ed. Norwood, MA: Artech House, 2013.

Gallo, Carmine. *The Presentation Secrets of Steve Jobs.* New York: McGraw-Hill, 2012.

Handley, Ann. "Uncovering New Territories." *Entrepreneur* 40, no. 4 (April 2012), p. 62.

Isson, Jean-Paul, and Jesse Harriott. *Win with Advanced Business Analytics: Creating Business Value from Your Data.* Hoboken, NJ: Wiley and SAS Business Series, 2012.

Jalkala, Anne, and Risto T. Salminen. "Communicating Customer References on Industrial Companies' Web Sites." *Industrial Marketing Management* 38, no. 7 (October 2009), pp. 825–37.

Lazkani, Nancy. "Harness the Power of Demonstration and Persuasion." *Response* 20, no. 8 (May 2012), p. 2.

Leonard, Devin. "The Last Pitchman." *Bloomberg Businessweek*, no. 4183 (June 14, 2010), pp. 4–5.

London, Jonathan, and Martin Lucas. *Using Technology to Sell: Tactics to Ratchet Up Results*. New York City: Apress, 2012.

McGaulley, Michael. *Sales Presentations and Demonstrations*. New York: Champlain House Media, 2010.

Sant, Tom. *Persuasive Business Proposals: Writing to Win More Customers, Clients, and Contracts*. New York: AMACOM, 2012.

Theriault, Michel. *Win More Business—Write Better Proposals*. Guelph, Ontario: WoodStone Press, 2010.

Urbaniak, Anthony. "The Demonstration." *American Salesman* 56, no. 1 (January 2011), pp. 3–5.

Williams, Robin. *The Non-Designer's Presentation Book*. San Francisco, CA: Peachpit Press, 2009.

chapter **10**

RESPONDING TO OBJECTIONS

SOME QUESTIONS ANSWERED IN THIS CHAPTER ARE

- How should salespeople sell value and build relationships when responding to objections?
- When do buyers object?
- What objections can be expected?
- Which methods are effective when responding to objections?
- How do you deal with tough customers?

PROFILE

PROFILE My name is Renee Miles. I received my bachelor's and master's degrees from Texas State University–San Marcos. I had the privilege of being taught professional selling by Mrs. Vicki West. I currently work as a medical device sales representative for Johnson & Johnson and have been with them for the last seven and a half years.

When I started out in sales, I did a lot of cold calling and knocking on doors. I heard objections and would get nervous and instantly think that this person does not want to be sold to.

What I have since come to learn is this: People hate to be sold to, but they love to buy! So my job is to make them love to buy from me and my company. How do you do that? By becoming an amazing listener and embracing objections.

Selling is a career about educating and building value. People don't know what they don't know—until they know it! How do prospects tell you what they don't know? They *object*! For example:

DOCTOR: "Renee, I'm happy with what I've been doing."

ME: "That is wonderful! Tell me about what you like about your process. Is there anything that can be improved? Doctor, after everything we've discussed, I would recommend stocking our lenses for improved efficiency. I have several offices that have found stocking lenses to be helpful with regard to increasing profitability, customer satisfaction, and saving staff time."

DOCTOR: "Renee, I don't want to pay that up-front cost."

ME: "Doctor, let's take a look at what your costs are right now and put pen to paper, as there are several ways to alleviate that up-front cost. But ultimately, I think you might be pleasantly surprised at what this will do for your practice profitability."

Objections are the key to "unlocking the door" to the prospect's business. I always have a pen and notepad—lean forward, listen to what the person is saying, ask good open-ended questions, and keep a pleasant demeanor.

As I present a solution, an objection (or two or three) will always come up. I write them down on the upper right corner of my notebook. I then ask if there is anything else they have a concern or question about that I can address. This gives the prospect an opportunity to see that you are there as a consultant—to address their concerns—not there just for your own agenda. Finally, it is important to confidently educate the person on why you are right!

There are usually the same four or five objections (give or take a few) that I hear the most often, so I need to know how to address each and also know how to roll in additional benefits. Forestalling is critical, and it allows me to proactively address objections that I have consistently heard.

Sales would be really boring and very difficult without objections! If you didn't hear an objection, it would make it hard to know what points to sell to. You know how to sell to the person because he or she tells you—if you take the time to listen.

One of my managers once told me, "Renee, objections are inevitable, but it is how you handle them that counts. The best salespeople are the ones you can look at from across the room and never know if they are talking business or just carrying on a conversation. They keep the same pleasant demeanor whether they are handling an objection, talking about their kids, dealing with a rude customer, or closing the biggest sale of their career!"

Take the time to listen, be engaging, and don't take objections personally, as objections are your key to uncovering the prospect's real need. If you can uncover it, they will love you and love to buy from you!

Visit our Web site at:
www.jnj.com

THE GOAL IS TO BUILD RELATIONSHIPS AND SELL VALUE •

An **objection** is a concern or a question raised by the buyer. Salespeople should do everything they can to encourage buyers to voice concerns or questions. The worst type of objection is the one the buyer refuses to disclose because a hidden objection cannot be dealt with. Many sales have been lost because salespeople didn't find out the objections or didn't helpfully respond to them.

Salespeople should keep in mind that the goal with regard to objections is the same as with every other part of the sales call: to sell real value to the buyer. Having a positive attitude about objections is paramount in this regard. Proper attitude is shown by answering sincerely, refraining from arguing or contradicting, and welcoming—even inviting—objections. Objections should be expected and never taken personally.

Simply pretending to be empathetic is useless; buyers can easily see through such pretense. Also, once the buyer gets the idea that the salesperson is talking for effect, regaining that buyer's confidence and respect will be almost impossible. Empathy shows as much in the tone of voice and facial expressions as in the actual words spoken.

The greatest evidence of sincerity comes from the salesperson's actions. One successful advertising agency owner states, "I have always tried to sit on the same side of the table as my clients, to see problems through their eyes." Buyers want valid objections to be treated seriously; they want their ideas to be respected, not belittled. They look for empathetic understanding of their problems. Real objections are logical to the prospect regardless of how irrational they may appear to the salesperson. Salespeople must assume the attitude of helper, counselor, and advisor and act accordingly. To do so, they must treat the prospect as a friend, not a foe. In fact, buyers will feel more comfortable about raising objections and will be much more honest the more they trust the salesperson, the better the rapport, and the stronger the partnering relationship.

The reality is that salespeople run into more rejection in a day than most people have to absorb in weeks or months. Because of the emotional strain, many see selling as a tough way to make a living. However, salespeople must remember that objections present sales opportunities. People who object have at least some level of interest in what the salesperson is saying. Further, objections provide feedback about what is really on the prospect's mind. Only when this openness exists can a true partnering relationship form. This attitude shows in remarks such as the following:

I can see just what you mean. I'd probably feel the same way.

That's a great question!

If I were purchasing this product, I'd want an answer to that same question.

WHEN DO BUYERS RAISE OBJECTIONS? •

Salespeople can expect to hear objections at any time during the buyer–seller relationship (see Chapter 3 for a review of the buying process). Objections are raised when the salesperson attempts to secure an appointment, during the approach, during the presentation, when the salesperson attempts to obtain commitment, and during the after-sale follow-up. Objections can also be made during formal negotiation sessions (see Chapter 12).

SETTING UP AN INITIAL APPOINTMENT

Prospects may object to setting the appointment times or dates that salespeople request to introduce the product. This type of objection happens especially when products, services, or concepts are unfamiliar to the buyer. For example, a commercial benefits salesperson for CLS Partners might hear the buyer make the following statement when asked to meet and learn more about a cafeteria-style benefits package: "No, I don't need to see you. I've not heard many good things about the use of cafeteria-style packages for dental products. Most employees just get confused!"

THE PRESENTATION

Buyers can offer objections during the beginning of the presentation (see Chapter 8). They may not like or believe the salesperson's attention-getting opening statement. They may not wish to engage in small talk or may not agree with statements made by the seller attempting to build rapport. Buyers may object to the salesperson's stated goals for the meeting.

Objections often come up to points made in the presentation. For example, a computer disaster recovery salesperson for Rackspace Hosting might hear this objection: "We've never lost a lot of computer data files before! Why should I pay so much money for a service I may never use?"

Such objections usually show the prospect's interest in the topic; thus, they can actually be desirable. Compared to a prospect who just says, "No thanks," and never raises his or her concerns, selling is easier when buyers voice their concerns because the salesperson knows where the buyers stand and that they are paying attention.

ATTEMPTING TO OBTAIN COMMITMENT

Objections may be voiced when the salesperson attempts to obtain commitment. For example, an AK Steel salesperson who has just asked the buyer's permission to talk to the buyer's chief engineer may hear this objection: "No, I don't want you talking to our engineers. My job is to keep vendors from bugging our employees."

Skill in uncovering and responding to objections is very important at this stage of the sales call. Also, knowing the objections that are likely to occur helps the salesperson prepare supporting documentation (letters of reference, copies of studies, and so on).

Salespeople who hear many objections at this point in the sales call probably need to further develop their skills. An excessive number of objections while obtaining commitment may indicate a poor job of needs identification and the omission of significant selling points in the presentation. It may also reveal ineffective probing during the presentation to see whether the buyer understands or has any questions about what is being discussed.

AFTER THE SALE

Even buyers who have agreed to purchase the product or service can still raise objections. During the installation, for example, the buyer may raise concerns about the time it is taking to install the equipment, the quality of the product or service, the customer service department's lack of friendliness, or the credit department's refusal to grant the terms the salesperson promised. To develop long-term relationships and partnerships with buyers, salespeople must carefully respond to these objections. After-sale service is more fully discussed in Chapter14.

COMMON OBJECTIONS

Prospects raise many types of objections. Although listing every objection is impossible, this section attempts to outline the most common buyer objections.[1]

It should be noted that some buyers like to raise objections just to watch salespeople squirm uncomfortably. (Fortunately, most buyers aren't like that!) Seasoned buyers, especially, sometimes like to make life difficult for sellers—particularly for young, nervous sellers. For example, Peggy, a manufacturer's salesperson for Walker Muffler, used to call on a large auto parts store in an attempt to have the store carry her line of mufflers. Jackie, the store's buyer, gave Peggy a tough time on her first two calls. At the end of her second call, Peggy was so frustrated with the way she was being treated that she decided never to call there again. However, as she was walking out of the store, she ran into a Goodyear rep who also called on Jackie to sell belts and hoses. Because the two salespeople were on somewhat friendly terms, Peggy admitted her frustrations to the Goodyear rep. He replied, "Oh, that's just the way Jackie operates. On the third call he is always a nice guy. Just wait and see." Sure enough, Peggy's next call on Jackie was not only pleasant but also productive! Buyers like Jackie usually just want to see the sales rep work hard for the order.

The following sections examine the five major types of objections (objections related to needs, product, source, price, and time), which are summarized in Exhibit 10.1, as well as several other objections that salespeople sometimes hear.

OBJECTIONS RELATED TO NEEDS

I Do Not Need the Product or Service

A prospect may validly state that the company has no need for what the salesperson is selling. A manufacturer that operates on a small scale, for example, may have no use for expensive machinery designed to handle large volumes of work. Similarly, a salesperson who is selling an accounts receivable collection service will find that a retailer that sells for cash does not require a collection service.

Salespeople may encounter such objections as "My business is different" or "I have no use for your service." These objections, when made by an accurately qualified buyer, show that the buyer is not convinced that a need exists. This problem could have been prevented with better implication and need payoff questions (see Chapter 8).

If the salesperson cannot establish a need in the buyer's mind, that buyer can logically be expected to object. In **pioneer selling**—selling a new and different product, service, or idea—the salesperson has more difficulty establishing a need in the buyer's mind. For example, salespeople for Alken-Murray often hear "I don't think we need it" when the buyer is asked to carry a line of biodegradable citrus degreasers.

I've Never Done It That Way Before

Most human beings are creatures of habit. Once they develop a routine or establish a custom, they tend to resist change. Fear of a new product's failure may be the basis for not wanting to try anything new or different. For example, Target Corporation's buyers are evaluated annually on the products they choose to buy, including such metrics as sales results, gross margins, and guest experience surveys.

Habits and customs also help to insulate the prospect from social risks to some degree. For example, suppose you are selling a new

Exhibit 10.1
Five Major Types of Objections

Objections Related to Needs
I do not need the product or service.
I've never done it that way before.

Objections Related to the Product
I don't like the product or service features.
I don't understand.
I need more information.

Objections Related to the Source
I don't like your company.
I don't like you.

Objections Related to the Price
I have no money.
The value does not exceed the cost.

Objections Related to Time
I'm just not interested today.
I need time to think about it.

line of marine engines to Newton, a newly promoted assistant buyer. If Jane, the previous assistant buyer and now the senior buyer, bought your competitor's product, Newton would appear to take less risk by continuing to buy from your competitor. If Newton buys from you, Jane may think, "I've been doing business with the other firm for 15 years. Now, Newton, you come in here and tell me I've been doing it wrong all these years? I'm not sure you're going to be a good assistant buyer."

OBJECTIONS RELATED TO THE PRODUCT

I Don't Like the Product or Service Features

Often the product or service has features that do not satisfy the buyer. At other times the prospect will request features currently not available. Customers may say things like these: It doesn't taste good to me! I was looking for a lighter shade of red. It took a month for us to receive our last order.

This buyer doesn't understand what the seller is saying.

I Don't Understand

Sometimes objections arise because customers do not understand the salesperson's presentation. Because these objections may never be verbalized, the seller must carefully observe the buyer's nonverbal cues. (See Chapter 4 for a discussion of nonverbal communication.) Misunderstandings frequently occur with customers who are unfamiliar with technical terms, unaware of the unique capabilities of a product, or uncertain about benefits arising from services provided with the product, such as warranties. Unfortunately buyers often will not admit that they do not understand something.

I Need More Information

Some buyers offer objections in an attempt to get more information. They may have already decided that they want the product or service but wish to fortify themselves with logical reasons they can use to justify the purchase to others. Also, the salesperson may not have provided enough credible proof about a particular benefit.

Conflict may also exist in the buyer's mind. One conflict could be a struggle taking place between the dictates of emotion and reason. Or the buyer may be concerned about the risk, and the seller hasn't sufficiently sold value. The buyer may be trying to decide between two competitive products or between buying and not buying. Whatever the struggle, buyers who object to get more information are usually interested, and the possibility of obtaining commitment is good.

OBJECTIONS RELATED TO THE SOURCE

I Don't Like Your Company

Most buyers, especially industrial buyers, are interested in the sales representative's company because the buyer is put at risk if the seller's firm is not financially sound, cannot continually produce the product, and so forth. These buyers need to be satisfied with the selling company's financial standing, personnel, and business policies. Buyers may ask questions such as these: How do I know you'll be in business next year? Your company isn't very well known, is it? Why does your company have a bad image in the industry?

Of course buyers who don't want to be rude may not actually voice these concerns. But unvoiced questions about the sales rep's company may affect their decisions and the long-term partnerships the sales rep is trying to establish.

I Don't Like You

Sometimes a salesperson's personality clashes with a prospect's. Effective salespeople know they must do everything possible to adjust their manner to please the prospect. At times, however, doing business with some people appears impossible.

Prospects may object to a presentation or an appointment because they have taken a dislike to the salesperson or because they feel they cannot trust the salesperson. Candid prospects may say, "You seem too young to be selling these. You've never worked in my industry, so how can you be trained to know what I need?" More commonly, the prospect shields the real reason and says, "We don't need any."

In some situations, the buyer may honestly have difficulty dealing with a particular salesperson. If the concern is real (not just an excuse), the seller's firm sometimes institutes a **turnover (TO)**, which simply means the account is given to a different salesperson. Unfortunately, TOs occasionally occur because the buyer has gender, racial, or other prejudices or because the salesperson is failing to practice adaptive selling behaviors.

ethics

thinking it through

Assume that you have worked as a salesperson for an industrial chemical firm for six months. You have attended a two-week basic selling skills course but have not yet attended any product knowledge training classes. You are making a sales call with your sales manager. The buyer says, "Gee, you look too young to be selling chemicals. Do you have a chemistry degree?" Before you get a chance to respond, your manager says, "Oh, he [*meaning you*] has already completed our one-month intensive product knowledge course. I guarantee he knows it all!" What would you say or do? What would you do if the buyer later asked you a technical question?

OBJECTIONS RELATED TO THE PRICE

I Have No Money

Companies that lack the resources to buy the product may have been misclassified as prospects. As indicated in Chapter 6, the ability to pay is an important factor in lead qualification. An incomplete or poor job of qualifying may cause this objection to arise.

When leads say they cannot afford a product, they may have a valid objection. If so, the salesperson should not waste time; new prospects should be contacted.

The Value Does Not Exceed the Cost

Buyers usually object until they are sure that the value of the product or service being acquired more than offsets the sacrifice. Exhibit 10.2 illustrates this concept. The question of value received often underlies customers' objections.

Whatever the price of a product or service, somebody will object that it is too high or out of line with the competition. Here are some other common price objections: I can beat your price on these items. We can't make a reasonable profit if we have to pay that much for the merchandise. I'm going to wait for prices to come down.

A more complete discussion of dealing with price objections appears later in this chapter. Implicit in many price objections is the notion of product or service

Exhibit 10.2

Value: The Relationship between Costs and Benefits

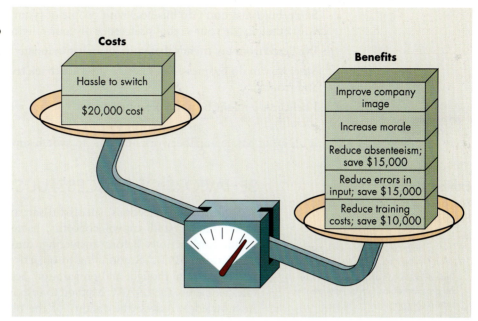

Note: If costs outweigh benefits, the decision will be not to buy. If benefits outweigh costs, the decision will be to buy.

quality. Thus, the buyer who states that your price is too high may actually be thinking, "The quality is too low for such a high price."

OBJECTIONS RELATED TO TIME

I'm Just Not Interested Today

Some prospects voice objections simply to dismiss the salesperson. The prospect may not have enough time to devote to the interview, may not be interested in the particular product or service, may not be in the mood to listen, or may have decided because of some unhappy experiences not to face further unpleasant interviews.

These objections occur when salespeople are cold calling (see Chapter 6) or trying to make an appointment. Particularly aggressive, rude, impolite, or pesky salespeople can expect prospects to use numerous excuses to keep from listening to a presentation.

I Need Time to Think about It

Buyers often object to making a decision "now."[2] Many, in fact, believe that postponing an action is an effective way to say no. Salespeople can expect to hear objections such as the following, especially from analyticals and amiables (see Chapter 5): I haven't made up my mind. I'd like to talk it over with my partner. Just leave me your literature; I'll study it and then let you know what we decide.

OTHER OBJECTIONS

Listing every possible objection that could occur under any situation would be impossible. However, following are a number of additional objections that salespeople often hear:

We have no room for your line.

There is no demand for your product.

Sorry, but I just don't do business with people of [your gender or your race or your ethnicity or your sexual preference or your religion and so forth].

I've heard from my friends that your insurance company isn't the best one to use.

Sure, we can do business. But I need a little kickback to make it worth my time and trouble.

I believe we might be able to do business if you are willing to start seeing me socially.

It's a lot of hassle in paperwork and time to switch suppliers.

Exhibit 10.3

Responding to Objections: Behaviors of Successful Salespeople

They anticipate objections and prepare helpful responses.

They address known problems before the prospect does; that is, they forestall known concerns.

They relax and listen and never interrupt the buyer.

They make sure that the objection is not just an excuse.

They always tell the truth.

BEHAVIORS OF SUCCESSFUL SALESPEOPLE

With regard to objections, successful salespeople anticipate objections and forestall known concerns, listen without interrupting, evaluate objections before answering, and always tell the truth (see Exhibit 10.3).[3] Responding to objections in a helpful manner requires careful thought and preparation. Some trainers suggest that salespeople use the **LAARC Method** to respond to objections: Listen, Acknowledge, Assess (the validity of the objection), Respond, and Confirm (that the objection has been answered).[4]

ANTICIPATE OBJECTIONS

Salespeople must know that at some time, objections will be made to almost everything concerning their products, their companies, or themselves. Common sense dictates that they prepare helpful, honest answers to objections that are certain to be raised, as "From the Buyer's Seat 10.1" describes.

Many companies draw up lists of common objections and helpful answers and encourage salespeople to become familiar with these lists. Most firms also videotape practice role plays to help salespeople become more proficient in anticipating objections and responding effectively in each situation. Successful sales representatives may keep a notebook and record new objections they encounter.

FORESTALL KNOWN CONCERNS

Good salespeople, after a period of experience and training, know that certain features of their products or services are vulnerable, are likely to be misunderstood, or are materially different from competitors' products. The salesperson may have products with limited features, may have to quote a price that seems high, may be unable to offer cash discounts, may have no service representatives in the immediate area, or may represent a new company in the field.

In these situations, salespeople often forestall the objection. To **forestall** is to prevent by doing something ahead of time. In selling, this means salespeople raise objections before buyers have a chance to raise them. For example, one salesperson forestalled a concern about the different "feel" of a split computer keyboard (the ones that are split down the middle to relieve stress and strain on the hands and wrists):

I know you'll find the feel to be different from your old keyboard. You're going to like that, though, because your hands won't get as tired. In almost every split keyboard I've sold, typists have taken only one day to get accustomed to the new feel, and then they swear that they would never go back to their old-fashioned keyboards again!

From the BUYER'S SEAT

THAT TASTES PRETTY AWFUL!

Being part of a buying team for Cub Food Stores, I've heard lots of presentations and offered plenty of objections. Due to the fact that how much someone likes a food product is based solely on their personal preferences, you can have some people who absolutely love the product, while others think it is the worst possible thing in the world, sometimes saying they would never even feed it to their dog.

If I were a salesperson, the first thing I would do is to know as many possible objections as people might have to my food product. Some of the most common objections that salespeople face when pitching a product to us are the following:

- Too spicy.
- It doesn't seem to have as much flavor as some of the comparable products that we already carry.
- Too salty.
- We are trying to get healthier options in our stores due to the growing health-conscious trend in our society.

- We have a strict profit margin that we stick to with all products, and yours isn't good enough.

Offering samples to all those involved in the buying process is a great way for salespeople to allow everyone to get their own opinion and discuss it amongst themselves. However, salespeople can actually create objections if they are unable to prep their samples effectively. If a product is supposed to be served hot and crispy and salespeople arrive with them premade in something to keep them warm, a lot of times they tend to become soggy and ultimately undesirable. Instead of having a salesperson say, "I'm sorry! The product is actually supposed to be hot and crispy, not soggy and barely warm, but this is the best I can do!" the salesperson can simply get in contact with us beforehand and find out that we have all of the appliances needed to prep the product in our office on arrival.

Source: Kathleen Griffin, Cub Foods; all names changes to protect anonymity; used with permission.

A salesperson might bring up a potential price concern by saying, "You know, other buyers have been concerned that this product is expensive. Well, let me show you how little it will really cost you to get the best."

Some salespeople do such a good job of forestalling that buyers change their minds without ever going on record as objecting to the feature and then having to reverse themselves.[5] Buyers are more willing to change their thinking when they do not feel constrained to defend a position they have already stated. Although not all objections can be preempted, the major ones can be spotted and forestalled during the presentation. Forestalling can be even more important in written proposals (see Chapter 9) because immediate feedback between buyer and seller is not possible. Such forestalled objections can be addressed throughout the proposal. For example, on the page describing delivery terms, the seller could insert a paragraph that begins this way: "You may be wondering how we can promise an eight-day delivery even though we have such a small production capacity. Actually, we are able to . . . because. . . ." Another option for forestalling objections in written proposals is to have a separate page or section titled something like "Concerns You May Have with This Proposal." The section could then list the potential concerns and provide responses to them.

This person is listening carefully.

RELAX AND LISTEN—DO NOT INTERRUPT

When responding to an objection, listen first and then answer the objection. Allow the prospect to state a position completely. A wise man said, "He that answereth a matter before he heareth it, it is folly and shame unto him."[6]

Do not interrupt with an answer, even if the objection to be stated is already apparent to you. Listen as though you have never heard that objection before.

Unfortunately too many salespeople conduct conversations somewhat like the following:

SALESPERSON: Mr. Clark, from a survey of your operations, I'm convinced you're now spending more money repairing your own motors than you would by having us do the job for you—and really do it right!

CUSTOMER: We're probably doing it fine right now. Now, I'm sure your repair service is good, but you don't have to be exactly an electrical genius to be able to...

SALESPERSON: Hang on! It isn't a matter of anyone being a genius. It's a matter of having a heavy investment in special motor repair equipment and supplies like vacuum impregnating tanks and lathes for banding armatures, boring bearings, and turning new shafts.

CUSTOMER: Yeah I know all that, but you missed my point. See, what I'm driving at...

SALESPERSON: I know what you're driving at, but you're wrong! You forget that even if your own workers are smart cookies, they just can't do high-quality work without a lot of special equipment.

CUSTOMER: But you still don't get my point! The maintenance workers that we now have doing motor repair work...

SALESPERSON: Could more profitably spend their time on plant troubleshooting! Right?

CUSTOMER: That isn't what I was going to say! I was trying to say that between their troubleshooting jobs, instead of just sitting around and shooting the bull...

SALESPERSON: Now wait a minute, Mr. Clark. If you think that a good motor rewinding job can be done in someone's spare time, you're wrong!

Obviously attitudes and interruptions like these are likely to bring the interview to a quick end.

Salespeople should plan to relax as buyers offer objections. It's even OK to plan on using humor in your answers to objections. For example, if the buyer objects to the standard payments and asks how low your company could go, you could respond as follows: "Well, if I could get the bank to send you money each month, would you buy it?"

After laughing, the seller could talk about the various payment options. Using humor, as in this example, may help defuse the nervousness that both buyer and seller are feeling during this part of the process. For more insight into the use of humor, see Chapter 4.

What if the buyer asks a question for which you've already covered the material? Don't say, "I've already covered that!" Instead let the buyer finish asking the question and then answer the question with enthusiasm.

EVALUATE OBJECTIONS

To truly sell value and establish a relationship, the seller must evaluate objections before answering.[7] Objections may be classified as unsatisfied needs (that is, real objections) or excuses. **Excuses** are concerns expressed by the buyer that mask the buyer's true objections. Thus, the comment "I can't afford it now" would simply be an excuse if the buyer honestly could afford it now but did not want to buy for some other reason.

A buyer seldom says, "I don't have any reason. I just don't want to buy." More commonly the buyer gives a reason that appears at first to be a real objection but is really an excuse: "I don't have the money" or "I can't use your product." The tone of voice or the nature of the reason may provide evidence that the prospect is not offering a sincere objection.

Salespeople need to develop skill in evaluating objections. No exact formula has been devised to separate excuses from real objections. Sometimes it is best to follow up with a question:

> BUYER: I just wish your company sold the full range of insurance products, you know, things like variable annuities.

> SELLER: If we did offer variable annuities, would you be interested in having all of your insurance needs met by me?

If the buyer says yes, you know the concern is real. If the buyer says no, you know the buyer is just offering the objection about annuities as an excuse.

Circumstances can also provide a clue to whether an objection is a valid concern. In cold calling, when the prospect says, "I'm sorry, I don't have any money," the salesperson may conclude that the prospect does not want to hear the presentation. However, the same reason offered after a complete presentation has been made and data on the prospect have been gathered through observation and questioning may be valid. Salespeople must rely on observation, questioning, knowledge about why people buy (see Chapter 3), and experience to determine the validity of reasons offered for objections.

ALWAYS TELL THE TRUTH

In dealing with prospects and customers, truthfulness is an absolute necessity for dignity, confidence, and relationship development. Recall that our purpose is not to manipulate but to persuade so that the buyer can make the most effective decision. Lying and deception are not part of a successful long-term relationship. Over time it will be hard to remember which lie you told to which customer. Salespeople should avoid even white lies and half-truths when they answer objections.

Salespeople who tell lies, even small ones, need to recognize they have a problem and then find ways to change. One way to avoid lies is to spend more time gaining knowledge about their products and the products of their competitors. Sellers who do so aren't as tempted to lie to cover up the fact that they don't know some information requested by the prospect. Sellers also should commit to tell the truth, even if competitors don't follow suit. It is simply the right thing to do.

EFFECTIVE RESPONSE METHODS

Any discussion of specific methods for responding to objections needs to emphasize that no perfect method exists for answering all objections completely. Some prospects, no matter what you do, will never believe their objections have been adequately addressed.

In some instances, spending a lot of time trying to convince the prospect may not be wise. For example, when an industrial recycling salesperson contacts a prospect who says, "I don't believe in recycling," the salesperson may better spend available time calling on some of the vast number of people who do.

This section describes seven common methods for responding to objections. As Exhibit 10.4 indicates, the first two, direct denial and indirect denial, are used only when the prospect makes an untrue statement. The next five methods—compensation, referral, revisiting, acknowledgment, and postponement—are useful when the buyer raises a valid point or offers an opinion.

Before using the methods described in this section, salespeople almost always need to probe to help the prospect clarify concerns and to make sure they understand the objection. This method is often called the **probing method.** If the prospect says, "Your service is not too good," the salesperson can probe by saying, "I'm not sure I understand," or by asking a question. For example, the seller could ask one or more of the following: Not too good? What do you mean by not too good? Exactly what service are you referring to? Is service very important to you? Can you explain what you mean?

While this probing is usually verbal, it can also include nonverbal probing. For example, Professor Donoho at Northern Arizona University teaches a method called the **friendly silent questioning stare (FSQS)** to encourage buyers to elaborate or explain more fully what their concerns are.

Many serious blunders have occurred because a salesperson did not understand a question, answered the wrong question, or failed to answer an objection fully. For example, a sales training manager was listening to a representative for a consulting firm talk about her services. At one point in the conversation,

Exhibit 10.4
Common Methods for Responding to Objections

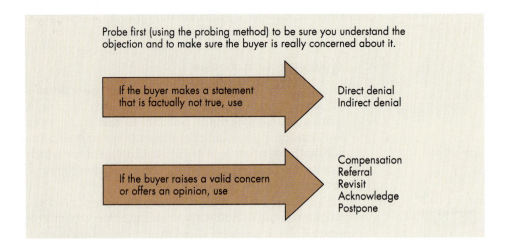

the manager asked, "Has anyone in the electrical products industry ever used this training package before?" The consultant answered, "Sure, we have sold this package to several firms. Why, just last week I received a nice letter from Colgate that had nothing but good things to say...." The manager did not buy the training package; he figured that if the consultant did not even know how to listen, the sales training package she was selling could not be very good either. (Chapter 4 provides many helpful suggestions regarding the art of questioning and probing.)

A salesperson who doesn't know the answer to the buyer's objection might say, "I don't know the answer to that question. But I'll find out and get the answer to you." The seller should paraphrase the buyer's question, write it down (this step helps jog the seller's memory as well as demonstrate to the buyer that the seller really intends to follow up), gather the information, and follow up quickly and exactly as promised. If you call the customer with the information and he or she is not available, leave the information on voice mail and then call later to verify that the prospect got the information. And don't forget that it is your responsibility to know most facts, so be prepared the next time for similar and additional questions and concerns. You can be sure your competitor is going to try to have complete answers ready.

thinking it through

How can the use of technology (such as databases, computers, and communication technology) help prevent a seller from having to answer, "I don't know the answer to that question. But I'll find out and call you with the information as soon as I can get it"?

DIRECT DENIAL

At times salespeople face objections based on incomplete or inaccurate information of the buyer. They should respond by providing information or correcting facts. When using **direct denial,** the salesperson makes a relatively strong statement to indicate the error the prospect has made. For example:

> BUYER: I am not interested in hearing about your guidance systems. Your firm was one of the companies recently indicted for fraud, conspiracy, and price fixing by a federal grand jury. I don't want to do business with such a firm.

> SALESPERSON: I'm not sure where you heard that, but it simply is not true. Our firm has never been involved in such activity, and our record is clean. If you would care to tell me the source of your information, I'm sure we can clear this up. Maybe you're confusing us with another firm.

No one likes to be told that he or she is wrong, so direct denial must be used with caution. It is appropriate only when the objection is blatantly inaccurate and potentially devastating to the presentation. The salesperson must also possess facts to back up such a denial. Direct denial should never be used if the prospect is merely stating an opinion or if the objection is true. For example, direct denial would be inappropriate to this objection: "I don't like the feel of simulated leather products." Direct denial should be avoided even for a false statement if the objection is of little importance to the buyer. An indirect denial would be more appropriate in that case.

INDIRECT DENIAL

In the **indirect denial method,** the salesperson denies the objection but attempts to soften the response. The salesperson takes the edge off the response by agreeing with the prospect that the objection is an important one. Prospects expect salespeople to disagree; instead, a salesperson who recognizes the sincerity of the objection will carefully respect the prospect's view. This approach avoids a direct contradiction and confrontation. To begin an answer, a salesperson would do well to agree with the prospect, but only to the extent that the agreement does not weaken the validity of the salesperson's later denial. For example:

> BUYER: Your machines break down more often than those of most of your major competitors.
>
> SALESPERSON: I can see why you might feel that way. Just 10 years ago that statement would have been right on target. However, things have changed with our new quality assurance program. In fact, just last year Syncos Ratings, a well-respected independent evaluator of quality in our industry, rated us as number one for fewest breakdowns.

The important features of indirect denial are that salespeople recognize the position of the customer who makes the objection and then continue by introducing substantial evidence. The beginning statement should always be true and assure the prospect that the question is a good one. Examples of such statements follow:

> With the market the way it is today, I can certainly see why you're concerned about that.

> I'll bet 90 percent of the people I call on voice the same concern.

> That's really an excellent question, and it allows me to clear up a misconception that perhaps I've given you.

Indirect denial should never be used if the prospect has raised a valid point or is merely expressing an opinion. It can be used for all personality types and is especially effective for amiables and analyticals because they like less assertive salespeople.

COMPENSATION METHOD

Every product has some advantages and some disadvantages compared to competing products. Also, an absolutely perfect product or service has never been developed; the firm always has to make cost–benefit decisions about what features to include.

Buyers note these trade-offs and often object because the salesperson's product is less than perfect. The wise salesperson will admit that such objections are valid and then proceed to show any compensating advantages. This approach is called the **compensation method** of responding to objections. Here is an example:

> PROSPECT: This machine has only four filling nozzles. Your competitor's has six nozzles.
>
> SALESPERSON: You're absolutely right. It has only four nozzles, but it costs $4,000 less than the competitor's models, and you said you needed a model that is priced in the lower range. Also, our nozzles are designed for easy maintenance. You have to remove only four screws to get to the filter screens. Most other models have at least 10 screws.

PREPARE FOR OBJECTIONS USING THE INTERNET

Objections can be very hard to overcome during a sales presentation if they are not prepared for. Sitting down and thinking about what objections a buyer may have about your product or service can lead to many possible objections, but there is a strong chance that you will have a bias toward your product and may miss certain things that may come up from a different point of view. With that being said, potential objections need to come from third parties as well.

For example, you are attempting to sell a new line of televisions to Target Corporation for them to sell in their stores. While they are not currently carrying your product, they do carry a wide variety of televisions. By searching their current products, you can now find a product that is comparable to the one that you are going to be presenting to their buyers. Once you find that comparable line, by simply clicking on the product, you will be able to find reviews that customers have posted. Some reviews will be positive and might very well help you discover points that the buyer will bring up in the sales call. If you know some of the specific product strengths that Target's current products have in the eye of the consumer, you can take these and emphasize the fact that your product will do the same thing for their customers.

You can also read reviews to learn what consumers dislike about the current products carried by the prospect. This information can help you determine the features you will discuss when objections arise (by indicating that your product also provides features that the current products do not).

Technology is growing at such a rapid pace that new, updated information is constantly available to anyone who has access to the Internet. By putting in the time and effort to do some background research on current product offerings of a company, you will find where their offerings are lacking and your product can help them but also where their products are excelling and know how to present your product in a way that will help you overcome the objection of "my current products have these features that my customers really like." This information can aid you in using the compensation method of responding to objections.

The compensation method is an explicit use of the multiattribute model discussed in Chapter 3. A low score on one attribute can be compensated for by a high score on another attribute. In fact, the compensation method is often referred to as the **superior benefit method** because the benefit of one attribute overcomes a concern about a less important attribute. The method can be effective for many objections and concerns. It seems most appropriate for analyticals, who are accustomed to conducting trade-off analyses. However, it is useful for all other personality types as well. "Sales Technology 10.1" describes how to use the Internet to help gather information that will be useful with this method.

Of course the buyer may not value the compensating advantages. The buyer may really need the features at issue (perhaps the machine must have six nozzles to work with another piece of the prospect's equipment). In such cases salespeople can recommend a different product (from their own line, if available, or from a competitor) or search for other prospects.

Another time that the compensation method may be used is when the prospect says, "I'm just going to think about it. I'll be in touch with you later." The seller can show how acting today more than compensates for the "pain" of making a decision today. These reasons usually include explaining the hidden costs of delaying the decision (it will go off sale, you will be saving money over your current system each month that you have our proposed system, our product may be out of stock when you need it, summer is a particularly good time to install a new system, or the like).

REFERRAL METHOD

When buyers' objections reflect their own attitudes or opinions, the salesperson can show how others held similar views before trying the product or service. In this method, called the **referral method** or the **feel–felt–found method**, the salesperson goes on to relate that others actually found their initial opinions to be unfounded after they tried the product:

> PROSPECT: I don't think my customers will want to buy a DVD player with all these fancy features.
>
> SALESPERSON: I can certainly see how you feel. Bob Scott, down the road in Houston, felt the same way when I first proposed that he sell these. However, after he agreed to display them next to his current DVD line, he found that his customers were very interested. In fact, he called me four days later to order more.

A buyer may question the credibility and knowledge of a salesperson. In this situation the salesperson can use the referral method to help resolve those concerns.

Those who teach this as the feel–felt–found method highlight the importance of the proper sequence, as well as the person or people identified in each stage. The sequence should be as follows: I can see how *you* feel . . . *others* felt the same way . . . yet *they* found. . . . Inexperienced salespeople often mix up the order or the parties identified (for example, by saying ". . . yet you will find").

Proof of the salesperson's assertion in the form of a testimonial letter strengthens the method; in fact, some trainers refer to this approach as the **third-party-testimony method.** If a letter is not available, the salesperson might be able to supply the name and phone number of the third party. The salesperson should always secure the third party's permission first, however. (See Chapter 9 for suggestions about testimonials and references.)

Although the referral method can be used for all personality types, it seems most appropriate for expressives and amiables. Both types tend to care about what other people think and are doing.

REVISIT METHOD

When using the **revisit method** (also called the **boomerang method**) of responding to objections, the salesperson turns the objection into a reason for buying the product or service. This method can be used in many situations (when making an appointment, during the presentation, when attempting to secure commitment, and in postsale situations):

> BUYER: I don't think these would sell in my gun shop. They're really drab looking.
>
> SALESPERSON: It's interesting that you mention that. In fact, their drab color is probably their best selling point and the reason you should carry them. You see, when a hunter is in the field, the last thing she wants to do is attract attention to herself. Thanks to the finish we use on this gear . . .

The revisit method requires care. It can appear very pushy and "salesy." This method does have useful applications, however. Often the product or service is actually designed to save the buyer substantial amounts of time or money. If the buyer objects to spending either the time to listen or the money, the revisit method may be a powerful tool to help the buyer see the benefit of investing these resources.

This method works with most personality types. Drivers may require the revisit method more often than other buyers because drivers tend to erect time constraints and other barriers and are less willing to listen to just any salesperson's presentation.

ACKNOWLEDGE METHOD

At times the buyer voices opinions or concerns more to vent frustration than anything else. When this occurs, the best strategy may be to use the **acknowledge method**, also called the **pass-up method**. Simply let the buyer talk, acknowledge that you heard the concern, pause, and then move on to another topic.

> BUYER: Hey, you use Beyoncé in your commercials, don't you? Sure you do. Now I want to tell you that I don't like what she stands for! Kids today need a role model they can look up to. What happened to the kind of role models we used to have?

> SALESPERSON: I certainly understand your concern. I remember my dad talking about some of his role models and the respect he had for them. [*Pause*] What were we talking about? Oh, yes, I was telling you about the coupon drop we are planning.

In this example the salesperson used the acknowledge method because the buyer apparently was just blowing off steam. A buyer who really wanted some response from the salesperson would have used the salesperson's pause to ask a direct question (Can't you change your commercials?) or make a statement (I refuse to do business with companies that use stars like Beyoncé in their commercials!).

In reality a salesperson often can do little about some prospects' opinions. What are the chances that this salesperson's firm will pull a $5 million ad campaign because one buyer objects? It is doubtful that a firm would take such action unless the buyer had tremendous power in the relationship.

Sometimes the salesperson can use the acknowledge method by simply agreeing with the prospect and then moving on, which suggests to the buyer that the concern really should not be much of an issue. For example:

> BUYER: You want $25 for this little plastic bottle?!

> SELLER: Uh-huh. That's what they cost...[*Pause*] Now do you see the switch on this side? It's used if you ever need to...

The acknowledge method should not be used if the objection raised is factually false. Also, it should not be used if the salesperson, through probing, could help clarify the buyer's thinking on the topic. Experience is the key to making such a determination. In general, though, the acknowledge method should be used sparingly.

POSTPONE METHOD

In the early part of a sales interview, the prospect may raise objections that the salesperson would prefer to answer later in the presentation, after discovering the prospect's needs. Using the **postpone method,** the salesperson would ask permission to answer the question at a later time:

> BUYER [*very early in the call*]: How much does the brass engraving equipment cost?
>
> SALESPERSON: If you don't mind, I would prefer to answer that question in a few minutes. I really can't tell you how much it will cost until I learn more about your engraving needs and know what kinds of features you are looking for.

The prospect will seldom refuse the request if the sales representative appears to be acting in good faith. The sales representative then proceeds with the presentation until the point at which the objection can best be answered.

Some objections are best answered when they occur; others can be responded to most effectively by delaying the answer. Experience should guide the sales representative. The salesperson should take care not to treat an objection lightly or let it appear that he or she does not want to answer the question. Another danger in postponing is that the buyer will be unable to focus on what the salesperson is saying until the concern is addressed. On the other hand, the salesperson is responsible for helping the buyer to critically evaluate the solution offered, and often the buyer can process information effectively only after learning preliminary facts.

Salespeople make the most use of the postponement method when a price objection occurs early in the presentation. However, this method can be used for almost any type of objection or question. For example, postponing discussions about guarantees, delivery schedules, implementation time frames, and certain unique product features until later in the presentation is often preferable.

What if the buyer is convinced that he or she needs the answer right now? Then the salesperson should answer the objection now. Salespeople usually have more to lose by demanding that the buyer wait for information than by simply providing the answer when the buyer strongly requests it. For example:

> PROSPECT: What are the delivery schedules for this new product?
>
> SALESPERSON: I would really prefer to discuss that after we talk about our unique production process and extensive quality control measures.
>
> PROSPECT: No, I want to know now!
>
> SALESPERSON: Well, keep in mind that my later discussion about the production process will shed new light on the topic. We anticipate a four- to five-month delivery time after the contract reaches our corporate headquarters.

USING THE METHODS

The seven methods just discussed appear in sales training courses across all industries and geographic boundaries. To help you more easily distinguish the differences among the various methods, Exhibit 10.5 provides an example of the use of each method for the objection, "Your product's quality is too low."

Salespeople often combine methods when answering an objection. For example, a price objection may initially be postponed and then be discussed later using

Exhibit 10.5

Responding to
Objections: Using
Each Method

Objection: Your product's quality is too low.

Responses*

Direct denial: That simply is not true. Our product has been rated as the highest in the industry for the last three years.

Indirect denial: I can certainly see why you would be concerned about quality. Actually, though, our product quality has been rated as the highest in the industry for the last three years.

Compensation: I agree that our quality is not as high as that of some of our competitors. However, it was designed that way for consumers who are looking for a lower-priced alternative, perhaps just to use in a weekend cottage. So you see, our somewhat lower quality is actually offset by our much lower price.

Referral: I can certainly understand how you feel. Mortimer Jiggs felt the same way before he bought the product. But after using it, he found that the quality was actually equal to that of other products.

Revisit: The fact that the quality is lower than in other products is probably the very reason you should buy it. You said that some of your customers are looking for a low-priced product to buy for their grandchildren. This product fills that need.

Acknowledge: I understand your concern. You know, one of the things I always look for is how a product's quality stacks up against its cost. [Pause] Now, we were talking about . . .

Postpone: That's an interesting point. Before discussing it fully, I would like to cover just two things that I think will help you better understand the product from a different perspective. OK?

*These are not necessarily good answers to the stated objection. Also, the choice of method would depend on whether the objection is factual. Thus, the replies given here are designed simply to differentiate the various methods.

the compensation method. At other times several methods can be used in one answer. Here is an example:

BUYER: I don't think this product will last as long as some of the other, more expensive competitive products.

SALESPERSON: That's probably the very reason you should buy it [*revisit method*]. It may not last quite as long, but it is less than half the cost of competitive products [*compensation method*]. I can certainly understand your concern, though. You know, Mark Hancock felt the way you do. He was concerned about the product's life. But after he used our product for one year, he found that its life expectancy didn't create any problems for his production staff [*referral method*].

Sometimes the buyer will ask multiple questions at once—for example, "How much did you spend on R&D last year, what percentage of your revenue does that represent, and what is your R&D model going forward?" What is a seller to do? Remembering the questions so they don't get lost, the salesperson answers them one by one.

CONFIRMING THAT THE OBJECTION HAS BEEN ANSWERED

Before moving on with the presentation, the salesperson needs to make sure that the buyer agrees that all objections have been completely answered. Without

Make sure the buyer agrees before moving on.

this commitment, the salesperson does not know whether the buyer understands the answer or whether the buyer's concerns have been fully addressed. To achieve this commitment, the salesperson can use one or more of the following types of phrases: Did I answer your question? Does that make sense? Do you see why that issue is not as important as you originally thought? Did that resolve your concern?

OBJECTIONS WHEN SELLING TO A GROUP OF BUYERS

Selling to a group of buyers (see Chapter 8) requires some extra care. If one person offers an objection, the seller should try to get a sense of whether other buyers share the concern. At times it may make sense to throw the issue back to the group. For example, if a buyer says that the people in his or her department won't attend the type of training sessions being proposed, the seller might respond as follows: Does anyone else have that same problem in their department? You all know your organizational climate better than I do. Have any of you found a way to deal with that issue that you would like to share with us? Any response from the seller should usually be directed to all buyers, not just the one who asked the question. After responding, the seller needs to make sure that all buyers are satisfied with the answer before moving on.

THE PRICE OBJECTION

Price is the perhaps the most frequently mentioned obstacle to obtaining commitment, as "Building Partnerships 10.1" describes. In fact, about 20 percent of buyers are thought to buy purely on the basis of price (which means that a full 80 percent buy for reasons other than price). As a result, all salespeople need to prepare for price objections. This section relates the concepts covered in this chapter to this common objection.

Price is still an issue even between partnering firms. One leading firm in its industry has estimated that only 3 percent of its orders are sold at list price; the rest are price discounted.[8]

Unfortunately the first response of many salespeople to a price objection is to lower the price. Inexperienced salespeople, desiring to gain business, often quote the lowest possible price as quickly as possible. They forget that for a mutually beneficial long-term relationship to exist, their firm must make a fair profit. Also, by cutting prices the firm has to sell more to maintain profit margins, as Exhibit 10.6 clearly illustrates.

When faced with a price objection, salespeople should ensure that they have up-to-date information, establish the value of the product, and use communication tools effectively.

USE UP-TO-DATE INFORMATION

Successful salespeople make sure they have the most current pricing information available to them. They know not only their prices but competitors' prices as well. Firms are helping salespeople in this regard. For example, many firms have developed intranet sites for their salespeople. If a salesperson finds that the company's price points are a little higher than the competition, the salesperson can use the intranet site to look for some sales or trade-in program that she or he can leverage to get the deal. It is important for sellers to have correct pricing facts.

ESTABLISH THE VALUE

The product's value must be established before the salesperson spends time discussing price. The value expected determines the price a prospect is willing to pay. Unless

OBJECTIONS CAN HELP YOU ASSESS YOUR SKILLS

The way we see it, objections tend to arise primarily when you have failed to adequately cover something in your presentation. If any of our salespeople are giving a sales presentation and at the end the buyer is still concerned with the fact that our product pricing may be higher than that of our competitors, this is a red flag that we have gone wrong somewhere in the presentation.

In such a large and developed industry as ours, pricing does not tend to vary too widely, and if we are much more expensive than our competitors, our salespeople need to reassess the situation and the product being offered. Many times, when there is a large disparity in price between the products we are attempting to sell and those which the competitor is selling to solve the same problem, either we are selling the wrong product or the competitor is. With that being said, prices between our products and comparable products that our competitors offer do not vary too widely, and therefore the price factor should have been completely eliminated in the decision-making process for our client throughout the sales presentation. We offer very high quality products that provide value to our clients. When the cost

objection arises at the end, it is crucial that our salespeople take a step back and try to figure out where they went wrong in demonstrating and communicating the value that the products and services we offer have.

Another objection that tends to be a tough one to overcome is that of "I am not sure how I feel about doing business with your company; I worked with so and so a few years back and had a terrible experience." In this situation, it is essential that salespeople emphasize that they are not the same person and that it would be an honor to correct the wrongdoings that they have had to deal with in the past and that we really are an outstanding company to do business with. At this point, the sales call regresses more toward that relationship-building stage as opposed to "get the sale and close the deal."

I'll end with one of my favorite quotes: "Everyone has a reason that they do not want to buy from you—as a salesperson, it is your job to give them the reasons that they need to buy from you."

Source: Kim Guay, AT&T; names changed to protect anonymity; used with permission.

---

the salesperson can build value to exceed the price asked, a sale will not occur.[9] As a rule, value cannot be established during the early stages of the presentation.

Price objections are best handled with a two-step approach. First, the salesperson should try to look at the objection from the customer's viewpoint, asking questions to clarify the customer's perspective: "Too high in what respect, Mr. Jones? Could you tell me how much we are out of line? We are usually quite competitive on this model, so I am surprised you find our price high.... Are the other quotes you have for the same size engine?"

After learning more about the customer's perspective, the next step is to sell value and quality rather than price (see Chapter 9 for a full discussion of the customer value proposition). Most customers prefer to buy less expensive products if they believe they will receive the same benefits. However, many customers will pay more for higher quality when the quality benefits and features are pointed out to them. Many high-quality products appear similar to lower-quality products; thus, salespeople need to emphasize the features that justify a difference.

For example, a salesperson who sells industrial fasteners and supplies may hear this objection: "That bolt costs $750! I could buy it elsewhere for $75." The salesperson should reply, "Yes, but that bolt is inside your most important piece of production equipment. Let's say you buy that $75 bolt. How much employee

Exhibit 10.6
Look before You Cut
Prices! You Must Sell
More to Break Even

Cut Price	Present Gross Profit					
	5.0%	10.0%	15.0%	20.0%	25.0%	30.0%
1%	25.0	11.1	7.1	5.3	4.2	3.4
2	66.6	25.0	15.4	11.1	8.7	7.1
3	150.0	42.8	25.0	17.6	13.6	11.1
4	400.0	66.6	36.4	25.0	19.0	15.4
5	—	100.0	50.0	33.3	25.0	20.0
6	—	150.0	66.7	42.9	31.6	25.0
7	—	233.3	87.5	53.8	38.9	30.4
8	—	400.0	114.3	66.7	47.1	36.4
9	—	1,000.0	150.0	81.8	56.3	42.9
10	—	—	200.0	100.0	66.7	50.0
11	—	—	275.0	122.2	78.6	57.9
12	—	—	400.0	150.0	92.3	66.7
13	—	—	650.0	185.7	108.3	76.5
14	—	—	1,400.0	233.3	127.3	87.5
15	—	—	—	300.0	150.0	100.0
16	—	—	—	400.0	177.8	114.3
17	—	—	—	566.7	212.5	130.8
18	—	—	—	900.0	257.1	150.0
19	—	—	—	1,900.0	316.7	172.7
20	—	—	—	—	400.0	200.0
21	—	—	—	—	525.0	233.3
22	—	—	—	—	733.3	275.0
23	—	—	—	—	1,115.0	328.6
24	—	—	—	—	2,400.0	400.0
25	—	—	—	—	—	500.0

A business truism says that you can cut, cut, cut until you cut yourself out of business. This can certainly apply to cutting prices in an effort to increase profits. The two don't necessarily go together. For example, select the gross profit being earned at present from those shown at the top of the chart. Follow the left column down until you line up with the proposed price cut. The intersected figure represents the percentage of increase in unit sales required to earn the same gross profit realized before the price cut. Obviously it helps to know this figure so you don't end up with a lot of work for nothing.

See for yourself: Assume that your present gross margin is 25 percent and that you cut your selling price 10 percent. Locate the 25 percent column under Present Gross Profit. Now follow the column down until you line up with the 10 percent cut in selling price in column 1. You will need to sell 66.7 percent more units to earn the same margin dollars as at the previous price.

time and production downtime would it take to disassemble the machine again and replace that one bolt?" The salesperson can then engage in a complete cost–benefit analysis (see Chapter 9) to solidify the point.

A supplier of integrated circuits (ICs) was competing with another company whose price was 10 cents less. The buyer asked for a price concession, noting that the competitor's product was obviously less expensive. Unbeknownst to the supplier, however, the buyer had already examined the value propositions of the two companies and determined that the higher-priced one was actually worth 12 cents more than the less expensive one, due to services offered. Thus, in reality, the buyer had already realized that the higher-priced one was actually less expensive in terms of value (12 cents more in value minus the 10 cents higher in price = 2 cents higher in value per IC). The higher-priced supplier caved in and gave the buyer a 10 cent reduction in price, costing his firm $500,000 (5 million units at 10 cents each) in potential profits! And the sad fact is that the buyer was already planning on going with the higher-priced supplier.[10]

Intangible features can also provide value that offsets price. Some of these features are services, company reputation, and the salesperson:

- Good service in the form of faster deliveries, technical advice, and field assistance is but one of the many intangibles that can spell value, savings, and profits to a customer. For example, one company cut its prices in response to buyers' demands. However, the company later found that what the customers really wanted was technical support. As the company cut its prices, it had only reinforced its image as low priced with little technical support.

- For a customer tempted to buy on price alone, salespeople can emphasize the importance of having a thoroughly reliable source of supply: the salesperson's company. It has been demonstrated time and again that quality is measured by the reputation of the company behind it.

- Customers value sales representatives who go out of their way to help with problems and promotions—salespeople who keep their word and follow through when they start something. These services are very valuable to customers.

USE COMMUNICATION TOOLS EFFECTIVELY

One pharmaceutical salesperson often hears that her company's drug for migraines is too expensive. Her response is to paint a word picture:[11]

> DOCTOR: How much does this product cost?
>
> SALESPERSON: It costs about $45.... There are 15 doses per bottle, so it ends up about $3 per dose.
>
> DOCTOR: That's too much money!
>
> SALESPERSON: Consider your patients who have to lie in the dark because their headaches are so bad they can't see straight, can't think straight, and are nauseated by migraine pain. A price of $3 is really inexpensive to relieve these patients' pain, wouldn't you agree?

Just telling customers about quality and value is not enough; they must be shown. Top salespeople use the communication tools discussed in Chapter 9 to describe more clearly the quality and value of their products. This process includes activities such as demonstrating the product, showing test results and quality control procedures, using case histories, and offering testimonials.

Salespeople must learn to deal with tough prospects and customers.

DEALING WITH TOUGH CUSTOMERS

Sellers need to maintain the positive attitude discussed earlier, even with rude, hard-to-get-along-with prospects. It's not easy, and it's not fun.

Sellers need to realize that we all have bad days. Maybe the buyer is having one. If the rudeness is quite blatant and the seller believes that this behavior is just due to the timing of the visit, the seller might say, "I'm sensing that this might not be the best time to talk. Should we reschedule for another time?"

If the buyer continues to communicate aggressively, being downright rude, you probably need to call attention to the fact.[12] After all, to develop a long-term win–win relationship and partnership, you both need to be on the same footing. Perhaps saying something like this will clear the air: "I'm sorry, Joe. I don't know quite how to say this. But it seems to me that you wish to argue more than learn about my products. I'll gladly continue if you think we can both approach this problem with professionalism and courtesy." By doing so, you are asserting yourself and confronting the issue head-on. At the same time, you are avoiding an emotional reaction of anger. Of course it is important to keep in mind the various personalities that buyers can have (see Chapter 5) and the adjustments suggested for each.

Also remember that the buyer's culture often dictates how he or she will respond to a seller. For example, Germans are known as being thorough, systematic, and well prepared, but they are also rather dogmatic and thus lack flexibility and the desire to compromise. As a result, sellers not accustomed to such a culture could have difficulty dealing with a German prospect who raises a price objection in a strong tone of voice.

Believe it or not, some of the toughest customers aren't those who are noisy and boisterous. Rather, they are often the passive ones, the quiet ones—the ones who don't object, don't question, and don't buy. What should a seller do? Be open, direct, and honest. Stop talking. Ask questions. Try your best to get the buyer involved. Establish trust so the buyer can feel confident enough to ask questions. If the buyer is still quiet, use a trial close. If this doesn't result in gaining commitment, ask the prospect what he or she would like to do at this point.

Believe it or not, the hardest prospects can be the quiet ones.

SELLING YOURSELF

Every day of your life, you will have objections. People love to tell me what isn't going to work or why I am wrong about things or why my product is all wrong for their business.

But when I get an objection from a friend about our weekend plans or I get questioned about whether I'm a good fit for the job during an interview or a doctor about why my product isn't going to work in his or her practice, the same techniques work. Listen to what the person is saying, ask good open-ended questions, keep the same pleasant demeanor, make note of what they are objecting to, and confidently educate the other person on why what you are telling them is the right answer!

Here's an example:

INTERVIEWER: You don't have a lot of experience in this field. Why should we consider you?

ME: Great question. You should hire me because I am trainable. I have a great background of different sales experiences, I'm well educated, and I am very coachable. You would be able to teach me any new process, and I will execute it exactly as you would like—unlike someone with already established "habits" that would come from having had experience in this field.

INTERVIEWER: Good point.

Objections can help you better understand people, situations, and life. Asking good open-ended questions always gives you an opportunity with any situation, to uncover the real need. If you don't take objections personally and learn how to make them into positives, you will be successful.

Source: Renee Miles; used with permission.

SUMMARY

Responding to objections is a vital part of a salesperson's responsibility. Objections may be offered at any time during the relationship between buyer and salesperson. They are to be expected, even welcomed, and they must be handled with skill and empathy.

Successful salespeople carefully prepare effective responses to buyers' concerns. Salespeople need to develop a positive attitude, commit to always telling the truth, refrain from interrupting, anticipate and forestall known objections, and learn how to evaluate objections.

Buyers object for many reasons. They may have no money, or they may not need the product. They may need more information or misunderstand some information already offered. They may be accustomed to another product, may not think the value exceeds the cost, or may not like the product's features. They may want to get rid of the salesperson or may not trust the salesperson or his or her company. They may want time to think or may object for many other reasons.

Effective methods of responding to objections are available, and their success has been proved. Methods exist both for concerns that are not true and for objections that either are true or are only the buyer's opinion. Sensitivity in choosing the right method is vital. Salespeople need to develop skill in responding to price objections and in dealing with tough customers. Nothing will substitute for developing skill in these areas.

KEY TERMS

ETHICS PROBLEMS

1. Your product has become the victim of industry price erosion. To remain competitive, your company has decided to allow all sales reps to drop all prices by 25 percent. However, you have a number of clients who are paying the original prices and seem happy. Do you tell them about the 25 percent price reductions or keep prices the same for them?
2. One student in a selling class once said, "Why are we learning these objection-handling methods? These techniques are just to help us manipulate our buyers!" How would you respond?

QUESTIONS AND PROBLEMS

1. Categorize each of the following responses into the five basic types of objections. Then illustrate one way to handle each:
   a. After a sales presentation, the physician says, "You've made some good points, but your competitor's drug can do just about everything yours can do."
   b. After the salesperson answers an objection, the prospect remarks, "I guess your product is all right, but as I told you when you walked in, things are going pretty well for us right now without your product."
   c. After a thorough presentation, the prospect answers, "Are you kidding me? You want how much money for that thing?"
   d. The customer says, "I can buy that online for a lot less than what you're selling it for."
2. Marjorie Kemps spent considerable time working with a prospective buyer. She thought a good order would be forthcoming on her next call. A portion of her conversation with the buyer went as follows:

   BUYER: You know, I like what I hear about your scaffolding and aerial lift service. But how can I be sure it will be available on the days that we need it for our next project?

   MARJORIE: We've never had any real complaints before. I'm pretty sure they will be easily available.

   BUYER: You are sure of that?

   MARJORIE: Well, I've never heard of any problems that I can remember.

   BUYER: [appearing unconvinced and looking at some papers on his desk without glancing up]: I'll let you know later what I plan to do. Thanks for dropping by.

   How can you improve on Marjorie's answer to the buyer's concern?
3. Describe the differences between postponing an objection and forestalling an objection. Then provide a clear example of appropriate postponing for this objection: "This iPad is way too expensive. I can buy Google tablets much cheaper than buying your iPad!"
4. Occasionally a buyer will offer several objections at one time. How would you respond if a buyer made the following comments without pausing? "Say, how long does it take your lab to get the results back to us? And what if we need same-day service sometime? Are your technicians certified? That's important, you know!"
5. In "Building Partnerships 10.1," you learned that some buyers don't want to do business with you because the last seller in your position was not very good. Make a list of questions you could ask someone you might go to work for that will help you ascertain this before you work for them.
6. Choose a restaurant in your town. Assume that you work at that restaurant and are planning to make calls to campus club organizations. Assume that the restaurant has a private meeting room available that will seat 25 people. Your objective is to have officers of the clubs schedule their meetings at the restaurant.
   a. Make a list of objections you may expect to encounter.
   b. What can you do to meet these objections effectively? List the answers you would propose, and label the methods used.
7. In "From the Buyer's Seat 10.1," you learned about a number of complaints that food buyers

have for new food products. How would you respond to a buyer who said, "Your new product is way too spicy for me!"

8. You have been describing to a retail security officer and his boss a new security camera that your firm just introduced. The camera has tracking features that make it easier for security officers to review tapes. The security officer says, "I would really like that!" The boss says, "Well, if it's what you think we need, OK. How much does it cost?" At your reply, "This one is $2,498," the boss exclaims, "For that little thing?" What should you say or do?

9. For each of the following objections, provide answers that clearly demonstrate the direct denial and indirect denial methods. Assume each objection is not true:
   a. My interior design customers wouldn't be impressed with the ability to see their proposed design plan in 3D. It's enough for me to just explain it to them and show them two-dimensional drawings.
   b. The cost of replacing the filter will be more than just buying a new unit.
   c. I heard that the resins used in manufacturing your unit might cause cancer.
   d. I can buy this cheaper online.

10. For each of the following objections, provide answers that clearly demonstrate the compensation method and referral method. Assume all the objections are either true or are the prospect's opinion:
   a. Your repossession service costs a lot of money!
   b. I don't think our customers will like the new fitness machines you're selling.
   c. Your repair mechanics aren't certified by the ATSG.
   d. My customers have never asked for this brand of recreational vehicle.

CASE PROBLEMS

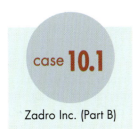

case **10.1**

Zadro Inc. (Part B)

There are many harmful germs found in the home, in public places, and in hotels while traveling. The Programmable UV Sanitizing Wand, made by Zadro, can effectively kill up to 99.99 percent of germs and viruses in just 10 seconds. It can also kill dust mites in mattresses, pillows, and carpets. Since the wand is portable, it can travel with you wherever you travel, removing harmful substances regardless of where you are. The user simply waves the scanner within a quarter inch of the surface for 10 seconds to kill the substances.

The scanner is 1½ inches high × 20 inches wide × 1¾ inches deep and runs on three C batteries. An optional AC adapter is sold separately. The scanner includes an electronic child lock to prevent misuse. A stand is provided and is used to go over keyboards, butcher blocks, and so on for hands-free operation. The programmable unit can be set for 10-, 20-, 40-, and 60-second times as well as two to five minutes, depending on the surface area that needs to be scanned. The unit is not designed to be used on humans or animals. The scanner, which is laboratory certified and tested, retails for $99, and all units come with a 90-day limited warranty. Resellers are offered the units for $60, with a quantity discount of $50 for all units over 100 in a single order.

Assume that you are selling the Programmable UV Sanitizing Wand to Target Corporation for them to resell.

Questions

1. What objections could the buyer raise? Make any assumptions necessary to develop this list.
2. Provide a response to each objection you listed in question 1 (make any assumptions necessary to create your responses). Include the name of the method you recommend for each objection.

Source: http://www.zadroinc.com/health-solutions-nano-technology-c-43_44.html; discount information is for illustration purposes only.

Hometown Focus is a small, locally owned and operated free weekly newspaper operated in Virginia, Minnesota. The paper was established in 2007 and is available in print and online. It is a community-driven newspaper that allows members in the community to share their stories, recipes, and photos. It is a small business that employs only nine people, but they do have over 400 contributors from 40 local communities. You can view more details about the paper at their Web site: http://www.hometownfocus.us.

Carlos Rivera is a salesperson for *Hometown Focus* and has made an appointment with Vijay Patel, a sales manager at Iron Trail Motors, a Chevrolet and Toyota dealership located in Virginia, Minnesota. Iron Trail offers quality new and preowned cars, trucks, and SUVs with a strong service department. Iron Trail already does advertising with a competing local newspaper called *Mesabi Daily News,* a daily, paid-subscription newspaper. Carlos is planning to discuss having Iron Trail Motors place ads in both its online and its print version of the paper.

Questions

1. List objections you think might occur during this first meeting with Vijay. Make any assumptions necessary to develop this list.
2. Describe how you would respond to each objection listed in question 1. Be sure to label the methods. Make any assumptions necessary to create your responses.

Sources: http://www.hometownfocus.us, http://www.virginiamn.com/site/forms/subscription_services, and http://www.irontrailchevrolet.com.

ROLE PLAY CASE

Today you will repeat your role play presentation from Chapter 9. (If you have not done role plays before, you will need to review the information about the various role play customers that can be found at the end of Chapter 3. If you didn't do the role play for Chapter 9, you will need to review that material also, which can be found at the end of Chapter 9.) When you act as the observer today, you should identify what objection-handling method the seller used and if it was done effectively. The professor will give you a sheet to use as a buyer, listing objections for you to use during the role play. When you sell, try to use a variety of objection-handling methods.

Note: For background information about these role plays, please see page 26.

To the instructor: Additional information needed to complete the role play is available in the Instructor's Manual.

ADDITIONAL REFERENCES

Boe, John. "Overcome Objections and Close the Sale." *American Salesman* 56, no. 8 (August 2011), pp. 10–14.

Bud, Peter Paul. *How to Be a Best Seller: 18 Simple and Proven Steps You Must Know to Succeed*. Raleigh, NC: Lulu, 2009.

Fisher, Leo D'Angelo. "Wind in the Sales." *BRW* 34, no. 1 (January 19, 2012), pp. 36–37.

Hunter, Mark. *High-Profit Selling: Win the Sale without Compromising on Price*. New York: AMACOM, 2012.

Kahle, Dave. "Preventing the Price Objection." *American Salesman* 54, no. 6 (June 2009), pp. 24–27.

McGaulley, Michael. *How to Sell: Face-to-Face Survival Guide*. New York: Champlain House Media, 2010.

Mulvey, Richard. *Handling Objections/Closing the Sale*. Durban, South Africa: Perception Business Skills, 2010.

Reilly, Tom. *Crush Price Objections: Sales Tactics for Holding Your Ground and Protecting Your Profit*. New York: McGraw-Hill, 2010.

Rutherford, Brian N., Nwamaka A. Anaza, and Adrienne Hall Phillips. "Predictors of Buyer-Seller Firm Conflict." *Journal of Marketing Theory and Practice* 20, no. 2 (Spring 2012), pp. 161–72.

Schiffman, Stephan. *25 Toughest Sales Objections—and How to Overcome Them*. New York: McGraw-Hill, 2011.

Shaltz, Gerry. *The DNA of Selling: What You Won't Learn in Business School*. Bloomington, IN: iUniverse, 2009.

Thull, Jeff. "The Three Traps of Selling." *American Salesman* 57, no. 9 (September 2012), pp. 15–19.

OBTAINING COMMITMENT

SOME QUESTIONS ANSWERED IN THIS CHAPTER ARE

- How much emphasis should be placed on closing the sale?
- Why is obtaining commitment important?
- When is the best time to obtain commitment?
- Which methods of securing commitment are appropriate for developing partnerships?
- How should pricing be presented?
- What should a salesperson do when the prospect says yes? When the prospect says no?
- What causes difficulties in obtaining commitment, and how can these issues be overcome?

PROFILE

PROFILE "What do you want to be when you grow up?" We've all heard that question. A doctor, a firefighter, or maybe even a prince. For me, the answer was always a vet. Growing up in Connecticut and being close to an aunt who lived on a farm, my childhood was filled with interesting animals: dogs, snakes, and even geckos. This love for animals led to seeking an education at Texas A&M, where I received a degree in biomedical science and then completed veterinary training. However, little did I know, sales would be where I found my true passion.

One summer afternoon before my senior year, a friend shared his experience he had in the sales world with me; I quickly became intrigued by how well he had done for himself and decided to get involved. Shortly after, I landed my first sales position with Vector Marketing. After that first sales job, I have found myself in the exciting, fast-paced world of selling and have never looked back since. While my degree may not have been in sales, I found that mastering the art of sales and performing veterinary surgeries were not all that different.

Both closing up a patient and closing a deal are important final steps to any surgery or sales meeting. One deal in particular taught me how to be effective at the close. A lucrative opportunity to help my company and a client arose early on in my career. After building a strong relationship with the director of operations, I felt confident I had an "in" with the company. Although my contact was not the final decision maker, I felt certain she would help make the deal happen. I felt assured that following her advice, her process, and her approach would seal the deal for me. I did follow her process, and when the time came to make the close, I *lost* the business!

Unfortunately, not following the sales process is an all-too-common mistake. I felt sure the relationship I had built would be enough for smooth sailing to the close, but regrettably it wasn't. Without earning the right to earn the prospect's business by following the sales approach, obtaining commitment at the close is nearly impossible. As I learned that

day, following the sales process is an irreplaceable part of successfully closing a deal. Every step brings the buyer to the closing point, and skipping even one step can throw the process out of balance, leaving an unsatisfied customer and a confused salesperson. If you find yourself scratching your head in confusion when a deal that looked certain turns south, you may just have skipped a step in the process. The hardest part to gaining commitment from the prospect simply comes when one of the steps has been skipped.

I can relate to this situation. I know what it is like to get excited, inch to the edge of your seat, feel the enthusiasm from the buyer, and sense a close. At that point, it's easy to skip a step and jump to the end. But being patient and following *all* the steps is a road map to success at the close. The best part is when the process has been followed, the closing actually becomes automated—the buyer ultimately ends up asking *you* for the business!

Being honest and open is also critical to an effective close. Whether you call yourself a consultant, an advisor, or any other title, at the end of the day the prospect knows you're a salesperson. I find freedom in this. Being sincere, honest, and open to the prospect has allowed me to gain respect and trust from my clients. At the end of the day, I just want my prospects to know "I'm here to earn the right to earn your business."

Whether you're a veterinarian or a salesperson, following the right process is the key to a successful close. Just as a vet would never skip a step in a surgery, a salesperson should never skip a step in a sales meeting to be successful. Following the right process will ultimately lead to one happy dog owner and one happy customer.

Visit our Web site at:
www.kmbs.com

SECURING COMMITMENT TODAY

Asking for the buyer's business, often called **closing**, has always received a great deal of emphasis in sales training. Hundreds of books, DVDs, CDs, and seminar speakers have touted the importance of closing—just Google "close sales" at Amazon, and over 8,000 book titles will appear. Almost all are devoted to a method or methods that will make the decision maker say yes.

Look a little closer at those titles, however, and you'll notice that most of them are old. Some of the books may even be older than your parents! Today's sales professionals recognize that securing a sale is the reason for their existence, but getting that sale should be due to the value created, not the technique used.

Rob Keeney, training director for Frosty Acres Brands, says this about closing:

> I don't see good closers as being "pushy." Assertive, yes. Direct, yes. "Pushy" implies the customer being somehow compelled to do something they really don't want to do. By contrast, a good closer helps a customer make the decision they really want or need to make. And sooner rather than later.

Charles Cohon, president of Prime Devices and an influential speaker in the manufacturer's representation industry, agrees, saying,

> Closing an order is not the end of a process, it is the beginning. Concentrate just on closing that order, and it will be the last order you get from that customer. Concentrate instead on developing a relationship with that customer that leads naturally to an order and you will earn not only that order, but also that customer's orders for many years to come.

Others also believe the traditional emphasis on getting the sale no matter what damages trust, insults the buyer's intelligence, and raises the possibility of losing commitment altogether. Customers make a buying decision, rather than the salesperson closing the sale. Buyers want to buy, not to be sold.

Solid research provides strong evidence that questions the value of closing techniques. The research, based on more than 35,000 sales calls over 12 years, has found that in a major sale, reliance on closing techniques actually reduces the chances of making a sale.[1] Further, salespeople who were specifically trained in closing actually closed fewer sales. For very low-priced products (as in door-to-door magazine sales), however, closing techniques may increase the chances of a sale.

So why even cover closing at all? Because there are nonmanipulative and trustworthy ways to gain commitment and because obtaining commitment is critical for the success of salespeople and their firms. Without a buyer's commitment, no sale takes place. As Dave Brock points out in "From the Buyer's Seat 11.1," salespeople who fail to gain the right commitment simply end up annoying the customer and failing to generate business. Also, buyers rarely volunteer to make a purchase even when that decision is obviously the right thing to do. This chapter covers the topic of obtaining commitment in a manner that is consistent with the theme of the book: developing and building long-term partnerships.

PART OF THE PROCESS

The process of obtaining commitment occurs throughout the natural, logical progression of any sales call. Recall from Chapter 3 that creeping commitment occurs when a customer becomes committed to a particular course of action throughout the buying process. Salespeople actually gain commitment repeatedly: when asking for an appointment, when checking to see whether the customer's entire needs have been identified, and when asking whether the prospect would like to see a demonstration or receive a proposal. Commitment, of course, is more than just

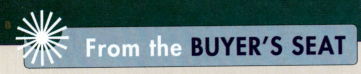

From the BUYER'S SEAT

SILLY ME, I THOUGHT SELLING WAS SUPPOSED TO GENERATE REVENUE!

I am president of Partners in Excellence, a company that consults with Fortune 500 clients in sales effectiveness. I have a keen eye in what to look for when I'm being sold to in my role as president, and I don't always like what I see.

I've always been under the impression that revenue generation (quota) was the key objective for salespeople. Therefore, I've always focused my time on finding customers that are interested in my solutions, who want to make a change, and who are willing to invest money in achieving the results they expect. That's a fundamental principle in qualifying. It's always seemed to be very important—I don't want to waste the customer's time, and, greedily, I don't want to waste my time.

Recently, however, I think I've been badly mistaken—at least based on the vast majority of sales calls I get. I always thought the goal was to find and qualify opportunities that could ultimately generate revenue, but that no longer seems to be the priority. I have to admit to being a little embarrassed. I try to keep at the forefront of best practices and emerging trends in sales effectiveness. However, I've missed this major new trend.

It seems the key goals for salespeople are (1) getting a customer to accept a piece of literature—a case study, a brochure, a catalog—and (2) getting a meeting, even if the prospect is not a fit in any possible scenario where they might buy a product.

I've been fielding a lot of prospecting calls from hopeful salespeople. They astound me! They must be on quota to send me a piece of literature. I've gotten calls from small businesses, from very large technology salespeople, various professional services organizations, and others. The salespeople are singular in their focus—"Can I send you [insert the right word—a cases study, a catalog, our brochure, etc.]?"

Most of the salespeople don't even ask questions. They have a well-rehearsed opening sentence (most of which have little meaning to me) culminating in "Can I send you some information?" My response is, "Why would I even be interested in that?" Most are not able to handle the objection. Their usual response? "Well, it's free!"

A few ask me a questions about me and my business, then somehow it gets to "Can I send you some information?" I struggle in these conversations. I try to connect the dots. I think to myself, "We were talking about this and that, how did we get to 'Can I send you some information?'" I can never figure it out; I don't know how my responses to the questions led to needing a piece of literature. In fact, a few times, the next action might have been a meeting—I was more than casually interested in what they were offering, but rather than picking up on the "buying signal," they wanted to send me a piece of literature.

Then there are the others: "We're going to be in the neighborhood and would like to meet." When I respond, "We don't buy that stuff—that's never a requirement in our business," they come back, "Well we'd just like the opportunity to meet." I always go back with, "If I never intend to buy anything you sell, why do you want to meet? What's the purpose?" They can never answer this, but they persist: "Are you available next Monday or Tuesday?"

I think I've figured it out. I'm a little ashamed. I've missed the trend. Apparently, revenue is no longer a key metric for salespeople. In sales training sessions, they are told, "Ignore buying signals, ignore whether the customer is qualified, ignore whether they are even in our sweet spot—get the meeting! The more meetings you have, the more successful you will be! Make sure you find some excuse to get a meeting, everything will work out once you get the meeting!"

I have always been of the impression that we are most effective when our activities are purposeful and create value for the customer. I've thought it better to reduce the number of calls required to close—not increase them. I've thought it not good to waste the customer's time or my time on things that are meaningless.

Have I missed something?

securing an order. As Exhibit 11.1 illustrates, salespeople will attempt to obtain a commitment that is consistent with the objectives of the particular sales call.

Obtaining commitment is also important in moving the account through the relationship process. Once a sale is made, salespeople begin to plan for the next sale or for the next level of commitment that indicates a deepening relationship.

Exhibit 11.1
Examples of
Commitments
Salespeople May
Attempt to Obtain

Examples of Presale Commitments

- To have the prospect agree to come to the Atlanta branch office sometime during the next two weeks for a hands-on demonstration of the copier.
- To set up another appointment for one week from now, at which time the buyer will allow me to do a complete survey of her printing needs.
- To inform the doctor of the revolutionary anticlotting mechanism that has been incorporated into our new drug and have her agree to read the pamphlet I will leave.
- To have the buyer agree to pass my information along to the buying committee with his endorsement of my proposal.
- To have the prospect agree to call several references that I will provide to develop further confidence and trust in my office-cleaning business.
- To have the prospect agree on the first point (of our four-point program) and schedule another meeting in two days to discuss the second point.
- To have the prospect initiate the necessary paperwork to allow us to be considered as a future vendor.

Examples of Commitments That Consummate the Sale

- To have the prospect sign an order for 100 pairs of Levi's jeans.
- To schedule a co-op newspaper advertising program to be implemented in the next month.
- To have the prospect agree to use our brand of computer paper for a trial period of one month.
- To have the retailer agree to allow us space for an end-of-aisle display for the summer presentation of Raid insect repellent.

At the same time, commitment is a two-way street. Salespeople also make commitments to buyers when the sale is made.

THE IMPORTANCE OF SECURING COMMITMENT

Overall, gaining commitment tells the salesperson what to do next and defines the status of the client. For example, gaining a needs identification appointment may mean that you have a "suspect"; at the end of that call, gaining commitment for a demonstration means you have a prospect. Gain an order and you gain a customer. Without gaining commitment, the salesperson may waste time doing the wrong things.

Salespeople need to become proficient in obtaining commitment for several other good reasons. First, if they fail to obtain commitment, it will take longer (more sales calls) to obtain a sale, if a sale occurs at all. Taking more time with one sale means fewer sales overall because you lose time for prospecting and other important activities. Second, assuming the product truly satisfies the prospect's needs, the sooner the prospect buys, the sooner she or he can realize the benefits of the product or service. Third, the company's future success depends on goodwill and earning a profit. Finally, securing commitment results in financial rewards for the salesperson; in addition, meeting needs is also intrinsically rewarding for the seller.

One thing to remember is that if you have done your job well and you have a product that the buyer truly needs, then you deserve the sale. The buyer is not doing you a favor by buying, and he or she expects you to ask for the sale if you've

thinking it through

Think for a moment about a major purchase that you or a family member made, such as a new TV or a car. During the shopping process, what were some of the worst closes you experienced? What salesperson behavior really angers you when you try to shop for major purchases? What made the difference between those experiences and the ones you found satisfying?

done your work professionally. Not only is gaining commitment important for you and your company, it is the professional thing to do. What is not professional is a high-pressure close; typically, high-pressure closing is necessary (and inappropriate) when the salesperson has not done a good job throughout the entire process.[2]

Before we get into how to obtain commitment, some time should be spent on the importance of terms and conditions of the sale and how these influence the total cost. Sometimes terms are an important need and may be presented early in the call. But we present the credit terms here because often a buyer decides what to buy and then explores the financial terms that are available.

FINANCIAL TERMS AND CONDITIONS

Most salespeople try to hold off on presenting price until the end. Yet price is often the first question asked. The final price is really a function of the terms and conditions of the sale and depends on several factors.

Cash flow is an issue for many buyers and can stop a sale. No matter how badly they may want or need the product, not having the cash can delay or even prohibit a sale. Santosh Natarajan, of SSI-India, experienced such a challenge when developing a software application for Korcett. The company was growing so fast that all cash was being used up in production, leaving no cash for an important software upgrade. Santosh worked out a payment plan that matched his invoices to receipt of payments from customers. There was added risk for SSI-India, but it was worth it.

Factors that affect price are the use of quantity and other discounts, as well as credit and shipping terms. Figuring out the final actual price can be difficult, especially in situations with many options and packages rather than standardized products.

DISCOUNTS

Discounts are given for many reasons and may be based on the type of customer (such as wholesaler or retailer, senior citizen or younger adult), quantity purchased, or some other factor. The most common type of discount is the quantity discount.

Quantity discounts encourage large purchases by passing along savings resulting from reduced processing costs. Businesses offer two types of quantity discounts: (1) the single-order discount and (2) a cumulative discount. An office equipment company offering a 10 percent discount on a single order for five or more facsimile machines is an example of a single-order discount. When offering a **cumulative discount,** that same company might offer the 10 percent discount on all purchases over a one-year period, provided the customer purchases more than five fax machines. The customer may sign an agreement at the beginning of the year promising to buy five or more machines, in which case the customer will be billed for each order at the discounted price (10 percent off). If the customer fails to purchase five fax machines, a single bill will be sent at the end of the year for the amount of the discount (10 percent of the single-unit price times the number of fax machines actually purchased). Another method is to bill the customer at the full price and then rebate the discount at the end of the year, based on the actual number of fax machines purchased.

CREDIT TERMS

Most U.S. sales are made on a credit basis, with **cash discounts** allowed for early payment. These cash discounts are the last discount taken, meaning that if a

TECHNOLOGY THAT CLOSES THE SALE

Salespeople today are often involved in highly complex sales that involve customized solutions. Technology is often thought of as supporting customer contact management or supporting customer service, but there is also technology that helps close the deal, too.

For example, product configurators are solutions that help salespeople at the close. Anritsu, a company that makes highly technical communication devices, uses Configure One's Concept software to allow customers to configure their own products online. Salespeople can use the software, too, and the software frees salespeople to focus on selling, not on product configuration. Katherine van Diepen, Anritsu's marketing communications manager, estimates that this software saves salespeople about 45 minutes per configuration, or the equivalent of adding one sales call per day per salesperson. Increased accuracy in configuration also means more satisfied customers.

Similar software can aid salespeople in converting proposals into sales. These systems, such as Quotegine

(quotegine.com) and ProposalSoftware.com, help salespeople save and reuse components of successful sales proposals. Like product configurators, these systems also help manage complex purchases from the sales process into the implementation process. The same data used to generate the proposal become the data that are then input automatically into the accounting system to generate accurate invoices as well as put automatically into production systems so that the right solutions are built and then input into the customer service system so that service documentation can be created.

One extra sales call per day may not seem like a lot, but for some sales settings, that may mean a 10 percent increase in sales. These systems, in the right settings, can significantly improve a salesperson's performance!

Sources: Matt Moore and Keith De La Rue, "Closing the Deal with the Help of Knowledge," *Knowledge Management Review* 11, no. 3 (July/August 2008), pp. 14–19; "Anritsu Case Study," http://www.configureone.com/pdf/ConfigureOnecasestudy-Anritsu.pdf, accessed March 3, 2010.

quantity discount is also offered, the cash discount is calculated after the quantity discount is taken off. A common discount is 2/10, n/30, which means that the buyer can deduct 2 percent from the bill if it is paid within 10 days from the date of invoice. Otherwise the full amount must be paid in 30 days. Another common discount is 2/10, EOM, which means that the 10-day period begins at the end of the month. For example, if the customer receives $1,000 worth of supplies on February 15 with terms of 2/10, EOM and pays the bill on March 5, the customer would pay $980 (that is, $1,000 at 2% = $20 discount for paying cash; $1,000 − $20 = $980). But if the customer pays on March 11, the bill would be the full $1,000.

Credit terms can be very important in capital equipment sales. Capital purchases have long lives and cost more than a buyer can afford to pay all at once. For example, the HVAC (heating, ventilation, and air conditioning) industry relies heavily on financing to sell heating and cooling systems. Johnson Controls offered a six months with no interest plan, called "same as cash." "Most consumers need some type of bridge financing to handle an unplanned $8,000 HVAC expense. That is why we feel we've seen so much business in the same-as-cash programs."[3] Easy credit terms can help salespeople close sales, but sales aren't complete until the buyer takes delivery. One home builder noticed that buyers were willing to put contracts on houses that hadn't been built yet in order to fix their credit during the nine months it took to complete the homes. So many "buyers" were unable to actually get credit and canceled sales that he quit taking orders on prebuilt homes.[4]

SHIPPING COSTS

The terms and conditions of sale include shipping costs. Recall from Chapter 2 that the term *free on board (FOB)* is used to determine the point at which the buyer assumes responsibility for both the goods and the costs of shipping them. Thus, FOB destination means the buyer will take responsibility for the goods once they reach the buyer's location, and the seller will pay the freight.

Suppose Hormel quotes an FOB origin price. It will load the truck at its Chicago plant, but the buyer will pay for shipping. If Hormel sold a truckload of pepperoni to Coppoli's Deli under terms of FOB destination, Hormel would pay for shipping and would have the pepperoni delivered to Coppoli's Deli's warehouse, where warehouse personnel would unload the truck.

If Hormel quotes a price for pepperoni that's FOB origin, then Coppoli's Deli pays for shipping. If the price is FOB destination, then Hormel pays for shipping.

Another form of FOB is *FOB installed*, meaning that title and responsibility do not transfer until the equipment is installed and operating properly. In some instances FOB installed can also mean that operator training must be provided before title transfers. These are important terms because there are significant costs associated with the technical installation and operator training for many pieces of sophisticated equipment. Buyers want to know the total price and what it includes.

The terms and conditions of a sale, including but not limited to price, can often play as important a role as the product itself in determining what is purchased. Creative salespeople understand the terms and conditions they have to work with so they can meet the needs of their buyers while also meeting the profit objectives of their own companies.

PRESENTING PRICE

Price is often discussed at the end of the presentation simply because the salesperson may not know what that price will be until the final solution is agreed on. Because price is so important to the buyer, it is worth considering how price should be presented.

Most firms set prices after careful study of competitors' offerings, the value delivered by the product or service, and the cost of providing the product or service. For these reasons the price should represent a reasonable and fair picture of the product's or service's value. Therefore, never apologize for a price or present the price apologetically; rather, present it with confidence.

Bruce Culbert, now chief service officer with the Pedowitz Group, says that salespeople sometimes negotiate against themselves. When he was at IBM,

I had an account manager who was under pressure to make quota for the quarter. In presenting a proposal to a prospective customer, the salesperson did as was agreed and sent the proposal via e-mail a full two weeks prior to quarter end because the client said they would be able to make a decision by the end of the month. If this deal closed, the salesperson would hit quota. Several days went by, and there was no response from the prospect. A follow-up e-mail and phone went unanswered. In a panic the salesperson began to submit revised proposals each time, lowering the price in an attempt to get the prospect to respond positively.

A week went by with no response. During the week two revised proposals had been submitted, each time lowering the price almost 10 percent. On the Tuesday before the quarter closed the client responded favorably to the original proposal with their apologies that they had not responded sooner but they were on vacation the past week and were just now catching up on e-mail. Needless to say the salesperson was ecstatic to learn of the good fortune just prior to quarter close. About 10 minutes later the salesperson received an additional e-mail from the client informing them to ignore the previous note and that they would like to accept proposal revision 2, which was almost 20 percent less than the original proposal.[5]

As Bruce says, here is a salesperson who panicked and lost the company 20 percent. Sometimes, companies can add to the pressure on salespeople, as you can see in Building Partnerships 11.1.

In addition to presenting the price with confidence, remember that price is not the focus of your presentation. The real issue is satisfying the needs of the buyer, of which budget is only one. True, a budget limitation can halt progress toward a sale. The real issue, though, is the total cost of ownership, which means the buyer should also factor in the value of the benefits delivered.

WHEN TO ATTEMPT TO OBTAIN COMMITMENT

Novice salespeople frequently ask themselves these questions: Is there a right time to obtain commitment? How will customers let me know they are ready to buy? Should I make more than one attempt? What should I do if my first attempt fails?

The right time to attempt to gain commitment is when the buyer appears ready, as evidenced by buying signals. Some salespeople say that one psychological moment in each sales presentation affords the best opportunity to obtain commitment, and if this opportunity is bypassed, securing commitment will be difficult or impossible. This belief is not true, however. Seldom does one psychological moment govern the complete success or failure of a sales presentation.

Most buyers will commit themselves only when they clearly understand the benefits and costs of such a decision. At times this point occurs early in the call. A commitment to purchase a large system, however, usually will not occur until a complete presentation and several calls have been made and all questions have been answered.

Buying signals, or indications that the buyer is ready to buy, can be evidenced both in the buyer's comments and nonverbally. Buying signals are also called **closing cues.**

BUYER COMMENTS

A customer's comments often are the best indication that he or she is considering commitment. A prospect will seldom say, "All right, I'm ready to endorse this product to our buying committee." Questions about the product or terms of sale and comments in the form of requirements or benefit statements signal readiness to buy, as do responses to trial closes.

Buyer Questions

Here are some examples of questions that signal readiness to buy:

If I agree to go with this cooperative advertising program, do you have any ads already developed that I could use?

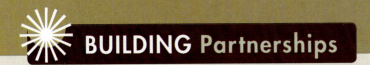
BUILDING Partnerships

TIMING AND PRICING

What's it like to be closed—especially for a big deal? Steve Schlesinger is a sales guy who tells this story: "Just last week, we had a significant purchase to make, not just because it was an expensive or large purchase but because it represented a major change in strategy. Our strategy for information technology has been to build our own. In many ways, we were ahead of the market, and off-the-shelf programs did not fit our needs." His company reconsidered this approach when it came time to upgrade their customer management software. "Our first thought was that it was too expensive. Two years ago, we had looked at software for customer management, and it just didn't make sense."

He called a friend at Salesforce.com, and they went to work on a solution. "The development meeting was excellent, the integration piece was developed, and then they came back with a good cost/benefit analysis." But then the decision got tougher. "With offices across the United States and United Kingdom, we realized we needed everyone who works with clients would need access to the software. This decision increased our license from 10 users to 70 or 80. That raises the costs substantially, and suddenly, that cost/benefit analysis wasn't looking so good." But it was two days before the end of the fiscal year for Salesforce.com, so they slashed the price and got the deal done.

Steve says it wasn't a hard, aggressive sale. The Salesforce.com team was transparent, "they needed to get it done and told us, and they gave me the leeway in the terms that I needed. They were very professional." But Steve clearly believes he got a better deal because of the timing.

LeeAnne Pearson conducted a study for a company that asked for anonymity. During the study, salespeople complained that top management would slash prices at the end of each quarter in order to get sales up and look good on Wall Street. "These salespeople were frustrated that they were giving up margin and commission in order for top management to look good and stock prices to go up. Worse yet, they also said buyers recognized the practice and purposively timed purchases and negotiated fiercely, knowing they could get bargains by waiting until the end of the quarter." These are sales of half a million dollars or more—yet salespeople are under the same pressure to close deals that car salespeople face every month!

Sources: LeeAnne Pearson, "Sales Practices: A Comparison of Top and Bottom Salespeople," Research Paper 11-1, Baylor University's Center for Professional Selling (September 1, 2011); Steve Schlesinger's quotes are from personal interview, February 5, 2010.

Do you have any facilities for training our employees in the use of the product?

How soon would you be able to deliver the equipment?

Not all questions signal a readiness to buy. But if the question concerns implementing the purchase and points toward when, not if, the purchase is implemented, the prospect may be getting ready to buy.

Requirements

Requirements are conditions that have to be satisfied before a purchase can take place. For example:

We need a cash discount for a supply order like this.

We need to get this in weekly shipments.

Requirements that are stated near the end of the presentation are need statements that reflect a readiness to buy when they relate to how the purchase will be consummated. As the examples illustrate, requirements relating to financial terms or shipping indicate that the decision to buy the product has been made and now it is time to work out the details.

Benefit Statements

Sometimes prospects offer their own benefit statements, such as these:

Oh, I like the way this equipment is serviced—it will make it much easier on my staff.

Good, that color will match our office decor.

Such positive statements reflect strong feelings in support of the purchase—a sign that the buyer is ready.

Responses to Trial Closes

Salespeople can solicit such comments by continually taking the pulse of the situation with **trial closes,** which are questions regarding the prospect's readiness to buy (first discussed in Chapter 8). Throughout the presentation, the salesperson should be asking questions:

How does this sound to you so far?

Is there anything else you would like to know at this point?

How does this compare with what you have seen of competing products?

Such questions are an important element of any sales process because trial closes serve several purposes, including identifying the customer's proximity to making the decision, gaining agreement on minor points, and creating a true dialogue in which the ultimate close is a natural conclusion. Note that these are more general questions than simply gaining agreement on benefits (discussed in Chapter 8), say as part of a FEBA.

One approach is to try a soft third-party trial close, such as by asking, "At this point, do you feel comfortable in recommending our product/service to others in your organization?" If you know that the buying process is likely to involve others, you can ask the question more specifically, such as, "Are you comfortable in bringing this to the [insert the appropriate title or name] attention?"

When a seller asks a trial close question, the buyer responds, thus creating a dialogue. Issues can be raised as objections or questions by the buyer, which tell the seller what to cover. Then, because the salesperson has been asking closing questions all along, the final close is just a natural part of the ongoing dialogue, as it should be.

NONVERBAL CUES

As in every phase of the presentation, nonverbal cues serve as important indicators of the customer's state of mind, as discussed in Chapter 4. While attempting to gain commitment, the salesperson should use the buyer's nonverbal signals to better identify areas of concern and see whether the buyer is ready to commit. Facial expressions most often indicate how ready the buyer is to make a commitment. Positive signals include eyes that are open and relaxed, face and mouth not covered with hands, a natural smile, and a relaxed forehead. The reverses of these signals indicate that the buyer is not yet ready to commit to the proposal.

Customers' actions also often indicate readiness to buy or make a commitment. For example, the prospective buyer of a fax machine may get a document and operate the machine or place the machine on the table where it will be used. The industrial buyer may refer to a catalog to compare specifications with competing products. A doctor, when told of a new drug, may pick up the pamphlet and begin carefully reading the indications and contraindications. A retailer considering whether to allow an end-of-aisle display may move to the end of an aisle and scan the layout. Any such actions may be signals for obtaining commitment; they should be viewed in the context of all available verbal and nonverbal cues.

HOW TO SUCCESSFULLY OBTAIN COMMITMENT

Do the two buyers on the right look like they are ready to commit to a purchase?

To obtain commitment in a nonmanipulative manner, salespeople need to follow several principles, including maintaining a positive attitude, letting the customer set the pace, being assertive instead of aggressive, and selling the right product in the right amounts.

MAINTAIN A POSITIVE ATTITUDE

Confidence is contagious. Customers like to deal with salespeople who have confidence in themselves, their products, and their companies. On the other hand, unnecessary fear can be a self-fulfilling prophecy. The student who fears essay exams usually does poorly; golfers who believe they will miss short putts usually do. So it is with salespeople: If they fear customers will not accept their proposals, the chances are good they will be right.

One manager related the example of a salesperson selling laundry detergent who unsuccessfully tried to convince a large discount chain to adopt a new liquid version of the product. When the rep's sales manager stopped by the account later in the week to follow up on a recent stockout problem, the buyer related his reasons for refusing the Liquid Tide: "Listen, I know you guys are sharp. You probably wouldn't come out with a new product unless you had tons of data to back up your decision. But honestly, the sales rep who calls on me is always so uptight and apprehensive that I was afraid to adopt the new product! Don't you guys teach them about having confidence?"

LET THE CUSTOMER SET THE PACE

Attempts to gain commitment must be geared to fit the varying reactions, needs, and personalities of each buyer. Thus, the sales representative needs to practice adaptive selling. (See Chapter 5 for a complete discussion of adaptive selling.)

Some buyers who react slowly may need plenty of time to assimilate the material presented. They may ask the same question several times or show they do not understand the importance of certain product features. In these circumstances the salesperson must deliver the presentation more slowly and may have to repeat certain parts. Trying to rush buyers is unwise when they show they are not yet ready to commit.

As we discussed earlier in the book, buyers' decision-making styles vary greatly. Japanese and Chinese buyers tend to move more slowly and cautiously when evaluating a proposition. In contrast, buyers working for *Fortune 500* firms located in the largest U.S. cities often tend to move much more quickly. The successful salesperson recognizes such potential differences and acts accordingly.

BE ASSERTIVE, NOT AGGRESSIVE

Marvin Jolson has identified three types of salespeople: aggressive, submissive, and assertive.[6] Exhibit 11.2 summarizes the differences among assertive, aggressive, and submissive salespeople's handling of the sales interview. **Aggressive** salespeople control the sales interaction but often fail to gain commitment because they prejudge the customer's needs and fail to probe for information. Too busy talking to do much listening, they tend to push the buyer too soon, too often, and too vigorously. They might say, "I can't understand why you are hesitant," but they do not probe for reasons for the hesitancy. A recent study found that

Exhibit 11.2

How Aggressive, Submissive, and Assertive Salespeople Handle Sales Activities

Selling Activity	Selling Style		
	Aggressive	Submissive	Assertive
Defining customer needs	Believe they are the best judge of customer's needs.	Accept customer's definition of needs.	Probe for need-related information that customer may not have volunteered.
Controlling the presentation	Minimize participation by customer.	Permit customer to control presentation.	Encourage two-way communication and customer participation.
Closing the sale	Overwhelm customer; respond to objections without understanding.	Assume customers will buy when ready.	Respond to objections, leading to somewhat automatic close.

aggressive salespeople negatively impacted overall customer satisfaction, even when customers were satisfied with the product itself.[7]

Submissive salespeople often excel as socializers. With customers they spend a lot of time talking about families, restaurants, and movies. They establish rapport quite effectively. They accept the customers' statements of needs and problems but do not probe to uncover any latent needs or opportunities. Submissive salespeople rarely try to obtain commitment, perhaps because they may fear rejection too much.

Assertive salespeople, the third type, are self-confident and positive. They maintain the proper perspective by being responsive to customer needs. Rather than aggressively creating new "needs" in customers through persuasion, they look for buyers who truly need their products and then use questions to acquire information. Their presentations emphasize an exchange of information rather than a one-way presentation.

SELL THE RIGHT ITEM IN THE RIGHT AMOUNTS

The chance of obtaining commitment improves when the right product is sold in the right amount. Although this principle sounds obvious, it often is not followed. Sometimes salespeople try to get the biggest order they can. Customers have long memories, they will refuse to do business again with someone who oversells, and they may also lack confidence in someone who undersells.

For example, before attempting to sell two copiers, the office equipment sales representative must be sure that these two copiers, instead of only one copier or perhaps three, best fit the needs of the buyer's office. The chemical company sales representative selling to an industrial firm must know that one tank car of a chemical is more likely to fit the firm's needs than 10 55-gallon drums. The Johnson Wax sales rep who utilizes the firm's Sell to Potential program knows the importance of selling not too few units (the store will run out of stock during the promotion) and not too many units (the store will be stuck with excess inventory after the promotion). The chances to obtain commitment diminish rapidly when the salesperson tries to sell too many or too few units or the wrong grade or style of product.

Also, salespeople should not rely solely on trial orders. A **trial order** is a small order placed by a buyer to see if the product will work and should not be confused with a trial close. A trial order is no commitment, and all too often a buyer will agree to a trial just to get rid of the salesperson. Further, if any learning curve is necessary, a customer who agrees to a trial might be unwilling to invest the time necessary to fully learn the product and will not fully realize the benefits.

The product will be rejected often because customers don't have time to give fair trials. Trial orders can work well when the product is easy to implement (such as selling a new product to a retailer for resale) or when the benefits can be realized only by seeing the product in use.

EFFECTIVE METHODS

"If closing is seen by so many sales experts as manipulative and insulting, are effective methods those that are manipulative but not insulting?" asked one of our students. It is a fair question, and the answer has two elements. First, the salesperson's purpose is to sell the right product in the right amounts. If the prospect does not need what is being sold, the salesperson should walk to the next door and start again. Thus, there should never be a need for manipulation (review Chapter 2 for a discussion of manipulation). Second, in addition to selling only what the customer needs, the salesperson should also sell in a fashion consistent with the way the buyer prefers to buy. Therefore, the salesperson should gain commitment in a manner that will help the buyer make the choice, consistent with the principle of persuasion. We use the word *choice* here to mean that the buyer can say no. Salespeople do try to persuade buyers, but with persuasion, the choice remains with the buyer. Manipulative techniques are designed to reduce or eliminate choice; partnering methods are not.

ethics

Studying successful methods and techniques enables salespeople to help prospects buy a product or service they want or need. Buyers sometimes have a need or a want but still hesitate to buy the product or service that will satisfy it. For example, an industrial buyer for a candy manufacturer refused to commit to a change in sweeteners, even though she needed better raw material. Why? Because the sweetener rep had met with her on four separate occasions, and the buyer had difficulty remembering all that was said and agreed on. (Apparently this salesperson was not using a software program like NetSuite very effectively.) Had the salesperson used the appropriate method (the benefit summary method, discussed later in this section), commitment might have been obtained. This section describes several of the most important methods for gaining commitment.

DIRECT REQUEST

The most straightforward, effective method of obtaining commitment is simply to ask for it, called the **direct request method.** However, salespeople need to be wary of appearing overly aggressive when using this direct request method. Decisive customers, such as drivers, appreciate getting down to business and not wasting time. Here are some examples:

Can I put you down for 100 pairs of model 63?

Can we meet with your engineer next Thursday to discuss this further?

Will you come to the home office for a hands-on demonstration?

Can you call the meeting next week?

BENEFIT SUMMARY

Early in the interview salespeople discover or reiterate the needs and problems of the prospect. Then, throughout the presentation, they show how their product can meet those needs. They do this by turning product or service features into benefits specifically for that buyer. As they present each benefit, they ask if that benefit meets the need. When using this approach, called the **benefit summary method,** the salesperson simply reminds the prospect of the agreed-on benefits of the proposal. This nonmanipulative method helps the buyer synthesize points covered in the presentation to make a wise decision. For example, a salesperson attempting to obtain a buyer's commitment to recommend a proposal to a buying committee might say this:

> You stated early in my visit that you were looking for a product of the highest quality, a vendor that could provide quick delivery, and adequate engineering support. As I've mentioned, our fasteners have been rated by an independent laboratory as providing 20 percent higher tensile strength than the closest competitor, resulting in a life expectancy of more than four years. We also discussed the fact that my company can deliver fasteners to your location within 3 hours of your request and that this promise holds true 24 hours a day. Finally, I discussed the fact that we have four engineers on staff whose sole responsibility is to provide support and develop specifications for new fasteners for existing customers. Would you be willing to give the information we discussed to the buying committee along with your endorsement of the proposal?

One advantage of the benefit summary method over the direct request method is that the seller can help the buyer remember all the points discussed in the presentation. The summary becomes particularly important in long presentations and in selling situations involving several meetings prior to obtaining commitment. The salesperson cannot assume that the buyer will remember all the major points discussed in the presentation.

BALANCE SHEET METHOD

Sometimes referred to as the *Ben Franklin method* because Franklin described using it to make decisions, the **balance sheet method** aids prospects who cannot make a decision, even though no reason for their behavior is apparent. Such a prospect may be asked to join the salesperson in listing the pros and cons of buying now or buying later, of buying the salesperson's product or that of a competitor, or of buying the product or not buying it at all.

However, like many nonmanipulative sales techniques, this method can insult a buyer's intelligence if used inappropriately. The salesperson may start to obtain commitment with the following type of statement:

> You know, Mr. Thacker, Ben Franklin was like you, always determined to reach the right decisions and avoid the wrong ones. I suppose that's how you feel. Well, he suggested taking a piece of paper and writing all the reasons for deciding yes in one column and then listing the reasons for deciding no in a second column. He said that when you make this kind of graphic comparison, the correct decision becomes much more apparent.

That close may seem manipulative; it certainly sounds silly. A more effective start may be to simply draw a T on a plain piece of paper, place captions on each side of the crossbar, and leave space below for the insertion of specific benefits or sales points. Then ask the buyer to list pros and cons of making the purchase. For example, assume the product is National Adhesives' hot-melt adhesive used to attach paper labels to plastic Coke bottles. Coca-Cola is currently using a liquid adhesive made by Ajax Corporation. The top of the T might look like this:

Benefits of Adopting the National Adhesives Hot-Melt Method	Benefits of Staying with the Ajax Liquid Adhesives

The salesperson may say something like, "Making a decision like this is difficult. Let's see how many reasons we can think of for your going with the National

Adhesives system." The salesperson would write the benefits (not features) in which the customer has shown interest on the left side of the T. Next the salesperson would ask the customer to list reasons to stay with the Ajax adhesive on the right side. When completed, the T lists should accurately reflect all the pros and cons of each possible decision. At that point the buyer is asked, "Which method do you think is the wisest?"

When used properly, the balance sheet method can help hesitant buyers express their feelings about the decision in a manner similar to the multiattribute matrix (see the appendix of Chapter 3), which gives the salesperson an opportunity to deal with those feelings. It is especially appropriate for a buyer who is an analytical but would make less sense for an expressive. However, the balance sheet approach takes time and may appear "salesy," particularly if relatively unimportant benefits are considered to be equal to more important reasons not to buy. Also, the list of benefits of the product being sold will not always outnumber the list on the other side of the T.

PROBING METHOD

In the **probing method** sales representatives initially attempt to obtain commitment by another method, perhaps simply asking for it (the direct request method). If unsuccessful, the salesperson uses a series of probing questions designed to discover the reason for the hesitation. Once any reason becomes apparent, the salesperson asks a what-if question. (What if I could successfully resolve this concern? Would you be willing to commit?) An illustrative dialogue follows:

SALESPERSON: Could we make an appointment for next week, at which time I would come in and do a complete survey of your needs? It shouldn't take more than three hours.

PROSPECT: No, I don't think I am quite ready to take that step yet.

SALESPERSON: There must be some reason why you are hesitating to go ahead now. Do you mind if I ask what it is?

PROSPECT: I'm just not convinced that your firm is large enough to handle a customer of our size.

SALESPERSON: In addition to that, is there any other reason why you would not be willing to go ahead?

PROSPECT: No.

SALESPERSON: If I can resolve the issue of our size, then you would allow me to conduct a survey?

PROSPECT: Well, I wouldn't exactly say that.

SALESPERSON: Then there must be some other reason. May I ask what it is?

PROSPECT: Well, a friend of mine who uses your services told me that often your billing department sends him invoices for material he didn't want and didn't receive.

SALESPERSON: In addition to that, is there any other reason for not going ahead now?

PROSPECT: No, those are my two concerns.

SALESPERSON: If I could resolve those issues right now, would you be willing to set up an appointment for a survey?

PROSPECT: Sure.

This dialogue illustrates the importance of probing in obtaining commitment. The method attempts to bring to the table all issues of concern to the prospect. The salesperson does not claim to be able to resolve the issues but simply attempts to find out what the issues are. When probing has identified all the issues, the salesperson should attempt to resolve them as soon as possible. After successfully dealing with the concerns of the buyer, the salesperson should then ask for a commitment.

There are many modifications of the probing method. Another way to achieve the same results is the following:

SALESPERSON: Are you willing to buy this product today?

PROSPECT: No, I don't think so.

SALESPERSON: I really would like to get a better feel of where you are. On a scale of 1 to 10, with 1 being absolutely no purchase and 10 being purchase, where would you say you are?

PROSPECT: I would say I'm about a 6.

SALESPERSON: If you don't mind my asking, what would it take to move you from a 6 to a 10?

Also, it is important to always keep cultural differences in mind. For example, if a Japanese businesswoman wants to tell an American salesperson that she is not interested, she might state, "Your proposal would be very difficult," just to be polite. If the seller attempts to use the probing method, the Japanese businesswoman may consider the seller to be pushy or a poor listener. In the same way, an Arab businessperson will never say no directly, a custom that helps both sides avoid losing face.[8]

This Frosty Acres Brands salesperson is using the alternative choice close, giving the buyer an option between a name brand (Domino) and their own brand of sugar.

Photography by Lynn Conn, used with permission

ALTERNATIVE CHOICE

In many situations a salesperson may have multiple options to present to a buyer. For example, Teo Schaars sells diamonds directly from cutters in the Netherlands to consumers in the United States. When he started in sales, he would display several dozen diamonds on a purple damask–covered table. Sales were few until his father, a Dutch diamond broker, suggested that he limit his customers' choices; there were simply too many diamonds to choose from, overwhelming the buyer. Schaars found his father's comments to be wise advice. Now Schaars spends more time probing about budget and desires and then shows only two diamonds at a time, explaining the key characteristics of each. Then he allows the customer to express a preference. Schaars may have to show half a dozen or more diamonds before a customer makes the final decision, but he rarely shows more than two at a time (www.anschardiamonds.com).

TRIAL OFFERS

One strategy that can be effective but is also very tricky is the trial offer. This approach is also called "the puppy dog close," based on the idea that once you take a puppy home, you won't want to give it up. If your product is simple to use and the benefits are obvious only in use, a trial offer can be effective. If the product is complicated, however, prospects may not want to make the investment in learning how to use it and conclude it is too difficult to learn. A fear that some sales managers have is that salespeople will rely too much on the approach as a way to avoid actually asking for the order.

If you plan to use the approach, it's best to do the following:

- Set a specific time for training, if needed, and make sure the user is comfortable with the product.
- Document that the decision criteria are concrete—and that the trial is needed to achieve those criteria.
- Agree on when a decision will be made.

Some salespeople, such as in the car or office equipment business, find that prospects may use trials as a way to simply borrow the product and solve a short-term need. Setting proper expectations at the outset can aid in avoiding those situations.

OTHER METHODS

Literally hundreds of techniques and methods to obtain commitment have been tried. Exhibit 11.3 lists a number of traditional methods. Most of them, however, tend to be ineffective with sophisticated customers; nevertheless, many can be

Exhibit 11.3
Some Traditional Closing Methods

Method	How It Works	Remark
Minor-point close	The seller assumes it is easier to get the prospect to decide on a very trivial point than on the whole proposition: What color do you like, blue or red?	This method can upset a prospect who feels he or she is being manipulated or tricked into making a commitment. Even unsophisticated buyers easily spot this technique.
Continuous *yes* close	Throughout the presentation, the seller constantly asks questions for which the prospect most logically would answer yes. By the end of the discussion, the buyer is so accustomed to saying yes that when the order is requested, the natural response is yes.	This method is based on self-perception theory. As the presentation progresses, the buyer begins to perceive himself or herself as being agreeable. At the close, the buyer wants to maintain this self-image and almost unthinkingly says yes. Use of this method can destroy long-term relationships if the buyer later feels manipulated.
Assumptive close	The seller, without asking for the order, simply begins to write it up. A variation is to fill out the order form as the prospect answers questions.	This method does not even give the buyer the courtesy of agreeing. It can be perceived as being very pushy and manipulative.
Standing-room-only close	The seller attempts to obtain commitment by describing the negative consequences of waiting. For example, the seller may state, "If you can't decide now, I'll have to offer it to another customer."	This method can be effective if the statement is true. However, if the prospect really does need to act quickly, this deadline should probably be discussed earlier in the presentation to reduce possible mistrust and the feeling of being pushed.
Benefit-in-reserve close	First the seller attempts to obtain commitment by another method. If unsuccessful, the seller says, "Oh, if you order today I can offer you an additional 5 percent for your trade-in."	This method can backfire easily. The buyer tends to think, "If I had agreed to your first attempt to obtain commitment, I would not have learned about this new enticement. If I wait longer, how much better will your offer be?" The buyer may then seek additional concessions in every future sale attempt.
Emotional close	The seller appeals to the buyer's emotions to close the sale. For example, the seller may say, "This really is a good deal. To be honest with you, I desperately need to secure an order today. As you know, I work on a straight commission basis. My wife is going to have surgery next week, and our insurance just won't cover . . ."	Many obvious problems arise with this method. It is an attempt to move away from focusing entirely on the buyer's personal needs. It does not develop trust or respect. Do not use this close!

used in a nonmanipulative manner if appropriate. For example, the minor-point close can be appropriate if there really is a need to make a choice between two options; the factor that makes the method manipulative is the assumption that the minor choice is the equivalent to making the sale.

No method of obtaining commitment will work if the buyer does not trust the salesperson, the company, and the product. Gaining commitment should not require the use of tricky techniques or methods to force buyers to do something they do not want to do or to manipulate them to buy something they do not need.

IF COMMITMENT IS OBTAINED

The salesperson's job is not over when commitment is obtained. In fact, in many ways the job is just beginning. This section describes the salesperson's responsibilities that accrue after the buyer says yes.

NO SURPRISES

Customers do not like surprises, so now is the time to go over any important information they will need to fully enjoy the benefits of the product or service. For example, if you are selling life insurance and a physical is required, give the customer as much detail as possible to prepare him or her for that experience. Or if a company is going to lease a piece of heavy equipment, let the customer know that delivery will occur after a credit check and how long that credit check will take. John Branton, president of Safe Harbor Financial, requires his salespeople to make sure the client understands how the product works and, if any negative consequences can occur, make sure the client is prepared for it. No customer wants to be surprised with a tax bill later, for example, even if the purchase was still the best choice available.[8]

CONFIRM THE CUSTOMER'S CHOICE

Customers like to believe they have chosen intelligently when they make a decision. After important decisions, they may feel a little insecure about whether the sacrifice is worth it. Such feelings are called **buyer's remorse** or **postpurchase dissonance**. Successful salespeople reassure customers that their choice was the right one. For example:

I know you will enjoy using your new office machines. You can plan on many months of trouble-free service. I'll call on you in about two weeks to make sure everything is operating smoothly. Be sure to call me if you need any help before then. Or

Congratulations, Mr. Jacobs. You are going to be glad you decided to use our service. There is no finer service available. Now let's make certain you get off to the right start. Your first bulletin will arrive on Tuesday, March 2.

Or

You've made an excellent choice. Other stores won't have a product like this for at least 30 days.

GET THE SIGNATURE

The buyer's signature often formalizes a commitment. Signing the order is a natural part of a well-planned procedure. The order blank should be accessible, and the signing should be treated as a routine matter. Ordinarily the customer has decided to buy before being asked to sign the order. In other words, the signature on the order blank merely confirms that an agreement has already been reached. The decision to buy or not to buy should not focus on a signature.

The salesperson needs to remember several important points: (1) Make the actual signing an easy, routine procedure; (2) fill out the order blank accurately and promptly; and (3) be careful not to exhibit any excess eagerness or excitement when the prospect is about to sign.

SHOW APPRECIATION

All buyers like to think that their business is appreciated even if they purchase only small quantities. Customers like to do business with salespeople who show that they want the business.

Salespeople may show appreciation by writing the purchaser a letter. This practice especially develops goodwill after large purchases and with new customers. In some situations a small gift, such as a pen with the selling company's name on it, may also be an effective thank-you. Salespeople should always thank the purchaser personally; the thanks should be genuine but not effusive.

Is an e-mail message adequate? Eleanor Brownell doesn't think so. She says, "It (a handwritten note) makes you memorable."[9]

CULTIVATE FOR FUTURE CALLS

In most fields of selling, obtaining commitment is not the end of a business transaction; rather, it is only one part of a mutually profitable business relationship. Obtaining commitment is successful only if it results in goodwill and future commitment. Keep in mind that research shows that it is how the salesperson treats the customer that is the biggest determinant of future sales. How the customer gets treated determines loyalty, which then influences repurchase.[10]

Customers like to do business with salespeople who do not lose interest immediately after securing commitment. What a salesperson does after achieving commitment is called **follow-up.** As Jeffrey Bailey, sales director for Oracle, recognizes, "Making the sale is only the beginning." After making the sale, the salesperson must follow up to make sure the product is delivered when promised, set up appropriately, and so forth. We talk more about follow-up in later chapters. The point here is that the sale does not end with the customer's signature on the order form. Research shows that the quality of follow-up service is an important contributing factor in perceptions of salesperson quality and long-term relationships.[11]

REVIEW THE ACTIONS TO BE TAKEN

An important step, particularly when commitment is next in the buying process, is to review what each party has agreed to do. In the case of a multiple-visit sales cycle, the salesperson must review not only what the client will do but also what the salesperson will do to prepare for the next meeting. To be welcomed on repeat calls, salespeople must be considerate of all the parties involved in buying or using the product. They must pronounce and spell all names correctly, explain and review the terms of the purchase so no misunderstandings will occur, and be sociable and cordial to subordinates as well as those in key positions. In addition, the buyer or user must get the service promised. The importance of this point cannot be overemphasized. Chapter 13 provides detailed information about how to service the account and build a partnership.

IF COMMITMENT IS NOT OBTAINED

When asking for commitment, salespeople can often encounter objections. One important consideration is to recognize that these objections are no different than any others; they just happen at a time when you might think they're more important because the process is near the end. One approach is to respond with a question that checks the importance of the objection. For example, if the buyer objects to price, ask, "If price weren't an issue, is there anything else preventing us from moving forward?" If the answer is yes, then you probe to determine what those issues are, as price was likely just a screen for the real concerns. If the answer is no, then you can explore financial terms and other financial options. Other objections can serve as excuses to screen the real one, but price is the most often used screen.

Naturally the salesperson does not always obtain the desired commitment. The salesperson should never take this situation personally (which is easier said than done). Doing everything right does not guarantee a sale. Situations change, and customers who may have really needed the product when everything started may find that other priorities make a purchase impossible.

Many times, when a buyer says no, the seller is wise to treat it as "No, not now" rather than "No, never." Kenneth Young, CEO of Tymco, once told a salesperson that he just didn't have the budget to make the decision now but that he'd consider it again the following year. "The salesperson stayed in touch, and when it came time to plan the budget, I made sure she was given a chance to give us all of the cost details so we could plan for the purchase."

thinking it through

Many students report that asking for the order is the hardest part of selling. Why is it difficult? Does the customer need you to ask for the sale? Have you ever needed a salesperson to ask you to buy? Why or why not?

This section describes some of the common reasons for failing to obtain commitment and offers practical suggestions for salespeople who encounter rejection.

SOME REASONS FOR LOST OPPORTUNITIES

In this discussion, we are assuming that the salesperson did an appropriate qualifying job and understood the buyer's needs. As you saw in "From the Buyer's Seat 11.1," some buyers are being asked to take a meeting or take the next step in the purchase process when no need is present. Clearly asking for commitment when there's no need is foolish. So why would you lose a sale if the customer clearly had a need? Here's a few reasons.

Wrong Attitudes

As discussed earlier in the chapter, salespeople need to have a positive attitude. A fear that obtaining commitment will be difficult may be impossible to hide. Inexperienced salespeople naturally will be concerned about their ability to obtain commitment; most of us have an innate fear of asking someone else to do anything. Some salespeople even fail to ask for the sale because if they never ask, they will never hear no. As a result, they always have more prospects but fewer customers than everyone else. But all salespeople know they need to focus on obtaining commitment to keep their jobs.

Some salespeople display unwarranted excitement when they see that prospects are ready to commit. Research suggests that nonverbals are very important cues and can signal trustworthiness or a lack thereof to buyers. A salesperson who appears excited or overly eager may display nonverbal cues that suggest dishonesty or a lack of empathy.[12] At this point wary buyers may change their minds and refuse to commit.

One of the main reasons for salespeople's improper attitudes toward obtaining commitment is the historical importance placed on closing the sale. Closing has often been viewed as a win–lose situation (if I get the order, I win; if I don't get the order, I lose). Until salespeople see obtaining commitment as a positive occurrence for the buyer, these attitudes will persist.

Poor Presentation

Prospects or customers who do not understand the presentation or see the benefits of the purchase cannot be expected to buy. The salesperson must use trial closes (see Chapter 8) and continually take the pulse of the interview.

A boring presentation can be one reason for failure to obtain commitment.

A poor presentation can also be caused by haste. The salesperson who tries to deliver a 60-minute presentation in 20 minutes may skim over or omit important sales points. Forgoing the presentation may be better than delivering it hastily. Further, a sales presentation given at the wrong time or under unfavorable conditions is likely to be ineffective.

Another reason for not obtaining commitment is lack of product knowledge. In fact, lack of product knowledge is often cited as an important barrier to obtaining commitment.[13] If the salesperson does not know what the product does, you can be certain the buyer will not be able to figure it out either.

Poor Habits and Skills

Obtaining commitment requires proper habits and some measure of skill. The habit of talking too much rather than listening often causes otherwise good presentations to fail. Knowing when to quit talking is just as important as knowing what to say. Some salespeople become so fascinated by the sound of their own voices that they talk themselves out of sales they have already made. A presentation that turns into a monologue is not likely to retain the buyer's interest.

DISCOVERING THE CAUSE

The real reasons for not obtaining commitment must be uncovered. Only then can salespeople proceed intelligently to eliminate the barriers. Some firms have developed sophisticated systems to follow up on lost sales. Sales software, such as NetSuite or salesforce.com, can also identify points in the selling process where a salesperson may be having difficulty. If the sales cycle involves a demonstration, for example, and the salesperson turns fewer leads into demonstrations, the fault may lie in the needs identification skills of that salesperson.

Dave Alexander, account executive for SGA, Inc., says his company does a postsale analysis whether it wins or loses the sale. This discipline causes the sales team to focus on the factors that really lead to success.[14] Dave Stein, author of *How Winners Sell,* says that all too often salespeople will lay the blame for failure on price or the product but will take personal credit for any successes.[15] Both Stein and Alexander agree, however, that an effective win/loss system forces the salesperson to examine the real causes and, if the sale was not won, consider personal strategies for improvement.

SUGGESTIONS FOR DEALING WITH REJECTION

Maintain the Proper Perspective

Probably the inexperienced salesperson's most important lesson is that when a buyer says no, the sales process has not necessarily ended. A no may mean

"Not now," "I need more information," "Don't hurry me," or "I don't understand." An answer of no should be a challenge to seek the reason behind the buyer's negative response.

In many fields of selling, most prospects do not buy. The ratio of orders achieved to sales presentations may be 1 to 3, 1 to 5, 1 to 10, or even 1 to 20. Salespeople may tend to eliminate nonbuyers from the prospect list after one unsuccessful call. This practice may be sound in some cases; however, many sales result on the second, third, fourth, or fifth call. Tim Pavlovich, sales executive for Dell, had one client require over 50 sales calls before closing. Of course, the sale was worth over $100 million annually, so it was pretty complicated. When an earlier visit has not resulted in commitment, careful preparation for succeeding calls becomes more crucial.

Another perspective is that when a buyer says no it is because the buyer is not yet fully informed; otherwise the buyer would have said yes. Consequently, if the buyer has given the salesperson the opportunity to make a presentation, the buyer recognizes that a need exists or is going to exist. What has not happened yet is that match between the offering and the need. At the same time, however, no does not mean "Sell me again right now." As we discussed earlier, "No" may mean "Sell me again later."

The salesperson should have a clear objective for each sales call. When commitment cannot be obtained to meet that objective, the salesperson will often attempt to obtain commitment for a reduced request (a secondary or minimum objective). For example, the salesperson may attempt to gain a trial order instead of an actual order, although, as we discussed earlier, this opportunity should be offered as a last resort.

Recommend Other Sources

A sales representative who uses the consultative selling philosophy (as described in Chapter 5) may recommend a competitor's product to solve the prospect's needs. When recommending other sources, the sales rep should explain why his or her product does not meet the prospect's needs and then provide the name of the competitive product. The goodwill generated by such a gesture should lead to future opportunities when the timing and needs are right.

After recommending other sources, the salesperson usually should ask the prospect for names of people who might be able to buy the seller's product. Also, the salesperson should emphasize the desire to maintain contact with the prospect in the event the seller's firm develops a competitive offering.

Good Manners Are Important

If obtaining commitment fails for any reason, the salesperson should react goodnaturedly. Salespeople have to learn to accept no if they expect to call on prospects again. Even if salespeople do not obtain commitment, they should thank prospects for their time. Arguing or showing disappointment gains nothing. The salesperson may plan to keep in contact with these prospects through e-mail, an occasional phone call, a follow-up letter, or product literature mailings. One salesperson likes to make the following statement at the conclusion of any meeting that does not result in commitment: "I'll never annoy you, but if you don't mind, I'm going to keep in touch."

Many salespeople consider leaving something behind that will let the prospect contact the salesperson in the future. Some firms use promotional products, such as a pen with the company's name and phone number, as a gift after each call to remind the prospect of the salesperson's company. Others may simply use brochures and business cards.

BRINGING THE INTERVIEW TO A CLOSE

Few buyers are interested in a prolonged visit after they commit. Obviously the departure cannot be abrupt; the salesperson should complete the interview smoothly. But goodwill is never built by wasting the buyer's time after the business is concluded.

Remember that most sales take several calls to complete. If an order wasn't signed (and often getting an order isn't even the objective of the call; see Chapter 7) and the prospect wishes to continue considering the proposal, the salesperson should leave with a clear action plan for all parties. An example of the kind of dialogue the salesperson might pursue follows:

> SALESPERSON: When will you have had a chance to look over this proposal?
>
> BUYER: By the end of next week, probably.
>
> SALESPERSON: Great, I'll call on you in about 10 days, OK?
>
> BUYER: Sure, set up something with my secretary.
>
> SALESPERSON: Is there anything else I need to do for you before that next meeting?

The salesperson should always make sure the next step is clear for both parties. Therefore, review what you will do next, what the customer will do next, and when you will meet again.

Follow up promptly with a thank-you and reminder note after the sales call. If you are following up after a sales call in which you gained commitment for the next sales call, an e-mail message is not only sufficient but the best idea. For example, Bruce Culbert of the Pedowitz Group follows up each sales call with an e-mail that summarizes what happened, what each person promised to do (including what the buyer promised), and when the next meeting is. The sales cycle may take months, and such documentation is necessary to avoid losing momentum. Even when he is told no, his follow up e-mail includes a simple thank-you for the opportunity, along with a time frame for a follow-up. When he finally gets the sale, he'll follow up with a handwritten note and, in some cases, a "launch" dinner with the client to celebrate the new relationship.

Shirley Hunter, an account executive with Teradata, will follow up a sale with a handwritten thank-you note. She may also personally present a thank-you gift (her product costs half a million dollars, so a sale is worth celebrating). Her choice of a gift, though, will reflect the situation—a box of Lifesavers for the executive who got behind the purchase, a box of crayons for an architect, or something equally creative.

SELLING YOURSELF

When Carter Simon felt his fraternity needed a stronger recruiting program to attract new members, he had to gain the support of the senior leadership of the chapter. In addition, he had to convince the older members to take on a more active role with the recruiting process. "Getting someone to say they will do something is a lot easier than actually getting them to do it," says Simon.

Corey Bergstrom and others at Cabela's faced a similar challenge when they realized that the company needed a new direction in how it sold through technology. Corey presented his plan to the executive team, who then asked him to present it to the board of directors. Corey, who is an IT guy and not a salesperson, successfully proved his business case. A year later, the board is very happy with the results, as Corey's team has grown sales significantly. The stock market also likes the results, with stock prices up over 35 percent.

When selling internally, in your fraternity now or in your company later, gaining real commitment can mean the difference between a program's success or failure. Just because the choice seems obvious to you—"It's the best decision for our customer and our company!"—doesn't mean that others in the company see it the same way. Nor can someone always order an employee to do something and expect the task to be done well. Commitment skills when selling yourself are critical to a successful career, whether you go into sales or something else altogether.

As with external customers, though, understanding and selling to others' needs has to come first. If you are interested only in your own needs, no closing skills will carry you.

What's also important to remember is that when selling internally, you have to live with the consequences of the selling process much more intimately than when selling to a customer. Using pushy or cheesy techniques contributes to a reputation that makes future decisions or actions more difficult to secure.

Earlier we noted Shirley Hunter's perspective on thanking a customer for a sale. She also believes, though, that internal celebrations are necessary to say thank you to those who contributed either to a sale or to a successful customer implementation. Cultivating for future calls or decisions is also important. You may not win on this decision, but there will be other opportunities to use your closing skills when selling yourself.

SUMMARY

Commitment cannot be obtained by some magical or miraculous technique if the salesperson has failed to prepare the prospect to make this decision throughout the presentation. Salespeople should always attempt to gain commitment in a way that is consistent with the objectives of the meeting. Obtaining commitment begins with the salesperson's contact with the prospect. It can succeed only when all facets of the selling process fall into their proper place. All sellers need to keep in mind this old saying: "People don't buy products or services; they buy solutions to their problems!"

The process of obtaining commitment is the logical progression of any sales call. Commitment is important for the customer, the seller's firm, and the seller. Commitment should result in a win–win situation for all parties concerned.

Pricing is an important element of any sale and is usually presented at the time of closing. Quantity discounts, payment terms, and shipping terms can affect the final price charged to the buyer as well as influence the decision.

There is no one "right" time to obtain commitment. Salespeople should watch their prospects closely and recognize when to obtain commitment. Successful salespeople carefully monitor customer comments, their buyers' nonverbal cues and actions, and their responses to probes. Comments can be in the form of questions, requirements, benefits, and responses to trial closes.

To successfully obtain commitment, the salesperson needs to maintain a positive attitude, allow the customer to set the pace, be assertive rather than aggressive, and sell the right item in the right amounts. Engaging in these practices will result in a strong long-term relationship between buyer and seller.

No one method of obtaining commitment works best for all buyers. The direct request method is the simplest to use; however, the prospect often needs help in evaluating the proposal. In those instances other methods may be more appropriate, such as the alternative choice, the benefit summary, the balance sheet method, or the probing method. No method of obtaining commitment will work if a buyer does not trust the salesperson.

If commitment is obtained, the salesperson should immediately assure the buyer that the choice was judicious. The salesperson should show genuine appreciation as well as cultivate the relationship for future calls.

If commitment is not obtained, the salesperson should analyze the reasons. Difficulties in obtaining commitment can be directly traced to wrong attitudes, a poor presentation, and/or poor habits and skills. Even if no commitment is obtained, the salesperson should thank the prospect for his or her time.

KEY TERMS

aggressive   293
assertive   294
balance sheet method   296
benefit summary method   295
buyer's remorse   300
buying signals   290
cash discount   287
closing   284
closing cues   290

cumulative discount   287
direct request method   295
follow-up   301
postpurchase dissonance   300
probing method   297
requirements   291
submissive   294
trial close   292
trial order   294

ETHICS PROBLEMS

1. One buyer stated, "All closing methods are devious and self-serving! How can a salesperson use a technique but still keep my needs totally in mind?" Comment. Integrate into your discussion the concepts of persuasion versus manipulation.
2. A customer asked the salesperson, "How do you intend to solve my problem?" The salesperson told the customer his approach and provided a time line on when each step would be completed. When asked for the sale, the customer said, "Oh, I'll just do it myself." Now that she had the process spelled out for her, she felt that she no longer needed the salesperson. Was her behavior appropriate? Why or why not? And, whether appropriate or not, how can salespeople avoid such situations?

QUESTIONS AND PROBLEMS

1. Review Exhibit 11.3 and discuss which social style would be best suited to which method of closing. Note that some of the methods are appropriate for multiple styles if worded differently. Give an example of how you would word one differently to address two different styles.
2. "The ABCs of closing are 'Always be closing.'" Another version is "Close early—close often." What is your reaction to these time-honored statements?
3. Harold Bumpurs, a professional purchasing agent, says he has never noticed any tricky closes. His perception is due not to the smooth closing skills of the salespeople who call on him but to the total skill sets they have developed. Prioritize a list of selling skills, from most important to least. How much time should be spent improving commitment-gaining skills as opposed to developing other skills? Why?
4. You've made six sales calls over a month with one prospect, qualifying needs with three separate influencers, and you finally get through to the decision maker. You make your presentation and it seems to go well. All of the

influencers are there; they are all nodding yes, so as you wrap up, you ask when they'd like to get started. The decision maker replies, "I'd like to think this over." Two of the influencers look surprised while the third looks confused. "OK," you reply, "is next Tuesday OK to check back?" How could you improve on your answer? Be specific; what exactly would you say?

5. One sales manager who worked for a refrigeration equipment company taught his salespeople the following close: Ask questions that allow you to fill out the contract. Assume the sale is made and hand the contract to the buyer, along with a pen. If the buyer doesn't immediately take the pen, drop it and make the buyer pick it up. Once the buyer has the pen in hand, he or she is more likely to use it to sign the contract, so just wait silently until the buyer does.

    a. Would you label this seller as assertive or aggressive?

    b. Is this a trick (manipulative) or merely dramatization (persuasive)?

    c. How would you respond to this behavior if you were the buyer?

6. You've identified a process by which your company could recycle packaging material, saving the company about 10 percent of the packaging costs. But when you talk this over with the person in charge of shipping, he says, "You're just a sales rep! Go sell something and let me do my job!" What do you think is driving his reaction? How would you respond? What would you do next?

7. What makes a Mercedes-Benz worth more than a Volkswagen? How would you convince someone that it is worth more if she or he knew nothing about the various brands of cars? How would the buyer's lack of knowledge influence how you try to gain commitment?

8. Todd Pollock, while in ticket sales for the San Francisco 49ers, says he heard "no" at least 10 times for every "yes," sometimes 20 times. How do you deal with rejection? What strategies would you try if you were in Todd's situation?

9. What would you say to a friend to gain his or her commitment to go on a spring break trip? Describe exactly what you would say to your friend using each of the following methods (make any assumptions necessary):

    a. Alternative choice.

    b. Direct request.

    c. Benefit summary.

    d. Balance sheet.

    e. Probing.

10. A customer is willing to order 100 cases listed at $20 per case to get a 15 percent quantity discount. Terms are 2/10, n/30. The customer pays five days after receiving the invoice. How much did the customer pay?

CASE PROBLEMS

case **11.1**

Closing Euro_LED

Using radio frequency identification (RFID) technology, Matya manufactures inventory management and tracking systems. Used in any environment where tracking inventory location is important, these devices track movement of products within a warehouse, within a manufacturing facility, and even while on the truck or train. Patsy Moorman was calling on Dave Daugherty, senior purchasing director for Euro-LED, a company that makes low-energy lighting for commercial applications. Dave has global responsibility for purchasing standardization, and developing a common inventory management system across all of Euro-LED's 24 locations in eight countries is a task he has to complete this year. Patsy's primary call objective was to have Dave agree to set up an appointment in the next several weeks for Patsy to present to the supply chain committee that will review proposals and narrow the choices down to three systems.

PATSY: Our scanning systems can support the digital standards of both the United States and Europe, which means that, with some engineering changes in your computer network, your locations can use the same scanners.

DAVE: Patsy, I've really been thinking that the RFID scanners made by Alcatel are industry standard, and I'm concerned about our China plant. What has Matya done differently with these scanners?

PATSY: Quality is something we take very seriously at Matya, but having the best-built old product isn't enough, is it? So we've also built probably the finest engineering staff over the past five years that you'll find anywhere. The result is a product line that was just awarded the Dubai Engineering Innovation World Cup award only last month.

DAVE: That's impressive, and you're right. A well-built product using yesterday's technology is of no benefit to us. But how important is bicontinental use at the scanning level? It's not like we ship from our European plants to the States; seems to me we could use local-made products and just merge data later when we need to.

PATSY: Yes, you can, but that's really inconsistent with the overall strategy of minimizing the number of vendors and having global suppliers. How do you serve Latin America or Africa?

DAVE: Well, we don't have a lot of business in Africa, yet but it's growing. And in Latin America, we supply both from China and the United States, so I see your point.

PATSY: Then you may have seen a report issued by DataMark that indicates some users have had data problems that were difficult to identify until something goes horribly wrong. Just merging data from disparate systems isn't always the best option.

DAVE: I've seen that data from DataMark as well as an article in the last issue of *Supply Chain Management*. But we've had no plans for a global RFID process.

PATSY: Why is that?

DAVE: We don't know that it is necessary—we don't think we've got that many locations where scanning is a necessity.

PATSY: What would be considered a significant percentage—of your total sites, I mean?

DAVE: I would guess 50 percent would be acceptable. What are others experiencing?

PATSY: We've got several, maybe four, that have standardized with us globally and another group of about two dozen that use us in the United States or Europe. How does that sound?

DAVE: Intriguing, though we're not the same as others.

PATSY: I know. That's why I'd like to set up a meeting with your supply chain team in the near future. But we'll probably also need someone there from logistics, right?

DAVE: Yes, I suppose we would.

PATSY: Will I have your endorsement at the meeting?

DAVE: We'll have to wait and see. I'll need some documentation on the figures you've given me, and I'd like that before we set up the meeting.

Questions

1. What form of closing did Patsy use to gain Dave's commitment to the idea? Was that appropriate? Why or why not?

2. List how you would attempt to obtain commitment using three other methods of your choice. Write out exactly what you would say for each method (and be sure to identify the method).

3. Although you have been shown only a portion of the conversation, evaluate Patsy's performance in terms of the following:
   a. Selling benefits, not features
   b. Using trial closes
   c. Using communication aids to strengthen the presentation
   d. Responding to objections
   e. Attempting to gain commitment at the proper time

case 11.2

Blue Onion

Blue Onion is a systems integrator, meaning that it helps companies integrate new software into the old systems and the customer's processes. So when a customer buys SAP software, for example, Blue Onion customizes the software to fit the customer's work processes and to work with the customer's old software.

Sean Thornton just joined the company as an account executive. After five years of systems analysis and sales support for Oracle, a major software provider, he wanted to earn a salesperson's living, so he made the switch. As part of his training he spent some time working with several experienced salespeople. One such salesperson was Mary Kate Danaher.

She filled him in on the client they were about to see as they entered a large office building. "They are buying a system called BOSS," she said. "This is going to be a massive change for them, and it looks like they'll implement in three phases over a two-year period."

"In other words, a big sale for us, right?" replied Sean.

"Yup. And I'm not going to let them get away. They are considering doing the integration on their own, using temporary employees, and that never works well. So I've already filled out a contract and today, when we meet with the CEO, we'll get it signed." The determination in her voice matched the purpose in her step as she strode to the bank of elevators in the center of the lobby.

Once in the CEO's office, sitting around a small conference table with the head of MIS and the CFO, Mary Kate reviewed the key points of the agreement, saying, "Shirley, you know that this is a critical implementation and you can't afford any mistakes. That's why you should rely on Blue Onion," and handed the contract to the CEO.

The head of MIS squirmed uncomfortably. Shirley looked at him, and he said, "Shirley, I really think we can do this ourselves and save a lot of money."

"With all due respect, Jack, my experience would say that you can't. Temporaries just don't care as much as your own people do, nor as much as our people do," said Mary Kate, with conviction.

Silence draped over the table. Sean could hear an antique clock ticking away on the shelf behind Shirley's desk. After what seemed like an hour but was probably only a few seconds, Shirley looked at the CFO, who nodded almost imperceptibly. She took out her pen, signed the contract, and handed it back to Mary Kate.

"Thank you, Shirley. I will personally see this project through to completion, on time and on budget, and at the end, you'll get all you hoped for and more," said Mary Kate.

The MIS director stood, looking at the CEO and then the CFO, then back to the CEO. Then he stuck out his hand, saying, "Congratulations, Mary Kate and good luck." Then he turned, and left the room.

An awkward pause was broken first by Mary Kate. "Shirley, I will set up a meeting with our engineering manager and Jack for next week so that we can lay out the plan for integration. I'm sure that Jack will enjoy meeting her." Small talk ensued, and within five minutes, Mary Kate and Sean were back in the lobby.

"Well, rookie, we got it!" exclaimed Mary Kate. They exchanged high fives and headed to the parking lot.

Questions

1. Assess Mary Kate's style. Is her style something Sean should emulate?
2. Blue Onion's implementation team will need to work very closely with Jack and his people, and it doesn't appear that Jack wants to be helpful. What could Mary Kate have done to avoid this situation? Assume this meeting was called by Shirley. How could Mary Kate have handled it differently?

ROLE PLAY CASE

Once again you will give your presentation to the same buyer (BancVue, GelTech, and High Point Solutions) that you did after Chapters 9 and 10 (if you did not do role plays after those chapters, review that material now). This time you will complete your presentation, first summarizing the needs and going all the way to asking for the sale. You will have an opportunity to work on presentation, objection handling, and closing skills.

If two people are involved in the sale (a seller and a buyer) while a third observes, the observer should do the following:

1. Identify any objection-handling methods used.

2. Determine whether the seller is focused on benefits or only features.

3. Note when trial closes are used.

4. Identify the closing method used.

The professor will pass out new buyer sheets.

ADDITIONAL REFERENCES

Agnihotri Raj, Adam Rapp, and Kevin Trainor. "Understanding the Role of Information Communication in the Buyer-Seller Exchange Process: Antecedents and Outcomes." *Journal of Business and Industrial Marketing* 24, no. 7 (2009), pp. 474–89.

Baumgarth, Carsten, and Lars Binckebanck. "Sales Force Impact on B-to-B Brand Equity: Conceptual Framework and Empirical Test." *Journal of Product and Brand Management* 20, no. 6 (2011), pp. 487–98.

Bradford, Kevin D., J. Michael Crant, and Joan M. Phillips. "How Suppliers Affect Trust with Their Customers: The Role of Salesperson Job Satisfaction and Perceived Customer Importance." *Journal of Marketing Theory and Practice* 17, no. 4 (Fall 2009), pp. 383–94.

Fu, Frank, Willy Bolander, and Eli Jones. "Managing the Drivers of Organizational Commitment and Salesperson Effort: An Application of Meyer and Allen's Three-Component Model." *Journal of Marketing Theory and Practice* 17, no. 4 (Fall 2009), pp. 335–50.

Gough, Orla, and Mohamed Nurullah. "Understanding What Drives the Purchase Decision in Pension and Investment Products." *Journal of Financial Services Marketing* 14, no. 2 (September 2009), pp. 152–72.

Pettijohn, Charles E., and Linda Pettijohn. "An Exploratory Analysis of Student Exposure to Personal Selling: An MBA Perspective." *Academy of Educational Leadership Journal* 14, special issue (2010), pp. 35–46.

Pinar, Musa, J. Russell Hardin, and Zeliha Eser. "Applicant Perceptions of the Gender Effect on the Selling Process and on Targeting Customers: Does Gender Matter?" *Academy of Marketing Studies Journal* 15, no. 1 (2011), pp. 107–24.

Rutherford, Brian N., James S. Boles, Hiram C. Barksdale Jr., and Julie T. Johnson. "Buyer's Relational Desire and Number of Suppliers Used: The Relationship between Perceived Commitment and Continuance." *Journal of Marketing Theory and Practice* 16, no. 3 (Summer 2008), pp. 247–57.

Singh, Ramendra, and Abraham Koshy. "Determinants of B2B Salespersons' Performance and Effectiveness. *Journal of Business and Industrial Marketing* 25, no. 7 (2010), pp. 535–46.

Turner, Roger, Christophe Lasserre, and Pascal Beauchet. "Marketing Metrics: Innovation in Field Force Bonuses: Enhancing Motivation through a Structured Process-Based Approach." *Journal of Medical Marketing* 7, no. 2 (2007), pp. 126–35.

Weber, John A. "Business Ethics Training: Insights from Learning Theory." *Journal of Business Ethics* 70, no. 1 (2007), pp. 61–85.

Zallocco, Ronald, Ellen Bolman Pullins, and Michael L. Mallin. "A Re-Examination of B2B Sales Performance. *Journal of Business and Industrial Marketing* 24, no. 8 (2009), pp. 598–614.

chapter

12

FORMAL NEGOTIATING

SOME QUESTIONS ANSWERED IN THIS CHAPTER ARE

- What is negotiation selling? How does it differ from nonnegotiation selling?

- What items can be negotiated in selling?

- What type of planning needs to occur prior to a negotiation meeting? How should a seller set objectives?

- How can the negotiation session be effectively opened? What role does friendly conversation play?

- Which negotiation strategies and tactics do buyers use? How should negotiators respond?

- What are the salesperson's guidelines for offering and requesting concessions?

PROFILE

PROFILE My name is Evans Adonis. I graduated from Northern Illinois University (NIU) with a bachelor of science in marketing and a certificate in professional sales while on a full football scholarship. I received my master's in sports management while working for the NIU Intercollegiate Athletics Department as a marketing/sales assistant. During my time at NIU, I learned professional sales under the tutelage of Dr. Rick Ridnour, my lead business professor. Currently, I am a sales executive for the Dallas Cowboys Football Club. My focus is selling suites and premium inventory for Cowboys games and third-party events. This is accomplished by making calls, conducting personal meetings, and negotiating with C-level executives to establish a favorable deal.

Almost every outbound sales process has a negotiation phase where the seller probes to uncover the prospects' needs. The key to being a successful negotiator is asking the right questions to discover how your product adds value to their company. Partnering with the Dallas Cowboys has numerous benefits for XYZ Company, such as the opportunity to entertain clients in the luxurious $1.3 billion venue. This is one of the many tactics used to create a value proposition and help the prospect think differently about how they are currently growing their business. That's the difference between mediocre and expert negotiators.

Bad negotiators are easily appeased, dishonest, and closed-minded and tend to fear conflict, whereas great negotiators are patient, probers, and challengers. Challengers are not afraid to ask uncomfortable questions at the negotiation table (e.g., "On a scale of 1 to 10, how close are we to getting a deal done, with 5 not being an option?"). This type of unsettling question allows the seller to determine the buyer's position and handle any objections before moving forward. Keep in mind that successful salespeople are not always successful negotiators. The power to influence one's perception versus the ability to reconfigure one's thinking process is completely different.

Preparation and planning are the two most important parts of the negotiation process. Knowing information about your prospect's company *and* the individuals at the table indicate you have done your research. In the sports industry, learning about what school the CEO attended or the CFO's favorite sport is vital to building rapport and leveraging the sale. Some facts are online, but it is best to ask the executive assistants after befriending them and gaining their trust. In addition, planning includes creating an agenda, having the correct documents on hand, and having resolutions to their objections.

Lastly, once both parties agree to a deal, *always* ask one more confirming question, such as, "Can we receive the signed paperwork by 5:00 p.m. today?" Sounds simple, right? However, most sales reps are complacent after a verbal agreement and forget to hold the buyer accountable for finishing the deal. The agreement is not complete until the money exchanges hands and all necessary paperwork is submitted. From experience, time kills sales! Do not allow the buyer to leave the meeting without an agreement to purchase, a "no," or a follow-up meeting to further discuss details. The buyer will respect your assertiveness and negotiation skills, and a relationship will be built regardless of the outcome.

Visit our Web site at:
www.dallascowboys.com

We have all engaged in negotiations of some type. Most of these were informal (such as with your parents about attending a concert) and dealt with relatively minor issues, although they may have been intensely important to you at the time. This chapter discusses formal negotiations that occur between buyers and salespeople. The skills you will learn can also be used in your day-to-day negotiations with friends, parents, and people in authority positions.

THE NATURE OF NEGOTIATION

The bargaining process through which buyers and sellers resolve areas of conflict and arrive at agreements is called **negotiation.** Areas of conflict may include minor issues (like who should attend future meetings) as well as major ones (such as cost per unit or exclusive purchase agreements). The ultimate goal of both parties should be to reduce or resolve the conflict.

Two radically different philosophies can guide negotiations. In **win–lose negotiating** the negotiator attempts to win all the important concessions and thus triumph over the opponent. This process resembles almost every competitive sport you have ever watched. In boxing, for example, one person is the winner, and the other is, by definition, the loser.

In the second negotiating philosophy, **win–win negotiating,** the negotiator attempts to secure an agreement that satisfies both parties. You have probably experienced social situations similar to this. For example, if you want to attend a football game and your friend wants to attend a party, you may negotiate a mutual agreement that you both attend the first half of the game and still make it to the party. If this arrangement satisfies both you and your friend, you have engaged in win–win negotiating.

The discussion in this chapter assumes that your goal as a salesperson is to engage in win–win negotiating. In fact, this entire book has emphasized developing relationships, which is a win–win perspective. Partners attempt to find solutions that benefit both parties because each party is concerned about the other party's welfare.

However, the buyer may be using a win–lose strategy, whereby the buyer hopes to win all major concessions and have the seller be the loser. To help you spot and prepare for such situations, we discuss many of these tactics as well.

NEGOTIATION VERSUS NONNEGOTIATION SELLING

How does negotiation differ from the sales presentations we have discussed up to this point? This textbook has already covered many aspects of negotiating an agreement between buyer and seller. For example, in Chapter 10 we discussed the negotiations that occur as the seller is helping the buyer deal with objections. And in Chapter 11 we talked about obtaining commitment, which often requires negotiating on some key points. Importantly, however, we assumed that many, if not most, factors during a regular sales call are constrained, and not open to change or negotiation. For example, the price of Allsteel Energy brand ergonomic seating has been set at $499. The Allsteel salesperson will not lower that price unless, of course, the buyer agrees to purchase large quantities. Even then the buyer will receive just a standard quantity discount as outlined in the seller's price manual. In essence, the salesperson's price book and procedure manual form an inflexible set of rules. If the buyer objects, an attempt to resolve the conflict will occur by using techniques discussed in Chapter 10 (such as the compensation method or the revisit method).

Formal negotiations usually involve multiple buyers and multiple sellers.

In contrast, if the Allsteel seller enters formal negotiations with the same buyer, the price and delivery schedules will be subject to modification. The buyer neither expects nor wants the seller to come to the negotiation meeting with any standard price book. Instead the buyer expects most policies, procedures, and prices to be truly negotiable.

Negotiations also differ from regular sales calls in that they generally involve more intensive planning and a larger number of people from the selling firm. Pre-negotiation planning may go on for six months or more before the actual meeting takes place. Planning participants usually represent a wide spectrum of functional areas of the firm, such as production, marketing, sales, human resources, accounting, purchasing, and executive officers.

Finally, formal negotiations generally take place only for very large or important prospective buyers. For example, Hormel might negotiate with some of the largest food chains, such as Walmart Foods and Cub Foods, but would not engage in a large, formal negotiation session with small local or mom-and-pop grocery stores. Negotiating is an expensive endeavor because it uses so much of so many important people's time. The firm wants to invest the time and costs involved in negotiating only if the long-term nature of the relationship and the importance of the customer justify the expense.

WHAT CAN BE NEGOTIATED?

If the customer is large or important enough, almost anything can be negotiated. Salespeople who have not been involved in negotiations before often find it hard to grasp the fact that so many areas are subject to discussion and change. Exhibit 12.1 lists some items that are often negotiated between buyers and sellers. But in reality, no single negotiation session covers all the areas listed. Each side comes to the bargaining table with a list of prioritized issues; only important points for which disagreement exists are discussed.

ARE YOU A GOOD NEGOTIATOR?

All of us are negotiators; some of us are better than others. We have negotiated with parents, friends, professors, and, yes, sometimes even with opponents. However, the fact that you have engaged in many negotiations in your lifetime does not mean you are good at negotiating.

The traits necessary to successfully negotiate vary somewhat, depending on the situation and the parties involved. Some characteristics, however, are almost universal. For example, a good negotiator must have patience and endurance; after two hours of discussing the same issue, the negotiator needs the stamina and willingness to continue until an agreement is reached. Also, a willingness to take risks and the ability to tolerate ambiguity become especially critical in business negotiations because it is necessary to both accept and offer concessions during the meeting without complete information.

Successful salespeople do not always make great negotiators. In fact, negotiating may be the most difficult skill for any salesperson to develop. Many managers have to coach reps on their negotiating skills because many reps don't want to risk ruining a relationship they worked hard to build. The unconscious reaction of most salespeople in negotiations often ends up being the opposite of the correct thing to do. For example, what if, in preparation for the upcoming negotiation session,

Exhibit 12.1

Items That Are Often Negotiated between Buyers and Sellers

Inventory levels the buyer must maintain.

Inventory levels the seller must keep on hand to be able to restock the buyer quickly.

Details about the design of the product or service.

Web page development.

How the product will be manufactured.

Display allowances for resellers.

Advertising allowances and the amount of advertising the seller does.

Sales promotion within the channel of distribution.

Delivery terms and conditions.

Retail and wholesale pricing points for resellers.

Prices and pricing allowances for volume purchases.

Amount and location of shelf positioning.

Special packaging and design features.

Service levels after the sale.

Disposing of unsold or obsolete merchandise.

Credit terms.

How complaints will be resolved.

Order entry and ease of monitoring orders.

Type and frequency of communication between the parties.

Performance guarantees and bonds.

the customer asks for detailed specifications about your product? Most salespeople would gladly supply reams of technical data, full glossy pictures, an offer of plant tours, and the like. The problem with that approach lies in the possibility that the customer will pick several features that he or she does not need and then pressure for price concessions. (Look, I don't need that much memory capacity and don't want to pay for something I'm not going to use. So why don't you reduce your price? I shouldn't have to pay for something I'm not planning on ever using!) A salesperson who is a good negotiator would avoid this situation by supplying information to the customer only in exchange for the right to ask the customer more questions and thus gain more information.

People who fear conflict usually are poor negotiators. In fact, some negotiating strategies are actually designed to increase the level of conflict to bring all the issues to the table and reach an equitable settlement. Along the same lines, people who have a strong need to be liked by all people at all times tend to make very poor negotiators. Other undesirable traits include being closed-minded, unorganized, dishonest, and downright belligerent.

Of course cultural differences do exist. For example, Brazilian managers may believe competitiveness is more important in a negotiator than integrity. Chinese managers in Taiwan may emphasize the negotiator's rational skills less than his or her interpersonal skills.

As this discussion indicates, being a truly excellent negotiator requires a careful balance of traits and skills. Take a moment and complete the questionnaire in Exhibit 12.2 to rate your negotiating skills. Don't be discouraged by a low score. You cannot easily change personality traits, but the rest of this chapter suggests ways to improve your skills.

PLANNING FOR THE NEGOTIATION SESSION

Preparation and planning are the most important parts of negotiation, according to many expert sources.[1] And that planning includes preparing ourselves emotionally for the stress that will occur within a negotiation session. In Chapter 7 we discussed how to gather precall information and plan the sales call. All of that material is equally relevant when planning for an upcoming negotiation session—for example, learning everything possible about the buying team and the buyer's organization.

The meetings the salesperson will have with the buyer before the actual negotiation session facilitate this learning. The buyer may also be, or have been, a customer of the salesperson, with the upcoming negotiation session designed to review contracts or specify a new working relationship. Even in such scenarios, negotiators will want to carefully review the players and learn as many facts about the situation as possible.

LOCATION

Plan to hold the negotiation at a location free from distraction for both teams. A neutral site, one owned by neither party, is usually best; it removes both teams from interruptions by business associates, and no one has a psychological ("home court") advantage. Experienced negotiators find the middle of the workweek best for negotiations and prefer morning to afternoon or evening (because people are more focused on their jobs rather than after-hours and weekend activities).

Some negotiations are now occurring online. Research shows that using these new forms can affect the behavior of negotiators.[2] For example, reciprocity doesn't occur as frequently or in the same way. Those who are the first to offer a concession

Exhibit 12.2
Negotiation Skills
Self-Inventory

Place a check by each item that accurately reflects your personality and traits on an average, normal day.

_____ 1. Helpful	_____ 20. Receptive
_____ 2. Risk taker	_____ 21. Easily influenced
_____ 3. Inconsistent	_____ 22. Enthusiastic
_____ 4. Persistent	_____ 23. Planner
_____ 5. Factual	_____ 24. Stingy
_____ 6. Use high pressure	_____ 25. Listener
_____ 7. Self-confident	_____ 26. Controlled
_____ 8. Practical	_____ 27. Think under pressure
_____ 9. Manipulative	_____ 28. Passive
_____ 10. Analytical	_____ 29. Economical
_____ 11. Arrogant	_____ 30. Gullible
_____ 12. Impatient	_____ 31. Afraid of conflict
_____ 13. Seek new approaches	_____ 32. Endurance
_____ 14. Tactful	_____ 33. Tolerate ambiguity
_____ 15. Perfectionist	_____ 34. Have strong need to be liked
_____ 16. Stubborn	_____ 35. Organized
_____ 17. Flexible	_____ 36. Honest
_____ 18. Competitive	_____ 37. Belligerent
_____ 19. Gambler	

How to score the checklist:

All of the traits listed are positive except for the following negative traits: 3, 6, 9, 11, 12, 15, 16, 19, 21, 24, 28, 30, 31, 34, and 37. To arrive at a total score, give yourself one point for all positive traits and subtract one point for all negative traits. To interpret your total score: 19–22 = excellent; 15–18 = good; 11–14 = fair.

often don't find the other party giving a similar one in return, regardless of the power in the relationship. Furthermore, contrary to face-to-face negotiations, having more power in a relationship doesn't result in the other party giving larger concessions.

TIME ALLOTMENT

As you are probably aware, negotiations can take a tremendous amount of time. Some business negotiations take years. But how much time should be set aside for one negotiation session? The answer depends on the negotiation objectives and the extent to which both sides desire a win–win session. Studies have shown that high time pressure will produce nonagreements and poor outcomes when one or more sides take a win–lose perspective, but if both sides have a win–win perspective, high outcomes are achieved regardless of time pressure.

Sales reps need to set aside time to plan for a negotiation session.

NEGOTIATION OBJECTIVES

Power is a critical element when developing objectives. The selling team must ask, Do we need them more than they need us? What part of our service is most valuable to them? Can they get similar products elsewhere? Optimally both parties share balanced power, although this situation is rare in practice.

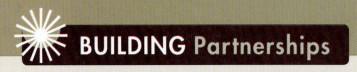

SOME THOUGHTS FROM A SEASONED NEGOTIATOR

Many facets of the planning process lay the groundwork for the negotiation phase of the sales process. I must fully understand the strengths and weaknesses of my own products as well as those of my competitors. I must understand the market and factors that could affect the success of the complete sale. I cannot promise a lead time that I know my factory cannot deliver on. I cannot promise a quality level that does not meet the expectations of the customer. We must also realize that if you are in this business for the long term, there may be times that it is best to walk away from the sale if there is a risk that could lead to an unhappy customer and jeopardize your relationship with the customer and future business. I have had to walk away several times, but my customer has always been very appreciative of my honesty and consideration for their business, and I have benefited from this by future business that has come to my company.

With this in mind, the formal negotiation is a time to clearly spell out to your customer all the pertinent details of the sale, including pricing, detailed specifications, warranty, lead time, and, most important, why they should give you the order. In many cases, you and your competition may be very similar in all the details noted above. This is where the relationship comes into play, and it is important to convey that you will be here after the sale for the service and follow up as needed. I have heard the statement many times that "people buy from people they like and trust." I have found this to be very true and go back to developing a relationship of trust with your customers. Many buyers often don't care as much about what factory made the product; they want someone to be there for them if an issue arises and take care of any problems that may occur.

Pricing will always be a factor, and you are blind to think that having a great relationship with a buyer will allow you to be a lot higher in price and still make the sale. If you know that your pricing is much higher, you must be prepared to clearly explain the features and benefits of your product compared to the low-cost alternative. The Internet has brought a whole new wrench in pricing and negotiating in the past five to eight years. I have found that if we can explain the value that I bring to the sale and the service level that will be included from my company, the "price war" with the Internet companies becomes less of an issue. When someone buys from an Internet company, often the burden of service and resolving issues if the product has problems falls on the ultimate customer. There is no local dealer salesperson to help them resolve the issue. For example, if a restaurant buys a commercial toaster from an Internet dealer and it breaks down, they must send the toaster to a service center of the Internet company across the country and likely be out of their toaster for three to four weeks. By purchasing from me on a local level, if they have an issue, we can get them a loaner unit within a day so that they can continue operating their business smoothly. I can offer a service that a low-cost Internet dealer cannot, and most restaurant owners want to have this assurance so that their business can operate without interruption.

In summary, the formal negotiation is the time to lay all your cards on the table, be honest with your customer, and rely on your preparation and overall salesmanship to close the sale.

Source: RDM; confidentiality as requested; used with permission.

In developing objectives for the session, keep in mind that the seller will almost certainly have to make concessions in the negotiation meeting. Thus, setting several objectives, or positions, is extremely important, as "Building Partnerships 12.1" describes.

The **target position** is what your company hopes to achieve at the negotiation session. Your team should also establish a **minimum position,** which is the absolute minimum level you will accept. Finally, an **opening position**—the initial proposal—should be developed.

For example, for a Fenwal salesperson negotiating the price for a blood collection and transfusion system at a blood bank, the target position could be $2.5 million, with a minimum position of $2 million and an opening position of $3 million. In negotiations over service levels by Gallovidian Fresh Foods in the United Kingdom with Morrisons grocery stores with regard to fresh vegetables, the seller's opening position might be weekly delivery, the target position delivery twice a week, and the minimum position (the most the seller is willing to do) delivery three times a week.

To allow for concessions, the opening position should reflect higher expectations than the target position. However, the buyer team may consider a very high opening position to be unrealistic and may simply walk away. You have probably seen this happen in negotiations between countries that are at war. To avoid this problem, negotiators must be ready to support that opening position with solid information. Suppose the opening position for a Colgate-Palmolive negotiating team is to offer the grocer a display allowance of $1,000 (with a target position of offering $1,500). The team must be ready to prove that $1,000 is reasonable. When developing objectives, negotiators need to sort out all issues that could arise in the meeting, prioritizing them by importance to the firm. Then the negotiators should develop contingency plans to get a good idea, even before the meeting begins, of their planned reactions and responses to the buyer's suggestions.

Talking over these issues beforehand helps the negotiation team avoid "giving away the store" during the heat of the negotiation session. It also allows the team to draw on the expertise of company experts who will not be present during the session.

The buyer team also develops positions for the meeting. Exhibit 12.3 presents a continuum that shows how the two sets of positions relate. With the positions illustrated, the parties can reach an agreement somewhere between the seller's minimum (S_M) and the buyer's maximum (B_M). However, if B_M falls to the left of S_M (has a lower maximum acceptable price), no agreement can be reached; attempts at negotiation will be futile. For example, if the buyer is not willing to pay more than $200 ($B_M$) and the seller will not accept less than $250 ($S_M$), agreement is impossible. In general, the seller desires to move as far to the right of S_M (as high a price) as possible, and the buyer desires to move as far to the left of B_M (as low a price) as possible.

Negotiators need to try to anticipate these positions and evaluate them carefully. The more information collected about what the buyer hopes to accomplish, the better the negotiators will be able to manage the meeting and arrive at a win–win decision.

Negotiators create a plan to achieve their objectives. However, the chance of failure always exists. Thus, planners need to consider strategy revisions if the

Exhibit 12.3
Comparing Buyer and Seller Price Positions

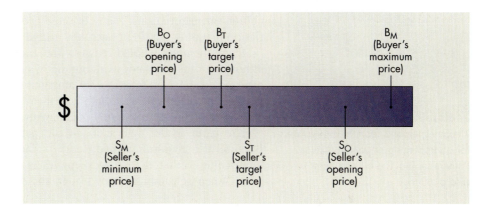

B_O (Buyer's opening price) B_T (Buyer's target price) B_M (Buyer's maximum price)

S_M (Seller's minimum price) S_T (Seller's target price) S_O (Seller's opening price)

original plan should fail. The development of alternative paths to the same goal is known as **adaptive planning.** For example, a firm may attempt to secure a premium shelf position by using any of the following strategies:

- In return for a 5 percent price discount
- In return for credit terms of 3/10, n/30
- In return for a 50–50 co-op ad campaign

The firm would attempt to secure the premium shelf position by using, for example, the first strategy; if that failed, it would move to the second strategy; and so forth. Fortunately, with laptops and spreadsheets such as Excel, negotiators can quickly calculate the profitability of various package deals for their firms.

Many firms will engage in a brainstorming session to try to develop strategies that will meet the firm's objectives. A **brainstorming session** is a meeting in which people are allowed to creatively explore various methods of achieving goals. Once again, cultural differences exist. For example, Chinese and Russian businesspeople habitually use extreme initial offers, whereas Swedish businesspeople usually open with a price close to their target position.

TEAM SELECTION AND MANAGEMENT

So far we have discussed negotiation as though it always involves a team of both buyers and sellers. Usually this is the case. However, negotiations do occur with only two people present: the buyer and the salesperson.

Teams offer both pros and cons. Because of team members' different backgrounds, the group as a whole tends to be more creative than one individual could be. Team members can help one another and reduce the chances of making a mistake. However, the more participants, the more time generally required to reach agreement. Also, team members may voice differing opinions among themselves, or one member may address a topic outside his or her area of expertise. Such things can make the seller's team appear unprepared or disorganized.

In general the seller's team should be the same size as the buyer's team. Otherwise the sellers may appear to be trying to exert more power or influence in the meeting. Whenever possible, strive for the fewest team members possible. Unnecessarily large teams can get bogged down in details; and the larger the team, the more difficult reaching a decision generally becomes.

Each team member should have a defined role in the session. For example, experts are often included to answer technical questions; executives are present as more authoritative speakers on behalf of the selling firm. Exhibit 12.4 lists the types of team members often chosen for negotiations. Many of these people take part in prenegotiation planning but do not actually attend the negotiation session.

Team members should possess the traits of good negotiators, although it often does not work out that way. For example, many technical experts have no tolerance for ambiguity and may fear conflict. As a result, the team leader needs to help them see clearly what their role is, as well as what they should not get involved in, during the session.

The team leader will manage the actual negotiation session. Because of their intimate knowledge of the buyers and their needs, salespeople, rather than the executives on the team, often fill this post. When selecting a team leader, the seller's management also

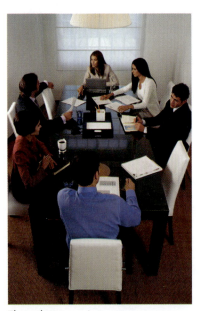

The salesperson's team must prepare for an upcoming negotiation session. Remember that the buyer's team is also planning.

Exhibit 12.4

People Who May
Serve on the Selling
Negotiation Team

Title	Possible Role
Salesperson	Coordinates all functions.
Field sales manager (district manager, regional manager, etc.)	Provides additional local and regional information. Secures necessary local funding and support for planning and presentations. Offers information about competitors.
National sales manager/ vice president of sales	Serves as a liaison with corporate headquarters. Secures necessary corporate funding and staff support for planning and presentation. Offers competitor information.
National account salesperson/national account sales manager	Provides expertise and support in dealing with issues for important customers. Offers information about competitors.
Marketing department senior executives, product managers, and staff	Provide suggestions for product/service applications. Supply market research information as well as information about packaging, new product development, upcoming promotional campaigns, etc. Offer information about competitors.
Chief executive officer/ president	Serves as an authority figure. Facilitates quicker decisions regarding changes in current policy and procedures. As a peer, can relate well with buyer's senior officers.
Manufacturing executives and staff	Provide information about current scheduled production as well as the possibility/cost of any modifications in the schedule.
Purchasing executives and staff	Provide information about raw materials inflows. Offer suggestions about possible quantity discounts from suppliers.
Accounting and finance executives and staff	Source of cost accounting information. Supply corporate target returns on investment, cost estimates for any needed changes in the firm under various buying scenarios, and information about order entry, billing, and credit systems.
Information technology executives and staff	Provide information about current information systems and anticipated changes needed under various buying scenarios. Help ensure that needed periodic reports for the buyers can be generated in a timely fashion.
Training executives and staff	Provide training for negotiation effectiveness and conduct practice role plays. Also provide information about and suggestions for anticipated necessary buyer training.
Outside consultants	Provide any kind of assistance necessary. Especially helpful if the firm has limited experience in negotiations or has not negotiated with this type of buyer before.

needs to consider the anticipated leader of the buyer team. It is unwise to choose a leader for the selling team who may be intimidated by the buyer's leader.

The team usually develops rules about who will answer what kinds of questions, who should be the first to respond to a concession offered by the buyers, who will offer concessions from the seller's standpoint, and so on. A set of nonverbal and verbal signals is also developed so team members can communicate with one another. For example, they may agree that when the salesperson takes out a breath mint, all team members are to stop talking and let the salesperson handle all issues; or when the executive places her red book inside her briefcase, the team should move toward its target position, and the salesperson should say, "OK, let's look at some alternatives."

To ensure that team members really understand their respective roles and that all rules and signals are clearly grasped, the team should practice. This process usually involves a series of videotaped role play situations. Many firms, such as Standard Register, involve their sales training department in this practice.

USING SKYPE IN PREPARATION FOR NEGOTIATION

Formal negotiating can be a very difficult process, especially for a salesperson who is particularly new to the organization or to the sales field. The saying "practice makes perfect" is a great way to think of negotiating. Salespeople who know how others in their organization would handle a negotiation situation are much better off than those going in blind. However, in large organizations, it may be hard to get in face-to-face with someone who may be able to help you in your techniques and skills in negotiating the products that you are selling.

Technology helps to take away the time limitations that may put a constraint on your ability to meet with someone who may be able to help you. Imagine you are a new salesperson preparing for a final sales negotiation with a large corporation and you know that your opening price is going to be negotiated. Your boss is 500 miles away in your company's corporate office, but you know

he has been dealing with this company for a long time. You talk with your boss and schedule a time to do a mock presentation and negotiation session via Skype. In this Skype conversation you give your planned presentation to your boss, and at the end he is acting as the buyer you are presenting to. With his knowledge of your potential customer, he will be able to bring up things that the buyer may try to negotiate.

Using Skype in this situation is more beneficial than talking over the phone or communicating via e-mail because the person you are talking with will be able to tell you what your nonverbal facial expressions are telling him or her (e.g., you are nervous, you are unsure if you are saying the right thing, and so on). Buyers will pick up on these weaknesses and do their best to take advantage of them while negotiating because, in the end, it is their job to get the best possible price for their company.

Trainers, using detailed information supplied by the team, realistically play the roles of the buying team members. Firms can also use technology to train, as "Sales Technology 12.1" describes.

The selling team will likely have many meetings before the negotiation session. These will be internal meetings, with members of the selling team, and also meetings with the buyers. Because not every selling team member can be at all meetings, sometimes it is hard for team members to keep abreast of developments.

INDIVIDUAL BEHAVIOR PATTERNS

The team leader needs to consider the personality style of each member of both teams to spot any problems and plan accordingly. Of course one method would be to sort the members into analyticals, amiables, expressives, and drivers based on the dimensions of assertiveness and responsiveness (see Chapter 5 for a full discussion). Some researchers have developed personality profiles specifically for negotiations. This section presents one of the most widely used sets of negotiation profiles.

After studying actual conflict situations, a number of researchers arrived at a set of basic conflict-handling modes based on the dimensions of assertiveness and cooperativeness.[3] Exhibit 12.5 presents these five modes: competing, accommodating, avoiding, compromising, and collaborating. Note that these five styles are different from the social styles (drivers, amiables, expressives, and analyticals) that we have been using throughout the book. Because all negotiations involve some

Exhibit 12.5
Conflict-Handling
Behavior Modes

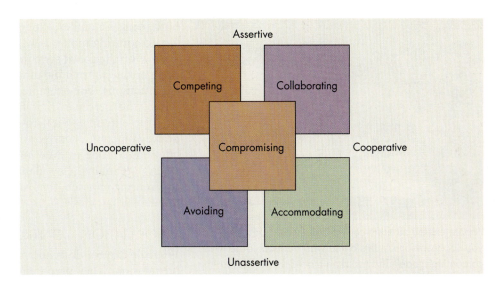

Source: Adapted from Kenneth Thomas, "Conflict and Conflict Management," in *The Handbook of Industrial and Organizational Psychology,* ed. Marvin Dunnette (Skokie, IL: Rand McNally, 1976).

degree of conflict, this typology is appropriate for use by salespeople preparing for a negotiation session.

People who resolve conflict in a **competing mode** are assertive and uncooperative. They tend to pursue their own goals and objectives completely at the expense of the other party. Often power oriented, they usually surround themselves with subordinates (often called "yes-men") who go along with their ideas. Team members who use the competing mode look for a win–lose agreement: They win, the other party loses.

Individuals in the **accommodating mode** are the exact opposite of competing people. Unassertive and highly cooperative, accommodators focus on the needs and desires of the other party and seek primarily to satisfy the concerns of the other party.[4] Although they do not necessarily wish to lose, they do want to make sure the other side gets all they want. Accommodators can be spotted by their excessive generosity; their constant, rapid yielding to another's point of view; and their obedience to someone else's order, even if it is obviously not something they desire to do.

Some people operate in the unassertive and uncooperative **avoiding mode.** These people do not attempt to fulfill their own needs or the needs of others. In essence, they simply refuse to address the conflict at all. They do not strive for a win–win agreement; in fact, they do not strive for any agreement.

The **compromising mode** applies to people "in the middle" in terms of cooperativeness and assertiveness. A compromiser attempts to find a quick, mutually acceptable solution that partially satisfies both parties. A compromiser gives up more than a competing person but less than an accommodating person. In many ways the compromiser attempts to arrive at a win–win solution. However, the agreement reached usually does not maximize the satisfaction of the parties. For example, a compromising person might quickly suggest, "Let's just split the difference." Although this sounds fair, a better solution—one that would please both parties more—may be reached with further discussion.

Finally, people in the **collaborating mode** are both assertive and cooperative. They seek to maximize the satisfaction of both parties and hence to reach a truly win–win solution. Collaborators have the motivation, skill, and determination to really dig into an issue or a problem and explore all possible solutions. The best situation, from a negotiation standpoint, would be to have on

People exhibit different conflict-handling modes. Can you spot someone in this photo who appears to be in the competing mode? The avoiding mode? The collaborating mode?

both teams a number of people who generally use a collaborating mode.

As with the social style matrix described earlier, one person can exhibit different modes in different situations. For example, a buying team negotiator who perceives that his or her position on an issue extremely vital to the long-term welfare of the company is correct may revert from a collaborating mode to a competing mode. Likewise, when potentially heavy damage could occur from confronting an issue, that same buyer might move to an avoiding mode.

INFORMATION CONTROL

What do buyers do while selling teams engage in preparation? They prepare too! Keep in mind that buyers have read as many books and attended as many seminars about negotiation as sellers have because this training is one of their best negotiating tools. Buyers try to learn as much as they can about the seller's team and plans, including the seller's opening, target, and minimum positions. Buyers also are interested in the seller's team membership and decision rules. As a result, the selling team leader needs to emphasize the need for security: Don't give everyone access to all information. In fact, many team members (such as technical support) do not need to have complete and exhaustive knowledge of all the facts surrounding the negotiation.

As an example, one *Fortune* 500 firm was negotiating a $15 million deal with one of its customers. The selling team's leader had to leave the room for a few minutes, and while he was gone, the plant manager for the selling firm came in. The plant manager, though intending to do no harm, bragged about how his company had already invested $2 million in a prototype and retooling just to prepare for the customer's expected commitment. Needless to say, when the seller's team leader returned to the room, the buyer said he had all the information he needed. Two days later the buyer was a very tough negotiator, armed with the knowledge that the seller had already committed to the project. It pays to control the flow of information!

THE NEGOTIATION MEETING

Before discussing what occurs in the negotiation meeting, we should note that some buyers will attempt to engage in a win–lose tactic of beginning to negotiate when the other party does not expect it.[5] This tactic has been called **ambush negotiating** or a **sneak attack.** It can occur during meetings prior to the negotiation meeting or even during installation of the new product. For example, during the first week of installation of a new telecommunications system, the buyer may state, "We're going to have to renegotiate the price of this system. Since we signed that contract, we have learned of a new system being introduced by one of your competitors." The seller should never negotiate in such a situation until prepared to deal with the issue completely.

At the negotiation meeting the buyer team and seller team physically come together and deliberate about topics important to both parties, with the goal of arriving at decisions. As mentioned earlier, this meeting usually has been preceded by one or more smaller buyer–seller meetings designed to uncover needs and explore options. Informal phone conversations probably were used to set some aspects of the agenda, learn about team members who will be present, and so on. Also, the negotiation itself may require a series of sessions to resolve all issues.

PRELIMINARIES

Engaging in friendly conversation to break the ice before getting down to business is usually a good idea. Use this time to learn and use the names of all members on the buyer team. This preliminary activity is especially important in many international negotiation meetings. For example, Japanese businesspeople usually want to spend time developing a personal relationship before beginning negotiations, and alcohol is usually a part of this. Not so in Saudi Arabia, where customs dictate strict abstinence.

Every effort should be made to ensure a comfortable environment for all parties. Arranging ahead of time for refreshments, proper climate control, appropriate size of room, adequate lighting, and correct layout of furniture will go far to establish an environment conducive to negotiating.

Most negotiations occur at a rectangular table. Teams usually sit on opposite sides, with the team leaders at the heads of the table. If possible, try to arrange for a round table or at least a seating arrangement that mixes members from each team together. This seating plan helps the parties feel that they are facing a common task and fosters a win–win atmosphere.

If the buyer team has a win–lose philosophy, expect all kinds of ploys to be used. For example, the furniture may be too large or too small or may be uncomfortable to sit in. The buyers may sit in front of large windows to force you to stare directly into sunlight. You may discover that the sellers' seats are all placed beneath heat ducts and the heat is set too high. You should not continue with the meeting until all unfavorable physical arrangements have been set right.

As far as possible the selling team should establish a win–win environment. This environment can be facilitated by avoiding any verbal or nonverbal threatening gestures, remaining calm and courteous, and adopting an attitude of investigation and experimentation. The leader might even comment,

> I can speak for my team in saying that our goal is to reach agreements today that we can all be proud of. We come to this meeting with open minds and look forward to exploring many avenues toward agreement. I am confident that we will both prosper and be more profitable as a result of this session.

thinking it through

What if you do everything in your power to establish a win–win relationship with the buyer team, but the buyers insist on viewing the negotiation session as a series of win–lose maneuvers? That is to say, your team consists mostly of collaborators who are trying to see that both sides are winners, whereas the buyers are mostly in the competing mode where they hope to win and hope you lose. Since they won't play by win–win "rules," should you?

An **agenda,** a listing of what will be discussed and in what sequence, is important for every negotiation session. It helps set boundaries and keeps everyone on track. Exhibit 12.6 offers an example of a negotiation agenda. The selling team should come to the meeting with a preliminary typed agenda. Don't be surprised when the buyer team also comes with an agenda; in that case the first thing to be negotiated is the agenda itself. In general, putting key issues not at the very first in the agenda is advantageous. This approach allows time for each party to learn the other's bargaining style and concession routines. Moreover, agreement has already been reached on some minor issues, which, in a win–win situation, supports an atmosphere for reaching agreement on the major issues.

Exhibit 12.6

Preliminary Negotiating Session Agenda

Preliminary Agenda

Meeting between FiberCraft and Rome Industrial Inc.

Proposed New Spin Machine for 15 FiberCraft Plants

November 21

1. Introductions by participants.
2. Agree on the meeting agenda.
3. Issues:
   a. Who will design the new machine?
   b. Who will pay the costs of testing the machine?
   c. Who will have ownership rights to the new machine (if it is ever built for someone else)?
   d. Who will be responsible for maintaining and servicing the new machine during trial runs?
   e. Who will pay for any redesign work needed?
4. Coffee break.
5. Issues:
   a. How and when will the machines be set up in the 15 locations? Who will be responsible for installation?
   b. What percentage will be required for a down payment?
   c. What will the price be? Will there be any price escalation provisions? If not, how long is this price protected?
6. Summary of agreement.

GENERAL GUIDELINES

To negotiate effectively, the seller team must put into practice the skills discussed throughout this book. For example, listening carefully is extremely important. Careful listening involves not only being silent when the buyer talks but also asking good probing questions to resolve confusion and misunderstanding.

The team leader must keep track of issues discussed or resolved. During complicated negotiations many items may be discussed simultaneously. Also, some issues may be raised but not fully addressed before someone raises a separate issue. The leader can provide great assistance by giving periodic status reports, including what has been resolved and the issues being discussed. More important, he or she can map out what still needs to be discussed. In essence this mapping establishes a new agenda for the remainder of the negotiation session.

Once again, cultural differences are important in negotiations. For example, most Canadians and Americans are uncomfortable with silence; most Japanese, on the other hand, are much more comfortable with extended periods of silence. North Americans negotiating with Japanese businesspeople usually find this silence stressful. Negotiators must prepare themselves for such probabilities and learn ways to reduce stress and cope in this situation.

If negotiations require an interpreter, carefully select someone well qualified for the job. And don't expect everything you say to be translated correctly. Here are some items that have been translated into English from another language (so you can get a sense of the problem of translation errors):[6]

- In a family-style restaurant in Hong Kong: Come broil yourself at your own table.

- From an Italian hotel in the mountains: Standing among the savage scenery, the hotel offers stupendous revelations. There is a French window in every room. We offer commodious chambers, with balcony imminent to a romantic gorge. We hope you want to drop in. In the close village you can buy jolly memorials for when you pass away.

- In a Moscow newspaper under the heading "INTERPRETING": Let us you letter of business translation do. Every people in our staffing know English like the hand of their back. Up to the minute wise-street phrases, don't you know, old boy!

- In a Sarajevo hotel: Guests should announce abandonment of their rooms before 12 o'clock, emptying the rooms at the latest until 14 o'clock for the use of the room before 5 at the arrival or after the 16 o'clock at the departure will be billed as one more night.

Finally, keep in mind that during negotiations, people need to save **face**, which is the desire for a positive identity or self-concept. Of course not all people strive for the same face (some want to appear "cool," some "macho," some "crass," and so on). Negotiators will at least try to maintain face and may even use the negotiation session to improve or strengthen this identity.

Exhibit 12.7

What to Do When the
Buyer Turns to Win–Lose
Strategies

Detach yourself.	Don't respond right away. Instead give yourself time to think about the issue. Say something like "Hold on, I'm not sure I follow you. Let's go back over what you just said again." Use the time you have gained to rethink your positions and what would be in the best interests of both parties.
Acknowledge their position and then respond.	In using this tool, you are trying to create a favorable climate for your response. You would start off by mentioning that you agree with them by saying something like "Yes, you have a good point there when you said . . ." After agreeing, you then make your point. For example, you might conclude by saying, "and I would like to make sure you continue to have minimal downtime. And for that to happen, you know, we really need to have someone from your firm attend the training." This tool is somewhat similar to the indirect denial and revisit techniques discussed in Chapter 10.
Build them a bridge.	Come up with a solution that incorporates the buyer's suggestion. For example, "building on your idea, what if we . . ." or "I got this idea from something really neat you said at our meeting last Friday." This approach helps the buyer save face.
Warn, but don't threaten.	Sometimes you may have to help a buyer understand the consequences of his or her position. For example, if the buyer indicates that she or he must have a cheaper fabric for the furniture in an office building, you can say, "I know how important the choice of fabric is to your firm's image, but if you choose that fabric, you won't achieve the image you're really looking for. How much will that cost you in lost clients who might not get a sense that you are very successful?" A warning is not the same thing as a threat. A threat is what will happen if you don't get *your way;* a warning is what will happen if they do get *their* way.

DEALING WITH WIN–LOSE NEGOTIATORS

Many books have been written and many consultants have grown rich teaching both buyers and sellers strategies for effective negotiating. Unfortunately many of these techniques are designed to achieve a win–lose situation. We describe several to illustrate the types of tactics buyers might engage in during negotiations. This knowledge will help the negotiating team defend its position under such attacks.

Both buyers and sellers occasionally engage in the win–lose strategies described here. However, because we are assuming that sellers will adopt a win–win perspective, this section focuses on how to handle buyers who engage in these techniques. Exhibit 12.7 presents an effective overall strategy for dealing with win–lose negotiators.

Good Guy–Bad Guy Routine

You have probably seen the **good guy–bad guy routine** if you watch police movies or TV shows.[7] A tough police detective interrogating the suspect gets a little rough. The detective uses bright lights and intimidation. After a few minutes a second officer (who has been watching) asks his companion to "go out and get some fresh air." While the tough detective (the "bad guy") is outside, the other detective (the "good guy") apologizes for his partner's actions. The good guy goes on to advise the crook to confess now and receive better treatment rather than wait and have the bad guy harass him or her some more. The routine works on the "hurt and rescue" principle: The bad guy offers discomfort and tension, and then the good guy offers escape and a way to bring closure to the situation.

Negotiators often try the same routine. One member of the buyer team (the bad guy) makes all sorts of outlandish statements and requests:

> Look, we've got to buy these for no more than $15 each, and we must have credit terms of 2/10, net 60. After all the business we've given you in the past, I can't believe you won't agree to those terms!

Then another member of the buyer team (the good guy) takes over and appears to offer a win–win solution by presenting a lower demand:

> Hang on, Jack. These are our friends. Sure, we've given them a lot of business, but remember they've been good to us as well! I believe we should let them make a decent profit, so $15.50 would be more reasonable.

According to theory, the sellers are so relieved to find a friend that they jump on the good guy's suggestion.

As an effective defense against such tactics, the selling team must know its position clearly and not let the buyer's strategy weaken it. Obviously the selling team needs the ability to spot a good guy–bad guy tactic. A good response might be the following:

> We understand your concern. But based on all the facts of the situation, we still feel our proposal is a fair one for all parties involved.

Lowballing

You may also have experienced **lowballing,** which occurs when one party intentionally underestimates or understates a cost.[8] Car dealers have used it for years. The salesperson says, "This car sells for $19,613." After you agree to purchase it, what happens? "Oh, I forgot to tell you that we have to charge you for dealer prep and destination charges, as well as an undercoating already applied to the car. So let's see, the total comes to $20,947. Gee, I'm sorry I didn't mention those expenses before!" Most people go ahead and buy. Why? They have already verbally committed themselves and do not want to go against their agreement. Also, they do not want to start the search process again.

The technique is also used in buyer–seller negotiations in industrial situations. For example, after the sellers have signed a final agreement with the buyer team, one of the buyer team members says, "Oh, I forgot to mention that all of our new contracts must specify FOB destination, and the seller must assume all shipping insurance expenses."

The best response to lowballing is just to say no. Remind the buyer team that the agreement has been finalized. The threat of lowballing underscores the importance of getting signatures on contracts and agreements as soon as possible. If the buyers insist on the new items, the selling team will simply be forced to reopen the negotiations. (Try this tactic on car dealers too!)

A variation of lowballing, **nibbling,** is a small extra, or add-on, the buyer requests after the deal has been closed. Compared to lowballing, a nibble is a much smaller request. For example, one of the buyers may state, "Say, could you give us a one-time 5 percent discount on our first order? That would sure make our boss happy and make us look like we negotiated hard for her." Nibbling often works because the request is so small compared to the entire agreement.

The selling team's response to the nibble depends on the situation. It may be advantageous to go ahead and grant a truly small request that could be easily met. On the other hand, if the buyer team uses nibbling often, granting these requests may need to be restricted. Again, the best strategy is to agree on the seller's position before the meeting begins and set guidelines for potential nibbles. Often the seller grants a nibble only if the buyer agrees to some small concession in return.

Emotional Outbursts

How do you react when a close friend suddenly starts crying, gets angry, or looks very sad? Most of us think, What have I done to cause this? We tend to feel guilty, become uneasy, and try to find a way to make the person stop crying. That is simply human nature.

Occasionally buyer teams will appeal to your human nature by engaging in an **emotional outburst tactic.** For example, one of the buyers may look directly at you, shake his or her head sadly, slowly look down, and say softly,

> I can't believe it's come to this. You know we can't afford that price. And we've been good partners all these years. I don't know what to say.

This statement is followed by complete silence among the entire buyer team. Members hope you will feel uncomfortable and give in to their demands. In an extreme case one or more buyers would actually walk out of the room or begin to shout or cry.

The selling team, once again, needs to recognize this behavior as the technique it is. Assuming no logical reason exists for the outburst, the negotiators should respond with a gentle but firm reminder of the merits of the offer and attempt to move the buyer group back into a win–win negotiating frame of mind.

If a member of the buying team engages in an emotional outburst tactic, the seller should never respond in like fashion.

Budget Limitation Tactic

In the **budget limitation tactic,** also called a **budget bogey,** the buyer team states something like the following:

> The proposal looks great. We need every facet of the program you are proposing in order for it to work in our business. But our budget allows us only $250,000 total, including all costs. You'll have to come down from $300,000 to that number, or I'm afraid we can't afford it.

This statement may be absolutely true. If so, at least you know what you have to work with. Of course claims of budget ceilings are sometimes just a ploy to try to get a lower price.

The best defense against budget limitations is to do your homework before going into the negotiation session. Learn as much as you can about budgets and maximums allowed. Have alternative programs or proposals ready that incorporate cost reduction measures. After being told of a budget limitation during the negotiation session, probe to make sure that the claim is valid. Check the possibility of splitting the cost of the proposal over several fiscal years. Probe to find out whether the buyer would be willing to accept more risk for a lower price or to have some of the installation work done by the buyer's staff. You can also help forestall this tactic by working closely with the buyer before the negotiation meeting, providing reasonable ballpark estimates of the cost of the proposal.

Browbeating

Sometimes buyers will attempt to alter the selling team's enthusiasm and self-respect by **browbeating** them. One buyer might make a comment like the following:

> Say, I've been reading some pretty unflattering things about your company in *The Wall Street Journal* lately. Seems like you can't keep your unions happy or your nonunion employees from organizing. It must be tough to get out of bed and go to work every day, huh?

If the selling team feels less secure and slightly inferior after such a comment, the tactic was successful.

You should not let browbeating comments influence you or your proposal. That's easier said than done, of course. Presumably you were able to identify in prenegotiation meetings that this buyer had this type of personality. If so, you could prepare by simply telling yourself that browbeating will occur but you will not let it affect your decisions. If you can make it through one such comment, buyers usually will not offer any more because they can see that browbeating will not help them achieve their goals.

One response to such a statement would be to practice **negotiation jujitsu.**[9] In negotiation jujitsu the salesperson steps away from the opponent's attack, rather than attacking his or her position, and then directs the opponent back to the issues being discussed. Instead of striking back, the seller breaks the win–lose attempt by not reacting negatively. The seller may even ask for clarification, advice, or criticism, but will not try to defend her ideas. The goal in all of this is to calm the buyer, giving the person a chance to release anger or frustration and make his or her position more clear while helping the seller maintain control of her own emotions. For example, the salesperson may say,

> I hear what you're saying. We're concerned about our employees and are working to resolve all problems as quickly as we can. If you have any ideas that would help us in this regard, we'd sure like to hear them. . . . Now, we were discussing price . . .

Other Win–Lose Tactics

Of course many other tactics are used, and it is beyond the purpose of this book to list them all. However, here are a few more:

- Limited authority: "Sorry, but we don't have the authority to make that decision here today." Solution: Verify the truth of that statement. If true, get the person with authority to the table.

- **Red herring** (bringing up a minor point first to distract the other side from considering the main issue): "We're going to have to have Saturday delivery in our agreement." Solution: Ask to set it aside temporarily until more substantive issues are dealt with.

- **Trial balloons** (floating an idea without really offering it as a concession or agreement; the goal is just to get information): "So have you considered going to a deferred shipping plan?" Solution: Don't just supply the information; ask "Well, if we did, what would your offer be?"

- Total silence by the buyer after you make an offer (most salespeople are uncomfortable with silence and will start offering some solution to break the buyer's silence): [Buyers just sit there and stare at the sellers.] Solution: Restate your offer, but don't offer new suggestions until they have acted on what you suggested. Just repeat your terms.

MAKING CONCESSIONS

One of the most important activities in any negotiation is the granting and receiving of concessions from the other party. One party makes a **concession** when it agrees to change a position in some fashion. For example, if your opening price position was $500, you would be granting a concession if you agreed to lower the price to $450.

Based on many successful negotiations in a wide range of situations, a number of guidelines have been formulated to make concessions effectively:[10]

1. Never make concessions until you know all of the buyer's demands and opening position. Use probing to help reveal these.

2. Never make a concession unless you get one in return and don't feel guilty about receiving a concession.

3. Concessions should gradually decrease in size. At first you may be willing to offer "normal size" concessions. As time goes on, however, you should make much smaller ones; for example, use a pattern like the following: 300–245–220–205–201–200. This approach helps the prospect see that you are approaching your target position and are becoming much less willing to concede.

4. If a requested concession does not meet your objectives, don't be afraid to simply say, "No. I'm sorry, but I just can't do that."

5. All concessions you offer are tentative until the final agreement is reached and signed. Remember that you may have to take back one of your concessions if the situation changes.

6. Be confident and secure in your position and don't give concessions carelessly. If you don't follow this advice, your buyers may lose respect for your negotiating and business skills. Everyone wants to conduct business with someone who is sharp and who will be in business in the future. Don't give the impression that you are not and will not.

7. Don't accept the buyer's first attempt at a concession. Chances are the buyer has built in some leeway and is simply testing the water.

8. Help the buyer to see the value of any concessions you agree to. Don't assume the buyer will understand the total magnitude of your "generosity."

9. Start the negotiation without preconceived notions. Even though the buyers may have demanded certain concessions in the past, they may not do so in this negotiation meeting.

10. If, after making a concession, you realize you made some sort of mistake, tell the buyer and begin negotiating that issue again. For example, if you made a concession of delivery every two weeks instead of every four weeks but then realize that your fleet of trucks cannot make that route every two weeks, put the issue back on the table for renegotiation.

11. Don't automatically agree to a "let's just split the difference" offer by the buyers. Check out the offer to see how it compares to your target position.

12. If the customer says, "Tell us what your best price is, and we'll tell you whether we are interested," remain noncommittal. Respond, "In most cases, a price of $X is the best we can do. However, if you want to make a proposal, we'll see what we can do."

13. Know when to stop. Don't keep trying to get more, even if you can.

14. Use silence effectively. Studies have shown cultural differences in the negotiator's ability to use silence. For example, Brazilians make more initial

concessions (use less silence early) than North Americans, who make more than the Japanese.

15. Plan the session well. Know your **best alternative to a negotiated agreement (BTNA)**, the best alternative to a negotiated agreement. What will be the result if you don't come to agreement? This is the standard or guide against which to evaluate the agreement you are trying to achieve. Sometimes it just makes sense to not come to an agreement rather than come to an agreement that makes the seller's team worse off. This concept is sometimes called **consequences of no agreement (CNA)**, the consequences of no agreement.

The granting and receiving of concessions is often very complex and can result in the negotiations taking months or years to complete. Setting the proper environment early in the meeting puts you well on the way to a successful negotiation. Remember to develop an agenda and be aware of win–lose strategies that buyers may use. Offer concessions strategically.

RECAP OF A SUCCESSFUL NEGOTIATION MEETING

This chapter discussed win–win and win–lose negotiation sessions. Seasoned veterans will note that in some situations, the session could more accurately be classified as **win–win not yet negotiating**. In win–win not yet, the buying team achieves its goals while the selling team doesn't. However, the sellers expect to achieve their goals in the near future, thanks to the results of that negotiation session. For example, Antonio Willars in Monterrey, Mexico, relates the following:

> I was working for the magazine *Revista Motor y Volante* and negotiating with Gonher, a lubricating oil company. At that time, no oil companies advertised in my magazine. So I negotiated an agreement with Gonher with a lower price than I had hoped to achieve, based on the belief that that sale would result in increased business over the long term. Although I didn't achieve my pricing goals in that session, I took a longer-term view. It paid off. That was the first of many, consistent sales to Gonher, all at our regular rates. Plus, many oil companies, such as Quaker State, now advertise in the magazine. So although I had a "win not yet" outcome in that first meeting, we have now achieved a complete win–win situation.

When the session is over, be sure to get any negotiated agreements in writing. If no formal contract is possible, at least summarize the agreements reached. And don't forget to do postnegotiation evaluation and learn from your mistakes.

thinking **it** through

How can the use of information technology help keep track of issues during a negotiation session and ensure that all agreements reached during a negotiation session are included in the final written agreement?

Studies have shown that more cooperation exists if both sides expect future interactions. Keep in mind that your goal is to develop a long-term partnership with your buyer, as "From the Buyer's Seat 12.1" illustrates. This process can be aided by being levelheaded, courteous, and, above all, honest. Also, do not try to get every concession possible out of your buyer. If you push too hard or too long, the buyer will get irritated and may even walk out. Never lose out on an agreement by being too greedy. Remember your goal: to reach a win–win settlement.

HOW WE NEGOTIATE

I have been a buyer at a major U.S. retailer for a year and half and prior to my current role worked for two years on a team that supported and helped buyers with business partnerships and negotiations. In my buyer role, I'm responsible for running the profit and loss for multiple categories of products and make decisions ranging from what assortment we will carry in all stores to what promotions we will run on my items. As part of these decisions, I end up spending a lot of my time meeting and talking with our vendor partners to make sure that we have the right products on the shelves at the right prices for our customers while also making a profit for the company.

Negotiations happen on a very frequent basis in my company, whether this is for something very small, such as getting a good cost on a new item, or for large things, such as negotiating an entire program or contract for multiple years. At the core, we negotiate to get the right program for our customers while making a profit for our shareholders. Many times we are negotiating costs of goods with the vendors and other financial terms; however, there are other items outside of cost that we ask for as well. These might include a unique item produced just for our company or a "first to market" deal where our company will be the first to carry the new product.

For large product categories or when the dollars being negotiated are large, buyers at our company go through a specific process to ensure that we are getting the best deal for the company. The process starts by determining a strategy and goals of the negotiation. With the help of our support teams, we'll ask ourselves questions like "Do you want just the lowest product cost, or is product quality important?" "What will taking the business away from the incumbent vendor 'X' mean to our overall relationship with them?" and "What financial goals do you need to hit during the upcoming year?" Having a team to help us think through the strategy and goals is very important and leads to better ending outcomes. After we determine the strategy and goals, we will communicate these along with a time line and process overview to the competing vendors. The vendors then have a period of time to submit their initial proposals; after we get them, we will review them and provide feedback via conference calls or e-mail. The vendors can listen to our feedback and make adjustments to their proposals.

For large and important categories, at this point we may invite the vendors to our office for a formal competitive line review. The vendors will be there with all the other vendors competing for the business, and after a series of meetings we will award the business to the winning vendor. Having a formalized process at our company gives us the best chance of getting the best all-around deal.

In my buying and support role experiences, I have seen a lot of different outcomes to the negotiations process. The following are examples of situations that I've seen happen and the impact that they can have on the business and relationships that are formed between buyers and vendors.

Example 1:

I was in a formal negotiation negotiating a fairly large portion of my business. After eliminating some vendors early on due to either poor costing or poor product quality, it was narrowed down to the incumbent vendor and a new vendor that had done business elsewhere in our company but not with me personally. The new vendor was coming in with a significantly lower cost than the incumbent for a product that was essentially the same as our incumbent. We gave the feedback to our incumbent that they were getting beat in cost and asked them to go back and see what else could be done. The incumbent came back and said that they could go no lower and were very surprised that any vendor could get better costing on the same items. This got me thinking that maybe the new vendor was not being completely honest, so I called a buyer in another area of the company and asked his opinion of the vendor. He said that he was in a similar situation as I was in last year and ended up giving the business to the new vendor. This turned out to be a big mistake because about six months into the program, the new vendor came back and said that they could no longer support the quoted cost and needed to pass along a cost increase. At this point the buyer was stuck and had to take the cost increase. After hearing this I kept the business with the incumbent vendor and did not take the risk of going with the new vendor.

This is a great example of how sometimes in negotiations, something looks very appealing on the outside, but once you start to peel back the layers, you may find

(Continued)

something that you do not like. It is the buyer's job to make sure that they are looking at all aspects and using all the resources available to make the most informed decisions.

Example 2:

In another negotiation we had a vendor partner selected for a large part of the business and needed the vendor to come down in cost to help us hit our profit goals. We asked for more movement, but the vendor said that was as low as they could go, and we believed them. We started to get creative and thought about what else we could offer the vendor to get the cost we wanted. We had a smaller piece of the business that originally wasn't going to be negotiated, as it wasn't a key focus for us, but we knew that if we could give the salesperson additional placement, that would give him leverage at his company to get us the better deal on the bigger part of the business. So we offered that, and sure enough he was able to come back and get us the deal we needed to hit our goals. This is a great example of where the buyer needed to get creative and actually sell the salesperson on an idea instead of just being sold to.

Source: Jimmy Aldridge; all names changed to protect anonymity; used with permission.

SELLING YOURSELF

Negotiation occurs during nearly every interaction with another person. Whether it is with your boss discussing pay raises, your parents and curfew times, or an aggressive used car salesman with price, you find yourself attempting to establish a win–win scenario. Let us say you were interviewing for a marketing position at Nike, arguably the top sports apparel company in the world, and need to create an ad campaign to unveil their new partnership with the National Football League (NFL). How do you come up with a compelling presentation? What factors are necessary to convey the proper message? Why should Nike select you over other candidates? Understanding the Nike philosophy will help you earn that position. Here's how.

First, find out everything about Nike, the NFL, and its new partnership. Review Nike's historical ad campaigns and identify their direction for the future. Other important factors are your target market, goals and strategies, knowing the industry trends, and essentially covering the five Ps: promotion, price, place, product, and people. Part of negotiating is having a sufficient amount of background knowledge to showcase your expertise in the appropriate field. Interviewing for a job is no different. Preparation and planning prior to the meeting will allow you to convey the appropriate message in a confident and concise manner.

How do you convey this message? Simple: teach, tailor, and take control of your presentation. Teach your listeners something new about your product's value. Tailor your message and effectively position your pitch to the audience. Finally, take control of your presentation with conviction and assertiveness. Good negotiators are able to entice the customer within the first six seconds of the meeting through their appearance, persona, and diction. Nonverbal cues such as smiling, hand gestures, and posture can depict the direction of the conversations. With all influences in use, you will leave Nike with a tough decision to make.

Finally, the moment of truth has arrived. Nike offers you the marketing position, and with great jubilation you accept the position without hesitation. Good move or bad move? The answer is bad move, mainly because the second part of the negotiation phase has just begun, and you accepted before dealing. Remember, *everything* can be negotiated: salary, benefits, relocation fees, reimbursement items, office space, company apparel, work hours, and many more facts. All of the above should be discussed prior to the acceptance to ensure that both parties clearly understand the expectations and requirements to succeed together. Once a win–win agreement is confirmed, accept the position and celebrate.

Successful salespeople have one thing in common: passion. Truly enjoying your work and having that uncanny ability to positively enhance another person's business is powerful. Negotiating deals to generate revenue for your company is a self-fulfilling process, as it allows you to hit goals and/or possibly pocket a portion of the profits (commission-based jobs only). Nevertheless, selling yourself should be a part of your daily lifestyle. Being recognized as someone who is invaluable to a group is one of the most credible accomplishments one can achieve.

Source: Evans Adonis; used with permission.

SUMMARY

This chapter described how to engage in win–win negotiating. It also described how buyers may engage in win–lose negotiating.

Almost anything can be negotiated. The areas of negotiation will depend on the needs of both parties and the extent of disagreement on major issues.

A successful salesperson is not necessarily a good negotiator. Important negotiator traits include patience and endurance, willingness to take risks, a tolerance for ambiguity, the ability to deal with conflict, and the ability to engage in negotiation without worrying that every person present will not be on one's side.

As in regular sales calls, careful planning counts. This step involves choosing the location, setting objectives, and developing and managing the negotiating team. The salesperson does not act alone in these tasks, but instead draws on the full resources of the firm.

Preliminaries are important in sales negotiation sessions. Friendly conversation and small talk can help to reduce tensions and establish rapport. Agendas help to set boundaries and keep the negotiation on track. Win–lose strategies that buyers use include a good guy–bad guy routine, lowballing, emotional outbursts, budget limitation, browbeating, and other tactics. As much as possible, the salesperson should respond to any win–lose maneuvers calmly and with the intent of bringing the other side back to a win–win stance.

Concessions, by definition, will occur in every negotiation. Many guidelines have been established to help negotiators avoid obvious problems. For example, no concession should be given unless the buyer gives a concession of equal value. Also, any concessions given are not formalized until the written agreement is signed; thus, all concessions are subject to removal if appropriate.

KEY TERMS

accommodating mode 323
adaptive planning 320
agenda 325
ambush negotiating 324
avoiding mode 323
BATNA (best alternative to a
    negotiated agreement) 332
brainstorming session 320
browbeating 330

budget bogey 329
budget limitation tactic 329
CNA (consequences of no agreement) 332
collaborating mode 323
competing mode 323
compromising mode 323
concession 331
emotional outburst tactic 329
face 326

ETHICS PROBLEMS

1. "Try to get a big concession from your opponent by giving away a small, insignificant concession yourself." Comment.

2. "If your opponent begins to use an unethical tactic, walk out of the room." Comment on this statement.

QUESTIONS AND PROBLEMS

1. Based on the situations described in "From the Buyer's Seat 12.1," list three things salespeople should do to ensure successful negotiations.

2. Suppose you're a salesperson with a local milk producer, and you're negotiating with a regional grocer over the number of deliveries you will make to its stores in a given week. Your maximum is six times a week, your opening is three times a week, and your target is five times a week. After negotiating for some time, the grocer states, "Look, we're not willing to accept anything less than 14 times a week." What do you do now?

3. Assume you're a salesperson who is known for your excellent negotiating skills. You're a true collaborator in every sense of the word. Today you're supposed to engage in a negotiation with an important client. It's taken three months to set up this meeting, and your team of five, including your vice president, is assembled and ready to walk into the meeting. You are your team's designated leader. Your cell phone rings, and it's a relative, telling you that a close loved one has passed away unexpectedly. With the news comes a desire to just quit everything. What do you do now?

4. In "Sales Technology 12.1," you learned how salespeople are using Skype to prepare for upcoming negotiation sessions. What are some potential problems with using this technology in this way?

5. According to the text, engaging in friendly conversation to break the ice before getting down to business is usually a good idea. When would it not be a good idea?

6. Assume you are going to have your fourth and final job interview with Fastenal, a distributor of fasteners and other construction-related materials, next Friday. Knowledgeable friends have told you that because you passed the first three interviews, you will be offered the job during the fourth interview. Also, you know that Fastenal likes to negotiate with its new hires.
   a. Think about your own needs and desires for your first job (such as salary, expense reimbursement, benefits, geographic location, and promotion cycle).
   b. For each need and desire listed, establish your target position, opening position, and minimum position.
   c. Fastenal has probably also developed positions that might meet each of your needs and desires. Describe how you could discover these positions before next Friday's meeting.

7. Stephanie Bolen, a salesperson for Nestlé, is preparing for an important negotiation session with Cub Foods, a large national food chain, regarding an upcoming promotional campaign. Her boss has strongly suggested that he attend the meeting with her. The problem is that her boss is not a good negotiator; he tends to get angry, is unorganized, and tries to resolve conflict by talking nonstop and thus wearing down the buyer team with fatigue. Her boss definitely has a win–lose negotiating philosophy. What should Stephanie do?

8. "You are the worst possible person to have to negotiate for yourself. You care too much about the outcome. Always let someone else negotiate for you."

State your reaction to this statement. What implications does it have in industrial sales negotiations?

9. During negotiation, buyers make all kinds of statements. What would be your response to the following, assuming each occurred early in the meeting?

   a. We refuse to pay more than $15,000 each. That's our bottom line—take it or leave it!

   b. Come on, you've got to do better than that!

   c. You know, we're going to have to get anything we decide here today approved by our international headquarters before we can sign any kind of a contract.

   d. One of our buyers can't make it here for another hour. But let's go ahead and get started and see what progress we can make.

   e. Tell you what, we need to see a detailed cost breakdown for each individual item in your proposal.

10. "As a salesperson negotiator, my buyer's problem becomes my problem." Comment.

CASE PROBLEMS

case **12.1**

DoubleTree Hotels

DoubleTree has more than 300 hotels in 23 different countries. The chain is owned by Hilton and strives to create what they term CARE (Create A Rewarding Experience) for all of their guests. The CARE system starts with a warm chocolate chip cookie to welcome each guest. That is followed with stylish guest rooms, each including the Sweet Dreams® by DoubleTree Sleep Experience. Most guest rooms offer the higher-quality CITRON bath products by Crabtree & Evelyn. Double-Tree also offers Fitness Rooms for their guests.

Julie, a salesperson for Micros, was attempting to negotiate with DoubleTree with regard to Micros's OPERA Reservation System (ORS). ORS, a central reservation system, is a part of an enterprise-wide room inventory management system offered by Micros. ORS has many outstanding features, including the following: It supports multicurrency and multilanguage situations; it lets you set up rate structures for individual properties or groups of properties; it can easily handle complicated situations, such as shared reservations, frequent-flyer, and loyalty program memberships, negotiated rates, and rate discounts; and it conveniently searches for room availability across all of the properties.

Julie met with the DoubleTree buyers on eight different occasions before the formal negotiation meeting. She had created a win–win proposal that she was sure would meet the needs of DoubleTree and Micros. Her boss had even congratulated her on her hard work and the proposed solution. "You're going to get it, I'm sure!" she had said. "And then we can start talking about that raise you've been asking for!"

Everything was going great in the negotiation meeting until Julie was startled to hear Kevin Tarnoski, the key negotiator for DoubleTree, practically shout, "Listen, Julie! I can't believe you're asking that much for this little reservation system! The recession hit all of us in the hospitality industry very hard. Come to think of it, that's probably why you're trying to stick it to us with this price. Knock it off! Lower your price, or we'll go elsewhere!" He then proceeded to tell her how much he was willing to pay to lease her system.

Julie didn't know what to say. The price cut being requested by Kevin was 5 percent less than Micros's minimum price objective.

Questions

1. Evaluate the negotiation meeting to this point. How could Julie have better planned for the meeting?

2. What should Julie do now? Be explicit and give reasons for your answers. Make any necessary assumptions.

Sources: This is a fictitious scenario. Information about DoubleTree came from http://doubletree3.hilton.com/en/about/doubletree/index.html. Information about Micros came from http://www.micros.com/Solutions/ProductsNZ/OPERAReservationSystemORS.

This chapter described a number of basic conflict-handling modes that people use in negotiation. These include competing, collaborating, compromising, avoiding, and accommodating.

Carefully reread the section that describes these modes. For each mode, identify someone you know who falls into the mode and answer the following questions. It will probably help to think of a specific situation that you have observed or have experienced with the person.

Questions

1. How do you know this person has this conflict-handling mode? Identify specific behaviors that you have observed or heard about to support your assertion about this person.
2. How do you (and others) interact with this person during a conflict situation? In other words, what do you do? How do you respond to this person's behavior? Is your approach effective?
3. Would you like to have this person on your team during an important negotiation session? Why or why not?

ROLE PLAY CASE

Break up into pairs; one person will serve as a buyer and the other as a NetSuite salesperson. The buyer is the VP of sales for the Atlanta regional office of UPS shipping. UPS is an international carrier that does overnight express package delivery, package delivery, and international shipping. It can ship anything anywhere. There are 54 salespeople employed, with six sales managers reporting to the VP. The salespeople use a card system, whereby they get the buyer's business card and staple it to an index card on which they can keep their notes. The company plans to add five salespeople per year until it doubles in size, with a new sales manager every other year. Sales force turnover is 15 percent per year, and often the cards are not turned over or are incomplete. One other problem is that growth is not meeting targets. Managers train their sales teams, but reps complain that it isn't what they need. Managers don't know what they need because they don't know where in the sales process the reps are not effective. NetSuite can provide pipeline analysis as well as better reporting of activity and results, a key need. Each rep generates about $1 million in shipping revenue per year.

About half the reps are not particularly computer literate and don't use computers to keep track of their accounts now. About half the reps have software they use to record call information, but that information is not tied to the company's computers or database. All salespeople have laptops, which they can use to access shipping records via a wireless Internet connection.

As a rep or as a buyer, take a few minutes to determine your opening and target positions on such factors as price, training, service, and anything else you can think of. Both of you can use information about NetSuite found in the role play section at the end of the book or on the NetSuite Web site to determine your positions and negotiating strategies. In your planning, include the use of a win–lose tactic, but be willing to move back to win–win if the other person responds appropriately. No additional information will be provided by the instructor.

Note: For background information about these role plays, please see page 26.

To the instructor: Additional information that will help you with this exercise is available in the Instructor's Manual.

ADDITIONAL REFERENCES

Asherman, Ira G. *Negotiation at Work: Maximize Your Team's Skills with 60 High-Impact Activities*. New York City: AMACOM, 2012.

Benoliel, Michael. *Negotiation Excellence: Successful Deal Making*. Singapore: World Scientific Publishing, 2011.

Challagalla, Goutam, R. Venkatesh, and Ajay K. Kohli. "Proactive Postsales Service: When and Why Does It Pay Off?" *Journal of Marketing* 73, no. 2 (2009), pp. 70–87.

Chang, Cheng-Wen, David M. Chiang, and Fan-Yun Pai. "Cooperative Strategy in Supply Chain Networks." *Industrial Marketing Management* 41, no. 7 (October 2012), pp. 1114–24.

Chang, Shu-Hao, Kai-Yu Wang, Wen-Hai Chih, and Wen-Hsin Tsai. "Building Customer Commitment in Business-to-Business Markets." *Industrial Marketing Management* 41, no. 6 (August 2012), pp. 940–50.

"Defend Yourself against Influence Strategies." *Negotiation* 15, no. 5 (May 2012), pp. 5–7.

Gates, Steve. *The Negotiation Book: Your Definitive Guide to Successful Negotiation*. Hoboken, NJ: Wiley, 2011.

"Giving Outsiders a Voice in Your Negotiation." *Negotiation* 15, no. 6 (June 2012), pp. 1–4.

Hames, David S. *Negotiation: Closing Deals, Settling Disputes, and Making Team Decisions*. Thousand Oaks, CA: Sage, 2011.

Harvard Business Review on Winning Negotiations. Harvard Business Review Press, Cambridge, MA: Harvard Business Review Paperback Series, 2011.

Herbst, Uta, Markus Voeth, and Christoph Meister. "What Do We Know about Buyer–Seller Negotiations in Marketing Research? A Status Quo Analysis." *Industrial Marketing Management* 40, no. 6 (2011), pp. 967–78.

Hutson, Don, and George Lucas. *The One Minute Negotiator: Simple Steps to Reach Better Agreements*. San Francisco, CA: Berrett-Koehler Publishers, 2010.

Lammers, Frauke. "Fairness in Delegated Bargaining." *Journal of Economics and Management Strategy* 19, no. 1 (2010), pp. 169–85.

Latz, Marty. "The Golden Rules of Negotiation." *Sales and Marketing Management*, January/February 2009, p. 24.

Leung, T. K. P., Ricky Yee-Kwong Chan, Kee-hung Lai, and Eric W. T. Ngai. "An Examination of the Influence of Guanxi and Xinyong (Utilization of Personal Trust) on Negotiation Outcome in China: An Old Friend Approach." *Industrial Marketing Management* 40, no. 7 (2012), pp. 1193–205.

Lewicki, Roy, Bruce Barry, and David Saunders. *Essentials of Negotiation*. New York City: McGraw-Hill/Irwin, 2010.

Lum, Grande. *The Negotiation Fieldbook, Second Edition: Simple Strategies to Help You Negotiate Everything*. New York City: McGraw-Hill, 2010.

Moon, Yongma, Tao Yao, and Sungsoon Park. "Price Negotiation under Uncertainty." *International Journal of Production Economics* 134, no. 2 (December 2011), pp. 413–23.

"Negotiators: When Overwhelmed by Choices, Find Order in Chaos." *Negotiation* 15, no. 9 (September 2012), pp. 1–4.

Nyden, Jeanette. *Negotiation Rules: A Practical Guide to Big Deal Negotiation*. Cape Coral, Florida: Sales Gravy Press, 2009.

Thompson, Leigh. *The Mind and Heart of the Negotiator*. Upper Saddle River, New Jersey: Prentice Hall, 2011.

Thorn, Jeremy G. *How to Negotiate Better Deals*. Lake Charles, LA: Global Management Enterprises, 2009.

Visentin, Marco, and Daniele Scarpi. "Determinants and Mediators of the Intention to Upgrade the Contract in Buyer–Seller Relationships." *Industrial Marketing Management* 41, no. 7 (October 2012), pp. 1133–41.

chapter

13

BUILDING PARTNERING RELATIONSHIPS

SOME QUESTIONS ANSWERED IN THIS CHAPTER ARE

- What different types of relationships exist between buyers and sellers?
- When is each type of relationship appropriate?
- What are the characteristics of successful partnerships?
- What are the benefits and risks in partnering relationships?
- How do relationships develop over time?
- What are the responsibilities of salespeople in partnerships?

PROFILE

PROFILE My current career position as a medical device sales representative at Applied Medical is most enjoyable during those critical times when I am building *true* relationships with my customers. Getting to know their families, why they chose their careers, the stresses of their day, and their current goals all huge motivators to me. And here is the real kicker— I genuinely do care! There are countless times when I find that I am talking with customers almost entirely about them as individuals with almost no discussion of "business." I sincerely love working with people, and it was this love that initially drew me to sales. The opportunity to meet new people every day completely energizes me. When I really begin building a new relationship, most often my natural enthusiasm comes through to that prospect or customer. However, as noted by Jill Konrath of *SNAP Selling*, not all contacts are interested in building relationships beyond the basic transactions at the start.

As a member of the Professional Selling Program while at the University of Central Florida, I initially learned so much through my various classes and mentorships. Since then, my starter collegiate text, *Selling: Building Partnerships*, has proven to be an excellent handbook on effectively communicating with customers and building solid relationships. Notably, determining my clients' social styles has really helped me to be able to more quickly connect with my customer. By now I am able to determine fairly quickly whether I am dealing with a "driver" or "amiable" or other personality type and to quickly adjust my product introduction accordingly.

In my current position as a medical device sales representative, I have to adapt my sales approach to two completely different classifications of customers. The first is the surgeon, who generally has very little time to talk during the day, let alone allowing his or her sales representative to build a professional friendship. The second customer group is made up of people within the hospital administration. They usually have time to talk, listen to more complete product demonstrations, and can better communicate their own goals with sales representatives. Of course, I have a much easier time building relationships with people in administration, but I have to adapt my style to both customer classifications. Interestingly, I find that the people with whom I often have a naturally easier time building relationships are those who are willing to ultimately help me with the more difficult "driver"-style customers within the purchasing mix. I find that even the customers who are initially the most difficult in our dealings are frequently the ones who will eventually warm up and exhibit significant trust. That is an ever-fascinating process.

In my initial medical device sales assignment, I would often worry that I would not be able to build a large enough portfolio of new business to even meet my quota. Honestly, I would envy those salespeople who would come back from lunch breaks to several messages from customers needing something from them. I wanted to be needed. I wanted to be a resource to my customers. But I was new, and most of my customers didn't know who I was or what I could provide to them as a solutions source. My colleagues and supervisors would point out that the business would come in time but that my customers first needed to see that they could trust me to provide a value-added solution. I had to continually call on account after account until some finally agreed that they needed something from me. Once I was perceived as accomplishing various tasks for them swiftly and correctly, I was then given growing levels of trust. Those initial bits of trust opened the doorway for them to reach out for other things of increasing priority (overnight orders, last-minute quotes, discounts on shipping, and so on), which then led into trusting me with even larger projects and orders. Throughout that process, I began a special niche relationship with my hard-to-reach driver customers. I find that these particular people are now much more willing to work and talk to me. I have proven my reliability to them. They have gone on to trust that I am able to truly help them meet or exceed their needs.

With anyone in my personal life, the more I trust them, the more open I usually am with them and vice versa. This is true with most relationships, especially the one between the salesperson and the client. I must first earn their trust over time with proven service and ability and always relate to them in their social style as best as I can. In conclusion, every chance customers give you to earn their trust and prove your knowledge and ability, seize it! Over time, I am confident that you can bring a large number of even the most opposed and nonconforming style client to your side. Employ the art and science of selling as found in this text, so embrace the sales challenge. It will be rewarding in financial, emotional, and other ways as well.

Visit our Web site at:
www.appliedmedical.com

THE VALUE OF CUSTOMERS

Many people believe the emphasis in selling is on getting the initial sale. For most salespeople, however, sales increases from one year to the next are due to increasing the revenue from existing accounts, not just from getting new accounts. Even in industries where purchase decisions are made infrequently, salespeople gain a competitive advantage by maintaining strong relationships with their customers. Eventually, when buying decisions need to be made, those customers look to people they know and trust. Christina Harrod, for example, discussed in the opening profile the importance of being trustworthy because people want to buy from people they know and trust.

Customers are, of course, the primary revenue source for companies. Some customers are worth more in terms of revenue than some salespeople recognize. For example, a car salesperson may think only of the immediate sale, but each customer is potentially worth hundreds of thousands of dollars in revenue over the salesperson's lifetime. Exhibit 13.1 illustrates the value of a small attorney's office over a 20-year period for just a few salespeople. For example, if an office equipment/supply salesperson sold all the copiers and office supplies needed during that 20-year period, total revenue would be almost $100,000! This is an example of **customer lifetime value (CLV), which is the combined total of all future sales (typically discounted back into current dollars)**. If the salesperson thinks in terms of just one sale, however, the customer is worth no more than $5,000.

Exhibit 13.1

Selected Expenses for a Small Law Firm over a 20-Year Period

Item	Cost	Total
Computers	7 @ $2,000	$14,000
Copiers	5 @ $5,000	25,000
Copying supplies	$50 per month	12,000
Printer/scanner/fax	5 @ $2,000	10,000
Fax supplies	$20 per month	4,800
Telephone systems	3 @ $1,000	3,000
Other office supplies	$100 per month	24,000
Office furniture	$5,000	5,000
Total over 20 years		$97,800

How much do you spend on clothing each month? Now multiply that figure by 12. Assuming that you shop in the same places during the four years you will be in college, multiply that result by 4. The total is the amount of your clothing purchases over your college career. Does anyone treat you like a $1,000 customer, or are you treated like a $20 customer? What would you expect to be different in how you are treated if the store recognized your true value?

Research shows that successfully retaining customers is important to all companies. Using a consultative customer-oriented sales approach has been shown to improve both customer retention and firm profitability, even with commodity products.[1] Yet another study finds that the average company loses 20–50 percent of its customer base every year, and the rate is increasing.[2] Salespeople are critical to the process of keeping customers: Another study finds that the relationship quality between the salesperson and the buyer is one driver of financial performance. The better the relationship, the better the firm's performance.[3]

We have already discussed the importance of good service in generating referrals and of becoming a trusted member of the community in which your buyers operate so you can acquire more customers (see Chapter 6). The value of satisfied customers is so high that it makes good business sense to build the strongest possible relationships. Some sales experts believe that is takes, on average, seven visits to conclude an initial solo exchange, but only three to achieve the first re-order. Whether it is actually 7 + 3 in your business, or some other ratio, the reality is that the first sale is often merely a test. In fact, many companies now don't celebrate the first sale as much as they celebrate the first reorder! In this chapter we discuss the nature of relationships and the types of relationships that can be built, and we begin to explore how to build those relationships over time. In the next chapter we focus on strategies to build longer-term relationships.

RELATIONSHIPS AND SELLING

Many students may have heard of relationship marketing or customer relationship management (CRM) and wonder how these compare with building partnerships. *Relationship marketing* is a term with several meanings, but all reflect companies' attempts to develop stronger relationships with their customers. The premise is that loyal customers buy more, are willing to pay more, influence friends to also buy, and are willing to help develop new products.[4] Building a stronger relationship is accomplished through building loyalty. For example, American Airlines may think of its Aadvantage frequent flyer program as the heart of relationship marketing; loyalty is rewarded with air miles that can be redeemed for free flights. But in professional selling, **relationship marketing** refers to creating the type of relationship that best suits the customer's need, which may or may not require a partnership.

There are two types of loyalty: behavioral and attitudinal.[5] **Behavioral loyalty** refers to the purchase of the same product from the same vendor over time. When someone purchases out of habit, for example, that pattern is behavioral loyalty. Recall that earlier

Buyers who are attitudinally loyal to Apple and its computers may also be behaviorally loyal, buying products like the iPad when they are introduced.

we pointed out that buyers calculate profit by subtracting both price and shopping costs from the benefits received. Buying out of habit can reduce shopping costs and increase profit when past experience can indicate future satisfaction. **Attitudinal loyalty** is an emotional attachment to a brand, company, or salesperson. For example, some computer users develop an emotional attachment to Apple; they may also exhibit behavioral loyalty by buying only Apple products whenever possible or even buying a new iPad just because it is an Apple product.

Companies prefer buyers who are both attitudinally and behaviorally loyal; moreover, companies want loyal customers who stay customers forever. Companies want to receive as much of a buyer's lifetime value, or CLV, as possible. Further, not every customer's CLV is the same. Recall the attorney firm in Exhibit 13.1—not every firm of that size will spend money on equipment the same way. Some firms will need more, others less. Thus, companies want loyal customers who are also bigger spenders. Lower lifetime value customers may not be as important to the company.

Customer lifetime value is influenced by more than just that customer's purchases, though. How much more might that attorney be worth as a customer to an office equipment dealer in terms of referrals, sales to the associates who leave and open their own offices, and additional repeat business if the dealership really kept the attorney as a customer for life? What about the value of a new product idea generated by the attorney? All these elements can add value to the company.

There are entire books written about loyalty; the important element to recognize here is that the emphasis in this book is on building long-term relationships, in part to capture as much CLV as possible. Salespeople with the longer-term view recognize the power of CLV and consider both behavioral and attitudinal loyalty as an objective sell in a different way than if focused only on making the next sale. There are, however, different types of relationships, as we discuss next.

TYPES OF RELATIONSHIPS

Each time a transaction occurs between a buyer and a seller, the buyer and the seller have a relationship. Some relationships may involve many transactions and last for years; others may exist only for the few minutes during which money is exchanged for goods.

This section describes two basic relationship types: market exchanges and partnerships.[6] There are two types of each, summarized in Exhibit 13.2.

MARKET EXCHANGES

A **market exchange** is a transaction between a buyer and a seller in which each party is concerned only about its own benefit. The seller is concerned only with making the sale, the buyer with getting the product at the lowest possible price. Most business transactions are market exchanges, and there are two types: solo exchanges and functional relationships.

Solo Exchanges

Suppose you are driving to the beach for spring break. A warning light on your car's dashboard comes on. You stop at the next gas station, and the service attendant says your car needs a new alternator. The alternator will cost $650, including installation. At this point you might pay the quoted price, bargain with the service attendant for a lower price, or drive to another service station a block away and get a second opinion. After you select a service station, agree on a price, have the alternator replaced, and pay for the service, you have completed a

Exhibit 13.2

Types of Relationships between Buyers and Sellers

Factors Involved in the Relationship	Type of Relationship			
	Solo Market Transaction	Functional Relationship	Relational Partnership	Strategic Partnership
Time horizon	Short term	Long term	Long term	Long term
Concern for other party	Low	Low	Medium	High
Trust	Low	Low	High	High
Investments in the relationship	Low	Low	Low	High
Nature of the relationship	Conflict, bargaining	Cooperation	Accommodation	Coordination
Risk in relationship	Low	Medium	High	High
Potential benefits	Low	Medium	High	High

one-shot market exchange. Neither you nor the service station attendant expects to engage in future transactions.

Because the parties in the transaction do not plan on doing business together again, both the buyer and the seller in a **solo exchange** pursue their own self-interests. In this example, you try to pay the lowest price for the alternator, and the service station tries to charge the highest price for it. The service station is not concerned about your welfare, just as you are not concerned about the service station's welfare. Or perhaps more accurately, the service station calculates profit from the relationship immediately after the transaction. The issue is not an ethical one; there is no intent to maliciously hurt the other party. At the same time, however, there is no future consideration to worry about in terms of whether the transaction was worthwhile.

Functional Relationships

Functional relationships are long-term market exchanges characterized by behavioral loyalty; the buyer purchases the same product out of habit or routine. Buyers in this type of relationship tend to have the same orientation as they do in solo exchanges, but the previous purchase influences the next purchase. As long as the buyer is satisfied and the product is available at a reasonable price and does what it is supposed to do, the buyer will continue to buy.

Sometimes firms buy from the same supplier for a long time because it is easier than searching for a new supplier every time they need an item. In functional relationships (as in any long-term buyer–seller relationship), customer satisfaction is very important. Without customer satisfaction, behavioral loyalty cannot develop. **Customer satisfaction** occurs when the buyer's expectations are met and needs are fulfilled (we discuss this in detail later in this chapter).[7] When satisfied, a buyer is less likely to shop around for the next purchase because less hassle means more value to the buyer.

For example, a buyer for your school purchases janitorial supplies—paper towels, soap, cleanser, and mops—for the cleaning crew. However, the buyer and the janitorial supply distributor have little interest in working closely together. The relationship between the buyer and the distributor's salesperson is not critical to the school's success as an educational institution. The buyer can decide to deal with another distributor if service is poor, the product fails to perform, or another distributor works harder to get the business—in other words, if the buyer becomes dissatisfied.

Another example is your grocery store. You shop there because it is convenient both in terms of how close it is to your home and in terms of how well you know the store and can find what you want easily. You go back, but you'd consider going elsewhere for a special sale or to find something you want. A relationship, if you can call it that, is simply functional: As long as they have what you want at a competitive price, you'll keep shopping there.

Even in these long-term market exchanges, both parties are interested primarily in their own profits and are unconcerned about the welfare of the other party. In market exchanges price may be the critical decision factor. It serves as a rapid means of communicating the bases for the exchange. Basically the buyer and the salesperson in a market exchange are always negotiating over how to "split up the pie," or how to make more in the transaction. Each calculates profit at the end of each transaction or at least on a frequent basis, usually reflective of the billing cycle. If the janitorial supply company invoices the university monthly, for example, then each side will calculate profit monthly. If the school's buyer gets an invoice that seems too large, it may cause the buyer to shop around next time because there was insufficient "profit" or value for the buyer.

On the positive side, market exchanges offer buyers and sellers a lot of flexibility. Buyers and sellers are not locked into a continuing relationship, and thus buyers can switch from one supplier to another to make the best possible deal. However, these minimal relationships do not work well when buyers and sellers have an opportunity to increase the size of the pie by developing products and services tailored to their needs. These more complex transactions cannot be conducted solely on the basis of price. High levels of trust and commitment are needed to manage these types of relationships because buyers and sellers need to share sensitive information.[8]

PARTNERSHIPS

There are two types of partnerships: relational and strategic. In a partnership both parties are concerned about each other's welfare and about developing a **win–win relationship.** By working together, both parties benefit because the size of the pie increases.

Relational Partnerships

Many times the buyer and the salesperson have a close personal relationship that allows them to communicate effectively. These friendships create a cooperative climate between the salesperson and the customer. When both partners feel safe and stable in the relationship, open and honest communication takes place. Salesperson and buyer work together to solve important problems. The partners are not concerned about small details because they trust each other enough to know these will be worked out. These types of partnerships are not necessarily strategic to either organization, although they may be to the individuals involved, and are called **relational partnerships.**

How would you shop for a new car? If you knew someone in the car business, you'd probably go there first in order to work with someone you know and could trust. Now flip that relationship: If you bought cars regularly, you might want to build a friendship with a dealer's salesperson in order to rely on that friendship for protection against overly aggressive negotiating and other negative factors you might be concerned about. You'd feel confident you were getting a good deal from a friend, and you'd be happy that she or he could make a sale.

The benefits of a relational partnership go beyond simple increased short-term profits. Although both partners are striving to make money in the relationship, they are also trying to build a working relationship that will last a long time.

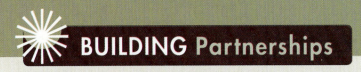

DO COMMODITIES NEED RELATIONSHIPS?

Customer service and relationships is obviously important when you sell something complex. But what about when you sell something that is a commodity, and you get paid straight commission so that you earn something only when you sell something? That's the scenario that faced Kevin Clonch, account executive for Total Quality Logistics (TQL), a shipping company, and, frankly, he was bit skeptical that service and relationships mattered.

But he quickly learned that what separated TQL from other shipping companies was the quality of service built through strong relationships. As Kevin points out, "The reason Ken Oaks started TQL traces back to his prior job in the produce industry. He found reliable transportation extremely difficult to find." That's why Oaks made service and relationships the foundations of his company—because that's what customers needed most. "While price might also be a determinant, especially in this economy, if you can show the value and go above and beyond on service, then the customers will always return. I always explain to my customers that you can't have champagne service with Coca-Cola prices, though. They usually get a good laugh out of that one, but it generally holds pretty true especially in transportation," says Kevin.

"Transportation makes customers extremely anxious because there are so many things that can go wrong, from pickup to delivery. So many aspects are out of the customer's control, such as weather, truck breakdown, theft, accidents, and in some cases temperature control throughout a shipment's travel. Communication keeps customers feeling secure; my main service component is letting the customer know at any moment if something goes wrong. We are available literally 24/7/365 and occasionally deal with issues at 2:00 a.m. or even on Christmas Day. This level of service, though, is necessary because we always say that doing the right thing is always better than trying to cover up a mistake that actually makes it worse."

Yes, TQL may pick up a load and take it to another location, but what Kevin sells isn't just transportation—it's peace of mind. Through building a relationship based on trust, Kevin enjoys success in a very competitive field. "By following these simple steps I have built long lasting customer relationships, but I can honestly call many of my customers very good friends due to the relationships that we have built throughout the years."

Kevin Clonch, featured in "Building Partnerships 13.1," says, "I have built long-lasting customer relationships, but I can honestly call many of my customers very good friends due to the relationships that we have built throughout the years." Relational partnerships can occur between a buyer and seller not only because of personal ties but also because each is important to the other professionally. For example, a trade show program may not be important enough to the organization to demand a strategic partner but is very important to the trade show manager. That manager may seek a relational partnership with a supplier, complete with personal investment of time and departmental resources, rather than a strategic organizational investment and commitment.

In Asian countries, the personal relationship is an important precursor to strategic partnerships. Several studies have found that social bonding and interpersonal commitment are necessary ingredients to any long-term partnership between Asian organizations.[9] In several studies examining relationships between buyers and sellers in China, interpersonal commitment was a precursor to organizational relationships; so without friendship, there was no partnership.[10]

In this chapter we talk about relationships between buyers and sellers, but these concepts also apply to personal relationships. A relational partnership is like a close friendship. In a close friendship you are not concerned with how the pie is split up each day because you are confident that, over the long run, each of you will get a fair share; further, the pie will be bigger because of your friendship. You trust your friend to care about you, and she or he trusts you in return. The founder of the country's largest department store chain, James Cash Penney, once said, "All great businesses are built on friendship."

Strategic Partnerships

Strategic partnerships are long-term business relationships in which the partner organizations make significant investments to improve the profitability of both parties. In these relationships the partners have gone beyond trusting each other to "putting their money where their mouths are." They take risks to expand the pie and to give the partnership a strategic advantage over other companies.

Strategic partnerships are created for the purpose of uncovering and exploiting joint opportunities. Members of strategic partnerships have a high level of dependence on and trust in each other, share goals and agree on how to accomplish those goals, and show a willingness to take risks, share confidential information, and make significant investments for the sake of the relationship.

One of the oldest strategic partnerships is that between HP and Disney, dating back to 1938, when Disney purchased test equipment for work on the movie *Fantasia*. Since then, the two companies have shared engineering resources to address needs that both have. Disney benefits from early advantages in engineering and HP from gaining customer insight that translates into new products.

Another example is Keyser Group and McDonald's. Think about what has to happen when McDonald's launches a new product—signs have to be changed in 37,000 stores all at the same time. That's Keyser's job: to make sure those signs are properly implemented all over the world, often on the same day. At the same time, Keyser works with McDonald's to test sign designs that help drive sales. Keyser, thanks to its work with McDonald's, has developed expertise in signage that few companies can claim, an expertise that others find valuable. McDonald's has also benefited with sales growth due to signage support. These two organizations have worked and grown together for decades.

Many salespeople are involved in both solo exchanges and functional relationships. Some customers buy once and are never heard from again. Others become loyal as long as everything goes smoothly. A few become friends, but strategic partnerships are rare. Exhibit 13.3 illustrates the differences in the nature of selling in market exchanges and long-term relationships.

Each type of relationship has its pluses and minuses. Companies cannot develop a strategic advantage from a market exchange, but they do get the flexibility to buy products from the supplier with the lowest cost when the order is placed. On the other hand, strategic partnerships create a win–win situation, but the companies are committed to each other and flexibility can be reduced. In the next section we talk about the characteristics of successful relationships—relationships that have the potential to develop into strategic partnerships.

thinking it through

Think about how you are treated when you walk into a clothing store. How much do you spend on average per month for clothing? How much would that be during your time in school? Does the store treat you on the basis of your value as a solo exchange? How would your treatment change if the store considered your lifetime value as a customer? What form of relationship would be needed for it to capture your CLV?

Exhibit 13.3
Selling in Market Exchanges and Long-Term Relationships

Market Exchange Selling Goal: Making a Sale	Long-Term Relationship Selling Goal: Building Trust

Making Contact
• Find someone to listen.
• Make small talk.
• Ingratiate and build rapport.
 	
Closing the Sale
• Deliver a sales pitch to
  • Get the prospect's attention.
  • Create interest.
  • Build desire.
  • Get the prospect to take action.
• Stay alert for closing signals.
• Use trial closes.
• Overcome objections.
• Close early and often.
 	
Following Through
• Reestablish contact.
• Resell self, company, and products.
	Initiating the Relationship
	• Engage in strategic prospecting and qualifying.
	• Gather and study precall information.
	• Identify buying influences.
	• Plan the initial sales call.
	• Demonstrate an understanding of the customer's needs.
	• Identify opportunities to build a relationship.
	• Illustrate the value of a relationship with the customer.
	
	Developing the Relationship
	• Select an appropriate offering.
	• Customize the relationship.
	• Link the solution to the customer's needs.
	• Discuss customer concerns.
	• Summarize the solution to confirm benefits.
	• Secure commitment.
	
	Enhancing the Relationship
	• Assess customer satisfaction.
	• Take actions to ensure satisfaction.
	• Maintain open, two-way communication.
	• Expand collaborative involvement.
	• Work to add value and enhance mutual opportunities.

Source: Adapted from Thomas Ingram, "Relationship Selling: Moving from Rhetoric to Reality," *Mid-American Journal of Business* 11 (1996), p. 6.

MANAGING RELATIONSHIPS AND PARTNERING

Salespeople are usually responsible for determining the appropriate form of relationship and for making sure that their companies develop the appropriate types of relationships with customers. In other words, some customers want and need, a market exchange, others need a functional relationship, and still others need a strategic partnership. As salespeople identify customer needs for product benefits, they also identify needs for relationship benefits and select the appropriate strategy as a result. Salespeople are likely to manage a portfolio of relationships, some of which may be strategic and others functional.[11] With some accounts, a strategic partnership may be called for. With others, it may be a relational partnership or functional relationship. The salesperson must determine which relationship type is appropriate for optimizing the customer's lifetime value.

CHOOSING THE RIGHT RELATIONSHIP

As you can see from the discussion about what makes for a strategic relationship, at least one factor that influences a salesperson's choice of relationship is the type of relationship the customer desires. Becoming a strategic partner requires investment by both parties, and if the customer isn't willing to make that investment, then another type of relationship is called for. Even then, not every customer who

Size matters! Most strategic partnerships involve larger customers like Saks 5th Avenue rather than O. F. Trump because their size makes the investment in the partnership worthwhile.

wants a strategic partnership should become your strategic partner. Some of the factors to consider are size of the account, access and image in the market, and access to technology.

Size

JCPenney has a strategic partnership with Martha Stewart. Would Martha Stewart have a similar partnership with Jordans, a single store? Probably not. The return could not be great enough to justify the investment. The thought is that by partnering with large accounts, the accounts invest in the supplier and become locked in. Economies of scale can often justify lower prices and higher investments. Size of the account, then, is one aspect to consider. But that doesn't mean that one should partner only with the largest accounts. In some cases larger accounts are not necessarily the most profitable, particularly when the seller's investments are factored in.[12] In other cases smaller accounts provide important benefits that larger accounts cannot, as we will discuss.

Access and Image

A strategic partnership may be called for if an account can provide access to a specific, desired market or can enhance the image of the seller. For example, SRI is a software company that has carefully selected initial customers in each market it serves. By first selling to customers with strong reputations, SRI is likely to gain other customers.

Access to Innovation

Some companies are called **lead users** because they face and resolve needs months or years ahead of the rest of the marketplace. These companies often develop innovations that the supplier can copy, either in the way it uses a product or by altering a product. Korcett, for example, needed to develop a site survey tool so that their technicians could more effectively manage inventory of Korcett equipment installed at customer locations. They teamed up with SRI (mentioned above) to develop a solution that SRI can then sell to other companies. Korcett, in this situation, was a lead user.

Note that one important function salespeople provide is the ability to listen to customers and deliver that knowledge back to the company so better products can be developed.[13] That function is important in new product development, but does not necessarily require deep relationships. What lead users provide is more than information; they provide the opportunity to co-create innovations that can then be converted into products. Note also that this contributes to the customer lifetime value of such customers.

Other lead users may develop innovations in other areas of the business, such as logistics, that suppliers can copy. For example, HEB is a grocery chain covering Texas and Mexico that has led the development of radio frequency identification (RFID), a technology used in logistics. Several suppliers such as Campbells have spent time with HEB logistics engineers to learn how RFID can make logistics more efficient. Astute salespeople can identify such companies and develop strategic partnerships that lead to joint development of new products or technologies—important outcomes regardless of the size of the account.

SALES Technology

CRM SOFTWARE: BOON OR BUST?

Would you take a class if you knew that more than half of the students failed it? Probably not. Yet 55 percent of CEOs and chief sales officers grade out their customer relationship management (CRM) software as a low F. So what's the problem?

Like most business situations, there isn't just one problem. Poor data entry by salespeople (often due to a poor data plan), a lack of understanding of how to use the data, and a separation of responsibilities between sales and marketing are three of the primary causes—but by no means all of the problems—according to a study by Baylor University sales professor Jeff Tanner. In spite of these challenges, many businesses are finding greater sales success by incorporating CRM technology into their sales processes.

Gallery Furniture, the leading furniture retailer in Houston, Texas, uses CRM to track shoppers after a visit. Gallery has learned that the belief that if a customer leaves without buying, the sale is lost forever is a myth. By using the CRM software to remind salespeople to follow up, more than 10 percent of all sales are made on the second or third visit.

Sales to consumers, though, are not the only situation where companies benefit from CRM. United Rentals, which rents commercial construction equipment to construction companies, used its CRM system to reestablish dormant accounts. The system directed salespeople to dormant accounts, which were then called. The program was so successful that the company found it needed to hire nine new salespeople just to handle the increased sales volume.

The challenge isn't the software; it's using CRM software properly. When used properly, relationships with customers can be maintained and strengthened, leading to stronger sales.

Sources: Anonymous, "Sales Lead Management Association Study Finds 64.9% of B2B Marketers Cannot Track ROI," *Marketing Weekly News*, March 6, 2010, p. 14; Jeff Tanner, "Data Strategies in B2B," Baylor University Center for Professional Selling, March 2012.

USING TECHNOLOGY TO INCREASE EFFICIENCY

Companies are using technology to drive two key areas of salesperson performance. The first is the use of technology to help salespeople manage all the information required to be effective, a type of **knowledge management technology.** Such knowledge management technology might include product catalogs and all the detailed specifications of those products, but knowledge management technology also includes customer records and transaction/service histories.

The second is relational management technology, which can build on customer knowledge management systems to create models that can be used to develop strategy. Some companies have struggled with such technologies, but "Sales Technology 13.1" shows how two companies have used such software to grow business.

Companies are also creating direct links with their customers and suppliers. Xerox and Baxter have developed electronic ordering mechanisms with their customers, and IBM uses private Web sites and Lotus Notes to enable suppliers to communicate with each other and with IBM buyers.

PHASES OF RELATIONSHIP DEVELOPMENT

Although not all relationships should become partnerships, strategic partnerships tend to go through several phases: (1) awareness, (2) exploration, (3) expansion, (4) commitment, and sometimes (5) dissolution.[14] Recent research indicates that the middle three stages are most important.[15] Cultural differences may alter the way buyers and sellers move through these phases, but strategic partnerships go through these stages in most situations.

AWARENESS

In the **awareness** stage it is likely that no transaction has taken place. During the awareness phase salespeople locate and qualify prospects, while buyers identify various sources of supply. Buyers may see a booth at a trade show, an ad in a magazine, or some other form of marketing communication and seek additional information. Reputation and image in the marketplace can be very important for sellers at this point. One important trend is toward **supplier relationship management (SRM),** which is the use of technology and statistics to identify important suppliers and opportunities for cost reduction, greater efficiency, and other benefits. Thus, awareness may result from analyzing current suppliers to identify those with whom a partnership may be possible.

Recognize, though, that relationships do not necessarily move from solo exchange to functional relationship to relational partnership to strategic partnership. Customers may actively seek partnerships for key areas of the firm's purchases, which may mean working to develop a strategic partnership with a new vendor. Or the relationship may develop over time and may involve one or more of the other forms of relationship. There is no requirement, however, that a partnership must start out as a solo exchange.

EXPLORATION

The **exploration** stage is a search and trial phase for both buyer and seller. Both parties may explore the potential benefits and costs of a partnership. At this point the buyer may make purchases, but these are likely in the form of market exchanges because neither side has committed to the relationship. Each purchase can be thought of as a test of the supplier's capability.

Satisfaction is key for the relationship to move beyond exploration. We focus on satisfaction in Chapter 14; however, several points about satisfaction should be understood in the context of relationships. First, keep in mind that both satisfaction with the salesperson and satisfaction with the company and its products and services influence the development of the relationship.[16] Such salesperson characteristics as dependability and competence are tested in the exploration phase and improve satisfaction. Second, buyers will object during the exploration phase to characteristics of the salesperson's offer. How those objections are handled (the topic of Chapter 10) is an important factor in successfully negotiating the exploration stage.[17]

EXPANSION

At this point the supplier has passed enough tests to be considered for additional business. The **expansion** stage involves efforts by both parties to investigate the benefits of a long-term relationship. The relationship can still devolve into a functional relationship rather than a strategic partnership, but the intention of both parties is to develop the appropriate type of relationship. The buyer's dependence on the seller as a primary source of supply grows and may lead to the purchase of additional products. Further, both sides begin to probe regarding interest in a partnership; such probing is both internal and external. Remember that the decision for a strategic partnership requires credible commitments, so many in the selling organization may need to review the opportunity.

COMMITMENT

In the **commitment** stage the customer and seller have implicitly or explicitly pledged to continue the relationship for a period of time. Commitment represents the most advanced stage of the relationship. Investments are made in the relationship, especially in the form of sharing proprietary information, plans, goals, and the like.

In Chapter 11 we discussed obtaining commitment as a stage in the sales process. In that sense we are talking about asking the buyer to make a decision—a decision either to buy the product or to take the next step in the decision process. The commitment stage in a relationship involves promises by both buyer and seller to work together over many transactions, not just a single decision.

DISSOLUTION

Dissolution can occur at any time in the relationship process, though it doesn't necessarily have to occur at all. Dissolution is the process of terminating the relationship and can occur because of poor performance, clash in culture, change in needs, and other factors. When dissolution occurs in latter stages of the relationship, the loss of investments made in the relationship can be significant and have an impact throughout both organizations.

CHARACTERISTICS OF SUCCESSFUL PARTNERSHIPS

Successful relationships involve cultivating mutual benefits as the partners learn to trust and depend on each other more and more. As trust develops, buyer and salesperson can resolve conflicts as they arise, settle differences, and compromise when necessary. Without trust there is no loyalty, and unhappy customers leave. While trust is important, other elements also characterize successful long-term relationships. The five foundational elements of strategic partnerships are (1) mutual trust, (2) open communication, (3) common goals, (4) commitment to mutual gain, and (5) organizational support (see Exhibit 13.4).

MUTUAL TRUST

The most important element in the development of successful long-term customer relationships is trust. **Trust** is a belief by one party that the other party will fulfill

Exhibit 13.4
Foundations of
Successful Relationships

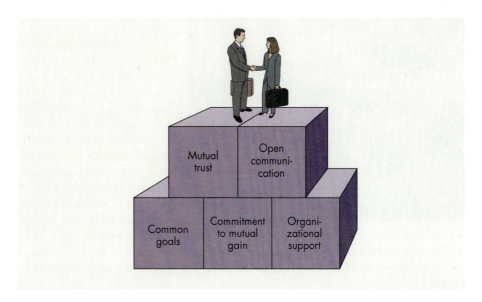

its obligations in a relationship. That trust has to be mutual, however. When salespeople and buyers trust each other, they are more willing to share relevant ideas, clarify goals and problems, and communicate more efficiently. Information shared between the parties becomes increasingly comprehensive, accurate, and timely. There is less need for salesperson and buyer to constantly monitor each other's actions because both believe the other party would not take advantage of them if given the opportunity.

Trust is an important building block for long-term relationships. A study of partnerships in both Latin America and Europe found trust to be the most important variable that contributes to the success of the relationship.[18] Trust is a combination of five factors: dependability, competence, customer orientation, honesty, and likability. In this section we discuss these factors and how salespeople demonstrate their own trustworthiness.

Dependability

Dependability, the buyer's perception that the salesperson, and the product and company he or she represents, will live up to promises made, is not something a salesperson can demonstrate immediately. Promises must be made and then kept. Early in the selling process, a salesperson can demonstrate dependability by calling at times agreed to, showing up a few minutes early for appointments, and providing information as promised.

Third-party references can be useful in proving dependability, especially if the salesperson has not yet had an opportunity to prove it personally. If the seller can point to a similar situation and illustrate, through the words of another customer, how the situation was resolved, the buyer can verify the seller's dependability. Some companies also prepare case studies of how they solved a particular customer's problem to aid salespeople in proving the company's dependability.

Product demonstrations, plant tours, and other special types of presentations can also illustrate dependability. A product demonstration can show how the product will work, even under difficult conditions. A buyer for appliance component parts was concerned about one company's ability to produce the large volumes required. The salesperson offered a plant tour to prove that the company could live up to its promises of on-time delivery. When the buyer saw the size of the plant and the employees' dedication to making quality products, she was convinced.

The salesperson's prior experience and training can also be used to prove dependability. For a company (and a salesperson) to remain in business, there must be some level of dependability. Length of experience, however, is a weak substitute for proving dependability with action.

As time goes on and the relationship grows, the buyer assumes dependability. For example, a buyer may say, "Well, let's call Sue at Mega. We know we can depend on her." At this point the salesperson has developed a reputation within the account as dependable. But reputations can spread beyond that account through the buyer's community. A reputation for dependability, however, can be quickly lost if the salesperson fails to continue to deliver as promised.

A tour of the manufacturing facility can be a sales tool to show dependability, as well as give prospective customers an opportunity to meet key manufacturing personnel.

Competence

Salespeople demonstrate **competence** when they can show that they know what they are talking about. Knowledge of the customer, the product, the industry, and the competition are all necessary to the success of the salesperson; in fact, recent research suggests that competence is a key component in developing trust.[19] Through the use of this knowledge, a salesperson demonstrates competence. For example, when a pharmaceutical representative can discuss the treatment of a disease in medical terms, the physician is more likely to believe that the rep is medically competent.

ethics

Salespeople recognize the need to appear competent. Unfortunately their recognition of the importance of competence may lead them to try to fake knowledge. Because buyers test the trustworthiness of a seller early in the relationship, they may ask questions just to see the salesperson's response. Salespeople should never make up a response to a tough question; if you don't know, say so but promise to get the answer quickly and then do it. At the same time, salespeople should try to present information objectively. Buyers can tell when salespeople are exaggerating the performance of their products.

Product knowledge is the minimum; customers expect salespeople to know everything about their own products and their company. That's why company training is so important. Johnson and Johnson's Vistakon division, which serves the contact lens market, provides eight weeks of training to new salespeople as you can see in Exhibit 13.5. One-fourth of that training is devoted to products, but a significant amount of additional training covers competitors, customers, and other market factors that salespeople need to know to be competent members of the industry. In addition to product competence, though, selling competence is also important. Much of the training focuses on increasing salespersons' selling competence so they can deliver the appropriate solutions to meet customers' needs. The result is a highly competent sales force that works in partnership with customers, helping them to run their businesses more successfully.[20]

Customer Orientation

Customer orientation is the degree to which the salesperson puts the customer's needs first. Salespeople who think only of making sales are sales oriented rather than customer oriented. Buyers perceive salespeople as customer oriented when sellers stress benefits and solutions to problems over features. Buyers who perceive that a product is tailored to their unique requirements are likely to infer a customer orientation. Stating pros and cons can also be perceived as being

Exhibit 13.5
Vistakon New Hire Training and Development

- On-boarding: 4 weeks
  - Week 1: District manager orientation and home study.
  - Week 2: Work with peer coach and home study.
  - Week 3: Work with field sales trainer in trainer's territory.
  - Week 4: Attend preceptorship and work with district manager to get certification.
- Primary sales school
  - Weeks 5 and 6: Attend primary sales school.
- Sales development
  - Week 7: Work with district manager in own territory.
  - Week 8: Field sales trainer works with rep in the rep's territory.
- Advanced sales development seminar
  - 2 weeks.

customer oriented because understanding the cons also indicates that the salesperson understands the buyer's needs.

Emphasizing the salesperson's availability and desire to provide service also indicates a customer orientation. For example, the statement "Call me anytime for anything that you need" indicates availability. Offering the numbers for toll-free hotlines, voice mail, and similar concrete information indicates a desire to respond promptly to the buyer and can serve as proof of a customer orientation. Christina Harrod's customers, for example, have her cell number and expect to be able to call her whenever there is an issue.

Several studies show that customer orientation is vital to achieving sales performance and customer satisfaction. One survey of salespeople showed customer orientation as a critical variable in predicting sales success;[21] similarly, several studies of buyers found that buyers are more loyal and more willing to tell others when their salesperson is customer oriented.[22]

Honesty

Honesty is both truthfulness and sincerity. While honesty is highly related to dependability ("We can count on you and your word because you are honest"), it is also related to how candid a salesperson is. For example, giving pros and cons can increase perceptions of honesty as well as a customer orientation.

Honesty is also related to competence. As we said earlier, salespeople must be willing to admit that they do not know something rather than trying to fake it; buyers consider salespeople who bluff to be dishonest.

The opposite, of course, is lying. Buyers figure out pretty quickly when they've been lied to; one salesperson lied to his customer about the expected response to the marketing program he sold. When it failed, not only did the customer refuse to purchase again, but he threatened to blow up the salesperson's house![23] Although not every customer who has been lied to will threaten physical harm, without honesty, a customer cannot trust a salesperson. In "From the Buyer's Seat 13.1," one purchasing professional says that even phony insincerity raises concerns about a salesperson's honesty. As discussed in Chapter 2, lying will not just cost a salesperson business in the short term; the long-term damage can be quite serious to the success of the business and may bring on lawsuits or criminal charges.

Likability

According to research, likability may be the least important component of trust because most people can be nice, although in some countries other than the United States, likability is much more important.[24] Likability refers to behaving in a friendly manner and finding a common ground between buyer and seller. Although likability is not as important as other dimensions, salespeople should still attempt to find a common ground or interest with all buyers. Buyers resent any attempts, though, of insincere rapport building. Do not feign interest if you truly aren't interested.

Likability can also be influenced with personal communications such as birthday cards, handwritten notes, and so forth. Many businesses send holiday cards and gifts to all customers, but personal touches make these gestures meaningful.

As you have probably noticed, the five dimensions of trust are tightly interrelated. Honesty affects customer orientation, which also influences dependability, for example. Salespeople should recognize the interdependence among these factors rather than simply focusing on one or two. For example, at one time many salespeople emphasized only likability. In today's market, professional salespeople must also be competent, dependable, honest, and customer oriented.

ethics

From the BUYER'S SEAT

THE PHONY REP PROBLEM

"Spend the first few minutes chatting about something personal—a picture, a trophy, anything, just show you're interested in what they're interested." That's the old-school way of selling. Today's buyers are skeptical of salespeople to begin with, and in today's time-starved business world, they mistrust these insincere efforts at creating a relationship.

Ed Braig, purchasing director for Central Texas Iron Works, says this about the practice: "You are not my best friend. We do not share a common bond the day you notice I have a deer mount on my wall or you see I drink coffee from an A&M mug. In fact, the deer could have been left here by my predecessor and the coffee mug handed me by the salesperson who just walked out as you walked in. It may not even be my office!"

Ed goes on to say, "My motto is make friends out of suppliers, not suppliers out of friends." His point is that you first have to earn his business and prove your worth. Then, and only then, is a friendship possible.

"Learn what my company does before you call. Learn my industry before you walk in. I love my job and am proud of my business, but I am not in this world to explain to you what it is that we do," he says. With the Internet making so many sources available, the salesperson who relies on a questioning technique instead of adequate precall planning to learn about Ed's company is immediately in trouble. "I actually enjoy and remember salespeople who take the time and effort to know me and what I do."

As Ed says, "Never, ever lie! Lie once to me, and that's it. And that starts with being phony with sincerity."

OPEN COMMUNICATION

Open and honest communication is a key building block for developing successful relationships. Buyers and salespeople in a relationship need to understand what is driving each other's business, their roles in the relationship, each firm's strategies, and any problems that arise over the course of the relationship. (Chapter 4 focuses on approaches for improving communication.) Such understanding comes through listening carefully to buyers. In fact, research shows that listening is important for building both trust and customer satisfaction.[25]

Open communication should lead to stronger relationships, though Suzanne Morgan, president of Print Buyers Online (a buying group for commercial printers), worries that concern for the other party may make customers reluctant to share their opinions when something goes wrong. Buyers, perhaps more so than sellers, may worry about hurting the salesperson's feelings and thus not be as open as the situation requires. She recommends, as does David Dennis of SBC Advertising, that salespeople make it as easy as possible for the buyer to speak up.[26]

One difference between a relational partnership and a strategic partnership is the strength and number of lines of communication. In a relational partnership, most communication between the buyer and the selling organization goes through the salesperson. In a strategic partnership, there will be more direct communication ties between the buying organization and the selling organization. For example, the selling company's shipping department may talk directly with the buying organization's receiving department when a problem arises with a shipment.

Cultural differences in communication style can be easily misunderstood and thus hinder open and honest communication. For example, all cultures have ways to avoid saying no when they really mean no. In Japan maintaining long-lasting, stable relationships is very important. To avoid damaging a relationship, customers rarely say no directly. Some phrases used in Japan to say no indirectly are "It's very difficult," "We'll think about it," and "I'm not sure"; alternatively, customers may leave the room with an apology. In general, when Japanese customers do not say yes or no directly, it means they want to say no.

COMMON GOALS

Salespeople and customers must have common goals for a successful relationship to develop. Shared goals give both members of the relationship a strong incentive to pool their strengths and abilities. When goals are shared, the partners can focus on exploiting opportunities rather than arguing about who will benefit the most from the relationship.

Shirley Hunter is an account executive for Teradata (a division of NCR) and has only one account, CapGemini. Her primary job is to help CapGemini sell Teradata as a part of the solutions CapGemini offers its clients. Hunter spends most of her time coordinating the efforts of Teradata and CapGemini salespeople selling to end users, but it is important that she understands CapGemini's goals and that she makes sure that everyone in Teradata understands and shares those goals.

Shared goals also help sustain the partnership when the expected benefit flows are not realized. If one Teradata shipment fails to reach an CapGemini customer on time because of an uncontrollable event, such as misrouting by a trucking firm, CapGemini will not suddenly call off the whole arrangement. Instead CapGemini is likely to view the incident as a simple mistake and will remain in the relationship. CapGemini knows that it and Teradata are committed to the same goal in the long run.

Clearly defined, measurable goals are also very important. Hunter has a sales budget she has to meet, but more important, the two organizations set joint goals such as sales revenue, on-time delivery, service response time, and others. Performance is assessed monthly to determine if these goals are being met so the two organizations can work together to rectify any problems quickly.

Effective measuring of performance is particularly critical in the early stages of the partnership. The achievement of explicitly stated goals lays the groundwork for a history of shared success, which serves as a powerful motivation for continuing the relationship and working closely together into the future.

COMMITMENT TO MUTUAL GAIN

Members of successful partnerships actively work to create win–win relationships by making commitments to the relationship. For example, SRI provides scanning services to GRM, one of the largest box storage companies in the world. GRM then sells these services to its customers. SRI arranged free sales training for the GRM salespeople. While this training would increase sales of all of GRM's services, SRI also knew that more scanning services would get sold, too.

In a partnership, commitment to mutual gain means that one does not take advantage of the other. One party is always more powerful than the other party, but in a partnership, it does not exercise that power over the other. Mutual dependence creates a cooperative spirit. Both parties search for ways to expand the pie and minimize time spent on resolving conflicts over how to split it.

Mutual Investment

As a successful relationship develops, both parties make investments in the relationship. **Mutual investments are tangible investments in the relationship by both parties.** They go beyond merely making the hollow statement "I want to be a partner." Mutual investment may involve spending money to improve the products and services sold to the other party, though research says that sellers tend to invest more in relationships than buyers.[27] For example, a firm may hire or train employees, invest in equipment, and develop computer and communication systems to meet the needs of a specific customer. These investments signal the partner's commitment to the relationship in the long run and are important to securing loyalty.[28]

Thus, it is not enough to say that you are committed to the relationship; actions of commitment must follow to signal that the commitment is real. These actions make the commitment believable. Mutual investments are also called **relationship-specific assets**; in other words, these are resources specific to the relationship and cannot be easily transferred to another relationship.

ORGANIZATIONAL SUPPORT

Another critical element in fostering good relationships is giving **boundary-spanning employees**—those employees who cross the organizational boundary and interact with customers or vendors—the necessary support. Some areas of support are training, rewards that support partnering behavior, and structure and culture. We start with structure and culture because these elements foster the others.

Structure and Culture

The organizational structure and management provide the necessary support for the salespeople and buyers in a partnering relationship. All employees in the firm need to "buy in"—in other words, accept the salesperson's and buyer's roles in developing the partnership. Partnerships created at headquarters should be recognized and treated as such by local offices, and vice versa. Without the support of the respective companies, the partnership is destined to fail.

The issue isn't just creating a culture among salespeople, however. The entire firm must have an orientation to building partnerships. Recall that strategic partnerships are characterized by direct, open communication between multiple members of both firms. If those nonselling members of the selling firm do not have a customer orientation, then the partnership may be doomed.

Training

Special training is required to sell effectively in a relationship-building environment. Salespeople need to be taught how to identify customer needs and work with customers to achieve better performance.

Steve Trerotola, of Alfa Color Imaging Inc., constantly trains his salespeople in relationship skills, needs identification skills, and other sales skills. In fact, he regularly puts salespeople in situations where he knows customers might need services the company can't offer and then waits to see if the rep overpromises or exaggerates company capabilities. These opportunities are used to train the rep how to respond in ways that improve, not damage, the relationship.[29]

Training is vital in helping salespeople identify ways to make it easier for customers to do business with them. At Alcoa Aluminum sales representatives are trained to look at what their customers do to a product that Alcoa could make for them. For example, one salesperson noticed that customers stack materials in skids in various size stacks, sometimes 10 feet tall. When an order is pulled from inventory, a forklift driver must go into the stacks and pull a particular skid. Sometimes the skids are not stacked with a packing ticket on the outside, so the driver has a hard time identifying the right skid. Alcoa began to put packing tickets on both ends of skids so drivers can always see the package numbers, no matter how the skids are stacked.

Rewards

Reward systems on both sides of the relationship should be coordinated to encourage supportive behaviors. In market exchanges buyers are rewarded for wringing out concessions from the salespeople, and salespeople are rewarded on the basis of sales volume. In a partnering relationship, rewarding short-term behaviors can be detrimental. For example, recent research regarding sales contests indicates that these short-term compensation events lead to short-term behaviors, such as getting sales at the expense of relationships.[30]

SELLING YOURSELF

Relationships are important in every area of life. As your faculty can tell you, some students want a transactional relationship (just come to class and get the grade) while others want a deeper relationship. If you use the Selling Partners mentor group on LinkedIn, you'll meet many sales professionals, many of whom are former students of instructors who use this book. These sales professionals developed deeper relationships with their sales instructors.

Faculty, though, are like customers in the sense that not all faculty want to develop deeper relationships with students. When they do want deeper relationships, it is likely to be with students who show an interest in the class and who are worthy of the professor's trust. That means students who are dependable, competent, honest, and likable. A professor with a deeper relationship will understand your job interests more completely, putting you in line for positions not directly available, providing access to job markets in the same way a customer may provide a salesperson with access to markets. While the concepts of this chapter are derived directly from research into business relationships, you can see how these concepts can apply now in your relationships with others.

SUMMARY

As we discussed in Chapter 1, many businesses are moving toward partnering strategies. A key premise is that long-term relationships can enable sellers to capture much, if not all, of a customer's lifetime value. Loyal buyers buy more and are willing to work more closely with sellers in mutually beneficial ways. However, most transactions between buyers and sellers will not be strategic partnerships. Many exchanges will continue to be market transactions and functional relationships.

Functional relationships and strategic partnerships are characterized by a mutual concern of each party for the long-run welfare of the other party. Both types of long-term relationships are based on mutual trust. However, strategic partnerships involve the greatest commitment because the parties are willing to make significant investments in the relationship.

Mutual trust, open communication, common goals, a commitment to mutual gain, and organizational support are key ingredients in successful relationships. These five factors form the foundation for win–win relationships between customers and salespeople.

Customers trust salespeople who are dependable, capable, and concerned about the customers' welfare. To build trust, salespeople need to be consistent in meeting the commitments they make to customers. Salespeople also need to demonstrate their concern for the well-being of customers.

KEY TERMS

ETHICS PROBLEMS

1. If partnerships are win–win, does that mean that market exchanges are win–lose? Is there an ethical difference between win–win and win–lose? Does the customer's value equation [recall from Chapter 1 that Value = Benefits − (Selling price + Time and effort)] have to be equal in profit to the seller's profit equation for a transaction to be ethical?

2. A customer is loyal to one of your competitors, but the contract is expiring soon. A request for proposals (RFP) has been written and issued; but the way it is written, only that competitor can win the contract renewal. You know that your product and service could satisfy the needs of the company better. Is there an ethics problem here? If so, what is it and why? If not, why not?

QUESTIONS AND PROBLEMS

1. When might relational partnerships become potentially dangerous for selling companies? Or should companies encourage salespeople to develop relational partnerships with all accounts? Why or why not?

2. Which is more important to the seller: attitudinal or behavioral loyalty? Why? What can a salesperson do to increase loyalty in buyers? How does loyalty relate to customer lifetime value?

3. Read "From the Buyer's Seat 13.1." Do you think most business buyers have a similar motto? Contrast Braig's perspective with the JC Penney quote in the text that all great business relationships are based on friendships. Who is right and why? Why is understanding this question of friendship/relationship important to

salespeople? What is the importance of precall planning to building relationships?

4. What company does the best job of building a relationship with you? Describe what they do to strengthen that relationship and why you like them so much. Identify five concepts from the chapter that are illustrated by your relationship with that company.

5. Which factors should a salesperson consider when deciding the type of relationship formed with a customer? How would these factors change when considering functional relationships versus strategic partnerships? What factors should the customer consider?

6. How do buyers calculate profit, or value? What is the role of the relationship type in increasing

buyer profit? What role does satisfaction play in calculating profit?

7. Christina Harrod, in the opening profile, describes several factors in her business that seem to make deeper relationships between customers and vendors more important. What are they?

8. Read "Sales Technology 13.1." In both examples, you could argue that the salespeople should be doing those activities without the software.

So why is the software needed, and what other things could be done to increase sales and strengthen relationships with the information that these salespeople gather and put into the CRM software system?

9. There are five foundational elements to strategic partnerships. How do these differ for relational partnerships? Functional relationships? What if four of the five are strong—what type of relationship is that?

CASE PROBLEMS

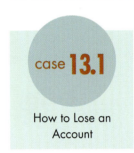

case **13.1**

How to Lose an Account

Robert Lawrence was aghast. Despite practicing the sales call four times, despite being told before the sales call exactly what to say when the question arose, and despite being directed by the account manager how to respond while in the sales call, the regional director of service still blew it—and away walked a $5.5 million customer.

Robert, branch manager for Mobile Connections, knew that the customer, Health Resources of Texas (HRT), was having problems with two of the copiers provided by Mobile. Further, these were reoccurring problems that should be resolved by replacing the equipment. To make matters worse, one of the problem copiers was used by Sharon Collins, one of the decision makers. He knew that Sharon was going to raise the issue of how Mobile would handle "lemons" and whether Mobile would honor its replacement promise. The service director was also aware of the problems but had not processed the request to replace them yet, so he didn't know with certainty whether the free replacement copiers would be approved. But Robert had rehearsed with Tony Lagera, the service director, to say that the company was reviewing the request and the copiers would either be replaced in the week or shifted to areas with less volume.

Sharon raised the question, just as Robert expected. And Tony flubbed it. He hemmed. He hawed. He did everything but answer the question directly. Unfortunately Robert couldn't just answer for Tony—the service area was Tony's responsibility, not Robert's. Robert and the account manager sat in stunned silence.

After the call, Robert asked, "So, Tony, how do you think it went?"

"Fine, Robert!" he replied with a smile. "You were right on target about Sharon's question."

"And you think you handled it?"

"Oh yes—I think she really liked my response!"

Robert didn't respond, though he thought about asking Tony why she repeated the question four times. Two weeks later, Robert got a copy of the letter that went to his salesperson, thanking Mobile for the presentation but informing them that Mobile would not be allowed to bid on the job. After serving HRT for three years without any hitch other than those two machines (and there were over 100 machines), Mobile wasn't even going to get a chance to bid.

Questions

1. Things had gone well with this account overall. What, though, were the critical issues in determining the customer's satisfaction that led to the loss of the customer? Was the problem simply a lack of satisfaction with the product? Using concepts from the chapter, describe how the customer's value

equation was influenced by the experiences both before the call and during the call. Consider, too, the role that the buying center makeup played in the situation.

2. Was there anything the sales rep or his boss, Robert Lawrence, could have done after the sales call to save the business?

3. Not only were there no other problems during the previous three-year contract, but Mobile had originally won the business away from a competitor and significantly improved HRT's situation. Why didn't those results enter the picture?

Source: This really happened, but the names have been changed to protect privacy. Used with permission.

case **13.2**

Southwest Tools

Southwest Tools is a manufacturer of specialized tools used in the drilling and maintenance of oil wells. The company has about 10 percent of a highly competitive market in which no other competitor has more than 12 percent. There are three other companies that specialize in oil field tools, along with hundreds of others that offer general purpose tools and a handful of oil field tools.

Marjorie Roberts, chief marketing officer, was contemplating how to increase sales in such a crowded market. The data suggested that 5 percent of all customers were responsible for 62 percent of the company's sales, but, more important, she saw that one customer, Prufrock Drilling, hadn't purchased anything in more than a year. When that was her old account back when she was a salesperson, it was a midsize account but growing. She decided to give them a call.

"Jack, I'm so delighted to find you're still with Prufrock," she said, as Jack Henderson answered his phone. "We've not talked since, what, that trade show in Houston three years ago?"

"Marjorie, great to hear from you," he replied. "What's up? I've not heard from your company in a couple of years!"

Marjorie was shocked. As they talked, she realized that, when her replacement left the company, a new rep had taken over the account but had never called on them. Curious as to the story on other dormant accounts, she called a few more. In every case, they gave the reason for switching as the new company salesperson called on them, but no one from Southwest had.

She took the findings from her short survey to Mark Linus, head of sales, and explained what she had found. "I'm not surprised," he said. "You have to make some choices on who you call. What I'm encouraging my reps to do is to find another account like one in that top 5 percent—that's where our real growth is."

Questions

1. Which group would you focus on—finding another account for the top 5 percent or reviving midlevel accounts that are dormant?

2. Assume that Southwest's CEO has said, "Do both." What is marketing's role in helping salespeople find and grow very large accounts? In reviving dormant accounts? Specifically describe what actions you would take in each segment. How can salespeople support the dormant account revival strategy without giving up on growing the very large accounts? What other options should be explored?

ROLE PLAY CASE

As with other role plays, you are a salesperson for Netsuite software. For additional information about Netsuite, you may want to review the information in the Netsuite role play at the end of Chapter 1; additional information can also be found at the end of the text and on the Web at www.netsuite.com.

Cor-Plus is a manufacturer and distributor of packing materials, such as corrugated boxes, custom plastic packaging, bottles (both plastic and glass), and other products. They have 24 salespeople who call on distributors who then sell to manufacturers who package their products in the Cor-Plus products. There are two sales managers and one national sales vice president.

Seller: You are calling on the national sales vice president, and you would like to understand that person's interest in relationship type. Take a few minutes and prepare some questions that you think will help you determine which relationship will be appropriate. After you are finished, tell the buyer what relationship type (choose only one) you thought you were dealing with and why. See if you were right!

Buyer: As you role-play the buyer, pick one of the relationship types. Before the role play starts, think about how you would answer the questions you developed. Also consider what your expectations would be in terms of after-sale service, pricing, and the like based on the relationship type you select.

Note: There is no additional information provided in the Instructor's Manual for this assignment. However, teaching notes are provided.

ADDITIONAL REFERENCES

Aeron, Harsha, Ashwani Kumar, and Janakiraman Moorthy. "Data Mining Framework for Customer Lifetime Value-Based Segmentation." *Journal of Database Marketing and Customer Strategy Management* 19, no. 1 (March 2012), pp. 17–30.

Babu, K. Sharath, and B. Raj Kumar. "Customer Service Management—Turning Customer Loyalty into Profitability." *Synergy* 8, no. 2 (July 2010), pp. 93–98.

Cui, A., R. Calantone, and D. Griffith. "Strategic Change and Termination of Interfirm Partnerships." *Strategic Management Journal* 32, no. 4 (2010), pp. 402–23.

Evanschitzky, Heiner, Arun Sharma, and Prykop Catja. "The Role of the Sales Employee in Securing Customer Satisfaction." *European Journal of Marketing* 46, no. 3/4 (2012), pp. 489–508.

Guenzi, Paol, and Laurent Georges. "Interpersonal Trust in Commercial Relationships: Antecedents and Consequences of Customer Trust in the Salesperson." *European Journal of Marketing* 44, no. 1/2 (2010), pp. 114–38.

Holm, Morten, V. Kumar, and Carsten Rohde. "Measuring Customer Profitability in Complex Environments: An Interdisciplinary Contingency Framework." *Academy of Marketing Science Journal* 40, no. 3 (May 2012), pp. 387–401.

Homburg, Christian, Michael Müller, and Martin Klarmann. "When Does Salespeople's Customer Orientation Lead to Customer Loyalty? The Differential Effects of Relational and Functional Customer Orientation." *Academy of Marketing Science Journal* 39, no. 6 (December 2011), pp. 795–812.

Kilic, Ceyhan, and Turkan Dursun. "The Effect of Organizational Culture on Customer Orientation." *Journal of the Academy of Business* 15, no. 2 (2010), pp. 1–7.

Musalem, Andrés, and Yogesh V. Joshi. "How Much Should You Invest in Each Customer Relationship? A Competitive Strategic Approach." *Marketing Science* 28, no. 3 (May/June 2009), pp. 555–67.

Palmatier, Robert W., Lisa K. Scheer, Jan-Benedict, and E. M. Steenkamp. "Customer Loyalty to Whom? Managing the Benefits and Risks of Salesperson-Owned Loyalty." *Journal of Marketing* 44, no. 2 (2007), pp. 185–99.

Priyanko Guchait, Karthik Namasivayam, and Lei Pui-Wa. "Knowledge Management in Service Encounters: Impact on Customers' Satisfaction Evaluations." *Journal of Knowledge Management* 15, no. 3 (2011), pp. 513–27.

Schwepker, Charles H., and David J. Good. "Moral Judgment and Its Impact on Business-to-Business Sales Performance and Customer Relationships." *Journal of Business Ethics* 98, no. 4 (February 2011), pp. 609–25.

Storbacka, K., L. Ryals, I. Davies, and S. Nenonen. "The Changing Role of Sales: Viewing Sales as a Strategic, Cross-Functional Process." *European Journal of Marketing* 43, no. 7/8 (2009), pp. 890–906.

Van Triest, Sander, Maurice J. G. Bun, Erik M. van Raaij, and Maarten J. A. Vernooij. "The Impact of Customer-Specific Marketing Expenses on Customer Retention and Customer Profitability." *Marketing Letters* 20, no. 2 (June 2009), pp. 125–38.

chapter 14

BUILDING LONG-TERM PARTNERSHIPS

SOME QUESTIONS ANSWERED IN THIS CHAPTER ARE

- How important is service after the sale?
- How should salespeople stay in contact with customers?
- Which sales strategies stimulate repeat sales and new business in current accounts?
- Which techniques are important to use when handling complaints?

PROFILE

PROFILE Good customer service is not just something you do after the sale to keep people happy—it's a sound sales strategy. In my case, delivering good customer service is how I built my territory into one of the leading sales markets for Concentra Urgent Care.

I graduated with a double major in entrepreneurship and real estate about two years ago. I also ran my own sales business, tearing down old barns and selling the wood while I was in college. This experience had me thinking that I wanted to start in a small business with an eye to eventually running my own firm. That's why I joined a start-up company based out of Atlanta that was trying to expand into Texas and the surrounding states. My time with them was a great learning experience, but when they struggled to pay the bills and me, it was time to do something else.

Through a professor at school, I learned about the position at Concentra, and I've been with the company for about a year. We provide occupational health care services, ranging from drug tests and employment physicals to physical therapy and injury care, for companies and their employees. Like most companies, Concentra wants to grow and has plans to grow the number of clinics substantially over the next few years. That growth was one reason why I joined because I knew there would be opportunity to grow my career.

But when I took over my territory, I quickly realized there were few *new* customers to be had. At the same time, though, the clinic was underperforming—sales had declined significantly over the past few years. For me to be successful, I had to find out where the greatest leakage was and turn it around, that is, which accounts had reduced the most in how much business they gave us. These current but shrinking accounts became my prospecting list. This strategy ran contrary to the company strategy of growth through new customers, but I knew that's where the biggest opportunity lay.

Service was the primary reason we were losing business. In fact, we're really a service business, so we have no choice but to deliver good service. For my accounts, though, service starts with me. When they realized they could count on me to follow up and do what I said I'd do, we began getting opportunities to win their business back. For example, it took nearly a year just to get in the door of one midsize account. In the course of talking with them before actually meeting them, I discovered that some of the prices my competitor was charging were as much as 30 percent less. Price, though, wasn't the issue—service was. When I finally got an appointment, I began by saying, "I can't touch some of the prices you are paying, but I can address your needs for better service." And, since I brought several staff members who actually deliver services with me, the client could see we were serious about it. In spite of our higher prices, our commitment to outstanding service won us the account back.

Our stronger reputation for patient satisfaction then enabled me to get into the large accounts where we never had the business. But my ability to serve my clients isn't just about the experience their employees have when they visit our clinic. My company also backed me up with research that I can use to prove to my clients how they can cut worker injuries with us and help them build a safer workplace. I work with my clients on a regular basis to review their injury and other occupational health history so that we can find ways to reduce health care expenses and improve the health of their employees. This type of service is unmatched in the industry. Knowing that I am improving the quality of life for workers in my area while helping their companies succeed motivates me to make sure I deliver the best service possible.

Visit our Web site at:
www.concentra.com

Exhibit 14.1
Stages of Partnerships

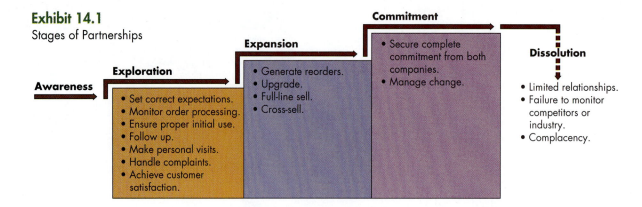

As we discussed in the previous chapter, relationships go through several stages, beginning with awareness and ending in dissolution. In this chapter we focus on the three stages between awareness and dissolution—exploration, expansion, and commitment—as illustrated in Exhibit 14.1. From the Buyer's Seat 14.1 describes how important customer experiences are in building a partnership. As you read the rest of the chapter, you will see how trust is built and maintained throughout the life of the partnership.

EXPLORATION

In the exploration stage, the relationship is defined through the development of expectations for each party. The buyer tests the seller's product, how the seller responds to requests, and other similar actions after the initial sale is made. A small percentage of the buyer's business is given to minimize the risk in case the vendor cannot perform. When the vendor performs well, trust is developed, as is a personal relationship.

Beginning the relationship properly is important if the relationship is going to last a long time. Keep in mind that the customer is excited about receiving the benefits of the product as promised by the salesperson. An unfavorable initial experience with the product or with the company may be extremely difficult to overcome. Beginning the relationship properly requires that the salesperson set the right expectations, monitor order processing, ensure proper use of the product, and assist in servicing the product.

SET THE RIGHT EXPECTATIONS

The best way to begin a relationship is for each party to be aware of what the other expects. To a large degree, customers base their expectations on sales presentations.

Salespeople should make sure customers have reasonable expectations of product performance. If the salesperson exaggerates the capabilities of the product or the company, the customer will be disappointed. Admitting there has been a misunderstanding will not satisfy a customer who has registered a complaint. Avoiding complaints by setting proper expectations is best. Long-term relationships are begun by making an honest presentation of the product's capabilities and eliminating any misconceptions before the order is placed.

MONITOR ORDER PROCESSING

Although many people may work on an order before it is shipped, the salesperson is ultimately responsible, at least in the eyes of the customer, for seeing that the product is shipped when promised. Salespeople should keep track of impending

From the BUYER'S SEAT

BENCHMARKING

Quick—who has served you in a way that really went way beyond your expectations? Some will say Nordstrom's, others might mention a hotel experience or an evening at a restaurant. Whatever that wonderful consumer experience was, you just had a reset experience—an experience that reset the standard for what you consider excellence in service.

Steve Hinsch, fleet management superintendent for the Clarke County government in Georgia, has a pretty high standard for after-sale service. He says, "Service after the sale (along with my other points of criteria, quality of product and price) is essential. Sometimes references don't really pan out to an acceptable level because we stay in heavy pursuit of service after the sale. The quickest way to our blacklist is to become readily unavailable postsale."

Hinsch goes on to say, "I have one specific tire vendor that has provided retreads and new tires to us for 20-plus years. This man knows how serious I am about being frugal with taxpayer dollars and appreciates it as a local citizen. He knows that there are many vendors in this field that court our business, so he remains highly competitive. He comes to our shop once a week, and if he will be unavailable for any reason, he gives us notice of an alternate contact." This high level of service is now the minimum that Steve expects—from all important vendors.

Kenneth Young, CEO of Tymco, a manufacturer of street sweepers, agrees that a reset occurs. "When you see a salesperson really do things right, you realize what you could and should expect from others—even if that salesperson is someone you deal with in your personal life and not at business."

That new standard holds across all settings. "When a salesperson goes above and beyond what you expect, you start to expect that from everyone. I realize not everyone can be a service superstar—but that's now the standard I hold my salespeople to and hope for the same from all of our vendors," says Young.

For salespeople, this benchmarking against the best means that you're not just compared to your competitors; you are also compared to all of the salespeople your customer works with now and has ever worked with in the past. Young agrees with Hinsch: "Standards are high, but service is how you earn the right to have my business now and into the future."

---

orders and inform buyers when the paperwork is delayed in the customer's plant. Orders placed directly with a salesperson should be transmitted to the factory immediately. Also, progress on orders in process should be closely monitored. If problems arise in filling the order, the customer should be informed promptly; on the other hand, if the order can be filled sooner than promised, the customer should be notified so the proper arrangements can be made.

Fortunately computers have made the sales representative's job easier. Salespeople can use handheld terminals and notebook PCs to check inventory and order status. Progressive firms have introduced automated order systems that allow the customer to sign a pad on the computer; the signature is sent to the company electronically, avoiding delays that might result if the contract were mailed.

Many firms, such as GE and Baxter Healthcare, facilitate the automatic placement of orders by having their own computers talk to customers' computers. This technology, called **electronic data interchange,** boosts the productivity of both the salespeople and the purchasing managers they call on. As a result, salespeople spend less time writing orders and more time solving problems; buyers save on ordering and inventory costs. Computerized com munication for order placement is particularly useful when managing a customer's needs worldwide. Problems arising from elements such as time zones and language barriers are minimized.

Monitoring order processing and other after-sale activities is critical to developing a partnership. Studies continually show that buyers are most often displeased with salespeople in this respect. Rossignol, the French ski and snowboard company, uses its CRM system to monitor order processing, ski shop inventories, and other data so salespeople can provide better after-sale service. Because skiing is a seasonal activity, sales are seasonal too. The company takes orders six months before shipping in order to plan ahead for the ski sale season, which is the early part of winter. But stores don't pay for the skis and snowboards until six months after shipping, or when orders are taken for the next year. Although it sounds like there is a lot of time to make sure things go smoothly, what is ordered for next year is a function of what is sold this year. The CRM system helps salespeople stay on top of how well their customers are doing in selling current inventory, so they can help sell that inventory out and make room for more. Thus, the partnership is created by helping both parties achieve their goals.[1]

This salesperson is training the customer in how to use the product properly. Getting customers off to the right start is essential to building long and satisfying relationships.

ENSURE PROPER INITIAL USE OF THE PRODUCT OR SERVICE

Customer dissatisfaction can occur just after delivery of a new product, especially if the product is technical or requires special installation. Customers unfamiliar with the product may have problems installing or using it. They may even damage the product through improper use. Many salespeople visit new customers right after initial deliveries to ensure correct use of the product. In this way they can also help the customer realize the full potential benefits of the product.

Some buyers may be knowledgeable about how to use the basic features of a product or service, but if it is not operating at maximum efficiency, the wise salesperson will show the buyer how to get more profitable use out of it. Many firms have staffed a customer service department to aid salespeople in this task. The salesperson is still responsible, however, to make sure the customer service department takes proper care of each new customer.

To be most effective, the salesperson should not wait until the user has trouble with the product. The fewer the difficulties allowed to occur, the greater will be the customer's confidence in the salesperson and the product.

FOLLOW UP

The first follow-up a salesperson should perform after the sale is a call to say thank you and to check to see that the product is working appropriately. Some salespeople use specialty advertising, or gifts imprinted with their company's name, to say thanks. These items are generally small enough to avoid concerns about bribery and can include desk clocks, pens, and the like. Chuck Gallagher, COO for American Funeral Financial, says the choice of a thank-you method is dependent on the buyer's social style. An analytical may prefer a concise e-mail message, whereas an expressive may enjoy a small gift. Rob Truss at DMG Construction also adds that the type and stage of relationship affect the choice of how thank you is said. Because his company builds buildings, the thank you may involve a big opening ceremony. Bob Hall's company hosts a thank-you cookout for their customers, and more than half usually attend.[2]

Follow-up, though, doesn't stop with thank you. Salespeople should also follow up regularly with their accounts to identify any changing needs or possible problems. In fact, failing to follow up is a major complaint that buyers have about salespeople. One recent study indicated that 80 percent of sales executives believed their company provides great service, but only 8 percent of their customers agreed.[3] Why the mismatch in perceptions? Because salespeople all too often fail to follow up.

Recall, too, that different functional areas and members of the buying center had different needs to start with. Follow-up with only the users or those most directly involved with the product may result in other members of the buying center becoming dissatisfied. The nature of the follow-up should reflect their needs, which means, for example, that for a purchasing agent, follow-up should reflect the agent's concerns with the financial aspects and return on investment.[4]

Personal visits can be the most expensive form of follow-up because of the time it takes to travel and because the sales call will last longer than one conducted through other means. A personal visit, though, can be extremely productive because the salesperson can check on inventories or the performance of the machine or other aspects that can be accomplished only at the customer's site. Plus, a customer may be more likely to disclose more information, such as a minor complaint or compliment, in a personal setting than over the phone. Regular personal visits can also build trust, a key component needed to move the relationship forward. But these visits aren't just niceties; they require planning and sales objectives as you prepare for the next sale. As illustrated in "Building Partnerships 14.1," some salespeople have learned, to their chagrin, that just running out to make a call can be unproductive.

Between personal visits, it is often a good idea to make contact via telephone. A salesperson can make 12 or more such calls within an hour, efficiently checking on clients. Telephone calls are two-way communication, giving the customer an opportunity to voice any concerns and minimizing intrusion. Contact management software, such as NetSuite, can help salespeople schedule telephone follow-ups.

Few salespeople turn to the mail as a way to say thank you or follow up on a sale. Sometimes, though, sending a thank-you by real mail (as opposed to e-mail) can set a salesperson apart. But for regular contact, e-mail may be sufficient. Aprimo and Marketo are two software offerings that automate e-mail follow-up, with e-mails triggered to follow up any number of events, such as a service call by a technician. The e-mails are signed by the salesperson and customized based on data from the CRM solution.

Following up with customers signals that the salesperson is dependable and customer oriented. Although the objective may be to create a functional relationship rather than a strategic partnership, such follow-up is still necessary to remind the customer that you are the salesperson with whom they want to do business.

HANDLE CUSTOMER COMPLAINTS

Handling complaints is critical to developing goodwill and maintaining partnerships. Complaints can occur at any time in the partnering process, not just during the exploration stage, but they may be more important in the early stages of a partnership. Attempts to establish partnerships often collapse because of shortsightedness in handling customer complaints. Some firms spend thousands of dollars on advertising but make the mistake of insulting customers who attempt to secure a satisfactory adjustment.

Complaints normally arise when the company and its products do not live up to the customer's expectations. Assuming the proper expectations were set, customers can be disappointed for any of the following reasons: (1) the product

BUILDING Partnerships

14.1

DOES "NOW" MEAN "NOW"?

The phone rings, and no matter what's happening, we pick it up. We might be having an important conversation with a loved one, but, even without knowing who it is, we'll put that on hold to answer the call.

The same is true when a customer says, "Come see me! Now!" Most salespeople rush off to answer the call without stopping to think about what *should* happen during the call and making sure they're ready.

Vicky Cayetano, vice president of sales for United Rental Laundry, believes that such urgency often results in the salesperson being unprepared. Vicki, who won the Sales and Marketing Executives Salesperson of the Year award for the Hawaii chapter, says, "I really get mad at myself if I know I lost a sale because I didn't do my very best, that I just ran in there and wasn't well prepared. Those moments don't happen very often. The reason you are not well prepared is often because you are dancing to the customer's tune. They say, "I need to see you, like today." And I am so anxious to please that I say "OK" and have not done my homework. So you have to be responsive, but you can't dance to their tune."

Bill Howell, while with IBM, said he had one customer who taught him the importance of preparation. "I had a customer for four years who bought regularly. After the second year, I'm afraid I took things for granted. When she wanted to reorder, I'd happily take the sale. It wasn't until near the end of my fourth year of handling that account that I learned that I was getting only about a third of their business. Had I done more preparation for each call, I would have had a better chance to win it all."

Ernie Bendele, with Rush Enterprises, also been recognized in his industry as a master salesperson, and he agrees that preparation is needed, even with repeat calls on good customers. He believes that while buyers want responsive salespeople, they really need and appreciate salespeople who will take the time to be prepared and know their stuff. "People like me who have been in the business for a long time have a good repeat customer base. We've built up relationships and trust. People come back to a salesperson because they feel comfortable doing business with them," says Ernie.

Sources: Anonymous, "Salesperson of the Year Shares Her Sales Secrets: Vicky Cayetano, *Hawaii Business 57*, no. 9 (March 2012), p. 12; Wendy Leavitt, "Master Salesperson," *Fleet Owner 105*, no. 9 (September 2010), p. 1.

---

performs poorly, (2) it is being used improperly, or (3) the terms of the sales contract were not met. Although salespeople usually cannot change the product or terms, they can affect these sources of complaints, minimizing them by setting proper expectations and ensuring proper use.

We've long known that people tell more friends about bad experiences than they do good experiences. Studies repeatedly show that when a company fails in its dealings with a complainant, the latter will tell twice as many people as when the experience is good. For every dissatisfied person who complains, an estimated 50 more simply stop buying the product, but handle the situation well, and repurchase intentions increase.[5] One study found that half of those told about a bad experience refused to ever consider the offending vendor.[6] In fact, a bad experience is far more likely to result in no future purchase than a good experience is to result in repurchase. Companies that can improve customer satisfaction will see positive financial results, mostly by avoiding negative experiences.[7]

Most progressive companies have learned that an excellent way to handle customer complaints is through personal visits by sales representatives. Thus, the salesperson may have total responsibility for this portion of the company's public relations. Salespeople who carry this burden must be prepared to do an effective job.

Complaints cannot be eliminated; they can only be reduced in frequency. The salesperson who knows complaints are inevitable can learn to handle them as a

Exhibit 14.2
Responding to Complaints

- Encourage buyers to tell their story.
- Determine the facts.
- Offer a solution.
- Follow through with action.

normal part of the job. The following discussion presents some techniques for responding to complaints; Exhibit 14.2 provides an overview.

Encourage Buyers to Tell Their Story

Some customers can become angry over real or imaginary grievances. They welcome the salesperson's visit as an opportunity to voice complaints. Other buyers are less emotional in expressing complaints and give little evidence of irritation or anger, but the complaint is no less important. In either case customers need to tell their stories without interruption. Interruptions add to the irritation of emotionally upset buyers, making it almost impossible to arrive at a settlement that is fair to all parties.

Customers want a sympathetic reaction to their problems, whether real or imagined. They want their feelings to be acknowledged, their business to be recognized as important, and their grievances handled in a friendly manner. An antagonistic attitude or an attitude that implies the customer is trying to cheat the company seldom paves the way for a satisfactory adjustment. You can probably relate to this feeling if you have ever had to return a defective product or get some kind of adjustment made on a bill. Exhibit 14.3 suggests ways to handle irate customers.

Good salespeople show they are happy the grievance has been brought to their attention. After the customer describes the problem, the salesperson may express regret for any inconvenience. An attempt should then be made to talk about points of agreement. Agreeing with the customer as far as possible gets the process off to the right start.

Determine the Facts

It is easy to be influenced by a customer who is honestly making a claim for an adjustment. An inexperienced salesperson might forget that many customers make their case for a claim as strong as possible. Emphasizing the points most likely to strengthen one's case is human nature. But the salesperson has a responsibility to his or her company too. A satisfactory adjustment cannot be made until all the facts are known.

Whenever possible, the salesperson should examine, in the presence of the customer, the product claimed to be defective. Encouraging the customer to pinpoint the exact problem is a good idea. If the defect is evident, this step may be unnecessary. In other instances, make certain the complaint is understood. The purpose of getting the facts is to determine the cause of the problem so the proper solution can be provided.

Experienced salespeople soon learn that products may appear defective when actually nothing is wrong with them. For example, a buyer may complain that paint was applied exactly as directed but repainting became necessary in a short

Exhibit 14.3
Handling Rude or Irate Customers

1. Follow the Golden Rule—treat your customer the way you would like to be treated, no matter how difficult the client becomes.
2. Prove you listened—paraphrase the customer's concern, recognizing the customer's feelings along with the facts.
3. Don't justify, excuse, or blame others—be positive and thank the customer for bringing the problem to your attention so that you can resolve it.
4. Do the hard things first—the faster they get done, the more your customer will appreciate you and your efforts.
5. Call back if the customer hangs up.
6. Give the customer someone else to call, but only in case you are not available—don't pass the buck!

time; therefore, the paint was no good. However, the paint may have been spread too thin. Any good paint will cover just so much area. If the manufacturer recommends using a gallon of paint to cover 400 square feet with two coats and the user covers 600 square feet with two coats, the product is not at fault.

On the other hand, salespeople should not assume product or service failure is always the user's fault. They need an open mind to search for the facts in each case. In one instance, the paint spilled out of the bucket all over the buyer's truck while the customer took it back to Home Depot to register a complaint that the paint was too thin—like painting with milk. The Home Depot customer service representative refused to believe the buyer that the paint had spilled (even though the paint-covered truck was in the Home Depot parking lot), assuming the buyer used it and was trying to get it for free. The buyer agreed that it was reasonable to require him to take the claim up with the manufacturer, but the Home Depot clerk's assumption that the buyer lied about the missing paint cost Home Depot a $10,000 per year customer. Some companies have the policy that the customer is always right, in which case there is no need to establish responsibility. While there is still a need to determine what the cause was so the right solution can be offered, do not assume the customer is to blame.

In this phase of making an adjustment, salespeople must avoid giving the impression of stalling. The customer should know that the purpose of determining the facts is to permit a fair adjustment—that the inquiry is not being made to delay action or avoid resolution.

Offer a Solution

After the customer tells his or her story and the facts are determined, the next step is to offer a solution. At this time the company representative describes the process by which the company will resolve the complaint, and the rep should then gain agreement that the proposed solution is satisfactory. Recent research suggests that offering several solutions and allowing a customer to choose one is far more effective than telling the customer what the solution will be. Giving the customer a choice puts the customer in control, which increases satisfaction with how the compliant was handled.[8]

Company policies vary, but many assign the responsibility for settling claims to the salesperson. Other companies require the salesperson to investigate claims and recommend a settlement to the home office. Salespeople are in the best position to make adjustments fairly, promptly, and satisfactorily, especially if the customer and salesperson are geographically distant from the home office. Permitting salespeople to only recommend a course of action, though, assures the customer of attention from a higher level of management, increasing the likelihood that the customer will accept the action taken.

Whatever the company policy, the customer desires quick action and fair treatment and wants to know the reasons for the action. Most customers are satisfied if they quickly receive fair treatment. Customers are seldom convinced of the fairness of a solution that isn't exactly what they wanted unless the reasoning behind the decision is explained to them. Nothing discourages a customer more than having action postponed indefinitely or being offered vague promises. Although some decisions may take time, the salesperson should try to expedite action. The opportunity to develop a partnership may be lost if the time lapse is too great, even though action is taken in the customer's favor.

Some salespeople make disparaging remarks about their own companies or managers in an effort to shift the blame. Blaming someone else in the company is a poor practice because this behavior can cause the customer to lose faith in both the salesperson and the company. Moreover, if the customer does not like the proposed solution, the salesperson trusted to make an adjustment or recommendation should shoulder the responsibility. Any disagreement on the action taken should be ironed out between the salesperson and the home office staff. When reported to the customer, the action must be stated in a sound, convincing manner.

The action taken may vary with the circumstances. Some possible settlements when a product is unsatisfactory are the following:

1. Replace the product without cost to the customer.

2. Replace the product and share the costs with the customer.

3. Instruct the customer on how to proceed with a claim against a third party (for example, the paint manufacturer in the Home Depot situation).

4. Send the product to the factory for a decision.

Occasionally customers make claims they know are unfair. Although they realize the company is not at fault, they still try to get a settlement. Fortunately, relatively few customers do this.

To assume that a customer is willfully trying to cheat the company would be unwise. He or she may honestly see a claim as legitimate even though the salesperson can clearly tell that the company is not at fault. The salesperson does well, then, to proceed cautiously and, if any doubt exists, to treat the claim as legitimate.

A salesperson convinced that a claim is dishonest has two ways to take action. First, he or she can give the buyer an opportunity to save face by suggesting that a third party may be to blame. For example, if a machine appears not to have been oiled for a long time, a salesperson may suggest, "Is it possible that your maintenance crew neglected to oil this machine?" Second, the salesperson can unmask the fraudulent claim and appeal to the customer's sense of fair play. This procedure may cause the loss of a customer. In some cases, however, the company may be better off without that customer.

Answers to the following questions often affect the action to be taken:

- What is the dollar value of the claim? Many firms have established standard procedures for what they classify as small claims. For example, one moving and storage firm considers any claim under $200 to be too insignificant to investigate fully; thus, a refund check is issued automatically for a claim under this amount. Firms may also have a complete set of procedures and policies developed for every size of claim.

- How often has this customer made claims? If the buyer has instituted many claims in the past, the company may need to not only resolve the specific complaint but also conduct a more comprehensive investigation of all prior claims. Such a probe may reveal systematic flaws in the salesperson's company, product, or procedures. For example, Agria (a Swedish commercial insurance company) routinely examines customer complaints to determine if new services should be developed. One result is that Agria is one of the fastest-growing insurance companies in Europe.[9]

- How will the action taken affect other customers? The salesperson should assume that the action taken will be communicated to other prospects and customers. If the complaining customer is part of a buying community (discussed in Chapter 6), chances are good that others will learn about the resolution of the claim. Thus, the salesperson must take actions necessary to maintain a positive presence in that community, possibly even providing a more generous solution than the merits of the case dictate.

The solution that will be provided must be clearly communicated to the customer. The customer must perceive the settlement as being fair. When describing the settlement, the salesperson should carefully monitor all verbal and nonverbal cues to determine the customer's level of satisfaction. If the customer does not agree with the proposed course of action, the salesperson should seek ways to change the settlement or provide additional information about why the settlement is fair to all parties.

Follow Through with Action

A fair settlement made in the customer's favor helps to resell the company and its products or services. The salesperson has the chance to prove what the customer has been told for a long time: that the company will devote time and effort to keeping customers satisfied.

The salesperson who has authority only to recommend an adjustment must take care to report the facts of the case promptly and accurately to the home or branch office. The salesperson has the responsibility to act as a buffer between the customer and the company. After the claim is filed, contact must be maintained with the customer to see that the customer secures the promised settlement.

The salesperson also has a responsibility to educate the customer to forestall future claims. After a claim has been settled to the customer's satisfaction is a fine time to make some suggestions. For example, the industrial sales representative may provide a new set of directions on how to oil and clean a machine.

Achieve Customer Satisfaction

Although complaints always signal customer dissatisfaction, their absence does not necessarily mean customers are happy. Customers probably voice only 1 in 20 of their concerns. They may speak out only when highly dissatisfied, or a big corporation's buyer may not be aware of problems until the product's users vent their frustration. Lower levels of dissatisfaction still hurt sales especially in today's high tech environment when a tweeted complaint can reach hundreds of followers. Salespeople should continuously monitor customers' levels of satisfaction and perceptions of product performance because customer satisfaction is the most important reason for reordering at this stage in the relationship. Many companies also monitor Twitter, as you can see in "Sales Technology 14.1."

When the customer is satisfied, an opportunity for further business exists. Complaints and dissatisfaction can occur at any time during the relationship, but handling complaints well during the exploration stage is one way to prove that the salesperson is committed to keeping the customer's business. When customers sense such commitment, whether through the handling of a complaint or through other forms of special attention, they may be ready to move to the expansion stage.

EXPANSION

The next phase of the buyer–seller relationship is expansion. When a salesperson does a good job of identifying and satisfying needs and the beginnings of a partnership are in place, the opportunity is ripe for additional sales. As mentioned in the previous chapter, some companies celebrate the first reorder more than they do an initial purchase because the reorder signals a long and profitable relationship. For example, Brian George of the Houston Texans of the National Football League closed a small promotion with Mattress Mack (Jim McIngvale) of Gallery Furniture. But Brian really celebrated when Mack expanded into a full-season sponsorship, including hosting Texans running back Arian Foster's radio show at the Gallery Furniture store. With greater trust, the salesperson can focus on

TODAY'S EMPOWERED CUSTOMER

Social media have broadened the audience for complaining customers. Between YouTube, Facebook, Twitter, and all of the others, an upset consumer can reach literally thousands of friends with a single complaint.

Yet one recent study shows that less than 30 percent of complaints on Twitter receive a response. The hope must be that these complaints don't carry much weight with others, but even if there is little or no impact on others, the reality is that if these complaints are handled, there is a strong favorable impact on the complainer who is much more likely to repurchase. Moreover, more than half of those who tweet a complaint expect a response; failure to respond does have a negative impact on that customer.

For example, the European company Carphone Warehouse monitors Twitter to quickly identify when a customer tweets a complaint. Then a customer service representative will respond directly back to the customer, either through Twitter or by e-mail, depending on what will be quickest.

Twitter is not the only online method for identifying customer service issues. Other microblogging sites, like Yammer.com, are also gaining ground as a place where customers can post comments about a company's performance. Phone Works founder Anneke Seley says, "Fundamentally, it's important to understand whether your customers are using social media or not...if you're in sales and trying to be of service to other people, it's about understanding what's going to help them. If they want to use Twitter, then let them communicate with you via Twitter."

Individual salespeople can also benefit from staying in touch with customers via social media. Dan Harding, a regional sales director, uses LinkedIn to find out what's important to his customers. If a service issue arises through a posting on LinkedIn, on Twitter, or in a customer's blog, Dan finds it quickly and responds quickly. Additionally, though, he has a better sense of what's important to each customer now and can identify sales opportunities too.

HubSpot salespeople not only use Twitter and LinkedIn to monitor customer issues but also use these sites find out how their prospects reacted to the sales pitch. Says Ellie Merman, "What do they say when they turn around to their friends and colleagues? Twitter gives you the opportunity to 'listen in' on this conversation. In fact, we did just that recently and used that feedback to actually improve our pitch going forward."

Sources: Ellie Merman, "Five Ways Salespeople Can Use Twitter," http://blog.hubspot.com/blog/tabid/6307/bid/5209/5-Ways-Sales-People-Can-Use-Twitter.aspx#ixzz28uOkXBDH (October 20, 2009), accessed October 10, 2012; Lisa Gschwandtner, "It's All about Strategy," *Selling Power*, January/February 2010, pp. 32–36; Natalie Petouhoff, "The Social Customer Economy," *Customer Relationship Management*, March 2010, p. 14; Anonymous, "Maritz & Evolve24 Twitter Study," September 2011, http://www.maritzresearch.com/~/media/Files/MaritzResearch/e24/ExecutiveSummaryTwitterPoll.ashx, accessed October 10, 2012.

identifying additional needs and providing solutions. In this section we discuss how to increase sales from current customers to expand the relationship. Keep in mind, however, that the activities of the exploration stage (monitoring order processing, handling complaints, and so on) still apply.

There are several ways to maximize the selling opportunity each account represents. These include generating reorders, upgrading, full-line selling, and cross-selling.

GENERATING REPEAT ORDERS

In some situations the most appropriate strategy is to generate repeat orders. For example, Cargill provides salt and other cooking ingredients to Kellogg's. The best strategy for the Cargill salesperson may be to ensure that Kellogg's continues to buy those ingredients from Cargill. Several methods can be used to improve the likelihood of reorders. We discuss each method in turn.

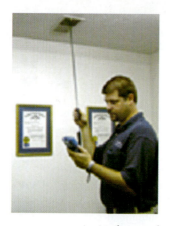

Contractor David Richardson, owner of Richardson Heating and Air Conditioning in Louisville, Kentucky, is measuring wet bulb and dry bulb temperatures from a supply register as part of making sure that a new installation is meeting customer requirements.

Be Present at Buying Time

One important method of ensuring reorders is to know how often and when the company makes decisions. NetSuite and other CRM software can provide order histories for accounts and give you a customer's buying cycle. For example, if you know that a particular customer reorders every 90 days, you can call on the 80th day with an offer and increase reorders.

Buyers do not always have regular buying cycles, which can make it difficult for salespeople to be present at buying time. In these situations the seller still wants to be present in the buyer's mind. One way to remain in front of customers is with specialty advertising items, useful items that are imprinted with the company name. Pharmaceutical companies may give prescription pads to keep a drug's brand in front of the doctor, while a technology company may imprint a webcam with its name to go on top of the desktop screen. In both instances, the goal is to keep the brand name at the top of the buyer's mind so that when a purchase is made, that's the brand thought of first.

Help to Service the Product

Most products need periodic maintenance and repair, and some mechanical and electronic products require routine adjustments. Such service requirements offer salespeople a chance to show buyers that the seller's interest did not end with the delivery of the product. Salespeople should be able to make minor adjustments or take care of minor repairs. If they cannot put the product back into working order, they must notify the proper company representative. They should then check to see that the repairs have been completed in a timely manner and to the customer's complete satisfaction.

As we discuss in Chapter 16, part of the salesperson's job is getting to know the company's maintenance and repair people. These repair people can act as the salesperson's eyes and ears when they make service calls. The same can be said in some settings with getting to know delivery people. At Office Depot, delivery people look for empty offices when delivering furniture because these offices mean future sales. When a good relationship is established with service personnel, salespeople can learn of pending decisions or concerns and take the necessary action.

thinking it through

Some customers take advantage of salespeople by trying to have them perform almost all the routine maintenance on a product for free. What can you as a salesperson do to curb such requests? How do you know where to draw the line?

Provide Expert Guidance

An industrial buyer or purchasing agent may need help in choosing a proper grade of oil or in selecting a suitable floor cleaner. A buyer for a retail store may want help developing sales promotion ideas. Whether the buyer needs help in advertising, selling, or managing, good salespeople are prepared to offer worthwhile suggestions or services.

The salesperson usually prospers only if the buyer prospers. Obviously, unless buyers can use a product or service profitably or resell it at a profit, they have no need to continue buying from that product's seller. One expert suggests finding non-selling-related ideas to offer your customers. When you use your industry expertise to solve problems or develop opportunities for your clients that do not involve the sale of your product, you add value to the relationship, which can ultimately help you expand your business within the account.

Many firms have developed a team approach to providing guidance and suggestions. For example, Verizon uses a systems approach to help develop and maintain the communication systems of its major accounts. The major account service team (MAST) is composed of marketing (as chairperson), engineering, service, supply, and traffic representatives. This interdepartmental approach brings together all skills required to provide expert guidance and suggestions to meet the expanding, sophisticated needs of large customers.

Standard Register's philosophy for success in the highly competitive field of selling business forms includes expert advice. Its forms management program makes the company a business partner with, rather than merely a supplier to, its major accounts. Customers are shown how to control the costs of buying and using forms by such practices as redesigning existing forms, grouping forms for more economical ordering, keeping records of quantities on hand and on order, and keeping track of the dollar value of the inventory. Standard Register's customers welcome such advice, and the result is a high reorder rate.

Provide Special Assistance

Salespeople are in a unique position to offer many types of assistance to the buyer. This section briefly mentions a few of the types of assistance salespeople can give their customers.

Salespeople engage in many activities to provide special assistance. For example, salespeople for Cott Beverages, a Canadian maker of private-label soft drinks for companies like Walmart, work as consultants, offering advice on product design and store layout. Salespeople at Simmons help set up mattress displays in furniture stores. Makita power tool salespeople provide free demonstrations for customers of hardware stores. Most salespeople who sell to resellers will tidy up the shelves and physically restock them from the stockroom supplies. Salespeople also help train the reseller's employees in how to sell the products to the final consumers.

Gail Walker of Marquis Communications, a trade show and special events service agency, worked in the customer's booth at a trade show when one of the customer's salespeople got sick. She worked as hard as if she were one of the firm's employees. Providing such special assistance is one hallmark of excellence in selling. Good relationships are built faster and made more solid by the salesperson who does a little something extra for a customer, performing services beyond his or her normal responsibilities.

UPGRADING

Similar to generating reorders is the concept of upgrading. **Upgrading,** also called *upselling,* is convincing the customer to use a higher-quality product or a newer product. The salesperson seeks the upgrade because the new or better product serves the needs of the buyer more effectively than the old product did.

Upselling is critical to companies like Oracle. According to the CFO of Oracle, almost all of their customers buy support services at the time of the system purchase. When Oracle acquired Sun, they quickly introduced a plan to upgrade as many Sun customers to added support because so few Sun customers were buying support from Sun. Many were buying support from other vendors, so upselling those customers was an immediate opportunity for revenue growth.[10]

When you upgrade, it is a good idea to emphasize during the needs identification phase that the initial decision was a good one. Now, however, technology or needs have changed, and the newer product fits the customer's requirements better. Otherwise the buyer may believe that the seller is trying to take advantage of the relationship to foist a higher-priced product.

FULL-LINE SELLING

Full-line selling is selling an entire line of associated products. For example, a Xerox copier salesperson may sell the copier but also wants to sell the dry ink and paper the copier uses and a service contract. Or a Campbell Soup Company salesperson will ask a store to carry cream of potato soup as well as tomato soup.

The emphasis in full-line selling is on helping the buyer realize the synergy of owning or carrying all the products in that line. For example, the Xerox salesperson may emphasize the security in using Xerox supplies, whereas the Campbell rep will point out that sales for all soups will increase if the assortment is broader.

CROSS-SELLING

Cross-selling is similar to full-line selling except the additional products sold are not directly associated with the initial products. For example, cross-selling occurs when the Xerox salesperson attempts to sell a fax machine to a copier customer or when a Campbell Soup Company rep sells spaghetti sauce to a soup buyer. Cross-selling involves leveraging the relationship with a buyer to identify needs for additional products; one reason is that it can cost much less to cross-sell to an existing client than to acquire a new client.[11] Again, trust in the selling organization and the salesperson already exists; therefore, the sale should not be as difficult as it would be with a new customer, provided the needs exist. Cypress Care sells health care plans and services to companies and has two distinct sales forces. The products differ, and often the buyers are different. But in some instances, the same buyer buys plans and services. In these instances, Cypress Care salespeople work across team lines to jointly serve the client and cross-sell the other offerings.[12]

Cross-selling (and full-line selling) requires additional training, as illustrated in Exhibit 14.4. Some attempts at cross-selling, though, can resemble the initial sale because the buying center may change. For example, the spaghetti sauce buyer may not be the same person who buys soups. If that is the case, the salesperson will have to begin a relationship with the new buyer, building trust and credibility.

Convincing a retailer to carry all Stubbs barbecue sauce flavors is full-line selling; convincing the retailer to also carry Stubbs marinades and rubs is cross-selling. Cross-selling leverages existing relationships to increase account share, or the percentage of a customer's business that you can earn.

COMMITMENT

When the buyer–seller relationship has reached the commitment stage, there is a stated or implied pledge to continue the relationship, as we discussed in the last chapter. Formally this pledge may begin with the seller becoming a **preferred supplier,** which is a much greater level of commitment than the levels discussed in Chapter 11. Although preferred-supplier status may mean different things in different companies, in general it means that the supplier is assured of a large percentage of the buyer's business and will get the first opportunity to earn new business. For example, at John Deere, only preferred suppliers are eligible to bid on new product programs. Thus, preferred supplier is one term used for "partnership."

Exhibit 14.4
Seven Tips for Effective
Cross-Selling

1. *Product knowledge:* Salespeople have to know all their company's products. When companies introduce new cross-selling opportunities, training is needed to learn the new product lines.
2. *Cross-selling skills:* Salespeople must know how to identify the appropriate decision maker, how to leverage current relationships, and how to use other cross-selling skills. Cross-selling often requires additional training.
3. *Incentives:* Many salespeople are afraid of losing the first piece of business by asking for too much, so incentives can help make it worthwhile to ask.
4. *Reasonable quotas or goals:* The first goal when implementing a cross-selling strategy is to get salespeople to simply ask for the opportunity. Goals that are too tough encourage salespeople to force the cross-sale.
5. *Results tracking:* Effective organizations track results by individual and by sales team to identify cross-selling success. Many companies use contact management software like NetSuite or salesforce.com for results tracking.
6. *Timing:* Creating a promotion campaign to support cross-selling efforts, particularly when seasonality is an issue, can make a cross-selling strategy successful. Timing also refers to making sure training occurs before the program starts.
7. *Performance appraisals:* Salespeople need feedback to identify where and how in the process to improve.

Source: Vicki West, PhD, and Jan Minifie, PhD. Used with permission.

DaimlerChrysler classifies its relationships with suppliers into four categories. The first is transactional, or what we called *solo exchange* in the previous chapter. The second is coordinative, in which DaimlerChrysler may sign an annual contract. These two types of relationships are market exchanges. The next two are more strategic, with selective partnership being the first level. Suppliers are integrated into product development processes and work closely with DaimlerChrysler to develop effective interfaces. Alliances, or strategic partnerships, go even further, with integration of departments across the two companies, investment in joint assets, and joint concept development taking place. Such commitment is rare; few companies are strategic partners.

What does it take to become a preferred supplier? PPG, as part of its Supplier Added Value Effort (SAVE) program, uses several criteria (listed in Exhibit 14.5). In some cases a PPG preferred supplier is a distributor, not a manufacturer. In these situations the supplier and PPG work in tandem to find the best manufacturers at the lowest prices, with the result being increased sales volume and better volume discounts. PPG gets the lowest price possible at the required service level, and the distributor makes more profit. Clearly this is a win–win opportunity.

Note that upgrading, full-line selling, cross-selling, and handling complaints will continue to occur during the commitment stage. Because a commitment has been made by both parties to the partnership, however, expectations are greater. Handling complaints properly, appropriately upgrading or cross-selling, and fulfilling new needs are even more important because of the high level of commitment made to the partner.

Many buyers evaluate suppliers on criteria similar to those used by PPG (see Exhibit 14.5). Although the salesperson may not be able to influence corporate culture, she or he plays an important role in managing the relationship and leading both sides into commitment.

SECURING COMMITMENT TO A PARTNERSHIP

When firms reach the commitment stage, elements in addition to trust become important. Trust may be made operational in the form of shared risk, such as Baxter International's agreements with some customers to share savings or expenses for

Exhibit 14.5
Examples of Supplier
Criteria to Sell to PPG

Hard Savings
- Payment terms, such as cash discounts.
- Improve process:

  Cycle time reduction (shorter order/delivery cycles, for example).
- Inventory management:

  Vendor inventory management.
- Quality and innovation:

  Variability reduction—no defects and no adjustments needed to make products fit our applications.
- Supply chain management:

  Optimum packaging—light packaging that reduces shipping costs while still protecting the product.

Soft Savings
- Commercial:

  Minority-owned vendors.
- Global initiatives:

  New markets—provide access to new markets, either by partnering into new markets or by adjusting products to fit needs of new markets.
- Improve process:

  Improve safety or environmental procedures.
- Quality and innovation:

  Training.
- Supply chain management:

  Bar coding—can reduce the time our employees take to process a shipment.

Source: www.ppg.com/crp_purchasing/$ave/measurement_grid.htm (accessed March 1, 2008).

joint programs. Along with the dimensions of trust such as competence and dependability and honesty (or ethics), there must be commitment to the partnership from the entire supplying organization, a culture that fits with the buyer's organizational culture, and channels of communication so open that the seller and buyer appear to be part of the same company.

COMMITMENT MUST BE COMPLETE

Commitment to the relationship should permeate both organizations, from top management to the secretary who answers the phone. This level of commitment means devoting the resources necessary to satisfy the customer's needs and even anticipating needs before the buyer does.

The salesperson owns the responsibility to secure commitment from his or her own company. Senior management must be convinced of the benefits of partnering with a specific account and must be willing to allow the salesperson to direct the resources necessary to sustain the partnership. (Chapter 16 explores the process of building the internal partnerships the salesperson needs to coordinate those resources.)

Commitment also requires that all employees be empowered to handle the needs of the customer. For example, if the customer has a problem with a billing process, administration should be willing to work with the partner to develop a more satisfactory process. In a partnership the customer should not have to rely on only the salesperson to satisfy its needs. For Mike Power, sales manager for Lovejoy Inc., a big part of the equation is making sure that someone in the organization is always accessible to provide an answer or solve an opportunity.

"Accessibility means that we can respond quickly to customer or distributor emergencies. For example, recently we received a call about a coupling breakdown at a steel mill at 1 a.m. From the time the mill's maintenance supervisor called the distributor's sales representative to the time we loaded the coupling on the truck for delivery, less than four hours had passed."[13] Accomplishing this feat took many more employees than just a salesperson.

COMMUNICATION

In the exploration stage, availability must be demonstrated (we already discussed the example of toll-free hotlines and voice mail to allow the seller's organization to respond quickly to customer calls). But in the commitment phase of a partnership, the seller must take a proactive communication stance. This approach means actively seeking opportunities to communicate at times other than when the salesperson has something to sell or the customer has a problem to resolve.

Partners are usually the first to learn about each other's new products, many times even codeveloping those products.[14] Part of the commitment between suppliers and their customer partners is the trust that such early knowledge will be kept confidential. Partners want to know what is coming out soon so they can make appropriate plans.

Salespeople should also encourage direct communication among similar functional areas. In previous stages the two firms communicated through the buyer and the salesperson. If multilevel selling occurred, it occurred at even levels—that is, vice presidents talking to one another. But when two firms commit to a partnership, the boundaries between them, at least in terms of communication, should blur, as illustrated in Exhibit 14.6.

The buyer's production department, for example, should be able to communicate directly with the seller's engineering department rather than going through the salesperson, if production needs to work on a change in the product design. Although the salesperson would want to be aware of a product design change and ensure that engineering responded promptly to the customer's concern, direct communication means more accurate communication and a better understanding of the customer's needs. A better solution is more likely to result when there is direct communication.

CORPORATE CULTURE

Corporate culture is the values and beliefs held by senior management. A company's culture shapes the attitudes and actions of employees and influences the development of policies and programs.[15] For example, consider the following scene. In a large room with concrete floors are a number of cubicles built from plywood. Each cubicle has a card table, two folding chairs, and a poster that says, "How low can you go?" Such is the scene in Bentonville, Arkansas, the corporate headquarters of Walmart, where salespeople meet their buyers for Sam's Club and Walmart. That room reflects Walmart's culture of the lowest possible price.

A similar culture of constantly seeking ways to drive down costs is necessary for a seller to develop a partnership with Walmart. A single salesperson will not change a company's corporate culture to secure a partnership with a buyer, but the salesperson must identify the type of culture both organizations hold and make an assessment of fit. Although a perfect match is not necessary, the salesperson must be ready to demonstrate that there is a fit. Offering lavish entertainment to a Walmart buyer, for example, would not demonstrate a fit. Telling the buyer that you are staying at a Circle 6 Motel might.

Exhibit 14.6

Direct Communication
between Partners

In traditional settings,
companies communicate
through a single buyer
or purchasing agent
and the salesperson.
Partners, though, allow
direct communication
between members of
the selling and buying
companies.

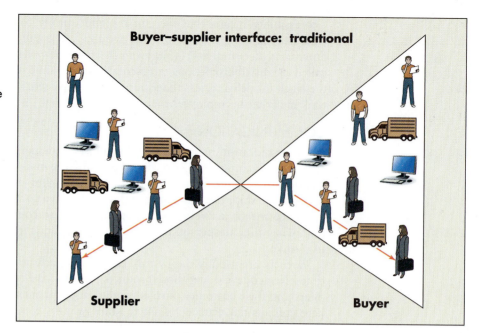

Buyer–supplier interface: traditional

Supplier   Buyer

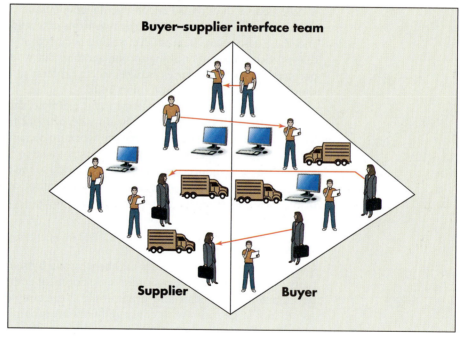

Buyer–supplier interface team

Supplier   Buyer

Companies have often sought international partners as a way to enter foreign markets. Walmart partnered with Cifra when the U.S. retailer entered the Mexican market. Cifra provides distribution services and products to Walmart for Sam's Club and Walmart stores located in Mexico City, Monterrey, and Guadalajara. When partnering with companies from other countries, country culture differences as well as corporate culture differences can cause difficulties.

Though not attempting to change a company's culture, the salesperson who seeks a partnering relationship seeks change for both organizations. In the next section we discuss what types of changes salespeople manage and how they manage those changes.

THE SALESPERSON AS CHANGE AGENT

To achieve increasing revenue in an account over time, the salesperson acts as a **change agent,** or a cause of change in the organization. Each sale may involve some type of change—perhaps a change from a competitive product or simply a new version of the old one. Partnering, though, often requires changes in both the buying and selling organizations.

For example, American Distribution Systems (ADS), a pharmaceutical distributor, and Ciba-Geigy, a pharmaceutical manufacturer, took six months to implement a joint operating plan that integrated systems of both companies. ADS created a cross-functional team that re-created ADS systems to function as part of Ciba-Geigy. At the same time Ciba-Geigy had to share information and other resources to take full advantage of the benefits of the relationship. In this instance both buyer and seller had to change significantly for the partnership to work.

Change is not easy, even when it is obviously beneficial. The objective is to manage change, such as changing from steel to iron pipe, in the buyer's organization while giving the appearance of stability. Two critical elements to consider about change are its rate and scope. The **rate of change** refers to how quickly the change is made; the **scope of change** refers to the degree to which the change affects the organization. Broad changes affect many areas of the company, whereas narrow changes affect small areas. In general, the faster and broader the change, the more likely it will meet with resistance, as illustrated in Exhibit 14.7.[16]

To overcome resistance to change, the salesperson should consider several decisions. The first decision involves finding help in the buying organization for selling the proposal. Other important decisions are positioning the proposal, determining the necessary resources, and developing a time-based strategy.

Champions

First, the choice of one or more champions must be made. **Champions,** also called advocates or internal salespeople, work for the buying firm in the areas most affected by the proposed change and work with the salesperson to make the proposal successful. These champions can build momentum for the proposal by selling in arenas or during times that are off limits to the salesperson. For example, a champion may sell for the salesperson during a company picnic in a casual conversation with a coworker.

Exhibit 14.7
Change and Resistance

Resistance to change is greatest when the scope is broad and the rate of change is fast.

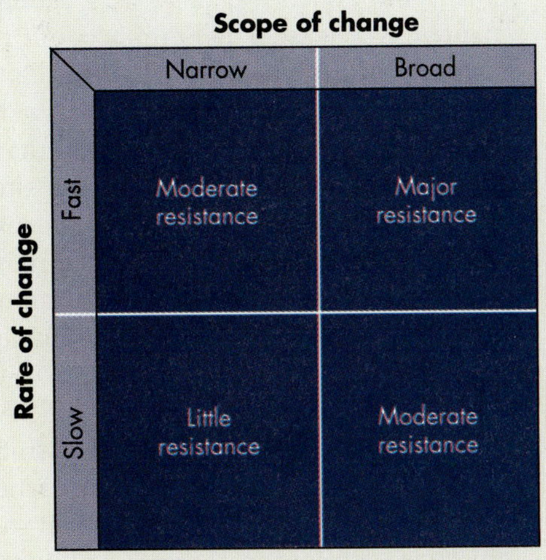

Scope of change

	Narrow	Broad
Fast	Moderate resistance	Major resistance
Slow	Little resistance	Moderate resistance

Rate of change

It is also important to recognize that the change in status from preferred supplier to strategic partner may also require a champion. Champions not only help persuade the firm to change but also help implement the change once the decision has been made. Such was the case at Tyco when the company wanted to revamp how it purchased services and maintenance products. Not only did the situation call for a complete review of vendors, it also required changing how these products and services were purchased. Getting the changes through to all the departments required identifying champions who would lead the change.[17] Thus, champions are important to salespeople.

Salespeople can help potential champions by providing them with all the knowledge they will need. Knowledge builds confidence; champions will have the courage to speak up when they are certain they know what they are talking about. Salespeople can also motivate champions to participate fully in the decision process by showing how the decision meets their needs as well as the overall needs of the company.

Positioning the Change

Positioning a change is similar to positioning a product in mass marketing, as you may have learned in your principles of marketing course. In this case, however, the salesperson examines the specific needs and wants of the various constituencies in the account to position the change for the greatest likelihood of success.

Because salespeople are highly proactive in finding areas for improvement (or change) in their partners' organizations, positioning a change may determine who is involved in the decision. For example, suppose the Dell representative who calls on your school recognizes that the student computer labs are getting out of date. Is a proposal for new equipment primarily the domain of the computer services department, or is it the domain of faculty who teach computing classes? If the computer services department favors Dell but the users favor Apple, the Dell rep will be better served by positioning the change as the responsibility of the computer services department. Positioning the proposed change appropriately may spell success or failure for the proposal.

Determining the Necessary Resources

The customer's needs may be beyond the salesperson's expertise. For example, Fram, a maker of auto parts, may be working with CarQuest, an auto parts retailer, to develop a major advertising program that will highlight their growing partnership. Such a change may require some selling to the advertising department at CarQuest. The Fram account representative will use the expert advice of Fram's own advertising department, its marketing research department, and probably its marketing management as well. These experts may visit CarQuest with the account rep and aid in securing that change in CarQuest's advertising focus.

The salesperson must assess the situation and determine what resources are needed to secure the buyer's commitment. Although the preceding example discusses allocation of personnel, salespeople must manage other resources as well, such as travel and entertainment budgets or sample supplies. (We discuss how to build internal partnerships to effectively coordinate company resources in Chapter 16.)

Developing a Time-Based Strategy

The salesperson must determine a strategy for the proposed change and set that strategy against a time line. This action accomplishes several objectives. First, the strategy is an outline of planned sales calls, with primary and minimum call objectives determined for each call. Second, the time line estimates when each call should occur. Of course objectives and planned times will change depending on the

Exhibit 14.8
Time Line for Fram/CarQuest

Month 1	Month 2	Month 3	Month 4	Month 5	Month 6
Visit director of marketing.	Visit merchandising manager and director of advertising.	Visit director of marketing.	Arrange tour of Fram facilities for VP of retail, director of marketing, and advertising and merchandising managers.	Submit plan to director of marketing.	Implement advertising program.
Primary objective: Determine marketing needs.	Primary objective: Secure support in principle.	Primary objective: Specify objectives for new advertising plan and secure commitment in principle.	Primary objective: Obtain commitment for review of plan.		
Minimum objective: Secure permission to see merchandising and advertising.					

results of each call, but this type of planning is necessary to give the salesperson guidance for each call, determine when resources are to be used, and make sure each call contributes to strategic account objectives.

For example, the Fram salesperson may determine that calls need to be made on five individuals at CarQuest. A time-based strategy would indicate which person should be visited first and what should be accomplished during that visit, as well as the order of visits to the remaining four members of the buying center. The strategy would also alert the salesperson as to when the advertising personnel were needed. Exhibit 14.8 illustrates such a time line.

DISSOLUTION

Too often salespeople believe that once a customer has committed to a partnership, less work is needed to maintain that relationship. That belief is untrue. Moreover, the recognition that everyone who touches the account has to continue to strengthen the account is important. Those who fail to strengthen the relationship may inadvertently weaken it.[18] Salespeople who subscribe to the belief that partnerships require less work fall victim to one or more common problems. As discussed in the previous chapter, the final stage for partnerships is dissolution, or breakup, but this stage can occur at any point, not just after commitment. Several potential problems, including maintaining few personal relationships, failing to monitor competitor actions or the industry, and falling into complacency, can lead to dissolution.

LIMITED PERSONAL RELATIONSHIPS

Salespeople tend to call on buyers they like; it is natural to want to spend time with friends. The result is that relationships are cultivated with only a few individuals in the account. Unfortunately for such salespeople, buyers may leave the organization, transfer to an unrelated area, or simply not participate in some decisions. Truly effective salespeople attempt to develop multiple relationships within an account.

Darryl Lehnus, noted sales professional in the sports sales profession, advocates a *3-by-3 strategy*. What he means is make sure you have three personal relationships at three levels of the organization (at least nine relationships total). When you maintain a 3-by-3 strategy, the chances of getting surprised and losing an account are substantially reduced.[19]

FAILING TO MONITOR COMPETITOR ACTIONS

No matter how strong the partnership is, the competition will want a piece of the business. And no matter how good the salesperson is, there will still be times when the account is vulnerable to competitor action. Accounts are most vulnerable when a personnel change occurs (especially if the rep has developed relationships with a limited number of people in the account), when technology changes, or when major directional changes occur, such as a company starting a new division or entering a new market.

The successful salesperson, however, monitors competitor action even when the account seems invulnerable. For example, an insurance agency had all the insurance business at a state university in Texas for more than 10 years but failed to monitor competitor action at the state capital and lost the account when another insurance agency found a sympathetic buyer in Austin. The loss of this one account cut annual earnings by more than 70 percent.

Monitoring competitor action can be as simple as checking the visitor's log at the front desk to see who has dropped by or keeping up with competitor actions and asking buyers for their opinions. Frequently, developing relationships with the many potential influencers in an account will also keep salespeople informed about competitor actions. As each person is visited, questions and comments about competitors will arise, indicating the activity level of competition.

Monitoring competition also means thinking about the benefits competitors offer, what their products do, and what their selling strategies are. When salespeople understand what the competition offers, they can position their own company's unique capabilities more effectively. It is not enough to know where competitors have made calls; good salespeople also know what the competition is saying.

FAILING TO MONITOR THE INDUSTRY

Similar to failing to monitor competition is a failure to monitor the industry in which either the salesperson or the customer operates. Salespeople often assume that the responsibility of monitoring the industry lies with someone else—either higher-ups in their own company or the customer. But salespeople who fail to monitor both industries may miss opportunities that change creates. As an extreme example, what would happen to an advertising agency's account executive if the Internet were ignored?

How does a professional salesperson monitor the industry? By reading trade magazines, blogs, and e-newsletters and by attending trade shows and conferences. The NetSuite sales representative who handles the John Deere account has to read not only Paul Greenberg's blog to know what's going on in the CRM industry but also Beauchamp McSpadden's blog on agribusiness and farm insurance. It's not enough to know your company's industry; with strategic partners, you must also know their industry.

FALLING INTO COMPLACENCY

Perhaps the most common thief of good accounts is complacency. In sales terms, **complacency** is assuming that the business is yours and will always be yours. It is failing to continue to work as hard to keep the business as you did initially to earn the business. For example, Coca-Cola was the sole supplier to El Volcan, the stadium for the professional soccer team Los Tigres in Monterrey, Mexico. After many years the stadium's concessions manager began to become annoyed with Coca-Cola because service seemed lackadaisical. As a result, the contract was put out to bid; Pepsi responded with a significantly better offer and won the business.

Monty Covington, vice president of sales for Grocery Supply Co. (GSC), schedules annual account reviews with key accounts. In these reviews, he and the account manager ask the customer to evaluate GSC's performance and to identify strategies that can help both companies continue to grow. These annual reviews do not allow GSC to become complacent.

To avoid complacency, salespeople should regularly audit their own customer service. Some of the questions a salesperson may want to consider are these:

- Do I understand each individual's personal characteristics? Do I have these characteristics in my computer file on each account?
- Do I maintain a written or computerized record of promises made?
- Do I follow up on every customer request promptly, no matter how insignificant it may seem?
- Do I follow up on deliveries, make sure initial experiences are positive, and ensure that all paperwork is done correctly and quickly?
- Have I recently found something new that I can do better than the competition?

CONFLICT

Not all dissolution is the result of conflict, as you can see from the types of reasons that most often lead to dissolution. But conflict between buyer and seller can occur, and when it does, the issues can be much more complex than the "usual" complaint.

Customer–supplier conflict is sometimes the result of conflicting policies within the customer's organization and even conflict between parts of the organization. For example, members of a buying center may not agree on what is best; whoever doesn't get his or her way may then take it out on the salesperson. Or the conflict may be a long-standing dispute unrelated to the salesperson that results in poor purchasing policies. A salesperson can moderate such conflict by helping the customer develop appropriate policies; one salesperson even brought in her own purchasing VP to consult with one of her clients so the client could get some ideas on better purchasing policies.

Trust-destroying conflicts can be avoided with several steps. First, start with a clear product description. If the product is a component part or critical for other reasons and the potential for ambiguity exists, write out a clear description. Services providers are especially vulnerable to ambiguity in the sales process because services are intangible. Specifying those services as completely as possible helps avoid later conflict. Another important element is to define who has authority to do what—both for the customer and for the selling organization. For example, it has to be clearly understood who can authorize change orders if the product specs have to be modified. Both these ideas require clear documentation, but good documentation is critical should such a dispute reach the courts.

Recognize that complaints can be the beginning of major conflict. Pathology Associates Medical Laboratories (PAML) lost a million-dollar client simply because small complaints added up over time. There was no major problem, at least at the start: an error on a bill, a late shipment, or a lost product. But these escalated into major conflict and the loss of the account, in part because PAML was unable to track the complaints. It now uses Microsoft Dynamics (CRM

Failing to monitor industry trends and changes is often a cause for losing a customer. One way to monitor the industry is to visit trade shows and see what the competition is offering.

software like NetSuite) to track complaints so it can both attack and solve any problems while also maintaining stronger customer relationships.[20] We discussed complaint handling as part of the exploration stage, but keep in mind that poor handling of complaints leads to the dissolution stage! Complaints in later stages are likely to lead to full-blown conflict if trust is not carefully salvaged. To repair damage to trust in a conflict, one consultant recommends the following seven steps (compare to the complaint-handling process discussed earlier):

1. Observe and acknowledge what has happened to lead to the loss of trust.
2. Allow your feelings to surface but take responsibility for your actions.
3. Gain support—offer your peer a chance to save face and gain agreement on any mitigating circumstances.
4. Put the experience in the larger context to affirm your commitment to the relationship.
5. Shift the focus from assigning blame to problem solving.
6. Implement the solution.
7. Let go and move on.

Keep in mind that while the relationship may be between two organizations, even the deepest strategic partnership is ultimately the responsibility of two people.

Whatever the reason for dissolution, all is not necessarily lost. Customers who defect, or buy from other vendors, sometimes return. In fact, seeking to woo customers back is an important strategy for many companies. Trevose, a Philadelphia-based weight loss management clinic, has a salesperson whose job is devoted to winning back clients. While dieters may be notorious as on-again off-again customers, every company has business potential among former customers, and that potential can be great.

SELLING YOURSELF

In the previous chapter we discussed how the concept of different types of relationships can also be applied to the relationships between students and professors and why you might want to work toward different relationships with different instructors. The focus is on how to build strong partnerships, which will apply to only certain situations.

One such situation is when you are involved in an organization on campus. Your organization will need to work with other organizations, both on campus and off. If you have big ideas you want to sell to others, the changes those will necessitate may also be big. That means identifying potential champions for change—people who will represent your ideas well to members in their own organizations or their departments of the school. Further, documenting decisions as part of the follow-up process will help avoid any conflict later, as well as demonstrate your professionalism and competence. Such follow-up will certainly set you apart!

Similarly, your organization may organize a fund-raising project or have T-shirt sales or some other sales transaction. How will you monitor orders (in the case of a T-shirt sale), how will you handle delivery, and will you engage in any postsale follow-up? If so, how?

In many different chapters in this book, you'll find references to the competitive advantage gained by having a personal reputation for integrity and competence. When opportunities for on-campus awards, scholarships, and postgraduation jobs arrive, your personal reputation will influence your ability to capitalize on those opportunities. In this chapter you've learned ways to demonstrate integrity and competence to satisfy and retain customers; apply those to your school environment, and you'll enjoy the type of personal reputation that leads to success.

SUMMARY

Developing partnerships has become increasingly important for salespeople and their firms. Salespeople can develop partnerships and generate goodwill by servicing accounts properly and by strategically building relationships. Both salespeople and buyers benefit from partnering.

Many specific activities are necessary to ensure customer satisfaction and to develop a partnering relationship. The salesperson must maintain the proper perspective, remember the customer between calls, build perceptions of trust, monitor order processing, ensure the proper initial use of the product or service, help to service the product, provide expert guidance and suggestions, and provide any necessary special assistance.

The best opportunities to develop goodwill are usually provided by the proper handling of customer complaints. Sales representatives should encourage unhappy customers to tell their stories completely, fully, and without interruption. A sympathetic attitude to a real or an imaginary product or service failure cannot be overemphasized. After determining the facts, the salesperson should implement the solution promptly and monitor it to ensure that proper action is taken.

The appropriate solution will depend on many factors, such as the seriousness of the problem, the dollar amount involved, and the value of the account. A routine should be developed to handle all complaints fairly and equitably.

In the expansion phase of the relationship, key sales activities are generating repeat orders, upgrading, cross-selling, and full-line selling. The goal is to achieve a partnership, in which case the seller is often designated a preferred supplier.

At this level of relationship, it is important that both organizations commit to the relationship from top to bottom and open communication directly between appropriate personnel in both organizations. At this point, salespeople become change agents as they work in both organizations to seamlessly integrate the partnership.

Sometimes relationships break up. When partnerships dissolve, usually there are multiple reasons for the breakup. For example, when a salesperson leans too heavily on a few personal relationships and those people leave or when the salesperson fails to monitor competitive actions, then the buying organization may feel less commitment to the relationship. Other reasons for dissolution include failing to monitor changes in the industry and becoming complacent. Winning a customer back is still a possibility and should be pursued when appropriate.

KEY TERMS

champion 385
change agent 385
complacency 388
corporate culture 383
cross-selling 380
electronic data interchange 369

full-line selling 380
preferred supplier 380
rate of change 385
scope of change 385
upgrading 379

ETHICS PROBLEMS

1. A customer is claiming you misrepresented a product in order to get the sale, so the contract should be voided. You know from other sources that the customer is in dire financial straits. You did not, at least in your mind, misrepresent the product. If your company agrees to cancel the contract, it is the same as saying you did misrepresent the product, and you could face termination or less drastic negative consequences. What should be done? (This is based on an actual event.)

2. The fairest solution to a customer's complaint is one that turns out to be against company policy, though certainly not against the law or unethical in any way. If you tried to do it, the chances are you could get away with it; but if caught, you would be terminated. What would you do?

QUESTIONS AND PROBLEMS

1. Your company sells manufacturing equipment, and a new machine had a control problem that affected about 20 percent of customers. The problem was written about in several magazines before your company fixed it. The problem turned out be a software glitch that could be fixed by downloading a patch from your company Web site, which could be done by customers. How would you deal with this problem if a customer brought it up? How would you respond if a prospect brought it up? Once the patch was written, what would you do?

2. Explain how active listening can be applied to a situation in which a customer makes a complaint. What can applying this art accomplish? What forms of active listening might actually cause *more* problems?

3. Read through "From the Buyer's Seat 14.1" and "Building Partnerships 14.1." These seem to be advocating opposite perspectives. How do you reconcile these two seemingly opposite positions?

4. The Miami Heat, like lots of sports teams, has a sales force that sells season tickets. Once someone is sold a season ticket package, the customer becomes someone else's responsibility. Every person in the office, no matter his or her regular job, has responsibility for a group of current customers; management believes this makes everyone more responsive to customer needs. But some customers complain; they would rather have the same salesperson who sold the tickets fix any problems. When should salespeople handle all complaints? When is it better to have everyone in the company take on some customer responsibility? When is it best to have one customer service department? Justify each response.

5. Some research suggests that how salespeople handle complaints is more important than whether there are problems. In fact, handling complaints well is one way to win loyalty. So should a company not fix a problem that it knows will lead to some minor complaints, thus giving its reps a chance to satisfy those complaints?

6. What is your reaction to the statement "The customer is always right"? Is it a sound basis for making adjustments and satisfying complaints? Can it be followed literally? Why or why not?

7. In the chapter-opening profile, John Tanner says that service was essential to his strategy. Is that just because he's in a service business? In what types of situations involving products would service after the sale be a strategic sales factor?

8. How do you know when full-line selling, upgrading, or cross-selling strategies are appropriate?

9. What are the various ways a salesperson can provide a potential champion with knowledge to build confidence? What types of knowledge will the champion need?

CASE PROBLEMS

case **14.1**

Digital Test & Equipment

Digital Test & Equipment (DTE) is a distributor of test equipment used in mining and oil applications. When Mark Polonsky, of Albany Manufacturing, got the call from Amy Sheppard at DTE, he was excited. For over a year he worked to get DTE to carry Albany's geothermal test equipment, but there was no progress—until today, when Amy asked if the Albany Geo-Core Xcel would handle conditions in the North Sea oil fields.

"I don't know," Mark replied. "I've personally not had any customers drilling in that area, but I will ask our senior engineer and find out. What's the situation?"

"We've got a really good shot at landing some business from British Petroleum, but we've got some holes in our product line," she replied. "I'm really thinking of making this an all-Albany pitch, which would be about a $400,000 contract. Or I may give them two solutions, one all Albany and one a mix of other products." She went on into detail about the conditions in which the Geo-Core would have to work so Mark would know what questions to ask.

After the call, Mark called the senior engineer and asked if the product would work. Assured that it would, he went to work on a great proposal. Not only would a $400,000 sale represent a month's quota, he knew that DTE was good for five times that in its other accounts. This opportunity was huge!

Amy called Mark immediately when she got his e-mail with the proposal attached. "This looks great, Mark! I think the all-Albany approach is best, so that's what we'll go with. I'll submit this to BP tomorrow."

Two months later the first Geo-Cores were installed and operational. But within a week it was obvious that they weren't up to the demanding weather conditions of the North Sea. The machines were breaking down on average about every four hours. Allison called Mark, quite upset with the results, particularly because BP now wanted to cancel the entire agreement.

Questions

1. Assume you are Mark. What should you do?

2. Does the stage of the buyer–seller relationship matter? Which buyer is most important, British Petroleum or DTE?

3. Your first call after hanging up with Allison is with the senior engineer who gave you the wrong information. He claims there is a simple fix, but a DTE engineer will have to make the trip there to do it, and that will be about a $5,000 trip. First, what would you say to your manager who has to sign off on that expense? Second, how do you handle Allison?

Nash Bagby, CEO of CSP Services, was livid. For the third time in two days, a customer called him to complain of a defect—the same defect. He called Mack McGuire, senior VP of operations. "Mack, what's the deal? I've had three customers call me about the feed mechanism not working properly in a brand-new Quantum."

"Really?" Mack replied. "I've not heard anything. Let me check it out and get back to you." Mack hit disconnect on the phone, then dialed Sara Marshall, director of customer service.

"Mack, I don't really know what you're talking about. Let me ask around with some of the customer service reps." Sara hung up and walked around the cubicles, where each of the 32 service reps was busily taking phone calls, handling instant messages on the service chat desk, and e-mailing customers. She managed to catch four reps between calls and quickly learned that each had taken a call on the Quantum's feed mechanism that morning. But one said the issue was due the operator not reading the instructions, while another had used some unauthorized supplies that could affect the feeder's operation.

As she returned to her office, she thought about how upset Mack seemed to be and why. The last thing she wanted to do was create problems for Bagby, CEO of the firm, or for Mack. But she was proud of her team's ability to resolve customer problems. After all, customer reports indicated a first-time call resolution (meaning the problem was fixed the first time) rate of 73 percent, well ahead of the industry rate of 58 percent. And she was operating the center at 12 percent under budget. What could she do to identify issues that crop up quickly like the Quantum feeder, and how could she help others in the company craft a better customer experience to avoid problems in the first place?

ROLE PLAY CASE

Today you will receive a telephone call from one of your accounts. The account is Fournier Equipment, a company that manufactures small construction equipment sold worldwide. There is one plant in St. Albans, Vermont; one in Montpellier, France; and one in Canberra, Australia. With 12 salespeople in the United States, 6 in Latin America, 4 in Australia/Asia, and 6 in Europe, the company does about $450 million a year in gross revenue. Fournier bought 40 licenses from you, which it began using about two weeks ago. Training was done through four different independent certified NetSuite trainers, one in each country. The vice president of sales was the decision maker and the only person you met. The primary needs were to get better forecasting so the plant would not fall behind or schedule things wrong, leading to stockouts or overruns; to get more customer information so it can market directly to customers and get them to prefer Fournier for all of their needs; and to reduce the amount of time spent on paperwork by salespeople.

Each of you will take turns being the buyer and the seller. If divided into teams of three, the third person will observe. Your professor will give you a sheet to use when you are the buyer.

ADDITIONAL REFERENCES

Anisimova, Tatiana, and Felix Mavondo. "The Performance Implications of Company–Salesperson Corporate Brand Misalignment." *European Journal of Marketing* 44, no. 6 (2010), pp. 771–95.

Cheng, Loyalty. "Comparisons of Competing Models between Attitudinal Loyalty and Behavioral." *International Journal of Business and Social Science* 2, no. 14 (August 2011), pp. 149–66.

Christ, Paul, and Rolph Anderson. "The Impact of Technology on Evolving Roles of Salespeople." *Journal of Historical Research in Marketing* 3, no. 2 (2011), pp. 173–93.

Dagger, Tracey S., and Meredith David. "Uncovering the Real Effect of Switching Costs on the Satisfaction-Loyalty Association: The Critical Role of Involvement and Relationship Benefits." *European Journal of Marketing* 46, no. 3/4 (2012), pp. 447–68.

Homburg, Christian, and Michael Klarmann Müller. "When Does Salespeople's Customer Orientation Lead to Customer Loyalty? The Differential Effects of Relational and Functional Customer Orientation." *Journal of the Academy of Marketing Science* 39, no. 6 (2011), pp. 795–812.

Hunt, C. Shane. "The Emerging Influence of Compensation Plan Choice on Salesperson Organizational Identification and Perceived Organizational Support." *Journal of Leadership, Accountability and Ethics* 9, no. 1 (February 2012), pp. 71–80.

Johnson-Busbin, Julie, James Busbin, and Jim DeConinck. "A Study of the Effect of Customer Orientations and Compensation Plans on Salesperson Ratings." *GSTF Business Review* 1, no. 4 (April 2012), pp. 143–48.

Le Meunier-FitzHugh, Kenneth, Jasmin Baumann, Roger Palmer, and Hugh Wilson. "The Implications of Service-Dominant Logic and Integrated Solutions on the Sales Function." *Journal of Marketing Theory and Practice* 19, no. 4 (Fall 2011), pp. 423–40.

Lin, Su-Hsiu. "Effects of Ethical Sales Behavior Considered through Transaction Cost Theory: To Whom Is the Customer Loyal?" *Journal of International Management Studies* 7, no. 1 (April 2012), pp. 31–40.

Malms, Olive, and Christian Schmitz. "Cross-Divisional Orientation: Antecedents and Effects on Cross-Selling Success." *Journal of Business to Business Marketing* 18, no. 3 (2011), p. 253.

Marshall, Norman W. "Commitment, Loyalty and Customer Lifetime Value: Investigating the Relationships among Key Determinants." *Journal of Business and Economics Research* 8, no. 8 (August 2010), pp. 67–84.

Piercy, Nigel F. "Evolution of Strategic Sales Organizations in Business-to-Business Marketing." *Journal of Business and Industrial Marketing* 25, no. 5 (2010), pp. 349–59.

Singh, Ramendra, and Abraham Koshy. "A New Conceptualization of Salesperson's Customer Orientation." *Marketing Intelligence and Planning* 30, no. 1 (2012), pp. 69–82.

Zboja, James J., and Michael D. Hartline. "An Examination of High-Frequency Cross-Selling." *Journal of Relationship Marketing* 11, no. 1 (2012), pp. 41–56.

Zhang, Lida L., Long W. Lam, and Clement S. F. Chow. "Segmenting the Customer Base in a CRM Program according to Customer Tolerance to Inferiority: A Moderator of the Service Failure–Customer Dissatisfaction Link." *Journal of Consumer Satisfaction, Dissatisfaction and Complaining Behavior* 22 (2009), pp. 68–87.

chapter

15

MANAGING YOUR TIME AND TERRITORY

SOME QUESTIONS ANSWERED IN THIS CHAPTER ARE

- Why is time so valuable for salespeople?
- What can you do to "create" more selling time?
- What should you consider when devising a territory strategy?
- How does territory strategy relate to account strategy and building partnerships?
- How should you analyze your daily activities and sales calls?
- How can you evaluate your own performance so you can improve?

PROFILE

PROFILE Window seats, early check-ins, and upgrades to roomier seats are airline essentials any frequent business traveler craves. These are just some of the requests I make whenever possible when I am covering my territory—the western half of the United States.

I've held many sales roles for the 3M Infection Prevention Division since graduating from college seven years ago. I studied sales as an undergraduate and also completed an internship with 3M in the Infection Prevention Division. My division manufactures products used in operating room and clinic settings. Currently, I am a surgery center specialist managing our relationship with a vendor partner and their sales team. I also work on internal cross-functional marketing, sales management, and sales learning and development teams. With this much responsibility, the way I manage my territory and time is critical to my effectiveness.

I usually like to travel with my vendor reps at least twice a year in their respective territories for at least two days a week. We meet with customers and distribution partners, creating plans for how to grow their business. We also travel to many industry and customer trade shows throughout the year around the country in their territories. With these sales expectations and customer interactions, one has to develop an effective plan and tactics to receive the most value for their time. Here are a couple of my time and territory management tactics and tools I employ to be effective. I encourage you to develop your own tactics that are effective for you in your territory:

1. *You have to spend time on the opportunities that have the greatest potential.* We all have finite time in most instances with our customer. For example, when I make a trip to the western half of the United States to work with my sales team, I try to direct our efforts to our largest sales opportunities while I am in the territory. Of course, we do meet with our medium to small opportunities, but we just want to make sure we are maximizing our time in the field. In addition to meeting with these customers while I am out working in the West, I try to meet with my western distributor partners, product/clinical specialist, and regional sales directors from my organization. The more points we can touch, the more information and knowledge we can have to manage our time and territory better.

2. *Delegate items to your sales support team.* That team can include sales analyst, product specialist, contract specialist, and so on. These team players have specific skill sets and experience that will help you along the way in closing and completing the sales process. We love to employ our clinical specialists (who are nurses) to educate nurses like themselves on the benefits of using our products in the operating room. It lends great credibility to us, the sales reps, as well as our organization. Even if you don't have specific resources assigned to you, finding people who can help you is important. Teaming and delegation is essential in any sales process, as it will free you to spend your time where it will pay off the most.

3. *Use digital tools such as e-mail, text messages, product webinars, and instant messaging wisely.* These tools have allowed me to manage my territory virtually from anywhere. We most recently used a combination of webinars over three weeks to present a sterilization class to over 150 customers throughout the country. Because of these webinars, we were able to secure a nice amount of new business for Q3 without having to do as many individual presentations in someone's clinic or hospital. These are great easy-to-use applications, and I would advise you to add them to your repertoire to maximize your time and territory management.

I suspect these recommendations would apply in principle to many jobs, but you can see how you have to manage your territory as you embark on your sales career. The great thing about time and territory management is that you can personalize it to fit your and your customer's schedule. Time and territory management is an ever-evolving concept that I am quite sure will look different 10 years from now, and this makes sale roles exciting and makes for more progressive careers. Well, I have to go out check in for flight now, as I think I am running late!

Visit our Web site at:
www.3m.com

THE VALUE OF TIME

The old axiom "Time is money" certainly applies to selling. If you work 8 hours a day for 240 days of a year, you will work 1,920 hours that year. If you earn $50,000, each of those hours will be worth $26.05. An hour of time would be worth $31.25 if your earnings climb to $60,000. Looking at your time another way, you would have to sell $260 worth of product per hour to earn $50,000 if you earned a 10 percent commission!

The typical salesperson spends only 920 hours a year in front of customers. The other 1,000 hours are spent waiting, traveling, doing paperwork, or attending sales meetings. Thus, as a typical salesperson, you really have to be twice as good, selling $520 worth of products every hour to earn that $50,000 commission.

The lesson from this analysis is clear: Salespeople must make every hour count to be successful. Time is a resource that cannot be replaced if wasted. But time is just one resource, albeit a critical resource, at the salesperson's disposal.

Managing time and territory is often a question of how to allocate resources. Allocating resources such as time is a difficult management process, but when done well, it often spells the difference between stellar and average performance. Many times it is difficult to know what is really important and what only seems important. In this chapter we discuss how to manage your time. Building on what you have learned about the many activities of salespeople, we also provide strategies for allocating resources among accounts—that is, managing your territory.

Salespeople have to carefully allocate resources such as time. Although every job will occasionally require burning the midnight oil, carefully planning one's time can make for a more balanced and enjoyable life.

THE SELF-MANAGEMENT PROCESS

The self-management process in selling has four stages. The first stage is setting goals, or determining what is to be accomplished. The second stage is allocating resources and determining strategies to meet those goals. In the third stage the salesperson implements the time management strategies by making sales calls, sending e-mail or direct mail pieces, or executing whatever action the strategy calls for. In the fourth and final stage, the salesperson evaluates performance to determine whether the goals will be reached and the strategies are effective or whether the goals cannot be reached and the strategies must change. This process is illustrated in Exhibit 15.1 and will serve as an outline for this chapter.

Exhibit 15.1
The Self-Management
Process

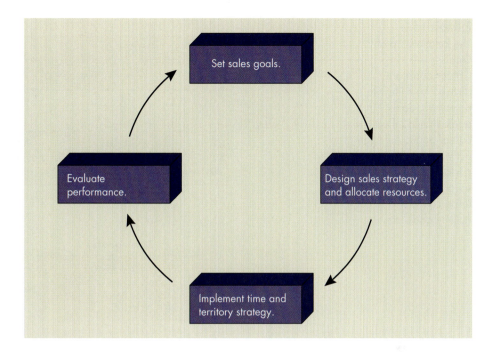

SETTING GOALS

THE NEED FOR GOALS

The first step in managing any worthwhile endeavor is to consider what makes it worthwhile and what you want to accomplish. Salespeople need to examine their careers in the same way. Career goals and objectives should reflect personal ambitions and desires so the individual can create the desired lifestyle, as illustrated in Exhibit 15.2. When career goals reflect personal ambitions, the salesperson is more committed to achieving those goals.

To achieve career objectives, salespeople must set sales goals. These sales goals provide some of the means for reaching personal objectives. Sales goals also guide the salesperson's decisions about which activities to perform, when to perform those activities, whom to see, and how to sell.

The salesperson lacking goals will drift around the territory, wasting time and energy. Sales calls will be unrelated to objectives and may be minimally productive or even harmful to the sales process. The result will be poor performance and, eventually, the need to find another job.

In Chapter 7 you learned that salespeople should set call objectives so the activities performed during the call will bring them closer to those objectives. The same can be said for setting sales goals: When sales goals are set properly and adhered to, the salesperson has a guide to direct his or her activities.

THE NATURE OF GOALS

As you read in Chapter 7, goals should be specific and measurable, achievable yet realistic, and time based (SMART). Goals should be specific and measurable so the salesperson knows when they have been met. For example, setting a goal of making better presentations is laudable, but how would the salesperson know if the presentations were better or worse? A more helpful goal would be to increase the number of sales resulting from those presentations. The best goal would be a specific increase, such as 10 percent. Then there would be no question about the achievement of the goal.

Exhibit 15.2

The Relationship of Goals

Career goals are devised from lifestyle objectives. Sales goals should reflect career goals. Although activities lead to sales, performance goals are usually set first. Then, using conversion goals, activity goals are set.

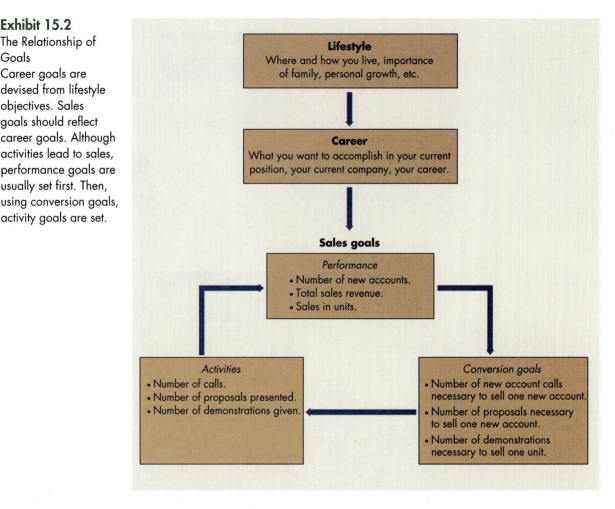

Lifestyle
Where and how you live, importance of family, personal growth, etc.

Career
What you want to accomplish in your current position, your current company, your career.

Sales goals

Performance
- Number of new accounts.
- Total sales revenue.
- Sales in units.

Activities
- Number of calls.
- Number of proposals presented.
- Number of demonstrations given.

Conversion goals
- Number of new account calls necessary to sell one new account.
- Number of proposals necessary to sell one new account.
- Number of demonstrations necessary to sell one unit.

Goals should also be reachable yet challenging. One purpose of setting personal goals is to motivate oneself. If goals are reached too easily, little has been accomplished. Challenging goals, then, are more motivating. But if the goals are too challenging or if they are unreachable, the salesperson may give up.

Goals should be time based; that is, goals should have deadlines. Putting a deadline on a goal provides more guidance for the salesperson and creates a sense of urgency that can be motivating. Without a deadline, the goal is not specific enough, and the salesperson may be able to drag on forever, never reaching the goal but thinking progress is being made. Imagine the motivational difference between setting a goal of a 10 percent increase in sales with no deadline and setting a goal of a 10 percent increase for the next month. The first instance lacks a sense of urgency, of needing to work toward that goal now. Without a deadline, the goal has little motivational value.

One problem some people have is periodically creating goals and then forgetting them. Goals should be written down and then posted. For

Some salespeople keep a reminder, like a photo of a new house, of their personal goals in front of them to help motivate themselves.

example, each month Will Pinkham has a goal for selling five new accounts (Will sells office equipment for Ikon Office Solutions). At the start of each month, he puts a new list on the wall over his desk, and as he sells each new account, he adds it to the list starting at the bottom. He starts the list at the bottom to remind him that his goal is to sell five, so when he sells one, his goal becomes four, and so forth. Probably not all goals should be posted in highly public areas, but the idea is to keep the goal in front of you so it continues to direct your activities.

TYPES OF SALES GOALS

Salespeople need to set three types of sales goals: performance, activity, and conversions (refer back to Exhibit 15.2). Although many salespeople focus only on how many sales they get, setting all three types of goals is necessary to achieve the highest possible success.

Performance Goals

Goals relating to outcomes are **performance goals.** In sales, outcomes such as the size of a commission or bonus check, the amount of sales revenue generated or number of sales generated, and the number of prospects identified are common performance goals. For example, the salesperson in Exhibit 15.3 set a performance goal of $6,000 in commissions and another performance goal of eight sales. Revenue quotas are an example of goals set by the company, but each salesperson should also consider setting personally relevant goals. For example, you may want to set higher goals so you can achieve higher earnings. People are more committed to achieving goals they set themselves; that commitment makes achieving them more likely. Performance goals should be set first because attaining certain performance levels is of primary importance to both the organization and the salesperson.

Personal development goals, such as improving presentation skills, are important to long-term professional growth and are a form of performance goals. Every person, whether in sales or other fields, should have some personal development goals. Reaching those goals will not only improve overall job performance but also increase personal satisfaction. Like all performance goals, however, these goals should meet the criteria of being specific, challenging, and time based. Further, it helps to make these goals measurable. For example, if you set improving presentation skills as a performance goal, some outcome such as increased sales or fewer objections should occur that you can measure to determine if your skills are truly improving.

Exhibit 15.3
Goal Calculations

Monthly earnings goal (performance goal):	$6,000
Commission per sale:	$750
$6,000 earnings ÷ $750 per sale = 8 sales	
Monthly sales goal (performance goal):	8
Closings goal (conversion goal):	10%
8 sales × 10 prospects per sale = 80 prospects	
Monthly prospects goal (performance goal):	80
Prospects per calls goal (conversion goal):	1 in 3
80 prospects × 3 calls per prospect = 240 calls	
Monthly sales calls goal (activity goal):	240
240 calls × 20 working days per month = 12 calls	
Daily sales calls goal (activity goal):	12

Activity Goals

Salespeople also set activity goals. **Activity goals** are behavioral objectives: the number of calls made in a day, the number of demonstrations performed, and so on. Activity goals reflect how hard the salesperson wants to work. The company may set some activity goals for salespeople, such as a quota of sales calls to be made each week. Exhibit 15.3 lists two activity goals: 240 sales calls per month and 12 calls per day.

All activity goals are intermediate goals; that is, achieving them should ultimately translate into achievement of performance goals. As Teradata discovered by auditing sales performance, activity goals such as a specific number of telephone calls per day are needed for the salespeople to achieve the overall performance goals.[1] Activity goals help salespeople decide what to do each day, but those goals must ultimately be related to making sales.

However, activity goals and performance goals are not enough. For example, a salesperson may have goals of achieving 10 sales and making 150 calls in one month. The salesperson may get 10 sales but make 220 calls. That salesperson had to work much harder than someone who managed to get 10 sales in only 150 calls. What caused the difference? Answer that question and you, too, can work smarter rather than harder, but the answer presupposes that you first measured conversions and then set goals based on what should be achieved.

Conversion Goals

Conversion goals are measures of a salesperson's efficiency. Conversion goals reflect how efficiently the salesperson would like to work, or work smarter. Unlike performance goals, conversion goals express relative accomplishments, such as the number of sales relative to the number of calls made or the number of customers divided by the number of prospects. The higher the ratio, the more efficient the salesperson. Exhibit 15.3 lists two conversion goals: closing 10 percent of all prospects and finding one prospect for every three calls. In the preceding example, a rep earning 10 sales while making 150 calls could close 4 or 5 more sales by making 220 calls because that rep gains a sale every 15 calls.

Conversion goals are important because they reflect how efficiently the salesperson uses resources, such as time, to accomplish performance goals. For example, Freeman Exhibit Company builds custom trade show exhibits. Customers often ask for booth designs (called speculative designs) before making the purchase to evaluate the offerings of various competitors. Creating a custom booth design is a lot of work for a designer, and the cost can be high, but it does not guarantee a sale. If a salesperson has a low conversion rate for speculative designs, overall profits will be lower because the cost for the unsold designs must still be covered. If the rep can increase the conversion rate, the overall costs for unsold designs will be lower, hence increasing profits.

Working harder would show up as an increase in activity; working smarter should be reflected in conversion goals. For example, a salesperson may be performing at a conversion rate of 10 percent. Reaching a conversion goal of 12 percent (closing 1 out of 8 instead of 1 out of 10) would reflect some improvement in the way the salesperson operates—some method of working smarter.

Measuring conversions tells salespeople which activities work best. For example, suppose a salesperson has two sales strategies. If A generates 10 sales and B generates 8 sales, the salesperson may think A is the better strategy. But if A requires 30 sales calls and B only 20, the salesperson would be better off using strategy B. Thirty sales calls would have generated 12 sales with strategy B.

Comparing your performance with the best in your organization is a form of **benchmarking**.[2] Benchmarking can help you see where you are falling short. For example, if your conversion ratio of leads to appointments (the number of leads needed to get one appointment) is the same as that of the top seller but you are closing only half of your spec designs and that person is closing 80 percent, you know you are losing sales at the spec design stage. You can then examine what that person does to achieve the higher conversion ratio.

SETTING SALES GOALS

Performance and conversion goals are the basis for activity goals. Suppose a sale is worth $500 in commission. A person who wants to earn $4,000 per month (a performance goal) needs to make eight sales each month. If the salesperson sees closing 1 out of 10 prospects as a realistic conversion goal, a second performance goal results: The rep must identify 80 prospects to yield eight closings. If the rep can identify one prospect for every three sales calls (another conversion goal), 240 sales calls (an activity goal) must be made. Assuming 20 working days in a month, the rep must make 12 sales calls each day (another activity goal). Thus, activity goals need to be the last type of goals set because they will be determined by the desired level of performance at a certain rate of conversion.

Even though the conversion analysis results in a goal of 12 calls each day, that conversion rate is affected by the strategy the salesperson employs. A better strategy results in a higher conversion rate and better allocation of time, one of many important resources that must be allocated properly to achieve sales goals. We discuss how to allocate resources in the next section.

ALLOCATING RESOURCES

The second stage of the time and territory management process is to develop a strategy that allocates resources properly. These resources are allocated to different sales strategies used with different types of accounts with the purpose of achieving sales goals in the most effective and efficient manner possible.

RESOURCES TO BE ALLOCATED

Salespeople manage many resources. Some of these are physical resources, such as free samples, demonstration products, trial products, brochures, direct mail budgets, and other marketing resources. Each of these physical resources represents a cost to the company, but to the salesperson they are investments. Salespeople consider physical resources as investments because resources must be managed wisely to generate the best possible return. Whereas financial investments may return dividends or price increases, the salesperson's investments should yield sales.

A key resource that salespeople manage is time. Time is limited, and not all of a salesperson's work time can be spent making sales calls. Some time must be spent attending meetings, learning new products, preparing reports for management, traveling to sales calls, and handling other nonselling duties; in fact, nonselling activities can take up to 70 percent of a salesperson's time. Thus, being able to manage time wisely is important. As we discuss in the next chapter, salespeople also coordinate many of the company's other departments to serve customers well. Salespeople must learn how to allocate these resources in ways that generate the greatest level of sales.

WHERE TO ALLOCATE RESOURCES

For salespeople the allocation of resources is often a question of finding the customers or companies that are most likely to buy and then allocating selling resources to maximize the opportunities they offer. As you may have learned in your principles of marketing course, some market segments are more profitable than others. And just as the company's marketing executive tries to determine which segments are most profitable so that marketing plans can be directed toward those segments, salespeople examine their markets to allocate their selling resources.

Maximizing the opportunity means finding profitable ways to satisfy the greatest number of customers, but not necessarily everybody. One study of services customers found that only 44 percent were profitable; the rest cost the company money.[3] In the following section we discuss how to analyze the market to identify potential customers that are most likely to buy so resources will be allocated properly.

ACCOUNT CLASSIFICATION AND RESOURCE ALLOCATION

Not all customers have the same buying potential, just as not all sales activities produce the same results. The salesperson has to concentrate on the most profitable customers and minimize effort spent with customers that offer little opportunity for profitable sales. The proportion of unprofitable accounts is usually greater than one would think. As a rule, 80 percent of the sales in a territory come from only 20 percent of the customers. Therefore, salespeople should classify customers on the basis of their sales potential to avoid spending too much time and other resources with low-potential accounts, thus helping to achieve sales goals.

Customer management is not just a time management issue. Managing customers includes allocating all the resources at the salesperson's disposal in the most productive manner. Time may be the most important of these resources, but salespeople also manage sample and demonstration inventories, entertainment and travel budgets, printed materials, and other resources.

ABC Analysis

The simplest classification scheme, called **ABC analysis,** ranks accounts by sales potential. The idea is that the accounts with the greatest sales potential deserve the most attention. Using the 80/20 rule, the salesperson identifies the 20 percent of accounts that (could) buy the most and calls those A accounts. The other 80 percent are B accounts, and noncustomers (or accounts with low potential for sales) are C accounts. Eli Lilly (a pharmaceuticals company) classifies physicians and SC Johnson Wax classifies retail stores this way. One use is planning sales calls; so for example, A accounts could be seen every two weeks, B accounts every six weeks, and C accounts only if there is nothing else to do. An example of an account analysis appears in Exhibit 15.4. As you can see, Sam Thompson has used estimated potential to classify accounts so he can allocate sales calls to accounts with the greatest potential.

ABC classification schemes work well only in industries that require regular contact with the same accounts, such as consumer packaged goods and pharmaceuticals. Some industries (plant equipment, medical equipment, and other capital products) may require numerous sales calls until the product is sold. After that sale, another sale may be unlikely for several years, and the number of sales calls may diminish. Then the A, B, and C classification may not be helpful.

Salespeople in some industries find grid and customer relationship analysis methods more useful than ABC analysis. They have learned that simply allocating sales activities on the basis of sales potential may lead to inefficiencies. For example, to maximize great potential, satisfied customers may need fewer calls than accounts of equal potential that are loyal to a competitor.

Grid Analysis

The **sales call allocation grid** classifies accounts on the basis of the company's competitive position with an account, along with the account's sales potential. As with ABC analysis, the purpose of classifying accounts through grid analysis is to determine which accounts should receive more resources. By this method, each

Exhibit 15.4

Account Classification

Salesperson: Sam Thompson   A. Analysis of Call Pattern: 2011

Customer Type	Number of Customers Contacted	Number of Calls	Average Calls per Customer	Sales Volume	Average Sales per Call
A	15	121	8.1	$212,515	$1,756
B	21	154	7.3	115,451	756
C	32	226	7.0	78,010	345
D	59	320	5.4	53,882	168
Total	127	821		$460,859	561

B. Annual Territory Sales Plan (dollars in thousands)

Account	Actual Sales 2009	2010	2011	2012 Estimated Potential Sales	Forecast	Number of Calls Allocated	Classification
Allied Foods	$100	$110	$150	$250	$150	48	A
Pic N-Save	75	75	90	300	115	48	A
Wright Grocers	40	50	60	175	90	24	B
H.E.B.	20	30	30	150	30	24	B
Piggly Wiggly	10	10	25	100	55	18	C
Sal's Superstore	0	0	30	100	80	18	C
Buy-Rite	0	0	0	80	75	18	C
Tom Thumb	0	10	20	75	70	18	C
Apple Tree	0	5	12	60	60	12	D
Buy Lo	0	0	10	60	50	12	D
Whyte's Family Foods	10	8	9	50	40	12	D

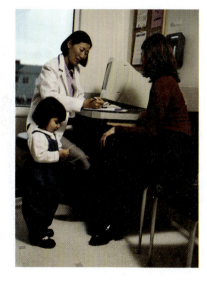

Although Dr. Liu's practice may appear smaller than that of the clinic on the right, the astute salesperson would determine each business's sales potential before classifying either as an A, B, or C account.

Exhibit 15.5

Sales Call Allocation Grid

	Strength of Position	
	Strong	**Weak**
High (Account Opportunity)	**Segment 1** Attractiveness: Accounts are very attractive because they offer high opportunity, and the sales organization has a strong position. Sales call strategy: Accounts should receive a high level of sales calls because they are the sales organization's most attractive accounts.	**Segment 2** Attractiveness: Accounts are potentially attractive because they offer high opportunity, but the sales organization currently has a weak position with accounts. Sales call strategy: Accounts should receive a high level of sales calls to strengthen the sales organization's position.
Low (Account Opportunity)	**Segment 3** Attractiveness: Accounts are somewhat attractive because the sales organization has a strong position, but future opportunity is limited. Sales call strategy: Accounts should receive a moderate level of sales calls to maintain the current strength of the sales organization's position.	**Segment 4** Attractiveness: Accounts are very unattractive because they offer low opportunity, and the sales organization has a weak position. Sales call strategy: Accounts should receive a minimal level of sales calls, and efforts should be made to selectively eliminate or replace personal sales calls with telephone sales calls, direct mail, etc.

Source: Raymond W. LaForge, Clifford E. Young, and B. Curtis Hamm, "Increasing Sales Productivity through Improved Sales Call Allocation Strategies," *Journal of Personal Selling and Sales Management,* November 1983, pp. 53–59.

account in a salesperson's territory falls into one of the four segments shown in Exhibit 15.5. The classification is determined by the salesperson's evaluation of the account on the following two dimensions.

First, the **account opportunity** dimension indicates how much the customer needs the product and whether the customer is able to buy the product. Some factors the salesperson can consider when determining account opportunity are the account's sales potential, growth rate, and financial condition. This rating is similar to the ABC analysis and is a measure of total sales potential. Again, the idea is that accounts with the greatest opportunity deserve the greatest resources.

Second, the **strength of position** dimension indicates how strong the salesperson and company are in selling the account. Some factors that determine strength of position are the present share of the account's purchases of the product, the attitude of the account toward the company and the salesperson, and the relationship between the salesperson and the key decision makers in the account. The strength of position helps the salesperson understand what level of sales is likely in the account. The account opportunity may be tremendous—say, $1 million. But if the account has always purchased another brand, the salesperson's strength of position is weak, and his or her real potential is something much less than $1 million.

Global accounts represent a difficult challenge in terms of determining potential and position. Position may be strong in one location and weak in another; potential may also vary. Marvin Wagner, an engineer with John Deere, has been working with Deere engineers and suppliers to Deere to standardize products globally. He's had to help suppliers negotiate with buying centers involving engineers in as many as four different countries, all with different expectations and preferences for different vendors. What may be preferred by engineers at the Arc-les-Gray plant in France may not even be considered by engineers in Ottumwa, Iowa.

The appropriate sales call strategy depends on the grid segment into which the account falls. Accounts with high potential and a strong position are very attractive because the salesperson should be able to sell large amounts relatively easily. Thus, these attractive accounts should receive the highest level of sales calls. For example, if you have an account that likes your product and has established a budget for it, and you know that the customer needs 300 units per year, you may consider that customer to be a segment 1 account (assuming 300 units is a high number) and plan to allocate more calls to that account. But if a competitor has a three-year contract with the account, you might be better off spending less time there. The account may buy 3,000 units per year, but you have little chance of getting any of that business. By classifying the account as a segment 2, you would recognize that the most appropriate strategy is to strengthen your position in the account. The sales call allocation grid, then, aids salespeople in determining where, by account, to spend time in order to meet sales goals.

THE GRID AND CURRENT CUSTOMERS The sales call allocation grid is a great tool for analyzing current customers. Recall the value of a customer that was discussed in Chapter 13; many businesses experience little or no profit in the first year of a customer's life. But over time profit grows if the salesperson can increase sales in the account, find ways to reduce the cost to serve the account (for example, shipping more can lower shipping costs), and so on.

In a landmark study of the paper and plastics industry, the key to a company's profit was found to be customer share, not market share. **Customer share,** also called **account share,** is the average percentage of business received from a company's accounts in a particular category. A similar term is **share of wallet,** which is the same thing but usually for an individual consumer. Over 15 years ago, an analysis of companies in that industry indicated that even if a company was the dominant supplier to a group of buyers, another company could be more profitable if it served fewer customers but had all their business.[4] Since that study, numerous studies have found similar insights. As a result, many companies are looking for how to increase account share, rather than the number of accounts.[5]

INVESTING IN ACCOUNTS

Planning based on customer analysis should result in more effective use of the opportunities presented by accounts. This improvement relates to better use of time, which is allocated to the appropriate accounts (see From the Buyer's Seat 15.1). But developing good strategies entails more than developing good time use plans; strategies require the use of other resources as well.

Salespeople invest time, free samples or trials, customer training, displays, and other resources in their customers. Companies such as IBM use predictive modeling to determine which accounts are likely to be more productive. This knowledge helps salespeople determine where to invest resources—time, samples, displays, and so forth. Sales costs, or costs associated with the use of such resources, are not always costs in the traditional sense but rather are investments in the asset called customers. This asset generates nearly all of a firm's revenue. Viewed from this perspective, formulating a strategy to allocate resources to maintaining or developing customers becomes vitally important.

Salespeople must determine not only which customers require sales effort, but also what activities should occur. CRM software can assist through

From the BUYER'S SEAT

SALES ACCORDING TO WOODY ALLEN

Woody Allen, the famous movie director, says that 80 percent of success is just showing up. Paul Tepfenhart, vice president of e-commerce for the grocer HEB, agrees. As one who has bought many technology solutions for HEB and formerly for Walmart.com, Paul has had a great deal of experience observing whether salespeople show up.

"There is no substitute for personal interaction," says Paul. He notes that "companies sell very little in the B2B environment. People buy from people." During the sales process, he emphasizes the importance of judging how a salesperson will take care of him after the sale by what happens during the sale. "Nothing damages credibility as a lack of dependability. Not showing up, being late, being unprepared are all symptoms of what might be poor execution later, something no buyer can afford. In sales, showing up, being prepared, optimistic, personable, and engaged is essential. It is the price of entry. It overcomes many other shortfalls. A successful start to a sales career begins with making an unwavering commitment to show up."

Greg May agrees. Greg is one of Honda's top dealers and chairs the company's dealer committee for technology. "I was looking at making a purchase of a technology platform to serve my customers more effectively and had scheduled an introductory call with a salesperson from an agency that would not only provide me the technology, they would also create the applications and campaigns using the technology. But then the salesperson stood me up for the call—no notice, no follow-up for 24 hours. I can't trust my customers' well-being and my business to someone who can't even answer the phone when they say they will."

Paul offers a more positive example. "A more recent one involved Sarah who worked for a CPG (consumer package goods) company for about three years. She was always on time and prepared with her company's view of the category and how we were performing versus our competitors. Her philosophy came across as 'I am here to help you win by growing your category relative to your competitors.'" Paul recognizes that "she wanted to grow her branded items and finding a common objective made it a shared mission between me (her buyer) and her." Paul says the door opened for her when her competitor failed to meet his commitments. "Because Sarah was diligent and dependable and showed up, she grew her shelf space, achieved better placement on the shelf, and got the promotion (to feature her product) she had presented repeatedly. Beating the competition is not always having the better offer, but it always is consistently being there and doing exactly what you commit. Sarah has double-digit growth, and her competitor is scrambling to make up for his lack of dependability."

Woody Allen was right—opportunities are there only for those who show up.

pipeline analysis: a process for identifying and managing sales opportunities, also known as *opportunity management*. Recall that in Chapter 6 we discussed how accounts can move through stages from lead to prospect to customer. NetSuite, for example, can complete a pipeline analysis, telling the salesperson how well she is moving accounts from one stage to the next. In addition to being useful in determining conversion ratios and ensuring that a salesperson is creating enough opportunities to reach sales goals, pipeline analysis requires identifying which stage an account is in. Recognizing the account's stage in the pipeline is useful to determine what steps are appropriate. You don't want to try to do a spec design with a prospect for whom you haven't finished identifying needs, for example.

IMPLEMENTING THE TIME MANAGEMENT STRATEGY

Time is a limited resource. Once spent, it cannot be regained. How salespeople choose to use their time often means the difference between superstar success and average performance. Susan Flaviano, a sales manager for Lonseal, offers the

SALES Technology

PRESALE TECHNOLOGY

There's no doubt that the last few minutes of the sales process are critical. That moment when the account goes from prospect to customer is a moment to enjoy, to savor, to celebrate. But so much leads up to that moment, and much of that presale effort is supported by technology.

The effects of technology are felt even before there is a territory! A sales territory can be optimally created using software such as GeoMetrx (www.geomtrx.com), just one of many that combine data on potential customers with mapping capabilities to create balanced and optimized sales territories. Centrix Pharmaceuticals, for example, uses the software not only to create sales territories but also to help salespeople generate call patterns that minimize time wasted driving from one doctor to the next.

Another important presale technology is lead nurturing software, also called marketing automation. Aprimo (www.aprimo.com), for example, is one program that allows marketers to communicate with leads before they are prospects. Because so many purchases now start with research on the Web, software helps sellers identify those who are browsing on the company's Web site. The same software can then apply marketing automation tools to "talk" via e-mail, chat, text, or any other digital channel to potential buyers early in the research process. Then, when the potential buyer has signaled sufficient interest, the lead is passed on to the salesperson. United Rentals (the largest construction equipment rental company in the world) uses Aprimo to follow browsers, offer additional material to help them make decisions, and then, when the time is right, introduce the salesperson.

Together, these two technologies mean more sales calls on higher probability accounts, resulting in more sales per salesperson. Most salespeople, though, are not even aware that their company uses such software. The Dwyer Group, for example, uses Eloqua (an Oracle product) for marketing automation, but the salespeople know only that their leads have already gotten certain information about the company's offerings and what information the leads have shared online. This above-the-funnel interaction means a lot fewer cold calls and more time spent with people who are ready to buy.

following tips for managing your time as a salesperson; keep these in mind as you read through this section:

- Start early. Get a jump start to the day before anyone else. Then you control the day without the day controlling you.
- Manage responsiveness. Although responsiveness is key to being successful, you cannot let customer calls, e-mail messages, and voice mail consume your day. We now have the ability to respond immediately, but it is important to choose specific times during the day to reply to correspondence.
- Schedule in advance. I set most of my appointments one week in advance, which helps me stay on target. Usually, if there is not a set commitment, it is easy to justify staying in the office to get caught up on paperwork.
- Use downtime wisely. If you have a canceled appointment or extra time over lunch, or you arrive to an appointment early, use this time to plan or follow up. With our laptops and sophisticated project tracking tools, you can use this time anywhere and reduce the amount of time spent in your office or at home on Saturday catching up on paperwork![6]

Remember that your time is worth $30 to $40 an hour, but only if you use it to sell. Your company has invested a great deal to get prospects ready to see you (see Sales Technology 15.1) but all of that goes for nought if no sales call is made. Use your time to hone a golf game or spruce up the yard, and opportunities to sell disappear. Although no manager really knows how a salesperson uses time, when the results are posted, accurate conclusions can be drawn.

DAILY ACTIVITY PLANNING

To be effective time planners, salespeople must have a good understanding of their own work habits. For example, some people tend to procrastinate in getting the day started, whereas others may want to knock off early. If you are a late riser, you may want to schedule early appointments to force yourself to get started. On the other hand, if your problem is heading for home too early, schedule late appointments so you work a full day.

Many salespeople have the opposite problem—they never seem to stop working. One study found that 81 percent of salespeople felt like they had to be available to their customers 24/7.[7] The iPad, iPhone, and other similar products make the Internet and phone ubiquitous, but that is no excuse for failing to plan adequately. Susan Flaviano, now a sales manager for Lonseal, believed quantity of calls was the most important thing. But after a while, she realized she had no personal life and, more importantly, no more success than anyone else. She backed off the quantity of calls and began to spend more time planning her activities; the result was an increase in both sales and personal time.[8]

GUIDELINES

Salespeople need to include time for prospecting and customer care in their daily activities. Some minimize the time for such activities because they think sales do not occur on such calls, but prospects and happy customers feed future sales. Ikon, an office equipment dealer, requires salespeople to handle customer care calls before 9 a.m. and after 4 p.m. and to schedule prospecting activities between 10 a.m. and noon and between 2 p.m. and 3 p.m. Scheduled appointments are worked in when customers require them. The company bases these guidelines on its experience with buyers and when they are available.

Such planning guides are designed to maximize **prime selling time**—the time of day at which a salesperson is most likely to see a buyer. One salesperson, Lee Brubaker with Sandler Systems, calls this "pay time."[9] Prime selling time depends on the buyer's industry. For example, a good time to call on bankers is late afternoon, after the bank has closed to customers. However, late afternoon is a bad time to call on physicians, who are then making rounds at the hospital or trying to catch up on a full day's schedule of patients. Prime selling time should be devoted to sales calls, with the rest of the day used for nonselling activities such as servicing accounts, doing paperwork, or getting information from the home office.

Prime selling time varies from country to country. In the United States prime selling time is usually 9 a.m. to 4 p.m. with the noon hour off for lunch. In Mexico lunch starts and ends later, generally from 12:30 to 2:00 p.m.; offices may not close until 7 p.m. or later. In Great Britain prime selling time starts later; a British Telecom rep may not begin making calls until 10 a.m.

PLANNING PROCESS

A process exists to help you plan your daily activities, with or without the aid of planning guides. This process can even help you now, as a student, take more control of your time and use it effectively.

As Exhibit 15.6 shows, you begin by making a to-do list. Then you determine the priority of each activity on your list. Many executives rank activities as A, B,

Exhibit 15.6
Activities Planning
Process

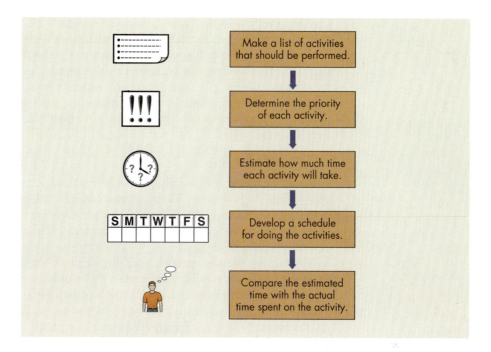

or C, with A activities requiring immediate action, B activities being of secondary importance, and C activities being done only if time allows. You can correlate these A, B, and C activities with the A, B, and C accounts discussed earlier, as well as activities such as paperwork and training. Prioritizing activities helps you choose which activities to perform first.

Note the difference between activities that seem urgent and activities that truly are important. For example, when the phone rings, most people stop whatever they are doing to answer it. The ringing phone seems urgent. Activities such as requests from managers or even customers may have that same sense of urgency; the desire to drop everything else to handle the request is called the "tyranny of the urgent." And the "urgent" can get overwhelming: The average businessperson receives 274 personal e-mail messages and 304 business e-mail messages weekly, and according to another study, that number will grow as marketers increase their use of e-mail marketing.[10] Of course these statistics do not include telephone requests from customers. Yet, like most phone calls, even requests from customers may be less important than other tasks. Successful businesspeople learn to recognize what is truly urgent and prioritize those activities first.

The next step in the planning process is to estimate the time required for each activity. In sales, as we mentioned earlier, time must be set aside for customer care and prospecting. The amount of time depends on the activity goals set earlier and on how long each call should take. However, salespeople often have unique activities, such as special sales calls, demonstrations, customer training, and sales meetings, to plan for as well. Time must also be set aside for planning and paperwork.

The next step, developing an effective schedule, requires estimating the amount of time such activities will require. As follow-up, be sure to compare how long an activity actually took with how long you thought it would take. Comparing actual time to planned time with the aid of calendaring tools in software systems like NetSuite can help you plan more accurately in the future.

Using the Computer for Planning

Many of the same customer management programs that salespeople use to identify and analyze accounts incorporate time-planning elements. This software can generate to-do lists and calendars through a tickler file or by listing certain customer types. A **tickler file** is a file or calendar that salespeople use to remember when to call specific accounts. For example, if customer A says to call back in 90 days, the computer will remind ("tickle") the salesperson in 90 days to call that customer. Or if the company just introduced a product that can knock out competitor B, the computer can generate a list of prospects with products from competitor B; the salesperson then has a list of prospects for the new product.

Need for Flexibility

Although working out a daily plan is important, occasions will arise when the plan should be laid aside. You cannot accurately judge the time needed for each sales call, and hastily concluding a sales presentation just to stick to a schedule would be foolish. If more time at one account will mean better sales results, the schedule should be revised.

To plan for the unexpected, your first visit of the day should be to a prime prospect (in the terms discussed earlier, this would be an A account or activity); then the next best potential customer should be visited (provided the travel time is reasonable); and so forth. If an emergency causes a change of plans, at least the calls most likely to result in sales will have been made.

MAKING MORE CALLS

Making daily plans and developing efficient routes are important steps toward better time use. But suppose you could make just one more call per day. Using our analysis from the beginning of this chapter and Exhibit 15.3, this change would mean 240 more calls per year, which is like adding one month to the year!

Some salespeople develop an "out Tuesday, back Friday" complex. They can offer many reasons why they need to be back in the office or at home on Monday and Friday afternoons. Such a behavior pattern means the salesperson makes 20 to 30 percent fewer calls than a salesperson who works a full week. John Plott, with DG Vault, got one large sale by working the full week. He was making cold calls on a Friday afternoon, trying to set up appointments for the following week, when he reached an attorney whose current vendor was unable to meet a deadline. The attorney said if he could get the software set up that afternoon, he could have the business. The result was a $30,000 account and $4,500 in commission.[11]

Salespeople who make calls in bad weather often find that their competition has taken the day off, leaving the field wide open for those who want to succeed.

To get the most out of a territory, the sales representative must make full use of all available days. For example, the days before or after holidays are often seen as bad selling days. Hence, while the competition takes those extra days off, the salesperson can be working and making sales calls he or she would otherwise miss. The same reasoning applies to bad weather: Bad weather reduces competition and makes things easier for the salesperson who doesn't find excuses to take it easy. On the other hand, good weather can tempt the salesperson to the golf course, doing yard work, or otherwise avoiding the job. No matter the weather, the professional salesperson continues to work.

Salespeople can use certain techniques to increase the time they spend in front of customers selling instead of traveling. We mentioned Susan Flaviano's (Lonseal sales manager) challenges in managing her time earlier. One of her solutions, in addition to planning her time more effectively, was to use GPS routing software to help her plan her travel time more efficiently. Using routing techniques means she spends less time in the car and more time in front of customers.[12]

Routing

Routing is a method of planning sales calls in a specific order to minimize travel time. Two types of sales call patterns, routine and variable, can be more efficient with effective routing. Using **routine call patterns,** a salesperson sees the same customers regularly. For example, Eli Lilly pharmaceutical salespeople's call plans enable them to see all important doctors in their territory at least once every six weeks. Some doctors (those who see large numbers of certain types of patients) are visited every two weeks. The salesperson repeats the pattern every six weeks, ensuring the proper call level.

Variable call patterns occur when the salesperson must call on accounts in an irregular order. In this situation the salesperson would not routinely call on each account within a specified period. Routing techniques are useful, but the salesperson may not repeat the call plan on a cyclical basis.

The four types of routing plans, **circular routing, leapfrog routing, straight-line routing,** and **cloverleaf routing,** are illustrated in Exhibit 15.7. If an Eli Lilly

Exhibit 15.7

Types of Routing Plans

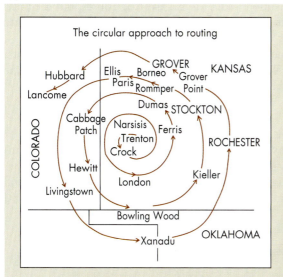

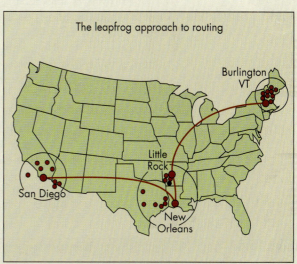

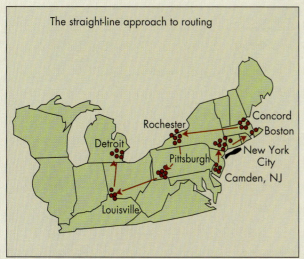

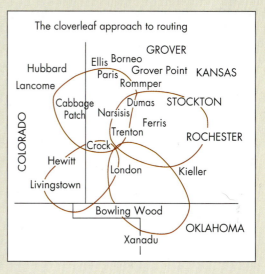

salesperson used the cloverleaf method (with six leaves instead of four) for a routine call pattern, every sixth Tuesday would find that salesperson in the same spot. But a salesperson with variable call patterns could use the cloverleaf method to plan sales calls for an upcoming week and then use the straight-line method the next week. The pattern would vary depending on the demands of the customers and the salesperson's ability to schedule calls at convenient times.

Zoning

Zoning means dividing the territory into zones, based on ease of travel and concentration of customers, to minimize travel time. First, the salesperson locates concentrations of accounts on a map. For example, an office supply salesperson may find that many accounts are located downtown, with other concentrations around the airport, in an industrial park, and in a part of town where two highways cross near a rail line. Each area is the center of a zone. The salesperson then plans to spend a day, for example, in each zone. In a territory zoned like the one in Exhibit 15.8, the salesperson might spend Monday in zone 1, Tuesday in zone 2, and so forth.

Zoning works best for compact territories or for situations in which salespeople do not call regularly on the same accounts. (In a large territory, such as the entire Midwest, a salesperson is more likely to use leapfrog routes, but the principle is similar.) Calling on customers that are in a relatively small area minimizes travel time between calls.

Salespeople can also combine zoning with routing, using a circular approach within a zone, for example. When zones are designed properly, travel time between accounts should be minimal.

Using E-Mail and Telephone

Customer contacts should not always be in-person sales calls—the phone or e-mail can be effective. For example, some customer care calls can be handled by simply sending the customer an e-mail message asking whether everything is OK. The customer may appreciate the e-mail more than a personal visit because it can be read and responded to when the customer has time and

Exhibit 15.8
Zoning a Sales Territory A salesperson may work in zone 1 on Monday, zone 2 on Tuesday, and so forth.

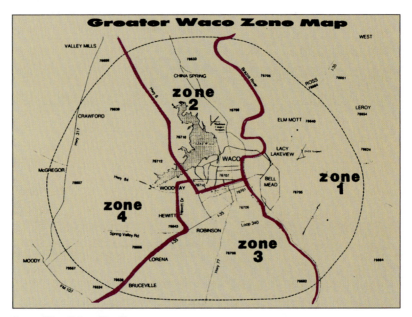

Source: *Waco Tribune Herald.*

doesn't interfere with other pressing responsibilities. The salesperson may be able to make more customer care calls by e-mail, increasing the number of contacts with customers. Keep in mind, though, that not all customer care activities should be handled by e-mail or phone. Recall from Chapter 14 that there are many reasons, such as reorders and cross-selling, to continue to make sales calls in person to current customers. For example, Sandra Kennedy, account executive for Spherion, has one account that she visits weekly. "It's my largest and most complicated account, and it just takes face time to make sure everything is going smoothly."[13]

Similarly, the telephone and direct mail can be used profitably for prospecting, as we discussed in Chapter 6. More calls, or customer contacts, can be made equally effectively with judicious use of e-mail and the telephone.

HANDLING PAPERWORK AND REPORTS

Every sales job requires preparing reports for management. All salespeople complain about such paperwork, but it is important. As we discuss later, paperwork can provide information that helps a salesperson determine what should be improved. The information also helps management decide what types of marketing plans work and should be used again. Therefore, every salesperson should learn to handle paperwork efficiently.

Paperwork time is less productive than time spent selling to customers, so completing it quickly is important. Salespeople can do several things to minimize the impact of paperwork on their prime selling time.

First, salespeople should think positively about paperwork. Although less productive than selling, it can increase their productivity and the productivity of the company's marketing programs by facilitating a detailed review of selling activities and marketing programs.

Second, salespeople should not let paperwork accumulate. We once knew of a salesperson who never did expense reports. He finally offered a summer intern 10 percent if she would complete his expense reports for the previous 12 months. This deal cost him $600; in addition, he was essentially lending the company $500 per month, interest free.

Routine reports should be completed daily. Nonproductive time (like time spent waiting for a customer) can be used for paperwork. Call reports and account records should be updated immediately after the calls so that important points are remembered and any follow-up actions can be planned.

Finally, salespeople should set aside a block of nonselling time for paperwork. The quickest way to do this job is to concentrate on it and avoid interruptions. Setting aside a small amount of time at the beginning or end of each day for writing thank-you and follow-up notes and completing reports saves prime selling time for selling activities while ensuring that the salesperson keeps up with paperwork.

Many companies now provide their salespeople with wireless notebook or pad computers so they can access customer information and complete paperwork in the field, sometimes even in a customer's office.

Using the Computer to Handle Paperwork and Communications

Many companies, such as McGraw-Hill, give their salespeople pad, laptop, or notebook computers. These computers can be hooked up to the company's network to access customer information and process other paperwork automatically. Salespeople who travel can thus complete their paperwork while in a hotel, an airport waiting area, and other places. Voice recognition systems enable salespeople to do paperwork without any paper. Companies such as Giant Eagle, a grocery distributor, use such systems to enable salespeople to call orders in and handle other paperwork from their cell phones.[14]

Salespeople calling on overseas accounts can also file reports or check the status of orders, even though the home office in another time zone may be closed for the night. Computers can help international selling organizations operate smoothly by reducing communication barriers between the field and the home office. Computers and fax machines enable salespeople to communicate with colleagues and customers all around the world, despite significant time differences.

Some customer relationship management packages, like NetSuite, include territory management capabilities. These packages allow salespeople to track their performance by calculating conversion rates, commissions, expenses, and other important figures. Such technology enables salespeople to file reports quickly. Salespeople for J&K Sales Associates (Manchester, New Hampshire) input detailed call information into a simple Outlook file. The detail includes the buyer's stage in the buying cycle (J&K uses five stages, from introduction to postsale follow-up) based on the purpose of the sales call. The company has seen greater than 20 percent productivity improvement throughout the organization simply because all company members, from the purchasing department to customer billing, have the information they need at their computers.[15]

To manage your time wisely, you must exploit a scarce resource in the most effective manner possible. Your objective is to make as many quality calls as possible by reserving prime selling time for selling activities. Routing, zoning, goal setting, and other methods of planning and scheduling time will help you maximize your prime selling time.

EVALUATING PERFORMANCE

Success in sales is a result of how hard and how smart a salesperson works. Unlike many other workers, salespeople have a great deal of control over both how hard and how smart they work. Evaluating performance is the component of self-management that provides direction for how hard the salesperson should be working as well as an opportunity to determine which strategies work best. Salespeople should evaluate each sales call individually but also look at which activity leads to desired outcomes and at what rate. Tom Jud expresses his perspective on evaluating performance in Building Partnerships 15.1, and the importance of recognizing what's important through self-evaluation. Let's examine each component in more detail.

POSTCALL ANALYSIS

At the end of each call, many salespeople take a moment to write down what occurred and what needs to be done, perhaps using a printed form or entering the information into a territory management program such as NetSuite. Information such as the customer's purchase volume, key people in the decision process, and current vendors is important to have, but so is personal information such as the fact that the buyer's three children play soccer. The salesperson can use that information when preparing for the next call.

Remember the plan you made for each sales call? That plan included one or more objectives. Postcall analysis should include reflecting on whether those objectives were reached. The professional salesperson not only looks for specific areas to improve but also evaluates the success of the overall sales call.

URGENT VERSUS IMPORTANT—NOT ALWAYS THE SAME

"We have a tendency to focus on the *urgent* things in life. But the more time we spend doing the *important* things, the greater success we can have," says Tom Jud, VP of inside sales at CA Technologies. Tom refers often to Dr. Stephen R. Covey, a highly recognized author and business consultant, who illustrates the difference between these two through his creation of the urgent-versus-important matrix. Urgent things are those crises, emergencies, and deadlines that monopolize our time. But the truth is that while these things seem so critically important, they really steal our attention away from the value activities that drive our businesses, like planning, prospecting, and meeting with customers. Learning to *manage* the urgent things and *focus* on the important things leads to greater efficiency and success.

Tom has been in sales and sales management for 16 years. Throughout those years he has seen how time management really can make or break a successful salesperson. He determined early on in his career that he would focus on the important things and manage time well, even if that meant doing administrative and clerical work during lunch or after hours. And many times it did. "I didn't want to waste a minute on anything that did not add value if I could be in front of a customer or prospect." He had witnessed how seemingly urgent activities could eat up a salesperson's day. "In sales, there is only a limited amount of time during a workday to connect and visit with your prospects and customers.

If you are not in front of them, your competition will be. Yet we let countless other things clog up our days and occupy our time. A lot of time we feel like we're being efficient and productive, but at the end of the day, we drive home from work wondering 'what did I even accomplish today?'"

Tom explains that this feeling of regret is a result of focusing on the urgent things during the day rather than the important activities. Forms may have been filled out, contracts drawn up, and e-mails replied to. These activities make us feel busy and productive, but did any of them really drive value creation or further long-term goals? Most likely not.

"Understanding that you only have a limited time to create value and do important things can revolutionize the way you work." Tom urges his salespeople to focus on the important things, like reaching customers during critical hours, planning sales call, and prospecting, to create value. He tells his salespeople, "When you manage the urgent things and focus on the important things, you'll quickly climb to the top. The drive home will no longer be filled with unsettling questions about productivity but rather, feelings of accomplishment and excitement."

"We are all given the same amount of time. We can't buy or add any minutes, hours, or days to our lives. But what we do with it and how we use that time is up to us."

Source: Brooke Borgias; used with permission.

ACTIVITY ANALYSIS

When planning their time, salespeople set certain activity goals. They use these goals not only as guidelines but also to evaluate their own performance. At the end of each day, week, and month, salespeople should review their activities in relation to the goals they set. Goals are written down or entered into NetSuite when they are set—say, Sunday evening when planning the following week. Then, on Friday evening, the actual activities from each day would be tallied and totaled for the week and compared to the goals. The salesperson could then evaluate whether more calls of a certain type are needed in the following week.

Merrill Lynch, for example, recommends that new brokers make 100 telephone calls each day (calls count even if no one answers). Frank Baugh, a new broker in central Texas, made 7,544 calls in his first 92 working days, or 82 calls per day. His goal is now 120 calls per day to bring his average up to 100 in the next quarter.

PERFORMANCE ANALYSIS

Salespeople also need to evaluate performance relative to performance goals set earlier. For example, they often evaluate sales performance in terms of percentage

Exhibit 15.9

Sales Evaluation
Measures

Evaluation Measure	Calculation	How to Use It
Conversion rate For total performance By customer type By product type	Number of sales —————————— Number of calls	Are your strategies effective? Do you need to improve by working smarter (i.e., a better strategy to improve your hit rate)? Compare yours to your company and/or industry average.
Sales achievement	$ Actual sales —————————— $ Sales goal	Is your overall performance where you believe it should be? Are you meeting your goals? Your company's goals?
Commission	$ Actual commission —————————— $ Earnings goal	
Sales volume (in dollars) By customer type		Where are you most effective? Do you need help with a customer type?
By product category		Are you selling the whole line?
By market share		How are you doing relative to your competition?
By new customers		Are you building new business?
By old customers		Are you servicing your accounts properly?
Sales calls Prospecting calls Account calls Sales presentations Call frequency by customer type		Are your efforts in the right place?

of quota achieved. Of course a commission or a bonus check also tells the salesperson if the earnings goal was met.

An earnings goal can be an effective check for overall performance, but salespeople also need to evaluate sales by product type, as outlined in Exhibit 15.9. Salespeople who sell only part of the product line may be missing opportunities for cross-selling or full-line selling, which means they have to work harder to achieve the same level of sales as the salesperson who successfully integrates cross-selling and full-line selling in the sales strategy.

PRODUCTIVITY ANALYSIS

Salespeople also need to identify which strategies work. For example, if using a certain strategy improved the ratio of appointments to cold calls made, that approach should be continued. Otherwise the salesperson should change it or go back to a previous approach. Frank Baugh, the Merrill Lynch broker, tried several approaches before settling on one that works well for him. Of course Baugh keeps good records, so he knows what works and what does not.

The **conversion ratio,** or number of sales per calls, is an important measure of effectiveness. Conversion ratios should also be calculated by account type; for example, a conversion ratio for type A accounts should be determined. Other conversion ratios can also pinpoint effective strategies and areas that need improvement.

Conversion ratios can also be calculated for each step of the sales cycle. Profiles International, for example, calculates the conversion ratio of leads to prospects to determine which marketing activities generate the highest number of qualified sales leads. These leads can be tracked all the way to the close, too, telling Dario Parolo, vice president of marketing, where to invest his marketing activities.

SELLING YOURSELF

A theme for this chapter is self-analysis to improve performance. As a student, engaging in self-analysis is important so you repeat activities that are successful (lead to good grades) and avoid those that are not. Did pulling an all-nighter improve your exam performance? Or did you do better when you studied for shorter periods each day beginning a week ahead?

Similarly, if you are in an organization and examine the organization's recruiting practices, you'll find that some methods work better than others. What method of finding leads worked best—posting a flyer in the dorms or posting an e-vite on Facebook? What events attracted the largest crowds, and which events provided the best prospective members? By applying what you've learned in this chapter to organizational recruiting (or fund-raising or other activities that mimic the sales process), you'll be able to improve your organization's performance.

But what about you? Do you set goals for your academic performance each semester? Do you track your progress toward those goals and keep the goals visible as a way to motivate yourself? Paul Lushin, a noted sales trainer based in Indianapolis, says, "Over the years, I've come to know myself very well: what makes me work harder and what I have to do to make myself do things I really don't want to do so that I can enjoy the performance I seek. I find that teaching this concept of knowing yourself is one of the most important things that can help salespeople succeed."[16] While he was talking about salespeople, the concept applies to students, too.

SUMMARY

A sales territory can be viewed as a small business. Territory salespeople have the freedom to establish programs and strategies. They manage a number of resources, including physical resources such as sample inventory, displays, demonstration equipment, and perhaps a company vehicle. More important, they manage their time, their customers, and their skills.

Managing a territory involves setting performance, activity, and conversion goals. Salespeople use these goals to allocate time to various activities and to manage customers.

To manage customers well, the salesperson must analyze their potential. Accounts can be classified using the ABC method or the sales call allocation grid. These analyses tell how much effort should be put into each account. Some organizations use CRM software to conduct these analyses on the entire customer database, which helps identify patterns within a territory. Salespeople can use these patterns to develop account sales strategies.

More calls (working harder) can be accomplished by moving nonselling activities, such as paperwork, to nonselling time. Also, selling time can be used more efficiently (working smarter). For example, routing and zoning techniques enable the salesperson to spend more prime selling time in front of customers instead of behind the steering wheel of a car.

Effective planning of the salesperson's day requires setting aside time for important activities such as prospecting and still making the appropriate number of sales appointments. Using the full workweek and employing technology such as telephones, computers, and fax machines can help the salesperson stay ahead of the competition.

Finally, salespeople must manage their skills. Managing skills involves choosing how to make sales calls and improving the way one sells. Improvement requires that salespeople first understand what they do well and what needs improvement. Evaluating their performance can provide them with that insight.

KEY TERMS

ETHICS PROBLEMS

1. A sales manager schedules all sales training and sales meetings on the weekend so salespeople lose no selling time. Is this ethical? Does your answer depend on how they get paid—straight salary, salary plus commission, or straight commission?

2. One company's culture is "flashy," meaning salespeople are expected to wear custom-tailored clothing, flaunt expensive jewelry and watches, and drive expensive cars. Assume you are about to graduate and go to work for this company. Consider this culture and relate it to your goals—how might this culture influence your goals? Is that influence healthy? Why or why not?

QUESTIONS AND PROBLEMS

1. Reread the chapter-opening profile, "From the Buyer's Seat 15.1," and "Building Partnerships 15.1". What themes run through all three essays?

2. Mike Rocker, Susan Flaviano, and many other salespeople work out of their homes. Rocker and Flaviano both recognize how tempting it is to work longer and to put off paperwork until the weekends because it is so convenient. What problems might succumbing to such temptation cause? What safeguards can they put into place?

3. Compare and contrast the special problems of self-management for Mike Rocker (this chapter's opening profile) and John Tanner (he was profiled in Chapter 14). Both work in health care sales, but one travels the western half of the United States and works out of his home, and the other manages a territory consisting of one small city and works out of the office.

4. Shakespeare wrote, "To thine own self be true." How would you apply this statement to your planning and development activities?

5. Which factors are important for classifying customers? Why? How would these factors change depending on the industry?

6. Distinguish between routing and scheduling and between routing and zoning. Explain how routing and scheduling can interact to complement the planning of an efficient day's work.

7. How might a pharmaceutical salesperson increase the number of calls made per day? A financial services representative selling pension plans to companies? A financial services representative selling retirement plans to consumers? A representative who sells golf clubs to retailers and pro shops?

8. One sales manager said, "Sales is a numbers game. To make more sales, make more sales calls." Should sales managers encourage salespeople to continually increase the number of calls made each week? Explain your answer. Reread "From the Buyer's Seat 15.1." How does this essay relate to your answer?

9. One recruiter told a class that students are used to getting feedback on how they are doing every couple of months, but salespeople do not get a "final grade" until a year has gone by. He claims that students have a hard time making that adjustment when they enter the work world.

What do salespeople do to know where they stand at any given time? What do you do now that helps you know where you stand in your classes? Why is such knowledge important?

10. How would you use the sales call allocation grid to determine a prospecting plan? Be specific, and number each step of the process you would use.

11. All semester so far, you've been selling Netsuite in practice role plays. List three benefits that Netsuite provides salespeople in self-management and three benefits for sales managers in supporting the sales team's time and territory management efforts.

CASE PROBLEMS

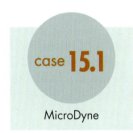

case **15.1**

MicroDyne

When Bill Maguire saw the headline that Micro-Automation and Dynamic Tools merged, he almost passed out. MicroDyne, the new company, would be his account, but what kind of account would it be?

Two years ago Bill landed the Dynamic Tools business after a hard-fought negotiation and sales process. First, the company had been using Bill's strongest competitor, Target Supply, for almost 10 years. Although some minor issues had arisen, overall Dynamic Tools was pretty satisfied. The director of manufacturing, Jack Reilly, really liked the Target Supply rep and fought hard against Bill. In one meeting Jack not only shouted at Bill, he told the head of purchasing that he resented Bill's company even getting a chance to bid! But in the end Bill's lower price and several customer testimonials, including one from a good friend of the CFO, won the business.

Over the two years since, Bill made a lot of progress in strengthening the relationship, except with Jack. But then, six months ago, Jack left Dynamic to take a position with Micro-Automation, also one of Bill's accounts. The first thing he did was call Bill. "Well, guess what, Bill. I'm canceling all outstanding orders with your company as of now. And that pallet of sweepers you sent yesterday? You can come get it. I switched all our business to Target."

Micro-Automation's business for Bill was much smaller than that of Dynamic, so the loss wasn't so bad. But Micro-Automation is bigger overall, and Dynamic Tool was acquired by Micro. Jack was back, as the movie promos say, "bigger and badder than ever."

Suddenly Bill's cell phone rang. The caller ID showed MicroDyne. Was Jack calling to cancel already?

Questions

1. Assess the new MicroDyne account in terms of the sales call allocation grid.

2. Assume the call is not from Jack but from the former Dynamic Tool CFO. She tells you that she is the new CFO, and they will be reviewing all vendors. You ask about Jack's responsibility and job title, and she laughs. "I know what you're thinking. But don't worry. You've done a great job for us. We just want to consolidate all purchases so we know we're getting the best deal." How should Bill respond? What should he do?

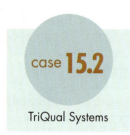

In January, Kevin Ludlum took over the sales team at TriQual Systems (TQS), a company that serves the cable TV industry. TQS installs cable TV equipment at apartment buildings, dorms, and similar high-intensity multitenant dwellings, then provides technical support service to the tenants.

At lunch on Kevin's first day, CEO Dave Dougherty said, "I want the company to expand significantly, but cash is tight, so hiring more salespeople isn't an option. But keep in mind we have a patented technology that our competitors can't match, so continuing our high growth rate seems likely."

"I think the first thing is to assess where we are with our top accounts," Kevin replied. "We don't have 100 percent penetration with any account, do we?" David shook his head no, then said, "We've not been able to get an exclusive agreement except with ACH; they'll use us in all of their new projects and any refurbishing projects. But elsewhere, each new complex is determined by a bid process."

David began to tick off names and discuss the top accounts. "With the exclusive agreement, ACH will be our largest customer by the end of the year. Next will be The Orchard." The Orchard is a company that owns and operates apartments near colleges and universities across the country. There are currently 32 such complexes, with 20 on the books to be built in the coming year. Of those 32, 14 were acquired, and the rest were built by Orchard; half of those built are served by TQS and the others by two other vendors. Of the 14 acquired sites, all were served by various other vendors, but TQS has expressed an interest in upgrading to new equipment over the next two years. "How quickly they refurbish," said David, "will be determined by how well they are able to build the new units within budget, but I'd like to get an exclusive with them because of the growth. But they seem reluctant to put all their eggs in one basket."

Third on the list was Pinetree Properties, a company that owns 64 properties across the South. "They've got us in five of their newer complexes, all of which serve colleges and universities. Our systems are best suited to the high data demands students put on their Internet cable systems. The company has seven older university properties and plans to refurbish two each year. I think we'll win that, as they really see our benefits in that environment. Where we've struggled with them is in their family properties because they don't think it's worth the price premium to get the higher-quality product."

Young & Family was fourth. This family-owned business operates a dozen apartment complexes in Florida, with four in Miami. "Frank Young loves us. He's totally bought into our system of billing and will use us in any new properties they build. Right now, they're looking at two smallish complexes, both in Miami. They put us in the last three properties they built."

Last on the list of top five is The Franklin Group, which owns 32 properties in the Pacific Northwest. "Like Young, they like us a lot, but their growth rate has slowed. We're also in their last three properties, and our best shot there is probably refurbishing the older properties. They should be doing a complete makeover in the next five years, but getting them to make that investment has been tough," said David. Kevin asked why, and David replied that the operations VP was in favor of it but the CFO was not. "Maybe we just need to find some new companies to work with."

Questions

1. Where would you place these accounts on the sales effort allocation grid? Justify your responses.
2. What is your sales strategy for each one? What is the order of priority?
3. If you were to look for new companies to work with, use the information from these descriptions and design the perfect prospect.

ROLE PLAY CASE

Six months ago, you went through your accounts and determined that how you've allocated your effort is not consistent with the potential of each account and your relative position. In one instance, National Barns, you've got a great relationship with the CIO (chief information officer or head of information technology) and have called on National Barns once or twice a month. There are, however, only 24 salespeople there, and the company isn't growing, so there isn't much opportunity. You decided that this is an account you no longer plan to visit in person but will check by phone.

Another account, Maguire Manufacturing, merited more calling. It had 34 salespeople six months ago and has 44 now. Because it continues to grow and has indicated that it may grow through acquisition of other companies, you've decided to visit it once or twice a month.

Grafton Gifts, a distributor of gifts and greeting cards, has been a tough account to understand. Its 120 salespeople who call on retailers around the country use a paper-based system to keep track of their accounts. Orders are placed on special handheld computers that are downloaded at night. The VP of sales says that's all the company needs, but the VP of marketing wants more information so a CRM marketing strategy can be used. Today you will visit the VP of marketing to determine whether you want to continue with this account.

Your professor will give you buyer sheets for your turn as a buyer.

ADDITIONAL REFERENCES

Berry, Julian. "How Should Goals for 'Contact Optimisation' Be Set, and How Should Contact Optimisation Be Managed in a Multi-Channel Inbound and Outbound Environment?" *Journal of Database Marketing and Customer Strategy Management* 16, no. 4 (2009), pp. 241–46.

Cespedes, Frank V., James P. Dougherty, and Ben S. Skinner III. "How to Identify the Best Customers for Your Business." *MIT Sloan Management Review* 54, no. 2 (Winter 2013), pp. 53–59.

Christ, Paul, and Rolph Anderson. "The Impact of Technology on Evolving Roles of Salespeople." *Journal of Historical Research in Marketing* 3, no. 2 (2011), pp. 173–93.

Eggert, Andreas, and Murat Serdaroglu. "Exploring the Impact of Sales Technology on Salesperson Performance: A Task-Based Approach." *Journal of Marketing Theory and Practice* 19, no. 2 (Spring 2011), pp. 169–85.

Eggert, Andreas, Wolfgang Ulaga, and Sabine Hollmann. "Benchmarking the Impact of Customer Share in Key-Supplier Relationships." *Journal of Business and Industrial Marketing* 24, no. 3/4 (2009), pp. 154–69.

Fleischer, Mark. "Key Account Management in the Managed Markets: Visibility and Collaboration for Greater Effectiveness." *Journal of Medical Marketing* 10, no. 1 (January 2010), pp. 53–60.

Hartmann, Nathaniel, N., Brian N. Rutherford, G. Alexander Hamwi, and Scott B. Friend. "The Effects of Mentoring on Salesperson Commitment." *Journal of Business Research* (forthcoming).

Koller, Monika, and Thomas Salzberger. "Benchmarking in Service Marketing: A Longitudinal Analysis of the Customer." *Benchmarking* 16, no. 3 (2009), pp. 401–20.

Lambert, Douglas M. "Customer Relationship Management as a Business Process." *Journal of Business and Industrial Marketing* 25, no. 1 (2010), pp. 4–17.

Sweet, Catherine, Tim Sweet, Beth Rogers, Valerie Heritage, and Mike Turner. "Developing a Benchmark for Company-Wide Sales Capability." *Industrial and Commercial Training* 39, no. 1 (2007), pp. 18–28.

Zallacco, Ronald, Ellen Bolman Pullins, and Michael L. Mallin. "A Re-Examination of B2B Sales Performance." *Journal of Business and Industrial Marketing* 24, no. 8 (2009), 598–611.

chapter **16**

MANAGING WITHIN YOUR COMPANY

SOME QUESTIONS ANSWERED IN THIS CHAPTER ARE

- Which areas of the company work with salespeople to satisfy customer needs?
- How do salespeople coordinate the efforts of various functional areas of the company?
- How do salespeople work with sales managers and sales executives?
- How do company policies, such as compensation plans, influence salespeople?
- How do salespeople work within the company to resolve ethical issues?
- What is the organizational structure, and how does it influence salesperson activities?

PROFILE

PROFILE First impressions are everything. We've all been told that since kindergarten. But I didn't fully understand how important impressions really were until I began working. "Brand building" is building a reputation that reflects who you are and how you work. We all know brand names of companies: Oracle, Nike, Timex. But individuals have brands as well. How you are branded determines not only how your customers see you but how your coworkers view you as well.

You start building your brand the moment you walk through the door on your first day. Your personal brand is determined by what you say and what you do. If you want to be known as a hard worker, then everything you do and say should be consistent with the brand "hard worker." Companies have all different brands within their workforces. There are the "workhorses," those who consistently turn out a large workload. There are those who have a brand of "big accounts." They regularly get and close the large deals. However, not every brand is good. There are the "procrastinators," "freeloaders," and "always late-ers" too. Having a negative brand can hurt your potential.

However, the best part is you get to choose your brand. Your words and actions build your brand. Unfortunately, many students don't understand this until it's too late. I've seen one too many coworkers fresh out of college come into Oracle and start off building a negative brand image. They don't do it on purpose. But they are not intentional in what they want their brand to be. They come in acting young and inexperienced and start building this brand of "I don't know anything." Brands travel quickly, and once a negative brand spreads, it will be hard to recruit people to work with you and your clients. You may be young and inexperienced, but if this is all you portray, coworkers will quickly begin to avoid working with you on accounts. Especially in a profession such as sales, having a good reputation within the company is critical to building an inside team that can meet your customer's needs.

As a sales consultant, building and maintaining positive relationships with my sales representatives and sales managers is key to serving my customers well. Without these relationships, I would not be able to serve my clients to the best of my ability, and neither would the sales representative or manager.

Oracle has a wide and useful but sometimes overwhelming product line. That's where I step in. Once the sales representative uncovers a need that Oracle can meet, I come in and investigate and identify which specific product best fits the customer's needs. I don't prospect or close any deals; I simply come alongside the customer and sales representative as a product expert and match needs and capabilities. I hold a position of trust from both the sales representative and the customer. That is where building my brand has been so impactful.

If I would have come into Oracle acting like I didn't know anything, there would be few representatives who would trust me to handle their valuable customers. It's the same with a salesperson. If a salesperson builds a bad personal brand, I'm not going to want to assist him or her with his or her clients if possible. Ultimately, you are not the only one harmed by a negative personal brand; your client will be too. You may have done the best prospecting, found a great client, and know that your product makes the best fit, but if you have built a negative personal brand, there will be few who will want to join your team from within. And having the support and knowledge of a team from within your company will help you best serve your client. Building strong relationships within your company starts with brand building.

It's okay to not know everything and have questions at your first job. But trust your training and experience and know that if you are a match for your company, you will be competent. So go in with an intentional brand in mind and start building it the moment you walk through the double glass doors on that first Monday morning.

Visit our Web site at:
www.oracle.com

BUILDING INTERNAL PARTNERSHIPS •————————

To effectively coordinate the efforts of various areas of a company, a salesperson must develop partnerships with the individuals in those areas. **Internal partnerships** are partnering relationships between a salesperson and another member of the same company. These partnerships should be dedicated to satisfying customer needs.

THE IMPORTANCE OF INTERNAL PARTNERSHIPS

By definition, a sales representative represents something. Students often think the title means that the salesperson represents only a company or a product, but at times the salesperson must represent the customer to the company. For example, the salesperson may have to convince the warehouse manager to ship a customer's product next to meet a special deadline. The salesperson does not have the authority to order the manager to ship the product, but he or she must use persuasion. Or the rep may have to negotiate with production to get a product manufactured to a customer's specifications. Sometimes success in landing a sale may depend on the salesperson's ability to manage such company efforts.

This ability to work with groups inside the company can directly affect the rep's pocketbook. One of the authors, while selling for a major corporation, had an opportunity to earn a large bonus by making 30 sales. He had 31 orders, but a sale didn't count until the product was delivered. Unfortunately two orders were delivered after the deadline, and he did not get the bonus. In tracking down the slow deliveries, the hapless salesperson learned that the order entry clerk had delayed processing the orders. A little probing uncovered the reason: She was upset with the way he prepared his paperwork! Her performance was evaluated on how quickly an order was delivered, but his sloppy paperwork always slowed her down and got her into trouble. Delaying work on his orders was her way of getting his attention.

It worked! For several months after that, he enlisted her help in filling out the paperwork properly before he turned it in. After that, she never had a problem with his orders. And when necessary to meet a customer's requirements, she would prioritize his orders.

THE ROLE OF SALES

Salespeople not only sell a company, its products, and its services to customers but also sell their customers' needs to their companies. Carrying the customer's voice across the organization is one of the most important functions of the sales force. Although many companies work to increase the customer contact time for support personnel so they will understand customers, often the only person who really understands what the customer needs and why is the salesperson. In fact, the ability to receive and act on customer knowledge brought back to the company by salespeople has been documented to positively influence market share, account share (or share of wallet), profit margins, and the customer's perceived value![1]

Nucor Fastener uses its CRM system to capture the voice of the customer. Salespeople's notes, along with a deep analysis of data from other systems, helped the company identify specific customer needs that required special treatment. For example, 50 percent of all rush orders were generated by only 12 customers. The account executives for those accounts were able to identify customer requirements that led to new service offerings, greater revenue, and higher customer satisfaction.[2]

But when companies do not have a formal voice of the customer process, salespeople still have a responsibility to their customers to ensure that the company is responsive to their changing needs. Jim Keller, account executive for Teradata and profiled in an earlier chapter, says, "You may not be able to directly alter a product's design right away. But I know my input, based on customer needs, has had an impact on when certain features were added and how certain functions were changed."

SELLING INTERNALLY

To service customers well, salespeople must often rely on personnel in other areas of the firm to do their respective jobs properly. Even in seemingly simple situations like selling shipping, it can take a lot of internal coordination, as Lillie Sanchez describes in Building Partnerships 16.1. But how well those other employees assist salespeople may be a function of the relationship the salesperson has already established with them. That relationship should be a partnership, just like the one the salesperson wants to establish with appropriate customers. To establish the appropriate partnership, the salesperson must invest time in understanding the customer's needs and then work to satisfy those needs.

thinking it through

Consider the impact electronic forms of communication have had on your life so far. How do such forms of communication help build internal partnerships, particularly when a salesperson is stationed far from company headquarters? How can such forms of communication hinder a salesperson's efforts to build internal partnerships?

As summarized in Exhibit 16.1, the first step of selling laterally is to recognize that it is the salesperson's responsibility to develop relationships with other departments. Rarely do other departments have an incentive to take the initiative. Salespeople who expect other workers to serve them are frustrated by the lack of support they receive. The better perspective is, How can I serve them so we can serve the customer better?

Use questioning skills such as SPIN to understand the personal and professional needs of personnel in other departments. Salespeople should have excellent communication skills but sometimes fail to use these skills when dealing with internal customers and support groups. SPIN and active listening are just as important to understanding the needs of colleagues as they are to satisfying customer needs. For example:

SALESPERSON: What do you do with these credit applications? (*Situation*)

CREDIT REP: We key the information into the computer system, and then it is processed by a credit company each night. The next morning we get a report that shows who has been approved and who hasn't. That's why it is so important to have a clean copy.

SALESPERSON: So the quality of the copy we give you is a problem? (*Problem*)

Exhibit 16.1
Seven Principles of Selling Internally

1. Understand that it's your problem. **Accept responsibility** for gaining the support of the internal staff.
2. **Appeal to a higher objective.** For example, show how what you are asking for meets an important company objective.
3. Probe to find out and **understand the personal and professional needs** of the internal customer. Use SPIN and active listening techniques.
4. Use arguments for support that adequately **address the internal customer's needs** as well as your own. Use your presentation skills.
5. Do not spend time or energy resenting the internal customers' inability to understand or accept your sense of urgency. Rather, spend this time fruitfully by trying to figure out how you can better communicate your needs in a manner that will **increase the internal customer's sense of urgency** to the level you need.
6. **Never personalize** any issues. Don't call names, blame the person in public, or hold a grudge.
7. Be prepared to **negotiate.**

IT'S LOGISTICS

UPS may be selling "logistics" in their commercials, but they aren't the only ones in the game. Whether the business is actually logistics or something else, it takes a lot of internal coordination—logistics—to make things happen.

Phoenix International is a privately owned freight forwarder and customs broker that supports companies involved in international trade. As a sales executive at Phoenix International, Lillie Sanchez says her role extends beyond selling new business. "On a daily basis my focus is to ensure my client's needs and wants are met. This may seem like an easy task, but it takes a solid relationship and strong management to be successful. Each client, commodity, and country I work with is a new canvass. Through active listening, research, and building a relationship with my clients, I am able to learn their business processes, specific requirements, frustrations, and wants. This knowledge allows me to create customized solutions that improve my customers' supply chain."

Once she signs up a new client, she becomes their advocate within Phoenix. "I ensure that all departments have an understanding of the company, the client's needs, and any specific handling instructions. I develop standard operating procedures with the operational staff to make the customer's needs transparent. I work with the credit department and account receivables to establish appropriate credit levels and payments terms. My information systems team and I work together to provide the customer real time visibility and reporting capabilities." These operational areas support the actual shipment of goods that the client wants, but without those support functions, the client's needs won't get met.

Sanchez's internal partnerships have to be strong because when something is delayed, the entire account could be lost. Sanchez offers this example: "Today I received a phone call from one of my clients, Jon. He was upset because his shipment was not going to arrive on the original estimated day due to a number of events. As I called his coordinator at Phoenix International to discuss various scenarios we could take to overcome the obstacle, the solution was simple and didn't take much time to resolve; with teamwork we were able to meet the customers' demands and make him happy."

Sanchez's preference is to learn of the problem from operations before the customer does. "I know that my next phone call will be from an angry customer. I like to take that call with a solution already in place, if possible." She points out that her strong relationships with her internal partners make these kinds of situations much easier to deal with. "When customers call with a concern and you have a logical explanation along with a solution, you save their day."

CREDIT REP: That's right.

SALESPERSON: What happens when you can't read the copy we give you? (*Implication*)

CREDIT REP: We put in incorrect information, which can result in a customer's credit application being rejected when it should have been accepted.

SALESPERSON: What happens when that happens? (*Implication*)

CREDIT REP: That's when we call you. Then we get the right information and reenter it. But we get in trouble because the approval cycle was made longer, and you know that the goal is to have a customer's order shipped in three days. We can't meet that goal if we're still working on its credit application.

SALESPERSON: So you need legible applications—and probably e-mail would be better than handwritten, right? (*Needs payoff*)

CREDIT REP: Yes, that would help a lot.

Keep in mind too that the salesperson cannot simply order a colleague to do what the salesperson wants, such as approving a customer's credit application. But if a salesperson can show that doing what he or she wants will also meet the needs of the colleague, the salesperson is more likely to receive the desired aid. Just as when selling to an external customer, persuasion requires the salesperson to meet the other person's needs as well. For example, if a salesperson can show a plant manager how an expedited order will result in a higher profit margin, thereby more than covering the plant manager's higher costs and helping that manager make production targets, both the plant manager's needs and the customer's needs will be met.

People from other departments, except for billing and customer service, do not have direct contact with the customer. Therefore, they do not feel the same sense of urgency the customer or the salesperson feels. Successful internal sellers can communicate that sense of urgency by relating to the needs of the internal customer. Just as they do with external customers, salespeople need to communicate the need to act now when they sell internally. They need to secure commitment to the desired course of action. Also, just as with external customers, the salesperson should be sure to say thank you when someone agrees to provide the support requested.

Selling to internal customers also means keeping issues professional. Personal relationships can and should be developed. But when conflicts arise, focus on the issue, not the person. Personalizing conflict makes it seem bigger and harder to resolve. For example, rather than saying, "Why won't you do this?" ask, "If you can't do this, how can we resolve the customer's concern?" This type of statement focuses the other individual on resolving the real problem rather than arguing about company policy or personal competence.

Be prepared to negotiate. Remember from Chapter 12 that negotiation is a set of techniques to resolve conflict. Conflicts between salespeople and members of the firm representing other areas will occur, and negotiation skills can be used to respond to conflicts professionally.

Salespeople must work with many elements of their organization. In fact, few jobs require the boundary-spanning coordination and management skill that the sales job needs. In the next section we examine the many areas of the company with which the salesperson works, what their needs are, and how they partner with the salesperson to deliver customer satisfaction.

COMPANY AREAS IMPORTANT TO SALESPEOPLE

The sales force interacts with many areas of the firm. Salespeople work with manufacturing, sales administration, customer service, and personnel. In some industries requiring customization of products, engineering is an important department for salespeople. Finance can get into the picture as well when that department determines which customers receive credit and what price is charged. In addition, salespeople work with members of their own department and the marketing department.

MANUFACTURING

In general, manufacturing is concerned with producing product at the lowest possible cost. Thus, in most cases, manufacturing wants long production runs, little customization, and low inventories. Customers, however, want their purchases shipped immediately and custom-made to their exact specifications. Salespeople may have to negotiate compromises between manufacturing and the customer.

Salespeople should also develop relationships with manufacturing so they can make accurate promises and guarantees to customers.

In addition, we've already discussed the importance of the salesperson in ensuring that customers' needs are heard and products designed that fit their needs. Research shows that close, collaborative relationships between salespeople and manufacturing yield better new product designs—better in the sense of greater market acceptance and sales volume.[3] Hose Master Inc., a manufacturer of industrial hoses, actually brings salespeople and customers together with manufacturing for training on products. Frank Caprio, major market specialist for Hose Master, says these training sessions always yield new ideas for products or product enhancements that manufacturing can implement quickly.[4]

Salespeople who develop internal partnerships with people in areas such as manufacturing and service can count on their internal partners for support.

ADMINISTRATION

The functions of order entry, billing, credit, and employee compensation require each company to have an administrative department. This department processes orders and sees that the salesperson gets paid for them. Employees in this area (as discussed earlier) are often evaluated on how quickly they process orders and how quickly the company receives customer payment. Salespeople can greatly influence both processes and realize substantial personal benefit for themselves.

The credit department is an important part of administration. Understanding the needs of the credit department and assisting it in collecting payments can better position the salesperson to help customers receive credit later. A credit representative who knows that you will help collect a payment when a problem arises is more likely to grant credit to one of your customers. Some companies do not pay commission until after the customer has paid to ensure that salespeople sell to creditworthy accounts. These companies, such as Ruhrpumpen Inc. (an industrial pump manufacturer) and General Electric, believe a close working relationship between sales and credit is critical to the financial health of the company. In fact, GE has a "Walk a Mile" program where salespeople spend a day in credit, and credit personnel spend a day in the field with salespeople. This program leads to greater understanding and communication that last long after the day of walking a mile in someone's shoes.[5]

SHIPPING

The scheduling of product shipments may be part of sales administration or manufacturing, or it may stand alone. In any case salespeople need the help of the shipping department. When salespeople make special promises to expedite a delivery, they actually must depend on shipping to carry out the promise. Shipping managers focus on costs, and they often keep their costs under control by planning efficient shipping routes and moving products quickly through warehouses. Expedited or special-handling deliveries can interfere with plans for efficient shipping. Salespeople who make promises that shipping cannot or will not fulfill are left with egg on their faces. That's why Andrea Kinnard, sales representative for Konica-Minolta in Fort Worth, has been known to help load a delivery truck so a customer could get a much-needed copier.

CUSTOMER SERVICE

Salespeople also need to interact with customer service. The need for this relationship should be obvious, but many salespeople arrogantly ignore the information obtained by customer service representatives. A technician who fixes the company's products often goes into more customers' offices or plants than the salesperson does. The technician often has early warning concerning a customer's switch to a competitor, a change in customer needs, or failure of a product to satisfy. For example, if an IBM technician spies a competitor's computer in the customer's office, the technician can ask whether the unit is on trial. If a good working relationship exists between the technician and the salesperson, the technician will warn the salesperson that the account is considering a competitive product. Close relationships and support of customer or technical service representatives mean not only better customer service but faster and more direct information flow to the salesperson. This information will help the salesperson gain and keep customers.

Salespeople, in turn, can help customer service by setting reasonable expectations for product performance with customers, training customers in the proper use of the product, and handling complaints promptly. Technicians are evaluated on the number of service calls they make each day and how long the product works between service calls, among other things. Salespeople can reduce some service calls by setting the right expectations for product performance. Salespeople can also extend the amount of time between calls by training customers in the proper use of the product and in preventive maintenance. An important byproduct of such actions should be higher customer satisfaction.

MARKETING

Sales is part of marketing in some firms and separate from marketing in others. Marketing and sales should be highly coordinated because their functions are closely related. Both are concerned with providing the right product to the customer in the most efficient and effective manner. Sales acts as the eyes and ears of marketing, while marketing develops the promotions and products that salespeople sell. Salespeople act as eyes and ears by informing the marketing department of competitor actions, customer trends, and other important market information. Marketing serves salespeople by using that information to create promotional programs or design new products. Marketing is also responsible for generating leads through trade show exhibiting, direct mail programs, advertising, and public relations.

Unfortunately not all marketing and sales departments just naturally get along. A study of Dutch firms found one reason to be simply that no one is responsible for interfacing between the departments.[6] Several other studies have shown that sales and marketing departments fail to communicate, don't trust each other, and even sabotage each other.[7] One study suggested that the biggest problem seems to be a lack of communication.[8] More recent studies, however, suggest that the differences run deeper than communication; the differences are driven by beliefs about what should be done and by whom, the perceived value of marketing versus sales, and other basic differences.[9] Proactive salespeople won't wait for marketing managers to make the first move. Rather than complain about poor marketing programs, proactive salespeople and sales managers prefer to participate in marketing decisions and keep communication lines open. When sales and marketing work together, salespeople have better programs with which to sell.[10]

SALES

Within any sales force, there may be several types of salespeople. As you learned in earlier chapters, global account managers may work with the largest accounts while other representatives handle the rest of the customers, and the salesperson must interact with certain sales executives and sales managers. How these people work together is the subject of the next section.

PARTNERS IN THE SALES ORGANIZATION

The sales function may be organized in many different ways, but no matter how it is organized, it is rarely perfect. Usually some customer overlap exists among salespeople, meaning several salespeople have to work together to serve the needs of one account. Customer needs may require direct customer contact with the sales executive as well as the salesperson. At the same time, the salesperson must operate in an environment that is influenced by the policies and procedures created by that same sales executive and executed by the salesperson's immediate manager. In this section we examine how the activities of sales management affect salespeople.

SALES MANAGEMENT

Salespeople should understand the roles of both sales executives and field sales managers. Salespeople who are able to develop partnerships with their managers will have more resources available to perform at a higher level.

The Sales Executive

The sales executive is the manager at the top of the sales force hierarchy. This person is a policy maker, making decisions about how the sales force will accomplish corporate objectives. Sales executives play a vital role in determining the company's strategies with respect to new products, new markets, sales forecasts, prices, and competition. The executives determine the size and organization of the sales force, develop annual and long-range plans, and monitor and control sales efforts. Sales executives also strive, or should strive, to create a corporate culture that supports appropriate behaviors by their sales managers and salespeople—behaviors that are both ethical and customer-oriented.[11] Duties of the sales executive include forecasting overall sales, budgeting, setting sales quotas, and designing compensation programs.

Size and Organization of the Sales Force

The sales executive determines how many salespeople are needed to achieve the company's sales and customer satisfaction targets. In addition, the sales executive must determine what types of salespeople are needed. For example, the sales executive determines whether global account management is needed. Many other types of salespeople can be selected, which we discuss later in this chapter. For now, keep in mind that the sales executive determines the level of customer satisfaction necessary to achieve sales objectives and then designs a sales force to achieve those goals. How that sales force is put together is important because salespeople often have to work together to deliver appropriate customer service and successfully accomplish sales goals.

Forecasting

Sales executives use a number of techniques to arrive at sales forecasts. One of the most widely used techniques is **bottom-up forecasting,** or simply adding each salesperson's own forecast into a forecast for total company sales. At each level of management, the forecast would normally be adjusted based on the manager's experience and broader perspective. This technique allows the information to come from the people closest to the market: the salespeople. Also, the forecast comes from the people with the responsibility for making those sales. But salespeople tend to be optimistic and may overestimate sales, or they may underestimate future sales if they know their bonuses depend on exceeding forecasts or if they think their quotas will be raised. Wise managers should quickly realize when salespeople are underestimating forecasts, though the salespeople may be able to obtain significant earnings the first time. Such behavior, though, not only is unethical but also creates many problems for the organization.[12]

Salespeople are especially important to the forecasting process when the executive is attempting to forecast international sales. Statistics used in the United States to forecast sales are often not available in other countries or, if available, may be unreliable. Companies in Europe operate in so many different countries that the only consistent numbers available may come from the sales force. One candy company found that its salespeople provided the best forecast possible, in part because they were closest to the customer but also because each country's data were collected and compiled in different ways, making comparisons impossible.[13] But even companies in the United States are pushing forecasting to the field. Coty Fragrance, makers of such fragrance brands as Jennifer Lopez, Vera Wang, and Kenneth Cole, began requiring salespeople to develop forecasts based on the data in their CRM system. Coty's forecasting improved, leading to a significant reduction in stockouts, which also accounted for an increase in sales when the industry was hit by the recession.[14] A recent study indicates that salespeople can forecast more accurately when given clear guidelines regarding their forecasting process. With such guidelines, greater consistency and accuracy can be achieved.[15]

Expense Budgets

Managers sometimes use expense budgets to control costs. An expense budget may be expressed in dollars (for example, the salesperson may be allowed to spend up to $500) or as a percentage of sales volume (such as expenses cannot exceed 10 percent of sales). A regional manager or salesperson may be awarded a bonus for spending less than the budget allocates. However, such a bonus may encourage the salesperson to underspend, which could hurt sales performance. For example, if a salesperson refuses to give out samples, customers may not be able to visualize how a product will work; thus, some may not buy. The salesperson has reduced expenses but hurt sales.

Although salespeople may have limited input into a budget, they do spend the money. Ultimately it is the salesperson's responsibility to manage the territorial budget. The salesperson not only has control over how much is spent and whether expenditures are over or under budget but also, and more important, decides where to place resources. Recall from Chapter 15 that these resources, such as samples and trial units or trips to the customers' location, are investments in future sales. If they are used unwisely, the salesperson may still meet the expense budget but fail to meet his or her sales quota.

Control and Quota Setting

The sales executive faces the challenge of setting up a balanced control system that will encourage each sales manager and salesperson to maximize his or her individual results through effective self-control. As we have pointed out throughout this text, salespeople operate somewhat independently. However, the control system management can help salespeople manage themselves more effectively.

Quotas are a useful technique for controlling the sales force. A **quota** represents a quantitative minimum level of acceptable performance for a specific period. A **sales quota** is the minimum number of sales in units, and a **revenue quota** is the minimum sales revenue necessary for acceptable performance. Often sales quotas are simple breakdowns of the company's total sales forecast. Thus, the total of all sales quotas equals the sales forecast. Other types of quotas can also be used. Understanding quotas is important to the salesperson because performance relative to quota is evaluated by management.

Profit quotas or **gross margin quotas** are minimum levels of acceptable profit or gross margin performance. These quotas motivate the sales force to sell more profitable products or to sell to more profitable customers. Some companies assign points to each product based on the product's gross margin. More points are assigned to higher-margin products. The salesperson can then meet a point quota by selling either a lot of low-margin products or fewer high-margin products. For example, assume an office equipment company sells fax machines and copiers. The profit margin (not including salesperson compensation) is 30 percent on copiers but only 20 percent on fax machines. Copiers may be worth three points each, whereas faxes are worth two. If the salesperson's quota is 12 points, the quota can be reached by selling four copiers, or six faxes, or some combination of both.

One challenge sales managers face is recognizing that performance quotas can negatively influence a customer orientation as salespeople put the need to make quota ahead of their customers' needs.[16] One type of quota that can avoid this dilemma is an activity quota. **Activity quotas,** similar to the activity goals we discussed in the preceding chapter, are minimal expectations of activities for each salesperson. The company sets these quotas to control the activities of the sales force. This type of quota is important in situations where the sales cycle is long and sales are few because activities can be observed more frequently than sales. For example, for some medical equipment, the sales cycle is longer than one year, and a salesperson may sell only one or two units each quarter. Having a monthly sales target in this case would be inappropriate, but requiring a certain minimum number of calls to be made is reasonable. The assumption made by management is that if the salesperson is performing the proper activities, sales will follow with the customer's needs in mind. Activities for which quotas may be established include number of demonstrations, total customer calls, number of calls on prospects, or number of displays set up.

Compensation and Evaluation

An important task of the sales executive is to establish the company's basic compensation and evaluation system. The compensation system must satisfy the needs of both the salespeople and the company. You, as a salesperson, need an equitable, stable, understandable system that motivates you to meet your objectives. The company needs a system that encourages you to sell products at a profitable price and in the right amounts.

Salespeople want a system that bases rewards on effort and results. Compensation must also be uniform within the company and in line with what competitors' salespeople receive. If competitors' salespeople earn more, you will want to leave and work for that competitor. But your company expects the compensation system to attract and keep good salespeople and to encourage you to do specific things. The system should reward outstanding performance while achieving the proper balance between sales results and costs.

Compensation often relates to quotas. As with quotas, salespeople who perceive the system as unfair may give up or leave the firm. A stable compensation system ensures that salespeople can reap the benefits of their efforts, whereas a constantly changing system may lead them to constantly change their activities but never make any money. A system that is not understandable will be ignored.

The sales executive decides how much income will be based on salary or incentive pay. The salesperson may receive a **salary,** which is a regular payment regardless of performance, or **incentive pay,** which is tied to some level of performance. There are two types of incentives: commission and bonus. A **commission** is incentive pay for an individual sale, whereas a **bonus** is incentive pay for overall

Exhibit 16.2
How Different Types of Compensation Plans Pay

| | | | | Amount Paid to Salesperson | | |
Month	Sales Revenue	Straight Salary	Straight Commission*	Combination†	Point Plan‡
January	$50,000	$3,500	$5,000	$1,500 (salary)	$3,800
	6 copiers			3,000 (commission)	
	10 faxes			4,500 (total)	
February	$60,000	3,500	6,000	1,500 (salary)	4,800
	6 copiers			3,600 (commission)	
	15 faxes			5,100 (total)	
March	$20,000	3,500	2,000	1,500 (salary)	1,600
	2 copiers			1,200 (commission)	
	5 faxes			2,700 (total)	

*Commission plan pays 10 percent of sales revenue.
†Commission portion pays 6 percent of sales revenue.
‡Copiers are worth three points, faxes are worth two, and each point is worth $100 in commission.
Note: These commission rates are used only to illustrate how compensation schemes work. Point plans, for example, do not necessarily always yield the lowest compensation.

Many companies offer incentives, such as special awards, bonuses, and other rewards, for outstanding sales performance.

performance in one or more areas. For example, a bonus may be paid for acquiring a certain number of new customers, reaching a specified level of total sales in units, or selling a certain amount of a new product.

Sales executives can choose to pay salespeople a straight salary, a straight commission, or some combination of salary, commission, and/or bonus. Most firms opt for some combination of salary and bonus or salary and commission. Fewer than 4 percent pay only commission, and slightly fewer than 5 percent pay only salary. Exhibit 16.2 illustrates how various types of compensation plans work.

Under the **straight salary** method, a salesperson receives a fixed amount of money for work during a specified time. The salesperson is assured of a steady income and can develop a sense of loyalty to customers. The company also has more control over the salesperson. Because income does not depend directly on results, the company can ask the salesperson to do things in the best interest of the company, even if those activities may not lead to immediate sales. Straight salary, however, provides little financial incentive for salespeople to sell more. For example, in Exhibit 16.2, the salesperson receives $3,500 per month no matter how much is sold.

Straight salary plans are used when sales require long periods of negotiation, when a team of salespeople is involved and individual results cannot be measured, or when other aspects of the marketing mix (such as advertising) are more important than the salesperson's efforts in generating sales (as in trade selling of consumer products). Most sales trainees also receive a straight salary.

A **straight commission** plan pays a certain amount per sale and includes a base and a rate but not a salary. The **commission base,** the item from which commission is determined, is often unit sales, dollar sales, or gross margin. The **commission rate,** which determines the amount paid, is expressed as a percentage of the base (such as 10 percent of sales or 8 percent of gross margin) or as a dollar amount (like $100 per sale). Exhibit 16.2 illustrates two straight commission plans: One pays 10 percent of sales revenue, and the other is a point plan that pays $100 per point (using the copier and fax example we discussed previously).

Exhibit 16.3

An Example of a Draw
Compensation Plan

Month	Draw	Commission Earned	Payment to Salesperson	Balance Owed to Company
January	$3,000	$0	$3,000	$3,000
February	3,000	5,000	3,000	1,000
March	3,000	4,500	3,500	

Commission plans often include a draw. A **draw** is money paid to the salesperson against future commissions—in essence a loan that guarantees a stable cash flow. For example, in Exhibit 16.3 the salesperson receives a draw of $3,000 per month. No commissions were earned during January, but the salesperson still received $3,000. In February the rep earned $5,000, but $2,000 went to pay back some of the draw from January, and the rep received only $3,000. In March the rep earned $4,500, of which $1,000 finished paying off the balance from January. Thus, the rep was given $1,500 in March.

Straight commission plans have the advantage of tying the salesperson's compensation directly to performance, thus providing more financial incentive for the salesperson to work hard. However, salespeople on straight commission have little company loyalty and certainly are less willing to perform activities, such as paperwork, that do not directly lead to sales. Xerox experimented with such a plan but found that customer service suffered, as did company loyalty among salespeople.

Companies that do not emphasize service to customers or do not anticipate long-term customer relationships (like a company selling kitchen appliances directly to consumers) typically use commission plans. Such plans are also used when the sales force includes many part-timers because part-timers can earn more when their pay is tied to their performance. Also, part-timers may need the extra motivation straight commission can provide.

Under a bonus plan, salespeople receive a lump-sum payment for a certain level of performance over a specified time. Bonuses resemble commissions, but the amount paid depends on total performance, not on each individual sale. Bonuses, awarded monthly, quarterly, or annually, are always used with salary and/or commissions in **combination plans.** Combination plans, also called salary-plus-commission plans, provide salary and commission and offer the greatest flexibility for motivating and controlling the activities of salespeople. The plans can incorporate the advantages and avoid the disadvantages of using any of the basic plans alone.

The main disadvantage of combination plans lies in their complexity. Salespeople confused by this complexity could unknowingly perform the wrong activities, or sales managers could unintentionally design a program that rewards the wrong activities. Using the earlier office equipment example, if faxes and copiers were worth the same commission (for example, $100 per sale), the salesperson would sell whatever was easiest to sell. If faxes were easier to sell than copiers, the firm may make less money because salespeople would expend all of their effort selling a lower-profit product unless the volume sold made up for the lower margin. Even then, however, the firm may be stuck with a warehouse of unsold copiers.

thinking **it** through

As a buyer, under which plan would you prefer your salesperson to work? Which would you prefer if you were a salesperson? What conflicts might occur between buyer and seller because of the type of compensation plan?

FIELD SALES MANAGERS

Salespeople report directly not to a sales executive but to a **field sales manager.** Field sales managers hire salespeople, evaluate their performance, train them, and perform other important tasks. Salespeople find it useful to partner with their managers because the managers often represent the salespeople to other parts of the organization. Also, the salesperson often has to sell the manager first on any new idea before the idea can be pitched to others in management. Building a partnering relationship with managers can go a long way toward getting ideas accepted.[17]

Evaluating Performance

Field sales managers are responsible for evaluating the performance of their salespeople. The easiest method of evaluating performance is to simply add up the amount of sales that the salesperson makes. But sales managers must also rate their salespeople's customer service level, product knowledge, and other, less tangible qualities. Some companies, such as Federal Express, use customer satisfaction surveys to evaluate salespeople. In other companies the manager rates each salesperson, using evaluation forms that list the desired aspects. (An example of an evaluation form appears in Exhibit 16.4.) Such evaluations help managers determine training needs, promotions, and pay raises.

The records and reports salespeople submit also play an important role in communicating their activities to the sales manager. The manager uses these reports to evaluate performance in a manner similar to the way the salesperson would. But these written reports are not enough; sales managers should also make calls with salespeople to directly observe their performance. These observations can be the basis for recommendations for improving individual performance or for commending outstanding performance. Other information, such as customer response to a new strategy, can be gained by making calls. This information should be shared with upper management to improve strategies.

Training

The sales manager trains new hires and provides refresher training for experienced salespeople. To determine what refresher training they need, managers often use information gathered while observing salespeople making sales calls.

Exhibit 16.4
Behavioral Observation Scale (BOS)

	Almost Never						Almost Always
1. Checks deliveries to see whether they have arrived on time.	1	2	3	4	5	6	7
2. Files sales reports on time.	1	2	3	4	5	6	7
3. Uses promotional brochures and correspondence with potential accounts.	1	2	3	4	5	6	7
4. Monitors competitors' activities.	1	2	3	4	5	6	7
5. Brushes up on selling techniques.	1	2	3	4	5	6	7
6. Reads marketing research reports.	1	2	3	4	5	6	7
7. Prospects for new accounts.	1	2	3	4	5	6	7
8. Makes service calls.	1	2	3	4	5	6	7
9. Answers customer inquiries when they occur.	1	2	3	4	5	6	7

Professional salespeople constantly need to upgrade their skills; here, a salesperson for Frosty Acres Brands is practicing how to open a sales call when she calls on a restaurant.

Content of training for new salespeople may be determined by a sales executive, but the field sales manager is often responsible for carrying out the training.

Most experienced salespeople welcome training when they perceive that it will improve their sales. Unfortunately salespeople often view training as an inconvenience that takes away from precious selling time. Dave Stein argues, though, that basic sales training is just that—basic—and if you want to sell to higher levels of the organization, if you want to work on bigger deals, and if you want to make more money, advanced skills are needed. Unfortunately he cites one study showing that less than half of companies surveyed offer any training, and of those, only half offer sales training. Thus, in some organizations, salespeople have to find advanced training on their own.[18] You should continue to welcome training, no matter how successful you are. It always offers the opportunity to improve your performance, or at least achieve the same level with less effort. Also, as you will see in Chapter 17, continuing to learn is important to the salesperson who is part of a learning organization.

MANAGING ETHICS IN SALES

Salespeople, particularly those within certain industries, have earned a reputation that is unfavorable. Most salespeople, though, want to act ethically. Because we have emphasized throughout this book methods of selling that help people solve problems and satisfy needs, we believe it is important to understand what companies do to encourage ethical behavior and how salespeople should work with their sales management partners to choose ethical options. First we discuss the sales executive's role in making ethics policy. Then we cover the roles of the field sales manager and the salesperson in implementing that policy.

ETHICS AND THE SALES EXECUTIVE

As mentioned earlier, sales executives should strive to create an ethical culture. While part of a sales executive's job is to determine corporate policy concerning what is considered ethical and what is not and how unethical behavior will be investigated and punished, it is also important that the sales executive support positive behaviors.[19] In addition, the sales executive must ensure that other policies, such as the performance measurement and compensation policies, support the ethics of the organization. Performance measurement and compensation policies that reward only outcomes may inadvertently encourage salespeople to act unethically because of pressure to achieve and a culture supporting the credo "the end justifies the means." But when behavioral performance measurement systems are in place, the compensation system can reward those who do things the right way. In addition, research shows that closer relationships with ethical managers support ethical behavior.[20] Although unethical behaviors may result in short-term gain (and therefore may accidentally be rewarded in an outcome-only compensation scheme), they can have serious long-term effects, such as loss of customers, unhappy salespeople who quit, and other negative outcomes.[21]

Sales executives must therefore develop a culture that creates behavioral norms regarding how things should be done and what behaviors will not be tolerated.

Such a culture can be enhanced through the development of formal policy, training courses in ethics, ethics review boards, and an open-door policy. **Open-door policies** are general management techniques that allow subordinates to bypass immediate managers and take concerns straight to upper management when the subordinates perceive a lack of support from the immediate manager. Open-door policies enhance an ethical culture because salespeople can feel free to discuss troublesome issues that involve their managers with someone in a position to respond. Two versions are **ethics review boards** and ethics officers, both providing expert advice to salespeople who are unsure of the ethical consequences of an action. Ethics review boards may consist of experts inside and outside the company who are responsible for reviewing ethics policies, investigating allegations of unethical behavior, and acting as a sounding board for employees.

Salespeople also have the right to expect ethical treatment from their company. Fair treatment concerning compensation, promotion policies, territory allocation, and other actions should be delivered. Compensation is probably the area with the most common concerns, although problems can arise in all areas. Compensation problems can include slow payment, hidden caps, or compensation plan changes after the sale.

For example, IBM published a brochure for its salespeople that said that there was no **cap,** or limit, on earnings. Yet the brochure also had, in bold letters, the statement that IBM had the right to modify the program—even after the sale—until the commission was paid. When a salesperson sold one major account $24 million worth of software, the company changed his commission plan so he received less than $500,000 instead of the $2.6 million he expected. The salesperson filed suit, but IBM won in part because of the modification statement in the letter.[22] IBM had every legal right to take the action it did, and caps are not unethical; what was questionable was that the salesperson was not made aware of the cap prior to making the sale.

thinking **it** through | Should schools have ethics review boards? What advantages would such boards have for the student? For the teacher? Would salespeople reap the same types of benefits if their companies had ethics review boards?

ETHICS AND THE FIELD SALES MANAGER

Salespeople often ask managers for direction on how to handle ethical problems, and the sales manager is usually the first person to investigate complaints of unethical behavior. Field sales managers can provide a role model for salespeople by demonstrating ethical behavior in role plays during training or when conducting sales calls in the field. Sales managers should also avoid teaching high-pressure techniques and manipulative methods of selling.

RESPONDING TO UNETHICAL REQUESTS

Salespeople may find themselves facing a sales manager who encourages them to engage in unethical behavior. When that situation occurs, a salesperson has several ways to avoid engaging in such behavior. Perhaps the most obvious option is to find another job, but that is not always the best solution. If the organizational culture supports the unethical request, however, finding another job may be the only choice. Exhibit 16.5 lists choices available to the salesperson.

Another way to handle unethical requests is to blow the whistle, or report the behavior, if the salesperson has adequate evidence (if adequate evidence is

Exhibit 16.5

Strategies for Handling Unethical Requests from a Manager

- Leave the organization or ask for a transfer.
- Negotiate an alternative course of action.
- Blow the whistle, internally or externally.
- Threaten to blow the whistle.
- Appeal to a higher authority, such as an ethics officer or ethics review board or a senior executive if ethics offices do not exist.
- Agree to the demand but fail to carry it out.
- Refuse to comply with the request.
- Ignore the request.

not available, sometimes simply threatening to blow the whistle may work). If this course of action is followed, the salesperson must be ready to accept a perception of disloyalty, retaliation by the manager, or other consequences. However, if senior management is sincere in efforts to promote ethical behavior, steps should be taken to minimize those negative outcomes. If an open-door policy or an ethics review board exists, the salesperson can take the concern to higher levels for review. For example, the salesperson could say, "I'm not sure that is appropriate. I'd like to get the opinion of the ethics review board." If the action is unethical, the sales manager may back down at that point. It is also possible that the manager will try to coerce the salesperson into not applying to the ethics review board; if that is the case, another course of action may prove to be a better choice.

Another strategy is to negotiate an alternative. This response requires the salesperson to identify an alternative course of action with a high probability of success. For example, if a sales manager tells the salesperson to offer a prospect a bribe, the salesperson should be prepared to prove that a price reduction would be just as effective. A similar tactic is simply to ignore the request. The salesperson may say to the manager that the request was carried out, when in fact it was not; the potential problem with this approach is that the salesperson has admitted to carrying out an unethical act (even though she or he did not), which can lead to future problems. Finally, the salesperson can simply deny the request. Denial can be a dangerous action in that it opens the salesperson to possible retaliation, particularly retaliation that is not obviously linked to the denial, such as denying access to training or reducing the size of the salesperson's territory.

thinking it through

Is it ethical to lie to your manager and say that you will engage in the unethical behavior that your manager demanded when you know you won't? Is all fair when you are combating a request to engage in unethical behavior?

The salesperson's choice of action will depend on how much proof is available, what alternative actions to the unethical action exist, and the type of relationship with the manager. Other factors to consider include the ethical climate of the organization and whether an open-door policy exists. The salesperson is always in control of his or her behavior and should never rationalize a behavior by placing responsibility on the sales manager.

SALESPEOPLE AS PARTNERS

Many types of salespeople exist, including telemarketing representatives, field salespeople, product specialists, and account specialists. Often there is some overlap in responsibilities; when overlap occurs, companies should have policies that facilitate serving the customer.

GEOGRAPHIC SALESPEOPLE

Most sales departments are organized geographically. A **geographic salesperson** is assigned a specific geographic territory in which to sell the company's products and services. Companies often combine geographic territories into larger branches, zones, or regions. For example, Eli Lilly has geographic regions that include 50 or more salespeople. Each Lilly salesperson has responsibility for a specific geographic area. For example, one rep may call on physicians in a portion of Dallas, using zip code boundaries to determine the territory; that rep may have all physicians in zip codes 75212, 75213, 75218, 75239, 75240, and 75252. Geographic salespeople may also work with account managers, product specialists, inside salespeople, and other members of the company's sales team.

ACCOUNT SALESPEOPLE

Companies may organize salespeople by account in several ways. The most extreme example is to give a salesperson the responsibility to sell to only one company but at every location of that company in the country or the world. In another common form of specialization, some salespeople develop new accounts while others maintain existing accounts. Developing new accounts requires skills different from maintaining an already sold account. For example, Holland 1916 recently reorganized around these lines. The decision was based on a desire to focus on larger accounts that could grow, recognizing that growing these accounts might require a different skill set than was needed to acquire the accounts. As a result of this thinking, Jim Humrichouse, CEO, developed a list of larger accounts with potential for more growth (recall the sales effort allocation grid from the previous chapter—these would be high opportunity/strong position current accounts), then assigned these to reps with a track record of success in growing current customers. He then hired new salespeople to take over those reps' geographic territories and tasked them with new account acquisition.[23]

Similar customers often have similar needs, whereas different types of customers may have very different needs for the same product. In such cases salespeople may specialize in calling on only one or a few customer types, although they sell the same products. NCR has different sales forces for calling on manufacturing companies, retailers, and financial companies. Andritz, an international heavy machinery company, has salespeople who sell only to paper producers and other salespeople who sell only to wastewater treatment plants, even though the same product is being sold. Some Procter & Gamble salespeople call on central buying offices for grocery store chains; others call on food wholesalers.

Companies also divide their customers on the basis of size. Large customers, sometimes called **key accounts,** may have a salesperson assigned only to that account; in some cases a small sales force is assigned to one large account. In some firms one company executive coordinates all the salespeople who call on an account throughout the nation or the world. These executives are called **national account managers (NAMs)** or **strategic account managers (SAMs).** These account managers are more than salespeople; they are business executives.

Strategic account managers sometimes manage large teams of salespeople. Account strategy for a global account may be determined by this strategic account manager, who has to rely on local salespeople to implement the strategy at the local level. For example, Hershey's has an account rep that calls on Walmart in Bentonville, Arkansas, but local salespeople work with individual stores and store managers. The local geographic rep's responsibility may involve coordinating delivery with the local customer. This coordination may also require customer training on the product (if the product is a machine or some other system) or working with a local store manager to set up displays, plan inventories, and so on. Local reps should also look for sales opportunities in the customer's location and provide this information to the SAM. They often become the eyes and ears of the SAM and provide early notice of opportunities or threats in the account, just

Exhibit 16.6

SAMs in the Sales Force

Although SAMs and geographic salespeople have different immediate managers, they still work together. SAMs coordinate the efforts of geographic reps within local buying offices of global accounts.

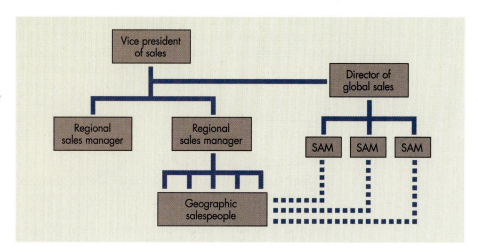

as a service rep does for the geographic rep. SAMs often report directly to the vice president of sales or to a director of global sales, as illustrated in Exhibit 16.6, but work with geographic reps.

As described in Chapter 6, a **house account** is handled by a sales or marketing executive in addition to that executive's regular duties, and no commission is paid on any sales from that account. House accounts are often key accounts, but not all key accounts are house accounts. The main difference is that house accounts have no "true" salesperson. Walmart has negotiated to be a house account with some suppliers with the expectation that those suppliers will pass on to Walmart what they do not have to pay in commission or salary. General Dynamics attempted the same strategy when buying, but abandoned the plan upon realizing that lower costs also meant reduced service.

Somewhat different is the mega-account strategy used at Motorola. The top 20 international accounts are actually managed by Motorola's CEO, who works directly with the CEO in each account. These accounts are a form of house account, but the CEO has sales responsibility and sales goals to achieve.

PRODUCT SPECIALISTS

When companies have diverse products, their salespeople often specialize by types of products. Johnson & Johnson, which sells baby products, has two specialized sales forces: the disposable products sales force and the toiletries sales force. Hewlett-Packard has separate sales forces that specialize in selling computers, electronic test instruments, electronic components, medical test equipment, or analytical test equipment. Each sales force has its own regional, district, and area sales managers. Insuror's of Texas has salespeople who specialize in auto insurance, others who specialize in home-owner's insurance, and still others who specialize in medical and disability insurance. However, all of Insuror's salespeople operate under the same sales management structure. Regardless of the management structure, sometimes the technical knowledge requirements are so great that organizing territories by product makes sense.

In addition to having management responsibilities similar to those for geographic reps, product salespeople must coordinate their activities with those of salespeople from other divisions. Success can be greater for all involved when leads and customer information are shared. For example, a Hewlett-Packard test instrument salesperson may have a customer who is also a prospect for electronic components. Sharing that information with the electronic components rep can help build a relationship that can pay off with leads for test instruments. In From the Buyer's Seat 16.1, Ben Becker describes how, as a buyer, he had to work with

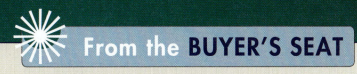

FAIL FAST, FAIL CHEAP

While working as a marketing manager for Continental/United Airlines, Ben Becker (now business intelligence manager at Direct Energy) was tasked with analyzing customer data to find new markets and new ways to generate revenue. "I had to think about how to generate new sales from existing customers, and I needed the right tools to understand my market and convince them to make additional purchases." In this role, Becker learned the "fail fast, fail cheap" way not only to make purchase decisions but also to convince internal partners that the right choices were being made.

One such situation involved software to capture Web browsing data of customers when on the company's Web site. The tools also changed the Web site content based on what the customer had looked at or might be considering. "This investment was well over a million dollars, not just for the software but also for the training and switchover costs," notes Becker.

Often in situations like this, the most difficult challenge in making the purchase isn't the budget. Rather, it's changing perceptions among senior leadership and getting buy-in from a wide group of people (recall the buying center from Chapter 3). For that reason, Becker adopted the "fail fast, fail cheap" approach. "I believe in pilots," says Becker, "not the pilots of our planes, although I believe in them too. No, I mean pilot tests." Among some of the leadership, the belief was that marketing doesn't influence demand—that if someone wants to fly, they will purchase it whether Continental/United markets to them or not. Says Becker, "If I sell my new tools on the premise that these tools will help us convince people to buy more, I'll lose the sale based on my premise. While I have a solid understanding of how these tools will help, not all of the leadership team does. Part of my job, then, is educating within the people I report to on how this will all work." Pilot tests do just that.

"Executives understand fail fast, fail cheap, meaning test everything, and if it isn't going to work, find out quickly and cheaply." Then, when things work, Becker lets the results speak for themselves. "I do everything I can to make sure I pick products and solutions that won't fail. A win for me is when I meet my business objectives and, at the same time, help other people in my organization achieve their objectives."

a broad array of people in his own organization, a time when he relied heavily on the vendor's product specialists.

INSIDE VERSUS OUTSIDE

Our discussion to this point has focused on outside salespeople, called **field salespeople**—that is, salespeople who sell at the customer's location. **Inside salespeople** (first identified in Chapter 1) sell at their own company's location. Inside salespeople may handle walk-in customers or work entirely over the telephone and Internet, or they may handle both duties. For example, a plumbing supply distributor may sell entirely to plumbers and employ inside salespeople who sell to those plumbers who come into the distributorship to buy products.

As we discussed in Chapter 6, the job of some inside salespeople is to provide leads for field salespeople. Other types of inside salespeople include account managers, field support reps, and customer service reps. An inside salesperson who is an account manager has the same responsibilities and duties as a field salesperson except that all business is conducted over the phone. Jean Heger, vice president of business development for Rail Europe, began her career in inside sales, where she managed relationships with tour and travel organizers.

A **field support rep** is a telemarketer who works with field salespeople and does more than prospect for leads. For example, field support reps at e-Rewards write proposals and price jobs, work directly with vendors to ensure satisfactory project completion, and interact with clients when needed. We discuss these representatives further when we address team selling strategies shortly.

Customer service reps (CSRs) are inbound salespeople who handle customer concerns. **Inbound** means they respond to telephone calls placed by customers, rather than **outbound,** which means the telemarketer makes the phone call (prospectors, account managers, and field support telemarketers are outbound reps). For example, if you call the 800 telephone number on the back of a tube of Crest toothpaste, you will speak with an inbound customer service rep. Many companies are now using customer service reps to identify cross-selling and up-selling opportunities, either by sending leads to field salespeople or closing the sales themselves. SuddenLink Communications, for example, has implemented a predictive model system that uses data from the CRM system to identify potential offers for customers who call about service. The customer service reps then make the sales pitch. Because the offers are more likely to be relevant to the buyer than a generic offer, customers don't seem to mind. In fact, they seem to like the approach—sales have increased over 20 percent since the launch of this system.[24]

SALES TEAMS

A growing number of companies are adopting a team approach to sales.[25] This concept is being used by companies that recognize they can best build partnerships by empowering one person, the account manager, to represent the organization. In **team selling** a group of salespeople support a single account. Each person on the team brings a different area of expertise or handles different responsibilities. As you see in Exhibit 16.7, each specialist can be called on to team up with the account managers.

Before adopting team selling, companies may have had one salesperson for each product line. Xerox, for example, once had separate copier, supplies, fax machine, printer, computer workstation,

Many companies use teams to work with large accounts. There may be members representing different functional areas of the company or, as in the case here, members of a global sales team meeting virtually.

Exhibit 16.7

Team Selling Organization

In team selling, product specialists work with account managers, who have total account responsibility. Product specialists are responsible for sales and service of only a limited portion of the product line and may work with several account managers.

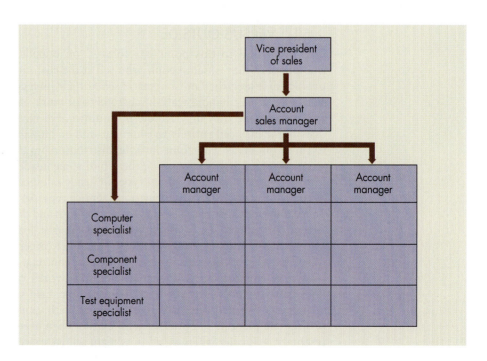

Exhibit 16.8
Forming Sales Teams for Multilevel Selling

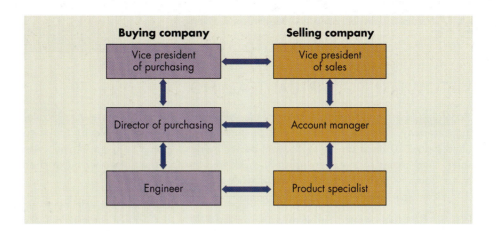

Exhibit 16.9
Inside–Outside Sales Team

Sometimes an inside rep or a field support rep works with accounts over the phone, and his or her partner, the field rep, makes calls at the customer's location.

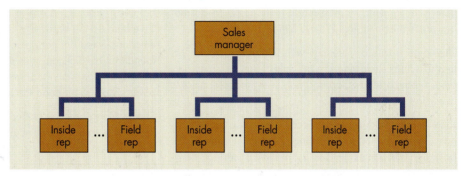

and communication network salespeople all calling on the same buyer. These reps would pass in customers' lobbies without recognizing one another. Customers grew tired of seeing as many as six salespeople from Xerox. Now one account manager calls on the buyer and brings in product specialists as needed.

Xerox uses permanent teams, whereas Teradata forms teams as needed. The data warehousing company will create a team that might include an expert in the vertical market in which the customer operates, a group of finance experts who can help develop the right financial measures for the decision, software engineers who make sure the Teradata product will work with the systems the customer already has in place, and the account manager.

In an extension of team selling, **multilevel selling,** members at various levels of the sales organization call on their counterparts in the buying organization. (As charted in Exhibit 16.8, for example, the vice president of sales calls on the vice president of purchasing.) Multilevel selling can take place without a formal multilevel sales team if the account representative requests upper-level management's involvement in the sale. For example, you may ask your company's vice president of sales to call on the vice president of operations at a prospect's company to secure top-level support for your proposal.

Another type of sales team is made up of the field rep and the field support rep (see Exhibit 16.9). Some companies use one telemarketer for each field salesperson, whereas other companies have several salespeople working with a telemarketer. The telemarketer performs as many selling tasks as possible over the telephone. But when a sales call is needed at the customer's location, the field support rep makes the appointment for the field rep. Such is the case with IBM.com, a division of IBM that provides software and technology consulting. Good communication and joint planning are necessary to avoid overbooking the field rep, as well as to prevent duplication of effort.

VIRTUAL SELLING, VIRTUAL TEAMING

According to Steve Richard, cofounder of the sales training company Vorsight, for every outside salesperson hired today, 10 more are being brought on for insides sales. And many of those are actually working from home. Some 17 percent work fully at home, while another 37 percent split time at the office and at home.

Patricia Sims, who started her sales career in the field, now works as an inside salesperson. "As time and technology progressed, it must made more sense to do that big presentation virtually," says Sims.

The same is true of meetings with internal partners. Virtual meetings, involving the full sales team or sales and other areas, are now part and parcel of the salesperson's everyday existence.

John Tanner, working as an account exec for Concentra, has a weekly Monday morning sales meeting with his boss and sometimes his boss's boss. "Our service delivery is local, so I see them every day. But my sales colleagues I may only see once a month, so these weekly meetings are my best chance to learn what others are doing," says Tanner.

Spencer Anderson, sales consultant with Oracle, says, "Certainly working on a national or global team is a challenge for collaborating. One way we have seen a steady increase in our collaboration and in turn quality of work is utilizing social networking sites to stay up to speed with each other. Also attending online training sessions together builds a educational connection within the team."

Collaboration with other functional areas can result in conflict that can escalate when people aren't face-to-face and make poor assumptions in the absence of nonverbal cues. Jackie Cruz, sales manager at Frye, Inc., said, "I've learned the hard way not to assume someone else's emotions when I'm not personally with them." One study found that conflict can arise unexpectedly when salespeople are involved in virtual teaming, and it takes a variety of behaviors to manage the conflict.

Shawn Naggiar, chief revenue officer at Act-On Software, says, "It is sometimes difficult to find the person with the right skill set." But collaborating via all of the communication tools, such as WebEx, GoToMeeting.com, Skype, Twitter, Facebook, and LinkedIn, is today's reality

Sources: Jeff Green, "The New Willy Loman Survives by Staying Home," *Bloomberg Businessweek* (January 14, 2013), pp. 16–17; Spencer Anderson, Jackie Cruz, and John Tanner, personal correspondence (January 15, 2013), used with permission; James I. F. Speakman and Lynette Ryals, "Key Account Management: The Inside Selling Job," *Journal of Business and Industrial Marketing* 27, no. 5 (2012), pp. 360–69.

Technology has played a key role in promoting good communication and joint planning. Companies can use CRM systems, for example, to give every member of the sales team access to all of the same customer records. This access means everyone knows what sales calls are planned and what happens as a function of the call. Another form of technology, represented by services like WebEx, enables someone to deliver a PowerPoint presentation to people scattered all over the world. Using WebEx, an account manager could present the account strategy, for example, to the sales team no matter where the members are located or present a proposal to a customer on another continent. See "Sales Technology 16.1" for additional insight into the use of technology to promote good communication and joint planning.

SELLING YOURSELF

Many times students have to engage in team projects, sometimes without much instruction in what makes an effective team. Yet the quality of the team is much more than just the sum of the individuals who are team members. Just as in team selling, each member of the team has to understand what the overall objective is, what each individual's role is, and what activities have to be undertaken when. But simply understanding what to do is a small part of making the team successful. More importantly, each individual has to perform and complete each task on time.

In addition, each class has a compensation plan—how grades are distributed. Sometimes the grades are team-based, just as in sales. Sometimes grades are entirely individual, and sometimes the overall grade is a function of both team and individual evaluations. But other motivations can entice students to learn. Recognition, the opportunity to work on real business problems, recognition of the relevance of the material being covered, and even monetary awards in competitions such as the National Collegiate Sales Competition can motivate different students to different levels of effort.

As you think about the courses you are taking, consider how you are compensated. Does the official compensation plan (grades, recognition, or the like) meet your motivational needs? In a group project, are your group members' needs being met? And are they living up to their responsibilities? These are real questions that plague professionals, whether they be salespeople or sales managers. Understanding how these questions apply to you now will help you select the right job later, as well as help you perform to your goals now.

SUMMARY

Successful salespeople manage resources and build internal partnerships with people in order entry, credit, billing, and shipping, as well as sales and marketing. These partnerships allow salespeople to keep the promises they make to customers when someone else must carry out those promises.

Salespeople in learning organizations also have a responsibility to carry the voice of the customer to other areas of the organization. Successful learning organizations are more adept at adapting to changing customer needs and developing successful products when salespeople fulfill their role of speaking for the customer.

In the sales organization salespeople work with and for a sales executive and a field sales manager. The sales executive determines policy and maintains financial control over the sales organization. Salespeople participate in the development of forecasts that the sales executive uses in the planning process.

Another policy decision involves the method of compensation for the sales force. The four basic methods are straight salary, straight commission, bonus, and a combination plan. Straight commission plans provide strong financial incentives for salespeople but give the company little control over their activities. Salary plans give greater control to the company but offer less incentive for salespeople to work hard.

Sales executives are also responsible for creating a culture that supports ethical activities. Policies (such as open-door policies) can encourage salespeople to act ethically. Ethical review boards are also useful in reviewing ethics policies, investigating potential ethics violations, and counseling salespeople who have concerns about the ethics of possible actions. Sometimes, however, salespeople face unethical requests from their managers. If that occurs, salespeople can choose from several courses of actions, such as blowing the whistle or appealing to an ethics review board.

Partnerships must be built within the sales force too. Some examples include team selling with product specialists, inside and outside teams, and multilevel selling.

KEY TERMS

ETHICS PROBLEMS

1. It took you four months to find a job, and you were almost out of money, when you finally landed your position. Today your boss asked you to do something you think is unethical, but she assures you that it is normal for this industry. You aren't sure what the corporate culture is yet because you are new at the company. How do you respond?

2. Your company pays straight commission based on gross margin, and you have some ability to determine the price, thereby influencing gross margin. The product is standard, and changes are not made to it when it is sold. What should determine how much you charge someone?

QUESTIONS AND PROBLEMS

1. Reread "From the Buyer's Seat 16.1." As a salesperson, what are the implications for how you might sell to Ben? How could you help Ben sell to others in his organization? Is his approach something you would welcome from your prospects or worry about? Why?

2. A company that rents office equipment to businesses pays its salespeople a commission equal to the first month's rent. However, if the customer cancels or fails to pay its bills, the commission is taken back, even if the customer cancels 10 months later. Is this policy fair? Why or why not? Why would the company have this plan?

3. Reread the chapter-opening profile of Kristen Scott and "Building Partnerships 16.1." What have they done to make their performance easier in working within their organization? What are some other things you can do to build stronger internal partnerships?

4. What is the role of the geographic salesperson in a national or strategic account? Assume that you are a NAM. What would you do to ensure the support of geographic reps? How would that support differ if you were a product specialist and worked in a team situation, with different NAMs on different accounts? As a product specialist, how would you get the support of the account manager?

5. Consider your own experience in group work at school. What makes groups effective? How can you translate what you have learned about group work into working as part of a sales team? Reread "Sales Technology 16.1." What do you think are the characteristics of effective sales teams that have to operate virtually? Could you use any technology tools to collaborate in school work groups more effectively?

6. Some companies are using contact management software to observe salespeople's activities and to supervise salespeople more closely. Some salespeople, though, are not supervised closely—as long as they close enough sales, the company is satisfied. To what extent should salespeople be allowed to manage themselves? What risks do you take as a sales manager when you allow self-management among salespeople? How can you minimize those risks?

7. A sales manager gets one too many complaints about pushy salespeople, poor follow-up after the sale, and a lack of customer care and wonders if the compensation plan is to blame. What can a manager do with compensation to promote greater customer service?

Are there other ways to motivate good customer service?

8. Many wise people say to worry about the things you can control and not to worry about the things you can't control. What does that mean for a salesperson, when so many promises a salesperson makes are actually fulfilled by someone else?

9. An experienced salesperson argues against salaries: "I don't like subsidizing poor performers. If you paid us straight commission, we'd know who could make it and who couldn't. Sure, it may take a while to get rid of the deadwood, but after that, sales would skyrocket!" Explain why you agree or disagree with this statement.

10. Salespeople are paid more than just about everyone in the company. This compensation difference can create jealousy, particularly among those who don't trust salespeople anyway and think salespeople just play golf and entertain their way to the big bucks. How can you combat these misperceptions? Does it really matter what others think about sales, or will the need to serve customers and thereby serve the company be enough?

CASE PROBLEMS

case 16.1

Energy Master Controls

Energy Master Controls, a manufacturer of heating and air-conditioning control systems for commercial properties, has the following compensation program. Reps are paid a $3,500 draw per month, with straight commission paid on a point system and a bonus based on quota performance. The SmartMeter, Energy Master's newest product, does much the same thing as the older FlexMeter but 30 percent faster and with greater accuracy. The point system is shown in Table 1.

Table 1

Product	Points/Sale	Quota (units per month)
SmartMeter	50	4
FlexMeter	40	5
HydraMeter	35	6
QuadraMeter	25	8
TriplexMeter	5	45

Reps are paid $5 per point, or $5,165 plus a bonus of $500, if they sell quota for each product, for a total of $6,675. The total number of points to reach each month is 1,035, but reps have to reach quota for each product to get the bonus. Tables 2–4 show the performance of the district.

Table 2

Product	Quota	Number Sold
SmartMeter	40	22
FlexMeter	50	78
HydraMeter	60	63
QuadraMeter	80	82
TriplexMeter	450	479

Table 3

Name	Smart-Meter	Flex-Meter	HydraMeter	QuadraMeter	Triplex-Meter	Total Points
Flores	3	11	7	9	52	1,320
McCoy	5	6	7	9	53	1,255
Smith	2	9	7	11	46	1,210
Nguyen	4	8	6	8	48	1,160
Ramamurthy	3	8	7	6	48	1,105
Longoria	2	8	6	7	48	1,045
Franks	1	8	6	8	48	1,020
Mills	1	7	7	8	47	1,010
Frasier	1	7	5	8	45	930
Tonga	0	6	5	8	44	835
Total	22	78	63	82	479	

Table 4
Total Sales Calls

Sales Call	Smart-Meter	Flex-Meter	HydraMeter	QuadraMeter	Triplex-Meter	Total Calls
Quota	20	20	10	10	10	70
Smith	28	16	11	9	10	75
Longoria	24	24	8	8	7	71
District average	27.2	18.6	9.5	10.4	9.7	75.4

Questions

1. Evaluate the district's sales performance. Draw conclusions ("Just where are we doing well? Doing poorly?") but don't fix anything yet. Justify your conclusions.
2. Compare the performance of Smith and Longoria. What are some possible explanations for the poor SmartMeter sales?
3. The VP of sales says the problem is a compensation plan problem. How would you fix it?
4. The company is planning to create a new position called product specialist. This salesperson will work with territory salespeople and will have a sales quota for SmartMeter only. The product specialist salesperson will work with one sales team (8 to 12 salespeople), and once a territory rep has identified a

SmartMeter prospect, the rep will bring in the product specialist. How should the compensation plan be adjusted? Why?

5. The VP of sales managed to get the product specialist idea approved by the CEO, even though the CEO argued that the salespeople were just too lazy to make the effort to sell the SmartMeter. "Lower the compensation on it to the territory reps, and everyone will sell the FlexMeter at its lower price," the CEO says. "The best way to get more SmartMeter sales is to cut compensation on the FlexMeter to 20 points." What do you think should be done? Why?

case **16.2**

IKOH Office

Karen Kennedy looked up, surprised to see her manager standing next to her. She had just hung up the phone after talking with Miranda in the Credit Department. "Um, did I get a little too loud, Rick?" she asked her manager.

"Why don't you come in my office and let's talk over what just happened," he replied, grimly.

"Great," she thought to herself. "First, the Kansas Hospital Resources order gets delayed to the point where they want to cancel it, then Credit wants me to get another form filled out, and now, the boss wants to talk over what just happened. Well, what just happened was I lost my temper, but they deserved it!" She sat down across the desk from Rick in his office, as he looked at her expectantly.

"I got a call this morning from Kansas Hospital Resources; you know, that's the 10-machine order I took two weeks ago." Rick nodded, so Karen continued. "They were upset because nothing has been delivered yet, but I had told them lead times were only a week. Which is what I was told."

"Yes, they are a week. Why hasn't this shipped?" he asked.

"That's what I wanted to know. So I called Frank and asked him." Frank Mangione is head of the warehouse in St. Louis that serves all of Kansas, Missouri, and a few other areas. "Frank said the order was a credit hold. What you heard was my conversation with Miranda in Credit. She tells me that it's on hold because a signature is missing on one of the forms. What gets me is no one called or e-mailed me about it. They let it sit, and I had to call and ask them. Rick, I'm tired of our Credit Department being a Sales Prevention Department. It's as if they do everything they can to screw us up. Now KHR is threatening to cancel the order if I can't get them a machine by Friday, but I've got to call them and say we missed a signature line and it will be a week after that before I can get them their first machine! Does IKOH want me to sell or what?"

Rick sat silently for a moment, then began to speak in a lower voice, trying to lower the tension in the room. But he knew she wouldn't like what he had to say. "Sounds like you have a problem to me."

Karen protested, "I have a problem? No, IKOH has a problem. It's just like trying to get paid. I can't get them to pay the right commission. And service. Don't get me started on our so-called service department! They never seem to want to fix my customers' machines!"

Rick said quietly, "Listen, we have 12 reps here in the Kansas City office. Of the 12, I have only one that keeps having problems with people in corporate or at the distribution center or with the service department. So I've got two questions for you. How are you going to handle KHR? And how are you going to fix your problems with everyone else?"

Questions

1. Answer Rick's questions as if you were Karen. To help you with your answer, consider that she and the service reps are in Kansas City, distribution is in St. Louis, and the corporate office (where credit, payroll, and other such functions are located) is in San Francisco. Regarding KHR, would it matter to your answer if this were a new customer versus a long-time customer? Why or why not, and if so, how?
2. What should or could Rick do to help Karen? Assume her sales performance is good, and he doesn't consider firing her an option.

ROLE PLAY CASE

You've just gotten back from KB Homes, one of the fastest-growing home builders in the United States. The KB Homes sales leadership team is considering NetSuite for all of their salespeople, and they've raised a number of questions that you need to get answered. If successful, this sale could be as big as 1,000 units. But they want to know several things:

1. Can you create a kiosk that will allow customers who visit KB's model homes to input their own data directly into a file that will load with NetSuite?
2. The buying center wants a license that includes all upgrades for three years.
3. They want permission to send a rep to your corporate headquarters to make a presentation to all the NetSuite employees about KB Homes. Employees who work in the field will be mailed a DVD presentation about KB Homes.

Each student will take turns playing the salesperson. The first question has to be addressed by the chief engineer. The second has to be addressed by the legal department. The final question has to be solved by the chief operations officer. If there are three people in a group, take turns observing. Your instructor will provide you with sheets for your role as one of the other NetSuite managers.

ADDITIONAL REFERENCES

Brehmer, Per-Olof, and Jakob Rehme. "Proactive and Reactive: Drivers for Key Account Management Programmes." *European Journal of Marketing* 43, no. 7/8 (2009), pp. 961–84.

Guenzi, Paolo, Laurent Georges, and Catherine Pardo. "The Impact of Strategic Account Managers' Behaviors on Relational Outcomes: An Empirical Study." *Industrial Marketing Management* 38, no. 4 (2009), pp. 300–12.

Joshi, Ashwin W. "Salesperson Influence on Product Development: Insights from a Study of Small Manufacturing Organizations." *Journal of Marketing* 74, no. 1 (January 2010), pp. 94–108.

Le Meunier-FitzHugh, Kenneth, Jasmin Baumann, Roger Palmer, and Hugh Wilson. "The Implications of Service-Dominant Logic and Integrated Solutions on the Sales Function." *Journal of Marketing Theory and Practice* 19, no. 4 (Fall 2011), pp. 423–40.

Le Meunier-FitzHugh, Kenneth, and Nigel F. Piercy. "Improving the Relationship between Sales and Marketing." *European Business Review* 22, no. 3 (2010), pp. 287–305.

Malshe, Avinash. "An Exploration of Key Connections within Sales-Marketing Interface." *Journal of Business and Industrial Marketing* 26, no. 1 (2011), pp. 45–57.

Paparoidamis, Nicholas G., and Paolo Guenzi. "An Empirical Investigation into the Impact of Relationship Selling and LMX on Salespeople's Behaviours and Sales Effectiveness." *European Journal of Marketing* 43, no. 7/8 (2009), pp. 1053–61.

Piercy, Nigel F., David W. Cravens, and Nikala Lane. "Sales Manager Behavior-Based Control and Salesperson Performance: The Effects of Manager Control Competencies and Organizational Citizenship Behavior." *Journal of Marketing Theory and Practice* 20, no. 1 (Winter 2012), pp. 7–22.

Rouziès, Dominique, Anne T. Coughlan, Erin Anderson, and Dawn Iacobucci. "Determinants of Pay Levels and Structures in Sales Organization." *Journal of Marketing* 73, no. 6 (November 2009), pp. 92–104.

Schwepker, Charles H., Jr., and David J. Good. "Sales Quotas: Unintended Consequences on Trust in Organization, Customer-Oriented Selling, and Sales Performance." *Journal of Marketing Theory and Practice* 20, no. 4 (Fall 2012), pp. 437–52.

Shepherd, C. David, Geoffrey L. Gordon, Rick E. Ridnour, Dan C. Weilbaker, and Brian Lambert. "Sales Manager Training Practices in Small and Large Firms." *American Journal of Business* 26, no. 2 (2011), pp. 92–117.

Smith, Brent, Trina Larsen, and Bert Rosenbloom. "Understanding Cultural Frames in the Multicultural Sales Organization: Prospects and Problems for the Sales Manager." *Journal of Transnational Management* 14, no. 4 (October 2009), pp. 277–92.

Speakman, James I. F., and Lynette Ryals. "Key Account Management: The Inside Selling Job." *Journal of Business and Industrial Marketing* 27, no. 5 (2012), pp. 360–69.

Steward, Michelle D., Michael D. Hutt, Beth A. Walker, and Ajith Kumar. "Coordination Strategies of High-Performing Salespeople: Internal Working Relationships That Drive Success." *Journal of Academy of Marketing Science* 38, no. 5 (2010), pp. 550–66.

Steward, Michelle D., Michael D. Hutt, Beth A. Walker, and Ajith Kumar. "Role Identity and Attributions of High-Performing Salespeople." *Journal of Business and Industrial Marketing* 24, no. 7 (2009), pp. 463–76.

MANAGING YOUR CAREER

SOME QUESTIONS ANSWERED IN THIS CHAPTER ARE

- Which entry-level jobs are available to new college graduates?
- Where do I find these jobs?
- How should I go about getting interviews, and what should I do when I have an interview?
- What selection procedures besides interviews might I go through?
- Which career paths are available in sales?
- How can I prepare myself for a promotion into management?

PROFILE

PROFILE While in college, I knew exactly what I wanted to do and had a three-year goal after graduation: medical sales and a certain income level. I started with an entrepreneurial company specializing in a cancerous tumor treatment, related mainly to urology and interventional radiology. My lifelong mentor was a part of it and gave me a shot to become part of the team with the title Business Development/Clinical Applications. There were only seven of us in the company at the time, with four of us traveling to develop business and consult during operations.

The small business I experienced had both its ups and its downs. I was traveling 100 percent of the time throughout the western United States. In the winters, I was able to travel with my skis and stay the weekend somewhere instead of head home. As a company we had a passion to work hard and had fun in everything we did. It was like a family at times. A negative was the nightmare of figuring out how to grow a business on a low budget, pushing that boundary as long as possible until more assets could be acquired. The long, strenuous travel hours ended up being more expensive than desired.

Two years later, I decided to change paths. At that time we had 12 total employees, and the owner and I started a small company on the side in South Texas. My experience in the entrepreneurial world was great. I lived in California for a while, traveled all over, made some great connections, and learned a ton about the medical industry. But I had goals that this small company would not allow me to hit.

I moved to a large orthopedic company selling medical devices/implants specializing in trauma orthopedics. We take care of broken bones after traumatic events like car accidents or other accidents leading to fractures, joint replacements after a hip or shoulder fracture, and limb deformities on children and adults with a genetic deformity. I joined a sales team of three, and the trauma life began. I went from traveling 100 percent of the time to being on call in one city 100 percent of the time. I quickly picked up on the business and earned my own territory within a few months. I really began to love what I do, and on top of that I hit my first financial goal.

Trauma life is crazy and cutthroat but fun: living on commission only with a pager and phone, no Caleber where you go, and getting called into surgery in the middle of the night and working 24/7. It's a way of life you have to commit to. Some people say you need a few screws loose to do trauma for more than a couple years and I agree. It's a passion.

I have been in trauma for four years with two large orthopedic companies, as I was recruited away by a competitor. My territory is my business. That is my only focus. Management has a sales team they focus on and are there to help you grow, support your growth, and act as sort of a buffer between you and corporate.

Are there more policies and procedures to go through with large corporations? Absolutely, but you have more resources to help you grow your own business/territory. The larger the company and more success you have, the more likely they are to invest in you and move you up if desired. I don't prefer a larger company to a small company or vice versa; both have their pluses and minuses.

One mantra I've heard and lived by has worked well for me: "If you work just for money, you'll never make it. But if you love what you are doing and always put the customer first, success will be yours." I believe it is extremely important to find something you have a passion for and run. As a sales rep, service/customer support should be priority. To service and support something you love will drive even more success. Second, "You don't close a sale; you open a relationship if you want to build a long-term, successful enterprise." A sale needs to be looked at as a long-term relationship. Work yourself up to the top of the totem pole. Don't follow success; rather, be excellent, and success will follow you.

Visit our Web site at:
www.stryker.com

Landing that first career position is an exciting moment! However, the job search is just the first task in managing your career. Like the chess player who is thinking two or three moves ahead, you too must think about subsequent opportunities. Also like the chess player, you must maintain some flexibility so you do not checkmate your career if one strategy does not work.

Sales is a great place to begin a career. Just ask Mark Hurd, CEO of Oracle. Hurd started in sales with NCR and became president of the Teradata subsidiary and then president of NCR. From there, he took over Hewlett-Packard, leading a turnaround based on improving their sales force. At each step of the way, Hurd has grown each company by focusing attention on the sales function.

OPPORTUNITIES IN SELLING

Selling offers many opportunities.

Corporate executives clearly recognize the importance of selling experience in any career, as evidenced by people like Mark Hurd and Spencer Ryan (profiled at the start of this chapter). Many people, though, have also found career satisfaction by staying in sales throughout their working lives.

Whether the career is sales or any other field, similar questions apply when searching for a job. In this chapter the focus is on the search for a sales position and how to land the first job. We examine how companies make hiring decisions and offer tips on how to build selling and management skills while managing a career.

MAKING A GOOD MATCH

The keys to being successful and happy lie in finding a good match between what you need and desire in a position and the positions companies offer.[1] The first step, then, is to understand yourself, what you need, and what you have to offer. Then you must consider what each company needs and what each has to offer. As Exhibit 17.1 illustrates, a good match means your needs are satisfied by what the company offers and what you offer satisfies the company's needs.

Exhibit 17.1

A Good Match between Salesperson and Company

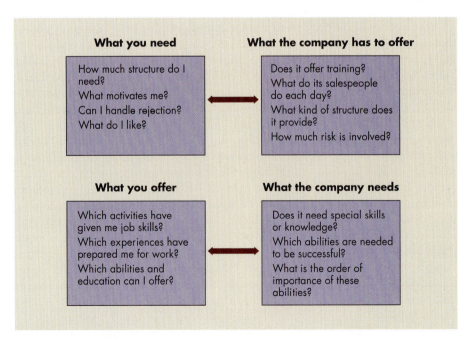

What you need

How much structure do I need?
What motivates me?
Can I handle rejection?
What do I like?

What the company has to offer

Does it offer training?
What do its salespeople do each day?
What kind of structure does it provide?
How much risk is involved?

What you offer

Which activities have given me job skills?
Which experiences have prepared me for work?
Which abilities and education can I offer?

What the company needs

Does it need special skills or knowledge?
Which abilities are needed to be successful?
What is the order of importance of these abilities?

Many companies, such as Konica-Minolta, Oracle, IBM, and others, use exotic trips as a reward for top performers.

UNDERSTANDING YOURSELF

Shakespeare said, "To thine own self be true," but to be true to yourself, you must know who you are, what you need, and what you can offer others.[2] Knowing these things about yourself requires substantial self-examination. We will pose some questions that can help you follow Shakespeare's suggestion.

Understanding Your Needs

The first step in making a good match between what you have to offer and a company's position is to determine what you need. Important questions to consider include the following:

1. *Structure:* Can you work well when assignments are ambiguous, or do you need a lot of instruction? Do you need deadlines that others set, or do you set your own deadlines? If you are uncomfortable when left on your own, you may need structure in your work life. Many sales positions, such as missionary and trade sales, are in a structured environment with well-defined procedures and routines. Other positions require the salesperson to operate with little guidance or structure.

2. *Motivation:* Will financial incentives, personal recognition, or simply job satisfaction get you going? Probably it will be some combination of the three, but try to determine the relative value of each to you. Then you can weigh compensation plans, recognition programs, and other factors when considering which sales position is right for you. You may want to review the section on compensation plan types in Chapter 16 to aid in determining which plan best suits your needs.

3. *Stress and rejection:* How much stress can you handle? Are you a risk taker, or do you prefer more secure activities? What do you do when faced with stress? With rejection? These are important questions in understanding what you need from a sales position. For example, capital equipment sales jobs can be high-stress positions because sales are few and far between. Other jobs may require you to wade through many rejections before landing a sale. If you thrive on that kind of challenge, the rewards can be gratifying. Some sales positions, though, involve working only with current customers, and salespeople incur little outright rejection. Every grocery store, for example, will carry at least some Procter & Gamble products so there is not the same stress placed on each individual sale.

4. *Interest:* What do you find interesting? Mechanical or technical topics? Merchandising? Art or fashion? You cannot sell something that bores you. You would just bore and annoy the customer.

Understanding What You Have to Offer

Other resources that can help you understand the person you are may be available through your college's placement center. You must also take inventory of what you bring to the job:

1. *Skills:* What activities and experiences taught you certain skills? What did you learn from those experiences and your education that you can apply to a career? Keep in mind that it is not the activities in which you

participated that matter to hiring companies; it is what you learned by participating that counts.

2. *Knowledge:* College has provided you with many areas of knowledge, but you have also probably learned much by participating in hobbies and other interests. For example, you may have special computer knowledge that would be useful in selling software, or you may have participated in a particular sport that makes you well suited to sell equipment to sporting goods stores. Kristen Scott, profiled at the start of Chapter 16, found that her course in CRM and her experience in selling NetSuite at the National Collegiate Sales Competition enabled her to compete against other salespeople with years of experience and win a sales position with Oracle straight out of college.

3. *Qualities and traits:* Every person has a unique personality. What parts of your personality add value for your potential employer? Are you detail oriented and systematic? Are you highly creative? In other words, what can you bring to the job that is uniquely you? Exhibit 17.2 lists traits of top salespeople, according to a study conducted for *Sales and Marketing Management* magazine.

Your answers to these questions will generate a list of what you have to offer companies. Then when you are in an interview, you can present features that make you a desirable candidate.

When to Ask These Questions

Unfortunately many students wait until just before graduation before seriously considering the type of career they desire. According to one career services director, students who start a search while in school will find a job three times faster than those who start after graduation. Although it is not always realistic to expect every student to map out a life plan prior to senior year, asking questions such as these as early as possible can guide a student to better course selection, better use of learning opportunities, and ultimately a better career decision. Then the student can begin actively searching for the job at the beginning of the senior year so that graduation signals the beginning of a career, not a career search.

Exhibit 17.2
Traits of Top Salespeople

1. Strong ego: able to handle rejection with healthy self-esteem.
2. Sense of urgency: getting it done now.
3. Ego driven: obsessive about being successful.
4. Assertive: being firm without being aggressive (see the discussion in Chapter 11).
5. Willing to take risks: willing to innovate.
6. Sociable: good at building relationships.
7. Abstract reasoner: able to handle complex selling situations and ideas.
8. Skeptical: a healthy bit of suspicion, not counting on commission until the sale is really a sale.
9. Creative: able to set oneself apart from the competition.
10. Empathic: able to place oneself in the buyer's shoes.

Source: Adapted from Erika Rasmusson, "The Ten Traits of Top Salespeople," *Sales and Marketing Management*, August 1999, pp. 34–37.

UNDERSTANDING THE COMPANY

While developing a good feel for who you are and what you have to offer companies, you should also explore what is available and which companies offer positions that appeal to you. As you can see in Exhibit 17.3, numerous sources provide information about positions and growth opportunities in various industries and specific companies. Don't forget, though, that the best sources are personal; be sure to talk over job opportunities with your friends, friends of your parents, and your professors. Use term papers as an excuse to call professionals in a field that interests you. Join trade and professional associations now because these offer great networking opportunities. As someone who has studied sales, you should use your prospecting skills too. Next let's discuss how to evaluate what you learn about the companies and their positions.

Exhibit 17.3

Sources of Job Information

Source	Example
Government	U.S. Industrial Outlook
Research services	Standard & Poor's Industry Surveys
Industry associations	Christian Booksellers' Association
Professional organizations	Sales and Marketing Executives International
General magazines	*BusinessWeek, Money*
Trade magazines	*Sales and Marketing Management, Selling Power*
Placement services	University placement office; nonfee private agencies such as Personnel One
Personal sources	Friends, relatives, industry association executives at trade shows, recruiters at career fairs
Web sites	marketingjobs.com

What the Company Has to Offer

When you meet a salesperson or sales manager, you should ask about compensation and recognition programs, training, career opportunities, and other information to determine whether the company truly offers benefits to satisfy your needs. You should also explore daily activities of the salesperson, likes and dislikes about the job, and what that person thinks it takes to succeed. This information will help you determine whether a match exists.

For example, if you need structure, you should look for a sales position in which your day is structured for you. Any industry that relies on repeated sales calls to the same accounts is likely to be highly structured. Industries with a structured sales day include consumer packaged goods sales (Procter & Gamble, Quaker Oats, and the like) and pharmaceutical sales (Novartis, Eli Lilly Company, and so forth). Even these sales positions offer some flexibility and independence. Office and industrial equipment sales provide much less structure when the emphasis is on getting new accounts.

Knowing your comfort level with risk and your need for incentives should help you pick a company with a compensation program that is right for you. If you need the security of a salary, look for companies in trade sales, equipment sales, pharmaceuticals, or consumer packaged goods. But if you like the risk of straight commission, which can often be matched with greater financial rewards for success, explore careers in areas such as convention sales, financial services, and other straight commission jobs.

Other factors to consider include the size of the company and its promotion policies, particularly if the company is foreign. Many companies have a "promote from within" policy, which means that whenever possible they fill positions with people who already are employees. One example is Worldwide Express, a company that sells shipping services in partnership with UPS. Alex BeMent was promoted after working at Worldwide Express for only six months to managing three salespeople, with responsibility for increasing the office to five or more. Such policies are very attractive if you seek career growth into management. A company that is foreign-owned, however, may prefer to staff certain positions with people from its home country.

Take advantage of interests you already have. If you are intrigued by medical science, seek a medical sales position. If merchandising excites you, a position selling to the trade would be appropriate. A bar of soap by itself is not exciting, but helping customers find ways to market that bar of soap is.

From the BUYER'S SEAT

WHAT THE RECRUITER SAYS

Dean Kyle, of Henry Schein, interviews dozens of graduating college students for sales jobs every year. Here's his advice to you if you're headed into sales.

"Probe, probe, probe. These three words may be some of the most important in my interviews. I have been interviewing hundreds of students for over 30 years. And they all make the same mistake. The funny thing is every candidate has been coached on it throughout his or her entire educational career.

I role-play with each one of my candidates in the interview; I tell them exactly what will happen. Students will immediately be met by an objection. Every time the buyer will shake his head and gruffly state, "Go away, we are already purchasing with company XYZ, we're happy, we don't need you." What would you say?

After I present this scenario, I lean over the desk and ask them that exact question. Ninety percent of my candidates answer the same way. After a little stuttering, stammering, and fidgeting, they product overload me. They spit fact after fact at me and go into a long, well-rehearsed list of product superiority.

This response is the opposite of what these students have been taught their whole sales education. Only 10 percent

of students get it right—they probe! If I'm the buyer, I do not want to listen to a speech about product superiority; I want to be understood and heard. You accomplish this by asking questions. The 10 percent that impress me immediately calm their composure and ask probing questions. "I've heard good things about Company XYZ. Can you tell me more?" When my candidates begin to ask questions and dig deeper, they find pain points and opportunities to build a successful presentation and ultimately a successful interview.

What puts someone in that 10 percent during the interview? The number one trait I look for while interviewing is a level of maturity. These students are calm under pressure, confident in their speech, and natural in their role play with a good personality, effective communication skills, sales acumen, and a high level of energy. The best way to gain this level of maturity portrayed during an interview is through life experiences, which often come from internships. But even with the best of life experiences, don't leave all your training at the door when you walk into my office! Remember, probe, probe, probe."

Source: Brooke Borgias, used with permission.

What the Company Needs

At this point in your job search, you may have narrowed your selection to a group of industries or companies. At a minimum you have a good picture of what a company should offer to land you as a salesperson. The next step is to find a company that needs you. Finding out what a company needs will require some research, but you will find this step fun and rewarding. Dean Kyle, sales manager for Henry Schein who has recruited college students and others for sales positions, provides his perspective on how to impress recruiters in "From the Buyer's Seat 17.1."

In general, companies look for three qualities in salespeople: good communication skills, self-motivation, and a positive and enthusiastic attitude. One sales consultant says these are reflections of the personality traits ego drive, ego strength, and empathy.[3] Recall from Exhibit 17.2 that other characteristics are important, such as a sense of urgency.

Companies in certain industries may also desire related technical skills or knowledge, such as medical knowledge for the field of pharmaceutical sales or insurance knowledge to enter that field. All companies need salespeople with computer skills because computers are increasingly being used to track and manage accounts, communicate internally, and perform other important activities.

Career fairs, such as this one at a hotel during spring break, can be a great opportunity to find internships or permanent sales positions.

If you want to enter a field requiring specialized knowledge or skills, now is the time to begin acquiring that knowledge. Not only will you already have the knowledge when you begin to search for a position, but you will also have demonstrated self-motivation and the right kind of attitude by taking on the task of acquiring that knowledge and skill.

THE RECRUITING PROCESS

Early in this book we discussed the buying process so you would understand the purchase decision buyers make. Now we will look at the recruiting process so you will understand how companies will view you as a candidate for a sales job or any other position.

SELECTING SALESPEOPLE

In recent years companies have made considerable progress in screening and selecting salespeople. Most have discarded the myth that there is one single "sales type" who will be successful selling anything to anybody. Instead they seek people who match the requirements of a specific position, using various methods to gain information and determine whether a good match will be made.

APPLICANT INFORMATION SOURCES

To determine whether a match exists between the job requirements and the applicant's abilities, information about the applicant must be collected. Companies use five important sources of information: application forms, references, tests, personal interviews, and assessment centers. We describe these five sources from the perspective of the company so you can understand how they are used to make hiring decisions. We also explain how you should use these sources of information so you can present yourself accurately and positively.

The **application form** is a preprinted form that the candidate completes. You have probably already filled these out for part-time jobs you have had. The form should include factual questions concerning the profile the company established for the position. Responses on the form are also useful for structuring the personal interview. Résumés provide much of the same information application forms do but are often too individualized for easy comparison. For this and other reasons, companies must supplement résumés with an application form (we discuss résumés in greater detail later in this chapter).

Contacting **references,** or people who know the applicant, is a good way to validate information on the application form. References can also supplement the information with personal observations. The most frequently contacted references are former employers. Other references are coworkers, leaders of social or religious organizations, and professors. You should be aware that some organizations try to develop relationships with faculty so they can receive leads on excellent candidates before visiting the placement office. Professors recommend students who have demonstrated the qualities the recruiting companies desire.

When you select references, keep in mind that companies want references that can validate information about you. Choose references that provide different information, such as one character reference, one educational reference, and one work-related reference.

Experienced sales managers expect to hear favorable comments from an applicant's references. More useful information may be contained in unusual comments, gestures, faint praise, or hesitant responses that may indicate a problem. Before you offer someone's name as a reference, ask that person for permission. At that time you should be able to tell whether the person is willing to give you a good recommendation.

Intelligence, ability, personality, and interest **tests** provide information about a potential salesperson that cannot be obtained readily from other sources. Tests can also correct misjudgments made by sales managers who tend to act on "gut feelings." Although tests were widely criticized in the early 1980s for failing to predict success better than other sources did, recent studies indicate that assessment tests are growing in popularity once more, in part because of their improved predictive power.[4] The new assessment tests, however, are more accurate when they are specifically related to sales and the situations potential salespeople may encounter.

Several types of tests may be given. H. R. Challey Inc. designs tests to determine a person's psychological aptitude for different sales situations. BSRP offers a test that measures a salesperson's call reluctance, or fear of initiating contact. IBM requires sales candidates to demonstrate technical aptitude through a test, while Skyline (a company that sells exhibition equipment for trade shows and other displays) requires a test that indicates the individual's ability to handle details. Like many companies, KB Homes requires candidates to pass a math test because of the importance of calculating price correctly. Still other tests indicate a candidate's ethical nature. Companies may require candidates to take tests in all these categories.

The important point to remember about tests is to remain relaxed. If the test is a valid selection tool, you should be happy with the outcome no matter what it is. If you believe the test is not valid—that is, does not predict your ability to succeed in that job—you may want to present your feelings to the recruiter. Be prepared to back up your line of reasoning with facts and experiences that illustrate why you are a good candidate for the position.

Interviews, or personal interaction between recruiter and candidate, are an important source of information for recruiters. Companies now give more attention to conducting multiple interviews in the selection process because sometimes candidates show only slight differences. Multiple interviews can improve a recruiter's chances of observing the differences and selecting the best candidate. We cover interviews in more detail later in the chapter.

Companies sometimes evaluate candidates at centrally located **assessment centers.** In addition to being used for testing and personal interviews, these locations may simulate portions of the job. Simulating the job serves two purposes. First, the simulation lets managers see candidates respond to a joblike situation. Second, candidates can experience the job and determine whether it fits them. For example, Merrill Lynch sometimes places broker candidates in an office and simulates two hours of customer telephone calls. As many as half the candidates may then decide that being a stockbroker is not right for them, and Merrill Lynch can also evaluate the candidates' abilities in a lifelike setting.

Companies use many sources of information in making a hiring decision, perhaps even asking for a copy of a videotaped presentation you may make for this class. These sources are actually selling opportunities for you. You can present yourself and learn about the job at the same time, continuing your evaluation of the match.

SELLING YOUR CAPABILITIES

With an understanding of the recruiting process from the company's point of view, you can create a presentation that sells your capabilities and proves you have the skills and knowledge the company wants. Preparing the résumé, gaining an interview, and presenting your capabilities in the interview are important activities that require sound planning to present yourself effectively.

PREPARING THE RÉSUMÉ

The résumé is the brochure in your marketing plan. As such, it needs to tell the recruiter why you should be hired. Tom Day, sales manager for Hormel, says he literally gets hundreds of résumés for sales positions, whether he has a position available or not. His company prefers to hire inexperienced salespeople right out of college, as do many companies, so don't let a lack of experience create anxiety or lead to misrepresentation on your résumé.[5] There are two broadly accepted formats for résumés: a conventional format and a functional style. In some career centers or if you choose to use an online résumé service, such as LiveCareer.com, you can choose from as many as 1,400 templates, but most follow the conventional style. Whether you choose the conventional style or the functional style of résumé, the purpose is to sell your skills and experience.

Conventional Résumés

Conventional résumés are a form of life history, organized by type of experience. The three categories of experience most often used are education, work, and activities/hobbies (see the example in Exhibit 17.4). Although it is easy to create conventional résumés, it is also easy to fail to emphasize important points. To avoid making this mistake, follow this simple procedure:

- List education, work experience, and activities.
- Write out what you gained in each experience that will help you prove you have the desired qualities.
- Emphasize what you learned and that you have the desired qualities under each heading.

For example, the résumé in Exhibit 17.4 is designed for a student interested in a sales career. Note how skills gained in this class are emphasized in addition to GPA and major. The candidate has also chosen to focus on customer service skills gained as a camp counselor, a job that a recruiter would otherwise overlook. Rather than just listing herself as a member of the soccer team, the candidate highlights the leadership skills she gained as captain.

Exhibit 17.4
Conventional Résumé
Example

Cheryl McSwain

After June 1:
435 Wayward View, Apt. B
State College, PA 10303
203/555-1289

Present Address:
612 Homer
Aurora, CO 86475
804/555-9183

Career Objective: Sales in the telecommunications industry

Education:

Colorado University, Boulder, Colorado
Bachelor of Business Administration, June 2013
Marketing
GPA: 3.25 on 4.0 scale

Major Subjects:
Personal Selling
Sales Management
Industrial Marketing

Other Subjects:
Microcomputing
Local Area Networks Management
Telecommunications

Emphasized selling and sales management in computing
and telecommunications. Learned SPIN, social styles, and
other adaptive selling techniques. Studied LANWORKS
and Novell network management.

Work Experience: Sales representative, *The Lariat* (CU campus newspaper)
Practiced sales skills in making cold calls
and selling advertising
Fall 2010 to present

Counselor, Camp Kanatcook
Learned customer service and leadership skills
Summers, 2010, 2011, 2012

Scholarships and Honors:
University Merit Scholar ($2,000/year, two years)
Top sales student, spring 2013
Dean's List, three semesters

Activities:

Member, Alpha Delta Pi Sorority
Rush chair, 2012
Motivated members to actively recruit; interviewed candidates
for selection
Homecoming float chair, 2011
Managed float building; sorority awarded second in float competition
Women's soccer team, four years
Captain, 2012–2013
Led team to conference championship, fall 2012

Functional Résumés

Functional résumés reverse the content and titles of the conventional résumé, organizing by what the candidate can do or has learned rather than by types of experience. As you can see in Exhibit 17.5, an advantage of this type of résumé is that it highlights more forcefully what the candidate can do.

When preparing a functional résumé, begin by listing the qualities you have that you think will help you get the job. Narrow this list to three or four qualities and then list activities and experiences to prove that you have those skills and abilities. The qualities are the headings for the résumé; the activities and experiences show that you have those qualities. One difficulty with this type of résumé is that one past job may relate to several qualities. If that is the case, emphasize the activity within the job that gave you the experience for each specific quality.

GAINING THE INTERVIEW

Students should begin examining different industries as early as possible, as we suggested earlier. As graduation looms closer and the time for serious job hunting arrives, your knowledge of the industries and companies that interest you will

Exhibit 17.5
Functional Résumé
Example

Cheryl McSwain

After June 1:
435 Wayward View, Apt. B
State College, PA 10303
203/555-1289

Present Address:
612 Homer
Aurora, CO 86475
804/555-9183

Career Objective: Sales in the telecommunications industry

Sales and Customer Service Experience:
Studied SPIN and adaptive selling techniques in personal selling.
Sold advertising in *The Lariat*, campus newspaper. Responsibilities included making cold calls, presenting advertising strategies, and closing sales.
Performed customer service tasks as camp counselor at Camp Kanatcook.
Served as the primary parent contact during drop-off and pick-up periods, answering parent queries, resolving parental concerns, and handling similar responsibilities.

Management and Leadership Experience:
Studied situational management in sales management.
Served as rush chair for sorority. Responsible for motivating members to recruit new members and developed and implemented a sales training seminar so members would present the sorority favorably within university guidelines.
Managed homecoming-float project. Sorority awarded second place in float competition.
Captained the women's varsity soccer team to a conference championship.

Telecommunications Skills and Experience:
Studied LANWORKS and Novell network management in telecommunications.
Designed, as a term project, a Novell-based LAN for a small manufacturing business.
Purchased and installed a six-computer network in a family-owned wholesaling business.

Scholarships and Honors:
University Merit Scholar ($2,000/year, two years)
Top sales student, spring 2013
Dean's List, three semesters

put you a step ahead. You will also understand the process the company will go through in searching for a new salesperson.

Using Personal Contacts

More important, you have already begun to make personal contacts in those fields—contacts you can now use to gain interviews. The same salespeople and sales managers who gave you information before to help you with term projects will usually be happy to introduce you to the person in charge of recruiting. Contacts you made at job fairs and trade shows can also be helpful.

thinking it through

Many students feel uncomfortable asking for favors from people they barely know, such as asking an acquaintance to forward a résumé to a decision maker or set up an interview. How can you overcome such feelings of discomfort? Why would someone want to help you find places to interview? What obligations do you have to people who give you the names of job contacts?

Using Employment Postings

Responding to Web postings or newspaper advertisements can also lead to job interviews. You will need to carefully interpret employment postings and then respond effectively to them.

All ads are designed to sell, and employment ads are no exception. But what sounds great may not be wonderful in reality. Here are some phrases often found in such ads and interpretations of them:

Independent contractor: You will work on straight commission with no employee benefits. You will probably receive no training and little, if any, support. Some experienced salespeople prefer this type of position, but it is probably not the best place to start.

Earn up to $ (or *unlimited income* or *our top rep made $500,000 last year*): You need to know what the average person makes and what the average first-year earnings are, not what the top rep made or the upper limit. The job could still be desirable, but you need to find out what reality is before accepting a position.

Sales manager trainee: This is another title for sales representative. Don't be put off or overly encouraged by high-sounding titles.

Bonuses paid weekly, daily commissions, or *weekly commissions:* These are high-pressure jobs and probably involve high-pressure sales.

Ten salespeople needed now! That's because everyone has quit. This company uses salespeople and then discards them.

You should look for two things in an ad: what the company needs and what it has to offer. The company should provide concrete information about training, compensation plan (although not necessarily the amount), amount of travel to expect, and type of product or service you will sell. You should also expect to find the qualifications the company desires, including experience and education. If this is a job you really want but you do not have the experience now, call and ask how to get it. Be specific: "What companies should I pursue that will give me the experience you are looking for?" If the ad requires e-mail response only, send an e-mail message and mention that you are a student. Many people are willing to help someone get started.

Responding to Postings

Many postings and ads will ask you to write or e-mail and may not list the company's name. A blind box number is given when the company name is not included in a newspaper ad; the box number is usually at the address of the newspaper. For example, the ad may say to send a résumé to Job Posting 943 at Monster.com. Don't be put off by the lack of company name; the posting or ad may be placed by a company such as IBM that would otherwise receive a large number of unqualified applicants. Companies use blind postings and blind box numbers for many legitimate reasons.

Writing the Cover Letter

When you write in response to a posting, you are writing a sales letter—even if you send it by e-mail. Like any sales letter, it should focus on what you can do for the company, not what you expect from it. The letter should start with an attention getter. Here is one example:

In today's economy, you need someone who can become productive quickly as a territory representative. Based on your posting at Monster.com, I believe that I am that person.

The Internet is a great source of leads for jobs; however, recruiters report receiving hundreds, and sometimes thousands, of résumés for every job they post. If you really want a job with a particular company, approach it like a sales opportunity and use your prospecting and relationship building skills.

This attention getter is direct, focuses on a probable need, and refers to the posting. The attention getter tells why you should be considered. The probability of getting a response to this e-mail is far greater than if you simply said,

> Please consider me for the territory representative position you posted at Monster.com.

The body of the letter should center on two or three reasons why you should be hired. For example, if you have the qualities of self-motivation and leadership, devote two paragraphs relating each to the position. Use your résumé as proof. For example:

> A territory representative position often requires self-motivation. As you can see from the attached résumé, I demonstrated self-motivation as a sales representative for the campus newspaper, as a volunteer for the local food bank, and as a member of the Dean's Honor Roll during two of the last four semesters.

The letter should close with a request for action. Ask for an interview and suggest times you are available. For example:

> Please call me to arrange an interview. My schedule allows me to meet with you on Tuesday or Thursday afternoon.

An alternative is to state that you will call:

> I will call you early next week to discuss my potential as a salesperson for XYZ Corporation.

No response does not necessarily mean you have been rejected; follow up with a phone call if you do not hear anything within a week. One former student got a job because he called to verify that the sales manager had received his résumé. She had never seen it but was impressed enough with the student's phone call to arrange an appointment. Sometimes e-mail is lost or delayed, goes to a junk mail file and gets deleted, or simply is deleted accidentally—and you would not want a company to miss out on the opportunity to hire you because of a computer glitch!

THE INTERVIEW

Many students do not realize how much competition exists for the best entry-level sales positions, or perhaps they do not know what companies look for in new employees. Students often act as though they are shopping for a job. Job shoppers, however, are not seriously considered by recruiters, who are usually astute enough to quickly pick up on the student's lack of interest. If the job shopper does become interested, it is probably too late because the recruiter has already discounted this applicant. Like it or not, you are really competing for a job. As in any competition, success requires preparation and practice.

Preparing for the Interview

Students who know something about the company and its industry lead the competition. You have already looked for company and industry information in the library, in business reference books, and in periodicals. You visited its Web site. You have also interviewed the company's customers, salespeople, and sales managers. You can use this knowledge to demonstrate your self-motivation and positive attitude—two of the top three characteristics sales managers look for in sales candidates. You will find it easier to demonstrate the third top characteristic, communication skills, with the confidence you gain from proper preparation.

In addition to building knowledge of the "customer," you must plan your responses to the questions you will be asked. Exhibit 17.6 lists standard interview questions.

Scenario questions are popular with recruiters. These questions ask what the candidate would do in a certain situation involving actions of competitors. (For example, what would you do if a customer told you something negative about your product that you knew to be untrue, and the customer's source of information was your competitor?) Such questions test ethics regarding competitors and the ability to handle a delicate situation. Scenario questions also test the candidate's response to rejection, ability to plan, and other characteristics. You can best prepare for these types of questions with this class and by placing yourself in the situations described in the cases and exercises in this book. You may also want to review the questions at the ends of the chapters.

The sales field has several unusual characteristics, such as travel, that influence the type of questions asked. For example, if significant travel is part of the position, you may be asked, "Travel is an important part of this job, and you may be away from home about three nights per week. Would you be able and willing to travel as the job requires?" However, some questions are illegal, and you do not have to answer

Exhibit 17.6

Frequently Asked Interview Questions

1. What are your long-range and short-range goals and objectives? When and why did you establish these goals, and how are you preparing yourself to achieve them?
2. What do you consider to be your greatest strengths and weaknesses?
3. Why did you choose the career for which you are preparing?
4. How do you think a friend or professor who knows you well would describe you?
5. Why should I hire you?
6. In what ways do you think you can make a contribution to our company?
7. Do you think your grades are a good indication of your academic achievement?
8. What major problem have you encountered, and how did you deal with it?
9. What do you know about our company? Why are you seeking a position with us?
10. If you were hiring a graduate for this position, what qualities would you look for?

Exhibit 17.7

Examples of Legal and
Illegal Questions

Subject	Legal Questions	Illegal Questions
Name	Have you ever used another name?	What is your maiden name?
Residence	Where do you live?	Do you own or rent your home?
Birthplace or national origin	Can you, after employment, verify your right to work in the United States?	Where were you born? Where were your parents born?
Marital or family status	Statement of company policy regarding assignment of work of employees who are related.	With whom do you reside? Are you married? Do you plan a family?
	Statement of company policy concerning travel: Can you accept this policy?	
Arrest or criminal record	Have you ever been convicted of a felony? (Such a question must be accompanied by a statement that a conviction will not necessarily disqualify the applicant.)	Have you ever been arrested?

Source: Baylor University Career Services Center.

them, such as "What is your marital status? Do you plan to have a family? Will that affect your ability to travel?" Exhibit 17.7 lists some questions that are illegal, as well as legal questions that you may have to answer.

So what do you do when you are asked an illegal question? One thing you should do is report the incident to your school's career services personnel if the interview is taking place on campus or as a result of the campus career services center. But when actually faced with the question, you have several choices. One is to ask, "Why do you ask? Is that important?" You may find that it is a question asked by an interviewer out of personal curiosity, and the interviewer may not have realized the question was inappropriate. Another response is to simply reply, "I'm sorry, I would prefer not to answer that question." If probed, you can state that you believe the question is not legal, but you will check with career services later; if the question is legal, you will answer it later. If the interviewer is simply ignorant, you will probably get an apology, and then the interview will move on. Otherwise you've identified a company where you may not wish to work. Your final option is, of course, to go ahead and answer the question.

At some point during the interview, the recruiter will ask whether you have any questions. In addition to using the standard questions concerning pay, training, and benefits, you should prepare questions that are unlikely to have been answered already. For example, suppose your research has uncovered the fact that the company was recently awarded the Malcolm Baldrige Award for Quality; you might plan to ask what the company did to win that award.

You may also want to plan questions about the interviewer's career, how it got started, and what positions he or she has held. These questions work best when you are truly interested in the response; otherwise you might sound insincere. Answers to these questions can give you a personal insight into the company. Also, you may often find yourself working for the interviewer, so the answers to your questions may help you decide whether you like and can work with this person.

Other important subjects to ask about are career advancement opportunities, typical first-year responsibilities, and corporate personality. You also need to know how financially stable the company is, but you can find this information for public firms in the library. If the firm is privately owned, ask about its financial stability.

Finally, it may seem trivial, but shine your shoes! You are interviewing for a professional position, so look professional. Recruiters have told us about students showing up for interviews dressed in cut off shorts and a T-shirt or looking hung over. Those interviews were over before they began. One interviewer even described how a student took a phone call from her mother during the interview. She told her mom that the interview was going great! Well, it was until she took the phone call. If you do not look the part now, an interviewer will not see you in the part.

During the Interview

The job interview is much like any other sales call. It includes an approach, needs identification, presentation, and gaining commitment. There are, however, several important differences because both parties are identifying needs and making presentations.

THE APPROACH Social amenities will begin the interview. You will not need the same type of attention getter that you would on a cold call. However, you may want to include an attention getter in your greeting. For example, use a compliment approach, such as "It must be very exciting to work for a Malcolm Baldrige award winner."

NEEDS IDENTIFICATION One difference between sales calls and job interviews is that both parties have needs they have individually defined before the meeting (in a sales call, SPIN helps you assist the buyer in defining needs). A question such as "Are you willing to relocate?" is used not to define needs so much as to determine whether the company's needs will be met. You should prepare questions that will help you learn whether the company's offer will meet your needs.

Take notes during the interview, especially when asking about the company, so you can evaluate whether your needs will be met. Carry a portfolio with extra résumés and blank paper and pens for note taking or use a pad computer, such as an iPad. You may want to ask, "Do you mind if I take notes? This information is important to me, and I don't want to forget anything."

Try to determine early whether your interviewer is a sales manager or a personnel manager. Personnel managers may have a difficult time telling you about the job itself, its daily activities, and so forth; they may be able to outline only things such as training and employee benefits. Sales managers can tell you a lot about the job, perhaps to the point of describing the actual territory you will work in.

Personnel managers do not like being asked about salary; you will find that many people will advise you not to ask about money on the first interview. On the other hand, you are making an important decision. Why waste your time or theirs if the salary is much lower than your other alternatives? Sales managers are less likely to object, but just in case, you may want to preface a question about earnings by saying, "Compensation is as important a consideration for me as training and other benefits when making a decision. Can you tell me the approximate earnings of a first-year salesperson?" You will probably get a range rather than a specific figure. You could also wait until a later meeting to ask about earnings.

People who prefer security desire compensation plans with an emphasis on salary. Other people like the potential rewards of straight commission. If either is important to you, ask about the type of compensation plan in the first meeting. For example, you should ask, "What type of compensation plan do you offer: salary, straight commission, or a combination of salary plus commission or bonus?"

PRESENTATION Features alone are not persuasive in interviews, just as features alone do not persuade buyers to purchase products. Recall the FEBA technique presented in Chapter 8, which stands for feature, evidence, benefit, agreement. Cheryl McSwain (see Exhibit 17.4) might say, "I was a camp counselor for two summers at Camp Kanatcook (*feature*), as you can see on my résumé (*evidence*). This experience taught me customer service skills that you will appreciate when I sell for you (*benefit*), don't you agree?"

If asked to describe yourself, use features to prove benefits. Recruiters will appreciate specific evidence that can back up your claims. For example, if you say you like people and that is why you think you would be a good salesperson, be prepared to demonstrate how your love of people has translated into action.

Many students carry portfolios into interviews. A **portfolio** is an organized collection of evidence of one's career.[6] For example, a portfolio might contain letters of reference, a résumé, thank-you letters from customers, a paper about an internship, a strategic plan created for a business policy class, or even photographs of the homecoming float for which you were chairperson. Some of our students offer videos of their sales calls from this class as part of their portfolios; these are often made available through YouTube to recruiters, along with digital portfolios that look like Web pages. Portfolios are one method of offering proof that you can deliver benefits.

thinking it through
How would you describe yourself in terms of features? What needs would be satisfied by those features so they could become benefits? What would go on your Web site or in your portfolio to prove your features? How could you use a Web site to market yourself?

Keep in mind that the interviewer also will be taking notes. Writing down answers takes the interviewer longer than it takes for you to speak. Once a question is answered sufficiently, stop and allow the interviewer time to write. Many applicants believe they should continue talking; the silence of waiting is too much to bear. Stay silent; otherwise, you may talk yourself out of a job.

GAINING COMMITMENT Because sales positions usually require skill at gaining commitment, sales managers will want to see whether the candidate has that skill. Be prepared to close the interview with some form of gaining commitment: "I'm very excited about this opportunity. What is our next step?"

Be sure to learn when you can expect to hear from the company, confirm that deadline, and write it down. You may want to say, "So I'll receive a call or a letter within the next two weeks. Let's see, that would be the 21st, right?"

Asking for commitment and confirming the information signal your professionalism and your organizational and selling skills.

SPECIAL TYPES OF INTERVIEWS

You can face many types of interviews: disguised interviews, stress interviews, and panel interviews, among others. **Disguised interviews,** or interviews in which the candidate is unaware that the interviewer is evaluating the candidate, are common at college placement offices. In the lobby you may meet a **greeter,** probably a recent graduate of your college, who will try to help you relax before a scheduled interview and offer you an opportunity to ask questions about the job and the company. Although you can obtain a lot of good information from a greeter, you may want to save some questions for the real interview. You may also want to repeat some questions in the interview to check for consistency. Keep in mind that the greeter is also interviewing you, even though the meeting seems like friendly conversation. Keep your enthusiasm high and your nerves low.

A **stress interview** is designed to place the candidate under severe stress to see how the candidate reacts. Stress interviews have been criticized as being unfair because the type of stress one experiences on a job interview often differs from the type of stress one would actually face on the job. Still, many reputable companies believe it is appropriate to try to determine how a candidate reacts to stress because stress is a real part of just about every sales position. One tactic is to ask three questions at once and see how the candidate answers; another is to ask, "How are you going to lose money for me?" (*translation:* What mistakes have you made in the past and what might you do in the future?) or other reversed versions of appropriate questions. Another strategy is to ask questions such as "What is 36 cubed?" or "What will the interest rates be on such and such a date (two years from now), to the exact one-hundredth please?"[7] While questionable in terms of measuring the appropriate form of stress, these methods are less questionable than the following: The interviewer asks the applicant to reveal something personal, such as a time when the person felt emotionally hurt. Once the situation has been described, the interviewer may mock the applicant, saying the situation wasn't that personal or that hurtful and surely the applicant can dig deeper. Another stress tactic is to ask the interviewee to sell something such as a pencil or a table; while this question is reasonable when used to observe selling style, being an unreasonable "customer" can turn the call into a stress interview.

You probably will not see stress interviews at a college placement office, but you could face one at some point in the job-hunting process. You may find it helpful to deal with a stress interview by treating it as a game (say to yourself, "She's just trying to stress me out; I wonder how far she will go if I don't react?"). Of course you may simply refuse to play the game, either by terminating the interview or by changing the subject. If you terminate the interview, you will probably not get the job.

In **panel interviews** you will encounter multiple interviewers. During a panel interview try to make eye contact with each interviewer. Focus on each person for at least three seconds at a time; anything less than that and you are simply sweeping the room. When asked a question, begin your answer by directing it to the questioner but then shift your attention to the group. By speaking to the group, you will keep all interviewers involved and avoid a two-person conversation. You may want to review how to sell to a group, described in Chapter 8.

Panel interviews require special tactics by the candidate to keep all interviewers involved. A focus on only the older gentleman may cost this young man a position.

Group interviews are similar to panel interviews, but they include several candidates as well as several interviewers. Group interviews may take place in a conference room or around a dinner table. If you find yourself in a group interview, avoid trying to top the stories of the other candidates.

Distinguish yourself by asking interviewers about their careers and what they find it takes to be successful.

Treat social occasions during office or plant visits as interviews, and avoid alcohol or overeating. As with stress interviews, the key is to maintain your cool while being yourself. You cannot do that if you overindulge. Remember that companies are still evaluating you during these "social" events.

FOLLOW-UP

Regardless of the type of interview, you should send a thank-you note shortly afterward. Send one to the greeter, if possible (thus, you will probably want to get this person's business card). If you had a panel interview, find out who the contact person is and write to that person. If you send a thank-you card, you'll stand out. Most people who write a follow-up will send an e-mail, which is the least you should do. If you send a card, thank the person in the first paragraph, then summarize the interview. Focus your summary on the reasons why you should be hired. In the final paragraph reiterate your thanks and end with an assumptive statement, such as "I look forward to seeing you again." Whether you send a card or an e-mail, it should be short and to the point.

If you do not hear by the target date, contact the person. One former student got his first job simply because he followed up. Sales managers will appreciate the saleslike perseverance; personnel managers may not so you may want to send them an e-mail. Within another week, call the personnel manager also. Simply ask for the status of your application rather than whether you got the job. The process of deciding may have taken longer than expected, or other situations may have caused delays. You need to know where you stand, however, so you can take advantage of alternatives, if possible.

INTERVIEWING NEVER ENDS

Even if you spend your entire career with one company, your job interviewing days are not over after you land that first job; you will interview for promotions as well. Some companies even interview candidates for admission to management development programs. The same techniques apply in all these cases. You will still need to prepare properly, conduct the interview professionally, close for some level of commitment, and follow up.

MANAGING YOUR CAREER GOALS

An important aspect of career management is to set life-based objectives and then use them to determine your career objectives. Balance between family and work goals is necessary, or one of several negative consequences could occur, such as divorce or success without fulfillment. One survey reported that a lack of work–life balance was one of the top reasons that managers resigned, were terminated, or were poorly evaluated.[8] Another study indicated that the recession of the late 2000s significantly impacted work–life balance for the worse. Nearly 50 percent of workers reported significant increases in stress due to work–life conflict.[9]

Balance, then, is important when setting career goals. Career decisions must be compatible with family and personal objectives. Keeping life goals in mind and remembering your reasons for setting those goals will help you map out a career with which you can be happy.

MAKING THE TRANSITION FROM COLLEGE TO CAREER

That first year after college is a unique and important time in anyone's life. How this transition is handled can have a big influence in whether you reach success

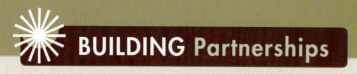
PERSONAL BRANDING AND THE BUSINESS PROFESSIONAL

Do you think personal branding matters? No? Then ask "RG3" or "Johnny Football." Both of those nicknames were creations by athletic departments that realized that their athletes needed branding to help them in their Heisman quest. In fact, not only did Baylor's athletic marketing department create the nickname, they also created an RG3 logo. Going into his Heisman-winning season, the knock on Robert Griffin was that he was a running quarterback; after all, his ESPN Top 10 plays were all running plays. So to counter that misperception, the team created a logo of Robert about to pass.

True, no amount of marketing would have overcome bad seasons for either Robert Griffin or Johnny Manziel. Neither would have won the Heisman had they not also had outstanding years.

What do you need for a personal brand?

1. Decide what your brand will mean. For RG3, it meant emphasizing his passing skills; for Johnny Football, it was the "all things football," the quintessential player who overcame his youth (he was the first freshman to win the Heisman).

2. Create hooks. A hook is something that helps people remember who you are. During the dot-com boom, consultant Dave Schrader called himself e-Dave, somewhat as a joke because every company was adding an "e" before its name (think e-Harmony). He's gone back to just plain "Dave," but people still remember him because of that e-Dave brand. Jackie Sherr, a realtor, always wears something bright red. Jeff Tanner, a consultant, always wears cowboy boots, and because he races thoroughbred horses, he also incorporates horse-racing images into his speeches. These hooks help people remember who you are.

3. Tie the hook to the purpose. Schrader helps companies make money through technology; the "e-Dave" is for "e-commerce." Sherr promotes putting your style into your home; the red shows her personal style. Tanner consults on sales and marketing performance; horse racing is all about performance.

4. Create a message. Some call it an elevator speech, meaning you should be able to describe yourself and your brand in the time it takes to ride an elevator. Develop a one-sentence description of who you are and what you can do.

5. Perform. Branding is about making a promise, so don't make a promise you can't or won't keep.

Personal branding is something you can and should start now. While your own brand will morph over time as you develop new skills and interests, starting now will help you land that first position and give you time to hone your brand.

or experience disappointment. Although a life's work is not created or ruined in the first months, a poor start can take years to overcome. It is not just a matter of giving up student attitudes and behaviors; making the transition also requires taking the time to understand and earn the rights, responsibilities, and credibility of being a sales professional. You will make mistakes during that transition; everyone does. But as many successful salespeople have learned, it isn't whether you make mistakes but rather whether you learn from them.

Many new hires want to make a great first impression, so they charge ahead and fail to recognize that the organization was there long before they were and has already developed its own way of doing things. The first thing to do is learn the organization's culture, its values, and the way things are done there.

Another important aspect of the first year is that you are under a microscope. Your activities are watched closely as management and your peers try to decide whether you are someone they can depend on. Demonstrate a mature willingness to learn, plus respect for those with experience. Part of this mature willingness to learn means you hold your expectations in check and keep your

Exhibit 17.8
Sales Advancement at Schneider Electric

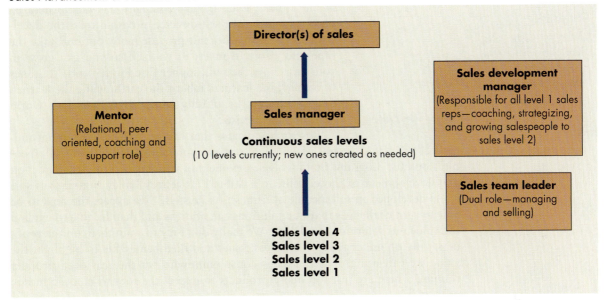

promote hopes realistic. Remember that recruiters tend to engage in puffery when presenting the opportunities and benefits of a company. Although the recruiter said it may be possible to earn a promotion in six months, the average may be much longer.

Seek a partnership with your manager. Although partnership implies a peer-level relationship and you do not have the experience to be a true peer with your manager, use the same partnering skills with him or her that you would use with customers. Find out what your manager needs and wants and then do it. Every workday is a test day except that you sometimes write the questions. Just like your professor, your manager wants the answers, not the problems. Give your boss solutions, and you will be well on the way to a partnership.

DUAL CAREER PATH

When you start out in sales, many career options are open. Career paths can alternate between sales and marketing or follow a route entirely within sales or entirely within marketing. You may even wind up as chief executive officer of a major global corporation, like Mark Hurd at Oracle. Exemplifying how you might pursue various positions, Exhibit 17.8 depicts the various career paths for salespeople at Schneider Electric. In addition to sales management opportunities, many companies also have opportunities in marketing and product development that begin in sales.

CONTINUE TO DEVELOP YOUR KSAs

Knowledge, skills, and abilities, or **KSAs,** are the package that you offer your employer. You just spent four or five years and a lot of money developing a set of KSAs, but like any asset, your KSAs will begin to decay if you do not continue to invest in them. Because you are the person in your company to whom your career means the most, many companies, such as Cisco, have recognized that ownership of development belongs to the person, not to the company, and have turned training into self-directed development programs. In addition to

Exhibit 17.9

Soft Skills Developed at Oracle

Negotiation
Value messaging
Competitive positioning
Reference selling
Working with partners
Prospecting skills
Best practices for how to lead a good sales cycle

self-directed training, much of the company's training has also gone virtual, meaning salespeople can access it online at any time.[10] Even if your company has not formalized development into a self-directed program or if the development program does not provide many options, take the time and effort to invest in yourself so you can grow in your career. As the philosopher Eric Hoffer said, "In times of change, the learners inherit the earth, while the learned find themselves beautifully equipped to handle a world that no longer exists."[11]

Research indicates that career development opportunities vary widely among companies, especially for salespeople. Look for programs that involve assessment of your skills, as well as direction and development of those skills. In Exhibit 17.9 Jeffrey Bailey summarizes soft KSAs developed in salespeople at Oracle. As he says, "We expect the reps to be able to spot challenges that our solutions can address and then be able to explain the value our solutions can deliver. We really don't try to train them on the products, only on understanding business issues and then being able to highlight the value we can bring. It is our sales consultants who get the real deep product training. There are just too many products to expect the reps to be deep in any of them."

Lifelong learning is important in today's learning organization. Although many companies have downsized, it is the versatile, well-educated employee who not only keeps a job but also develops a career.

Lifelong learning can be an important factor in not only improving your position but also enjoying what you do. Once you have a position within an organization, your objective will be to develop yourself to get a promotion and then to be successful in that promotion. (To get the promotion after that, you will need to do well in the job you are seeking.) You should take several significant actions in each position along the way. The first action is to understand your options because sales can often lead to various positions.

Sources of Improvement

Most companies continue to train their salespeople after basic sales training, but most training of experienced salespeople is product related rather than sales skills related. If you want to improve your selling skills, you may have to actively seek assistance.

The first place to start is with the field sales manager. When that person works with you in your territory, solicit feedback after each call. During these curbside conferences, you can learn a great deal about what you are doing from an objective observer. One warning, however: Make sure your manager only observes during the sales call and does not try to get into the act! As we discussed in the previous chapter, many sales managers are former salespeople who get excited in the heat of battle and may try to take over the sales call.

Peers provide another source. Who is successful in the company? When gathered together for a sales meeting, many successful salespeople pick one another's brains for new ideas and strategies. Offer to work with them in their territories for a day or so in order to learn from them. In most situations they will be flattered and helpful. Noncompeting salespeople in professional organizations such as Sales and Marketing Executives, an international organization of salespeople and marketing managers, will also be flattered to share their tips with you.

Learning doesn't end at graduation. This team of salespeople at Mechanical Service Company is learning about a new product.

Bookstores offer a wealth of material for developing sales skills. Many good books remind salespeople of the basics of selling and present advanced methods of selling and negotiating. Be sure to keep this book, too, because you will want to refer to it when you are in the field.

Sales seminars—in-person, online, or on DVDs and CDs—are also available. Seminars, such as those offered by Zig Ziglar, Dale Carnegie, Wilson Learning, and Tom Hopkins, can be very motivating. However, many experienced salespeople desire more than just motivation; they look for seminars that also teach new ways to present and gain commitment, as well as other sales skills. Some even learn to play golf because that's what their customers do.[12]

Another source of improvement is an industry association. Many industries and professions offer certification programs, which not only require that you improve and update your knowledge and skills but also offer proof to your customers that you have made that effort. Francisco Limas, sales representative with National Restaurant Supply in El Paso, sought certification in food safety and is now pursuing certification as a Foodservice Equipment Distributors Association Certified Salesperson. Though he's been recognized by the industry's top salespeople, he realizes that the certification provides both education and an assurance of quality to customers.[13] Certification was one measure of service quality that these buyers used when comparing suppliers.

Industry associations, though, can and do provide many training opportunities that may not lead to certification. For example, the National Association of Insurance and Financial Advisors (NAIFA) offers a number of professional development courses, including one called the NAIFA Sales System. The program is primarily delivered online, though it also includes a book and access to NAIFA mentors who will coach students through challenges that arise in their regular sales calls.[14]

In this course you have begun to develop your interpersonal persuasion, or selling, skills. Whether or not you plan a career in sales, you owe it to yourself to continue to develop these skills.

Learn Your Current Job

Learn all you can about the job you have now. Many people want promotions as fast as they can get them, regardless of their readiness. But consider that you will probably be managing the people who will be holding your current job. To be truly effective as their manager, you should learn all you can about the job of the people you hope to manage while in the best position to do so: while you are one of them.

Learn the Job You Want Next

A manager once said, "In order to become a manager, you must first be a manager." He meant that promoting someone is easier when that person already has the characteristics the position requires—that is, already acts like a manager—rather than having only potential.

SELF-PROMOTION VIA TECHNOLOGY

Are you LinkedIn? Most students are on Facebook and Twitter but seem to be slow to get a profile on LinkedIn or to start using the Internet for professional purposes through blogging and other activities.

Not every business professional needs a blog, but every business professional should have a profile on LinkedIn. Jeffrey Bailey, sales manager for Oracle, stated that the company wouldn't even consider hiring a salesperson who hasn't used social media personally. "If a prospective salesperson isn't using LinkedIn professionally already, then they can't sell in today's environment," believes Bailey. Like a Facebook for professionals, LinkedIn allows you to record your professional experience (like a résumé, only with more detail), provide opportunities for others to write recommendations for you (ask your professors), and endorse your abilities (ask your friends). However, Bruce Hurwitz, a professional staffer, cautions against reciprocal endorsements, or endorsing someone just because they endorsed you. "I won't [reciprocate] because it would be meaningless," and he has had requests for more information on people he has endorsed.

Another way to network is to read and comment on others' blogs. Reading your customers' blogs (or, for now,

the companies you may want to work for) is a good idea to see what's on their minds. Lisa Gschwandtner suggests being strategic about when to comment on what you read, choosing media (Twitter, blogs, LinkedIn status, and so on) and opportunities that fit the brand you are trying to build (see "Building Partnerships 15.1" in Chapter 15 on building a personal brand). Don't comment on every blog your customer or prospective employer writes and don't respond to every tweet; rather, comment only when you have something to say that contributes to the conversation. As a student, feel free to also ask questions in response to what you read. People are always happy to help students, and this is a way for you to build your network.

While it's important to contribute to online dialogues in ways that build your personal brand, it's also important to be personal. You can comment or tweet about a Red Sox/Yankee game if that's your interest. But commenting on how long it took to recover from the party at a trade show is probably not a good idea.

Sources: Lisa Gschwandtner, "It's All about Strategy," *Selling Power,* January–February 2010, pp. 32–36; Debra Donston-Miller, "LinkedIn Profiles: Not Just for Resumes Anymore," *Informationweek Online,* October 18, 2012); Jeffrey Bailey, personal interview, November 8, 2012.

Several ways exist for you to learn about the job you desire. First, solicit the help of people who hold the job now. Many companies expect managers to develop their people. Take advantage of that fact; ask for the help of such managers. Find out what they did to prepare themselves and what you should do.

Second, volunteer to take on special projects that will demonstrate your leadership and organizational abilities. Taking projects off the hands of your manager can also let you see the manager's responsibilities. Look for ways you can contribute to the overall sales team to show your commitment to the organization, your ability to lead and develop others, and your management skills.

In addition to improving your skills, many sales professionals also recommend building a personal brand—a professional reputation that is not only strong and positive but also widely recognized. Social media offer one outlet for building that brand, as discussed in "Sales Technology 17.1."

MANAGING STRESS

Selling can be a stressful career. For example, with three days left in the month, Richard Langlotz, then a sales manager at Konica-Minolta but now a regional vice president, faced a sales team that lost $100,000 in business. One sale alone, worth $60,000, would have made the team's quota, but that account delayed its order for a few months. The other prospects decided to go with the competition. Suddenly it looked as though Langlotz was going to finish the month well below quota. To top it off, one of his salespeople quit. What did he do? "I took my sales team to a pizza place," Langlotz says. He thought about calling a meeting and getting tough with his team, but he realized they already had enough stress and didn't need any more from him. At the pizza parlor, without any prompting from him, each salesperson examined his or her prospect lists and determined how the team was going to move sales forecast for the next month into the current month. The team was successful, and Langlotz says he learned a valuable lesson. "When you have good people doing their best, they don't need more stress from their manager." Many salespeople liken sales to a roller-coaster ride, with great emotional highs when sales are good but emotional lows when sales are poor. Research shows that support from the sales manager, such as that offered by Langlotz, can go a long way to reduce stress among salespeople.[15]

For some people, coping with stress results in changing jobs. Changing jobs may be the right thing for some people to do. Others turn to less healthful releases, such as absenteeism, drugs, alcohol, and so forth.[16] All jobs have some stress; managing that stress is important to leading a happy and healthy life. However, managing stress does not always mean removing the cause of stress. Sometimes, as with the loss of a loved one, most people find they must manage stress because they cannot remove or change its cause. Two types of stress common to salespeople because of the unique nature of sales positions are situational stress and felt stress.

SITUATIONAL STRESS

Situational stress is short-term anxiety caused by a situational factor.[17] You may face situational stress when waiting to make a sales presentation for your class, for example. The best strategy to deal with situational stress is to leave the situation or remove the situational factor causing the stress, but that approach is not always possible. You cannot, for example, simply tell your instructor that you are too stressed to sell in class today, so you are leaving! One technique for managing situational stress is to imagine that the situational factor has been removed (see Exhibit 17.10 for more ideas). In class, imagine that you have already finished your role play. Mentally consider that feeling of relief you get when you

Exhibit 17.10
Coping with Situational Stress

Use imaging: Close your eyes and imagine yourself past the source of stress. Try to feel the actual sensation of what it will be like when the stress is gone.

Exercise: Exercise can moderate feelings of stress. When situational stress occurs over a period of time, set time aside for exercise breaks.

Take breaks: Take a walk, phone a friend, do something. If working on a stressful project, take regular stress breaks. Combine imaging techniques with breaks to increase the stress-reducing power of breaks.

Rest: In addition to breaks, be well rested when the situation arises. If you have a major presentation, get a good night's rest beforehand.

Prepare: If the situation involves future performance, prepare and practice. Prepare for every contingency, but don't let the tension build by thinking only of things going wrong.

Recover: Plan time for postsituation recovery before you charge into the next high-stress situation. Doing two major presentations in one day, for example, may not provide you with the recovery time you need to do well in the second presentation.

know you have done a job well. Sometimes imaging success can reduce feelings of stress.

In sales situational stress may be caused by impending presentations, deadlines for closing orders (as in Richard Langlotz's case), and similar situations. Situational stress can cause stage fright in even the most experienced salespeople. One price of success is that situational stress will continue to occur, but successful salespeople learn to control their feelings of situational stress.

FELT STRESS

Felt stress lasts longer than situational stress because the causes are more enduring. **Felt stress** is psychological distress or anxiety brought about by job demands or constraints encountered in the work environment. For example, one study showed that when salespeople felt obliged to use coercive sales tactics, their levels of felt stress increased because they knew they were engaging in ethically questionable techniques.[18] Perhaps the most common form of felt stress is role stress, or feelings of stress caused by the salesperson's role.

Role stress is brought about by role conflict, role overload, and/or role ambiguity. **Role conflict** occurs when two partners demand incompatible actions of the salesperson. A common such occurrence is when the customer wants something that seems reasonable but the company won't allow it. Ted Howell represents a training company and was selling an e-learning training program. A customer wanted to see previous work, especially because he didn't like the demo version the company offered. Ted knew that the demo version didn't represent the client's solution, but his manager kept telling him that the demo should be sufficient. Ted's frustration level hit the boiling point in one call, to the point where his manager asked what was wrong. How do you tell your manager that he's the problem? Ted didn't, but he also gave the client another demo that was more in line with his needs. Seeing the right demo was all the client needed, and Ted got the sale.[19] Conflict occurred with the salesperson caught in the middle. **Role ambiguity** occurs when the salesperson is not sure what actions are required. The salesperson may not be sure what is expected, how to achieve it, or how performance will be evaluated and rewarded. **Role overload** is what happens when the role demands more than the person can perform. Asking a new salesperson to make the same types of presentations to high-level accounts that a veteran would make could cause role overload.

In general, the best way to handle role stress is to increase role accuracy (see Exhibit 17.11 for specific ideas). When the problem is role ambiguity, simply asking for further instruction or reviewing training materials may be helpful. Coaching and other management support can also be requested. Role conflict and role ambiguity require prioritizing activities. In the example of the salesperson who feels stress due to conflict between the customer's and the manager's demands,

Exhibit 17.11
Reducing Role Stress

Prioritize: Set your own priorities so that when different people place conflicting expectations on you, your preset priorities determine where your actions will go.

Seek support: Enlist support of your priorities from your spouse, your manager, and other key people. By focusing on goals and priorities, you can reduce conflict over specific activities.

Reset expectations: By prioritizing and seeking support, you can reset expectations of various constituencies so that they are in harmony. Communicate and gain agreement on what you are capable of doing so that others' expectations of you are realistic.

Act and move on: Once you have made a decision to act, don't dwell on the conflict. Act and move on.

the salesperson must decide whose needs will be met. Once that decision is made, further stress can be avoided by refusing to dwell on the conflict. Note that the conflict is still there (both parties have conflicting demands), but the effect on the salesperson is minimized.

In either case a strong partnership with the sales manager can greatly aid in reducing stress. When a partnership is formed between a sales manager and a salesperson, the salesperson has a better understanding of the demands of the job, which activities should receive priority, and how the job should be performed. Partners also have access to more resources and more information, which can help remove some of the organizational constraints that can bring about stress.[20]

Strong sales skills can also reduce feelings of stress. Mastery of the job will reduce feelings of stress because the salesperson is in control of the situation.

SELLING YOURSELF

This entire chapter is about selling yourself throughout your career. Here we focus on some aspects specific to college students looking for a career.

College students may not realize the competition they face. That company is interviewing not only at your school, but also probably at three or four others. At each school it may talk to 15 students, or about 75 total, all for one position. In addition, recruiters get hundreds and sometimes thousand of résumés if they also post the job on the Internet. The key is to make yourself stand out and still be truthful.

Keeping the résumé simple is one way to get noticed. According to Eric Ruiz, CEO of SalesJobs.com, one mistake college students make is to put in too much detail. "All they want to know is if you can sell and what kind of numbers you've produced. For recent graduates, that's just a matter of putting the right spin on your part-time job at the local burger shack; instead of saying you 'worked the order window,' write that your shift had the highest sales numbers of any shift, or that you increased ice cream sales by 6 percent by suggesting a weekly 'buy one get one half-off' day."[21]

When responding to a posting on the Internet, don't just cut and paste your résumé into an online form. Special formatting may not come across properly when the recruiter looks at it online unless the file is saved as rich text. Similarly, don't use an uncommon software format that few recruiters may have. Your résumé may come across as dots, blocks, and zeroes.

Ruiz also suggests that you don't write a cover letter for each online posting. "Writing a cover letter does not help you in the sales industry. The people reading your résumé are HR professionals and sales recruiters; they're generally overworked, and find cover letters superfluous. Again, they're only interested in seeing hard data regarding what you've sold, whom you sold it to, and what numbers you produced. They are focused on your previous performance because being successful in sales requires such a specialized skill set," says Ruiz.

He suggests creating an individually tailored version of your résumé for each industry in which you're seeking employment, emphasizing knowledge and experience that would transfer to different industries. For example, if you're working in food and beverage sales but you want to get into medical equipment sales, write that you "have a large percentage of hospital accounts" and are "familiar with the purchasing staff at all the local hospitals" and that you've "sold to doctors before."

E-mail addresses like *myvixen* and *partystupid* may be fine in college but not when you're looking for a job. "E-mail addresses should be professional—first name, last name, and a number is fine," notes Ruiz. While Ruiz recognizes that many people apply for sales jobs, "It's the little things, like a follow-up e-mail address, that can help you get that dream job." Once you create a professional address, be sure to check it often, don't change it again (some companies report being unable to track down a good candidate), and don't let the mailbox fill up.

And clean up your Myspace and Facebook pages. Many companies regularly review these pages before making a hiring decision. Similarly, create a professional voice mail message. It's time to get professional!

SUMMARY

A sales career offers many opportunities for growth and personal development, but that career has to start somewhere. That is the purpose of the job search: to find a good match between what you need and have to offer and what a company needs and has to offer.

To achieve a match that results in mutual satisfaction, you must first understand who you are—specifically what you need and what you have to offer. You can ask yourself a number of questions to stimulate your thinking about the type of person you are and what you will need from a sales position. In addition, as you review your experiences in school, work, and other activities, you can identify the skills and characteristics that you have to offer.

Finding industries and companies with the characteristics you desire will require you to apply your marketing research skills. The library contains many sources of information that will help you. Personal sources can also be useful in providing information as well as leads for interviews, as can the Internet.

Sources for job interviews include the campus placement office, personal contacts, and advertisements. Résumés are personal brochures that help sell a candidate. Writing effective cover letters will help you get interviews off campus, while the interview itself is similar to a sales call. Plan questions that demonstrate your knowledge of and interest in the company. Also, plan to ask for information that will help you make your decision. Follow up after the interview to demonstrate your desire and perseverance.

You are the person in the company to whom your career means the most. Therefore, you must actively manage your own career. Set career goals that are compatible with family and personal objectives. Keeping the reasons for these career goals in front of you will enable you to make better decisions.

Learn the job you have now. You may someday manage people who have this job; the better you know it, the better you will be at managing it. To become a manager, you must first be a manager. Learn the manager's job as well and volunteer for activities and projects that will let you demonstrate your management ability.

Stress can occur in any job. Situational stress is short term, whereas felt stress is longer term. For many people, the key to managing stress is to reduce the influence of stressors because the causes of stress often cannot be eliminated.

Sales offers a challenging and exciting career. The opportunities are so varied that almost anyone can probably fit into some sales position. Even if you choose a career in another field, take advantage of the material in this chapter. You should find these job search and career management tips helpful in any field. Good luck!

KEY TERMS

ETHICS PROBLEMS

1. You are interviewing for your dream job. Suddenly the interviewer notices your wedding ring and compliments you on it. But then he says, "You know, this job requires a lot of travel. What is your spouse going to say to that?" You answer the question, and he replies, "That's great, now, when you don't have kids. You don't have kids, do you? Because it is tough to be successful if you don't get the travel done." What do you do? What would you do if the interviewer said, "You know, handling conflict is an important part of this job. Describe a conflict you've had with your spouse and how you handled it."

2. Some people recommend signing up for as many interviews as possible, reasoning that the experience will be helpful when you find a company with a job you really want. (And who knows? You might find a job you like.) Is this practice ethical? Why or why not? If you answer that it depends, what does it depend on?

QUESTIONS AND PROBLEMS

1. What would you do differently if you were being interviewed by an amiable, a driver, an analytical, or an expressive? What about a panel interview with one driver and one amiable? One analytical and one expressive?

2. Spencer Ryan began his career in a small but rapidly growing company (look back at the opening profile). What were the advantages to his start? What do you think he may have missed out on by not working for a big, well-known company? Would you prefer to start out with a small or a large company, and why?

3. Now that you are at the end of the book, what traits do you have that would make you successful in sales? Are there specific industries or sales positions to which you are better suited? Why? Compare your list to that in Exhibit 17.2. How do you stack up? How would you prove that you have those traits?

4. Some interviews are conducted over the phone or by videoconference. What do you think is important and different about these types of interviews compared to face-to-face interviews? Do you think these difference carry over into selling by phone versus in person? Would you consider an inside sales position? Why or why not?

5. Reread "Building Partnerships 17.1." If a potential employer asked you today to describe your brand, what would it be? How do you make yourself memorable? What changes do you need to make to your social media presence to prepare for transitioning to a professional career and to build your personal brand?

6. Answer the questions in Exhibit 17.6 as you would in a sales job interview.

7. Your summer internship in a sales job was a bad experience. Your biggest complaint was that the sales manager seemed incompetent. Despite this negative experience, you like sales, so you are interviewing for a sales position. What would you say if asked why you do not

seek full-time employment with the summer internship firm?

8. One recruiter called a professor to check on a student that the professor referred. The recruiter said, "You gave this student my name last Wednesday and now it is Tuesday. Does this delay signal a lack of interest?" How would you answer that if the recruiter was asking you the question and you were the student? Why would a recruiter comment on the time it took to call? (Note that this is based on an actual situation.)

9. You are in an interview, and you think this is your dream job. How would you secure commitment? What would you say different in the first interview if it is a screening interview on campus versus the fourth interview at company headquarters? Is securing commitment more or less important for sales positions than for other types of positions?

10. What stresses do you have now? How do you deal with stress? What healthy ways to handle stress do you use? What are some ways you respond to stress that may not be so healthy?

CASE PROBLEMS

case **17.1**

Choices, Choices!

While studying for the final exam for the sales class, a group of students began talking about jobs. "I just don't think I could do sales," said Amanda. "I just don't think I could either go cold calling or try to call people on the phone I don't know and try to sell them something. But I like working with people."

"I think I could," replied Bill. "I just don't know what I want to sell. It has to be something I believe in." Murmurs of agreement followed. "And I want to have something different every day—I don't think I could sit behind a desk with the same old routine."

"I'm more like Amanda," said Emily. "I don't think I could do a lot of cold calling, but I'd like to be in sales anyway. Maybe something where they come to me or I see the same people. I'm good with people once I get to know them."

"I heard a lot of companies start you out on the phones first," Roger noted. "Like IBM. You start out on the phones, and if you're good, then you get to go out into the field."

Questions

1. What kinds of jobs would Bill be suited for? Emily? Can Emily's fears be overcome, or should she just find a job that doesn't involve cold calling?
2. Using the Web, find a position for each student to apply for. Print the ad and then on the same sheet (write on the back if you need to) justify your choice.
3. Pick one of the four positions you used in question 2 for yourself. Why is that a good fit for you?

case **17.2**

Mandy Baker's Interview

At 8:45 a.m., Mandy Baker arrived at her campus placement center for a 9:00 interview. She was surprised to be greeted by Caleb Washington, whom she had known in a marketing class. This conversation followed:

CALEB: Mandy, good to see you! I see that you are interviewing with us today. [shakes Mandy's hand and offers her a chair in the lobby]

MANDY: Caleb! Hi, how are you? I didn't know you were with HealthSouth. I've got the 9:00 spot.

CALEB: Great! I started with HealthSouth right after graduation, and it has been a great six months. Tell me, are you interviewing with many medical firms or just with HealthSouth?

MANDY: I'm very interested in pharmaceuticals, but I know that HealthSouth is doing real well. So I thought that I should consider all medical companies. One of the physicians at a sports medicine center recommended

HealthSouth. She said that your company does a lot of the rehabilitation services for the NFL as well as here at the university.

CALEB: That's right, we do! I'm glad to hear that others agree we are one of the best. [leans a little closer] Look, just relax in the interview. HealthSouth really likes to get people from State, and I'm sure you will do well. [looks up at the entrance of an older woman] Oh, here's Erin Rogers, my sales manager. She'll be interviewing you today. Erin, here's an old friend of mine, Mandy Baker.

ERIN: [stepping forward and offering her hand]: Mandy, it's nice to meet you.

MANDY: [shaking her hand firmly]: It's nice to meet you, too, Ms. Rogers. [turning to Caleb] Caleb, it was good to see you again. Perhaps we'll talk some more later. [Mandy and Erin seat themselves in the interviewing room; Erin has her iPad open with a small keyboard]

ERIN: Tell me about yourself, Mandy.

MANDY: I'm the oldest of three children, and we were raised in a small town in the eastern part of the state. As a kid, I was very interested in soccer and wanted to be an Olympic soccer player. But an ankle injury ended my soccer career. Still, I learned a lot about self-discipline and the importance of hard work to achieve success, and I am still involved in soccer as a coach for a youth team. In fact, I rehabbed my ankle at a HealthSouth center. Anyway, I chose State because it offers a strong marketing program. Marketing, and sales especially, seems to me to be a place where your success is directly related to your efforts. And I believe that more strongly now that I have taken the sales class here at State.

ERIN [types "h"]: I see. [momentary silence as she finishes the notes, then looks up] Tell me about a time when you were the leader of a group and things were not going your way. Perhaps it looked as if the group wasn't going to meet your objectives. What did you do?

MANDY: Let's see. There was the time when we were working on a group project for my marketing research class. Understand, though, that we had not elected a formal leader or anything. But no one in the group really wanted to do the project; everyone thought that research was boring. So at a group meeting, I suggested we talk about what we liked to do in marketing. After all, we were all marketing majors. Each person talked about why he or she had chosen marketing. Then I framed the project around what they wanted out of marketing. When they looked at it as a marketing project instead of a research project, it became something they wanted to do.

ERIN: Did you get an A?

MANDY: No, we got a B+. But more important, we were the only group that had fun, and I think we learned more as a result.

ERIN: I see. [momentary silence as she types] Tell me about your sales class—have you had any opportunity to use what you learned, and, if so, how'd you do?

MANDY: You mean other than this interview? [Erin smiles] I found that I use the questioning skills to learn about potential sorority members. These skills really helped me understand what they wanted in a sorority and whether we were a good fit. And the presentation skills I use with every in-class presentation, but I've not had a sales job, if that's what you mean.

The interview went on for nearly 30 minutes. Mandy thought she had done fairly well. She stopped in the lobby to write down her impressions and record Erin's answers to questions about the company. She smiled at Caleb, who was talking to another applicant.

Questions

1. What did Mandy do right? Why was that right? What did she do wrong? Why was that wrong?
2. What was Caleb's purpose at the interview? What do you think Caleb could tell Erin about Mandy?
3. HealthSouth is a publicly traded company. What sources of information could Mandy use to learn about the company? What information should she expect to get from those sources?

ROLE PLAY CASE

Congratulations, you just got promoted! Now you have to replace yourself by hiring a college graduate to take over your sales territory. Given everything you've learned about NetSuite this semester and what you know about sales, take a few minutes to identify the three most important features a salesperson should bring to the job and the questions you'd ask to determine if the candidate had those features. Then take turns interviewing each other in your group. There is no candidate information to be provided—each student will portray himself or herself when playing the candidate role.

ADDITIONAL REFERENCES

Alkhateeb, Fadi M., Patricia Baidoo, Marija Mikulskis Cavana, Danielle Gill, and Amanda Howell. "Is Certification for Pharmaceutical Sales Representatives Necessary?" *International Journal of Pharmaceutical and Healthcare Marketing* 5, no. 3 (2011), pp. 222–33.

Briggs, Elten, Fernando Jaramillo, and William A. Weeks. "Perceived Barriers to Career Advancement and Organizational Commitment in Sales." *Journal of Business Research* 65, no. 7 (July 2012), pp. 937–49.

Bristow, Denny, Douglas Amyx, Stephen B. Castleberry, and James J. Cochran. "A Cross-Generational Comparison of Motivational Factors in a Sales Career among Gen-X and Gen-Y College Students." *Journal of Personal Selling and Sales Management* 31, no. 1 (Winter 2011), p. 77.

Eesley, Dale T., and Phani Tej Adidam. "Mavenness and Salespeople Success: An Empirical Investigation." *Journal of Applied Business Research* 28, no. 5 (September/October 2012), pp. 903–12.

Hamwi, G. Alexander, Brian N. Rutherford, and James S. Boles. "Reducing Emotional Exhaustion and Increasing Organizational Support." *Journal of Business and Industrial Marketing* 26, no. 1 (2011), pp. 4–13.

Hawass, Hisham Hamid. "Committed Salesforce: An Investigation into Personality Traits." *International Journal of Business and Management* 7, no. 6 (March 2012), pp. 147–60.

Joo, Baek-Kyoo (Brian), and Sunyoung Park. "Career Satisfaction, Organizational Commitment, and Turnover Intention: The Effects of Goal Orientation, Organizational Learning Culture and Developmental Feedback." *Leadership and Organization Development Journal* 31, no. 6 (2010), pp. 482–500.

Karakaya, Fahri, Charles Quigley, and Frank Bingham. "A Cross-National Investigation of Student Intentions to Pursue a Sales Career." *Journal of Marketing Education* 33, no. 1 (April 2011), p. 18.

Lewin, Jeffrey E., and Jeffrey K. Sager. "An Investigation of the Influence of Coping Resources in Salespersons' Emotional Exhaustion." *Industrial Marketing Management* 38, no. 7 (October 2009), pp. 796–811.

Mallin, Michael L., Edward O'Donnell, and Michael Y. Hu. "The Role of Uncertainty and Sales Control in the Development of Sales Manager Trust." *Journal of Business and Industrial Marketing* 25, no. 1 (2010), pp. 30–42.

Marschke, Eleanor, Robert Preziosi, and William J. Harrington. "How Sales Personnel View the Relationship between Job Satisfaction and Spirituality in the Workplace." *Journal of Organizational Culture, Communication and Conflict* 15, no. 2 (2011), pp. 71–110.

Mayo, Michael, and Michael L. Mallin. "The Impact of Sales Failure on Attributions Made by 'Resource-Challenged' and 'Resource-Secure' Salespeople." *Journal of Marketing Theory and Practice* 18, no. 3 (Summer 2010), pp. 233–47.

Murray, Lynn M., and Arthur K. Fischer. "Staffing a New Sales Force: A Human Resource Management Case Study." *Journal of Business Case Studies* 7, no. 4 (July/August 2011), pp. 1–7.

Onvernah, Vincent. "The Effects of Coaching on Salespeople's Attitudes and Behaviors: A Contingency Approach." *European Journal of Marketing* 43, no. 7/8 (2009), pp. 938–51.

Rutherford, Brian N., Yujie Wei, JungKun Park, and Won-Moo Hur. "Increasing Job Performance and Reducing Turnover: An Examination of Female Chinese Salespeople." *Journal of Marketing Theory and Practice* 20, no. 4 (Fall 2012), pp. 423–36.

Sarathy, P. Sanjay. "Salespeople's Performance and Change in Career in Their Maintenance Stage." *International Journal of Organizational Innovation (Online)* 4, no. 3 (Winter 2012), pp. 216–34.

Schultz, Roberta J., Charles H. Schwepker Jr., and David J. Good. "Social Media Usage: An Investigation of B2B Salespeople." *American Journal of Business* 27, no. 2 (2012), pp. 174–94.

Shannahan, Kirby L., Alan J. Bush, and Rachelle J. Shannahan. "Are Your Salespeople Coachable? How Salesperson Coachability, Trait Competitiveness, and Transformational Leadership Enhance Sales Performance." *Journal of the Academy of Marketing Science* 41, no. 1 (January 2013), pp. 40–54.

Spillan, John E., Jeff W. Totten, and Manmohan D. Chaubey. "Exploring Personal Selling as a Career Option: A Case Study of the Perceptions of African-American Students." *Academy of Marketing Studies Journal, Special Issue 2*, no. 15 (2011), pp. 93–106.

Valenzuela, Leslier M., Jay P. Mulki, and J. Fernando Jaramillo. "Impact of Customer Orientation, Inducements and Ethics on Loyalty to the Firm: Customers' Perspective." *Journal of Business Ethics* 93, no. 2 (May 2010) pp. 277–93.

ROLE PLAY CASE 1

Instructor: See our book's website for a new Role Play Case 1.

STUBB'S BAR-B-Q

Stubb's Bar-B-Q is an Austin, Texas, manufacturer of barbecue sauces and marinades. Founder C. B. Stubblefield states on the Web site, "My recipes are known throughout Texas and the world as the best in barbecue, and I've put my heart and soul into each one. With my picture on the label and my recipe inside, you can be sure you're getting the finest quality available. Simply put, my life is in these bottles."

Stubb's offers a wide variety of products (see its Web site for the most up-to-date list of products and prices):

Product	Suggested Retail Price	Reseller Case Prices (When Buying Fewer Than 20 Cases in a Single Order)
Stubb's Bar-B-Q Sauce	$4.39	6 for $24
Stubb's Marinades (come in Pork, Beef, Teriyaki, and Chicken varieties)	$4.39	6 for $24
Stubb's Rubs (come in Bar-B-Q, Burger, Rosemary Ginger, Chilí Lime, and Herbal Mustard varieties)	$4.39	12 for $48

Marinade is usually used for about an hour, or a bit longer for more intense flavor, before cooking. Then the chef can baste the meat with fresh marinade as it cooks and serve it with one of the Stubb's Bar-B-Q Sauces. Rubs are spice mixtures applied to meat before it is grilled or smoked. Rubs are just like a marinade except that they add a layer of crust to the meat.

Stubb's offers noncumulative quantity discounts for resellers (the total number of cases can be based on mixed items; thus a reseller that buys 10 cases of Spice Rubs in any varieties and 11 cases of Moppin' Sauce in any varieties would get the additional 5 percent discount):

Quantity Purchased	Discount
Fewer than 20 cases	Standard reseller case prices
21–100 cases	An additional 5 percent off reseller case prices
Over 100 cases	An additional 10 percent off reseller case prices

Stubb's also offers a number of promotions for resellers. Resellers that set up an end-of-aisle display of at least 50 cases of a mix of sizes and flavors earn an extra $1 per case discount on all cases purchased. For resellers that advertise Stubb's products in the newspaper, there is a 50 percent co-op payment for the actual portion of the page cost of the advertisement. Thus if a grocery store runs a newspaper ad that includes one-eighth of a page for Stubb's products, Stubb's will reimburse the grocery store for 50 percent of the cost of the ad.

There are many competitive barbecue sauces, including such brands as K.C. Masterpiece, Porky's Gourmet, Cattlemen's Barbecue Sauce, and various flavors offered by Hunt's, Heinz, and Kraft.

Sources: http://stubbsbbq.elsstore.com; http://www.stubbsbbq.com. For more up-to-date information, please visit the Web sites. Information about discounts and promotions for retailers is fictitious but reflects the types of promotions allowed by manufacturers to retailers.

Situation 1: Safeway—Corporate Headquarters (Resell Situation)

Safeway is the second-largest supermarket chain in North America, after The Kroger Co., with over

1,600 stores located primarily through the western and central United States and western Canada. It also operates some stores in the mid-Atlantic region of the eastern seaboard. The company's headquarters is in Pleasanton, California. Safeway is one of the top 15 retailers in the United States and has sales of over $40 billion. (Source: www.safeway.com)

You are a salesperson for Stubb's. You are calling on a corporate headquarters grocery buyer of Safeway. Assume that Safeway has not carried Stubb's products in the past. Your goal is to have Safeway's corporate headquarters approve the offering of at least some Stubb's products in its stores and stock them in Safeway's distribution warehouses. Assume that the final decisions about which products will be offered in individual stores are up to the local store managers.

Situation 2: Safeway—Local Supermarket (Resell Situation)

Safeway is the second-largest supermarket chain in North America, after The Kroger Co., with over 1,600 stores located primarily through the western and central United States and western Canada. It also operates some stores in the mid-Atlantic region of the eastern seaboard. The company's headquarters is in Pleasanton, California. Safeway is one of the top 15 retailers in the United States and has sales of over $40 billion. (Source: www.Safeway.com)

You are a salesperson for Stubb's. You are calling on the grocery manager of a local Safeway. Assume that Safeway's corporate headquarters has approved the offering of Stubb's products and that Safeway carries them in its distribution centers. However, this SuperSafeway has never carried Stubb's products in the past. Your goal is to have this store manager approve the offering of at least some Stubb's products in his or her store. Note: If the store manager agrees to offer Stubb's, he or she will simply order the products from the Safeway distribution center.

Situation 3: Gourmet Garage Foods (Resell Situation)

Gourmet Garage was founded in 1981, a wholesaler serving the best restaurants in cities such as New York City. In 1992, they opened their New York warehouse to the public every day after the restaurant deliveries were finished. Consumers would shop at the warehouse looking for the same fresh ingredients that the best chefs of the city were using. Not long after that, Gourmet Garage was born. They now have five retail stores in Manhattan

neighborhood locations. Each store strives to offer the same quality and variety that New York's best chefs demand. (Source: www.gourmetgarage.com)

You are a salesperson for Stubb's. Your goal is to introduce Stubb's products to the grocery store manager and secure a sale of at least some of the products. The store carries several brands of barbecue sauce but has never carried Stubb's.

Situation 4: Mac's Convenience Stores (Resell Situation)

Mac's opened its first store in Richmond Hill, Ontario, in 1961 and has over 1,000 stores today. It is now a part of Couche-Tard, which is the second-largest convenience store chain in North America. Mac's Convenience Stores is recognized for its strong food service brands, including Seattle's Best Coffee and Frosters. All new locations have either a food service offering, a gas bar, or both. They also have Canada Post outlets in many locations, adding to the one-stop nature of their stores. Their innovative store design and merchandising is considered to be second to none. (Source: www.macs.ca)

You are a salesperson for Stubb's. Your goal is to introduce Stubb's Legendary Bar-B-Q sauce to a grocery buyer of Mac's and to secure at least a trial order.

Situation 5: Home Depot—Corporate Headquarters (Resell Situation)

Home Depot is an American retailer of home improvement and construction products and services. It operates stores in all 50 U.S. states as well as Puerto Rico, the Virgin Islands, and Guam; all 10 provinces of Canada; and Mexico and China. It sells a number of outdoor living products that include items such as barbecue grills, grill accessories, and grill cleaning and cooking tools. During grilling season, it carries a few of the best-selling brands of barbecue sauce next to the grills. (Source: www.homedepot.com)

You are a salesperson for Stubb's. You are calling on the corporate headquarters buyer for outdoors products at Home Depot. Home Depot has not carried Stubb's products in the past. Your goal is to have Home Depot corporate headquarters approve the offering of at least some of Stubb's products in its stores and carry the products in the Home Depot distribution warehouses. Assume that the final decisions about which products will be offered in individual stores are up to the local store managers.

Situation 6: Home Depot—Individual Store (Resell Situation)

Home Depot is an American retailer of home improvement and construction products and services. It operates stores in all 50 U.S. states as well as Puerto Rico, the Virgin Islands, and Guam; all 10 provinces of Canada; and Mexico and China. It sells a number of outdoor living products that include items such as barbecue grills, grill accessories, and grill cleaning and cooking tools. During grilling season, it carries a few of the best-selling brands of barbecue sauce next to the grills. (Source: www.homedepot.com)

You are a salesperson for Stubb's. You are calling on the outdoors department manager for one Home Depot store. Assume that the Home Depot corporate headquarters has approved the offering of Stubb's products and carries them in the Home Depot distribution centers. However, this Home Depot has never carried Stubb's products in the past. Your goal is to have this outdoors department manager approve the offering of at least some Stubb's products in his or her store. Note: If the store manager agrees to offer Stubb's, he or she will simply order the products from the Home Depot distribution center.

Situation 7: Whole Foods Market—Corporate Headquarters (Resell Situation)

Whole Foods Market, a supermarket chain based in Austin, Texas, that emphasizes natural and organic products, has been ranked among the most socially responsible businesses. Whole Foods Market sells only products that meet its self-created quality standards for being "natural," which the store defines as minimally processed foods that are free of hydrogenated fats as well as artificial flavors, colors, sweeteners, preservatives, and many others as listed on their online "Unacceptable Food Ingredients" list. Whole Foods started back in 1980 and now has over 300 stores in the United States and the United Kingdom (Source: Adapted from www.wholefoods market.com)

You are a salesperson for Stubb's. Your goal is to introduce Stubb's products to the grocery buyer of Whole Foods Market at corporate headquarters and secure an agreement that allows the offering of at least some Stubb's products in the stores. Assume that the final decisions about which products will be offered in individual Whole Foods Market stores are up to the local store managers. Also assume that the local store manager, if interested, would buy the products directly from Stubb's. For purposes of this role play, assume that Stubb's products meet Whole Foods Market's standards of "natural."

Situation 8: Whole Foods Market—Local Store (Resell Situation)

Whole Foods Market, a supermarket chain based in Austin, Texas, that emphasizes natural and organic products, has been ranked among the most socially responsible businesses. Whole Foods Market sells only products that meet its self-created quality standards for being "natural," which the store defines as minimally processed foods that are free of hydrogenated fats as well as artificial flavors, colors, sweeteners, preservatives, and many others as listed on their online "Unacceptable Food Ingredients" list. Whole Foods started back in 1980 and now has over 300 stores in the United States and the United Kingdom (Source: Adapted from www.wholefoods market.com)

You are the store manager of a local Whole Foods Market. Assume that the corporate headquarters of Whole Foods Market has approved the offering of Stubb's products. However, this Whole Foods Market has never carried Stubb's products in the past. Your goal is to have this local manager approve the offering of at least some Stubb's products in his or her store. Note: If the store manager agrees to offer Stubb's, he or she will need to purchase the products directly from Stubb's because the Whole Foods Market distribution center does not stock Stubb's products.

Situation 9: Applebee's Grill & Bar

Founded nearly three decades ago, Applebee's operates what is today the largest casual-dining chain in the world. The chain draws people of all ages and lifestyles with its fun, family-friendly atmosphere as well as its bar and grill menu. Currently, there are over 1,900 Applebee's restaurants operating around the world. Applebee's menu features beef, chicken, and pork items as well as burgers, pasta, and seafood, along with a selection of unique menu items found only at Applebee's. (Source: Adapted from www.applebees.com)

You are a salesperson for Stubb's calling on the corporate headquarters of Applebee's. Applebee's restaurants have never carried your sauce, and you have not called on the chain before. Your goal is to have Applebee's make Stubb's sauce available for customers to use with their meals either as a standard item placed on dining tables or available on request. Note: You are not requesting that Applebee's sell Stubb's products to customers.

Situation 10: Phil's BBQ

Since opening its doors in San Diego in 1998, Phil's BBQ has served over a million pounds of barbecue sauce. Serving thousands of customers a day across San Diego County, Phil Pace has built a group of three restaurants that focus on consistency, quality, freshness, and friendly service. (Source: Adapted from www.philsbbq.net)

You are a salesperson for Stubb's calling on the chef of Phil's BBQ. Your goal is to have the chef consider using Stubb's barbecue products as he or she prepares meals that use barbecue sauce and marinades. You would also like Stubb's products to be available if patrons request them during a meal. Note: You are not requesting that Phil's BBQ sell Stubb's products to customers.

ROLE PLAY CASE 2

NETSUITE

NetSuite is an award-winning contact management software package that integrates personal databases on accounts with calendar management, word processing, and other computer software applications. From the salesperson's perspective, NetSuite serves as a combination of a card file and calendar, and it enables salespeople to quickly identify prospects for new products, search for prospects in a given area, and perform other similar operations. In addition, all call records are maintained in a manner that enables salespeople to instantly recall personal information about any individual inside any account.

From the sales manager's perspective, the software's reporting features enable closer supervision of salespeople. The manager can observe who has made what calls on which prospects, intervene with helpful suggestions based on call notes provided by the salesperson, and create sales forecasts. Further, if a salesperson leaves, all of the territory information remains with the company because it is stored in NetSuite. Visit www.netsuite.com and, using the Products tab, click on the CRM+ button for more information.

The product sells for a suggested retail price of $129 per month per user or $1,548 per year per user. The minimum contract length is one year, and the price can be locked in for three years (with no more than a 5 percent increase) if a client wants to sign a three-year agreement. There is no installation cost. The software is a hosted product, meaning it resides on NetSuite servers and is maintained fully by NetSuite. No IT department is required! To use it, though, users must be able to access the Internet to download the account information and update it. Further, any customization has to be done by the user (or through a reseller).

NetSuite wins a lot of awards for its ease of use and functionality. The home page lists some of those awards and also has many reviews of NetSuite and other packages, so read it to understand the features and benefits more fully. In addition, you can watch several online demos to learn more about how salespeople use the software (click on the "Role-Based Demo" button).

NetSuite CRM+ Pricing	Base Package		
Features	Monthly	Annual	Included Units
Each full user	$129	$1,548	1 User
Customer self-service portal	—	—	Included
Partner relationship management module	—	—	Included
Technical support: Silver*	—	—	Included
Expense reporting + intranet + employee SS	—	—	For full users
Offline sales client	—	—	Included
Mail merge/e-mail communications	—	—	30,000 per month
E-mail marketing campaigns	—	—	10,000 per month

Netsuite's major competitors are Microsoft Dynamics and Salesforce.com, although there are many smaller competitors, such as Zoho, Aplicor, Pipeline Deals, and others. Spend some time at each of these Web sites not only to learn what they do differently or better, but to learn in general how CRM/SFA software works.

Resellers are also called value-added resellers, or VARs. To be a NetSuite VAR, the VAR has to agree to take a 16-hour training course to learn how to customize the software, which costs $495 per person. VARs can sell their customization services, though, at any price they want, which is how they can really make big money. They also get 15 percent commissions on anything they sell. Some VARs also package consulting on e-mail campaigns and similar services.

Reseller Situations

WORKFLOW SOLUTIONS Today, you are calling on the owner of Workflow Solutions. The company is a small VAR that specializes in software systems for manufacturers. You had a mutual friend set up a meeting with the owner. Your friend says that Workflow Solutions has been primarily a custom software provider. The owner of Workflow Solutions is a very talented businessperson and known for being very tough on everybody.

SALES INNOVATION Sales Innovation is a relatively new sales training organization that was established by two (married) former insurance company sales execs in Hartford, Connecticut. They specialize in working with independent insurance agencies. You are calling on the chief sales officer, whom you met at a Rotary function, but you don't know much else about them.

THE 48 GROUP Today, you are calling on the senior partner of The 48 Group, a new CRM consultancy. This person worked for Highland, a major consulting company, and left over a year ago to start this company with two junior partners who worked for client companies. All are very experienced in marketing automation and are well known in the industry. You heard the senior partner make a presentation at a conference and introduced yourself. In the brief conversation, you learned that they focus on SMBs (small to medium-sized businesses), primarily in the packaged food industry, and that they've not been a VAR for anyone. They have avoided pursuing prospects without CRM software thinking that if they don't have software, they don't need the help of a consultant, but at least the senior partner is willing to meet with you.

BANCMARK Today, you are calling on the information technology manager for BancMark, a national marketing consultancy that specializes in serving community banks. These are banks with fewer than 10 branches. You read a press release about the company, called, and got the appointment. On the phone call, you learned that BancMark manages marketing services for about 150 community banks, and they provide sales training for loan officers, although the banks prefer to use the term "business development" instead of "sales." They also sell several personality profile tests to companies for use in selecting new loan officers as well as other sales consulting services. They are also a VAR for SugarCRM already.

MACKIE OFFICE SUPPLY Today, you are calling on the owner of Mackie Office Supply. Mackie provides a range of office supplies for small businesses (furniture, paper, pens, and so on) as well as computers, computer repair, and printing services. You stopped by a store while in between appointments to pick up some toner for your home office printer and learned that there are six locations, one each in a different suburb of two metropolitan areas. Each location has a field salesperson, an inside salesperson who is on the phone most of the time, and the usual counter clerks. Most of their sales are delivered from the company's central warehouse, which is where the owner works.

Industrial User Situations

JAMES CONTRACT MANUFACTURING This company manufactures custom metal components that other companies design into their own products. Examples include the case used to make the milkshake machines used in McDonald's and the metal frames used in making airplane seating. The company serves a three-state area with 12 salespeople. The company was just taken over by the third generation of the James family, and the new president wants to grow the business aggressively. You learned about the aggressive growth plans when reading a feature on the company, so you called the president and made an appointment, saying that you could help the business grow.

FUTURIS DESIGN Today, you are calling on the president of Futuris Design, who happens to be the older sibling of one of your college classmates. Futuris Design makes commercial display systems used in showrooms and trade shows. The company has about 25 account execs and 20 project managers. There are approximately 50 projects that are "live" at any particular time. These projects generally last between two weeks and three months, with shorter projects being trade show booth designs and longer projects going into commercial showrooms. The projects require several meetings with clients, suppliers, and sometimes municipal building inspectors. The president wishes to increase the number of projects that the company can handle without additional personnel. You met the president at a charity golf tournament about three weeks ago.

INDEPENDENT BANK Today, you are calling on the founding CEO for Independent Bank. This young bank has been in business for about four years and only recently moved into its own building. While the banks started as an online bank, they quickly realized that they needed a more traditional outlet, too. You saw the new building open up and thought it would be a good idea to drop in. When you dropped in, you were told that there were two managers with seven loan officers each. Each officer was assigned about 200 clients. You were able to meet the CEO but scheduled an appointment for today, as the CEO was quite busy when you dropped in.

ANDRITZ Today, you are calling on the North America sales vice president for Andritz, a Swedish company that makes large industrial presses. The buyer has about 30 outside salespeople and 15 inside salespeople for the region, which includes Canada and Mexico. The machinery is used to make paper, clean water, and any other situation where you have a desire to press water out of mush. The sales supervisor called you after being told of your product by a friend of his.

AVIDYNE AviDyne is a communications engineering company that manufactures custom communications systems for use in global shipping. Essentially, the company takes a ship and rebuilds the communications systems, as they specialize in refurbishing ships. The communications systems include onboard communications as well as ship-to-shore. The buyer has about 100 engineers employed. Each of these engineers, to varying degrees, has meetings with management, clients, and suppliers. AviDyne recently adopted the notion that "everyone is a salesperson." You met the prospect at a trade show in Brussels about two months ago and scheduled an appointment to discuss your product.

PHOTO CREDITS

CHAPTER 1

Opener: © Comstock/PunchStock; p. 3: Courtesy of Amber Fischer; p. 8: © Custom Medical Stock Photo/Alamy; p. 10: © Royalty-Free/Corbis; p. 14: © Moodboard/Getty Images; p. 19: © Keith Brofsky/Getty Images; p. 20: © Jupiterimages/Comstock Premium.

CHAPTER 2

Opener: © Rubberball/Corbis; p. 29: Courtesy of Jim Keller; p. 36: © Purestock/SuperStock; p. 38: © Moodboard/Corbis; p. 41: © Royalty-Free/Corbis; p. 46: © Lynn Conn; p. 50: © Jupiterimages/Creatas/Alamy.

CHAPTER 3

Opener: © Andersen Ross/Getty Images; p. 59: Courtesy of Camille McConn; p. 62: Courtesy of STUBB's Legendary Kitchen; p. 65: Courtesy of Deere & Company; p. 72 (left): © Paul Burns/Blend Images/Corbis; p. 72 (top right): © LajosRepasi/Getty Images; p. 72 (bottom right): © Jon Feingersh/Blend Images LLC; p. 77: © Purestock/SuperStock.

CHAPTER 4

Opener: © E. Audras/PhotoAlto; p. 95: Courtesy of Sally Cook; p. 97: © S. Pearce/PhotoLink; p. 99: © Digital Vision/Getty Images; p. 103: © Keith Brofsky/Getty Images; p. 106 (top): © Gary Ombler/Getty Images; p. 106 (bottom): © Betsie Van Der Meer/Getty Images; p. 107 (all): Courtesy of Stephen B. Castleberry; p. 107 (all): Courtesy of Stephen B. Castleberry; p. 107 (all): Courtesy of Stephen B. Castleberry; p. 110: © Creatas Images/PictureQuest; p. 114: © Royalty-Free/Corbis; p. 117: © Pankaj Insy Shah/Getty Images.

CHAPTER 5

Opener: © Ryan McVay/Getty Images; p. 125: Courtesy of James Ellington; p. 130: © ColorBlind Images/Getty Images; p. 131: © Keith Brofsky/Getty Images; p. 134 (top left): Amn Devin Doskey/USAF; p. 134 (top right): © The McGraw-Hill Companies, Inc./Jill Braaten, photographer; p. 134 (bottom left): © Peter Macdiamid/Getty Images; p. 134 (bottom right): © Eric Thayer/Getty Images.

CHAPTER 6

Opener: © Mark Edward Atkinson/Blend Images LLC; p. 147: Courtesy of Angela Bertero; p. 152: © Corbis; p. 158: © AP Photo/Wally Santana; p. 161: © Jose Luis Pelaez Inc./Blend Images LLC; p. 165: © Dennis MacDonald/PhotoEdit; p. 166: © Jose Luis Pelaez/Getty Images.

CHAPTER 7

Opener: © Jose Luis Pelaez Inc./Blend Images LLC; p. 173: Courtesy of Brett Georgulis; p. 174: © Walter Hodges/Stone/Getty Images; p. 182: © Kim Steele/Getty Images; p. 184: © Purestock/SuperStock; p. 187: © Royalty-Free/Corbis; p. 188: © Paul Redman/Getty Images.

CHAPTER 8

Opener: © E. Audras/PhotoAlto; p. 195: Courtesy of David Maebane; p. 197: © Andersen Ross/Getty Images; p. 200: © John Cummings/Getty Images; p. 203: © Kaz Mori/Getty Images; p. 211: Courtesy of Huron Window Corp Manitoba, Canada; p. 213: © Eric Audras/Getty Images; p. 217: © Royalty-Free/Corbis.

CHAPTER 9

Opener: © Royalty-Free/Corbis; p. 225: Courtesy of Mike Buckland; p. 230: © Doug Menuez/Photodisc/Alamy; p. 231: Photo Courtesy of JELD-WEN Windows & Doors; p. 234: © The McGraw-Hill Companies, Inc./Jill Braaten, photographer; p. 235 (top): © Digital Vision/PunchStock; p. 235 (bottom): © Digital Vision/Getty Images; p. 237: © Creatas Images/PictureQuest; p. 242: © 2007 Getty Images.

CHAPTER 10

Opener: © Purestock/SuperStock; p. 253: Courtesy of Renee Miles; p. 257: © Michael Goldman/Getty Images; p. 262: © Royalty-Free/Corbis; p. 268: © Stockbyte/PunchStock Images; p. 271: © Jupiterimages/Brand X/Alamy; p. 275: © Getty Images/Stockbyte; p. 276: © Keith Brofsky/Getty Images.

CHAPTER 11

Opener: © Javier Pierini/Getty Images; p. 283: Courtesy of Danny Fernandez; p. 289: © Ariel Skelley/Blend Images LLC; p. 293: © Royalty-Free/Corbis; p. 298: Photography by Lynn Conn, used with permission; p. 303: © Big Cheese Photo/Jupiter Images.

CHAPTER 12

Opener: © Digital Vision/Getty Images; p. 313: Courtesy of Evans Adonis; p. 314: © Frank Herholdt/Getty Images; p. 317: © Brand X Pictures/Jupiterimages; p. 320: © Javier Pierini/Getty Images; p. 324: © Image Source Black/Alamy; p. 329: © Stockbyte/PunchStock Images.

CHAPTER 13

Opener: © Digital Vision/Getty Images; p. 341: Courtesy of Christina Harrod; p. 343 (top): © David Paul Morris/Getty Images; p. 343 (bottom): Courtesy of Apple, Inc.; p. 350 (top): The McGraw-Hill Companies, Inc./Andrew Resek, photographer; p. 350 (bottom): © Andrew Ward/Life File/Getty Images; p. 354: © Monty Rakusen/Getty Images.

CHAPTER 14

Opener: © Ronnie Kaufman/Larry Hirshowitz/Getty Images; p. 367: Courtesy of John Tanner; p. 369: Courtesy of John Tanner; p. 378: Courtesy of David Richardson Heating and Air Conditioning, Frankfort, KY; p. 380: Courtesy of Eddy Patterson, STUBB's Legendary Kitchen, Austin, TX; p. 390: Courtesy of Keith Reznick, Creative Training Solutions.

CHAPTER 15

Opener: © Royalty-Free/Corbis; p. 397: Courtesy of Mike Rocker; p. 398: © Andrea Chu/Getty Images; p. 400: © Patti McConville/Photographer's Choice/Getty Images; p. 405 (left): © Ryan McVay/Getty Images; p. 405 (right): © Stockbyte/PunchStock; p. 412: © Ablestock/Alamy; p. 415: Courtesy of John Tanner.

CHAPTER 16

Opener: © The McGraw-Hill Companies, Inc./Christopher Kerrigan, photographer; p. 425: Courtesy of Kristen Scott; p. 430: © Walter Hodges/Photodisc/Getty Images; p. 435: © Digital Vision/Getty Images; p. 438: Courtesy of John Tanner; p. 444: © Jon Feingersh/Getty Images.

CHAPTER 17

Opener: © Digital Vision/Getty Images; p. 455: Courtesy of Spencer Ryan; p. 457: © Glow Images; p. 461: © Robert Nickelsberg/Getty Images; p. 467: Courtesy of Sales Jobs Inc.; p. 472: © Upper Cut Images/SuperStock; p. 477: Courtesy of Mechanical Service Company Inc., Virginia Beach, VA.

ENDNOTES

CHAPTER 1

1. Wendell Berry, *The Unsettling of America*, 3rd ed. (San Francisco: Sierra Club Books, 1996).

2. Andrea L. Dixon and John F. Tanner, "Transforming Selling: Why It Is Time to Think Differently about Sales Research," *Journal of Personal Selling and Sales Management* 32, no. 1 (Winter 2012), pp. 9–14.

3. Sriram Dorai and Sanjeev Varshney, "A Multistage Behavioural and Temporal Analysis of CPV in RM," *Journal of Business and Industrial Marketing* 27, no. 5 (September 2012), pp. 403–11; Pankaj M. Madhani, "Value Creation through Integration of Supply Chain Management and Marketing Strategy," *IUP Journal of Business Strategy* 9, no. 1 (March 2012), pp. 7–26; Jaka Lindič and Carlos Marques da Silva, "Value Proposition as a Catalyst for a Customer Focused Innovation," *Management Decision* 49, no. 10 (December 2011), pp. 1694–708; Landy Chase, "Value, Selling, and the Social Media Sales Revolution," *American Salesman* 56, no. 7 (July 2011), pp. 3–5.

4. Jerry Mclaughlin, "The Loyalty Myth and Other Misunderstandings," *Brandweek* 52, no. 1 (January 10, 2011), p. 22.

5. Peter Fader, *Customer Centricity: Focus on the Right Customers for Strategic Advantage*, 2nd ed. (Philadelphia, PA: Wharton Digital Press, 2012); Chris Zane, *Reinventing the Wheel: The Science of Creating Lifetime Customers* (Dallas, TX: BenBella Books, 2011); Ted Triplett, "An Integrated Strategy Optimizes Customers' Lifetime Value," *ABA Bank Marketing* 44, no. 6 (July 2012) p. 35; Phillip E. Pfeifer and Anton Ovchinnikov, "A Note on Willingness to Spend and Customer Lifetime Value for Firms with Limited Capacity," *Journal of Interactive Marketing* 25, no. 3 (August 2011), pp. 178–89; Andreas Persson, "The Management of Customer Relationships as Assets in the Retail Banking Sector," *Journal of Strategic Marketing* 19, no. 1 (February 2011), pp. 105–19; Lauri Lehtonen, "Maintaining Customer Value," *Pulp and Paper International* 53, no. 2 (February 2011), pp. 29–32; Nicolas Glady, Bart Baesens, and Christophe Croux, "Modeling Churn Using Customer Lifetime Value," *European Journal of Operational Research* 197, no. 1 (2009), pp. 402–11; V. Kumar and Bharath Rajan, "Profitable Customer Management: Measuring and Maximizing Customer Lifetime Value," *Management Accounting Quarterly* 10, no. 3 (2009), p. 1.

6. Alan Wolf, "Best Buy's Dunn Endorses Multichannel Strategy," *TWICE: This Week in Consumer Electronics* 27, no. 2 (January 23, 2012), pp. 4-2; "Creating an Integrated Multichannel Strategy," *Baseline*, no. 112 (September 2011) p. 14; Lucinda Trigo-Gamarra and Christian Growitsch, "Comparing Single- and Multichannel Distribution Strategies in the German Life Insurance Market: An Analysis of Cost and Profit Efficiency," *Schmalenbach Business Review* 62, no. 4 (October 2010), pp. 401–17; Ambika Zutshi et al., "Marketers' Perceptions of the Implementation Difficulties of Multichannel Marketing," *Journal of Strategic Marketing* 18, no. 5 (August 2010), pp. 417–34.

7. For more insight into marketing communication programs, see Simone Barratt and Steve Davis, "Connected Commerce: The Intersection of E-Commerce and E-Communication," *Journal of Direct, Data and Digital Marketing Practice* 10, no. 3 (2009), pp. 249–61.

8. Even in virtual worlds, like Second Life, the presence of an avatar, rather than just advertising, is more effective. See Pierre Berthon, Leyland Pitt, Wade Halvorson, Michael Ewing, and Victoria L. Crittenden, "Advocating Avatars: The Salesperson in Second Life," *Journal of Personal Selling and Sales Management* 30, no. 3 (Summer 2010), pp. 195–208.

9. Gabriele Troilo, Luigi M. De Luca, and Paolo Guenzi," Dispersion of Influence between Marketing and Sales: Its Effects on Superior Customer Value and Market Performance," *Industrial Marketing Management* 38, no. 8 (November 2009), pp. 872–82.

10. Firms that do this are often said to exhibit service-dominant logic. See, for example, David Ballantyne, Pennie Frow, Richard J. Varey, and Adrian Payne, "Value Propositions as Communication Practice: Taking a Wider View," *Industrial Marketing Management* 40, no. 2 (2011), pp. 202–10; Yann Truong, Geoff Simmons, and Mark Palmer, "Reciprocal Value Propositions in Practice: Constraints in Digital Markets," *Industrial Marketing Management* 41, no. 1 (2012), pp. 197–206; and K. Le Meunier-FitzHugh, J. Baumann, R. Palmer, and H. Wilson, "The Implications of Service-Dominant Logic and Integrated Solutions on the Sales Function," *Journal of Marketing Theory and Practice* 19, no. 4 (2011), pp. 423–40. See also Karen E. Flaherty and James M. Pappas, "Expanding the Sales Professional's Role: A Strategic Re-Orientation?," *Industrial Marketing Management* 38, no. 7 (October 2009), pp. 806–13.

11. See Jürgen Kai-Uwe Brock and Josephine Yu Zhou, "Customer Intimacy," *Journal of Business and Industrial Marketing* 27, no. 5 (September 2012); Phil Osborne and David Ballantyne, "The Paradigmatic Pitfalls of Customer-Centric Marketing," *Marketing Theory* 12, no. 2 (June 2012), pp. 155–72; Carlos Castro, "The Power of Aggressive Analytics," *ABA Bank Marketing* 43, no. 4 (May 2011), pp. 30–34; Christoph Burmann, Jörg Meurer, and Christopher Kanitz, "Customer Centricity as a Key to Success for Pharma," *Journal of Medical Marketing* 11, no. 1 (February 2011), pp. 49–59; and Jaramillo Fernando and Douglas B. Grisaffe, "Does Customer Orientation Impact Objective Sales Performance? Insights from a Longitudinal Model in Direct Selling," *Journal of Personal Selling and Sales Management* 29, no. 2 (Spring 2009), pp. 167–78.

12. See Dave Rich, "New Routes to New Customers: A Customer-Centric Approach for Emerging Markets," *CRM Magazine* 13, no. 7 (2009), p. 14.

13. James I. F. Speakman and Lynette Ryals, "Key Account Management: The Inside Selling Job," *Journal of Business and Industrial Marketing* 27, no. 5 (September 2012), pp. 360–69.

14. Many studies have shown the value of salespeople working well with marketing (called the sales–marketing interface). See, for example, Douglas E. Hughes, Joël Le Bon, and Avinash Malshe, "The Marketing-Sales Interface at the Interface: Creating Market-Based Capabilities through Organizational Synergy," *Journal of Personal Selling and Sales Management* 32, no. 1 (Winter 2012), pp. 57–72. See also Matias G. Enz and Douglas M. Lambert, "Using Cross-Functional, Cross-Firm Teams to Co-Create Value: The Role of Financial Measures," *Industrial Marketing Management* 41, no. 3 (2011), pp. 495–507, and Tuba Üstüner and Dawn Iacobucci, "Does Intraorganizational Network Embeddedness Improve Salespeople's Effectiveness? A Task Contingency Perspective," *Journal of Personal Selling and Sales Management* 32, no. 2 (Spring 2012), pp. 187–206.

15. Excerpts from communication by Glenn R. Price; used by permission.

16. Adam Rapp, Raj Agnihotri, and Thomas L. Baker, "Conceptualizing Salesperson Competitive Intelligence: An Individual-Level Perspective," *Journal of Personal Selling and Sales Management* 31, no. 2 (Spring 2011), pp. 141–56.

17. This is important because salespeople can be instrumental in breaking down functional silos. See, for example, Avinash Malshe and Ravipreet S. Sohi, "Sales Buy-In of Marketing Strategies: Exploration of Its Nuances, Antecedents, and Contextual Conditions," *Journal of Personal Selling and Sales Management* 29, no. 3 (Summer 2009), pp. 207–26.

18. The newer the product, the more salespeople might be needed to explain the benefits. See, for example, S. Albers, M. Mantrala, and S. Sridhar, "Personal Selling Elasticities: A Meta-Analysis," *Journal of Marketing Research* 47, no. 5 (2010), pp. 840–53.

19. See, for example, Scott B. Friend, G. Alexander Hamwi, and Brian N. Rutherford, "Buyer-Seller Relationships within a Multisource Context: Understanding Customer Defection and Available Alternatives," *Journal of Personal Selling and Sales Management* 31, no. 4 (Fall 2011), pp. 383–96.

20. See, for example, John D. Hansen and Robert J. Riggle, "Ethical Salesperson Behavior in Sales Relationships," *Journal of Personal Selling and Sales Management* 29, no. 2 (Spring 2009), pp. 151–66.

21. Technical skills are important. See, for example, Peter A. Reday, Roger Marshall, and A. Parasuraman, "An Interdisciplinary Approach to Assessing the Characteristics and Sales Potential of Modern Salespeople," *Industrial Marketing Management* 38, no. 7 (October 2009), pp. 838–44, and Christian Homburg, Michael Müller, and Martin Klarmann, "When Should the Customer Really Be King? On the Optimum Level of Salesperson Customer Orientation in Sales Encounters," *Journal of Marketing* 75, no. 2 (March 2011), pp. 55–74.

22. See Harsha Aeron, Ashwani Kumar, and Janakiraman Moorthy, "Data Mining Framework for Customer Lifetime Value-Based Segmentation," *Journal of Database Marketing and Customer Strategy Management* 19, no. 1 (March 2012), pp. 17–30, and William McKnight, "Predictive Analytics: Beyond the Predictions," *Information Management* 21, no. 4 (July 2011), pp. 18–20.

23. M. Ahearne, S. MacKenzie, P. Podsakoff, J. Mathieu, and S. Lam, "The Role of Consensus in Sales Team Performance," *Journal of Marketing Research* 47, no. 3 (2010), pp. 458–69.

24. Francisca Castro, Jorge Gomes, and Fernando C. de Sousa, "Do Intelligent Leaders Make a Difference? The Effect of a Leader's Emotional Intelligence on Followers' Creativity," *Creativity and Innovation Management* 21, no. 2 (June 2012), pp. 171–82; Sojka, Jane ZView Profile; Deeter-Schmeiz, Dawn R., "Enhancing the Emotional Intelligence of Salespeople," *Mid-American Journal of Business* 17, no. 1 (Spring 2002), pp. 43–50; Malcolm Higgs and Scott Lichtenstein, "Is There a Relationship between Emotional Intelligence and Individual Values? An Exploratory Study," *Journal of General Management* 37, no. 1 (September 2011), pp. 65–79; R. Krishnaveni and R. Deepa, "Emotional Intelligence: A Soft Tool for Competitive Advantage in the Organizational Context," *IUP Journal of Soft Skills* 5, no. 2 (June 2011), pp. 51–62; Choi Sungwon, Donald H. Kluemper, and Kerry S. Sauley, "What If We Fake Emotional Intelligence? A Test of Criterion Validity Attenuation," *Journal of Personality Assessment* 93, no. 3 (May 2011), pp. 270–77; John Angelidis and Nabil Ibrahim, "The Impact of Emotional Intelligence on the Ethical Judgment of Managers," *Journal of Business Ethics* 99 (March 2, 2011), pp. 111–19; Jasbindar Singh, "Enhance Your EQ," *New Zealand Management* 58, no. 2 (March 2011), p. 48; M. Port, "The Human Approach," *Entrepreneur* 37, no. 9 (September 2009), p. 30; Guijun Zhuang, Youmin Xi, and Alex S. L. Tsang, "Power, Conflict, and Cooperation: The Impact of Guanxi in Chinese Marketing Channels," *Industrial Marketing Management* 39, no. 1 (January 2010), pp. 137–49.

25. See Harvey Deutschendorf, "EQ Boost," *T + D* 63, no. 10 (2009), pp. 92–93.

26. Nick Tasler and Lac D. Su, "The Emotional Ignorance Trap," *BusinessWeek Online*, January 19, 2009.

27. Blair Kidwell, David M. Hardesty, Brian R. Murtha, and Shibin Sheng, "Emotional Intelligence in Marketing Exchanges," *Journal of Marketing* 75, no. 1 (January 2011), pp. 78–95.

28. "The Business Case for Emotional Intelligence," *Talent Smart* (2009), http://www.talentsmart.com/media/uploads/pdfs/The_Business_Case_For_EQ.pdf, accessed August 30, 2012.

29. See Clifford Nass, "The Keyboard and the Damage Done," *Pacific Standard*, May/June 2012, pp. 22–25.

30. Rebecca Alexander, "The Dark Side of Emotional Intelligence," *Management Today* (April 2011), pp. 46–50.

31. Alison Damist, "Sales Hits the Big Time at Business Schools," August 13, 2012, http://mobile.businessweek.com/articles/2012-08-13/sales-hits-the-big-time-at-b-schools, accessed August 29, 2012.

32. Burnout can occur! See, for example, C. David Shepherd, Armen Tashchian, and Rick E. Ridnour, "An Investigation of the Job Burnout Syndrome in Personal Selling," *Journal of Personal Selling and Sales Management* 31, no. 4 (Fall 2011), pp. 397–410.

33. Jacquelyn Smith, "The Best- and Worst-Paying Sales Jobs," *Forbes.com*, June 2012, p. 32.

34. Ashley Post, "Pharmaceutical Sales Reps Can't Receive Overtime Pay under FLSA," *Insidecounsel* 23, no. 247 (July 2012), pp. 60–61.

CHAPTER 2

1. Lauren Etter, "Plenty of Spilled Milk to Cry Over for Dairymen Lured to US," and Mark Maremont and Leslie Scism, "Investors Recruit Terminally Ill to Outwit Insurers on Annuities," *The Wall Street Journal,* February 16, 2010, pp. A1, A4, and A16.

2. Douglas B. Grisaffe and Fernando Jaramillo, "Toward Higher Levels of Ethics: Preliminary Evidence of Positive Outcomes," *Journal of Personal Selling & Sales Management* 27, no. 4 (2007), pp. 355–71; F. Juliet Poujol and John F. Tanner Jr. (2010), "The Impact of Sales Contests on Salesperson Customer Orientation," *Journal of Personal Selling & Sales Management* 30 (1), 33–46.

3. J. Tsalikis and Walfried Lassar, "Measuring Consumer Perceptions of Business Ethical Behavior in Two Muslim Countries," *Journal of Business Ethics* 89 (2009), pp. 91–98.

4. American Medical Association, Opinion 8.061, Gifts to Physicians from Industry, http://www.ama-assn.org/ama/pub/physician-resources/medical-ethics/code-medical-ethics/opinion8061.page, accessed August 31, 2012; Anne Underwood, "Thanks but No Thanks," *Newsweek,* from the magazine issue October 2007, http://www.newsweek.com/id/57342, accessed February 15, 2010.

5. Thomas Wotruba, "The Evolution of Personal Selling," *Journal of Personal Selling & Sales Management* (Summer 1991), pp. 1–12; William C. Moncrief and Greg W. Marshall, "The Evolution of the Seven Steps of Selling," *Industrial Marketing Management* 34 (January 2005), pp. 13–22.

6. George W. Dudley and John F. Tanner Jr., *The Hard Truth about Soft Selling* (Dallas: Behavioral Science Research Press, 2005).

7. Sergio Roman and Salvador Ruiz, "Relationship Outcomes of Perceived Ethical Sales Behavior: The Customer's Perspective," *Journal of Business Research* 58 (April 2005), pp. 439–51.

8. John D. Hansen and Robert J. Riggle, "Ethical Salesperson Behavior in Sales Relationships," *Journal of Personal Selling & Sales Management* 29, no. 2 (2009), pp. 151–66.

9. Steve L. Grover and Cathy A. Enz, "The Influence of Company Rules, Ethical Climate, and Individual Characteristics," *Journal of Australian and New Zealand Academy of Management* 11, no. 2 (2005), pp. 27–36; Jay P. Mulki, Jorge Fernando Jaramillo, and William B. Locander, "Critical Role of Leadership on Ethical Climate and Salesperson Behaviors," *Journal of Business Ethics* 86 (2009), pp. 125–41; John W. Cadogan, Nick Lee, Anssi Tarkainen, and Sanna Sundqvist, "Sales Manager and Sales Team Determinants of Salesperson Ethical Behaviour," *European Journal of Marketing* 43 (2009), pp. 907–37.

10. Christophe Fournier, John F. Tanner Jr., Lawrence B. Chonko, and Chris Manolis, "Revisiting Antecedents of Salesperson Propensity to Leave: The Moderating Role of Ethical Climate," *Journal of Personal Selling & Sales Management* (2009), pp. 7–22.

11. Eberhard Schnebel and Marge Bienert, "Implementing Ethics in Business Organizations," *Journal of Business Ethics* 53 (2004), pp. 203–11; Jay Prakash Mulki, Fernando Jaramillo, and William B. Locander, "Effects of Ethical Climate and Supervisory Trust on Salesperson's Job Attitudes and Intentions to Quit," *Journal of Personal Selling & Sales Management* 26, no. 1 (2006), pp. 19–37.

12. Dennis N. Bristow, Rajesh Gulati, Douglas Amyx, and Jennifer Slack, "An Empirical Look at Professional Selling from a Student Perspective," *Journal of Education for Business* 81, no. 5 (May–June 2006), pp. 242–49.

13. Dudley and Tanner. See also Paul Milgrom, "What the Seller Won't Tell You: Persuasion and Disclosure in Markets," *Journal of Economic Perspectives* 22, no. 2 (2008), pp. 115–31.

14. Shirley Hunter, personal correspondence. Used with permission.

15. William Bearden, Thomas Ingram, and Raymond LaForge, *Marketing: Principles and Perspectives* (New York: McGraw-Hill/Irwin, 2004).

16. "Exclusive IOMA Survey: How Employers Address Sexual Harassment," *HR Focus* 78, no. 12 (2007), pp. 3–5.

17. Rich Kraus, personal correspondence. Used with permission.

18. Tara J. Radin and Carolyn E. Predmore, "The Myth of the Salesperson: Intended and Unintended Consequences of Product-Specific Sales Incentives," *Journal of Business Ethics* 36 (2002), pp. 79–92.

19. Andres Zoltners, Prakesh Sinha, and S. Lorimer, "Breaking the Sales Force Incentive Addiction: A Balanced Approach to Sales Force Effectiveness," *Journal of Personal Selling and Sales Management* 32, no. 2 (2012), pp. 171–86.

20. Stephanie Clifford, "Wal-Mart Concedes Bribery Case May Widen," *New York Times,* May 17, 2012, http://www.nytimes.com/2012/05/18/business/wal-mart-concedes-bribery-case-may-widen.html?pagewanted=all, accessed August 20, 2012.

21. Halliburton, "Sensitive Transactions," http://www.halliburton.com/AboutUs/default.aspx?pageid=2326, accessed August 31, 2012. If you go to the Halliburton main page and search "sensitive transactions," you'll find the same document in other languages.

22. Meryl Davids, "Global Standards, Local Problems," *Journal of Business Strategy,* January–February 1999, pp.22–35; James Murphy, "The Morality of Bargaining: Insights from 'Caritas in Veritate,'" *Journal of Business Ethics,* Supplement 100 (2011), pp. 79–88; Susanna Ripken, "Corporations Are People Too: A Multi-Dimensional Approach to the Corporate Personhood Puzzle," *Fordham Journal of Corporate and Financial Law* 15, no. 1 (2009), pp. 97–177. Check out all three of these; they are very different types of articles dealing with the ethical and philosophical issues of subordination, bribery, and culture.

23. O.C. Ferrell, Thomas N. Ingram, and Raymond W. LaForge, "Initiating Structure for Legal and Ethical Decisions in a Global Sales Organization," *Industrial Marketing Management* 29 (2000), pp. 555–64.

24. Evan Perez and Brent Kendall, "Twenty-Two Arrested in U.S. Bribery Probe," *The Wall Street Journal* (Eastern Edition), January 20, 2010, p. A3.

25. Edmund W. Searby and George P. Farragher, "Foreign Corrupt Practices Act Poses Risk for Middle Market Companies," *Marketing Weekly News,* January 2, 2010, p. 146.

26. Paulina Diosdado de la Pena and Presha Neidermeyer, "U.S. Businesses' Code of Ethics as an Instrument to Comply with the Federal Corrupt Practices Act," *International Business & Economics Research Journal* 8, no. 12, December 2009, pp. 67–73.

CHAPTER 3

1. Organization for Economic Cooperation and Development, "Size of Public Procurement Market," in *Government at a Glance 2011*, OECD Publishing, 2011, http://dx.doi.org/10.1787/gov_glance-2011-46-en, accessed September 27, 2012.

2. Marvin Wagner, interviewed October 1, 2012.

3. Becky Partida, "Global Sourcing Calls for Due Diligence," *Supply Chain Management Review* 15, no. 5 (2011), pp. 62–64.

4. Aaron Back, Jung-Ah Lee, and Charmian Kok, "Analysts Expect iPad to Give Lift to Asian Manufacturers," *The Wall Street Journal (online)*, January 29, 2010, http://online.wsj.com/article/SB10001424052748704878904575030633950504718.html, accessed February 26, 2010.

5. Stephen J. Bistritz, "Selling to the C-Suite," *BtoB* 95 (February 8, 2010), p. 7.

6. Alan Earls, "BASF Procurement Gets Deep into R&D," *Purchasing* 138 (June 18, 2009), p. 31.

7. Stephanie Wagner, "Tapping Supplier Innovation," *Journal of Supply Chain Management* 48, no. 2 (April 2012), pp. 37–52; Robert Dwyer and John F. Tanner Jr., *Business Marketing: Connecting Strategy, Relationships, and Learning*, 4th ed. (New York: McGraw-Hill/Irwin, 2009).

8. For a very interesting look at satisfaction by role in the buying center and by buy class, see Jeanne Rossomme, "Customer Satisfaction Measurement in a Business-to-Business Context: A Conceptual Framework," *Journal of Business and Industrial Marketing* 18 (February 3, 2003), pp. 179–96; another interesting study on lead conversion (and converting to straight rebuys) is by Jamie P. Monat, "Industrial Sales Lead Conversion Modeling," *Marketing Intelligence & Planning* 29, no. 2 (2011), pp. 178–94. See also Carol C. Bienstock and Marla B. Royne, "The Differential Value of Information in Industrial Purchasing Decisions: Applying an Economics of Information Framework," *International Journal of Physical Distribution and Logistics* 37 (2007), pp. 389–402; M. José Garrido Samaniego, Ana M. Gutiérrez-Arranz, and Rebeca San José-Cabezudo, "Determinants of Internet Use in the Purchasing Process," *Journal of Business & Industrial Marketing* 21 (2006), pp. 164–78.

9. Robert Dwyer and John F. Tanner Jr., *Business Marketing: Connecting Strategy, Relationships, and Learning*, 4th ed. (New York: McGraw-Hill/Irwin, 2009).

10. Goutam Chakraborty, Prashant Srivastava, and Fred Marshall, "Are Drivers of Customer Satisfaction Different for Buyers/Users from Different Functional Areas?" *Journal of Business & Industrial Marketing* 22, no. 1 (2007), pp. 20–39.

11. Robert B. Miller and Stephen E. Heiman, with Tad Tuleja, *Strategic Selling* (New York: Warner Books, 1985).

12. Alicia Young, "Lean, Mean, and Keen," *Supply Management* 12, no. 25 (2007), p. 38.

13. Ming Haw Leong and Jane Dunnett, "Customer Perceptions of Attribute Importance in Business-to-Business Environment," *The Business Review* 8, no. 1 (2007), pp. 40–45.

14. Robert T. Yoki, "If You Can Measure It, Then You Can Improve It," *Hospital Materials Management* 32, no. 12 (2007), pp. 10–11.

15. David Lenling, interviewed October 14, 2009.

16. M. José Garrido-Samaniego, A. María Gutiérrez-Arranz, and Rebeca San José-Cabezudo, Assessing the Impact of E-Procurement on the Structure of the Buying Centre, *International Journal of Information Management* 30 (April 2010), 135–51; Margy Conchar, George Zinkhan, Cara Peters, and Sergio Olavarrieta, "An Integrated Framework for the Conceptualization of Consumers' Perceived-Risk Processing," *Journal of the Academy of Marketing Science* 32, no. 4 (2004), pp. 418–37.

17. Anonymous, "Alcoa Posts Surprise Profit," *RTTNews*, April 10, 2012, accessed September 30, 2012.

18. Tobias Mettler and Peter Rohner, Supplier Relationship Management: A Case Study in the Context of Health Care," *Journal of Theoretical and Applied Electronic Commerce Research* 4 (December 2009), pp. 58–61; Hank Darlington, "How to Pick the Best Vendor Partners for Your Business," *Supply House Times* 46 (February 2004), pp. 52–53.

19. Tom Stundza, "One Way to Get a Raise: Take a Course," *Purchasing* 138 (December 2009), p. 50.

20. Susan Avery, "Bell Thinks outside the Box," *Purchasing* 136, no. 15 (2007), p. 60.

21. William Ho, Xiaowei Xu, and Prasanta Dey, "Multi-Criteria Decision Making Approaches for Supplier Evaluation and Selection: A Literature Review," *European Journal of Operational Research* 202 (April 2010), pp. 16–31.

CHAPTER 4

1. Jim Blythe, "Trade Fairs as Communication: A New Model," *Journal of Business and Industrial Marketing* 25, no. 1 (2010), pp. 57–62.

2. "89 Business Cliches That Will Get Any MBA Promoted and Make Them Totally Useless," *Investing*, April 25, 2012, http://www.forbes.com/sites/ericjackson/2012/06/19/89-business-cliches-that-will-get-any-mba-promoted-to-middle-management-and-make-them-totally-useless.

3. Rick Spence, "Tell the Tale, Get the Sale," *Profit* 31, no. 3 (Summer 2012), p. 14.

4. Grant Cardone, "The 50 Best Qualities of Great Salespeople," *Proofs* 95, no. 3 (June 2012), pp. 15–16.

5. Nicklas Salomonson, Annika Åberg, and Jens Allwood, "Communicative Skills That Support Value Creation: A Study of B2B Interactions between Customers and Customer Service Representatives," *Industrial Marketing Management* 41, no. 1 (2012), pp. 145–55.

6. See Dr. Lillian Glass, *The Body Language Advantage: Maximize Your Personal and Professional Relationships with This Ultimate Photo Guide to Deciphering What Others Are Secretly Saying, in Any Situation* (Minneapolis, MN: Fair Winds Press, 2012); Anita Raghavan, "Watch Your Body Language," *Forbes*, March 16, 2009, p. 92; and Shari Alexander, "Networking and Selling Using Body Language Secrets," *Sales and Marketing Management* (2009), p. 82.

7. Owen Hargie, *The Handbook of Communication Skills*, 2nd ed. (London: Routledge, 1997).

8. Clifford Nass, "The Keyboard and the Damage Done," *Pacific Standard*, May/June 2012, pp. 22–25.

9. John Perry, "Palm Power in the Workplace," *The American Salesman* 46 (October 2001), p. 22.

10. Carl Kinsey Goman, *The Silent Language of Leaders: How Body Language Can Help—or Hurt—How You Lead* (San Francisco: Jossey-Bass, 2011).

11. Marianne LaFrance, *Why Smile: The Science behind Facial Expressions* (New York: Norton, 2013).

12. See M. Bond, "Come-to-Work Eyes," *New Scientist* 204, no. 2731 (October 24, 2009), pp. 6–7.

13. See Linda Talley, "Louder Than Words: You've Got Plenty of Great Things to Say: Make Sure That Your Body Language Doesn't Betray Your Message," *T + D* 63, no. 11 (2009), pp. 30–32.

14. Mark Bowden, *Winning Body Language* (New York: McGraw-Hill, 2010).

15. Dale Carnegie, a noted sales training consultant, would disagree with this advice. He suggests that not offering a handshake shows a lack of assertiveness.

16. "Britons Waving Goodbye to Humble Handshake," http://www.indianexpress.com/news/britons-wavinggoodbye-to-humble-handshake/572050, accessed August 30, 2012.

17. All material presented in the five principles was written by Vicki L. West; used by permission.

18. See Andrea Godfrey, Kathleen Seiders, and Glenn B Voss, "Enough Is Enough! The Fine Line in Executing Multichannel Relational Communication," *Journal of Marketing* 75, no. 4 (July 2011), pp. 94–109, and Joan C. Curtis and Barbara Giamanco, *The New Handshake: Sales Meets Social Media* (Santa Barbara, CA: Praeger, 2010).

19. Renee P. Walkup and Sandra McKee, *Selling to Anyone over the Phone*, 2nd ed. (New York, New York: AMACOM, 2010).

20. See Terry Flynn, "Work with—and Around—Voicemail," *Multichannel Merchant*, June 1, 2009, p. 26.

21. Steve Johnson, "The Awesome Power of Social Media," *American Printer* 128, no. 3 (March 2011), p. 14.

22. Barbara Gregoire and Kent Gregoire, "Tweet Me, Friend Me, Make Me Buy," *Harvard Business Review*, July–August 2012, pp. 88–93.

23. See Jennifer Lai, "5 Twitter Tips for Your Company," CNN Money.com, July 22, 2009, http://brainstormtech.blogs.fortune.cnn.com/2009/07/22/5-twitter-tips-for-your-company, accessed August 30, 2012; "Twitter—Best Practices," https://business.twitter.com/en/basics/best-practices, accessed August 30, 3012.

24. For important differences to consider when translating into other languages, see http://www.transperfect.com.

CHAPTER 5

1. Subhra Chakrabarty, Gene Brown, and Roberte E. Widing II, "Demographic Antecedents to the Practice of Adaptive Selling," *Marketing Management Journal* 20, no. 2 (Fall 2010), pp. 108–18.

2. See Willem Verbeke, Bart Dietz, and Ernst Verwaal, "Drivers of Sales Performance: A Contemporary Meta-Analysis. Have Salespeople Become Knowledge Brokers?," *Journal of the Academy of Marketing Science* 39, no. 3 (June 2011), pp. 407–28, and Richard A. Lancioni and Rajan Chandran, "Managing Knowledge in Industrial Markets: New Dimensions and Challenges," *Industrial Marketing Management* 38, no. 2 (February 2009), pp. 148–51.

3. Name of company changed as required.

4. See Kimiz Dalkir and Jay Liebowitz, *Knowledge Management in Theory and Practice*, 2nd ed. (Cambridge, MA: MIT Press, 2011).

5. Dorit Nevo, Izak Benbasat, and Yair Wand, "Who Knows What?," *Wall Street Journal*, October 26, 2009, p. R4.

6. David Merrill and Roger Reid, *Personal Styles and Effective Performance* (Radnor, PA: Chilton, 1981).

7. For details, see http://wilsonlearning.com/capabilities/social_styles1.

8. See L. Romdhane, N. Fadhel, and B. Ayeb, "An Efficient Approach for Building Customer Profiles from Business Data," *Expert Systems with Applications* 37, no. 2 (March 2010), pp. 1573–85.

9. See James Andzulis, Nikolaos G. Panagopoulos, and Adam Rapp, "A Review of Social Media and Implications for the Sales Process," *Journal of Personal Selling and Sales Management* 32, no. 3 (Summer 2012), pp. 305–16.

CHAPTER 6

1. It is even important for nonprofit organizations.

2. Some organizations refer to their salespeople as hunters and farmers. Hunters go out and locate potential leads. Farmers are the ones who develop the leads into prospects and customers.

3. Brent Adamson, Matthew Dixon, and Nicholas Toman, "The End of Solution Sales," *Harvard Business Review* 90, no. 7/8 (July 2012), pp. 60–68.

4. V. Kumar, J. Andrew Petersen, and Robert P. Leone, "Driving Profitability by Encouraging Customer Referrals: Who, When, and How," *Journal of Marketing* 74, no. 5 (September 2010), pp. 1–17.

5. Jeff Zabin, *The ROI on Social Media Marketing: Why It Pays to Drive Word of Mouth* (San Carlos, CA: Aberdeen Group, 2009).

6. Michael Krause, "20 Ways to Recognize Your Star Clients," http://www.salessensesolutions.com, accessed September 10, 2012.

7. Phil Birt, personal correspondence; used by permission.

8. Al Slavin, "Network News: Agent Survey Shows a Growing Role for Online Sales Leads," *Best's Review* 110, no. 1 (2009), pp. 84–85.

9. See, for example, Howard Feiertag, "Networking Is Not Selling," *Hotel Management* 227, no. 3 (March 2012), p. 10.

10. Thanks to Karl Sooder for introducing this concept to the author.

11. James Andzulis, Nikolaos G. Panagopoulos, and Adam Rapp, "A Review of Social Media and Implications for the Sales Process," *Journal of Personal Selling and Sales Management* 32, no. 3 (Summer 2012), pp. 305–16.

12. Raj Agnihotri, Prabakar Kothandaraman, Rajiv Kashyap, and Ramendra Singh, "Bringing 'Social' into Sales: The Impact of Salespeople's Social Media Use on Service Behaviors and Value Creation," *Journal of Personal Selling and Sales Management* 32, no. 3 (2012), pp. 333–48.

13. For details, see http://www.salessensesolutions.com, accessed September 11, 2012.

14. See, for example, Michael Rodriguez, Robert M. Peterson, and Vijaykumar Krishnan, "Social Media's Influence on Business-to-Business Sales Performance," *Journal of Personal Selling and Sales Management* 32, no. 3 (Summer 2012), pp. 365–78; Bob Little, "Identifying Key Trends in Sales—From a Training Perspective." *Industrial and Commercial Training* 44, no. 2 (March 2012), pp. 103–8; Kevin J. Trainor, "Relating Social Media Technologies to Performance: A Capabilities-Based Perspective," *Journal of Personal Selling and Sales Management* 32, no. 3 (Summer 2012), pp. 317–31; Barbara Giamanco and Kent Gregoire, "Tweet Me, Friend Me, Make Me Buy," *Harvard Business Review* 90, no. 7/8 (July 2012), pp. 88–93; Landy Chase and Kevin Knebl, *The Social Media Sales Revolution: The*

New Rules for Finding Customers, Building Relationships, and Closing More Sales through Online Networking (New York: McGraw-Hill, 2011); Landy Chase, "The Power of Personal Branding," *American Salesman* 56, no. 6 (June 2011), pp. 7–9; Lynne Noella, "Ten Tips to Raise Your Business Visibility through Social Networks," *Financial Executive* 25, no. 9 (2009), p. 17; and Karen Schuele and Roland Madison, "Navigating the 21st Century Job Search," *Strategic Finance* 91, no. 7 (2010), pp. 49–53.

15. See Mike Krause, "3 Succinct Steps to Get Sales through Social Media," January 6, 2010, http://www.salessensesolutions.com, accessed March 1, 2010.

16. See Jennifer Lai, "5 Twitter Trips for Your Company," CNN Money.com, July 22, 2009, http://brainstormtech.blogs .fortune.cnn.com/2009/07/22/5-twitter-tips-for-your-company, accessed February 12, 2010.

17. Agnihotri et al., "Bringing 'Social' into Sales," p. 333.

18. Eddie B. Allen Jr., "Sheer Brilliance," *Deliver Magazine*, February 2012, pp. 20–21.

19. Mindy Charski, *Deliver Magazine*, February 2012, pp. 12–13.

20. Linda Armstrong, "Demo Day Camp," *Exhibitor Magazine*, October 2009, pp. 32–37.

21. See "Delivering Quality Leads, Not Just Quantity: The Interactive Value of Webinars," *CRM Magazine* 13, no. 3 (March 2009), pp. 3–6.

22. For information about SIC and NAICS codes, see the excellent listing of Web resources available at http://www.d.umn .edu.jvileta/naics.html.

23. Ted Sperides, personal correspondence; used with permission.

24. Mike Krause, "4 Telemarketing Questions Every Business Owner Needs to Ask," February 11, 2010, http://www .salessensesolutions.com, accessed September 8, 2012.

25. See, for example, Sandra Beckwith, "Going Deeper," *Deliver Magazine*, December 2009, pp. 13–17.

26. This is found in many places on the Web, including http:// www.answerology.com/index.aspx/question/2674611_ icdnuolt-blveiee-taht-I-cluod-aulaclty-uesdnatnrd-waht-Iwas-rdanieg-The-phaonmneal-pweor-of-the-.html, accessed September 9, 2012.

27. This poem is found in many places on the Web.

28. See http://www.salesleadmgmtassn.com.

29. See Adamson et al., "The End of Solution Sales," p. 64.

CHAPTER 7

1. See Alex Stein and Michael Smith, "CRM Systems and Organizational Learning: An Exploration of the Relationship between CRM Effectiveness and the Customer Information Orientation of the Firm in Industrial Markets," *Industrial Marketing Management* 38, no. 2 (2009), pp. 198–206.

2. Dawn Hedges, personal correspondence; names changed to protect confidentiality.

3. Neil Rackham, *Major Account Sales Strategy* (New York: McGraw-Hill, 1989), p. 39.

4. For their latest book on the topic, see Robert B. Miller, Stephen E. Heiman, Diane Sanchez, and Tad Tuleja, *The New Conceptual Selling: The Most Effective and Proven Method for Face-to-Face Sales Planning* (New York: Warner Business, 2005).

5. See Anne Stuart, "Create Order from Chaos," *Deliver Magazine*, July 2009, pp. 22–25.

6. Jim Hersma, personal correspondence; used with permission.

7. Special thanks to Karl Sooder for sharing this information.

8. Rackham, *Major Account Sales Strategy*.

9. Rackham, *Major Account Sales Strategy*, p. 30.

10. Brent Adamson, Matthew Dixon, and Nicholas Toman. "The End of Solution Sales." *Harvard Business Review* 61 (July–August 2012), pp. 60–68.

11. Phil Lauterjung, "The Best Days and Times to Cold Call," http://www.phillauterjung.com/the-best-days-and-times-to-cold-call, accessed April 1, 2012.

12. See Jan Ozer, "Webcasting for the Masses: Between Live Streaming Service Providers and Rich Media Communications Solutions, There Have Never Been More Options for Webcasting Live Events," *Streaming Media*, 2009, pp. 24–32. And salespeople should ensure quality sound, as this source suggests: Carmine Gallo, "Record Voice for Your Next Presentation," *Business Week Online*, January 7, 2010.

CHAPTER 8

1. Building partnerships and strong relationships is a process that starts when a lead is identified and continues throughout all postsale service and future calls.

2. John E. Cicala, Rachel K. Smith, and Alan J. Bush, "What Makes Sales Presentations Effective—A Buyer-Seller Perspective," *Journal of Business and Industrial Marketing* 27, no. 2 (April 2012), pp. 78–88.

3. Based on personal correspondence with Karl Sooder; used with permission.

4. Of course, many aspects of first impressions, such as race and gender, are outside the control of the salesperson.

5. Matt Leaf, personal correspondence; used with permission.

6. James Andzulis, Nikolaos G. Panagopoulos, and Adam Rapp, "A Review of Social Media and Implications for the Sales Process." *Journal of Personal Selling and Sales Management* 32, no. 3 (Summer 2012), pp. 305–16.

7. For more examples and tips on how to engage in small talk, see "How to Make Small Talk," http://www.ehow.com/ how_10812_make-small-talk.html, accessed October 19, 2012.

8. See Ken Dooley, "Conversation Topics That Kill Sales," March 9, 2010, http://www.businessbrief.com/conversa tiontopics-that-kill-sales-pass-this-list-on-to-your-newbies, accessed March 13, 2010.

9. R. Peterson and Y. Limbu, "The Convergence of Mirroring and Empathy: Communications Training in Business-to-Business Personal Selling Persuasion Efforts," *Journal of Business-to-Business Marketing* 16, no. 3 (July 2009), pp. 193–219.

10. Dan Seidman, "Hilarious Selling Mistakes," http://www .sellingpower.com/content/video, accessed March 16, 2010.

11. Neil Rackham, *SPIN Selling* (New York: McGraw-Hill, 1988).

12. Angie Main; used with permission.

13. Rackham, *SPIN Selling*.

14. Michael Port, "Take Out the Garbage," *Entrepreneur*, August 2009, p. 26.

15. Hank Darlington, "Learning to 'Sell' Features and Benefits," *Supply House Times* 54, no. 10 (December 2011), p. 44.

16. Neil Rackham, 2009, "Sales Strategies to Capture Market Share in a Down Economy," as viewed at http://www.thefreelibrary.com/Sales+strategies+to+capture+market+share+in+a+down+economy%3A+selling...-a0206465342, accessed on May 17, 2013.

17. Ray Hanson, personal correspondence; used by permission.

18. This can be found at many places on the Web, including http://www.davidpbrown.co.uk/psychology/smart-test.html, accessed October 16, 2012.

19. Cara Hale Alter, *The Credibility Code: How to Project Confidence and Competence When It Matters Most* (Meritus Books, 2012); Harry Labana, "Building Credibility on All Sides," Businessweek.com, http://www.businessweek.com/managing/content/oct2010/ca20101029_327671.htm?campaign_id=yhoo, accessed October 14, 2012.

20. Jim Hersma, personal correspondence; used with permission.

21. See, for example, "Increasing Sales with a Credibility Statement," http://silverbulletselling.com/increasing-sales-with-a-credibility-statement, accessed October 10, 2012.

22. Todd Graf, personal correspondence; used with permission.

23. Tracey Brill, personal correspondence; used with permission.

CHAPTER 9

1. Gordon Hester, "The Neuroscience behind Stories," *Direct Selling News*, October 2010, pp. 60–64.

2. A. Herasimchuk, "PowerPoint Is Not an Excuse," *Desktop* 64, no. 1 (February 2010), pp. 74–77.

3. "Points of Hue," https://delivermagazine.com/2010/02/points-of-hue/, accessed on, March 2010, p. 4.

4. "The Odd Slot: Loctite Hangs a Man for Charity," *Builders Merchants Journal*, October 2011, p. 50.

5. Suresh Goklaney, "How We Built a Door-to-Door Selling Machine," *Harvard Business Review* 90, no. 7/8 (July 2012), pp. 108–9.

6. Personal correspondence.

7. See, for example, http://www.qvidian.com.

8. Karl Sooder, "The Value Presentation," used with permission; Nicholas A. C. Read and Stephen Bistritz, *Selling to the C-Suite* (New York: McGraw-Hill, 2010).

9. Harri Terho, Alexander Haas, Andreas Eggert, and Wolfgang Ulaga, "'It's Almost Like Taking the Sales Out of Selling'—Towards a Conceptualization of Value-Based Selling in Business Markets," *Industrial Marketing Management* 41, no. 1 (2012), pp. 174–85.

10. The first example is adapted from an example from Read and Bistritz, *Selling to the C-Suite*, p. 135. The second example is provided by Karl Sooder.

11. See Jill Konrath, "How to Write a Value Proposition," http://www.sideroad.com/Sales/value_proposition.html, accessed October 20, 2012.

CHAPTER 10

1. See also "The 8 Objections," http://www.justsell.com/the-8-objections, accessed March 24, 2010.

2. Darin George, "'I Want to Think About It': How Salespeople Can Overcome the Biggest Objection in the Business," *Ward's Dealer Business* 46, no. 8 (August 20, 2012), p. 27.

3. See also "The Key to Eliminating Objections and Increasing Sales," http://www.powerhomebiz.com/vol147/sales.htm, accessed October 25, 2012, and Tom Hebrock,

"Selling 102: How to Handle Objections More Effectively," *TWICE: This Week in Consumer Electronics* 26, no. 15 (July 18, 2011), p. 28.

4. "LAARC Sales Resistance Mitigation Tactic," http://www.provenmodels.com/555/laarc-sales-resistance-mitigation-tactic, accessed October 25, 2012.

5. Salespeople can forestall known concerns but shouldn't bring up issues that aren't even a problem with a particular prospect. Thus the need for good precall information gathering becomes obvious.

6. Proverbs 18:13.

7. Howard Feiertag, "Clarify Client's Objection by Asking Questions," *Hotel Management* 227, no. 10 (August 2012), p. 12.

8. Personal correspondence; name of firm and industry withheld by request.

9. Gwen Moran, "Adapt to Survive," *Deliver Magazine*, July 2009, pp. 16–18.

10. James C. Anderson, Normalya Kumar, and James A. Narus (2008), "Become a Value Merchant," *Sales and Marketing Management*, May/June 2008, p. 21.

11. Tracey Brill, personal correspondence; used with permission.

12. See also "Dealing with Angry Customers," http://www.callcentrehelper.com/dealing-with-angry-customers-152.htm, accessed October 27, 2012, and Carmine Gallo, "Dealing with Angry Customers: How You Handle Mistakes and Improve Service Could Mean the Difference between Losing Customers and Keeping Their Business," *Business Week Online*, http://www.businessweek.com/stories/2007-06-20/dealing-with-angry-customersbusinessweek-business-news-stock-market-and-financial-advice, accessed October 25, 2012.

CHAPTER 11

1. Neil Rackham, *SPIN Selling* (New York: McGraw-Hill, 1988), pp. 19–51.

2. Mark Skaer, "Having Sales Awareness and Effectiveness," *Air Conditioning, Heating & Refrigeration News* 227, no. 1 (2006), pp. 50–52.

3. Joanna R. Turpin, "Financing Those Dream Systems," *Air Conditioning, Heating, & Refrigeration News* 237 (June 22, 2009), pp. 1–3.

4. Bill Lurz, "Qualifying Buyers a Big Problem," *Giants* 4 (September 2008), p. 14.

5. Bruce Culbert, personal correspondence, February 20, 2008; used with permission.

6. Marvin A. Jolson, "Selling Assertively," *Business Horizons*, September–October 1984, pp. 71–77.

7. Heiner Evanschitzky, Arun Sharm, and Prykop Catja, "The Role of the Sales Employee in Securing Customer Satisfaction," *European Journal of Marketing* 46, no. 3–4 (2012), pp. 489–508.

8. John Branton, "Closing Sales the Right Way," *National Underwriter, Life & Health* 113, no. 5 (March 2, 2009), p. 31.

9. Eleanor Brownell, "How to Make Yourself Memorable," *American Salesman* 55, no. 3 (March 2010), pp. 24–28.

10. Paolo Guenzi and Laurent Georges, "Interpersonal Trust in Commercial Relationships: Antecedents and Consequences of Customer Trust in the Salesperson," *European Journal of Marketing* 44, no. 1–2 (2010), pp. 114–29.

11. Stefanos Mousas, Stephan Henneberg, and Peter Naudé, "Trust and Reliance in Business Relationships," *European Journal of Marketing* 41, no. 9–10 (2007), pp. 1016–32; Nelson Oly Ndubisi and Christian N. Madu, "The Association of Gender to Firm–Customer Relationship," *The International Journal of Quality & Reliability Management* 26, no. 3 (2009), pp. 283–301.

12. Jasmin Bergeron and Michel Laroche, "The Effects of Perceived Salesperson Listening Effectiveness in the Financial Industry," *Journal of Financial Services Marketing* 14, no. 1 (June 2009), pp. 6–25.

13. Raj Agnihotri, Adam Rapp, and Kevin Trainor, "Understanding the Role of Information Communication in the Buyer–Seller Exchange Process: Antecedents and Outcomes," *Journal of Business & Industrial Marketing* 24, no. 7 (2009), pp. 474–99.

14. Mark Hunter, "What Did You Learn from the Last Sale You Lost?," *Agency Sales* 42, no. 3 (March 2012), pp. 27–28.

15. Dave Stein, "Smart Sales: Let's Role the Videotape," *Sales and Marketing Management* 160, no. 3 (May–June 2008), p. 8.

CHAPTER 12

1. Ken Dooley, "6 Tips for Negotiating in a Tough Economy," *Sales & Marketing Business Brief*, March 9, 2010, http://www.businessbrief.com/6-tips-for-negotiating-in-a-tougheconomy, accessed March 25, 2010.

2. Norman A. Johnson and Randolph B. Cooper, "Power and Concession in Computer-Mediated Negotiations: An Examination of First Offers," *MIS Quarterly* 33, no. 1 (2009), pp. 147–70.

3. The information in this section was developed from Kenneth Thomas, "Conflict and Conflict Management," in *The Handbook of Industrial and Organizational Psychology*, ed. Marvin Dunnette (Skokie, IL: Rand McNally, 1976); see also Robert M. Peterson and C. David Shepherd, "Negotiation Preparation Differences in Selling Situations: Collaborative versus Competitive Expectations," *Marketing Management Journal* 21, no. 2 (Fall 2011), pp. 103–14.

4. Roy Lewicki, Bruce Barry, and David Saunders, *Essentials of Negotiation* (New York: McGraw-Hill, 2010).

5. Charles Patton and P. V. (Sundar) Balakrishnan, "Negotiating When Outnumbered: Agenda Strategies for Bargaining with Buying Teams," *International Journal of Research in Marketing* 29, no. 3 (September 2012), pp. 280–91.

6. "Fractured English," *Have a Good Day*, January 1997, pp. 1–2.

7. See "Good Guy/Bad Guy," http://changingminds.org/disciplines/negotiation/tactics/good-bad_guy.htm, accessed October 28, 2012.

8. John Patrick Dolan, "How to Overcome the Top Ten Negotiating Tactics," http://www.myarticlearchive.com/articles/5/025.htm, accessed October 30, 2012.

9. See Roger Fisher and William Ury, *Getting to Yes: Negotiating Agreement without Giving In*, 2nd ed. (Boston: Houghton Mifflin, 1991).

10. See Roger Dawson, "Power Negotiating: Skills for Today's Tough Times," *Success*, 2009, pp. 90–91.

CHAPTER 13

1. Alfred Pelham, "Do Consulting-Oriented Sales Management Programs Impact Salesforce Performance and Profit?" *Journal of Business & Industrial Marketing* 21, no. 3 (2006), pp. 175–86; Zhen Zhu and Cheryl Nakata, "Reexamining the Link between Customer Orientation and Business Performance: The Role of Information Systems," *Journal of Marketing Theory & Practice* 15, no. 3 (2007), pp. 187–203; Mojtaba P. Salami, "Impact of Customer Relationship Management (CRM) in the Iran Banking Sector," *International Journal of Organizational Innovation* 2, no. 1 (Summer 2009), pp. 225–53; Alfred Pelham, "The Impact of Industry and Training Influences on Salesforce Consulting Time and Consulting Effectiveness," *Journal of Business & Industrial Marketing* 24, no. 8 (2009), pp. 575–89.

2. "Can Mobile Firms Ring the Changes and Slash Churn?" *Precision Marketing*, January 11, 2008, p. 12.

3. Robert W. Palmatier, Lisa K. Scheer, Mark B. Houston, Kenneth R. Evans, and Srinath Gopalakrishna, "Use of Relationship Marketing Programs in Building Customer–Salesperson and Customer–Firm Relationships: Differential Influences on Financial Outcomes," *International Journal of Research in Marketing* 24, no. 3 (2007), pp. 210–24.

4. V. Kumar and Denish Sha, "Can Marketing Lift Stock Prices?," *Sloan Management Review* 52, no. 4 (2011), pp. 24–26; Sofie Hansen, "The Global Diffusion of Relationship Marketing," *European Journal of Marketing* 42, no. 11/12 (2008), pp. 1156–70; Werner J. Reinartz, and V. Kumar, "The Impact of Customer Relationship Characteristics on Profitable Lifetime Duration," *Journal of Marketing* 67, no. 1 (2003), pp. 77–99; Rajkumar Venkatesan and V. Kumar, "A Customer Lifetime Value Framework for Customer Selection and Resource Allocation Strategy," *Journal of Marketing* 68, no. 4 (2004), pp. 106–25;.

5. P. Aurier and G. Sere de Lanauze, "Impacts of In-Store Manufacturer Brand Expression on Perceived Value, Relationship Quality and Attitudinal Loyalty," *International Journal of Retail and Distribution Management* 39, no. 11 (2011), pp. 810–35; Rebekah Russell-Bennett, Janet McColl-Kennedy, and Leonard V. Coote, "Involvement, Satisfaction, and Brand Loyalty in a Small Business Services Setting," *Journal of Business Research* 60, no. 12 (2007), pp. 1253–64.

6. Robert Dwyer, Paul Schurr, and Sejo Oh, "Developing Buyer–Seller Relationships," *Journal of Marketing*, April 1987, pp. 11–27; Sandy Jap and Barton Weitz, "A Taxonomy of Long-Term Relationships" (working paper, College of Business Administration, University of Florida, 1996); Lloyd M. Rinehart, James A. Eckert, Thomas J. Page Jr., and Thomas Atkin, "An Assessment of Supplier–Customer Relationships," *Journal of Business Logistics* 25, no. 1 (2004), pp. 25–63; Aurelia Lefaix-Durand, Robert Kozak, Robert Beauregard, and Diane Poulin, "Extending Relationship Value: Observations from a Case Study of the Canadian Structural Wood Products Industry," *The Journal of Business & Industrial Marketing* 24, no. 5/6 (2009), pp. 389–401.

7. Sunmee Choi and Anne S. Mattila, "Perceived Controllability and Service Expectations: Influences on Customer Reactions Following Service Failure," *Journal of Business Research* 61, no. 1 (2008), pp. 24–41.

8. Vishal Kashyap, Aurea H. P. Ribeiro, Anthony Asare, and Thomas G. Brashear, "Developing Sales Force Relationalism: The Role of Distributive and Procedural Justice," *Journal of Personal Selling & Sales Management* 27, no. 3 (2007), pp. 235–51; Tai Yi-Ming and Ho Chin-Fu, "Effects of Information Sharing on Customer Relationship Intention," *Industrial Management and Data Systems* 110, no. 9 (2010), pp. 1385–401.

9. Y. H. Wong, Humphry Hung, and Wing-ki Chow, "Mediating Effects of Relationship Quality on Customer Relationships: An Empirical Study in Hong Kong," *Marketing Intelligence and Planning* 25, no. 6 (2007), pp. 581–99; Brian Crombie, "Is Guanxi Social Capital?," *The ISM Journal of International Business* 1, no. 2 (2011), pp. 1–28.

10. Felix T. Mavondo and Elaine M. Rodrigo, "The Effect of Relationship Dimensions on Interpersonal and Interorganizational Commitment in Organizations Conducting Business between Australia and China," *Journal of Business Research* 52 (2001), pp. 111–21; Wen-Hung Wang, Chiung-Ju Liang, and Yung-De Wu, "Relationship Bonding Tactics, Relationship Quality, and Customer Behavioral Loyalty–Behavioral Sequence in Taiwan's Information Services Industry," *Journal of Services Research* 6, no. 1 (2006), pp. 31–57; Michael Trimarchi, Peter W. Liesch, and Rick Tamaschke, "A Study of Compatibility Variation across Chinese Buyer-Seller Relationships," *European Journal of Marketing* 44, no. 1–2 (2010), pp. 87–113.

11. Michael D. Johnson and Fred Selnes, "Customer Portfolio Management: Toward a Dynamic Theory of Relationships," *Journal of Marketing* 68, no. 2 (2004), pp. 1–17; Robert C. Dudley and Das Narayandas, "A Portfolio Approach to Sales," *Harvard Business Review* 84 (July–August 2006), pp. 16–24; Leff Bonney and Brian C. Williams, "From Products to Solutions: The Role of Salesperson Opportunity Recognition," *European Journal of Marketing* 43, no. 7/8 (2009), pp. 1032–45.

12. Dennis Campbell and Frances Frei, "The Persistence of Customer Profitability: Empirical Evidence and Implications from a Financial Services Firm," *Journal of Service Research* 7, no. 2 (2004), pp. 107–124; Morten Holm, V. Kumar, and Carsten Rohde, "Measuring Customer Profitability in Complex Environments: An Interdisciplinary Contingency Framework," *Journal of the Academy of Marketing Science* 40, no. 3 (2012), pp. 387–401.

13. Glen L. Urban and John R. Hauser, "Listening In to Find and Explore New Combinations of Customer Needs," *Journal of Marketing* 68, no. 2 (2004), pp. 72–87; Wadie Nasri and Lanouar Charfeddine, "Motivating Salespeople to Contribute to Marketing Intelligence Activities: An Expectancy Theory Approach," *International Journal of Marketing Studies* 4, no. 1 (2012), pp. 168–75.

14. Dwyer, Schurr, and Oh, "Developing Buyer–Seller Relationships."

15. Reinartz and Kumar, "The Impact of Customer Relationship Characteristics."

16. Brian N. Rutherford, James S. Boles, Hiram C. Barksdale Jr., and Julie T. Johnson, "Single Source Supply versus Multiple Source Supply: A Study into the Relationship between Satisfaction and Propensity to Stay within a Service Setting," *Journal of Personal Selling & Sales Management* 26, no. 4 (2006), pp. 371–84; Paolo Guenzi and Laurent Georges, "Interpersonal Trust in Commercial Relationships: Antecedents and Consequences of Customer Trust in the Salesperson," *European Journal of Marketing* 44, no. 1–2 (2010), pp. 114–28.

17. Kim Sydow Campbell, Lenita Davis, and Lauren Skinner, "Rapport Management during the Exploration Phase of the Salesperson–Customer Relationship," *Journal of Personal Selling & Sales Management* 26, no. 4 (2006), pp. 359–70; Anja Geigenmuller and Larissa Greschuchna, "How to Establish Trustworthiness in Initial Service Encounters," *Journal of Marketing Theory and Practice* 19, no. 4 (Fall 2011), pp. 391–405.

18. Constanza Bianchi and Abu Saleh, "On Importer Trust and Commitment: A Comparative Study of Two Developing Countries," *International Marketing Review* 27, no. 1 (2010), pp. 55–70.

19. Guenzi and Georges, "Interpersonal Trust in Commercial Relationships."

20. Alfred Pelham, "The Impact of Industry and Training Influences on Salesforce Consulting Time and Consulting Effectiveness," *Journal of Business and Industrial Marketing* 24, no. 8 (2009), pp. 575–84.

21. Mark E. Cross, Thomas G. Brashear, Edward E. Rigdon, and Danny N. Bellenger, "Customer Orientation and Salesperson Performance," *European Journal of Marketing* 33, 41, no. 7–8 (2007), pp. 821–39.

22. Gerrard Macintosh, "Customer Orientation, Relationship Quality, and Relational Benefits to the Firm," *Journal of Services Marketing* 21, no. 3 (2007), pp. 150–68; Jon C. Carr and Tara B. Lopez, "Examining Market Orientation as Both Culture and Conduct: Modeling the Relationship between Market Orientation and Employee Responses," *Journal of Marketing Theory & Practice* 15, no. 2 (2007), pp. 113–27.

23. Erin Strouth, "To Tell the Truth," *Sales & Marketing Management* 154, no. 7 (2002), pp. 40–48.

24. John M. Hawes, Kenneth Mast, and John E. Swan, "Trust Earning Perceptions of Sellers and Buyers," *Journal of Personal Selling & Sales Management* (Spring 1989), pp. 1–8; J. Tsalikis and Walfried Lassar, "Measuring Consumer Perceptions of Business Ethical Behavior in Two Muslim Countries," *Journal of Business Ethics* 89 (2009), pp. 91–98.

25. Jasmin Bergeron and Michel Laroche, "The Effects of Perceived Salesperson Listening Effectiveness in the Financial Industry," *Journal of Financial Services Marketing* 14, no. 8 (June 2009), pp. 6–25.

26. Lisa Cross, "Establishing Customer Loyalty," *Graphic Arts Monthly* 76, no. 9 (2004), pp. 39–42; Kimberly Scher, "Breaking Up Is Hard to Do: Knowing When a Customer Relationship Is Worth Keeping," *Catalyst,* September–October 2008, pp. 26–29.

27. Gilbert N. Nyaga, Judith M. Whipple, and Daniel F. Lynch, "Examining Supply Chain Relationships: Do Buyer and Supplier Perspectives on Collaborative Relationships Differ?" *Journal of Operations Management* 28, no. 2 (March 2010), pp. 101–15.

28. Constanza Bianchi and Abu Saleh, "On Importer Trust and Commitment: A Comparative Study of Two Developing Countries," *International Marketing Review* 27, no. 1 (2010), pp. 55–70.

29. Betsy Cummings, "Dodging Dishonesty," *Sales & Marketing Management* 157, no. 2 (2005), p. 10.

30. F. Juliet Poujol and John F. Tanner Jr., "The Impact of Contests on Salespeople's Customer Orientation: An Application of Tournament Theory," *Journal of Personal Selling & Sales Management* 30 no. 1 (Winter 2010), pp. 33–46.

CHAPTER 14

1. Dough Henschen, "SaaS-Based BI Tracks Rossignol Ski and Snowboard Sales," *Intelligent Enterprise Online,* January 5, 2010, http://intelligent-enterprise.informationweek.com/showArticle.jhtml;jsessionid=14FHIGTREQRNLQE1GHRSKH4ATMY32JVN?articleID=222200361, accessed March 24, 2010.

2. Bob Hall, "Saying Thanks," *Quick Printing* 33, no. 1 (October 2009), p. 6.

3. Samuel Greengard, "Keeping the Customer Satisfied," *CIO Insight* 109 (November 2009), pp. 32–35.

4. Goutam Chakraborty, Prashant Srivastava, and Fred Marshall, "Are Drivers of Customer Satisfaction Different for Buyers/Users from Different Functional Areas?" *Journal of Business & Industrial Marketing* 22, no. 1 (2007), pp. 20–32; Kenneth R. Lord and Pola Gupta, "Response of Buying-Center Participants to B2B Product Placements," *Journal of Business and Industrial Marketing* 25, no. 3 (2010), pp. 188–95.

5. Celso Augusto de Matos, Carlos A.V. Rossi, Ricardo T. Veiga, and Valter A. Vieira, "Consumer Reaction to Service Failure and Recovery: The Moderating Role of Attitude toward Complaining," *Journal of Services Marketing* 23, no. 7 (2009), pp. 462–75; Constantine Lymperopoulos and Ioannis E. Chaniotakis, "Price Satisfaction and Personnel Efficiency as Antecedents of Overall Satisfaction from Consumer Credit Products and Positive Word of Mouth," *Journal of Financial Services* 13, no. 1 (2008), pp. 63–71.

6. Rob Gerlsbeck, "Bad Reputation Can't Be Beat," *Marketing* 111, no. 14 (2006), p. 6.

7. Rajiv D. Banker and Raj Mashruwala, "Simultaneity in the Relationship between Sales Performance and Customer Satisfaction," *Journal of Consumer Satisfaction, Dissatisfaction and Complaining Behavior* 22 (2009), pp. 88–104; Tamilla Curtis, Russell Abratt, Dawna Rhoades, and Paul Diaon, "Customer Loyalty, Repurchase, and Satisfaction: A Meta-Analytical Review," *Journal of Consumer Satisfaction, Dissatisfaction and Complaining Behavior* 24 (2011), pp. 1–26.

8. Chia-Chi Chang, "When Service Fails: The Role of the Salesperson and the Customer," *Psychology & Marketing* 23, no. 3 (2006), pp. 203–14 Varela-Neira, Concepción, Rodolfo Vázquez-Casielles, and Víctor *The International Journal of Bank Marketing* 28, no. 2 (2010), pp. 88–112.

9. "Ikea: Not Sweden's Only Quality Company," *Strategic Direction* 22, no. 5 (2006), pp. 5–7.

10. Jeff Epstein, "Oracle+Sun Strategy Update," *Full Disclosure Wire* (January 27, 2010), http://search.proquest.com/docview/465978158/139B0C640C122A60263/11?accountid=7014, accessed October 10, 2012.

11. James J. Zboja and Michael D. Hartline, "An Examination of High-Frequency Cross-Selling," *Journal of Relationship Marketing* 11, no. 1 (2012), 41–56.

12. Robert Dwyer and John F. Tanner Jr., *Business Marketing: Connecting Strategy, Relationships, and Learning,* 4th ed. (Burr Ridge, IL: McGraw-Hill/Irwin, 2009).

13. Mike Power, "Accessibility Is Top Priority," *Industrial Distribution* 94, no. 10 (2005), p. 56.

14. Dwyer and Tanner, *Business Marketing.*

15. John W. Barnes, Donald W. Jackson Jr., Michael D. Hutt, and Ajith Kumar, "The Role of Culture Strength in Shaping Sales Force Outcomes," *Journal of Personal Selling &*
Sales Management 26, no. 3 (2006), pp. 255–70; Hassan Ghorbani, Seyedeh Masoomeh Abdollahi Demneh, and Arezoo Khorsandnejad, "An Empirical Investigation of the Relationship between Organizational Culture and Customer Orientation: The Mediating Effect of Knowledge Management (An Empirical Study in the Household Appliance Industry in Iran)," *International Journal of Marketing Studies* 4, no. 3 (June 2012), pp. 58–67.

16. John F. Tanner Jr., Jorge Wise, Christophe Fournier, and Sandrine Hollet, "Executives' Perspectives of the Changing Role of the Sales Profession: Views from France, the United States, and Mexico," *Journal of Business and Industrial Marketing* 23, no. 3 (2008), pp. 193–202.

17. Paul Teague, "Congratulations to Tyco International," *Purchasing* 138, no. 9 (September 17, 2009), p. 11.

18. J. Garry Smith and Donald P. Roy, "A Framework for Developing Customer Orientation in Ticket Sales Organizations," *Sport Marketing Quarterly, Suppl. Special Issue: Sales Force Management in Sport* 20, no. 2 (June 2011), pp. 93–102.

19. Darryl Lehnus, "Building the 3×3 Relationship Strategy," *Baylor University S3 Newsletter*, October 15, 2012.

20. Jessica Sebor, "CRM Gets Serious," *Customer Relationship Management,* February 2008, pp. 23–26.

CHAPTER 15

1. Leigh Anne Pearson, "Sales Performance at Teradata," Baylor University Center for Professional Selling Report, May 15, 2011; Jussi Hätönen and Mika Ruokonen, "Revising Marketing Strategies for Supplier Selection Criteria: Small Firm Approach from the Information and Communications Industry," *Journal of Business and Industrial Marketing* 25, no. 2 (2010), pp. 159–73.

2. Michael J. Barone and Thomas E. DeCarlo, "Performance Trends and Salesperson Evaluations: The Moderating Roles of Evaluation Task, Managerial Risk Propensity, and Firm Strategic Orientation," *Journal of Personal Selling and Sales Management* 32, no. 2 (Spring 2012), pp. 207–12; Oyvind Helgesen, "Customer Segments Based on Customer Account Profitability," *Journal of Targeting, Measurement, and Analysis for Marketing* 14, no. 3 (2006), pp. 225–37.

3. Lawrence Ang and Ben Taylor, "Managing Customer Profitability Using Portfolio Matrices," *Journal of Database Marketing & Customer Strategy Management* 12, no. 4 (2005), pp. 298–304.

4. Adel El-Ansary and Waleed A. El-Ansary, *Winning Customers, Building Accounts: Some Do It Better Than Others* (Jacksonville, FL: Paper and Plastics Education and Research Foundation, 1994).

5. Douglas Hughes, Joel LeBon, and Adam Rapp, "Gaining and Leveraging Customer-Based Competitive Intelligence: The Pivotal Role of Social Capital and Salesperson Adaptive Selling Skills," *Journal of the Academy of Marketing Science* 41, no. 1 (January 2013), pp. 91–110; Wagner Kamakura, "Cross-Selling: Offering the Right Product to the Right Customer at the Right Time," *Journal of Relationship Marketing* 6, no. 3/4 (January 2008), pp. 41–54.

6. Susan Flaviano, personal correspondence; used with permission.

7. "Survey Says Employees Feel Obligated 24/7," *Manufacturing Business Technology* 24, no. 9 (2006), p. 9.

8. Flaviano, personal correspondence.

9. Lee Brubaker, "Make Sure Pay Time Pays," *American Salesman* 51, no. 8 (2006), pp. 27–29.

10. E-mail receipt statistics are from Datran Media's "Marketing & Media Survey" (2008), and the increase in e-mail estimate is based on David Daniels (December 2007), Jupiter Research, with both sources available at http://www.emailstatcenter.com/Usage.html, accessed March 1, 2008. The increase in e-mail estimate is based on Merkle, "View from the Digital Inbox 2011," also at http://www.emailstatcenter.com/Usage.html, accessed January 8, 2013.

11. John Plott, personal correspondence, March 1, 2008; used with permission.

12. Flaviano, personal correspondence.

13. Sandra Kennedy, personal correspondence, January 2, 2013; used with permission.

14. Adam Boretz, "Freedom in the Field," *Speech Technology* 14, no. 3 (May 2009), pp. 15–19.

15. Jim Olsztynski, "Making Money by Mining Technology," *Supply House Times* 52, no. 4 (June 2009), pp. 34–36.

16. Paul Lushin, personal correspondence, September 7, 2013; used with permission.

CHAPTER 16

1. Douglas E. Hughes, Joël Le Bon, and Adam Rapp, "Gaining and Leveraging Customer-Based Competitive Intelligence: The Pivotal Role of Social Capital and Salesperson Adaptive Selling Skills," *Journal of the Academy of Marketing Science* 41, no. 1 (January 2013), pp. 91–110.

2. Neville May, "Communication Breakdown," *Sales & Marketing Management* 160, no. 4 (July–August 2009), pp. 12–13.

3. Ashwin W. Joshi, "Salesperson Influence on Product Development: Insights from a Study of Small Manufacturing Organizations," *Journal of Marketing* 74, no. 1 (January 2010), pp. 94–108.

4. Frank Caprio, "There Is Power in a Self-Assured Salesperson," *Industrial Distribution* 98, no. 6 (November 2009), p. 55.

5. Matthew Carr, "Stepping in Time: Unifying Cross-functional Relationships to Mitigate Risk and Improve Cash Flow," *Business Credit* 111, no. 5 (May 2009), pp. 56–58.

6. Wim G. Biemans and Maja Makovec Brencic, "Designing the Marketing–Sales Interface in B2B Firms," *European Journal of Marketing* 41, no. 3–4 (2007), pp. 257–71.

7. Kenneth Le Meunier-FitzHugh and Nigel F. Piercy, "Improving the Relationship between Sales and Marketing," *European Business Review* 22, no. 3 (2010), pp. 287–305; Robert Dwyer and John F. Tanner Jr., *Business Marketing: Connecting Strategy, Relationships, and Learning,* 4th ed. (Burr Ridge, IL: McGraw-Hill/Irwin, 2009).

8. "Selling Events Internally and to Customers," *Folio* 33 (November 2004), pp. 35–37.

9. Douglas E. Hughes, Joël Le Bon, and Avinash Malshe, "The Marketing-Sales Interface at the Interface: Creating Market-Based Capabilities through Organizational Synergy," *Journal of Personal Selling and Sales Management* 32. no. 1 (Winter 2012), pp. 57–69; Avish Malshe, "How Is Marketers' Credibility Construed within the Sales-Marketing Interface?," *Journal of Business Research* 63 (January 2010), pp. 13–19; Michael Beverland, Marion Steel, and G. Peter Dapiran, "Cultural Frames That Drive Sales and Marketing Apart: An Exploratory Study," *Journal of Business and Industrial Marketing* 21, no. 6 (2006), pp. 386–402.

10. Avinash Malshe, "An Exploration of Key Connections within Sales-Marketing Interface," *Journal of Business and Industrial Marketing* 26, no. 1 (2011), pp. 45–57; Philip L. Dawes and Graham R. Massey, "A Study of Relationship Effectiveness between Marketing and Sales Managers in Business Markets," *Journal of Business and Industrial Marketing* 21, no. 6 (2006), pp. 346–67; Paolo Guenzi and Gabriele Troilo, "The Joint Contribution of Marketing and Sales to the Creation of Superior Customer Value," *Journal of Business Research* 60, no. 2 (2007), pp. 98–113.

11. Christian Homburg, Jan Wieseke, Bryan A. Lukas, and Sven Mikolon, "When Salespoeple Develop Negative Headquarters Stereotypes: Performance Effects and Managerial Remedies," *Journal of the Academy of Marketing Science* 39, no. 5 (October 2011), pp. 664–82; Christophe Fournier, John F. Tanner Jr., Lawrence B. Chonko and Chris Manolis, "The Moderating Role of Ethical Climate on Salesperson Propensity to Leave," *Journal of Personal Selling and Sales Management* 30, no. 1 (2010), pp. 7–22; John W. Barnes, Donald W. Jackson Jr., Michael D. Hutt, and Aith Kumar, "The Role of Culture Strength in Shaping Sales Force Outcomes," *Journal of Personal Selling and Sales Management* 26, no. 3 (2006), pp. 255–70; Craig A. Martin and Alan J. Bush, "Psychological Climate, Empowerment, Leadership Style, and Customer-Oriented Selling: An Analysis of the Sales Manager-Salesperson Dyad," *Journal of the Academy of Marketing Science* 34, no. 3 (2006), pp. 419–38.

12. Richard Herrin, "The Politics of Forecasting," *The Journal of Business Forecasting* 29, no. 1, pp. 18–19.

13. Johanna Smaros and Markus Hellstrom, "Using the Assortment Forecasting Method to Enable Sales Force Involvement in Forecasting: A Case Study," *International Journal of Physical Distribution & Logistics Management* 34 (2004), pp. 140–57.

14. Doug Henschen, "A Matter of Survival," *InformationWeek* 1222, pp. 29–35.

15. F. Caniato, M. Kalchschmidt, and S. Ronchi, "Integrating Quantitative and Qualitative Forecasting Approaches: Organizational Learning in an Action Research Case," *Journal of the Operational Research Society* 62, no. 3 (March 2011), pp. 413–24.

16. Charles H. Schwepker Jr. and David J. Good, "Sales Quotas: Unintended Consequences on Trust in Organization, Customer-Oriented Selling and Sales Performance," *Journal of Marketing Theory and Practice* 20, no. 4 (Fall 2012), pp. 437–52; F. Juliet Poujol and John F. Tanner Jr., "The Impact of Sales Contests on Salespeople's Customer Orientation: An Application of Tournament Theory," *Journal of Personal Selling and Sales Management* 30 (Winter 2010), pp. 33–46.

17. Michael L. Mallin, Edward O'Donnell, and Michael Y. Hu, "The Role of Uncertainty and Sales Control in the Development of Sales Manager Trust," *The Journal of Business & Industrial Marketing* 25, no. 1 (2010), pp. 30–44; Thomas G. Brashear, Chris Manolis, and Charles M. Brooks, "The Effects of Control, Trust, and Justice on Salesperson Turnover," *Journal of Business Research* 58 (March 2005), pp. 241–57.

18. Dave Stein, "When Sales 101 Isn't Enough," *Sales and Marketing Management* 160, no. 6, p. 7.

19. Jay P. Mulki, Jorge Fernando Jaramillo, and William B Locander, "Critical Role of Leadership on Ethical Climate and Salesperson Behaviors," *Journal of Business Ethics* 86, no. 2 (May 2009), pp. 126–51; Nigel F. Percy, David W. Cravens, Nikala Lane, and Douglas W. Vorhies, "Driving Organizational Citizenship Behaviors and Salesperson In-Role Behavior Performance: The Role of Management Control and Perceived Organizational Support," *Journal of the Academy of Marketing Science* 34, no. 2 (2006), pp. 244–52.

20. Craig A. Martin, "An Empirical Examination of the Antecedents of Ethical Intentions in Professional Selling," *Journal of Leadership, Accountability and Ethics* 9, no. 1 (February 2012), pp. 19–26.

21. Poujol and Tanner, "The Impact of Sales Contests on Salespeople's Customer Orientation"; Sean Valentine and Gary Fleischman, "Ethics Training and Businesspersons' Perceptions of Organizational Ethics," *Journal of Business Ethics* 52 (July 2004), pp. 391–409.

22. Norman L. Tolle, "Brochure Setting Forth Sales Incentive Plan Did Not Create Binding Contract," *Employee Benefit Plan Review* 61, no. 5 (2006), pp. 26–27.

23. Jim Humrichouse, personal interview.

24. Heather Fletcher, "Suddenlink Calls for Change," *Target Marketing* 33, no. 2 (February 2010), p. 10.

25. Eli Jones, Andrea L. Dixon, Lawrence B. Chonko, and Joseph P. Cannon, "Key Accounts and Team Selling: A Review, Framework, and Research Agenda," *Journal of Personal Selling & Sales Management* 25, no. 2 (2005), pp. 181–98.

CHAPTER 17

1. Patricia V. Rivera, "The Birth of a Salesman," *Atlanta-Journal and Constitution,* August 12, 2007, p. 1D.

2. John Graham, "Ask the Right Questions before Taking Any Sales Job," *American Salesman* 53, no. 2 (2008), pp. 20–25.

3. Deborah Aarts, "The 3 Inherent Traits of Great Salespeople," *Profit* 29, no. 5 (November 2010), p. 38.

4. George W. Dudley and Shannon L. Goodson, *Earning What You're Worth? The Psychology of Sales Call Reluctance,* 2nd ed. (Dallas: Behavioral Science Research Press, 2008).

5. Tom Day, personal interview.

6. Ti Yu, "E-Portfolio, a Valuable Job Search Tool for College Students," *Campus-Wide Information Systems* 29, no. 1 (2012), pp. 70–76; Lucy Aitken, "Me and My Portfolio," *Campaign,* May 14, 2004, pp. 36–37; Denny E. McCorkle, Joe E. Alexander, James Reardon, and Nathan D. Kling, "Developing Self-Marketing Skills: Are Marketing Students Prepared for the Job Search?," *Journal of Marketing Education* 25 (December 2003), pp. 196–207.

7. Katie Carano, "Successful Interview and Negotiation Strategies: A Review," *Career Planning and Adult Development*

Journal 26, no. 4 (Winter 2010/2011), pp. 28–44; Laura Huag, "Intimidation and Stress: All in a Day's Interview," *Financial Times,* November 28, 2005, p. 14.

8. Heather N. Odle-dusseau, Thomas W. Britt, and Phillip Bobko, "Work-Family Balance, Well-Being, and Organizational Outcomes: Investigating Actual Versus Desired Work/Family Time Discrepancies," *Journal of Business and Psychology* 27, no. 3 (September 2012), pp. 331–43.

9. "Employee Satisfaction: Key to Recovery Success?" *HR Focus* 87, no. 4 (April 2010), pp. 1–5.

10. Susan Denny, personal interview.

11. Diane McGrath, "Continuous Learning," *Update,* Fourth Quarter 1998, p. 8.

12. Stefanie L. Boyer and Brian Lambert, "Take the Handcuffs off Sales Team Development with Self-Directed Learning," *T&D* 62, no. 11 (November 2008), pp. 62–67.

13. Lisa White, "Francisco Limas," *Foodservice Equipment & Supplies* 60, no. 7 (2007), p. 49.

14. Diane Powers, "Achieving Professional Sales Growth," *Advisor Today* 104, no. 5 (May 2009), p. 53.

15. Jay Prakash Mulki, Fernando Jaramillo, Shavin Malhotra, and William B. Locander, "Reluctant Employees and Felt Stress: The Moderating Impact of Manager Decisiveness," *Journal of Business Research* 65, no. 1 (January 2012), p. 77; Jeffrey E. Lewin and Jeffrey K. Sager, "Salesperson Burnout: A Test of the Coping-Mediational Model of Social Support," *Journal of Personal Selling and Sales Management* 28, no. 3 (Summer 2008), pp. 233–46.

16. Songqi Liu, Mo Wang, Yujie Zhan, and Junqi Shi, "Daily Work Stress and Alcohol Use: Testing Cross-Level Moderation Effects of Neuroticism and Job Involvement," *Personnel Psychology* 62, no. 3 (Autumn 2009), pp. 575–97; Anthony Urbaniak, "Managing Stress," *SuperVision* 67, no. 8 (2006), pp. 7–9.

17. Mulki et al., "Reluctant Employees and Felt Stress"; Neil McAdam, "Situational Stress and Restriction of Stylistic Repertoire in High Potential Managerial Aspirants: Implications for the Implementation of the 'New Organization,'" *Journal of Management and Organization* 12, no. 1 (2006), pp. 40–67.

18. Richard G. McFarland, "Crisis of Conscience: The Use of Coercive Sales Tactics and Resultant Felt Stress in the Salesperson," *Journal of Personal Selling & Sales Management* 23, no. 4 (2003), pp. 311–31.

19. Ted Howell, personal correspondence, March 4, 2008; used with permission.

20. Lewin and Sager, "Salesperson Burnout"; Praveen Aggarwal, John F. Tanner Jr., and Stephen B. Castleberry, "Factors Associated with Propensity to Leave the Organization: A Study of Salespeople," *Marketing Management Journal* 14, no. 1 (2004), pp. 90–102.

21. Eric Ruiz, personal interview; used with permission.

GLOSSARY

ABC analysis Evaluating the importance of an account. The most important is an A account, the second most important is a B account, and the least important is a C account.

accommodating mode Resolving conflict by being unassertive and highly cooperative. When using this approach, people often neglect their own needs and desires to satisfy the concerns of the other party.

account opportunity Another term for the sales potential dimensions of the *sales call allocation grid*.

account share See *customer share*.

acknowledge method Responding to an objection by letting the buyer talk, acknowledging that you heard the concern, and then moving on to another topic without trying to resolve the concern.

active listening Process in which the listener attempts to draw out as much information as possible by actively processing information received and stimulating the communication of additional information.

activity goals Behavioral objectives, such as the number of calls made in a day.

activity quota A type of quota that sets minimal behavioral expectations for a salesperson's activities. Used when the sales cycle is long and sales are few. Controls activities of salespeople.

adaptive planning The development of alternative paths to the same goal in a negotiation session.

adaptive selling Approach to personal selling in which selling behaviors and approaches are altered during a sales interaction or across customer interactions, based on information about the nature of the selling situation.

administrative law Laws established by local, state, or federal regulatory agencies, such as the Federal Trade Commission or the Food and Drug Administration.

advantages Reasons why a feature would be important to someone.

agenda List of what will be discussed, and in what sequence, in a negotiation session.

agent Person who acts in place of his or her company. See also *manufacturers' agents*.

aggressive Sales style that controls the sales interaction but often does not gain commitment because it ignores the customer's needs and fails to probe for information.

always a share A buyer who will always allocate only a share to each vendor, never giving one vendor all of the business. See also *lost for good*.

ambush negotiating A win-lose tactic used by a buyer at the beginning of, or prior to, negotiations when the seller does not expect this approach.

amiable Category in the social style matrix; describes people who like cooperation and close relationships. Amiables are low on assertiveness and high on responsiveness.

analogy Drawing a parallel between one thing and another.

analysis paralysis When a salesperson prefers to spend practically all his or her time analyzing the situation and gathering information instead of making sales calls.

analytical Category in the social style matrix; describes people who emphasize facts and logic. Analyticals are low on assertiveness and responsiveness.

annual spend The amount that is spent with each vendor and for what products.

application form Preprinted form completed by a job applicant.

articulation The production of recognizable speech.

assertive Sales manner that stresses responding to customer needs while being self-confident and positive.

assertiveness Dimension of the social style matrix that assesses the degree to which people have opinions on issues and publicly make their positions clear to others.

assessment center Central location for evaluating job candidates.

attitudinal loyalty An emotional attachment to a brand, company, or salesperson.

automatic replenishment (AR) A form of just-in-time inventory management where the vendor manages the customer's inventory, and automatically ships and stocks products at the customer's location based on mutually agreed-upon standards.

avoiding mode Resolving conflict in an unassertive and uncooperative manner. In this mode people make no attempt to resolve their own needs or the needs of others.

awareness The first phase in the development of a buyer–seller relationship, in which salespeople locate and qualify prospects and buyers consider various sources of supply.

backdoor selling Actions by one salesperson that go behind the back of a purchaser to directly contact other members of the buying center.

balance sheet method Attempts to obtain commitment by asking the buyer to think of the pros and cons of the various alternatives; often referred to as the Ben Franklin method.

balanced presentation Occurs when the salesperson shows all sides of the situation—that is, is totally honest.

barriers Buyer's subordinates who plan and schedule interviews for their superiors; also called screens.

BATNA (Best Alternative to a Negotiated Agreement) What will be the result if you don't come to negotiation agreement. This is a standard or guide against which to evaluate the agreement you are trying to achieve. Also called **CNA**, the consequences of no agreement.

behavioral loyalty The purchase of the same product from the same vendor over time.

benchmarking A process of comparing your activities and performance with those of the best organization or individual in order to improve.

benefit How a particular feature will help a particular buyer.

benefit opening Approach in which the salesperson focuses on the prospect's needs by stating a benefit of the product or service.

benefit summary method Obtaining commitment by simply reminding the prospect of the agreed-on benefits of the proposal.

bird dog Individual who, for a fee, will provide the names of leads for the salesperson; also called a spotter.

blitz Canvassing method in which a large group of salespeople attempt to make calls on all prospective businesses in a given geographic territory on a specified day.

body language Nonverbal signals communicated through facial expressions, arms, hands, and legs.

bonus Lump-sum incentive payment based on performance.

boomerang method A method of objection handling where the reason for objecting is turned into a reason to buy or move to the next phase.

bottom-up forecasting Forecast compiled by adding up each salesperson's forecast for total company sales.

boundary-spanning employees Employees who cross the organizational boundary and interact with customers or vendors.

brainstorming session Meeting in which people are allowed to creatively explore different methods of achieving goals.

bribes Payments made to buyers to influence their purchase decisions.

browbeating Negotiation strategy in which buyers attempt to alter the selling team's enthusiasm and self-respect by making unflattering comments.

budget bogey Negotiation strategy in which one side claims that the budget does not allow for the solution proposed; also called budget limitation tactic.

budget limitation tactic See *budget bogey*.

business defamation Making unfair or untrue statements to customers about a competitor, its products, or its salespeople.

buyer's remorse The insecurity a buyer feels about whether the choice was a wise one; also called post-purchase dissonance.

buying center Informal, cross-department group of people involved in a purchase decision.

buying community Small, informal group of people in similar positions who communicate regularly, often both socially and professionally.

buying signals Nonverbal cues given by the buyer that indicate the buyer may be ready to commit; also called closing cues.

canned sales pitch A scripted sales pitch to follow without deviation.

cap A limit placed on a salesperson's earnings.

capital equipment Major purchases made by a business, such as computer systems, that are used by the business for several years in its operations or production process.

cash discount Price discount given for early payment in cash.

center-of-influence method Prospecting method wherein the salesperson cultivates well-known, influential people in the territory who are willing to supply lead information.

champion Person who works for the buying firm in the areas most affected by the proposed change and works with the salesperson for the success of the proposal; also called advocate or internal salesperson.

change agent Person who is a cause of change in an organization.

circular routing Method of scheduling sales calls that includes using circular patterns from the home base in order to cover the territory.

closed questions Questions that can be answered with a word or short phrase.

closing Common term for obtaining commitment, which usually refers only to asking for the buyer's business.

closing cues See *buying signals*.

cloverleaf routing Method of scheduling sales calls that involves using loops to cover different portions of the territory on different days or weeks; on a map it should resemble a cloverleaf.

CNA The consequences of no agreement. What will be the result if you don't come to negotiation agreement. This is a standard or guide against which to evaluate the agreement you are trying to achieve. Also called BATNA (Best Alternative to a Negotiated Agreement).

coach Someone in a buying organization who can advise a salesperson.

cold call See *cold canvass method.*

cold canvass method Prospecting method in which a sales representative tries to generate leads for new business by calling on totally unfamiliar organizations; also called cold calls.

collaborating mode Resolving conflict by seeking to maximize the satisfaction of both parties and hence truly reach a win–win solution.

collateral Collection of documents that are designed to generate sales, and include such items as brochures, sales flyers and fact sheets, and short success stories.

collusion Agreement among competitors, made after contacting customers, concerning their relationships with customers.

combination plan Compensation plan that provides salary and commission; offers the greatest flexibility for motivating and controlling the activities of salespeople.

commission Incentive payment for an individual sale; often a percentage of the sale price.

commission base Unit of analysis used to determine commissions—for example, unit sales, dollar sales, or gross margin.

commission rate Percentage of base paid or the amount per base unit paid in a commission compensation plan—for example, a percentage of dollar sales or an amount per unit sold.

commitment The fourth stage in the development of a buyer–seller relationship in which the buyer and seller have implicitly or explicitly pledged to continue the relationship for an extended period.

common law Legal precedents that arise out of court decisions.

comparative cost–benefit analysis A comparison of the buyer's current situation's costs with the value of the seller's proposed solution. Can also be a comparison of the seller's product with a competitor's product.

compensation method Method used to respond helpfully to objections by agreeing that the objection is valid, but then proceeding to show any compensating advantages.

competence Whether the salesperson knows what he or she is talking about.

competing mode Resolving conflict in an assertive and noncooperative manner.

complacency The assumption that the business is yours and will always be yours.

compliment opening Approach in which the salesperson begins the sales call by complimenting the buyer in some fashion.

compromising mode Resolving conflict by being somewhat cooperative and somewhat assertive. People using this approach attempt to find a quick, mutually acceptable solution that partially satisfies both parties.

concession Agreement of one party in a negotiation meeting to change his or her position in some fashion.

conspiracy Agreement among competitors, made prior to contacting customers, concerning their relationships with customers.

contract to sell Offer made by a salesperson that received an unqualified acceptance by a buyer.

conventional résumé Form of life history organized by type of work experience.

conversion goals Measures of salesperson efficiency.

conversion ratio Similar to a batting average; calculated by dividing performance results by activity results (for example, dividing the number of sales by the number of calls).

corporate culture The values and beliefs held by a company and expressed by senior management.

creativity The trait of having imagination and inventiveness and using it to come up with new solutions and ideas.

credibility The characteristic of being perceived by the buyer as believable and reliable.

credibility statement A description of the seller and his or her company, offered to buyers to show that the seller can meet their needs.

credulous person standard Canadian law stating that a company is liable to pay damages if advertising and sale presentation claims and statements about comparisons with competitive products could be misunderstood by a reasonable person.

creeping commitment Purchase decision process that arises when decisions made early in the process have significant influence on decisions made later in the process.

cross-selling Similar to full-line selling except that the additional products sold are not directly associated with the initial products.

cultural relativism A view that no culture's ethics are superior to those of another culture's.

cumulative discount Quantity discount for purchases over a period of time; the buyer is allowed to add up all the purchases to determine the total quantity and the total quantity discount.

customer benefit proposition Statement showing how a product addresses the buyer's specific needs.

customer lifetime value (CLV) The sum of the customer's purchases over its entire life.

customer orientation Selling approach based on keeping the customer's interests paramount.

customer referral value (CRV) The monetary value of the a referrals as well as the costs to get and maintain the referral.

customer relationship management (CRM) A system to organize information about customers, their needs, company information, and sales information.

customer satisfaction Fulfillment of the buyer's expectations and needs.

customer service rep (CRP) Inbound salesperson who handles customer concerns.

customer share The percentage of business received from a company's accounts. Also called account share or share of wallet.

customer-centric Process of making the customer the center of everything that the selling firm does. See also *customer orientation.*

customer value proposition (also called value proposition) The way in which a salesperson's product or service will meet the prospect's needs and how that is different from the offerings of competitors, especially the next-best-alternative.

customized presentation Presentation developed from a detailed and comprehensive analysis or survey of the prospect's needs that is not canned or memorized in any fashion.

data mining The use of artificial intelligence and statistical tools to discover hidden insights in the volumes of data in a database.

databases Information about leads, prospects, and customers.

deception Unethical practice of withholding information or telling white lies.

deciders Buying center members who make the final selection of the product to purchase.

decoding Communication activity undertaken by a receiver interpreting the meaning of the received message.

dependability The act of the salesperson living up to promises made; is not something a salesperson can demonstrate immediately.

derived demand Situation in which the demand for a producer's goods is based on what its customers sell.

diagnostic feedback Information given to a salesperson indicating how he or she is performing.

digital collateral management Systems that archive, catalog, and retrieve digital media and text. Used by sales people to create presentation.

direct denial Method of answering objections in which the salesperson makes a relatively strong statement indicating the error the prospect has made.

direct request method Act of attaining commitment by simply asking for it in a straightforward statement.

disguised interview Discussion between an applicant and an interviewer in which the applicant is unaware that the interviewer is evaluating the applicant for the position.

dissolution The process of terminating the relationship; can occur because of poor performance, clash in culture, change in needs, and other factors.

distribution channel Set of people and organizations responsible for the flow of products and services from the producer to the ultimate user.

document cameras Cameras similar to traditional overhead projectors in their ability to display transparencies. However, because they are essentially cameras, document cameras are also capable of displaying any three-dimensional object without the use of a transparency. Also called *visual presenters.*

draw Advance from the company to a salesperson made against future commissions.

driver Category in the social style matrix; describes task-oriented people who are high on assertiveness and low on responsiveness.

economic influencer Someone who is concerned about the financial aspects of a purchase decision.

efficient consumer response (ECR) Distribution system that drives inventory to the lowest possible levels, increases the frequency of shipping, and automates ordering and inventory control processes without the problems of stockouts and higher costs.

80–20 listening rule A guideline that suggests salespeople should listen 80 percent of the time and talk 20 percent of the time.

electronic data interchange (EDI) Computer-to-computer linkages between suppliers and buyers for information sharing about sales, production, shipment, and receipt of products.

electronic whiteboard A digital version of an easel.

e-missives Timely, useful information that a seller provides to a buyer. This information might have nothing to do with the seller or the seller's product. The goal is to help make friends with the buyer and cement the relationship.

emotional intelligence The ability to effectively understand and use your own emotions and those of people with whom you interact. Includes four aspects: (1) knowing your own feelings and emotions as they are happening, (2) controlling your emotions so you do not act impulsively, (3) recognizing your customer's emotions (called empathy), and (4) using your emotions to interact effectively with customers.

emotional needs Organizational and/or personal needs that are associated with some type of personal reward and gratification for the person buying the product.

emotional outburst tactic Negotiation strategy in which one party attempts to gain concessions by resorting to a display of strong emotion.

encoding Communication activity undertaken by a sender translating his or her thought into a message.

end users Businesses that purchase goods and services to support their own production and operations.

endless-chain method Prospecting method whereby a sales representative attempts to get at least one additional lead from each person he or she interviews.

ethical imperialism The view that the ethical standards that apply locally or in one's home country should be applied to everyone's behavior around the world.

ethics Principles governing the behavior of an individual or a group.

ethics review board A group of experts inside and outside the company who are responsible for reviewing ethics policies, investigating allegations of unethical behavior, and acting as a sounding board for employees.

exclusive sales territories Method that uses a prospect's geographic location to determine whether a salesperson can sell to that prospect.

excuses Concerns expressed by the buyer that are intended to mask the buyer's true objections.

executive briefing center Presentation rooms set aside to highlight a company's products and capabilities.

executive summary In a written proposal, a summary of one page or less that briefly describes the total cost minus total savings, the problem to be solved, and the proposed solution.

expansion The third phase in the development of a relationship, in which it takes a significant effort to share information and further investigate the potential relationship benefits.

exploration The second phase in the development of a relationship, in which both buyers and sellers explore the potential benefits and costs associated with the relationship.

expressed warranty Warranty specified through oral or written communications.

expressive Category in the social style matrix; describes people who are both competitive and approachable. They are high on assertiveness and responsiveness.

extranet Secure Internet-based network connecting buyers and suppliers.

FAB When salespeople describe the features, advantages (why that feature is important), and benefits of their product or service.

face A person's desire for a positive identity or self-concept.

False Claims Act An 1863 law encouraging citizens to press claims against vendors that sell fraudulently.

feature (1) Quality or characteristic of the product or service. (2) Putting a product on sale with a special display and featuring the product in advertising.

feature dumping Talking about lots of features of little interest to the customer and wasting the buyer's time.

FEBA A method of describing a product or service where salespeople mention the feature, provide evidence that the feature actually does exist, explain the benefit (why that feature is important to the buyer), and then ask whether the buyer agrees with the value of the feature and benefit.

feedback See *diagnostic feedback*.

feel–felt–found method A method of objection handling where the salesperson acknowledges how the buyer feels, then relates how someone else felt the same but found that the objection was misguided.

felt stress Persistent and enduring psychological distress brought about by job demands or constraints encountered in the work environment.

field sales manager First-level manager.

field salespeople Salespeople who spend considerable time in the customer's place of business, communicating with the customer face-to-face.

field support rep Telemarketer who works with field salespeople and does more than prospect for leads.

FOB destination The seller has title until the goods are received at the destination.

FOB factory The buyer has title when the goods leave the seller's facility.

focus of dissatisfaction The person in the organization who is most likely to perceive problems and dissatisfactions; leads to the focus of power.

focus of power The person in the organization who can approve, prevent, or influence action.

focus of receptivity The person in the organization who will listen receptively and provide a seller with valuable information; leads to the focus of dissatisfaction.

follow-up Activity that a salesperson performs after commitment is achieved.

Foreign Corrupt Practices Act Law that governs the behavior of U.S. business in foreign countries; restricts the bribing of foreign officials.

forestall To resolve objections before buyers have a chance to raise them.

four A's The selling process, consisting of *a*cknowledge, *a*cquire, *a*dvise, and *a*ssure.

free on board (FOB) See *FOB destination* and *FOB factory*.

friendly silent questioning stare (FSQS) The act of silently waiting to encourage buyers to elaborate or explain more fully what their concern is.

full-line selling Selling the entire line of associated products.

functional relationship Series of market exchanges between a buyer and a seller, linked together over time. These relationships are characterized as win–lose relationships.

functional résumé Life history that reverses the content and titles of a conventional résumé and is organized by what a candidate can do or has learned rather than by types of experience.

gatekeepers Buying center members who influence the buying process by controlling the flow of information and/or limiting the alternatives considered. Sometimes called barriers or screens.

geographic salesperson Salesperson assigned a specific geographic territory in which to sell all the company's products and services.

good guy–bad guy routine Negotiation strategy in which one team member acts as the "good guy" while another team member acts as the "bad guy." The goal of the strategy is to have the opposing team accept the good guy's proposal to avoid the consequences of the bad guy's proposal.

go-to-market strategies The various options that firms have to sell their products. Examples include the Internet, franchises, telemarketers, agents, value added resellers, field salespeople, and so on.

greeter Interviewer who greets the applicant and may conduct a disguised interview.

gross margin quota Minimum levels of acceptable profit or gross margin performance.

group interview Similar to panel interview but includes several candidates as well as several interviewers.

halo effect How one does in one thing changes a person's perceptions about other things one does.

handouts Written documents provided to buyers before, during, or after a meeting to help them remember what was said.

honesty Combination of truthfulness and sincerity; highly related to dependability.

house accounts Accounts assigned to a sales executive rather than to the specific salesperson responsible for the territory containing the account.

implication questions Questions that logically follow one or more problem questions (in SPIN); designed to help the prospect recognize the true ramifications of the problem.

implied warranty Warranty that is not expressly stated through oral or written communication but is still an obligation defined by law.

impression management Activities in which salespeople engage to affect and manage the buyer's impression of them.

inbound Salespeople or customer service reps who respond to calls placed to the firm by customers rather than placing calls out to customers.

inbound telemarketing Use of the telephone, usually with a toll-free number, that allows leads and/or customers to call for additional information or to place an order.

incentive pay Compensation based on performance.

indirect denial method Method used to respond to objections in which the salesperson denies the objection but attempts to soften the response by first agreeing with the prospect that the objection is an important one.

inflection Tone of voice.

influencers Buying center members inside or outside an organization who directly or indirectly influence the buying process.

influential adversaries Individuals in the buyer's organization who carry great influence and are opposed to the salesperson's product or service.

initiator The person who starts the buying process.

inside salespeople Salespeople who work at their employer's location and interact with customers by telephone or letter.

insight selling A prospecting method whereby salespeople evaluate prospects who do not necessarily have a clear understanding of what they need but who are in a state of flux and have been shown to be quite agile in making changes (that is, they are able and willing to act quickly when a compelling case is made to them).

integrated marketing communications Coordinated communications programs that exploit the strengths of various communication vehicles to maximize the total impact on customers.

internal partnerships Partnering relationships between a salesperson and another member of the same company for the purpose of satisfying customer needs.

interview Personal interactions between candidates and job recruiters for the purpose of evaluating job candidates.

intimate zone That physical space around a buyer that is reserved primarily for a person's closest relationships. See also *social zone, public zone,* and *personal zone.*

introduction opening Approach method in which salespeople simply state their names and the names of their companies.

inventory turnover Measure of how efficiently a retailer manages inventory; calculated by dividing net sales by inventory.

invitation to negotiate The initiation of an interaction, usually a sales presentation, that results in an offer.

just-in-time (JIT) inventory control Planning system for reducing inventory by having frequent deliveries planned just in time for the delivered products to be assembled into the final product.

key accounts Large accounts, usually generating more than a specified amount in revenue per year, that receive special treatment.

kickbacks Payments made to buyers based on the amount of orders they place for a salesperson's products or services.

knowledge management technology Information technology that captures knowledge from people, organizes that knowledge, and makes it available to others.

KSAs Acronym for knowledge, skills, and abilities; the package that a candidate offers an employer.

LAARC method Method to respond to objections: Listen, Acknowledge, Assess (the validity of the objection), Respond, Confirm (that the objection has been answered).

lead A potential prospect; a person or organization that may have the characteristics of a true prospect.

lead management system The part of the lead process in which salespeople carefully analyze the relative value of each lead.

lead qualification system A process for qualifying leads.

lead user Company that faces and resolves needs months or years ahead of the rest of the marketplace.

leapfrog routing Method of scheduling calls that requires the identification of clusters of customers; visiting these clusters and "leaping" over single, sparsely located accounts should minimize travel time from the sales office to customers.

life-cycle costing Method for determining the cost of equipment or supplies over their useful life.

likability Behaving in a friendly manner and finding a common ground between the buyer and seller.

lost for good A buyer who gives all business to one vendor is considered lost for good for all of the out-suppliers because the buyer has cemented this relationship for a long period of time. See also *always a share*.

loudness Speech characterized by high volume and intensity.

lowballing Negotiation strategy in which one party voices agreement and then raises the cost of that agreement in some way.

lubrication Small sums of money or gifts, typically paid to officials in foreign countries, to get the officials to do their jobs more rapidly.

major sale Sale that involves a long selling cycle, a large customer commitment, an ongoing relationship, and large risks for the buyer if a bad decision is made.

manipulation Practice by a salesperson to eliminate or reduce the buyer's choice unfairly.

manufacturers' agents Independent businesspeople who are paid a commission by a manufacturer for all products and services the agents sell.

market exchange Relationship that involves a short-term transaction between a buyer and a seller that do not expect to be involved in future transactions with each other.

material requirements planning (MRP) Planning system for reducing inventory levels by forecasting sales, developing a production schedule, and ordering parts and raw materials with specific delivery dates.

merchandise market A form of exhibition or trade show used in fashion industries for manufacturers to sell products to retailers.

minimum call objective The minimum that a salesperson hopes to accomplish in an upcoming sales call.

minimum position Negotiation objective that states the absolute minimum level the team is willing to accept.

mirroring Where one person copies the nonverbals of another.

missionary salespeople Salespeople who work for a manufacturer and promote the manufacturer's products to other firms. Those firms buy products from distributors or other manufacturers, not directly from the salesperson's firm.

modified rebuy Purchase decision process associated with a customer who has purchased the product or service in the past but is interested in obtaining additional information.

MRO supplies Minor purchases made by businesses for maintenance and repairs, such as towels and pencils.

multichannel strategy The process of a firm using various go-to-market strategies at the same time.

multilevel selling Strategy that involves using multiple levels of company employees to call on similar levels in an account; for example, the VP of sales might call on the VP of purchasing.

multiple-sense appeals Method of attracting as many of the senses (hearing, sight, touch, taste, and smell) as possible.

mutual investment Tangible investments in the relationship by both parties (seller and buyer).

national account manager (NAM) Sales executive responsible for managing and coordinating sales efforts on a single account nationwide.

need payoff questions Questions that ask about the usefulness of solving the problem.

negative referral A customer who tells others about how poorly you or your product performed.

negotiation Decision-making process through which buyers and sellers resolve areas of conflict and arrive at agreements.

negotiation jujitsu Negotiation response in which the attacked person or team steps away from the opponent's attack and then directs the opponent back to the issues being discussed.

net present value (NPV) The investment minus the net value today of future cash inflows (discounted back to their present value today at the firm's cost of capital).

networking Establishing connections to other people and then using those networks to generate leads, gather information, generate sales, and so on.

new task Purchase decision process associated with the initial purchase of a product or service.

nibbling Negotiation strategy in which the buyer requests a small extra or add-on after the deal has been closed. Compared with *lowballing,* a nibble is a much smaller request.

noises Sounds unrelated to the message being exchanged between a salesperson and a customer.

nonverbal communication Nonspoken forms of expression—body language, space, and appearance—that communicate thoughts and emotions.

North America industry classification system (NAICS) A uniform classification system for all businesses for all countries in North America.

objection Concern or question raised by the buyer.

offer Specific statement by a seller outlining what the seller will provide and what is expected from the buyer.

office scanning Activity in which the salesperson looks around the prospect's environment for relevant topics to talk about.

open questions Questions for which there are no simple yes–no answers.

open-door policy General management technique that allows subordinates to bypass immediate managers and take concerns straight to upper management when the subordinates feel a lack of support from the immediate manager.

opening A method designed to get the prospect's attention and interest quickly and make a smooth transition into the next part of the presentation. Examples include introduction, product, question, referral, and so on.

opening position The initial proposal of a negotiating session.

opportunity cost The return a buyer would have earned from a different use of the same investment capital.

optimistic call objective The most optimistic outcome the salesperson thinks could occur in a given sales call.

orders Written orders that become contracts when they are signed by an authorized representative of a salesperson's company.

original equipment manufacturer (OEM) Business that purchases goods (components, subassemblies, raw and processed materials) to incorporate into products it manufactures.

outbound Salespeople, customer service reps, prospectors, account managers, and field support telemarketers who place phone calls out to customers.

outbound telemarketing Using the telephone to generate and qualify leads to determine whether they are truly prospects; also used to secure orders and provide customer contact.

outlined presentation Systematically arranged presentation that outlines the most important sales points. Often includes the necessary steps for determining the prospect's needs and for building goodwill at the close of the sale.

panel interview Job interview conducted by more than one person.

pass-up method A method of handling objections that essentially entails not handling the objection but ignoring it.

payback period Length of time it takes for the investment cash outflows to be returned in the form of cash inflows or savings.

performance feedback A type of feedback that salespeople often get from their supervisors that focuses on the seller's actual performance during a sales call.

performance goals Goals relating to outcomes, such as revenue.

personal selling Interpersonal communication process in which a seller uncovers and satisfies the needs of a buyer to the mutual, long-term benefit of both parties.

personal zone That physical space around a buyer that is reserved for close friends and those who share special interests. See also *public zone, social zone,* and *intimate zone.*

persuading Influencing someone to do something through reasoning or argument.

persuasion Practice by a salesperson designed to influence the buyer's decision, not manipulate it. See also *manipulation.*

pioneer selling Selling a new and different product, service, or idea. In these situations the salesperson usually has difficulty establishing a need in the buyer's mind.

pipeline analysis A process for identifying and managing sales opportunities; also called opportunity management. See also *sales funnel*.

poaching The unethical act of stealing a prospect from a salesperson in the same company.

portfolio Collection of visual aids that can be used to enhance communication during a sales call.

postpone method Objection response technique in which the salesperson asks permission to answer the question at a later time.

postpurchase dissonance See *buyer's remorse*.

preferred supplier Supplier that is assured a large percentage of the buyer's business and will get the first opportunity to earn new business.

prequalification Determination by firms whether leads are qualified before turning them over to the field sales force.

price discrimination Situation in which a seller gives unjustified special prices, discounts, or special services to some customers and not to others.

primary call objective Actual goal the salesperson hopes to achieve in an upcoming sales call.

prime selling time Time of day at which a salesperson is most likely to be able to see a customer.

privacy laws Laws that limit the amount of information that a firm can obtain about a consumer and specify how that information can be used or shared.

probing method Method to obtain commitment in which the salesperson initially uses the direct request method and, if unsuccessful, uses a series of probing questions designed to discover the reason for the hesitation.

problem questions Questions about specific difficulties, problems, or dissatisfactions that the prospect has.

producer Firm that buys goods and services to manufacture and sell other goods and services to its customers.

product opening Approach in which the salesperson actually demonstrates the product features and benefits as soon as he or she walks up to the prospect.

profit margin The net profit the reseller makes, expressed as a percentage of sales.

profit quota Minimum levels of acceptable profit or gross margin performance.

promoters Your most loyal customers who not only keep buying from you but also urge their friends and associates to do the same.

prospect A lead that is a good candidate for buying what the salesperson is selling.

prospecting The process of locating potential customers for a product or service.

public zone That physical space around a person in which listening to speeches and interacting with passersby is comfortable for that person. See also *personal zone, intimate zone,* and *social zone*.

push money See *spiffs*.

qualifying a lead The process of determining whether a lead is in fact a prospect.

quantifying the solution Showing the prospect that the cost of the proposal is offset by added value.

question opening Beginning the conversation with a question or stating an interesting fact in the form of a question.

quick response (QR) system System of minimizing order quantities to the lowest level possible while increasing the speed of delivery to drive inventory turnover; accomplished by prepackaging certain combinations of products.

quota Quantitative level of performance for a specific time period.

rapport Close, harmonious relationship founded on mutual trust.

rate of change The speed at which change is occurring; a critical element to consider about change.

rational needs Organizational and/or personal needs that are directly related to product performance.

reciprocity Special relationship in which two companies agree to buy products from each other.

red herring A minor point brought up to distract the other side from the main issue being negotiated.

references People who know an applicant for a position and can provide information about that applicant to the hiring company.

referral event Gatherings designed to allow current customers to introduce prospects to the salesperson in order to generate leads.

referral method Method of helpfully responding to objections in which the salesperson shows how others held similar views before trying the product or service.

referral opening Approach in which the name of a satisfied customer or friend of the prospect is used at the beginning of a sales call.

referred lead Name of a lead provided by either a customer or a prospect of the salesperson.

relational partnership Long-term business relationship in which the buyer and seller have a close, trusting relationship but have not made significant investments in the relationship. These relationships are characterized as win–win relationships.

relationship marketing Marketing that seeks to win customers by building the right type of relationship desired by those customers.

relationship-specific assets Resources that are specific to a relationship and cannot easily be transferred to another one.

request for proposal (RFP) Statement issued by a potential buyer desiring bids from several potential vendors for a product. RFPs often include specifications for the product, desired payment terms, and other information helpful to the bidder. Also called request for bids or request for quotes.

requirements Conditions that must be satisfied before a purchase can take place.

resale price maintenance Contractual term in which a producer establishes a minimum price below which distributors or retailers cannot sell their products.

resellers Businesses, typically distributors or retailers, that purchase products for resale.

response time The time between sending a message and getting a response to it.

responsiveness The degree to which people react emotionally when they are in social situations. One of the two dimensions in the social style matrix.

return on investment (ROI) Net profits (or savings) expected from a given investment, expressed as a percentage of the investment.

revenue quota The minimum amount of sales revenue necessary for acceptable performance.

reverse auction An auction, but instead of a seller offering a product and buyers bidding, a buyer offers a contract and sellers bid; prices fall as sellers compete to win the sale.

revisit method Process of responding to objections by turning the objection into a reason for acting now.

role ambiguity The degree to which a salesperson is not sure about the actions required in the sales role.

role conflict The extent to which the salesperson faces incompatible demands from two or more constituencies that he or she serves.

role overload A role (or job) demanding more than the person can perform.

role stress The psychological distress that may be a consequence of a salesperson's lack of role accuracy.

routine call patterns Method of scheduling calls used when the same customers are seen regularly.

routing Method of scheduling sales calls to minimize travel time.

salary Compensation paid periodically to an employee independently of performance.

sale The transfer of title to goods and services by the seller to the buyer in exchange for money.

sales asset management A system used to archive, catalog, and retrieve digital media and text.

sales call allocation grid Grid used to determine account strategy; the dimensions are the strength of the company's position with the account and the account's sales potential.

sales force–intensive organization Firms whose go-to-market strategy relies heavily on salespeople.

sales funnel A prospecting term that reflects that some leads do not become prospects and that some prospects do not become customers. One thousand leads might be needed, for example, to generate 200 prospects, of which only 15 might become prospects. This funnel of smaller and smaller numbers is called the sales funnel.

sales portals Online databases that include in one place many sources of information that the salesperson might need. Include items such as account data, competitor intelligence, and news about the industry, the company, and the economy.

sales puffery Exaggerated statements about the performance of products or services.

sales quota The minimum number of sales in units.

scope of change The extent or degree to which change affects an organization; a critical element to consider about change.

screens See *barriers.*

secondary call objectives Goals a salesperson hopes to achieve during a sales call that have somewhat less priority than the primary call objective.

seeding Sending the customer important and useful items or information prior to the meeting.

selective perception The act of hearing what we want to hear, not necessarily what the other person is saying.

selling analytics An attempt to gain insights into customers by using sophisticated data mining and analytic techniques.

selling center A team that consists of all people in the selling organization who participate in a selling opportunity.

selling deeper Selling more to existing customers.

services End-user purchases such as Internet and telephone connections, employment agencies, consultants, and transportation.

sexual harassment Unwelcome sexual advances, requests for sexual favors, and other, similar verbal (such as jokes) and nonverbal (such as graffiti) behaviors.

share of wallet See *customer share.*

simple cost–benefit analysis Simple listing of the costs and savings that a buyer can expect from an investment.

situation questions General data-gathering questions about background and current facts that are very broad in nature.

situational stress Short-term anxiety caused by a situational factor.

six sigma selling programs Programs designed to reduce errors introduced by the selling system.

small talk Talk about current news, hobbies, and the like that usually breaks the ice for the actual presentation.

sneak attack See *ambush negotiating*.

social media The technological component of the communication, transaction, and relationship-building functions of a business that leverages the network of customers and prospects to promote value cocreation.

social networking Using Web sites to interact.

social style matrix Method for classifying customers based on their preferred communication style. The two dimensions used to classify customers are assertiveness and responsiveness.

social zone The physical space around a person in which business transactions and other impersonal relationships are comfortable for the person. See also *public zone, intimate zone,* and *personal zone*.

solo exchange Both the buyer and the seller pursue their own self-interests because they do not plan on doing business together again.

speaking–listening differential The difference between the 120-to-160-words-per-minute rate of speaking versus the 800-words-per-minute rate of listening.

spiffs (push money) Payments made by a producer to a reseller's salespeople to motivate the salespeople to sell the producer's products or services.

SPIN Logical sequence of questions in which a prospect's needs are identified. The sequence is situation questions, problem questions, implication questions, and need payoff questions.

spotter See *bird dog*.

standard industrial classification (SIC) A uniform classification system for an industry. The SIC system is being replaced by the new *North America industry classification system (NAICS)*.

standard memorized presentation Carefully prepared sales story that includes all the key selling points arranged in the most effective order; often called a canned sales presentation.

statutory law Laws based on legislation passed by either state legislatures or Congress.

straight commission Compensation method of a certain amount per sale; plan includes a base and a rate but not a salary.

straight rebuy Purchase decision process involving a customer with considerable knowledge gained from having purchased the product or service a number of times.

straight salary Compensation method that pays a fixed amount of money for working a specified amount of time.

straight-line routing Method of scheduling sales calls involving straight-line patterns from the home base in order to cover the sales territory.

strategic account manager (SAM) A company executive who coordinates all the salespeople who call on an account throughout the nation or the world. Also called national account manager (NAM).

strategic partnership Long-term business relationship in which the buyer and seller have made significant investments to improve the profitability of both parties in the relationship. These relationships are characterized as win–win relationships.

strength of position Dimension of the sales call allocation grid that considers the seller's strength in landing sales at an account.

stress interview Any interview that subjects an applicant to significant stress; the purpose is to determine how the applicant handles stress.

style flexing Adjusting your behavior to mirror or match that of your customer.

submissive Selling style of salespeople who are often excellent socializers and like to spend a lot of time talking about nonbusiness activities. These people are usually reluctant to attempt to obtain commitment.

subordination Payment of large sums of money to officials to get them to do something that is illegal.

superior benefit method Type of compensation method of responding to an objection during a sales presentation that uses a high score on one attribute to compensate for a low score on another attribute.

supplier relationship management (SRM) The use of technology and statistics to identify important suppliers and opportunities for cost reduction, greater efficiency, and other benefits.

supply chain logistics The management of the supply chain.

supply chain management (SCM) Set of programs undertaken to increase the efficiency of the distribution system that moves products from the producer's facilities to the end user.

systems integrator Outside vendor who has been delegated the responsibility for purchasing; has the authority to buy products and services from others.

target position Negotiation objective that states what the team hopes to achieve by the time the session is completed.

team selling Type of selling in which employees with varying areas of expertise within the firm work together to sell to the same account(s).

technical influencer A person who makes sure that a purchase meets technical requirements.

telemarketing Systematic and continuous program of communicating with customers and prospects via telephone and/or other person-to-person electronic media.

testimonial Statement, usually in the form of a letter, written by a satisfied customer about a product or service.

tests Personality or skills assessments used in assessing the match between a position's requirements and an applicant's personality or skills.

third-party-testimony method Method of responding to an objection during a sales presentation that uses a testimonial letter from a third party to corroborate a salesperson's assertions.

tickler file File or calendar used by salespeople to remind them when to call on specific accounts.

trade fair The European term for *trade show*.

trade salespeople Salespeople who sell to firms that resell the products rather than using them within their own firms.

trade secrets Information owned by a company that gives it a competitive advantage.

trade show Short exhibition of products by manufacturers and distributors.

trial balloon An idea floated without being actually offered.

trial close Questions the salesperson asks to take the pulse of the situation throughout a presentation.

trial order A small order placed by a buyer in order to test the product or the vendor. Not to be confused with trial close.

trust Firm belief or confidence in the honesty, integrity, and reliability of another person.

turnover (TO) An account is given to another salesperson because the buyer refuses to deal with the current salesperson.

24/7 service A phrase that highlights the fact that customers expect a selling firm to be available 24 hours a day, 7 days a week.

two-way communication Interpersonal communication in which both parties act as senders and receivers. Salespeople send messages to customers and receive feedback from them; customers send messages to salespeople and receive responses.

tying agreement Agreement between a buyer and a seller in which the buyer is required to purchase one product to get another.

Uniform Commercial Code (UCC) Legal guide to commercial practice in the United States.

upgrading Convincing the customer to use a higher-quality product or a newer product.

users Members of a buying center that ultimately will use the product purchased.

value The total benefit that the seller's products and services provide to the buyer. Also, the customer's perceived benefit received minus the selling price and minus the costs and hassles of buying.

value analysis Problem-solving approach for reducing the cost of a product while providing the same level of performance. See *quantifying the solution*.

variable call patterns A nonsystematic method that a salesperson occasionally uses for calling on accounts.

vendor analysis A formal method used by organizational buyers to summarize the benefits and needs satisfied by a supplier.

vendor loyalty Commitment of a buyer to a specific supplier because of the supplier's superior performance.

versatility A characteristic, associated with the social style matrix, of people who increase the productivity of social relationships by adjusting to the needs of the other party.

videoconferencing Meetings in which people are not physically present in one location but are connected via voice and video.

virtual sales call See *Webcasting*.

visual presenters See *document cameras*.

voice characteristics The rate of speech, loudness, pitch, quality, and articulation of a person's voice.

warranty Assurance by the seller that the goods will perform as represented.

Webcasting Videoconferencing in which the meeting is broadcast over the Internet.

Webiner Online seminar.

win–lose negotiating Negotiating philosophy in which the negotiator attempts to win all the important concessions and thus triumph over his or her opponent.

win–win negotiating Negotiating philosophy in which the negotiator attempts to secure an agreement that completely satisfies both parties.

win–win not yet negotiating A negotiation session in which the buying team achieves its goals while the selling team does not. However, the sellers expect to achieve their goals in the near future, thanks to the results of that negotiation session.

win–win relationship Type of relationship in which firms make significant investments that can improve profitability for both partners because their partnership has given them some strategic advantage over their competitors.

word picture Story or scenario designed to help the buyer visualize a point.

zoning Method of scheduling calls that divides a territory into zones. Calls are made in a zone for a specified length of time and then made in another zone for the same amount of time.

COMPANY INDEX

SUBJECT INDEX